THE ROUGH GUIDE TO
CHILE
& EASTER ISLAND

This seventh edition updated by
**Nick Edwards, Anna Kaminski, Shafik Meghji and
Sorrel Moseley-Williams**

ROUGH
GUIDES

Contents

Introduction to
Chile

Clinging to the edge of South America, long, narrow Chile has a fantastical serpentine shape: some 4300km in length – equivalent to the distance between Norway and Nigeria – and with an average width of just 175km. Once you set foot here, however, these unlikely-sounding measurements make perfect sense, and it soon becomes apparent that Chile is a geographically self-contained unit – essentially an island. The Andes, the great mountain range that forms its eastern border, are a formidable barrier of rock and ice that cuts the country off from Argentina and Bolivia. The Atacama Desert, a 1000km stretch of parched wasteland, separates it from Peru to the north. And to the west, just a few islands dotted in the Pacific Ocean break the waves that roll onto Chile's coast from Australasia.

All this has created a country distinct from the rest of South America and one that defies many people's expectations. It is developed, relatively affluent, and – with the notable exception of the horrific Pinochet dictatorship of the 1970s and 1980s – boasts a tradition of **political stability**. Today, Chile – a place of geographical extremes – is one of the safest, easiest and most rewarding South American countries to travel in.

Chile's dazzling **diversity** is also reflected in its people – from the alpaca herders of the altiplano (the high Andean plain) and the huasos (cowboys) of Patagonia to the businessmen of Santiago and the hip young things in Valparaíso – and its cuisine, which runs the gamut from the sweet tropical fruit of the arid north to delicious king crab from the southern fjords. Above all, though, it is the country's remote and dizzyingly **beautiful landscapes** that draw visitors. With a population of around eighteen million largely confined to a handful of major cities, much of the country is made up of vast tracts of scarcely touched wilderness – where you can be days from the nearest tarmacked road.

CHILE AND EASTER ISLAND

metres
3658
2743
1828
914
457
183
0

Easter Island (Chile)

PERU
Arica
Iquique

BOLIVIA

PARAGUAY

Calama
San Pedro
de Atacama
Antofagasta

Copiapó

La Serena   Vicuña

ARGENTINA

Cordoba

Los Vilos
Viña del Mar
Valparaíso   Mendoza
SANTIAGO
Rancagua

Buenos Aires

Talca

Buenos Aires

Chillán
Concepción

*Juan Fernández
Archipelago (Chile)*

PACIFIC
OCEAN

Temuco   Pucón
Valdivia
Osorno
Puerto Varas
Puerto Montt
Ancud
Chiloé   Castro
Quellón   Chaitén
*Arch. de los
Chonos*

ATLANTIC
OCEAN

Puerto Aisén
Coyhaique

N

Cochrane
Golfo de Penas

Villa O'Higgins   El Chaltén

Isla Wellington   El Calafate

Puerto Natales
Strait of Magellan

*Tierra
del Fuego*
Punta Arenas
Porvenir

Ushuaia
Puerto
Williams
Cape Horn

0   250
kilometres

FACT FILE

- Chile lives and breathes **football**: the national team won the 2015 Copa América on home soil and the Copa América Centenario in 2016, but disappointingly failed to qualify for the 2018 World Cup.

- Around **18 million people** live in Chile, consisting of a fairly homogenous mestizo population with a few indigenous peoples: Mapuche in the Lake District, Aymara in the far north, Easter Island's Rapa Nui, and Yámana and Kawéskar in Patagonia and Tierra del Fuego.

- Chile's national **motto** is *"Por la razón o la fuerza"* meaning "By right or by might".

- In 2017, Tompkins Conservation and the government signed an historic agreement to expand the area protected by **national parks** by more than 40,000 square kilometres – roughly the size of Switzerland.

- In the longest recorded dry spell in Chile's **Atacama Desert**, it didn't rain for more than forty years.

- Chile legalized **divorce** in 2004 and **abortion** (in certain circumstances) in 2017.

Where to go

Few countries can match Chile's sheer diversity of scenery and range of climatic zones – from the world's driest non-polar desert to immense ice-fields and glaciers. Spread between these extremes is a kaleidoscope of panoramas, taking in sun-baked scrubland, lush **vineyards** and orchards, virgin **temperate rainforest**, dramatic **fjords** and endless **Patagonian steppes**. Towering above is the jagged spine of the Andes, punctuated by colossal peaks and **smouldering volcanoes**.

Given the huge distances involved, it's important to plan your **itinerary** (see page 22) before you go. The country splits roughly into two halves, with the capital, Santiago, the jumping-off point for both the sunny north, all vineyards, beaches and desert, and the capricious south, comprised of glaciers, mountains, forests and fjords.

Santiago boasts some fine monuments, museums and restaurants, and is handy for visiting a number of Chile's oldest **vineyards**. Nearby, the quirky port of **Valparaíso** provides an interesting contrast, with a bohemian but gritty vibe, and splendid bay views from its many hills. **North of Santiago**, highlights include the handsome colonial city of **La Serena** and the lush **Elqui Valley**, its hills ideal for horse treks and its distilleries perfect for pisco sampling. A succession of idyllic **beaches** lies spread out along the dazzling fringe of the **Norte Chico**, which comprises semi-arid landscapes and hardy vegetation that takes all the moisture it needs from sea mists. The mining city of **Copiapó** is a springboard for excursions to **Bahía Inglesa**, one of the country's most attractive seaside resorts, and east into the barely trodden cordillera, where you'll find the mineral-streaked volcanoes of **Parque Nacional Nevado de Tres Cruces** and the turquoise **Laguna Verde**.

Further north, the **Atacama Desert**, stretching for more than 1000km into southern Peru, presents an unforgettable, otherworldly landscape; sights include ancient petroglyphs, nitrate ghost towns, fertile oases and some of the world's most powerful telescopes – all the better to lose yourself in the clear night skies. Tiny **San Pedro de Atacama** makes an ideal base for exploring this arid, moonlike region. Up in the Andes, the vast plateau known as the **altiplano** encompasses snowcapped volcanoes, bleached-

CHILE'S WILDLIFE

Chile's diverse **animal kingdom** inhabits a landscape of extremes. The country's formidable natural barriers – the immense Pacific, lofty Andes and desolate Atacama – have resulted in an exceptional degree of **endemism**, with a third of the mammals that live here, such as the shy pudú (pygmy deer), found nowhere else on earth.

Four species of **camelid** alone live in the barren altiplano: the shaggy, domesticated **llama** and **alpaca** in the north, and their wild cousins – the Patagonia-dwelling **guanaco** and the delicate **vicuña** with its highly prized fur, restricted to the high altitudes. Chile's biggest cat is the elusive **puma**, another Patagonia resident, while smaller wildcats, from the **colo-colo** to the **guiña**, also stalk these grasslands. Endemic rodents, such as the mountain **vizcacha**, are found in the northern highlands, while several species of **fox** can be spotted in the desert, altiplano and coastal forest.

A haven for birdwatchers, Chile is home to a curious mix of the small and beautiful, such as **hummingbirds** (including the firecrown, endemic to the Juan Fernández islands), while at the other end of the scale is the mighty Andean **condor**, soaring over the mountains. High in the Andes near the Bolivian border, the **Chilean and James's flamingo** gather at remote saltwater lakes, while the long-legged **ñandú** propels itself over the Patagonian steppe. Equally impressive seabirds include the **Humboldt**, **Magellanic** and **king penguins**, while Chile's coastal waters host some spectacular mammals, such as the **blue whale** and several species of **dolphins**.

white salt flats, lakes speckled pink with flamingos, grazing llamas, alpacas and vicuñas, whitewashed churches and Aymara communities. The best points to head for up here are **Parque Nacional Lauca** – the highest of Chile's many national parks, and accessible from the city of Arica – and **Parque Nacional Volcán Isluga**, near the city of **Iquique**.

South of Santiago, the lush **Central Valley**, with its swathes of orchards and vineyards, dotted with stately haciendas, invites you to find Chile's best vintages, including Carmenère, the country's signature grape. Further south, the much-visited **Lake District** is a postcard-perfect landscape of conical volcanoes, iris-blue lakes, rolling pastureland and dense araucaria forests; the adventure sport capitals of **Pucón** and **Puerto Varas** offer a welcome injection of adrenaline, with trekking, volcano climbing, mountain biking, whitewater rafting and horseriding on offer. Just off the southern edge of the Lake District, the **Chiloé** archipelago is famous for its rickety houses on stilts, distinctive wooden churches and rich local mythology.

Back on the mainland, the **Carretera Austral** carves its way through virgin temperate rainforest and past dramatic fjords, two of which are the embarkation points for boat trips out to the sensational **Laguna San Rafael glacier**. Tiny **Futaleufú** is one of the world's top spots for whitewater rafting, the region's pristine rivers are a favourite for fly-fishing and **Parque Nacional Patagonia** gives you the opportunity to hike through gorgeous landscapes.

Beyond the Carretera Austral, cut off by the **Campo de Hielo Sur** (Southern Ice-Field), lies **Patagonia**, a land of bleak windswept plains bordered by the magnificent granite spires of the **Torres del Paine** massif, a magnet for hikers and climbers. Just over the border in Argentina are two of the region's star attractions: the **Fitz Roy Sector** of **Parque Nacional Los Glaciares**, a favourite for trekkers, and, to the south, the awe-inspiring **Glaciar Perito Moreno**. Across the Magellan Strait, **Tierra del Fuego**, also

ADVENTURE SPORTS

If you're looking to experience an adrenaline rush, you've come to the right place. Chile features some of the best **skiing** in the southern hemisphere; the finest resorts lie just 40km from Santiago, in Valle Nevado and Portillo, while the Termas de Chillán ski centre in the middle of the country allows you to combine the longest run in South America with steaming thermal pools for après-ski relaxation.

Spanning the 4320km length of the country, the hugely ambitious **Sendero de Chile** (Chile Trail) consists of numerous sections running through spectacularly varied scenery and skirting some splendid **volcanoes** – which are a defining feature of Chile's geography. In the far north, experienced trekkers can tackle behemoths such as Volcán Parinacota and Volcán Ojos del Salado – the world's tallest active volcano – while the Lake District's Volcán Villarrica and Volcán Osorno make spectacular day climbs for novices. The most challenging vertical ascents are the giant granite towers at the heart of Torres del Paine National Park. If the mountains aren't high enough, climb aboard a hot-air balloon or **paraglide** above Iquique's giant sand dune – a favourite with sandboarders.

Water junkies will undoubtedly be tempted by Chile's veritable playground of rivers and seas. While Río Trancura and Río Petrohue cater to beginners, Río Futaleufú remains Chile's most challenging river for **whitewater rafting** and **kayaking**, while the northern sector of Parque Nacional Pumalín Douglas R. Tompkins, the Gulf of Ancud, the southern fjords and the turbulent Magellan Strait are all prime **sea-kayaking** territory.

AVERAGE MONTHLY TEMPERATURES AND RAINFALL

	Jan	Feb	Mar	Apr	May	Jun	Jul	Aug	Sep	Oct	Nov	Dec
ARICA												
Max/Min (°C)	26/20	27/20	25/19	24/17	22/15	19/14	18/14	18/14	19/15	20/15	22/17	24/18
Max/Min (°F)	79/68	80/68	78/66	75/63	71/60	67/58	65/57	65/58	66/59	69/60	72/62	76/65
rainfall (mm)	1	0	0	0	0	0	0	3	0	0	0	2
PUNTA ARENAS												
Max/Min (°C)	15/7	14/7	12/5	10/4	7/2	5/1	4/1	6/1	8/2	11/3	12/4	14/6
Max/Min (°F)	59/45	57/45	54/41	50/39	45/36	41/34	39/30	43/34	46/36	52/37	54/39	57/43
rainfall (mm)	38	23	33	36	33	41	28	31	23	28	18	36
SANTIAGO												
Max/Min (°C)	29/12	29/11	27/9	23/7	18/5	14/3	15/3	17/4	19/6	22/7	26/9	28/11
Max/Min (°F)	84/54	84/52	81/48	73/45	64/41	57/37	59/37	63/39	66/43	72/45	79/48	82/52
rainfall (mm)	3	3	5	13	64	84	76	56	31	15	8	5

shared with Argentina, sits shivering at the bottom of the world, a remote place of harsh, desolate beauty, the lively city of **Ushuaia** on the Argentinian side giving easy access to the Beagle Channel, while Chile's southernmost town, **Puerto Williams**, is the gateway to one of the continent's toughest treks, the **Dientes de Navarino**.

Finally, there are the country's two Pacific possessions: **Easter Island** – one of the most remote places on earth, famed for its mysterious statues – and the little-visited **Isla Robinson Crusoe**, part of the Juan Fernández Archipelago, with dramatic volcanic peaks and a wealth of endemic wildlife.

When to go

Chile encompasses a wide range of **climates** (and micro climates). Its seasons are the reverse of those in Europe and North America, with, broadly speaking, winter falling in the June to September period and summer between December and March. Given the dramatic variety of its climate and geography, the country can be visited at any time of year, but there is, of course, an **ideal time to visit each region**. Santiago and the surrounding area, northern Chile and the Atacama Desert are year-round destinations, though temperatures tend to be hottest between January and March. Easter Island's climate is mild and warm all year, but February is the time to go to if you want to catch the **island's biggest festival**. If you have your heart set on **skiing** around Santiago or further south, the best time is from July through to September (also the perfect time to go husky sledding in the Lake District), when snow conditions are ideal. The **season for adventure sports** in the Lake District and northern Patagonia tends to be November through to March, when the weather is warmest, though kayaking is possible year-round. Patagonia and Tierra del Fuego are best visited in the warmer months of November to March; from June to September many places are closed and the area is difficult to navigate due to the snow, though it can also be a beautiful time to visit the southern national parks, which you'll have pretty much to yourself.

Author picks

Scaling the breathless heights of its lofty national parks, driving some of Chile's most challenging and isolated roads, and enduring the heat of the desert, Rough Guides' authors have covered every nook and cranny of this implausibly shaped country – from the wilds of southern Isla Navarino to the Atacama Desert in the north. Here are their personal favourites:

Best sunrise Chile has many contenders for this title, but the mesmerizing sight of the sun rising up behind the colossal *moai* of Ahu Tongariki (see page 450) on Easter Island is hard to beat.

Head south Experience life at the very end of the world in the remote, windswept but friendly town of Puerto Williams (see page 424), deep in Tierra del Fuego.

Ghost towns Explore the haunting nitrate towns of Humberstone and Santa Laura (see page 192) – once thriving centres of industry, but long since abandoned to the desert.

Drive that sled Step into the snow-shoes of a musher and bond with your own husky team during a multi-day expedition in the Andes (see page 270).

Put your trip in context Santiago's thought-provoking Museo de la Memoria y los Derechos Humanos (Museum of Memory and Human Rights; see page 70) is dedicated to the many victims of the brutal Pinochet dictatorship.

Stargazing Make the most of clear night skies and see the universe like you've never seen it before with potent telescopes and engaging astronomers at the mountaintop Del Pangue Observatory (see page 143).

Hit the road For the ultimate driving challenge, take on Chile's Carretera Austral (see page 348) through the land of cowboys and pioneers, admiring the waterfalls plunging down from the mountains around you.

Spend the night in a palafito A number of these brightly coloured, stilted fishermen's huts in Chiloé have been converted into idiosyncratic boutique hotels (see page 331).

> Our author recommendations don't end here. We've flagged up our favourite places – a perfectly sited hotel, an atmospheric café, a special restaurant – throughout the Guide, highlighted with the ★ symbol.

HUSKY-SLEDDING IN THE ANDES
MOAI, EASTER ISLAND

25

things not to miss

It's not possible to see everything Chile has to offer in one trip – and we don't suggest you try. What follows is a selective taste of the country's highlights: outstanding scenery, picturesque villages and dramatic wildlife. All highlights are colour-coded by chapter and have a page reference to take you straight into the Guide, where you can find out more.

1 SOUTHERN PATAGONIA
See page 382
Explore the tip of the Americas, where the country splinters into granite towers, glaciers and fjords.

2 WINE TASTING, COLCHAGUA VALLEY
See page 227
Sample some of the best red wines in the world as you taste your way along the "Ruta del Vino".

3 PARQUE NACIONAL LAUCA
See page 209
Behold Chile's highest national park, with altitudes between 4000m and 6000m, herds of llamas, remote geysers and altiplano lakes.

4 VALPARAÍSO
See page 96
This remarkable city sits perched by the sea, draped over a jumble of steep hills around a wide bay.

5 RODEOS AND HUASOS
See page 219
Witness expert horsemanship and a slice of national culture at the rodeos in the Central Valley.

6 PARAGLIDING IN IQUIQUE
See page 187
Soar over Iquique, one of South America's top paragliding destinations, and enjoy incredible views of the giant sand dune of Cerro Dragón far below.

7 PENGUINS
See page 392
Head to the thriving colony at Isla Magdalena for an up-close look at Magellanic penguins.

8 LAGUNA VERDE
See page 157
Massive active volcanoes surround these richly hued waters, making for an almost surreal landscape that's the perfect spot to enjoy the bubbling lakeside hot springs.

9 SURFING IN PICHILEMU
See page 228
Tackle the challenging Punta de Lobos break at Chile's best surfing spot, or learn to surf on beginner-friendly waves in Pichilemu.

10 CHINCHORRO MUMMIES
See page 208
Gape at these prehistoric, remarkably intact mummies, pulled from a 7000-year-old burial site near Arica.

11 HIKING VOLCÁN VILLARRICA
See page 280
Take a guided hike up this active volcano, the focal point of a park with excellent opportunities for trekking and camping.

12 TRACKING PABLO NERUDA
See pages 71, 103 and 110
The Nobel Prize-winning poet is one of Chile's best-known literary exports. Visit any of the three houses he lived in: La Chascona in Santiago, La Sebastiana in Valparaíso, or Isla Negra.

13 CURANTO
See page 320
In Chiloé, tuck into this delicious concoction of shellfish, smoked meat and potato dumplings, traditionally cooked in a pit in the ground.

14 BAHÍA INGLESA
See page 161
Dip into turquoise waters and soak up rays on the sands of this relatively unspoilt beach.

15 TERMAS DE PUYUHUAPI
See page 360
Isolated and largely inaccessible, the resort here is home to steaming hot springs, and is one of the great getaways along the Carretera Austral.

13

14

15

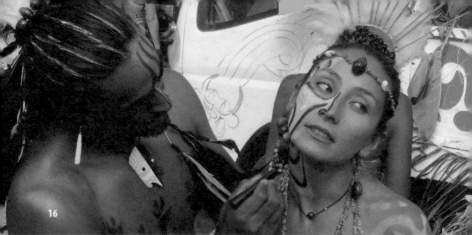

16 TAPATI, EASTER ISLAND
See page 449
Partake in the remote island's liveliest festival, complete with traditional dancing, woodcarving and surfing competitions, all amid the mysterious *moai* stone statues.

17 PARQUE NACIONAL TORRES DEL PAINE
See page 398
Without a doubt, this spectacular park draws most visitors to southern Chile, and it does not disappoint even after all the photos and hype.

18 BOAT TRIP ALONG THE BEAGLE CHANNEL
See page 434
If you make it all the way down to Tierra del Fuego, a trip through the Channel, spotting sea lions, penguins and whales, is a must.

19 STARGAZING
See pages 136 and 143
Chile's northern skies are the most transparent in the southern hemisphere, as testified by the many international observatories stationed here. Head to the Elqui Valley's Cerro Mamalluca observatory to play astronomer and gaze up at the stars.

20 VALLE DE LA LUNA
See page 183
Trek across this aptly named moonscape, just south of San Pedro de Atacama.

17

18

19

20

21

22

23

21 LAPIS LAZULI
See page 50
For a lovely Chilean souvenir, pick up jewellery made from lapis, the cool blue stone mined throughout the country and sold in local crafts markets.

22 CHURCHES OF CHILOÉ
See page 327
The archipelago's beautiful wooden churches rise over the heart of almost every small village.

23 PUERTO WILLIAMS
See page 424
Spend time in the most southerly town on earth, the jumping off point for the dramatic Dientes del Navarino hike.

24 SAN RAFAEL GLACIER
See page 367
Embark on an exhilarating boat ride alongside this stunning ice formation.

25 PISCO ELQUI
See page 145
Take a tour of a distillery, followed by a taste of a pisco sour, Chile's national cocktail.

Itineraries

The following itineraries span the entire length of this incredibly varied country, taking you from the icy fjords and snow-tipped mountains of the south to the fertile wine-growing valleys in the centre and parched desert and highland lagoons of the north. Given the vast distances involved, you may not be able to cover every highlight, but even picking a few from the itineraries below will give you a thrilling window onto Chile's geographical and cultural wonders.

THE GRAND TOUR

Allow at least three weeks if you wish to cover Chile from top to bottom; flying between some of the destinations will allow you to cover vast distances quickly.

❶ Atacama Desert Visit erupting geysers, crinkly salt plains and emerald lakes in the morning, and deep, mystical valleys by sunset in the driest desert on earth. See page 166

❷ Elqui Valley/stargazing near Vicuña Take advantage of some of the clearest skies in Chile and look at the universe through some of the world's most powerful telescopes. See page 140

❸ Santiago Chile's rapidly evolving capital boasts a vibrant eating out and nightlife scene, several fascinating museums, numerous cultural pursuits, and excellent ski resorts nearby. See page 56

❹ Easter Island Gazing down into the giant crater of the extinct Rano Kau volcano and visiting the magical *moai* at Ahu Tongariki and Rano Raraku truly are once-in-a-lifetime experiences. See page 440

❺ Valparaíso Valparaíso is a tangle of colourful houses, cobbled streets and bohemian hangouts spread across a series of undulating hills overlooking the Pacific. See page 96

❻ Central Valley wineries Visit the numerous traditional bodegas around Curicó and Santa Cruz, and try some of Chile's finest vintages. See pages 227 and 231

❼ Chiloé Sample one of the country's most memorable dishes, admire the *palafitos* (traditional fishermen's houses on stilts) or hike through temperate rainforest on Chile's mist- and myth-shrouded island. See page 314

❽ Parque Nacional Torres del Paine Hike the trails of Chile's most popular – and spectacular – national park or climb the granite towers that give the park its name. See page 398

NATURAL WONDERS

Since Chile's varied landscapes span the entire country, allow at least three weeks for this ambitious – and rewarding – trip.

❶ Parque Nacional Lauca Admire the volcanoes, high-altitude lagoons dotted with flamingos and grazing llamas and vicuñas in Chile's highest national park. See page 209

❷ Isla Robinson Crusoe With its endemic flora and fauna, extensive underwater attractions and demonic peaks, Isla Robinson Crusoe still has the edge-of-the-world castaway feel that inspired Daniel Defoe's famous book. See page 457

❸ Lake District hot springs Relax in the many thermal springs that dot the region – you can choose from rustic soaking pools or resort-style complexes with hotels and excellent restaurants. See page 271

❹ A boat trip around the San Rafael glacier Head out to the ice-filled lagoon that is Chile's fastest shrinking glacier and get close to the ice in a speedboat. See page 367

❺ Tierra del Fuego Explore the deserted roads running through steppe and dotted with guanacos and rheas, or fish in the pristine lakes and rivers of the most remote region in Chile (and Argentina). See page 416

❻ Beagle Channel Take a boat trip in the country's southernmost reaches, in search of penguins, sea lions and the occasional pod of Commerson's dolphins. See page 434

❼ Cape Horn Fly over some of the world's most treacherous waters or brave a sailing trip to Chile's southernmost group of weather-beaten islands. See page 428

ADVENTURE CHILE

With the exception of the treks, all the activities on this itinerary are doable as day-trips, so a couple of weeks should be sufficient.

❶ Paragliding/surfing in Iquique Ilquique's climate makes it one of the best places in the world to soar the skies or dance through waves. See pages 187 and 188

❷ Adrenaline sports around Pucón The Lake District's adventure capital offers skydiving, mountain biking, snowboarding and husky sledding. See page 280

❸ Climbing Volcán Osorno Tackle the Lake District's most perfect conical peak in a full-day ascent from Lago Llanquihue. See page 300

❹ Kayaking in Parque Nacional Pumalín Douglas R. Tompkins Explore the maze of tiny islands in the isolated fjords of this new national park. See page 350

❺ Whitewater rafting on Río Futaleufú Ride the waves of the most challenging river in Chile, navigating such rapids as the "Throne Room" and "Inferno". See page 356

❻ Trekking the Dientes de Navarino Hike one of South America's toughest treks at the very end of the world. See page 425

ROAD SIGN, ALTIPLANO

Basics

Getting there

Most people fly into Chile, arriving at Santiago's modern international airport, though some travel by land from neighbouring countries, and a handful arrive by sea.

Airfares depend on the **season**. You'll generally pay the most in the December–February and June–August periods, the southern and northern hemisphere's summer holiday months, respectively. Fares drop slightly during the "shoulder" months – March and November – and you'll normally get the best prices during the low seasons: April, May, September and October.

Note that if you plan to visit **Easter Island**, your flight there from Santiago is likely to be cheaper if bought in conjunction with a LATAM international flight (see below).

Flights from the US and Canada

American Airlines (W aa.com), Delta (W delta.com) and LATAM (W latam.com) offer **non-stop flights** to Santiago from US airports such as **Miami**, **Dallas-Fort Worth** and **Atlanta**. It is also possible to travel via other Latin American countries such as Colombia, Peru and Brazil. Typical **fares** are around US$950–1600 in the high season.

Air Canada (W aircanada.com) – and sometimes LATAM – has flights from Toronto to Santiago; typical high-season fares are around C$1450–1800. It is, however, often cheaper to fly via the US.

Flights from the UK and Ireland

British Airways (W britishairways.com) has direct flights from **London** to Santiago, but it's often cheaper to travel via a **European**, **Latin American** or **US city**; LATAM (W latam.com), Iberia (W iberia.com) and Air France (W airfrance.com) are among the options. High-season fares cost £750–1000. Unless you're flying with BA, pay attention to the route, as well as the price; even the shortest and most convenient indirect flights via Madrid or Buenos Aires entail a total travelling time of more than sixteen hours. Flying via the US takes longer still (though is often cheaper).

Round-the-world flights

If Chile is part of a longer journey, consider buying a **round-the-world** (RTW) ticket. An "off-the-shelf" itinerary including Santiago costs around £1300–1900. Alternatively, a travel agent can custom-make a RTW ticket for you, though this is more expensive. Trailfinders (W trailfinders.com), STA Travel (W statravel.com) and Round The World Flights (W roundtheworldflights.com) sell RTW tickets.

Flights from Australia, New Zealand and South Africa

Qantas (W qantas.com) and LATAM (W latam.com) offer direct flights from **Sydney** and **Auckland** to Santiago; cheaper indirect flights are also available. In the high season, expect to pay around Aus$2500–3300 or NZ$2300–3500.

South African Airways (W flysaa.com) and LATAM (W latam.com) have flights from **Johannesburg** to Santiago via São Paulo, Brazil. Expect to pay around ZAR14,000–17,000.

Air passes

If you plan to visit several South American destinations, **air passes** are another option,. The **Visit South America** pass (W oneworld.com) offered by the Oneworld alliance (which includes LATAM, British Airways, Iberia, Qantas and American Airlines) allows you to plan your own itinerary, with set flight prices depending on the distance travelled between (or within) countries; you must use a minimum of three flights. The **LATAM Pass** is similar. However, you may find that promotional fares online or within Chile are a better option than either.

RECIPROCITY CHARGE

Chile levies a **reciprocity charge** (aka an **arrival tax**), priced in US dollars, for citizens from the **US** (US$131), **Canada** (US$132), **Australia** (US$61), **Mexico** (US$23) and **Albania** (US$30) in reciprocation for similar taxes levied on Chilean citizens arriving in these countries. There has been talk of abolishing these fees – check with your Chilean consulate for the latest. For US and Canadian citizens, the payment is valid for the lifetime of the passport; for the other nationalities, it lasts for ninety days (regardless of how many times you cross the border during this period).

A BETTER KIND OF TRAVEL

At Rough Guides we are passionately committed to travel. We believe it helps us understand the world we live in and the people we share it with – and of course tourism is vital to many developing economies. But the scale of modern tourism has also damaged some places irreparably, and climate change is accelerated by most forms of transport, especially flying. All Rough Guides' flights are carbon-offset.

Buses from neighbouring countries

Several roads **connect Chile with Argentina** – from Mendoza to Santiago or Valparaíso via Los Andes; from Bariloche to Osorno and Puerto Montt, and from Río Gallegos to Puntas Arenas – all of which are served by buses. There are other routes, one of the most dramatic being from San Juan to La Serena, which goes leads over the mountains and through the Elqui Valley; the route only opens in the warmer months between October/November and April. All Andean routes, even the road from Mendoza, can be blocked by snow from April onwards. A decent road and regular buses link Peru to Chile from Tacna through to Arica. You can also catch buses from La Paz in Bolivia to Arica; this takes you through the stunning scenery of the Lauca National Park (see page 209). But if you're doing the journey in reverse beware: it means travelling from sea level up to 4500m in just a few hours – take plenty of water and expect to feel pretty uncomfortable. Many travellers cross from Uyuni in Bolivia to San Pedro de Atacama via a salt flats tour.

Trains from neighbouring countries

Chile has **international rail links** between Arica and Tacna in Peru (the line re-opened in 2016) and between Uyuni in Bolivia and Calama. Plans to construct a railway line between Arica and La Paz in Bolivia have been mooted.

AGENTS AND OPERATORS

Adventure Associates Australia ☏ 02 6355 2022, ⓦ adventureassociates.com. Established operator with tours and cruises to Antarctica, Chile and South America as a whole.

Anglatin Travel US ☏ 1 800 918 8580, ⓦ anglatin.com. A range of tours focusing on topics such as rural life, birdwatching, ancient cultures and even llamas.

Chimu Adventures UK ☏ 020 7403 8265, ⓦ chimuadventures.com. Offers off-the-rack and tailor-made itineraries throughout Chile (and beyond), plus Patagonia, Tierra del Fuego and Antarctic cruises.

Dragoman UK ☏ 01728 861 133, ⓦ dragoman.com. Overland journeys in purpose-built vehicles; shorter camping and hotel-based safaris, too.

Exodus UK ☏ 0845 240 5550, ⓦ exodus.co.uk. Adventure and activity tour operator taking small groups for specialist programmes including hiking, biking, overland jaunts and cultural trips.

Explore UK ☏ 1252 883616, ⓦ explore.co.uk. Small-group tours, treks, expeditions and safaris throughout Chile, including Easter Island.

Intrepid Travel UK ☏ 0808 274 5111, ⓦ intrepidtravel.com. Small-group tours with the emphasis on cross-cultural contact and low-impact tourism.

Journey Latin America UK ☏ 020 8747 8315, ⓦ journeylatinamerica.co.uk. Long-established Latin America specialists, with a huge choice of trips (package and tailor-made) across Chile, plus many multi-country tours.

Mountain Travel Sobek US ☏ 1 888 831 7526, ⓦ mtsobek.com. Trips include the "On the Smuggler's Trail in Patagonia" package, which features hiking and camping.

REI Adventures US ☏ 1 800 622 2236, ⓦ rei.com/adventures. Climbing, cycling, hiking, cruising, kayaking and multi-sport tours.

Ski.com ☏ 1 800 908 5000, ⓦ ski.com. Package skiing trips to Portillo, Valle Nevado and beyond.

South America Travel Centre Australia ☏ 03 9642 5353, ⓦ southamericatravelcentre.com.au. Large selection of tours and accommodation packages throughout the continent.

Tucan Travel UK ☏ 0800 804 8435, ⓦ tucantravel.com. Backpacker/budget group trips in Chile and neighbouring countries.

Wilderness Travel US ☏ 1 800 368 2794, ⓦ wildernesstravel.com. Specialists in hiking, cultural and wildlife adventures.

Wildlife Worldwide UK ☏ 020 8667 9158, ⓦ wildlifeworldwide.com. Customized trips for wildlife and wilderness enthusiasts.

World Expeditions Australia ☏ 02 8270 8400, ⓦ worldexpeditions.com.au, New Zealand ☏ 09 368 4161, ⓦ worldexpeditions.co.nz. A selection of adventure holidays.

Visas and red tape

Most foreign visitors to Chile do not need a **visa**. The exceptions are citizens of Cuba, Russia, Middle Eastern countries (except Israel) and African counties (except South Africa). Some nationalities also have to pay an arrival tax (see page 25).

Visitors of all nationalities are issued with a ninety-day **tourist entry card** (*Tarjeta de Turismo*) on arrival, which can be extended once for an additional ninety days. It will be checked by the

International Police at the airport or border post when you leave Chile – if it's expired you won't be allowed to leave the country until you've paid the appropriate fine at the nearest *Intendencia* (up to US$100). If this happens when you're trying to fly out of the international airport in Santiago, you'll have to go back downtown to Moneda 1342 (Mon–Fri 9am–1pm; ☎ 2 2672 5320).

If you lose your tourist card, ask for a duplicate immediately, either from the Fronteras department of the Policía Internacional, General Borgoño 1052, Santiago (☎ 2 2698 2211) or from the Extranjero's department of the Intendencia in any provincial capital. There's no charge for replacing lost or stolen cards.

If you want to **extend** your tourist card, you can either pay US$100 at the Intendencia of Santiago or any provincial capital, or you can simply leave the country and re-enter, getting a brand-new ninety-day *Tarjeta de Turismo* for free. Note that **under-18s** travelling to Chile without parents need written parental consent authorized by the Chilean Embassy, and that minors travelling to Chile with just one parent need the written, authorized consent of the absent parent.

CHILEAN EMBASSIES ABROAD

Australia 10 Culgoa Circuit, O'Malley, Canberra ACT 2606 ☎ 02 6286 2098, ⓦ chileabroad.gov.cl/australia/.

Canada 50 O'Connor St, suite 1413, Ottawa, ON K1P 6L2 ☎ 613 235 4402, ⓦ www.congechiletoronto.com.

New Zealand 19 Bolton St, Wellington ☎ 04 471 6270, ⓦ chileabroad.gov.cl/nueva-zelanda/.

South Africa 169 Garsfontein Rd Ashlea, Delmondo Office Park Block C, Gardens, Pretoria ☎ 012 460 1676, ⓦ chileabroad.gov. cl/sudafrica/.

UK 12 Devonshire St, London, W1N 2DS ☎ 020 7580 1023, ⓦ chileabroad.gov.cl/reino-unido/.

US 1732 Massachusetts Ave NW, Washington, DC 20036 ☎ 202 785 1746, ⓦ chileabroad.gov.cl/estados-unidos/en.

Getting around

Travelling in Chile is easy, comfortable and, compared with Europe or North America, relatively good value. Most Chileans travel by bus, and it's such a reliable, affordable option that you'll probably do likewise. However, internal flights are handy for covering long distances in a hurry. The country has a good road network, and driving is a quick, relatively stress-free way of getting around. Chile's rail network has fallen into decline and only limited services are available. South of Puerto Montt, ferry services provide a slow but scenic way of travelling.

By plane

Chile is a country of almost unimaginable distances (it's more than 5000km by road from Arica to Punta Arenas), making **flying** by far the quickest and most convenient way to take in both its northern and southern regions in a single trip. Fares are quite high, though you can find good promotions from time to time.

The leading airline is **LATAM** (ⓦ latam.com), which besides offering the widest choice of domestic flights, is Chile's principal long-haul carrier and the only one with flights to Easter Island. **Sky Airline** (ⓦ skyairline.com) has more limited routings but usually lower prices.

Air taxis and regional airlines such as DAP (ⓦ dapairline.com) operate services to smaller destinations between Puerto Montt and Puerto Williams, but they are more susceptible to weather delays and may not fly without a minimum number of passengers (usually six). There are also flights from Santiago to Isla Robinson Crusoe (see page 460).

By bus

Chile's **long-distance buses** offer an excellent service, far better than their European or North American counterparts – thanks mainly to the enormous amount of legroom, frequent departures and flexible itineraries. Facilities depend less on individual companies than on the class of bus you travel on, with prices rising according to comfort level. A **pullman** (not to be confused with the large company of the same name) or **clásico** contains standard semi-reclining seats; a **semicama** has seats with twice the amount of legroom that recline a good deal more; and a **salon cama**, at the top of the luxury range, has wide seats (just three to a row) that recline to an almost horizontal position à la first class on a plane. All buses have toilets. Many include meals or snacks, while others stop at restaurants where set meals might be included in the ticket price. DVDs, piped music and bingo games are also common. Check out the locations of the screens first and find yourself a seat that suits you.

Thanks to the intense competition and price wars waged between the multitude of bus companies,

fares are low. As a rule of thumb, reckon on around CH$1500–2000 per hour travelled on standard intercity buses; the most luxurious services cost at least four times that. It always pays to compare fares offered by the different companies serving your destination, as you'll almost certainly find a special deal. This price comparison is easily done at the central terminal used by long-distance buses in most cities, where you'll find separate booking offices for each company (though Tur Bus and Pullman Bus, the two largest companies, often have their own separate terminals). Some towns, however, don't have a **central terminal**, in which case buses leave from their company offices.

Buy your ticket at least a few hours in advance, preferably the day before travelling, especially if you plan to travel on a Friday; book further in advance if you plan to travel over public holidays. The bigger companies allow you to book via their websites, though don't always accept foreign cards; there are also **online booking services** such as Ⓦ recorrido. cl and Ⓦ voyhoy.cl.

An added advantage of buying ahead is that you'll be able to choose a seat away from the toilets, either by the aisle or window and, more importantly, the side of the bus you sit on. Even with a/c, seats on the sunny side can get extremely hot. There is little reason to buy a round-trip ticket unless you are travelling in peak season.

When it comes to **boarding**, make sure that the departure time on your ticket corresponds exactly to the time indicated on the little clock on the bus's front window, as your ticket is valid only on the bus it was booked for. Your luggage will be safely stored in lockers under the bus and the conductor will issue you a numbered stub for each article.

If you're travelling north of Santiago on a long-distance route, or crossing an international border, the bus and all luggage will be searched by Ministry of Agriculture officials at checkpoints, and all sandwiches, fresh fruit and vegetables will be destroyed.

By local bus, colectivo and taxi

Local buses, often called *micros*, connect city centres with suburbs and nearby villages. These buses are often packed, and travelling with a large rucksack can be difficult. The main points of the route and final destination are displayed on the inside of the front window, but it always helps to carry a street map and be able to point to your intended destination. Buses that leave the city for the countryside normally depart from their own *terminal rural*, usually close to the Mercado Municipal (market building).

Colectivos, shared taxis operating along a set route with fixed fares, are normally only slightly more expensive than local buses. Most look like regular taxis (apart from being all black, not black and yellow) and have their route or final destination marked on a roof-board, but in some cities *colectivos* are bright yellow cars, often without a roof-board.

Taxis are normally black with a yellow roof. Foreigners are often overcharged, so check the meter has been turned on before you start a journey and get an estimate for the fare, if possible in Spanish. Fares should be shown on the windscreen.

By car

While Chile's towns and cities are linked by plenty of buses, most visitors are here for the country's wilderness areas, which are often difficult, and sometimes impossible, to reach on public transport. Many remote attractions are visited by tour companies, but for more independence, your best bet is to **rent a car**. To do this, you need to be at least 21 years old and have a major credit card so you can leave a blank voucher as a guarantee. You're allowed to use your national driver's licence, but you're strongly advised to bring, in addition, an **international licence**. Chile's *carabineros* (police officers), who frequently stop drivers to check their documents, are often suspicious of unfamiliar foreign licences and are always happier when dealing with international ones. Traffic regulations are rarely enforced, except for speeding on the highways. The **speed limit** is 50km/h or less in urban areas and 100km/h on highways; radar speed traps are commonplace. If an oncoming vehicle flashes its headlights, you're being warned about *carabineros* lurking ahead. If you do get pulled over, exercise the utmost courtesy and patience, and under no circumstances do or say anything that could possibly be interpreted as bribery.

Rental outlets and costs

Several international car rental companies have offices throughout Chile. In addition to these, you'll find an abundance of local outlets which are often, but by no means always, less expensive than the international firms. Rates can vary significantly, so it's worth checking as many companies as possible online. **Basic saloon cars** go from around US$50 per day. Make sure the quoted price includes IVA (the nineteen percent Chilean value added tax), insurance and unlimited mileage. Your

ADDRESSES

Addresses in Chile are nearly always written with just the street name (and often just the surname, if the street is named after a person) followed by the number; for example, Prat 135. In the case of avenues, however, the address usually starts with the word *avenida*, eg Avenida 21 de Mayo 553. Buildings without a street number are suffixed by s/n, short for *sin número* ("without a number").

rental contract will almost certainly be in (legal and convoluted) Spanish – get the company to take you through it. In most cases your liability, in the event of an accident, is around the US$500 mark; costs over this amount will be covered in total by the company.

Driving in towns

Most towns are laid out on a grid plan, which makes navigation pretty easy. However, the country is obsessed with **one-way traffic** systems, and many streets, even in the smallest towns, are one-way only, the direction of traffic alternating with each successive street. The direction is usually indicated by a white arrow above the street name on each corner; if in doubt, look at the direction of the parked cars. **Parking** is normally allowed on most downtown streets (but on one side only), and around the central square. You'll invariably be guided into a space by a wildly gesticulating *cuidador de autos* – a boy or young man who will offer to look after your car in return for a tip. In larger towns there's a small half-hourly charge for parking on the street, administered by eagle-eyed traffic wardens who slip tickets under your wipers every thirty minutes then pounce on you to collect your money before you leave (a small tip is expected, too). If you can't find a space, look out for large *"estacionamiento"* signs, which indicate private car parks.

Driving on highways

The **Panamerican** highway, which runs through Chile from the Peruvian border to the southern tip of Chiloé, is known alternately as Ruta 5, la *Panamericana*, or *el longitudinal*, with *sur* (south) or *norte* (north) often added on to indicate which side of Santiago it's on. Thanks to a multi-billion-dollar modernization project, it is now quickly becoming a divided highway, with two lanes in each direction and a toll booth every 30km. This is undoubtedly a major improvement over most single-lane highways in Chile, which are prone to head-on collisions involving buses and trucks.

Backcountry and altiplano driving

You'll probably find that many places you want to get to are reached by dirt road, for which it's essential to rent a suitable vehicle, namely a **jeep** or **pick-up truck**. On regular dirt roads you rarely need a 4WD vehicle. For **altiplano driving**, however, you should pay extra to have 4WD (with the sturdiest tyres and highest clearance), as you can come across some dreadful roads, hundreds of kilometres from the nearest town. Make sure, too, that you take two spare tyres, not one, and that you always carry a funnel or tube for siphoning, and more than enough petrol. Also pick up several five-litre water jugs – it may be necessary for either the passengers or the engine at some point. It can be difficult to navigate in the *altiplano*, with so much open space and so few landmarks – if you don't have a GPS enabled device, make a careful note of your kilometre reading as you go along, so you can chart your progress over long roads with few markers. A compass is also helpful. Despite this tone of caution, it should be emphasized that *altiplano* driving is among the most rewarding adventures that Chile offers.

Finally, a general point on **punctures**. This is such a common occurrence in Chile that even the smallest towns have special workshops (bearing signs with a tyre painted white) where they are quickly and cheaply repaired.

Hitching

While we absolutely do not recommend **hitching** as a safe way of getting about, there's no denying that it's widely practised by Chileans themselves. In the summer it seems as though all the students in Chile are sitting beside the road with their thumb out, and in rural areas it's not uncommon for entire families to hitch a lift whenever they need to get into town.

By ferry

South of Puerto Montt, a network of **ferries** operates through the fjords, inlets and channels of Chile's far south, providing a more scenic and romantic alternative to flights and long-distance buses. Two ferries in particular are very popular with tourists: from Puerto Montt to Chacabuco and the San Rafael glacier; and between Puerto Montt and Puerto Natales. There are also ferry links with Quellón on Chiloé, and with Chaitén, on the Carretera Austral, plus a number of shorter routes forming a bridge along various points of the Carretera Austral (see page 348). In addition, there is a ferry across Lago Todos Los Santos, connecting Petrohué with Peulla, near the Argentine border (see page 296).

MAIN FERRY ROUTES

Petrohué–Peulla, across Lago Todos Los Santos Five hours; daily crossings (year-round) with Andina del Sud (W andinadelsud.com). See page 296.

Puerto Montt–Chacabuco 24 hours; one sailing per week with Navimag (year-round; W navimag.com) and TransMarChilay (year-round; W www.transmarchilay.cl). See pages 309 and 366.

Puerto Montt–Chacabuco–Laguna San Rafael Five days, four nights (returning to Puerto Montt); one sailing per week with Navimag (year-round) and two to four with TransMarChilay (year-round). See pages 309 and 366.

Puerto Montt–Chaitén Ten hours; one sailing per week with Navimag (Jan & Feb); three to four per week with TransMarChilay (year-round). See pages 309 and 354.

Puerto Montt–Puerto Natales Four days, three nights; one sailing per week with Navimag (year-round). See pages 309 and 395.

Quellón–Chaitén Five hours; weekly sailings with Naviera Austral (W navieraaustral.cl; Jan & Feb). See pages 338 and 354.

By bike

Travelling by **bike** can be incredibly rewarding. Your time is your own and you won't find yourself stuck to rigid timetables or restricted to visiting destinations only served by public buses.

Supplies in Chile can be unreliable, so bring as much as you can from home. A good, sturdy mountain bike is a must, along with the usual locks and chains, strong racks, repair kit, lights, waterproof panniers, jackets and over-trousers. All equipment and clothes should be packed in plastic to protect from dust and moisture. Your major problem will be getting hold of **spares** when you need them – bike shops tend to be found only in Santiago and a few major cities. When on the road, bear in mind that long stretches are bereft of accommodation options and even the most basic services, so you must be completely self-sufficient and prepared for a long wait if you require assistance. Some bus companies will not transport bicycles unless you wrap frame and wheels separately in cardboard. When you enter the country, you may well find that customs officials enter details of your bicycle in your passport to prevent you from selling it.

The main dangers when cycling on Chile's roads are drivers. Make sure you stand out in the traffic by wearing bright colours, good reflective gear and lights when the visibility is poor. It goes without saying that you should **wear a helmet**; it's actually illegal to ride in Chile without one. Before you set off get your hands on one of the many good guidebooks available on long-distance cycling. Alternately, British cyclists can contact the **Cyclists Touring Club** in the UK (T 01483 238301, W cyclinguk.org).

By train

Chile once possessed a huge network of **railways**, thanks largely to the nitrate boom. Now the nitrate days are over, no national railway lines operate north of Santiago, and what lines are left south of the capital are unable to compete with the speed, prices and punctuality offered by buses.

Accommodation

On the whole, the standard of accommodation in Chile is reasonable, though many visitors feel prices are high for what they get, especially in the mid- and top-range brackets.

Bottom-end accommodation starts at around CH$10,000 (US$16) for a dorm room, around CH$22,000 (US$36) for a double. You'll have to pay from around CH$35,000 (US$57) for a double or twin with a private bathroom in a decent **mid-range** hotel, and from CH$55,000 (US$90) for a smarter hotel. There's usually a wide choice in the major tourist centres and the cities on the Panamericana, but in more remote areas you'll invariably have to make do with basic *hospedajes* (modest rooms, often in family homes). Most places include **breakfast** in their rates.

The price of accommodation often increases dramatically in **high season** – January, February and mid-September – particularly in seaside resorts, where it can be as much as double or even triple. Outside high season it's always worth trying to negotiate a discount, especially in person. A simple *"¿tiene algo un poco mas económico?"* ("do you have anything a little cheaper?") or *"¿me puede dar un descuento?"* ("could you give me a discount?") will often get you a lower price on the spot. It's rarely necessary to make reservations, unless you've got your heart set on a particular hotel, in which case it can be a good idea to phone a few days in advance – especially at weekends, even more so if it's within striking distance of Santiago. Note that using a website like Booking.com sometimes secures you a cheaper deal than if you book directly.

ACCOMMODATION PRICES

Except where stated, the hotel prices we quote throughout the Guide are for the cheapest **double room** in high season and include breakfast. At the lower end of the scale, **single travellers** can expect to pay half this rate, but mid- and upper-range hotels usually charge the same for a single as for a double. A number of hotels, particularly top-end establishments, quote their rates in **US dollars**; where this is so, we follow the hotel's pricing system. (Bear in mind that even if a hotel quotes its rates in CH$ only, it is always worth asking if you can pay in US dollars, as that should exempt you from the 19 percent IVA; see below). All **Argentinian** accommodation is likewise quoted in US dollars due to the volatility of the peso. In **hostels**, dorm rates are quoted per person and private room rates are based on two people sharing, unless stated otherwise; similarly, rates for **campsites** are quoted per person, rather than per pitch, unless otherwise stated.

Note that the price of accommodation in many tourist centres drops significantly outside January and February.

Room rates are supposed to be quoted inclusive of **IVA** (a Chilean goods and services tax of nineteen percent), but you should always check beforehand (¿está incluido el iva?). Increasing numbers of budget and many mid- and most upper-range hotels give you the opportunity to pay for your accommodation in **US dollars** (sometimes this can be done by credit/debit card as well as cash), which exempts you from paying IVA. However, not all hotels will offer this discount as a matter of course – it is always worth asking. Often, though, if they can't take off IVA, they'll offer you a discount of ten percent if you pay cash.

In 2013 the Chilean government launched a **sustainable tourism** certification programme for hotels; for a list of establishments that have met the criteria visit ⓦchilesustentable.travel.

Hotels

Chilean hotels are given a one- to five-star **rating** by Sernatur (the national tourist board), but this only reflects facilities and not standards, which vary widely. In practice, then, a three-star hotel could be far more attractive and comfortable than a four-star and even a five-star hotel; the only way to tell is to go and have a look, as even the room rates aren't a reliable indication of quality.

Generally, **mid-range hotels** fall into two main categories: large, old houses with spacious, but sometimes tired, rooms; and modern, purpose-built hotels, usually with smaller rooms, no common areas and better facilities. You'll always get a private bathroom with a shower (rarely a bath), hot water and towels, and generally TV. As the price creeps up there's usually an improvement in decor and more space, and at the upper end you can expect room service, a mini-bar (frigobar), a safe, a hotel restaurant, private parking and sometimes a swimming pool. The standards of top-end **hotels** can still vary quite dramatically, however – ranging from stylish boutique hotels or charming haciendas to grim, impersonal monoliths.

Motels, incidentally, are usually not economical roadside hotels, but places where couples go to have sex (rooms are generally rented for three-hour periods).

Residenciales

Residenciales are the most widely available, and widely used, accommodation option. As with hotels, standards can vary enormously, but in general they offer simple, modestly furnished rooms, usually off a corridor in the main building, or else in a row arranged around the backyard or patio. They usually

ACCOMMODATION ALTERNATIVES

Airbnb (ⓦairbnb.com) hasn't quite cornered the market when it comes to finding alternatives to standard hotel and hostel accommodation – the following websites are also worth checking out:
CouchSurfing ⓦcouchsurfing.org.
Homestay.com ⓦhomestay.com.
Vacation Rentals by Owner ⓦvrbo.com.

5 GREAT PLACES TO STAY

Explora Rapa Nui Easter Island. See page 447.

Hotel Alaia Near Pichilemu. See page 229.

Hotel Ilaia Punta Arenas. See page 390.

Tierra Atacama San Pedro de Atacama. See page 180.

Tierra Chiloé Chiloé. See page 326.

contain little more than a bed, a rail for hanging clothes and a bedside table and lamp, though some provide additional furniture, and a few more comforts such as a TV. Most, but not all, have shared bathrooms.

Where places differ is in the upkeep or "freshness" of the rooms: some are dank and damp, others have good bed linen, walls that are painted every summer, and a clean, swept, feel to them. Some of the slightly more expensive *residenciales* are very pleasant, particularly the large, nineteenth-century houses. While some *residenciales* cater exclusively to tourists, many, especially in the mining towns of the north, fill mainly with workmen.

Hospedajes and casas de familia

The distinction between a *residencial* and a *hospedaje* or *casa de familia* is often blurred. On the whole, the term **hospedaje** implies something rather modest, along the lines of the cheaper *residenciales*, while a **casa de familia** (or *casa familiar*) offers, as you'd expect, rooms inside a family home. The relationship between the guest and the owner is nevertheless no different from that in a *residencial. Casas de familia* don't normally have a sign at the door, and if they do it usually just says "*Alojamiento*" ("lodging"); more commonly, members of the family might meet tourists at the bus stations. These places are perfectly safe and you shouldn't worry about checking them out. Sometimes you'll find details of *casas de familia* at tourist offices as well.

Cabañas

Cabañas are very popular in Chile, found in tourist spots up and down the country, particularly by the coast. They are basically holiday chalets geared towards families, and usually come with a kitchen, sitting/dining area, one double bedroom and a second bedroom with bunks. They range from the very rustic to the distinctly grand, complete with

daily maid service. Note that the price is often the same for two people as it is for four: i.e. charged by cabin rather than per person. That said, as they're used predominantly by Chileans, their popularity tends to be limited to January, February and sunny weekends; outside these times demand is so low that you can normally get a very good discount. Many *cabañas* are in superb locations, right by the ocean, and it can be wonderfully relaxing to self-cater for a few days in the off-season.

Refugios

Many of the ranger stations in the national parks have a limited number of bunk beds available for tourists, at a charge from around CH$5000 (US$8) per person. Known as **refugios**, these places are very rustic – often a small, wooden hut – but they usually have toilets, hot running water, clean sheets and woollen blankets. Some of them, such as those at the Salar de Surire and Lago Chungará, are in stunning locations. Most *refugios* are open year-round, but if you're travelling in winter or other extreme weather conditions it's best to check with the regional forestry (Conaf) office in advance. While you're there, you can reserve beds in the *refugio*. This is highly advisable if you're relying solely on the *refugio* for accommodation, but if you're travelling with a tent as a backup, it's not really necessary to book ahead.

Hostels

The range and quality of Chile's **hostels** has increased significantly in recent years, and it's relatively rare to find a town or tourist destination without one. Some are pretty smart, and a few even style themselves as "boutique hostels". In addition to dorms, most also have a selection of private rooms. Hostels also tend to be among the best informal networks for information about local guides and excursions. Many are affiliated to Hostelling International (⚫ hihostels. com), and offer discounts for members.

Camping

There are plenty of opportunities for **camping** in Chile, though it's not always the cheapest way to sleep. If you plan to do a lot of it, equip yourself with the annual Spanish-language guide, **Turistel Rutero Camping**, which has maps, prices and information. Official campsites range from plots of land with minimal facilities to swanky grounds with hot showers and private barbecue grills. The latter, often part of holiday complexes in seaside resorts, can be very expensive, and are usually only open between December and March.

It's also possible to **camp wild** in the countryside, but you'll really need your own transport. Most national parks don't allow camping outside designated areas. Instead they tend to have either rustic camping areas administered by Conaf (particularly in northern Chile), costing from around CH$5000 (US$8) per tent, or else smart, more expensive sites run by *concesionarios* (more common in the south) that charge around CH$20,000 (US$33) or more for two to four people. As for beaches, some turn into informal, spontaneously erected campsites in summer; on others, camping is strictly forbidden.

If you do end up camping wild on the beach or in the countryside, bury or pack up your excrement, and take all refuse with you when you leave. Note that butane gas and sometimes Camping Gaz are available in hardware shops in most towns and cities. If your stove takes white gas, you need to buy *bencina blanca*, which you'll find either in hardware stores or, more commonly, in pharmacies.

For details of **camping in Chile's national parks**, see page 43.

Food and drink

Chile boasts a vast array of quality raw produce, but many restaurants lack imagination, offering similar limited menus. That's not to say, however, that you can't eat well here, and the fish and seafood, in particular, are superb. There are also various traditional dishes, often called comida típica or comida criolla, still served in old-fashioned restaurants known as picadas. Furthermore, most cities have increasing numbers of smarter restaurants, with Santiago and Valparaíso particularly excelling.

On the whole, eating out tends to be relatively **good value**. In local restaurants you can expect to pay around CH$4000–7000 for a main course. If you're aiming to keep costs way down, rather than resort to the innumerable **fast-food outlets**, you could head for the **municipal markets** found in most towns; besides offering an abundance of inexpensive, fresh produce, they are usually dotted with food stalls. The best trick is to do as the Chileans do and make lunch your main meal of the day; many restaurants offer a fixed-price *menú del*

5 GREAT PLACES TO EAT

El Chiringuito Zapallar. See page 118.
El Hoyo Santiago. See page 82.
J. Cruz Malbrán Valparaíso. See page 108.
Kalma Resto Ushuaia. See page 433.
Rucalaf Putemún Chiloé. See page 326.

día, always much better value than the à la carte options.

As for the other meals of the day, **breakfast** at most *residenciales* and hotels is usually a disappointing affair of toasted rolls, jam and tea or coffee, though if your hosts are inclined to pamper you, this will be accompanied by ham, cheese and cake. The great tradition of **onces** – literally "elevenses" but served, like afternoon tea, around 5 o'clock – is a light snack consisting of bread, ham, cheese and biscuits when taken at home, or huge fruit tarts and cakes when out in a *salon de té*. Except during annual holidays or at weekends, relatively few Chileans go out to **dinner**, which leaves most restaurants very quiet through the week. Note, also, that most places don't open for dinner before 8 or 9pm.

Fish and seafood

Chile's **fish** and **seafood** rank among the best in the world. To sample the freshest offerings, head to one of the many *marisquerías* (fish restaurants), particularly those along the coasts of the Litoral Central and the Norte Chico.

A note of caution: never collect shellfish from the beach to eat unless you know for sure that the area is free of **red tide**, an alga that makes shellfish toxic, causing death within a few hours of consumption (see page 44). There is little danger of eating shellfish contaminated by red tide in restaurants.

Meat dishes

Chileans are tremendous carnivores, with **beef** featuring prominently on most restaurant menus and family dinner tables. The summertime **asado** (barbecue) is a national institution. Always slow, leisurely affairs, accompanied by lots of Chilean wine, *asados* take place not only in back gardens, but also in specially equipped picnic areas that fill to bursting on summer weekends. In the south, where the weather is less reliable, large covered grills known as *quinchos* provide an alternative venue for grilling; animals such as goats are often

MINGAS TO MAYOCAN: CHILE'S NOT SO HUMBLE POTATO

The **potato**, a staple in the Chilean diet, has long been the subject of traditions and superstitions. Nowhere is this truer than in Chiloé, where potatoes must be sown during a waning moon in August or September, unless large *macho* specimens are required for seeds, in which case they are sown at the full moon. Neighbours help each other in every aspect of cultivation, a communal labouring tradition known as a *minga*. There are three main *mingas*: *quechatún*, the turning of the earth; *siembra de papa*, the planting; and *cosecha* or *sacadura*, the harvest.

Among the mythology and traditional customs associated with the potato are "magic stones" (*piedras cupucas*), which are found on Cerro Chepu, a hill near Ancud in Chiloé. Believed to have been hidden by witches (*brujos*), these porous silicon stones are carefully guarded until the potato plants bloom, and then the flowers are placed on them and burned as a sacrifice.

Another potato myth holds that a small silver lizard, *el Lluhay*, feeds on potato flowers, and anyone who can catch one is guaranteed good fortune. Still another maintains that a maggot, *la coipone*, which lives in the potato root ball, will prevent babies from crying when placed under their pillows.

MASH IT UP: POPULAR AND TRADITIONAL POTATO DISHES

Chuchoca Mashed potato mixed with flour and pig fat, plastered onto a long, thick wooden pole (*chuchoquero*) and cooked over an open fire.

Colao Small cakes made from potato, wheat, pork fat and crackling, cooked in hot embers.

Mallo de papas Potato stew.

Mayo de papas Peeled, boiled potatoes mashed with onions, chillies, pepper and pig fat.

Mayocan A potato, seaweed and dried-shellfish stew traditionally eaten for breakfast.

Milcao Small cakes of grated and mashed potato that are steamed like dumplings, baked or deep fried.

Pan de papas Baked flat round cakes of mashed potato mixed with flour, eggs and pig fat.

Papas rellenas Sausage-shaped rolls of mashed potato mixed with flour and filled with meat or shellfish.

Pastel de papas A baked dish with alternating layers of mashed potato and meat or shellfish topped with more potato.

---

sliced in half and cooked in *quinchos* on long skewers, Brazilian-style. The restaurant equivalent of an *asado* is the **parillada** – a mixture of grilled steaks, chops and sausages, sometimes served on a hot grill by your table. Following beef in the popularity stakes is **chicken**, which is usually served fried, but can also be enjoyed oven- or spit-roasted. Chilean chickens are nearly all corn-fed and delicious when well cooked. Succulent, spit-roasted chicken is widely available and inexpensive in Arica, in the far north, owing to the locally based chicken-breeding industries. In central Chile, *pollo al coñac* is a popular, and very tasty, chicken casserole, served in large clay pots with brandy and cream. **Pork** also features on many restaurant menus, but **lamb** (*cordero*) is hardly ever available, except in the Lake District.

Traditional food

A wide range of older, traditional dishes – usually a fusion of indigenous and Hispanic influences – are still very much a part of Chilean home cooking and can, with a little luck, be found in the small, old-fashioned restaurants that survive in the hidden corners of town or out in the countryside. Though recipes vary from region to region, depending on the local produce available, there are a few core staples, including sweetcorn and potatoes. **Sweetcorn** forms the basis of two of the most traditional Chilean dishes: *humitas* – mashed corn, wrapped in corn husks and steamed – and **pastel de choclo**, a pie made of mince or chicken topped by pureed sweetcorn and sugar and then baked in the oven. The **potato**, meanwhile, is such an important staple in the Chilean diet that it has acquired its own mythology and folklore (see above).

Another great traditional dish (or snack) is the **empanada**, as symbolic as the national flag, although it was introduced by the Spanish and is popular throughout South America. Baked or fried, large or small, sweet or savoury, *empanadas* (which are not unlike Cornish pasties) can be filled with almost anything, but the most traditional filling is *pino*, a mixture of minced beef, loads of onions, a slice of hard-boiled egg and an olive, with the pit (beware, as this is a good way to leave a tooth in Chile!).

Also very typical are **soups** and **broths**. There are numerous varieties, of which the most famous, cropping up as a starter on many a set meal, is *cazuela*. Named after large Spanish saucepans, *cazuela* is celebrated as much for its appearance as for its taste, with ingredients carefully chosen and cooked to retain their colour and texture: pale yellow potato, orange pumpkin, split rice, green beans, peas and deep yellow sweetcorn swimming in stock, served in a large soup plate with a piece of meat on the bone, and sprinkled with parsley and coriander. Other favourite one-pot broths include *caldillo*, very similar to *cazuela* but with fish instead of meat, and *escabechado*, a stew made with fish steaks that have been fried then soaked in vinegar. Doubtless because it is so economical, **offal** enjoys a long (though waning) history in Chilean cookery.

Fast food

All of Chile's towns are well endowed with greasy-spoon cafés and snack bars – usually known as *fuentes de soda* or *schoperías* – serving draught beer and low-cost fast food. This usually consists of **sandwiches**, which are consumed voraciously by Chileans – indeed, one variety, the **Barros Luco** (beef and melted cheese), is named after a former president who is said to have devised the combination. **Barros Jarpa** (ham and cheese) is another dietary staple. The choice of fillings is firmly meat-based, with most options revolving around **churrasco** – a thin cut of griddle-fried beef, rather like a minute steak.

Chile is also the unlikely home of a variety of **hot dogs**. Sitting all by itself in a bun, the hot dog is simply called a *vienesa*, but it's called an *especial* when mayonnaise is squeezed along the top, and the addition of tomato, sauerkraut and avocado makes it a *dinámico*. The most popular version is the *italiano* – with tomato, mayonnaise and avocado, which together resemble the colours of the Italian flag. It is not until the sausage is buried under extra sauerkraut and chopped tomato that it becomes completely *completo*.

Drinking

Soft **fizzy drinks** can be found everywhere in Chile. Bottled **mineral water**, too, is widely available, both sparkling (*con gas*) and still (*sin gas*). It is

TIPPING

It's customary to **tip ten percent** in restaurants – service is rarely included in the bill. You are not, however, expected to tip taxi drivers.

getting easier to find good **coffee**, though instant is still far more common than it should be, particularly off the beaten track. **Herbal teas** are widely available and come in countless flavours. The most popular varieties are *manzanilla* (camomile), *menta* (mint) and *boldo* (a fragrant native plant). Where Chile really comes into its own, though, is with the delicious, freshly squeezed **fruit juices** (*jugos naturales*) available in many bars, restaurants and roadside stalls, especially in the Central Valley, and a few northern oases like Pica. Another home-grown drink is *mote con huesillo*, sold at numerous roadsides throughout the Central Valley and Lake District in summer. *Mote* is boiled or soaked barley grain, and *huesillos* are sun-dried peaches, though this sweet, gooey drink can be made with any fresh soft fruit.

Chilean **beer** comes in several varieties, with Cristal and Escudo dominating the market; smaller brewer Kunstman also has a national reach, and the range and quality of craft beers is rapidly expanding.

There's always a good selection of **wine**, on the other hand, though the choice on restaurant lists rarely reflects the vast range of wines produced for export. Regarded as the Chilean national drink, **pisco sour** is a tangy, refreshing aperitif made from pisco (a white brandy created from distilled Moscatel grapes, freshly squeezed lemon juice and sugar – see page 145). You may also come across a number of **regional specialities**, including *chicha de manzana* (apple cider), made at home by every *huaso* (see page 38) in the Central Valley. Further south, in the Lake District, a traditional element of many drinks is *harina tostada* (toasted maize flour), used by the Mapuche since pre-Spanish days. Today it's still common to see Mapuche sitting around a table with a large jug of frothy coffee-coloured

TAP WATER

Tap water is generally drinkable throughout Chile, with the exception of the Atacama, though the high mineral content in Santiago's supply upsets some people's stomachs.

liquid, which is dark beer mixed with *harina tostada*. The flour is also mixed with cheap wine, among other drinks, and is usually stocked by the sackful at local Lake District bars.

Festivals

Most of Chile's festivals are held to mark religious occasions, or to honour saints or the Virgin Mary. What's fascinating about them is the strong influence of pre-Spanish, pre-Christian rites, particularly in the Aymara communities of the far north and the Mapuche of the south. Added to this is the influence of colourful folk traditions rooted in the Spanish expeditions of exploration and conquest, colonization and evangelism, slavery and revolution.

In the *altiplano* of the **far north**, Aymara herdsmen celebrate Catholic holy days and the feasts of ancient cults along with ritual dancing and the offering of sacrificial llamas.

In **central Chile**, you'll witness the influence of colonial traditions. In the days of the conquest, an important ingredient of any fiesta was the verbal sparring between itinerant bards called *payadores*, who would compose and then try to resolve each other's impromptu rhyming riddles. The custom is kept alive at many fiestas in the Central Valley, where young poets spontaneously improvise *lolismos* and *locuciones*, forms of jocular verse that are quite unintelligible to an outsider. These rural fiestas always culminate in an energetic display of *cueca* dancing, washed down with plenty of wine and *chicha* – reminiscent of the entertainment organized by indulgent hacienda-owners for their peons.

In the **south**, the solemn Mapuche festivals are closely linked to mythology, magic and faith healing, agricultural rituals and supplications to gods and spirits. Group dances (*purrún*) are performed with gentle movements; participants either move around in a circle or advance and retreat in lines. Most ceremonies are accompanied by mounted horn players whose 4m-long bamboo instruments, *trutrucas*, require enormous lung power to produce a note. Other types of traditional wind instruments include a small pipe (*lolkiñ*), flute (*pinkulwe*), cow's horn (*kullkull*) and whistle (*pifilka*). Of all Mapuche musical instruments, the most important is the sacred drum (*kultrún*), which is only used by faith healers (*machis*).

For more on *altiplano* fiestas and ceremonies, see pages 199.

A festival calendar

JANUARY AND FEBRUARY

San Sebastián Jan 20. Spaniards brought the first wooden image of San Sebastián to Chile in the seventeenth century. After a Mapuche raid on Chillán, the image was buried in a nearby field, and no one was able to raise it. The saint's feast day has become an important Mapuche festival, especially in Lonquimay, where it's celebrated with horse racing, feasting and drinking.

La Candelaria Feb 1–3. Celebrated throughout Chile since 1780, when a group of miners and muleteers discovered a stone image of the Virgin and Child while sheltering from an inexplicable thunderstorm in the Atacama. Typical festivities include religious processions and traditional dances.

Festival Internacional de la Canción End Feb. This glitzy and wildly popular five-day festival is held in Viña del Mar's open-air amphitheatre, featuring performers from all over Latin America and broadcast to most Spanish-speaking countries.

EASTER

Semana Santa (Holy Week) Among the nationwide Easter celebrations, look out for Santiago's solemn procession of penitents dressed in black habits, carrying crosses through the streets, and La Ligua's parade of mounted *huasos* followed by a giant penguin.

Fiesta del Cuasimodo First Sun after Easter. In many parts of central Chile, *huasos* (see page 38) parade through the streets on their horses, often accompanied by a priest sitting on a float covered in white lilies.

MAY AND JUNE

Santa Cruz de Mayo May 3. Throughout the *altiplano*, villages celebrate the cult of the Holy Cross, inspired in the seventeenth century by the Spaniards' obsession with crosses, which they carried everywhere, erected on hillsides and even carved in the air with their fingers. The festivities have strong pre-Christian elements, often including the sacrifice of a llama.

Procesión del Cristo de Mayo May 13. A huge parade through the streets of Santiago bearing the *Cristo de Mayo* – a sixteenth-century carving of Christ whose crown of thorns slipped to its neck during an earthquake, and which is said to have shed tears of blood when attempts were made to put the crown back in place.

Noche de San Juan Bautista June 13. An important feast night, celebrated by families up and down the country with a giant stew, known as the *Estofado de San Juan*. In Chiloé, an integral part of the feast are roasted potato balls called *tropones*, which burn the fingers and make people "dance the *tropón*" as they jig up and down, juggling them from hand to hand.

Fiesta de San Pedro June 29. Along the length of Chile's coast, fishermen decorate their boats and take the image of their patron saint out to sea – often at night with candles and flares burning – to pray for good weather and large catches.

JULY AND AUGUST

Virgen de la Tirana July 12–18. The largest religious festival in Chile, held in La Tirana in the far north, and attended by more than eighty thousand pilgrims and hundreds of costumed dancers (see page 195).

Virgen del Carmen July 16. Military parades throughout Chile honour the patron saint of the armed forces; the largest are in Maipú, on the southern outskirts of Santiago, where San Martín and Bernardo O'Higgins defeated Spanish Royalists in 1818.

Jesús Nazareno de Caguach Aug 21–31. Thousands of Chilotes flock to the archipelago's tiny island of Caguach to worship at a 2m-high figure of Christ, donated by the Jesuits in the eighteenth century.

SEPTEMBER AND OCTOBER

Fiestas Patrias Sept 18. Chile's Independence Day is celebrated throughout the country with street parties, music and dancing.

Virgen de las Peñas First Sun of Oct. Each year, numerous dance groups and more than ten thousand pilgrims from Chile, Peru, Bolivia and Argentina make their way along a tortuous cliff path to visit a rock carving of the Virgin in the Azapa Valley, near Arica. There are many smaller festivals in other parts of Chile, too.

NOVEMBER AND DECEMBER

Todos los Santos (All Saints' Day) Nov 1. Traditionally, this is the day when Chileans tend their family graves. In the north, where Aymara customs have become entwined with Christian ones, crosses are often removed from graves and left on the former bed of the deceased overnight. Candles are kept burning in the room, and a feast is served for family members, past and present.

Día de los Muertos (All Souls' Day) Nov 2. A second vigil to the dead is held in cemeteries, with offerings of food and wine sprinkled on the graves. In some far north villages, there's a tradition of reading a liturgy, always in Latin.

La Purísima Dec 8. Celebrated in many parts of Chile, the festival of the Immaculate Conception is at its liveliest in San Pedro de Atacama, where it's accompanied by traditional Aymara music and dancing.

Fiesta Grande de la Virgen de Andacollo Dec 23–27. More than 100,000 pilgrims from all over the north come to Andacollo, in Norte Chico, to worship its Virgin and watch the famous masked dancers (see page 129).

Spectator sports

The Chileans are not a particularly exuberant people, but passions are roused by several national enthusiasms – chiefly football and rodeo, which at their best are performed with electrifying skill and theatricality.

Football

Fútbol reigns supreme as Chile's favourite sport. Introduced by British immigrants in the early 1800s, football in Chile can trace its history back to the playing fields of the Mackay School, one of the first English schools in Valparaíso, and its heritage is reflected in the names of the first clubs: Santiago Wanderers (who are actually from Valparaíso), Everton, Badminton, Morning Star and Green Cross.

Everton and Wanderers are still going strong, but the sport is now dominated by the Santiago teams of Colo Colo, Universidad Católica and Universidad de Chile. Matches featuring any of these teams are guaranteed a good turnout and a great atmosphere. There's rarely any trouble, with whole families coming along to enjoy the fun. And if you can't make it to a match, you'll still see plenty of football on the huge TVs that dominate most cafés and bars, including European games shown on cable channels.

Football hardly has a season in Chile. In addition to the league calendar, there are numerous other competitions of which the Copa de Libertadores is the most important. So you'll generally be able to catch the action whenever you visit.

Horse racing

There are two very different types of **horse racing** in Chile: conventional track racing, known as *hípica*, and the much rougher and wilder *carreras a la chilena*. Hípica is a sport for rich Santiaguinos, who don their tweeds and posh frocks to go and watch it at the capital's Club Hípico and Hipódromo Chile, which have races throughout the year. The most important of these are the St Leger at the Hipódromo Chile on December 14, and the Ensayo at the Club Hípico on the first Sunday in November.

Carreras a la chilena are held anywhere in the country where two horses can be found to race against each other. Apart from the organized events that take place at village fiestas, these races are normally a result of one *huaso* betting another that his horse is faster. Held in any suitable field, well away from the prying eyes of the *carabineros*, the two-horse race can attract large crowds (who bet heavily on the outcome).

Rodeo

Rodeos evolved from the early colonial days when the cattle on the large estancias had to be rounded up and branded or slaughtered by *huasos* (see page 38). The feats of horsemanship required to do so soon took on a competitive element, which eventually found an expression in the form of rodeos. Even though ranching has long declined in Chile,

THE CHILEAN HUASO

"Of the many cowboys of the Americas, none remains as shrouded in mystery and contradiction as Chile's *huaso*," writes Richard Slatta in *Cowboys of the Americas*. The *huaso* certainly holds a special place in Chile's perception of its national identity. But the definition of the *huaso* is somewhat confused and subject to differing interpretations. The one you're most likely to come across is that of the "**gentleman rider**", the middle-class horseman who, while not a part of the landed elite, is a good few social rungs up from the landless labourer. This is the *huaso* you'll see at rodeos and in *cueca* performances. The latter is **Chile's national dance** – a curious cross between English morris dancing and smouldering Sevillanas that can, in fact, be traced back to the African slave dances, which were also the basis of the Brazilian samba and Peruvian *zamacueca*.

Gentlemen riders are part of a romanticized image of the Chilean countryside and a far cry from the much larger and perhaps more authentic group who carried out the real horsework on the land. More akin to the Argentine gaucho and the Mexican *vaquero*, this other type of *huaso* was a landless, badly paid and poorly dressed ranch hand who worked on the large haciendas during the cattle round-up season. Despite the harsh reality of his lifestyle, the lower-class *huaso* is also the victim of myth-making, frequently depicted as a paragon of virtue and happiness.

All types of *huasos*, whatever their social status, were renowned for outstanding **horsemanship**, marvelled at for their practice of training their horses to stop dead in their tracks at a single command (*la sentada*). A skill mastered in the southern Central Valley was mastery of the *bolas* – three stones or metal balls attached to long leather straps, which were hurled at animals and wrapped around their legs, bringing them to the ground. *Huasos* also developed a host of equestrian contests including the *juego de cañas* (jousting with canes), the *tiro al gallo* (a mounted tug-of-war) and *topeadura* (a side-by-side pushing contest). Today these displays have a formal outlet in the regular **rodeos** (see page 219) in the Central Valley. As for the working *huaso*, you'll still come across him in the back roads of rural central Chile.

organized rodeos remain wildly popular, with many free competitions taking place in local stadiums (known as *medialunas*) from September to April. Taking in a rodeo not only allows you to watch the most dazzling equestrian skills inside the arena, but also to see the *huasos* decked out in all their traditional gear: ponchos, silver spurs and all.

Outdoor activities

Chile offers an enormous range of outdoor activities, including volcano-climbing, skiing, surfing, whitewater rafting, fly-fishing and horseriding. An increasing number of operators and outfitters have got wise to the potential of organized adventure tourism, offering one- or multi-day guided excursions.

Many of these companies are based in **Pucón**, in the Lake District, with a good sprinkling of other outfitters spread throughout the south. There are fewer opportunities for outdoor activities in the harsh deserts of the north, where *altiplano* jeep trips and mountain biking are the main options. If you do plan to take part in adventurous activities, be sure to check that you're covered by your travel insurance, or take out specialist insurance where necessary.

Rafting and kayaking

Chile's many frothy rivers and streams afford incomparable rafting opportunities. Indeed, the country's top destinations, the mighty **Río Bio Bío** and the **Río Futaleufú**, entice visitors from around the globe. Rafting trips generally range in length from one to eight days and, in the case of the Bio Bío, sometimes include the option of climbing 3160m Volcán Callaquén. In addition to these challenging rivers, gentler alternatives exist on the **Río Maipo** close to Santiago, the **Río Trancura** near Pucón and the **Río Petrohue** near Puerto Varas. The Maipo makes a good day-trip from Santiago, while excursions on the latter two are just half-day affairs and can usually be arranged on the spot, without advance reservations. In general, all rafting trips are extremely well organized, but you should always take great care in choosing your outfitter – this activity can be very dangerous in the hands of an inexperienced guide.

Chile's whitewater rapids also offer excellent **kayaking**, though this is less developed as an organized activity – your best bet is probably to contact one of the US-based outfitters that have camps on the Bío Bío and Futaleufú (see pages 245 and 356). **Sea kayaking** is becoming increasingly popular, generally in the calm, flat waters of Chile's southern fjords, though people have been known to kayak around Cape Horn. Note that the Chilean navy is very sensitive about any foreign vessels (even kayaks) cruising in their waters, and if you're planning a trip through military waters, you'd be wise to inform the Chilean consulate or embassy in your country beforehand.

Hiking

For the most part, Chile is a very empty country with vast tracts of wilderness offering potential for fantastic **hiking**. Chileans, moreover, are often reluctant to stray far from their parked cars when they visit the countryside, so you'll find that most trails without vehicle access are blissfully quiet. However, the absence of a national enthusiasm for hiking also means that, compared with places of similar scenic beauty like California, British Columbia and New Zealand, Chile isn't particularly geared up to the hiking scene, with relatively few long-distance trails (given the total area) and a shortage of decent trekking maps. That said, what is on offer is superb, and ranks among the country's most rewarding attractions.

The **north** of Chile, with its harsh climate and landscape, isn't really suitable for hiking, and most walkers head for the lush native forests of Chile's **south**, peppered with waterfalls, lakes, hot springs and volcanoes. The best trails are nearly always inside **national parks** or reserves, where the *guardaparques* (rangers) are a good source of advice on finding and following the paths. They should always be informed if you plan to do an overnight hike (so that if you don't come back, they'll know where to search for you). The majority of trails are for half-day or day hikes, though some parks offer a few long-distance hikes, sometimes linking up with trails in adjoining parks. The level of path maintenance and signing varies greatly from one park to another, and many of the more remote trails are indistinct and difficult to follow.

Few parks allow **wild camping**, while the few that do have a series of rustic camping areas that you're required to stick to – check with the *guardaparque*. If you do camp (the best way to experience the Chilean wilderness) note that **forest and bush fires** are a very real hazard. Take great care when making a campfire (check before that they're allowed; don't light fires in Torres del Paine). Also, never chop down

5 GREAT OUTDOOR ACTIVITIES

Dog sledding Villarrica. See page 270.
Kayaking Chiloé. See page 322.
Paragliding Iquique. See page 187.
Skiing Portillo. See page 92.
Trekking Parque Nacional Patagonia. See page 374.

vegetation for fuel, as most of Chile's native flora is endangered.

By far the most popular destination for hiking is **Torres del Paine** in the far south, which offers magnificent scenery but fairly crowded trails, especially in January and February. Many quieter, less well-known alternatives are scattered between Santiago and Tierra del Fuego, ranging from narrow paths in the towering, snow-streaked central Andes to hikes up to glaciers off the Carretera Austral.

If you go hiking, it's essential to be well **prepared** – always carry plenty of water, wear a hat and sun block, and carry extra layers of warm clothing to guard against the sharp drop in temperature after sundown. Even on day hikes, take enough supplies to provide for the eventuality of getting lost, and always carry a map and **compass** (*brújula*), preferably one bought in the southern hemisphere or adjusted for southern latitudes. Also, make a conscious effort to help preserve Chile's environment – where there's no toilet, bury human waste at least 20cm under the ground and 30m from the nearest river or lake; take away or burn all your **rubbish**; and use specially designed **ecofriendly detergents** for use in lakes and streams.

Climbing

The massive Andean cordillera offers a wide range of **climbing** possibilities. In the **far north** of Chile, you can trek up several volcanoes over 6000m, including Volcán Parinacota (6330m), Volcán Llullaillaco (6739m) and Volcán Ojos del Salado (6950m). Although ropes and crampons aren't always needed, these ascents are suitable only for experienced climbers, and need a fair amount of independent planning, with only a few companies offering guided excursions.

In the **central Andes**, exciting climbs include Volcán Marmolejo (6100m) and Volcán Tupungato (6750m), while in the **south**, climbers head for Volcán Villarrica (2840m) and Volcán Osorno (2652m), both of which you can tackle even with little mountaineering experience.

Throughout Chile there's a lot of tedious bureaucracy to get through before you can climb. To go up any mountain straddling an international border (which means most of the high Andean peaks), you need advance **permission** from the **Dirección de Fronteras y Límites del Estado** (DIFROL), Seventh Floor, Teatinos 180, Santiago (☎2 2827 5900, Ⓦwww.difrol.gob.cl). To get this, write to or email DIFROL with the planned dates and itinerary of the climb, listing full details (name, nationality, date of birth, occupation, passport number, address) of each member of the climbing team, and your dates of entry and exit from Chile. Authorization will then be sent to you on a piece of paper that you must present to Conaf before ascending (if the peak is not within a national park, you must take the authorization to the nearest *carabineros* station). If your plans change while you're in Chile, you can usually amend the authorization or get a new one at the *Gobernación* of each provincial capital. You can also apply through a Chilean embassy in advance of your departure, or print and send a form from their website. There's further **information** on climbing in Chile online at Ⓦtrekkingchile.com.

Fly-fishing

Chile has a well-deserved international reputation as one of the finest **fly-fishing** destinations in the world. Its pristine waters teem with rainbow, brown and brook trout, and silver and Atlantic salmon. These fish are not native, but were introduced for sport in the late nineteenth century; since then, the wild population has flourished and multiplied, and is also supplemented by generous numbers of escapees from local fish farms. The fishing **season** varies slightly from region to region, but in general runs from November to May.

Traditionally, the best sport-fishing was considered to be in the **Lake District**, but while this region still offers great possibilities, attention has shifted to the more remote, pristine waters of **Aisén**, where a number of classy fishing lodges have sprung up, catering mainly to wealthy North American clients. Fishing in the Lake District is frequently done from riverboats, while a typical day's fishing in Aisén begins with a ride in a motor dinghy through fjords, channels and islets towards an isolated river. You'll then wade upstream to shallower waters, usually equipped with a light six or seven weight rod, dry flies and brightly coloured streamers. Catches weigh in between 1kg and 3kg – but note that many outfitters operate only on a catch and release basis.

Skiing

Chile offers the finest and most challenging **skiing** in South America. Many of the country's top slopes and resorts lie within very easy reach of Santiago, including **El Colorado**, **La Parva**, **Valle Nevado** and world-renowned **Portillo**. A bit further south, but no less impressive, stands the popular **Termas de Chillán**.

Horse-trekking

Exploring Chile's dramatic landscapes on horseback is a memorable experience. The best possibilities are **around Santiago** and in the **Central Valley**. In addition to the spectacular scenery, you can also expect to see condors and other birds of prey. Trips are usually guided by local *arrieros*, who herd cattle up to high pastures in springtime and know the mountain paths intimately. You normally spend about five or six hours in the saddle each day; a lingering *asado* (barbecue), cooked over an open fire and accompanied by plenty of Chilean wine, will be part of the experience. At night, you sleep in tents transported by mules.

The only disadvantage of riding treks in the central Andes is that, due to the terrain, you're unlikely to get beyond a walk, and cantering is usually out of the question. If you want a faster pace, opt for the treks offered by some companies in Patagonia, where rolling grasslands provide plenty of opportunity for gallops – though the weather can often put a dampener on your trip.

Mountain biking

For most of Chile's length, there are extremely good and little-used dirt roads perfect for **cycling** – although the numerous potholes mean it's only worth attempting them on a **mountain bike**. For a serious trip, you should bring your own bike or buy one in Santiago – **renting** a bike of the quality required can be difficult to arrange. An alternative is to go on an organized cycling excursion, where all equipment, including tents, will be provided. Note that during the summer, cycling in Patagonia and Tierra del Fuego is made almost impossible by incessant and ferociously strong winds.

Surfing

Chile's beaches are pulling in an increasing number of surfers, who come to ride the year-round breaks that pound the Pacific shore. By unanimous consent, the **best breaks** – mainly long left-handers – are concentrated around Pichilemu, near Rancagua, which is the site of the annual National Surfing Championships. Further north, the warmer seas around Iquique and Arica are also popular.

Adventure tourism operators and outfitters

Below is a selection of operators and outfitters for various outdoor activities. The list is by no means comprehensive, and new companies are constantly springing up to add to it – you can get more details from the relevant regional Sernatur office.

ALL-ROUNDERS AND CLIMBING

Altue Active Travel Coyancura 2270, Providencia, Santiago ☏ 2 2333 1390, ⓦ altue.com. Reliable, slick operation whose options include rafting the Río Maipo, Aconcagua and Ojos del Salado expeditions, plus horse-treks. Ask about climbing tours up Volcán Osorno and Volcán Villarrica.

Azimut 360 Eliodoro Yañez 1437, Providencia, Santiago ☏ 2 2235 1519, ⓦ azimut360.com. Franco-Chilean outfit with a dynamic team of guides and a wide range of programmes, including helicopter tours, mountain biking, Aconcagua expeditions and climbs up Chile's highest volcanoes.

Cascada Expediciones Don Carlos 3227, Las Condes, Santiago ☏ 2 2232 9878, ⓦ cascada.travel. One of the pioneers of adventure tourism in Chile, with a particular emphasis on activities in the Andes close to Santiago, where it has a permanent base in the Cajón del Maipo. Programmes include rafting and kayaking the Río Maipo, horse-treks in the high cordillera and hiking and mountain biking.

Sportstour El Golf 99, Las Condes, Santiago ☏ 2 2589 5200, ⓦ www.sportstour.cl. This well-run operation offers balloon rides and flights, among other tours.

FLY-FISHING

Cumilahue Lodge PO Box 2, Llifen ☏ 2 2196 1601, ⓦ anglingtours.com. Very expensive packages at a luxury Lake District lodge run by Adrian Dufflocq, something of a legend on the Chilean fly-fishing scene.

Off Limits Adventures Av Bernardo O'Higgins 560, Pucón ☏ 09 9949 2481, ⓦ offlimits.cl. Half-day and full-day excursions, plus fly-fishing lessons. One of the more affordable options.

HORSE-TREKKING

See also Altue Active Travel and Cascada Expediciones in "All-rounders and climbing" (see above).

Chile Nativo Casilla 42, Puerto Natales ☏ 2 2717 5961, ⓦ chilenativo.com. Dynamic young outfit specializing in five- to twelve-day horse-trekking tours of the region, visiting out-of-the-way locations in addition to Parque Nacional Torres del Paine.

Hacienda de los Andes Río Hurtado, near Ovalle ☏ 53 269 1822, ⓦ haciendalosandes.com. Beautiful ranch in a fantastic location in the Hurtado Valley, between La Serena and Ovalle, offering exciting mountain treks on some of the finest mounts in the country.

Pared Sur Juan Esteban Montero 5497, Las Condes, Santiago ☏ 2 2207 3525, ⓦ paredsur.cl. In addition to its extensive mountain-biking programme, Pared Sur offers a one-week horse-trek through the virgin landscape of Aisén, off the Carretera Austral.

Rancho de Caballos Casilla 142, Pucón ☏ 09 8346 1764, ⓦ rancho-de-caballos.com. Ranch offering a range of treks from one to ten days.

Ride World Wide Staddon Farm, North Tawton, Devon, UK ☏ 01837 82544, ⓦ rideworldwide.com. UK-based company that hooks up with local riding outfitters around the world. In Chile, it offers a range of horseback treks in the central cordillera, the Lake District and Patagonia.

KAYAKING

Al Sur Expeditions Aconcagua 8, Puerto Varas ☏ 65 223 2300, ⓦ alsurexpeditions.com. One of the foremost adventure tour companies in the Lake District, and the first one to introduce sea kayaking in the fjords south of Puerto Montt.

Bío Bío Expeditions PO Box 2028, Truckee, CA 96160, US ☏ 562 196 4258, ⓦ bbxrafting.com. This US-based rafting outfitter organizes paddles down the Bío Bío or Futaleufú, as well as in Argentina.

¡ecole! Urrutia 592, Pucón ☏ 45 244 1675, ⓦ ecole.cl. Ecologically focused guesthouse/tour company offering, among other activities, sea kayaking classes and day outings in the fjords south of Puerto Montt and around Parque Nacional Pumalín Douglas R. Tompkins.

Expediciones Chile Gabriela Mistral 296, Futaleufú ☏ 65 272 1386, ⓦ exchile.com. River kayaking outfitter, operated by former Olympic kayaker Chris Spelius, catering to all levels of experience, especially seasoned paddlers.

MOUNTAIN BIKING

See also Azimut 360 and Cascada Expediciones in "All-rounders and climbing" (see above).

Pared Sur Juan Esteban Montero 5497, Las Condes, Santiago ☏ 2 2207 3525, ⓦ paredsur.cl. Pared Sur has been running mountain bike trips in Chile for longer than anyone else. It offers a wide range of programmes throughout the whole country.

SKIING

For full details of the resorts near Santiago, see page 92.

Sportstour El Golf 99, Las Condes, Santiago ☏ 2 2589 5200, ⓦ www.sportstour.cl. Among a wide-ranging national programme, including hot-air balloon rides and flights on cockpit biplanes and gliders, this travel agent offers inclusive ski packages at resorts near Santiago and Termas de Chillán.

TREKKING AND HIKING

See also "All-rounders and climbing" (see above).

Cascada Expediciones Don Carlos 3227, Las Condes, Santiago ☏ 2 2232 9878, ⓦ cascada.travel. Leading adventure operator, offering guided treks across Chile, including the Lake District, Patagonia and the Atacama Desert.

Cosmo Andino Caracoles s/n, San Pedro de Atacama ☎ 55 285 1069, ⓦ cosmoandino.cl. Focusing on the Atacama Desert, with several guided hikes and treks.

Erratic Rock Baquedano 719, Puerto Natales ☎ 61 241 4317, ⓦ erraticrock.com. Offering a wide range of standard and tailor-made treks in Patagonia and Tierra del Fuego.

WHITEWATER RAFTING

See also Cascada Expediciones (see page 41).

Bío Bío Expeditions PO Box 2028, Truckee, CA 96160, US ☎ 56 2196 4258, ⓦ bbxrafting.com. Headed by Laurence Alvarez, the captain of the US World Championships rafting team, this experienced and friendly outfit offers a range of trips on the Bio Bío and Futaleufú.

Turismo Trancura O'Higgins 211-C, Pucón ☎ 45 244 3436, ⓦ www.trancura.cl. Major southern operator with high standards and friendly guides, offering rafting excursions down the Río Trancura and the Bio Bío.

National parks and reserves

Around eighteen percent of Chile's mainland territory is currently protected by the state under the extensive Sistema Nacional de Areas Silvestres Protegidas (National Protected Wildlife Areas System), which is made up of thirty national parks, thirty-eight national reserves and eleven natural monuments – and this number is due to increase (see below). The protected areas inevitably include the country's most outstanding scenic attractions, but while there are provisions for tourism, the main aim is always to conserve and manage native fauna and flora. Given Chile's great biodiversity, these vary tremendously, and park objectives vary from protecting flamingo populations to monitoring glaciers. All protected areas are managed by the Corporación Nacional Forestal, better known as Conaf (ⓦ www.conaf.cl).

Definitions and terms

National parks (*parques nacionales*) are generally large areas of unspoiled wilderness, usually featuring fragile endemic ecosystems. They include the most touristy and beautiful of the protected areas, and often offer walking trails and sometimes camping areas too. **National reserves** (*reservas nacionales*) are areas of ecological importance that have suffered some degree of natural degradation; there are fewer regulations to protect these areas, and "sustainable" commercial exploitation (such as mineral extraction) is permitted. **Natural monuments** (*monumentos naturales*) tend to be important or endangered geological formations, or small areas of biological, anthropological or archeological significance.

In addition to these three main categories, there are a few **nature sanctuaries** (*santuarios de la naturaleza*) and **protected areas** (*areas de protección*), usually earmarked for their scientific or scenic interest. And as well as state-owned parks, there are several important private initiatives.

NEW PARKS AND RESERVES

In March 2017, Tompkins Conservation (see page 351) and President Michelle Bachelet signed an historic agreement to **expand the area protected by Chile's national parks** by more than 40,000 square km – roughly the size of Switzerland. The private foundation donated more than 4000 square km of protected land, the largest gift of its kind in South America, including their two flagship parks – Parque Pumalín and Parque Patagonia – while the government committed almost 36,000 square km of state-owned land. The agreement resulted in the creation of five new national parks (Pumalín Douglas R. Tompkins, Patagonia, Melimoyu, Cerro Castillo and Kawéskar) and in the expansion of three more (Corcovado, Isla Magdalena and Hornopirén), all of which form part of the new **Ruta de los Parques** (Route of Parks) – a chain of seventeen national parks that stretches down the spine of Chile for 2400km from Parque Nacional Alerce Andino to Parque Nacional Cabo de Hornos. "It's a culmination of our life's work," Kris Tompkins commented when asked about the historic handover. "This is what we've always intended."

In a separate move, later in 2017, the government also created a new **marine reserve** around Easter Island: the **Rapa Nui Rahui Marine Protected Area** (see page 445) spans some 740,000 square km and protects dozens of endemic species.

Park administration

The administration of Chile's protected areas is highly centralized with all important decisions coming from **Conaf's head office** in Santiago (see page 78). This is a good place to visit before heading out of the capital, as you can pick up brochures, books and basic maps. In addition, each regional capital has a Conaf headquarters, which is useful for more practical pre-visit information. The parks and reserves are staffed by **guardaparques** (park wardens), who live in ranger stations (*guarderías*). Most parks are divided into several areas, known as "sectors" (*sectores*), and the larger ones have a small *guardería* in each sector.

Visiting the parks

No permit is needed to visit any of Chile's national parks; you simply turn up and pay your **entrance fee**, though some parks are free. Ease of **access** differs wildly from one park to the next – a few have paved highways running through them, while others are served by dirt tracks that are only passable for a few months of the year. Getting to them often involves renting a vehicle or going on an organized trip, as around two-thirds of Chile's national parks can't be reached by public transport.

Arriving at the park boundary, you'll normally pass a small hut (called the Conaf control) where you pay your entrance fee and pick up a basic map. Some of the larger parks have more than one entrance point. The main ranger station is always separate from the hut; it contains the rangers' living quarters and administrative office, and often a large map or scale model of the park. The more popular parks also have a **Centro de Información Ambiental** attached to the station, with displays on the park's flora and fauna. A few parks have **camping** areas. These are often rustic sites with basic facilities, run by Conaf, which usually charge around CH$5000–10,000 per tent. In other parks, particularly in the south, Conaf gives licences to concessionaires, who operate campsites and *cabañas*, which tend to be very expensive. Some of the more remote national parks, especially in the north, have small **refugios** attached to the ranger stations. Some of them are in stunning locations, overlooking the Salar de Surire, for example, or with views across Lago Chungará to Volcán Parinacota. Sadly, however, they are unreliable.

Health

Chile is a fairly risk-free country to travel in as far as health problems are concerned. No inoculations are required, though you might want to consider a hepatitis A jab, as a precaution. Check, too, that your tetanus boosters are up to date. Many travellers experience the occasional stomach upset, and sunstroke is also quite common, especially at high altitudes.

Chile is well endowed with **pharmacies** (*farmacias*) – even smaller towns usually have at least a handful. If you need to see a **doctor**, make an appointment at the outpatient department of the nearest hospital, usually known as a *clínica*. The majority of *clínicas* are private, and expensive, so make sure your **travel insurance** (see page 46) provides good medical cover.

Rabies

Rabies, though only a remote risk, does exist in Chile. If you get bitten or scratched by a dog, you should seek medical attention *immediately*. The

MAREA ROJA

Chile's **shellfish** should be treated with the utmost caution. Every year, a handful of people die because they inadvertently eat bivalve shellfish contaminated by red tide, or *marea roja*, algae that becomes toxic when the seawater temperature rises. The government monitors the presence of this algae with extreme diligence and bans all commercial shellfish collection when the phenomenon occurs. There is little health risk when eating in restaurants or buying shellfish in markets, as these are regularly inspected by the health authorities, but it's extremely dangerous to collect shellfish for your own consumption unless you're absolutely certain that the area is free of red tide. Note that red tide affects all shellfish, cooked or uncooked.

disease can be cured, but only through a series of stomach injections administered before the onset of symptoms, which can appear within 24 hours or lie dormant for months, and include irrational behaviour, fear of water and foaming at the mouth. There is a vaccine, but it's expensive and doesn't prevent you from contracting rabies, though it does buy you time to get to hospital.

Altitude sickness

Anyone travelling in Chile's northern *altiplano*, where altitudes commonly reach 4500m – or indeed anyone going higher than 3000m in the cordillera – needs to be aware of the risks of **altitude sickness**, locally known as *soroche* or *apunamiento*. This debilitating and sometimes dangerous condition is caused by the reduced atmospheric pressure and corresponding reduction in oxygen that occurs around 3000m above sea level. **Basic symptoms** include breathlessness, headaches, nausea and extreme tiredness, rather like a bad hangover. There's no way of predicting whether or not you'll be susceptible to the condition, which seems to strike quite randomly, affecting people differently from one ascent to another. You can, however, take steps to avoid it by ascending slowly and allowing yourself to acclimatize. In particular, don't be tempted to whizz straight up to the *altiplano* from sea level, but spend a night or two acclimatizing en route. You should also avoid alcohol and salt, and drink lots of water. The bitter-tasting coca leaves chewed by many locals in the *altiplano* (where they're widely available at markets and village stores), can help ease headaches and the sense of exhaustion.

Although extremely unpleasant, the basic form of altitude sickness is essentially harmless and passes after about 24 hours (if it doesn't, descend at least 500m). However, in its more serious forms, altitude sickness can be dangerous and even life-threatening. One to two percent of people travelling to 4000m develop HAPO (high-altitude pulmonary oedema), caused by the build-up of liquid in the lungs. Symptoms include fever, an increased pulse rate and coughing up white fluid; sufferers should descend immediately, whereupon recovery is usually quick and complete. Rarer, but more serious, is HACO (high-altitude cerebral oedema), which occurs when the brain gets waterlogged with fluid. Symptoms include loss of balance, severe lassitude, weakness or numbness on one side of the body and a confused mental state. If you or a fellow traveller display any of these symptoms, descend immediately and get to a doctor; HACO can be fatal within 24 hours.

Sunburn and dehydration

In many parts of Chile, **sunburn** and **dehydration** are threats. They are obviously more of a problem in the excessively dry climate of the north, but even in the south of the country, it's easy to underestimate the strength of the summer sun. To prevent sunburn, take a **high-factor sunscreen** and wear a wide-brimmed hat. It's also essential to drink plenty of fluids before you go out, and always carry large quantities of water with you when you're hiking in the sun. You lose a lot of salt when you sweat, so make sure to add more to your food, or take a rehydration solution.

Hypothermia

Another potential enemy, especially at high altitudes and in Chile's far southern reaches, is **hypothermia**. Because early symptoms can include an almost euphoric sense of sleepiness and disorientation, your body's core temperature can plummet to danger level before you know what has happened. Chile's northern deserts have such clear air that it can drop to -20ºC (-4ºF) at night, which makes you very vulnerable to hypothermia while sleeping if proper precautions aren't taken. If you do get hypothermia, the best thing to do is take your clothes off and jump into a sleeping bag with someone else – sharing another person's body heat is the most effective way of restoring your own. If you're alone, or have no willing partners, then get out of the wind and the rain, remove all wet or damp clothes, get dry and drink plenty of hot fluids.

MEDICAL RESOURCES

Canadian Society for International Health Canada ☎ 613 241 5785, ⓦ csih.org. Extensive list of travel health centres.

Centers for Disease Control and Prevention US ☎ 1 800 232 4636, ⓦ cdc.gov/travel. Official US government travel health site.

Hospital for Tropical Diseases Travel Clinic UK ☎ 0845 155 5000, ⓦ www.thehtd.org. Leading travel clinic and hospital.

International Society for Travel Medicine US ☎ 1 404 373 8282, ⓦ istm.org. Has a full list of travel health clinics.

MASTA (Medical Advisory Service for Travellers Abroad) UK check ⓦ masta-travel-health.com for the nearest clinic.

Tropical Medical Bureau Ireland ☎ 1850 487 674, ⓦ tmb.ie. The TMB has 22 travel clinics across the country.

The Travel Doctor – TMVC Australia ☎ 1300 658 844, ⓦ traveldoctor.com.au. Lists travel clinics in Australia.

Culture and etiquette

Chile's social mores reflect the European ancestry of the majority of its population, and travellers from the West will have little trouble fitting in, especially if they have a good grasp of Spanish. Chileans are not especially ebullient and high-spirited – particularly when compared with their Argentine neighbours – and are often considered rather formal.

However, they are also known for their quick wit and wordplay, and considering its relatively small population, Chile has produced an impressive array of writers, poets, artists and musicians. The overwhelming majority of Chileans identify themselves as **Catholic**, and the church still has significant – though waning – influence. Unsurprisingly, then, this is a rather conservative country: divorce was legalized in 2004; the legalization of abortion (in certain circumstances) came thirteen years later; and attitudes towards homosexuality, though improving, are generally far from enlightened (see page 47). Chileans are very family-oriented: children are popular and travelling **families** can expect special treatment and friendly attention.

Although stereotypical Latin American **machismo** undoubtedly exists, it is not as strong as in some other countries in the region.

Travel essentials

Costs

Chile is expensive compared with most of South America. Accommodation is comparatively pricey, but eating out is relatively good value if you avoid the flashier restaurants and take advantage of set lunch menus. Transport is good value given the levels of comfort.

In general, per day, you'll need to allow US$55 to get by on a tight budget; around US$100 to live more comfortably, staying in mid-range hotels and eating in good restaurants; and upwards of US$150 to live fewln luxury.

The most widespread hidden cost in Chile is the **IVA** (Impuesto al Valor Agregado), a tax of nineteen percent added to most goods and services. Although most prices include IVA, there are many irritating exceptions. Hotel rates sometimes include IVA and sometimes don't; as a tourist, you're supposed to be exempt from IVA if you pay for your accommodation in US dollars. Car rental is almost always quoted without IVA. If in doubt, you should always clarify whether a price quoted to you includes the tax.

Once obtained, various official and quasi-official **youth/student ID cards** soon pay for themselves in savings. Full-time students are eligible for the International Student ID Card (ISIC; ⓦ isic.org).

The **exchange rate** at the time of writing was: £1 = CH$819; $1 = CH$605; €1 = CH$729. Check the latest rates at ⓦ oanda.com.

Crime and personal safety

Chile is one of the **safest** South American countries, and violent crime against tourists is rare. The kind

EMERGENCY NUMBERS

Air rescue 138 (for mountaineering accidents)
Ambulance 131
Carabineros 133
Coast Guard 137
Fire 132
Investigaciones 134 (for serious crimes)

of sophisticated tactics used by thieves in neighbouring Peru and Bolivia are extremely uncommon in Chile, and the fact that you can walk around without being gripped by paranoia is one of the country's major bonuses.

This is not to say, of course, that you don't need to be careful. Opportunistic pickpocketing and **petty theft** is common in Santiago and major cities such as Valparaíso, Arica and Puerto Montt, and you should take all the normal precautions to safeguard your money and valuables, paying special attention in bus terminals and markets – wear a money belt, and keep it tucked inside the waistband of your trousers or skirt, out of sight, and don't wear flashy jewellery, flaunt expensive phones or cameras, or carry a handbag. It's also a good idea to keep copies of your passport, tourist card, driving licence and credit card details separate from the originals (scanning and saving digital copies is also advisable) – whether it's safer to carry the originals with you or leave them in your hotel is debatable, but whatever you do, you should always have some form of ID on you, even if this is just a copy of your passport.

Chile's police force, the **carabineros**, has the whole country covered, with stations in even the most remote areas, particularly in border regions. If you're robbed and need a police report for an insurance claim, you should go to the nearest *retén* (police station), where details of the theft will be entered in a logbook. You'll be issued a slip of paper with the record number of the entry, but in most cases a full report won't be typed out until your insurance company requests it.

Electricity

220V/50Hz is the standard throughout Chile. The sockets are two-pronged, with round pins (as opposed to the flat pins common in neighbouring countries).

Insurance

Travel insurance is essential. Before buying a new policy, check whether you are already covered: some all-risks home insurance policies may cover your possessions when overseas, and many private medical schemes include cover when abroad.

After checking out these possibilities, you might want to contact a **specialist travel insurance company**, or consider the travel insurance deal offered by Rough Guides (see above). A typical travel insurance policy usually provides cover for the loss of baggage, tickets and – up to a certain limit – cash, as well as cancellation or curtailment of your journey. Most exclude so-called dangerous sports unless an extra premium is paid; in Chile this can mean scuba diving, whitewater rafting, windsurfing and trekking, though probably not kayaking or jeep safaris. If you take medical coverage, ascertain whether benefits will be paid as treatment proceeds or only after you return home, and if there is a 24-hour medical emergency number.

When securing baggage cover, make sure that the per-article limit will cover the most valuable possession you're bringing with you. If you need to make a claim, you should keep receipts for medicines and medical treatment, and in the event you have anything stolen, you must obtain an official statement from the police.

Internet

Chile is generally very well connected. Cybercafés are everywhere, and broadband (*banda ancha*) is common. Most hotels, hostels, cafes, bars and restaurants provide **wi-fi** access, normally for free.

As most accommodation offers free wi-fi, the reviews in this Guide only mention wi-fi in places where there is no service (or where it is limited by location, eg only in the lobby) or where you have to pay for it.

LGBT travellers

Chilean society is generally extremely **conservative**, and homosexuality is still a taboo subject for many. Outside Santiago – with the minor exceptions of some northern cities such as La Serena and Antofagasta – there are few LGBT venues, and sadly it is advisable for same-sex couples to do as the locals do and remain discreet, especially in public. Machismo, while not as evident as in other Latin American countries, is nevertheless deeply ingrained, but is increasingly being challenged. That said, gay-bashing and other homophobic acts are rare and the government has passed anti-discrimination legislation. The International Gay and Lesbian Association (W iglta.org) has information on LGBT-friendly travel companies in Chile and around the world.

Living and/or working in Chile

There are plenty of short-term work opportunities for foreigners in Chile; the difficultly lies in obtaining and maintaining a **work visa**.

A tourist card does not allow you to undertake any **paid employment** in Chile – for this, you need to get a work visa before you enter the country, which can either be arranged by your employer in Chile or by yourself on presentation (to your embassy or consulate) of an employment contract authorized by a Chilean public notary. You can't swap a tourist card for a work visa while you're in Chile, which means that legally you can't just go out and find a job – though many language schools are happy to ignore the rules when employing teachers.

If you're pre-planning a longer stay, consult **Overseas Jobs Express** (W overseasjobs.com) and the **International Career and Employment Center** (W internationaljobs.org); both list internships, jobs and volunteer opportunities across the world.

Many students come to Chile taking advantage of semester or **year-abroad programmes** offered by their universities. Go to W studyabroad.com for links and listings to study programmes worldwide.

Teaching English

Demand for native-speaking English teachers in Chilean cities is high and makes **language teaching** an obvious work option. Though it can be competitive, it's relatively easy to find work either teaching general English in private language schools or business English within companies. A lucky few get by with minimal teaching experience, but with an **EFL** (English Language Teaching), **TEFL** (Teaching English as a Foreign Language) or **CELTA** (Certificate in English Language Teaching to Adults) qualification you're in a far better position to get a job with a reputable employer. The most lucrative work is private, one-to-one lessons, which are best sought through word of mouth or by placing an ad in a local newspaper. The British Council website (W britishcouncil.org) has a list of vacancies.

Volunteering

You can easily **volunteer** in Chile, but you'll often have to pay for the privilege. Many organizations target people on gap years (at whatever stage in their lives) and offer placements on both inner city and environmental projects. For free or low-cost volunteer positions across South America takie a look at the excellent W volunteersouthamerica. net.

STUDY AND WORK PROGRAMMES

AFS Intercultural Programs W afs.org. Intercultural exchange organization with programmes in more than fifty countries.

Amerispan W amerispan.com. Highly rated educational travel company that specializes in language courses, but also runs volunteer programmes all over Latin America.

British Council W britishcouncil.org. Produces a free leaflet which details study opportunities abroad. The website has a list of current job vacancies for recruiting TEFL teachers for posts worldwide.

Council on International Educational Exchange (CIEE) W ciee.org. Leading NGO offering study programmes and volunteer projects around the world.

Earthwatch Institute W earthwatch.org. Scientific expedition project that spans more than fifty countries with environmental and archeological ventures worldwide.

Rainforest Concern W rainforestconcern.org. Volunteering opportunities protecting threatened habitats in South and Central America. The Chilean project is based in the Nasampulli Reserve in the south of the country.

Raleigh International W raleighinternational.org. Volunteer projects across the world for young travellers.

Volunteer South America W volunteersouthamerica.net. Free and low-cost volunteering opportunities across the continent.

Maps

The maps in this Guide will help you to navigate the main tourist destinations, but if you are driving, hiking or heading off the beaten track, you may require more detailed ones. No two **road maps** of Chile are identical, and none is absolutely correct, with the bulk of errors relating to the representation of dirt roads. Reliable country maps include the comprehensive **TurisTel** map, printed in the back of its guides to Chile and also published in a separate booklet. Sernatur produces a good fold-out map of the whole of Chile, on sale at the main office in Santiago, and an excellent map of the north, free from Sernatur offices in Santiago and the north. Other useful maps include **Auto Mapa**'s Rutas de Chile series, distributed internationally. Outside Chile, also look for the **Reise Know-How Verlag** and **Nelles Verlag** maps of Chile, which combine clear road detail along with contours and colour tinting.

You can pick up free and usually adequate **street plans** in the tourist office of most cities, but better by far are those contained in the Turistel guidebooks. The most comprehensive A–Z of Santiago appears in the back of the CTC phone directory.

The best maps to use for **hiking** are the series of **JLM** maps, which cover some of the main national parks and occasionally extend into Argentina. They're produced in collaboration with Conaf and are available in bookshops and some souvenir or outdoor stores.

The media

Media output in Chile is nothing to get excited about. If you know where to look, journalistic standards can be high but you might find yourself turning to foreign TV channels, websites or papers if you want an international view on events.

Newspapers

The Chilean **press** has managed to uphold a strong tradition of editorial freedom ever since the country's first newspaper, *La Aurora*, was published by an anti-royalist friar in 1812, during the early days of the independence movement. One year before *La Aurora* folded in 1827, a new newspaper, *El Mercurio* (W emol.com), went to press in Valparaíso, and is now the longest-running newspaper in the Spanish-speaking world. Emphatically conservative, and owned by the powerful Edwards family, *El Mercurio* is considered the most serious of Chile's dailies, but still has a minimal international coverage. The other major daily is *La Tercera,* which tends to be more sensationalist. The liberal-leaning *La Nación* is the official newspaper of the state, while the *Santiago Times* (W santiagotimes.cl), and online English-language paper, is a good read.

Chile also produces a plethora of racy **tabloids** as well as ¡*Hola!*-style clones. For a more edifying read, try the selection of *Private Eye*-style satirical papers, such as *The Clinic* (W theclinic.cl). In Santiago you can usually track down a selection of foreign papers, though elsewhere you'll generally have to rely on online editions.

TV and radio

Cable **TV** is widespread, offering innumerable domestic and international channels. CNN is always on offer, as are a range of (mainly US) sports and entertainment channels; BBC World is less common. Of the five terrestrial channels, top choice is Channel 7, the state-owned Televisión Nacional, which makes the best programmes in Chile. Generally, however, soap operas, game shows and football predominate.

In terms of international **radio**, Voice of America (W voanews.com) and Radio Canada (W rcinet.ca) can both be accessed but unfortunately the BBC no longer broadcasts its World Service in Chile.

Money

The basic unit of **currency** is the peso, usually represented by the $ sign (and by CH$ in this book, for clarity). Many hotels, particularly the more expensive ones, and some tour companies, accept US dollars cash (and will give you a discount for paying this way; see page 31). Apart from this, you'll be expected to pay for everything in local currency. You may, however, come across prices quoted in the mysterious **"UF"**. This stands for *unidad de fomento* and is an index-linked monetary unit adjusted (every minute) daily to remain in line with inflation. The only time you're likely to come across it is if you rent a vehicle (your liability, in the event of an accident, will probably be quoted in UFs on the rental contract). You'll find the exchange rate of the UF against the Chilean peso in the daily newspapers, along with the rates for all the other currencies.

Note that prices throughout this Guide are quoted in Chilean pesos, Argentine pesos or US dollars, according to how the establishment or company in question quotes them on the ground.

Credit and debit cards can be used either in **ATMs** (which have a CH$150,000–200,000 daily limit and usually charge a withdrawal fee). MasterCard, Visa and American Express are accepted just about everywhere, but other cards may not be recognized. Alternatively, pick up a pre-paid debit card such as Travelex's Cash Passport (ⓦ travelex.co.uk). While credit/debit cards are widely accepted by businesses in cities and major tourist destinations, this is not the case in more remote areas such as Tierra del Fuego and Easter Island, where it is advisable to bring plenty of cash.

Cities and tourist destinations usually have at least one **casa de cambio** (exchange bureau) for changing foreign currency. **Travellers' cheques** are now rarely accepted.

Opening hours and public holidays

Most **shops and services** open Monday to Friday from 9am to 1pm and 3pm to 6pm or 7pm, and on Saturday from 10am or 11am until 2pm. Supermarkets stay open at lunchtime and may close as late as 11pm on weekdays and Saturdays in big cities. Large shopping malls are often open all day on Sundays. **Banks** have more limited hours, generally Monday to Friday from 9am to 2pm, but *casas de cambio* tend to use the same opening hours as shops.

Many **tourist offices** only open Monday to Friday throughout the year, with a break for lunch, but in summer (usually mid-Dec to mid-March) some increase their weekday hours and open on Saturday and sometimes Sunday; note that their hours are subject to frequent change. Post offices don't close at lunchtime on weekdays and are open on Saturdays from 9am to 1pm.

February is the main holiday month in Chile, when there's an exodus from the big cities to the beaches or the Lake District, leaving some shops and restaurants closed. February is also an easy time to get around in Santiago, as the city appears half-abandoned.

MAJOR HOLIDAYS

January 1 New Year's Day (*Año nuevo*).
Easter Good Friday, Easter Saturday and Easter Sunday are the climax to Holy Week (*Semana Santa*).
May 1 Labour Day (*Día del Trabajo*).
May 21 *Combate Naval de Iquique*. A Remembrance Day celebrating the end of the War of the Pacific after the naval victory at Iquique.
June 15 Corpus Christi.
June, last Monday San Pedro and San Pablo.
August 15 Assumption of the Virgin.
September 18 National Independence Day (*Fiestas Patrias*), in celebration of the first provisional government of 1810.
September 19 Armed Forces Day (*Día del Ejército*).
October 12 Columbus Day (*Día de la Raza*), marking the discovery of America.

CALLING HOME FROM ABROAD

To **make an international call from Chile**, dial the "carrier code" (see page 49), then "00", then the destination's country code (see below), before the rest of the number. Note that the initial zero is omitted from the area code when dialling the UK, Ireland, Australia and New Zealand from abroad.
Australia 00 + 61 + area code minus initial zero
Ireland 00 + 353 + area code minus initial zero
New Zealand 00 + 64 + area code minus initial zero
South Africa 00 + 27+ area code
UK 00 + 44 + area code minus initial zero
US and Canada 00 + 1 + area code

November 1 All Saints' Day (*Todos los Santos*).
December 8 Immaculate Conception.
December 25 Christmas Day (*Navidad*).

Phones

Most **landline numbers** consist of seven or eight digits, preceded by the city/area code; if dialling from the same area, drop the city or area code and dial the seven or eight digits directly. If you are making a long-distance call you need to first dial a "carrier code" (for example "188" for Telefónica or "181" for Movistar), then an area code (for example "2" for the Santiago metropolitan region or "32" for the Valparaíso region) and finally the number itself. **Mobile phone numbers** have eight digits. When calling from a landline to a mobile, dial "09" and then the rest of the number (for mobile to mobile calls, the "09" is not necessary).

Using **phonecards** is a practical way to phone abroad, and it's worth stocking up on them in major cities, as you can't always buy them elsewhere. Alternatively, there are dozens of call centres or **centros de llamadas** in most cities. Another convenient option is to take along an **international calling card**. The least expensive way to call home, however, is via **Skype**.

The cheapest way to use your mobile (making sure it is unlocked first) is to pick up a **local SIM card**. You now need to register (for free) online – visit ⓦ multibanda.cl for more information. The main mobile operators in Chile are Movistar, Entel and Claro.

Post

The **postal service** is very reliable for international items, but can be surprisingly erratic for domestic items. A letter from Santiago takes about five days to reach Europe, a little less time to reach North America and usually no more than a couple of weeks to more remote destinations. Allow a few extra days for letters posted from other towns and cities. Do not send any gifts to Chile using regular post; theft is extremely common for incoming shipments. For important shipping to Chile try express services such as FedEx and DHL.

Post offices are marked by a blue Correos sign, and are usually on or near the Plaza de Armas of any town; postboxes are blue, and bear the blue Correos symbol.

Shopping

While Chile's **handicrafts** (*artesanía*) are nowhere near as diverse or colourful as in Peru or Bolivia, you can still find a range of beautiful souvenirs, usually sold in *ferias artesanales* (craft markets) on or near the central squares of the main towns. As for day-to-day **essentials**, you'll be able to locate just about everything you need in the main towns across the country.

The finest and arguably most beautiful goods you can buy in Chile are the items – mainly jewellery – made of **lapis lazuli**, the deep-blue semi-precious stone found only here and in Afghanistan. Note that the deeper the colour of the stone, the better its quality. Though certainly less expensive than lapis exports sold abroad, they're still pricey.

Most *artesanía* is considerably less expensive. In the **Norte Grande**, the most common articles are alpaca sweaters, gloves and scarves, which you'll find in *altiplano* villages like Parinacota, or in Arica and Iquique. The quality is usually fairly low, but they're inexpensive and very attractive. In the **Norte Chico**, you can pick up some beautiful leather goods, particularly in the crafts markets of La Serena. You might also be tempted to buy a bottle of pisco there, so that you can recreate that pisco sour experience back home – though you're probably better off getting it at a supermarket in Santiago before you leave, to save yourself carting it about. The **Central Valley**, as the agricultural heartland of Chile, is famous for its *huaso* gear, and you'll find brightly coloured ponchos and stiff straw hats in the numerous working *huaso* shops. The highlight in the **Lake District** is the traditional Mapuche silver jewellery, while the **far south** is a good place to buy chunky, colourful knitwear.

A range of these goods can also be bought in the major crafts markets in **Santiago**, notably Los Dominicos market. Also worth checking out are Santiago's little **flea markets** (see page 87).

Hard **haggling** is neither commonly practised nor expected in Chile, though a bit of bargaining is in order at many markets.

Time

Confusingly, Chile has frequently changed its **time zones** in recent years. As of early 2018, most of the mainland was three hours behind GMT in the summer (December–March) and four hours behind in the winter (June–Sept); the Magallanes region (which covers the extreme south of the country) was three hours behind GMT year round. Easter Island was five hours behind in the summer, and six hours behind in the winter.

Tourist information

The government-run tourist board, **Sernatur** (Ⓦ sernatur.cl), has a large office in Santiago, plus branches in every provincial capital. In smaller towns you're more likely to find a municipal **Oficina de Turismo**, sometimes attached to the Municipalidad (town hall). If there's no separate tourist office it's worth trying the Municipalidad itself.

USEFUL WEBSITES

Chile Travel Ⓦ chile.travel. The official government tourism site.

Latin America Bureau Ⓦ lab.org.uk. The website of this well-respected UK-based charity has the latest news, analysis and information from across Latin America, including Chile.

Turismo Chile Ⓦ chiletourism.travel. Info and news on the major attractions in each region, with some historical and cultural background.

Travellers with disabilities

Chile makes very few provisions for people with disabilities, and travellers with mobility problems will have to contend with a lack of lifts, high kerbs, dangerous potholes on pavements and worse. However, Chileans are courteous people and are likely to offer assistance when needed. Spacious, specially designed toilets are becoming more common in airports and the newer shopping malls, but restaurants and bars are progressing at a slower pace. New public buildings are legally required to provide **disabled access**, and there will usually be a full range of facilities in the more expensive hotels. It is worth employing the help of the **local tourist office** for information on the most suitable place to stay. **Public transport**, on the other hand, is far more of a challenge. Most bus companies do not have any dedicated disabled facilities so, given that reserved disabled parking is increasingly common, travelling with your **own vehicle** might be the easier option.

Travelling with children

Families are highly regarded in Latin American societies, and Chile is no exception. Chile's **restaurants** are well used to catering for children and will happily provide smaller portions for younger diners. The main health hazards to watch out for are the heat and sun. Always remember that the sun in Chile is fierce, so hats and bonnets are essential; this is especially true in the south where the ozone layer is particularly thin. Very high-factor **sunscreen** can be difficult to come by in remote towns so it is best to stock up at pharmacies in the bigger cities. **High altitudes** (see page 44) may cause children problems and, like adults, they must acclimatize before walking too strenuously above 2000m. If you intend to travel with babies and very young children to high altitudes, consult your doctor for advice before you leave.

Long-distances buses charge for each seat so you'll only pay less if a child is sitting on your knee. On **city buses**, however, small children often travel for free but will be expected to give up their seat for paying customers without one. Airline companies generally charge a third less for passengers under 12 so look out for last-minute **discount flights** – they can make flying an affordable alternative to an arduous bus ride.

Santiago
and around

SANHATTAN, SANTIAGO

1 Santiago and around

Set on a wide plain near the foot of the Andes, Santiago boasts one of the most dazzling backdrops of any capital city on earth. The views onto the towering cordillera after a rainstorm clears the air are truly magnificent, especially in winter, when the snow-covered peaks rise behind the city like a giant white rampart against the blue sky (though smog, unfortunately, often obscures such vistas). The city itself is a rapidly expanding metropolis of approaching seven million people, and though it has long hidden in the shadow of more famous South American cities, such as Buenos Aires and Rio de Janeiro, it nevertheless has its own proud identity.

Santiago is divided into 32 autonomous **comunas**, most of them squat, flat suburbs stretching out from the heart of the city. The **historic centre**, in contrast, is compact, manageable, and has a pleasant atmosphere. Part of the appeal comes from the fact that it's so **green**: tall, luxuriant trees fill the main square, and there are numerous meticulously landscaped parks. Above all, though, it's the all-pervading sense of energy that makes the place so alluring, with crowds of Santiaguinos constantly milling through narrow streets packed with shoe-shiners, fruit barrows, news kiosks and sellers of everything from coat hangers to pirated DVDs.

Architecturally, the city is a bit of a hotchpotch, thanks to a succession of earthquakes and a spate of haphazard rebuilding in the 1960s and 1970s. Ugly office blocks and shopping arcades (*galerías*) compete for space with beautifully maintained colonial buildings, while **east of the centre** Santiago's economic boom is reflected in the glittering new commercial buildings, skyscrapers and luxury hotels of the *comunas* of Vitacura, Providencia and Las Condes. These different faces are part of a wider set of contrasts – between the American-style shopping malls in the **barrios altos**, for example, and the old-fashioned shops in the historic centre; between the modish lounge bars and the simple cafés known as *fuentes de soda*; and, in particular, between the sharp-suited professionals and the scores of street sellers scrambling to make a living. It's not a place of excesses, however: homelessness is minimal compared with many other cities of its size, and Santiago is pretty safe.

It also makes a great base for exploring the surrounding region. With the **Andes** so close and accessible, you can be right in the mountains in an hour or two. In winter people go **skiing** for the day; in warmer months the **Cajón del Maipo** offers fantastic trekking, horseriding and rafting. The port city of Valparaíso (see page 96) and beach resorts in and around Viña del Mar (see page 110) are in day-trip territory from the capital, while nearby villages such as **Los Andes** and **Pomaire** can provide a relaxing antidote to Santiago's bustle. Still more tempting are the many **vineyards** within easy reach (see page 89).

BACK-COUNTRY SKIERS NEAR PORTILLO

Highlights

❶ Plaza de Armas Gaze at the colonial architecture surrounding Santiago's lively central plaza – or sit on a bench and take in the hustle and bustle. See page 57

❷ Museo Chileno de Arte Precolombino This exquisite collection of artefacts from dozens of pre-Hispanic civilizations features fine tapestries, intricate ceramics and dazzling jewels. See page 62

❸ Museo de la Memoria y los Derechos Humanos This large museum is dedicated to remembering the victims of Chile's dictatorship. It may not make comfortable viewing, but it is essential to understanding those dark years. See page 70

❹ Mercado Central and Feria Municipal La Vega Explore the city's two main markets and sample a selection of excellent fresh fish and seafood. See page 70

❺ Cerro San Cristóbal Ride the elevator to the top of this steep hill where, on a clear day, you have great views of the snowcapped Andes towering over the city. See page 72

❻ Andean skiing Skiers and snowboarders will delight in the world-class ski areas near Santiago, including the world-famous Portillo resort. See page 92

HIGHLIGHTS ARE MARKED ON THE MAPS ON PAGES 56 AND 58

1 Santiago

Increasingly becoming a destination in its own right rather than simply the entry point into Chile, **SANTIAGO** is a cultural, economic and historical hub, and the best place to get a handle on the country's identity. Dipping into the city's vibrant and constantly developing cultural scene, checking out its museums, and dining at its varied restaurants will really help you make the most of your time in this kaleidoscopic country.

You can get round many of Santiago's attractions on foot in two to three days. The historic centre has the bustling **Plaza de Armas** at its core, while north of downtown, on the other side of the Río Mapocho, it's an easy funicular ride up **Cerro San Cristóbal**, whose summit provides unrivalled views. At its foot, **Barrio Bellavista** is replete with cafés, restaurants, bars and clubs. West of the centre, the once glamorous *barrios* that housed Santiago's moneyed classes at the beginning of the twentieth century make for rewarding, romantic wanders, and contain some splendid old mansions and museums. As you move east into Providencia and Las Condes, the tone is newer and flasher, with shiny malls and upmarket restaurants, as well as the crafts market at **Los Dominicos**.

Brief history

In 1540, some seven years after Francisco Pizarro conquered Cuzco in Peru, he dispatched **Pedro de Valdivia** southwards to claim and settle more territory for the Spanish crown. After eleven months of travelling, Valdivia and his 150 men reached what

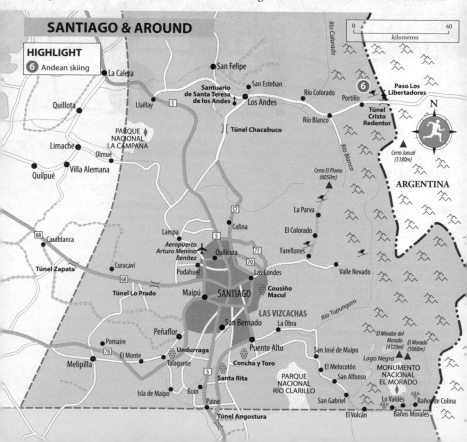

he considered to be a suitable site for a new city and, on February 12, 1541, officially founded "Santiago de la Nueva Extremadura", wedged into a triangle of land bounded by the Río Mapocho to the north, its southern branch to the south and the rocky Santa Lucía hill to the east. A native population of **Picunche** was scattered around the region, but this didn't deter Valdivia from getting down to business: with great alacrity the main square was established and the surrounding streets were marked out with a string and ruler, a fort was built in the square (thus named "Plaza de Armas") and several other buildings were erected. Six months later they were all razed in a Picunche raid.

The town was doggedly rebuilt to the same plans, and Santiago began to take on the shape of a new colonial capital. But nine years after founding it, the Spaniards, in search of gold, shifted their attention to Arauco in the south, and Santiago became something of a backwater. Following the violent Mapuche uprising in 1553, however, the Spaniards were forced to abandon their towns south of the Bio Bío, and many returned to Santiago. Nonetheless, growth continued to be very slow: settlers were never large in number, and what opportunities the land offered were thwarted by strict trade restrictions. Moreover, expansion was repeatedly knocked back by regular **earthquakes**.

Independence

Santiago started to look like a real capital during the course of the eighteenth century, as trade restrictions were eased, more wealth was created, and the population increased. However, it wasn't until after **independence** in 1818 that expansion really got going, as the rich clamoured to build themselves glamorous mansions and the state erected beautiful public buildings such as the Teatro Municipal.

Santiago today

As the city entered the twentieth century it began to push eastwards into the new *barrio alto* and north into **Bellavista**. The horizontal spread has gone well beyond these limits since then, gobbling up outlying towns and villages at great speed; Gran Santiago now stretches 40km by 40km. Its central zones have shot up vertically, too, particularly in **Providencia** and **Las Condes**, where the showy high-rise buildings reflect the country's rapid economic growth since the 1990s. Despite this dramatic transformation, however, the city's central core still sticks to the same street pattern marked out by Pedro de Valdivia in 1541, and its first public space, the Plaza de Armas, is still at the heart of its street life.

Plaza de Armas and around

The **Plaza de Armas** is the centre of Santiago and the country, both literally – all distances to the rest of Chile are measured from here – and symbolically. It was the first public space laid out by Pedro de Valdivia when he founded the city in 1541 and quickly became the nucleus of Santiago's administrative, commercial and social life. This is where the young capital's most important seats of power – the law courts, the governor's palace, and the cathedral – were built, and where its markets, bullfights (no longer allowed), festivals and other public activities took place. Four and a half centuries later, this is still where the city's pulse beats loudest, and half an hour's people-watching here is perhaps the best introduction to Santiago.

These days the open market space has been replaced by **flower gardens** and numerous trees; palms, poplars and eucalyptus tower over benches packed with giggling schoolchildren, gossiping old ladies, lovers, tourists and packs of uniformed shop girls on their lunch break. Thirsty dogs hang around the fountain; shoe-shiners polish the feet of businessmen clutching *El Mercurio*; and ancient-looking chess players hold sombre tournaments inside the bandstand. Against this is a backdrop of constant noise supplied by street performers, singers and evangelical preachers. Meanwhile, a constant ebb and flow of people march in and out of the great civic and religious buildings enclosing the square.

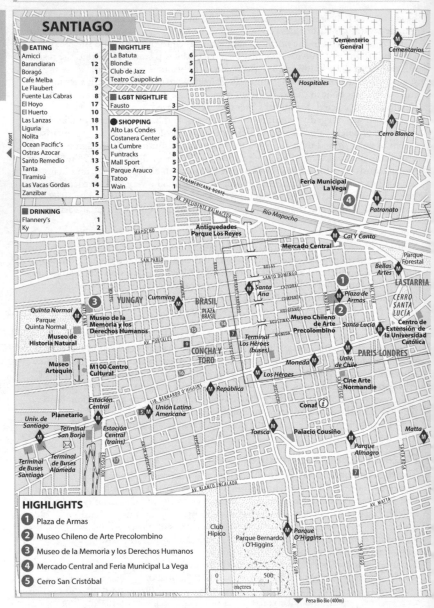

SANTIAGO

● EATING

Amicci	6
Barandiaran	12
Boragó	1
Cafe Melba	7
Le Flaubert	9
Fuente Las Cabras	8
El Hoyo	17
El Huerto	10
Las Lanzas	18
Liguria	11
Nolita	3
Ocean Pacific's	15
Ostras Azocar	16
Santo Remedio	13
Tanta	5
Tiramisú	4
Las Vacas Gordas	14
Zanzibar	2

■ DRINKING

Flannery's	1
Ky	2

■ NIGHTLIFE

La Batuta	6
Blondie	5
Club de Jazz	4
Teatro Caupolicán	7

● LGBT NIGHTLIFE

Fausto	3

● SHOPPING

Alto Las Condes	4
Costanera Center	6
La Cumbre	3
Funtracks	8
Mall Sport	5
Parque Arauco	2
Tatoo	7
Wain	1

HIGHLIGHTS

1. Plaza de Armas
2. Museo Chileno de Arte Precolombino
3. Museo de la Memoria y los Derechos Humanos
4. Mercado Central and Feria Municipal La Vega
5. Cerro San Cristóbal

Correo Central

Plaza de Armas 559 • Mon–Fri 8.30am–7pm, Sat 8.30am–1pm

On the northwest corner of the Plaza de Armas stands the **Correo Central** (central post office), whose interior, with its tiered galleries crowned by a beautiful glass roof, is every bit as impressive as its elaborate facade. It was built in 1882 on the foundations of what had been the Palacio de los Gobernadores (governors' palace) during

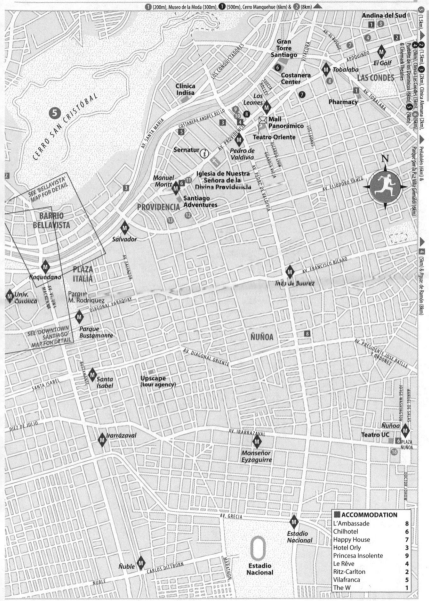

SEE 'BELLAVISTA' MAP FOR DETAIL

SEE 'DOWNTOWN SANTIAGO' MAP FOR DETAIL

■ ACCOMMODATION	
L'Ambassade	8
Chilhotel	6
Happy House	7
Hotel Orly	3
Princesa Insolente	9
Le Rêve	4
Ritz-Carlton	2
Vilafranca	5
The W	1

colonial times, and the Palacio de los Presidentes de Chile (presidential palace) after independence.

Municipalidad

Plaza de Armas s/n

On the northeast corner of the Plaza de Armas is the pale, Neoclassical edifice of Santiago's **Municipalidad**. The first *cabildo* (town hall) was erected on this site

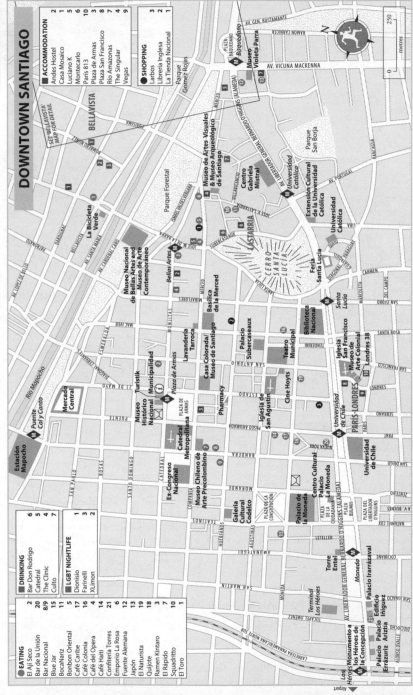

DOWNTOWN SANTIAGO

■ ACCOMMODATION
Andes Hostel	2
Casa Mosaico	1
Luciano K	5
Montecarlo	6
Paris 813	10
Plaza de Armas	3
Plaza San Francisco	8
Río Amazonas	7
The Singular	4
Vegas	9

● SHOPPING
Larbos	3
Librería Inglesa	2
La Tienda Nacional	1

● EATING
El Ají Seco	2
Bar de la Unión	20
Bar Nacional	8/9
Blue Jar	11
BocaNariz	
Bonbon Oriental	5
Café Caribe	17
Café Colonia	16
Café del Opera	4
Café Haití	14
Confitería Torres	21
Emporio La Rosa	6
Fuente Alemana	12
Japón	13
El Naturista	19
Quijote	18
Ramen Kintaro	3
El Rápido	7
Squadritto	10
El Toro	1

■ DRINKING
Bar Don Rodrigo	6
Catedral	5
The Clinic	4
Culto	7

■ LGBT NIGHTLIFE
Dionisio	1
Farinelli	3
XLimon	2

'SEE BELLAVISTA' MAP FOR DETAIL

back in the early seventeenth century and also contained the city's prison. Several reconstructions and restorations have taken place since then, most recently in 1895. A curious feature is that the basement is still divided into the original cells of the old prison, now used by the municipal tourist office (see page 78).

Museo Histórico Nacional

Plaza de Armas 951 • Tues–Sun 10am–6pm • Free • ☎ 2 2411 7010, ⓦ museohistoriconacional.cl

Wedged between the Correo and the Municipalidad is the splendid **Palacio de la Real Audiencia**, an immaculately preserved colonial building that's borne witness to some of Santiago's most important turns of history. Built by the Spanish Crown between 1804 and 1807 to house the royal courts of justice, it had served this purpose for just two years when Chile's first government junta assembled here to replace the Spanish governor with its own elected leader. Eight years later it was the meeting place of Chile's first Congress, and the building was the seat of government until 1846, when President Bulnes moved to La Moneda. The Palacio's grand old rooms, situated around a large central courtyard, today house the **Museo Histórico Nacional**. Arranged chronologically over two floors, the rooms are crammed with eclectic relics of the past, including furniture, city models and paintings of historic rather than artistic value – note the classic portrait of Bernardo O'Higgins upstairs, followed by a row of paintings of members of the Chilean elite, all of whom seem to be doing their best to imitate the independence hero. All of it is fun to look at, but it's a little too chaotic to be really illuminating, even if you can understand the Spanish-only information panels.

Catedral Metropolitana

Plaza de Armas • Mon 11am–7pm, Tues–Sat 10am–7pm, Sun 9am–7pm • Free • ☎ 2 2696 2777, ⓦ iglesiadesantiago.cl

The west side of the Plaza de Armas is dominated by the grandiose stone bulk of the **Catedral Metropolitana**. A combination of Neoclassical and Baroque styles, with its orderly columns and pediment and its ornate bell towers, the cathedral bears the mark of **Joaquín Toesca**, who was brought over from Italy in 1780 to oversee its completion. Toesca went on to become the most important architect of colonial Chile, designing many of Santiago's public buildings, including La Moneda (see page 64). This is actually the fifth church to be built on this site; the first was burned down by Picunche just months after Valdivia had it built, and the others were destroyed by earthquakes. Inside, take a look at the main altar, carved out of marble and richly embellished with bronze and lapis lazuli. Note also the intricately crafted silver frontal, the work of Bavarian Jesuits in the sixteenth century.

Casa Colorada

Merced 860 • Mon–Fri noon–6pm • Free • ☎ 2 2386 7400, ⓦ santiagocultura.cl/casa-colorada

Just off the southeast corner of the Plaza de Armas is the **Casa Colorada**, built in 1769 and generally considered to be Santiago's best-preserved colonial house. With its clay-tiled roof, row of balconied windows opening onto the street and distinctive, deep-red walls, the two-storey mansion certainly provides a striking example of an eighteenth-century town residence. The house is built around two large patios, and hosts the humble **Museo de Santiago**, dedicated to the history of the city from pre-Columbian to modern times.

Ex-Congreso Nacional

Morandé and Compañía • Not open to the public

The impressive white, classically built **Ex Congreso Nacional**, set amid lush gardens two blocks west of the Plaza de Armas, is where Congress used to meet until it was dissolved on September 11, 1973, the day of the coup d'état. In 1990, following the end of the military regime, a new congress building was erected in Valparaíso, although members of Congress still use this one for its library and meeting rooms.

1

Museo Chileno de Arte Precolombino

Compañía and Bandera • Tues–Sun 10am–6pm • CH$4500 • ☎ 2 2928 1500, ⓦ precolombino.cl

Just off the southwest corner of the Plaza de Armas stands the beautifully restored 1807 Real Casa de la Aduana (the old royal customs house), which now houses the **Museo Chileno de Arte Precolombino** – perhaps Chile's best museum.

The collection spans a period of about ten thousand years and covers an area stretching from present-day Mexico down to southern Chile, brilliantly illustrating the artistic wealth and diversity of Latin America's many cultures. The items were selected primarily on the basis of their artistic merit, rather than on their scientific or anthropological significance. Adding to the permanent exhibits in the basement and upstairs, the ground floor devotes three rooms to temporary exhibitions.

Chile antes de Chile

The basement houses the **Chile antes de Chile** (Chile before Chile) exhibition, which showcases items from pre-Columbian indigenous groups native to the sliver of land and islands that are now Chile. Highlights include **Aymara** silverware, wooden **Easter Island** statues and **Inca** tunics and bags with geometric designs that would not look out of a place in an Andes village market today, although these examples are hundreds of years old. The curious exhibit that looks like a grass skirt is also a relic from the Inca, who made it all the way down to central Chile during their expansion in the fifteenth century. Known as a **quipú**, it consists of many strands of wool attached to a single cord, and was used to keep records by means of a complex system of knots tied in the strands.

América Precolombina

The upstairs rooms – **América Precolombina** – hold works from around Latin America, arranged geographically. Many of the best items are grouped together in room 1, **Obras Maestras** (master works), including a beautifully fashioned Aztec ear ornament of pure gold, one of the few **Aztec** relics to escape being melted down by the Spanish *conquistadores*, and a huge bas-relief carving of a **Mayan** armed warrior with two small figures at his feet.

One of the most startling pieces is found in the **Mesoamérica** section (corresponding to present-day Mexico and central America) – a statue of **Xipé-Totec**. This god of spring is represented as a man covered in the skin of a monkey, exposing both male and female genitalia. At the time of the Spanish conquest, the cult of Xipé-Totec was widespread through the region, and was celebrated in a bizarre ritual in which a young man would cover himself with the skin of a sacrificial victim and wear it until it rotted off, revealing his young, fresh skin and symbolizing the growth of new vegetation from the earth.

In the **Área Intermedia**, covering what is now Ecuador, Colombia and central America, look out for wonderful **coca-leaf-chewing figures** known as *coqueros*, carved with a telltale lump in their mouth by the Capulí culture. The collection's best textiles, meanwhile, are preserved in the cool environment of the **Sala Textil**, illuminated by motion-sensitive lighting. Hanging here is a fragment of painted cloth depicting three human figures with fanged jaws. The oldest textile in the museum, it was produced by the Chavín culture almost three thousand years ago, and is still in astonishingly good condition.

South of Plaza de Armas

The bustling streets that spread out **south of Plaza de Armas** are where the bulk of the old city centre's commercial activity is to be found. One of the most packed pedestrian thoroughfares, **Ahumada**, runs south from the west side of the Plaza de Armas to the Alameda. Walking down, you'll pass sombre doorways leading into labyrinthine shopping arcades, *confiterías* and, between Agustinas and Moneda, the famous stand-up cafés **Caribe** and **Haiti**. Take a moment to pop into the **Banco de Chile**, between

Huérfanos and Agustinas; its vast hall, polished counters and beautiful old clock have barely changed since the bank opened in 1925.

Running parallel to Ahumada a block to the west, **Bandera** is another traffic-free street, whose pavement has been painted in colourful designs, with plenty of seating from where to admire the artwork. Another lively pedestrian street, **Huérfanos**, crosses Ahumada at right angles, one block south of the plaza, and is lined with numerous banks and cinemas. Several places of interest are dotted among the shops, office blocks and *galerías* of the surrounding streets.

Basílica de la Merced
Mac Iver 341 • Mon–Fri 10am–6pm • Free

The **Basílica de la Merced** is a towering, Neo-Renaissance structure just off Huérfanos, on the corner of Merced and Mac Iver, with a beautifully carved eighteenth-century pulpit. On the second floor of the church, the small **La Merced Museum** houses a collection of Easter Island artefacts, including a wooden **rongo rongo tablet**, carved in the undeciphered Easter Island script – one of just 29 left in the world.

Teatro Municipal
Agustinas 794 • ☎ 2 2463 1000, ⓦ municipal.cl

A splendid French-style Neoclassical building, the **Teatro Municipal** boasts a dazzling white facade of arches, columns and perfect symmetry. This has been the capital's most prestigious ballet, opera and classical music venue (see page 87) since its inauguration in 1857. It's worth asking to have a look around inside; the main auditorium is quite a sight, with its sumptuous red upholstery and crystal chandeliers.

Palacio Subercaseaux
Agustinas 741 • Not open to the public

Opposite the Teatro Municipal, and in the same French Neoclassical style, is the **Palacio Subercaseaux**, topped with a fine mansard roof. It was built at the beginning of the twentieth century for the Subercaseaux, one of the country's wealthiest families, after they had lived in Paris for twenty years, and it is said that Señora Subercaseaux would only agree to return to Santiago if her window looked out on to the Teatro Municipal. Today it is used by banks and the airforce officers' club.

Iglesia de San Agustín
Estado 180 • Daily 8am–8pm • Free • ☎ 2 2638 0978

The yellow **Iglesia de San Agustín** dates from 1608 but has been extensively rebuilt since. The chief interest within its highly decorative interior is the wooden carving of Christ, just left of the main altar as you face it (see below).

Galeria Cultural Codelco
Huérfanos 1270 • Mon–Fri 9am–6pm • Free

Copper is everywhere in the gleaming, appropriately burnished headquarters of the Corporacion Nacional del Cobre de Chile, usually known simply as **Codelco**. The

---

THE LEGEND OF THE SLIPPING CROWN

Known as the **Cristo de Mayo**, the wooden carving of Christ in the Iglesia de San Agustín (see above) is the subject of an intriguing local legend. The story goes that the crown of thorns around the figure's head slipped down to its neck during the 1647 earthquake, and that when someone tried to move the crown back up to its head, the carved face of Christ began to bleed. For this reason, the crown has remained untouched ever since, still hanging around the neck.

1

company – by far the world's largest producer of copper – was nationalized by Allende in the 1970s and has been a cash cow for the Chilean government ever since. Even the most pro-free market politicians have not seriously attempted to return it to private hands. The facade of the building has copper panels, the door handles are made with anti-microbial copper, and the metal lines the interior walls. Inside, the small **Galeria Cultural Codelco** offers changing exhibitions, usually themed on a slightly odd mixture of community outreach and – yes – copper.

Palacio de la Moneda and around

The presidential palace **La Moneda**, which can be approached either via the Alameda or the vast **Plaza de la Constitución**, is at the heart of the *centro cívico*, Chile's political centre. Ministers and their aides hurry back and forth between the ministry buildings in the area and the palace, while on the south side of La Moneda the newly landscaped Plaza de la Ciudadanía gives access to an underground cultural centre.

Palacio de La Moneda

Plaza de la Ciudadanía 26 • Guided tours (1hr) 4 daily, reserve in advance at ✉ visitas@presidencia.cl; changing of the guard Feb, March, June, July, Sept & Oct odd-numbered dates (ie 1st, 3rd, 5th etc); Jan, April, May, Aug, Nov & Dec even-numbered dates; Mon–Fri 10am, Sat & Sun 11am • Free, but bring your passport for identification

The perfect symmetry and compact elegance of the **Palacio de La Moneda**, one of Chile's best-known buildings, is spread across the entire block. The low-lying Neoclassical presidential palace was built between 1784 and 1805 by the celebrated Italian architect Joaquín Toesca for the purpose of housing the royal mint (hence the name *La Moneda* – literally, "the coin"). After some forty years it became the residential palace for the presidents of Chile, starting with Manuel Bulnes in 1848 and ending with Carlos Ibáñez del Campo in 1958. At this point it stopped being used as the president's home, but it continues to be the official seat of government. On September 11, 1973, President Salvador Allende committed suicide in his office in La Moneda rather than surrender to the encroaching military (see page 479), and photos of the airforce strafing the palace as Pinochet's coup closed in became among the most defining images of those troubled years.

Plaza de la Constitución

The **Plaza de la Constitución** is surrounded by important institutions, including the central bank, the foreign ministry and the finance ministry. In front of the justice ministry in the southeast corner of the square is one of Chile's few monuments to Allende, with his arm outstretched.

Centro Cultural Palacio La Moneda

Plaza de la Ciudadanía 26 • Daily 9am–8.30pm • 9am–noon CH$2500, noon–8.30pm CH$5000 • ☎ 2 2355 6500, 🌐 ccplm.cl

The **Centro Cultural Palacio La Moneda**, on the Alameda side of the Palacio de la Moneda, opened in advance of Chile's 2010 bicentennial celebrations. This flagship underground art gallery and cultural space has a huge modernist concrete central hall, which houses ever-changing exhibitions. The permanent displays in the adjacent galleries feature an eclectic array of artwork, jewellery, pottery, textiles and photography from across Chile (none of the exhibits is captioned in English). There's also an art cinema, film archive, craft store, bookshop, *Confitería Torres* branch (see page 81), restaurant and café.

Along the Alameda

Officially the **Avenida del Libertador General Bernardo O'Higgins**, Santiago's most vital east–west artery is universally known as the **Alameda**, a term used to describe a poplar-lined avenue used for strolling and recreation, and found in many Latin

American cities. This one began life as *La Cañada* (or "channel"), when a branch of the Mapocho was sealed off shortly before independence, and a roadway was created over the old riverbed. A few years later, when the Supreme Director Bernardo O'Higgins decided that Santiago required an *alameda*, La Cañada was deemed the best place to put it: "There is no public boulevard where people may get together for honest relief and amusement during the resting hours ... La Cañada, because of its condition, extension, abundance of water and other circumstances, is the most apparent place for an alameda." Three rows of poplars were promptly planted along each side, and the Alameda was born, soon to become *the* place to take the evening promenade.

Since those quieter times the boulevard has evolved into the city's biggest, busiest, noisiest and most polluted thoroughfare. Still, it's an unavoidable axis and you'll probably spend a fair bit of time on it or under it: the main metro line runs beneath it, and some of Santiago's most interesting landmarks stand along it.

Universidad de Chile and around
Southeast of the Palacio de la Moneda (see page 64), on the south side of the Alameda, is the **Universidad de Chile**, a fine French Neoclassical building dating from 1863. Opposite is the **Bolsa de Comercio**, Santiago's stock exchange, housed in a flamboyant, French Renaissance-style building that tapers to a thin wedge at the main entrance. One block west lies Plaza Bulnes, flanked by the **tomb** and massive **equestrian statue of Bernardo O'Higgins** to the south. Just further west is a 128m telecommunications tower, known as the **Torre Entel**, the focus of New Year's Eve fireworks displays.

Barrio París-Londres
Formed where Calle Londres intersects Calle París, **Barrio París-Londres** is tucked behind the Iglesia San Francisco on what used to be the monastery's orchards. These sinuous, cobbled streets lined with refurbished mansions, stylish hotels and busy hostels, look like a tiny piece of Paris's Latin Quarter. Created in 1923 by a team of architects, the *barrio* is undeniably attractive but feels incongruous to its surroundings. There is, however, a dark side to the area, at **Londres 38**

Londres 38
Londres 38 • Tues–Fri 10am–1pm & 3–6pm, Sat 10am–2pm; guided tours (45min) Mon–Fri noon & 4pm, Sat noon • Free • ☎ 2 2325 0374, ⓦ londres38.cl

The seemingly innocuous **Londres 38** building was one of the four main torture and detention centres in Santiago during the Pinochet dictatorship – and the only one not subsequently destroyed. Between September 1973 and September 1974, 96 people – considered opponents of the dictatorship – were killed here by the Dirección de Inteligencia Nacional (DINA). After a long battle by survivors, victims' families and human rights groups, the building was taken over and opened to the public in an effort to highlight the grave human rights abuses of the Pinochet years and the ongoing fight for justice. As well as displays on the building's history, Londres 38 also serves as a space for exhibitions, workshops and talks.

Iglesia San Francisco
Av O'Higgins 834 • Daily 8am–8pm • Free

The red **Iglesia San Francisco** is Santiago's oldest building, erected between 1586 and 1628. Take a look inside at the **Virgen del Socorro**, a small polychrome carving (rather lost in the vast main altar) brought to Chile on the saddle of Pedro de Valdivia in 1540 and credited with guiding him on his way, as well as fending off native attackers by throwing sand in their eyes. For all its age and beauty, the most remarkable feature of this church is its deep, hushed silence; you're just footsteps from the din of the Alameda but the traffic seems a million miles away.

1

Museo de Arte Colonial

Londres 4 · Mon–Fri 9.30am–1.30pm & 3–6pm, Sat & Sun 10am–2pm · CH$1000 · ⓦ museosanfrancisco.com

The monastery attached to the Iglesia San Francisco houses the **Museo de Arte Colonial**, which has a highly evocative collection of paintings, sculpture, furniture, keys and other objects dating from the colonial period, most of it religious and a good deal of it created in Peru, the seat of colonial government. Note the immense eighteenth-century **cedar door** of the first room you come to off the cloisters; carved into hundreds of intricately designed squares, this is one of the museum's most beautiful possessions. On the other side of the cloisters, across a peaceful, palm-filled garden, the Gran Sala hosts another highlight – an astonishing 54 paintings of the life of **St Francis of Assissi**. Dating from the seventeenth century, the paintings were all done by the Cuzco school in Peru, colonial South America's foremost art movement, who combined colourful religious imagery with indigenous motifs.

Cerro Santa Lucía and around

The lushly forested **Cerro Santa Lucía** is Santiago's most imaginative and exuberant piece of landscaping. Looking at it now, it's hard to believe that for the first three centuries of the city's development this was nothing more than a barren, rocky outcrop, completely ignored despite its historical importance – it was at the foot of this hill that Santiago was officially founded by Valdivia, on February 12, 1541. It wasn't until 1872 that the city turned its attention to Santa Lucía once more, when the mayor of Santiago, Vicuña Mackenna, enlisted the labour of 150 prisoners to transform it into a grand public park.

Quasi-Gaudíesque in appearance, with swirling pathways and Baroque terraces and turrets, this is a great place to come for panoramic views across the city. If slogging up the steps doesn't appeal, use the free lift on the western side of the park, by the junction with Huérfanos (erratic opening hours). While it's busy and safe by day, muggings have been reported in the Cerro Santa Lucía after dark.

Immediately west of the hill stands the massive **Biblioteca Nacional** (Mon–Fri 9am–7pm, Sat 9am–2pm), one of Latin America's largest libraries, with temporary exhibitions of rather specialist interest and free-to-use computers with internet.

Barrio Lastarria

ⓦ barriolastarria.com

Just east of Cerro Santa Lucía, squashed into a triangle between the hill, the Alameda and Parque Forestal, the quiet, arty **Barrio Lastarria** neighbourhood – sometimes referred to as Barrio Bellas Artes – is centred on the small, cobbled **Plaza Mulato Gil**, at the corner of Merced and Lastarria. As well as artists' workshops, galleries and bookshops, the neighbourhood is well known for its sparkling restaurant and bar scene (see pages 82 and 85).

Centro Gabriela Mistral

Av O'Higgins 227 · Exhibitions Tues–Sat 10am–9pm, Sun 11am–9pm · Free · ☎ 2 2566 5500, ⓦ gam.cl

Named after famous Chilean poet Gabriela Mistral, the enormous **Centro Gabriela Mistral** – an arts centre usually referred to as **GAM** – was an exciting new addition to Santiago's burgeoning cultural scene when it opened in 2010. Its ten large, airy halls still show off the best of Chile's art, literature, music and dance, while its plazas house contemporary sculptures, many relating to Chilean themes such as copper or the Mapuche. There's also an on site wine shop, bookshop and antiques fair (Tues–Sun 10am–8pm).

Museo de Artes Visuales and Museo Arqueológico de Santiago

José Victorino Lastarria 307 · Tues–Sun 10.30am–6.30pm · Tues–Sat CH$1000, Sun free · ☎ 2 2664 9337, ⓦ mavi.cl

The **Museo de Artes Visuales** in the centre of Lastarria features some of the best new sculptures, painting and photography by Chile's emerging artists. The buildig also houses the small but well-stocked **Museo Arqueológico de Santiago**, with hats, bags, jewellery, baskets and other items from all over the country.

Museo Violeta Parra

Vicuña Mackenna 37 • Tues–Fri 9.30am–6pm, Sat & Sun 11am–6pm • Free • ☎ 2 2355 4600, ⓦ museovioletaparra.cl

Although it's located a short way south of the Alameda, the **Museo Violeta Parra** is best visited while touring Lastarria. Violeta Parra (1917–67) was a half-indigenous folk singer and artist of humble origins, who became the first Chilean to have an exhibition at the Louvre. The large curved concrete structure encompasses an absorbing display of Parra's oil paintings, papier maché works and embroidery, as well as documentary videos and audio samples of the plaintive folk music for which she was most renowned.

South of the Alameda

South of the Alameda, along Line #2 on the metro, there's a clutch of interesting sights, including one of the best of Santiago's nineteenth-century French-style palaces, and, in a very different vein, a park that is a popular excursion for the city's more down-at-heel classes.

Palacio Cousiño

Dieciocho 438 • Tues–Fri 9.30am–1.30pm & 2.30–5pm, Sat & Sun 9.30am–1.30pm • CH$3000 • ☎ 2 2386 7448 • ⓜ Toesca

Now reopened and restored after being damaged in the 2010 earthquake (see page 487), the **Palacio Cousiño** was the most magnificent of the historic palaces that lie south of the Alameda, the one that dazzled Santiago's high society by the sheer scale of its luxury and opulence. It was built between 1870 and 1878 for Doña Isidora Goyenechea, the widow of Luis Cousiño, who had amassed a fortune with his coal and silver mines. All the furnishings and decoration were shipped over from Europe, especially France, and top European craftsmen were brought here to work on the house: Italian hand-painted tiles; Bohemian crystal chandeliers; mahogany, walnut and ebony parquet floors; a mosaic marble staircase; and French brocade and silk furnishings are just a few of the splendours of the palace.

Parque Bernardo O'Higgins

ⓜ Parque O'Higgins

Perhaps the best reason to come to **Parque Bernardo O'Higgins**, a few blocks southwest of Palacio Cousiño, is to soak up the Chilean family atmosphere, as it's one of the most popular green spaces in the city. It was originally the Parque Cousiño, commissioned by Luis Cousiño, the entrepreneurial millionaire, in 1869, and the place to take your carriage rides in the late nineteenth century. These days working-class families and groups of kids flock here on summer weekends to enjoy the picnic areas, outdoor pools (very crowded), roller rink, basketball court, gut-churning rides of amusement park **Fantasilandia** (ⓦ fantasilandia.cl), and concert venue Movistar Arena (ⓦ movistararena.cl). There is also **El Pueblito**, a collection of adobe buildings typical of the Chilean countryside and housing several cheap restaurants, a few craft stalls and a handful of small museums.

The western neighbourhoods

West of Los Héroes, the Alameda continues through the once-wealthy **neighbourhoods** abandoned by Santiago's well-heeled residents a few decades ago, when the moneyed classes shifted to the more fashionable east side of town. After falling into serious decline, these areas are finally coming into their own again, as a younger generation has started renovating decaying mansions, opening up trendy cafés and bookshops and injecting a new vigour into the streets.

1

PALACIOS OF THE ALAMEDA

Walk west of Torre Entel along the Alameda and you enter what was once the preserve of Santiago's moneyed elite, with several glorious mansions built around 1900 serving as reminders. The first to look out for is the French-style **Palacio Irarrázaval**, on the south side of the Alameda between San Ignacio and Dieciocho; built in 1906 by Cruz Montt, it now houses an old-fashioned restaurant. Adjoining it at the corner of Dieciocho, the slightly later and more ornate **Edificio Iñíguez**, by the same architect in league with Larraín Bravo, houses *Confitería Torres* (see page 81), said to be where the "national" sandwich, the Barros Luco, was invented in honour of a leading politician.

Then check out the 1917 **Palacio Ariztía**, being remodelled as the future home of Chile's constitutional court, a little further on in the next block; a fine copy of an Art Nouveau French mansion, again by Cruz Montt, it is set off by an iron-and-glass door canopy. Next door, the late nineteenth-century **Palacio Errázuriz** is the oldest of these Alameda mansions. It's looking a little sad these days, but its owners and previous occupants the Brazilian embassy have promised restoration work and plan to move back in once they're finished. Built for Maximiano Errázuriz, mining mogul and leading socialite, it is a soberly elegant two-storey building in a Neoclassical style. You're now standing opposite the triumphant **Monumento a los Héroes de la Concepción**, an imposing statue that borders the junction of the Alameda with the Avenida Norte Sur (the Panamericana); this is where metro lines #1 and #2 intersect at Los Héroes station.

Barrios Concha y Toro, Brasil and Yungay

One of the most beautiful neighbourhoods on the northern side of the Alameda, between avenidas Brasil and Ricardo Cumming, is **Barrio Concha y Toro**, a jumble of twisting cobbled streets leading to a tiny round plaza with a fountain in the middle. Further north you'll find **Barrio Brasil**, one of the liveliest of the newly revived neighbourhoods, centred on the large, grand Plaza Brasil, full of children playing at the amusing cement sculpture playground and among the old silk-cotton and lime trees. Bordering Barrio Brasil to the west and stretching over to Parque Quinta Normal, **Barrio Yungay** has a growing number of bohemian restaurants and bars, many housed in attractively crumbling buildings.

Estación Central

Less than a kilometre south of Yungay stands one of the Alameda's great landmarks: the stately **Estación Central**, featuring a colossal metal roof that was cast in the Schneider-Creusot foundry in France in 1896. It's the only functioning train station left in the city, with regular services to the south.

Parque Quinta Normal and around

Parque Quinta Normal is perhaps the most elegant and peaceful of Santiago's parks, created in 1830 as a place to introduce and acclimatize foreign trees and plants to the city. Today the park is packed with some beautifully mature examples: Babylonian willows, Monterey pine, cypress, Douglas fir and poplars, to name just a few. Additional attractions include a pond with rowing boats for rent, and several fine **museums**. Often deserted during the week, the park is packed on summer weekends.

Museo de Historia Natural

Parque Quinta Normal • Tues–Sat 10am–5.30pm, Sun 11am–5.30pm • Free • ☎ 2 2680 4603, ⓦ mnhn.cl • Ⓜ Quinta Normal

The grand, Neoclassical building near the entrance of Parque Quinta Normal houses the **Museo de Historia Natural**. Founded in 1830 and occupying its present building since 1875, this is Latin America's oldest natural history museum and still one of the most important. It has a colossal blue whale skeleton, and an Easter Island collection that features a *moai*, an upturned topknot or hat, and the famous Santiago Staff, inscribed with the mysterious, undeciphered *rongo rongo* script.

MUSEU NACIONAL DE BELLAS ARTES

1

Museo Artequin

Av Portales 3530 • Tues–Fri 9am–5pm, Sat & Sun 11am–6pm • Tues–Sat CH$1500, Sun free • ☎ 2 2681 8656, ⓦ artequin.cl • Ⓜ Quinta Normal

The wildly colourful glass-and-metal building standing opposite Parque Quinta Normal's Avenida Portales entrance was originally the Chilean pavilion in the Universal Exhibition in Paris, 1889. It now contains the engaging **Museo Artequin** – short for Arte en la Quinta – which aims to bring people, especially schoolchildren, closer to art by exposing them to reproductions of the world's greatest paintings in a relaxed, less intimidating environment. They're all here, from El Greco and Delacroix through to Andy Warhol and Jackson Pollock.

Museo de la Memoria y los Derechos Humanos

Matucama 501 • Tues–Sun: Jan & Feb 10am–8pm; March–Dec 10am–6pm • Free • ☎ 2 2579 9600, ⓦ museodelamemoria.cl • Ⓜ Quinta Normal

The **Museo de la Memoria y los Derechos Humanos** (Museum of Memory and Human Rights), housed in an large, eye-catching glass building just outside Parque Quinta Normal, is dedicated to the victims of human rights abuses during the years of the Pinochet dictatorship, a period in which an estimated three thousand people were killed or "disappeared", and thousands more tortured, detained or sent into exile, including current President Michelle Bachelet. Opened in 2010 at the time of Chile's bicentennial, the museum houses a powerful combination of multimedia displays, exhibits, photos, art, poetry and literature to tell the story of the military coup and its enduring impact. Exhibits include moving eyewitness accounts, TV footage from the time, and heartbreaking letters and personal items belonging to junta victims. The top floor holds temporary exhibitions, on related subjects such as workers' rights. Although a knowledge of Spanish and recent history is useful in understanding some of the archive material, it is not essential. A sight not to be missed.

Mercado Central and around

Puente and San Pablo • Daily 7am–5/6pm • Free

The **Mercado Cental** stands close to the southern bank of the Río Mapocho, four blocks north of Plaza de Armas. This huge metal structure, prefabricated in England and erected in Santiago in 1868, contains a very picturesque fruit, vegetable and fish market. The fish stalls are especially fascinating, packed with glistening eels, sharks and salmon, buckets of oysters, mussels and clams, and unidentifiable shells from which live things with tentacles make occasional appearances. The best time to come is at lunchtime, when you can feast at one of the many **fish restaurants** dotted around the market; the cheapest and most authentic are on the outer edge, while those in the centre are touristy and pricier. Keep an eye on your belongings, as pickpockets are not unknown here.

Feria Municipal La Vega

Antonio López de Bello and Salas • Mon–Sat 5.30am–6pm, Sun 6am–3pm • Free

The gargantuan **Feria Municipal La Vega** is a couple of blocks back from the riverbank opposite the Mercado Central. There's no pretty architecture here, and few tourists; just serious shoppers and hundreds of stalls selling the whole gamut of Central Valley produce, from cows' innards and pigs' bellies to mountains of potatoes and onions, at a fraction of the price charged in the Mercado Central. There is also a gallery of economical **seafood restaurants**, popular with locals and rarely visited by tourists. Few have alcohol licences, but if you ask for an "iced tea" (" *te helado* ") you'll be served either white wine in a Sprite bottle or red wine in a Coca-Cola bottle.

Estación Mapocho

Just west of the Mercado Central, right by the river, is the immense stone-and-metal **Estación Mapocho**, built in 1912 to house the terminal of the Valparaíso–Santiago railway line. With the train service long discontinued, the station is now a cultural centre, housing exhibitions, plays and concerts. Take a look inside at the great copper, glass and marble roof. The **Feria Nacional del Libro**, one of the continent's most important book fairs, is also held here in November.

Parque Forestal

The **Parque Forestal**, stretching along the southern bank of the Mapocho between Puente Recoleta and Puente Pío Nono, was created at the end of the nineteenth century on land that was reclaimed from the river after it was channelled. Lined with long rows of trees and lampposts, it provides a picturesque setting for the **Palacio de Bellas Artes**, built to commemorate the centenary of Chilean independence. The funky restaurant and bar scene of Barrio Lastarria (see page 85) backs on to this area.

Museo Nacional de Bellas Artes and Museo de Arte Contemporáneo
Parque Forestal s/n • Tues–Sun 10am–6.45pm • Free • ☎ 2 2499 1632, ⓦ mnba.cl

The **Palacio de Bellas Artes** houses the **Museo Nacional de Bellas Artes,** featuring predominantly Chilean works from the beginning of the colonial period onwards. The quality of the work is mixed, and none of the paintings equals the beauty of the building's vast white hall with its marble statues bathing in the natural light pouring in from the glass-and-iron ceiling. The displays change frequently, but look out for the surrealist paintings of Chilean master Roberto Matta and the close-up portrait photos of Jorge Brantmayer. The **Museo de Arte Contemporáneo**, accessed from the other side of the building, hosts temporary exhibitions focused on international or Chilean contemporary artists.

Barrio Bellavista

Originally – and sometimes still – known as *La Chimba*, which means "the other side of the river" in Quechua, **Barrio Bellavista** grew first into a residential area when Santiago's population started spilling across the river in the nineteenth century. Head across the Pío Nono bridge at the eastern end of the Parque Forestal and you'll find yourself on **Calle Pío Nono**, Bellavista's main street. Nestling between the northern bank of the Mapocho and the steep slopes of Cerro San Cristóbal, Bellavista is a warren of leafy streets, many boasting imaginative street art, and a centre for restaurants, bars and pubs. A popular night-time destination for both locals and visitors, the neighbourhood has a slightly edgy feel; it is generally safe, but it is wise to stay on your guard after dark. An evening **handicraft market** that spreads along the length of Pío Nono is held at weekends.

You might also be tempted by the dozens of **lapis lazuli** outlets running east along Avenida Bellavista from Puente Pío Nono, though there are few bargains to be found. **Patio Bellavista**, Pío Nono 73, is a modern shopping and dining complex – and a popular gringo hangout.

La Chascona
Marquéz de la Plata 0192 • Tues–Sun: Jan & Feb 10am–7pm; March–Dec 10am–6pm • CH$7000 • ☎ 2 2737 8712, ⓦ fundacionneruda.org

Tucked away in a tiny street at the foot of Cerro San Cristóbal is **La Chascona**, the house the poet Pablo Neruda shared with his third wife, Matilde Urrutia, from 1955 until his death in 1973. It was named *La Chascona* ("tangle-haired woman") by Neruda, as a tribute to his wife's thick red hair. Today it's the headquarters of the Fundación Neruda, which has painstakingly restored this and the poet's two other houses – La Sebastiana in Valparaíso (see page 103) and Isla Negra, about 90km down the coast (see page 110) – to their original condition. The admission price includes a worthwhile self-guided audio tour, available in English.

1

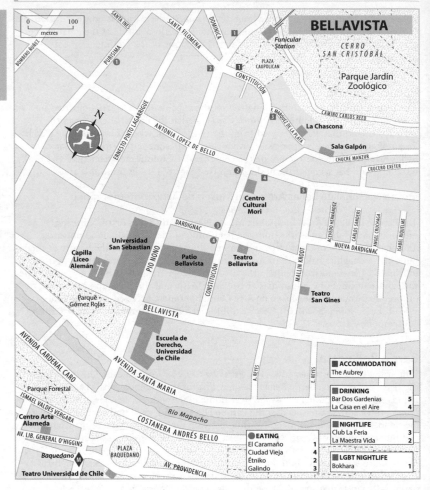

This house, split into three separate sections that climb up the hillside, is packed to the rafters with objects collected by Neruda, illuminating his loves, enthusiasms and obsessions. Beautiful African carvings jostle for space with Victorian dolls, music boxes, paperweights and coloured glasses; the floors are littered with old armchairs, stools, a rocking horse, exotic rugs and a sleeping toy lion. There are numerous references to Neruda's and Matilde's love for each other, such as the bars on the windows, in which their initials are entwined and lapped by breaking waves, and the portrait of Matilde by Diego Rivera, which has the profile of Neruda hidden in her hair. The third and highest level houses Neruda's library, containing more than nine thousand books, as well as the diploma he was given when awarded the Nobel Prize for Literature in 1971, and a replica of the medal.

Cerro San Cristóbal

Funicular Tues–Sun: Jan & Feb 10am–7.45pm; March–Dec 10am–6.45pm • Mon–Fri CH$2000 return, Sat & Sun CH$2600 return • Téléférique Tues–Sun: Jan & Feb 10am–8pm; March–Dec 10am–7pm • Mon–Fri CH$2510 return, Sat & Sun CH$3010 return • ☎ 2 2730 1331, ⓦ parquemet.cl

TREKS AROUND SANTIAGO

On a clear day, the mountains look so close to Santiago you feel as if you could reach out and touch them, and indeed it doesn't take long to reach at least the foothills if you want a walk that's a bit more challenging than Cerro San Cristóbal without leaving town. **Treks into the precordillera** pretty much all involve an upward climb – but will quickly reward you with fantastic views over the city and beyond (wear shoes with good grip). Within the confines of Santiago, **Cerro Manquehue** is an extinct volcano, whose woodcut-worthy cone towers over the *barrios altos*. It's a stiff but rewarding hike to the top (5hr return) – the path begins near the end of a road called Via Roja, which twists and turns up the fringes of Vitacura (the nearest metro is Manquehue; from there you'll need to take a taxi). Skirting the eastern edge of the city, a chain of nature reserves (ⓦ asociacionparquecordillera.cl) takes you further up into the Andes proper. The pick of these parks is probably **Aguas de Ramón** (daily: summer 8am–6pm; rest of year 8am–5pm; CH$1500), whose main route heads towards a river and series of small waterfalls. The park entrance is in Onofre Jarpa, in the neighbourhood of La Reina – the nearest metro is Príncipe de Gales, from where you can catch a taxi.

A trip to the summit of **Cerro San Cristóbal** – which includes parkland, botanical gardens, a dismal zoo and two **swimming pools** – is one of the city's highlights, particularly on a clear, sunny day when the views are stunning. The hill is, in fact, an Andean spur, jutting into the capital's heart and rising to a peak of 860m, a point marked by a 22m-high statue of the *Virgen de la Inmaculada*. The easiest way to get up is via the **funicular** from the station at the north end of Pío Nono in Bellavista, which takes up to the Terraza Bellavista. You can also take the newly refurbished **téléferique** from the Prodencia side of the hill, whose upper terminal is just 300m from the top of the funicular; combined tickets are available. From Terraza Bellavista, where there are a handful of food and craft stalls, it's a short but steep walk up to the huge white Virgin. If you are fortunate enough to be in Santiago after a rain in the winter, the usually hazy view of suburbs climbing into the surrounding mountains will be enhanced by a crisp vista of snowy mountain peaks. Trails wind through the woods to the base of the hill – ideal if you prefer a little exercise on the way up or down.

Piscina Tupahue and Piscina Antilén

Av Alberto Mackenna s/n • Jan to mid-March & mid-Nov to Dec Tues–Sun 10am–7.30pm • CH$6000–7500 • You can walk from the Terraza Bellavista, take a taxi from the bottom of the hill, or at weekends hop on a free shuttle bus from Pío Nono 450 (10.30am)

For an afternoon picnic and **swimming** in the summer months, there is no better place in Santiago than **Piscina Tupahue** and **Piscina Antilén**, the two **huge pools** atop the Cerro San Cristóbal. The jointly run pools offer cool, clean swimming and, at 736m above the city, wonderful views.

Los barrios altos

The **barrios altos** east of the city centre, spreading into the foothills of the Andes, are home to Santiago's moneyed elite; the farther and higher you get, the richer the people, the bigger the houses and the taller the gates. It's hard to believe that until the beginning of the twentieth century there was virtually no one here; it was for its isolation and tranquillity that the Sisters of Providencia chose to build their convent on what is now Avenida Providencia in 1853. Later, following a slow trickle of eastbound movement, there was a great exodus of wealthy families from their traditional preserves west of the city over to the new *barrio alto* in the 1920s, where they've been entrenched ever since. The parallel street running in the other direction from Avenida Providencia was originally called Avenida Nueva Providencia but was renamed Avenida 11 de Septiembre under the dictatorship to commemorate the date of the 1973 military coup; it is in the process of being changed back to its original name.

1

Providencia

Northeast of the city centre, **Providencia** has little in the way of sights as such, but is home to hotels, restaurants and travel agencies. Away from the main drags, you'll find attractive tree-lined streets, stylish stores and elegant cafés. At its eastern edge, around the border with Las Condes, a cluster of skyscrapers, offices and restaurants make up the buzzing financial and dining district nicknamed "**Sanhattan**", site of some of the most expensive real estate in Chile.

Sky Costanera

Av Andres Bello 2457 • Daily 10am–10pm (last entry 9pm) • CH$15,000 • ☎ 2 2916 9269, ⓦ skycostanera.cl • Ⓜ Tobalaba

Dominating the area, and indeed the entire Santiago skyline, is the 300m-high **Gran Torre Santiago**, Latin America's tallest skyscraper, designed by Argentine architect Cesar Pelli. Part of a complex that includes the equally enormous Costanera Center shopping mall (see page 88), its **Sky Costanera** viewing platform offers panoramic bird's eye views of the whole city and the surrounding Andes.

Las Condes

As you head east from Providencia towards **Las Condes**, the shops and office blocks gradually thin out into a more residential district, punctuated with the occasional giant shopping mall, such as **Alto Las Condes** (see page 88).

Pueblito de los Dominicos

Apoquindo 9085 • Daily: summer 10.30am–8pm; rest of year 10am–7pm • Ⓜ Los Dominicos

The best collection of arts and crafts in Santiago is found at the **Pueblito de los Dominicos** market, a large, lively and expensive craft fair. Held in a mock village in Las Condes, the market sits in the shadow of the lovely white Iglesia de los Dominicos, topped with greening copper cupolas, which looks colonial but was built by Dominican monks in the nineteenth century. The market sells a wide range of beautiful handicrafts, as well as antiques, books, fossil shark teeth and a decent restaurant; it's a quiet respite from the noise and grime of the city.

Museo de la Moda

Av Vitacura 4562 • Tues–Sun 10am–6pm • CH$3000 • ☎ 2 2219 3623, ⓦ museodelamoda.cl • Bus #112, #425, #425e, #419e or #C22 from Ⓜ Escuela Militar

The **Museo de la Moda** is an essential stop-off for fashionistas, its collection of more than ten thousand exhibits dating from the fifth century BC to the present day. Dresses worn by Princess Diana and Marilyn Monroe, Diego Maradona's football boots and Madonna's bra from her Blond Ambition tour are among the items held in the collection, although not all may be on display at any one time.

Parque Araucano

Presidente Riesco 5555 • Tues–Sun 9am–9pm • Free • 20min walk or taxi from Ⓜ Escuela Militar

Right opposite the Parque Arauco shopping mall (see page 88), **Parque Araucano** is a particularly lovely park to wander around, clean and well tended, with a rose garden and fountains. It's also a good place to come if you have youngsters to entertain, with a couple of attractions aimed at children or the young at heart (note that they get very crowded at weekends and holiday times). **Selva Viva** (Mon–Fri 9am–6pm, Sat & Sun 10am–7pm; CH$9950; ☎ 2 2944 6300) is a hot and humid "jungle" space, where butterflies and parrots fly overhead and you can stroke snakes, iguanas and toucans. **KidZania** (Mon–Sat 11am–9.30pm, Sun 11am–7pm; adults CH$11,950, children CH$17,950; online discounts available; ☎ 2 2964 4000, ⓦ santiago.kidzania.com) allows children to learn about different professions in a hands-on way, operating on "patients", making sushi or sitting in a real plane cockpit.

1

Peñalolén

On Santiago's outskirts, southeast of Las Condes, the mostly lower-middle-class neighbourhood **Peñalolén** was the site of **Villa Grimaldi**, one of the main torture and interrogation centres during the Pinochet years.

Parque por la Paz Villa Grimaldi

Av José Arrieta 8401 • Daily 10am–6pm; guided tours (Ihr 30min) Tues–Fri 10.30am, noon & 3pm • Free • ☎ 2 2292 5229, ⓦ villagrimaldi. cl • Bus #513 or #D09 from ⓜ Plaza Egaña

From mid-1974 to mid-1978, Villa Grimaldi – a privately owned country house that was taken over by the secret police – was used for the torture of people deemed to be political opponents of the Pinochet regime. Around five thousand were detained here; at least 240 were killed. The buildings have since been knocked down, and the grounds turned into the **Parque por la Paz Villa Grimaldi** (Peace Park Villa Grimaldi), with a series of monuments that include a wall listing names of victims and a re-creation of the huts prisoners were kept in. The park now serves as both a memorial to the victims and to educate future generations about the dictatorship. Bilingual audio guides are available.

ARRIVAL AND DEPARTURE   SANTIAGO

Santiago is one of the easiest and least intimidating South American capitals to arrive in. Connections from the **airport** and **bus terminals** to the city centre are frequent and straightforward, and while you should take normal precautions, you're unlikely to be hassled or feel threatened while you're finding your feet.

BY PLANE

Aeropuerto Arturo Merino Benítez International and domestic flights arrive at Arturo Merino Benítez airport in Pudahuel (the commune the airport is sometimes named after; ☎ 2 2690 1752, ⓦ aeropuertosantiago.cl), 26km northwest of Santiago. The smart international terminal has a tourist information desk, bureau de change (rates are fairly poor) and ATMs. There are flights from here throughout Chile and South America; most are operated by LATAM (central office Estado 82; ☎ 600 526 2000, ⓦ latam.com).

By bus The cheapest way to get between the airport and the city centre is by bus. Centropuerto (daily 6am–11.30pm; every 10min; CH$1800; ⓦ centropuerto. cl) runs to and from Los Héroes metro station, while Tur Bus (daily: 5am–midnight every 20min; midnight–5am hourly; CH$1800) uses the Terminal de Buses Alameda (see below). Both services also call at intermediate stops, including Pajaritos, useful for connections to Valparaíso and the coastal resorts. Minibus firms such as TransVIP (☎ 2 2677 3000, ⓦ transvip.cl), operating from the row of desks by the airport exit, offer door-to-door services from the airport to your hotel, charging around CH$10,000/person. You have to wait around until the bus is full, and you'll probably get an unwanted city tour as other passengers are dropped off before you reach your own hotel.

By taxi By the airport exit there's a desk where you can book official airport taxis, which cost at least CH$20,000 to the city centre. If you bargain with the private taxi drivers touting for business, you can usually pay less, but taking these taxis is at your own risk. Returning to the airport, the taxis charge a few thousand pesos less – it's a good idea to book a radiotaxi ahead (see page 78).

By car There are a number of car rental booths at the airport, including Avis (☎ 2 2795 3971, ⓦ avis.com), Rosselot (ⓦ rosselot.cl) and Dollar (ⓦ dollar.com).

Destinations Antofagasta (14–16 daily; 2hr); Arica 8–10 daily; 2hr 40min); Calama (12–15 daily; 2hr); Concepción (7–12 daily; 1hr); Copiapó (4–6 daily; 1hr 30min); Easter Island (1–2 daily; 5hr 40min); Iquique (12–16 daily; 2hr 30min); La Serena (6–9 daily; 1hr); Osorno (1 daily; 1hr 35min); Puerto Montt (12–15 daily; 1hr 45min); Punta Arenas (8–12 daily; 3hr 30min); Temuco 8–10 daily; 1hr 20min); Valdivia (10–15 daily; 1hr 30min).

BY BUS

By far the greatest majority of transport services are provided by buses, run by a bewildering number of private companies. These operate out of four main terminals. While you can normally turn up and buy a ticket for same-day travel, it's better to get it in advance, especially at weekends. For travel on the days around Christmas, New Year's Eve, Easter and the Sept 18 national holiday, you should buy your ticket at least a week ahead.

TERMINAL DE BUSES SANTIAGO

Terminal de Buses Santiago, also known as Terminal de Estación Central and Terminal Sur, just west of the Universidad de Santiago metro station, is the largest (and most chaotic) of the terminals, used by more than a hundred bus companies. Services south down the Panamericana from this terminal are provided by all the major companies, including Cóndor Bus (☎ 2 2680 6900, ⓦ condorbus.cl), Inter Sur (☎ 2 2779 6312) and Tas Choapa (☎ 2 2822 7561, ⓦ taschoapa.cl). Buses to the coastal

1

resorts of the Litoral Central are run by Cóndor Bus and Pullman Bus (☏ 600 600 0018, ⓦ pullman.cl).

Destinations Chillán (every 30min–1hr; 5hr); Concepción (every 30min; 6hr); Curicó (every 30min; 2hr 45min); Osorno (hourly; 10hr); Puerto Montt (every 30min; 14hr); Talca (every 15min; 3hr 30min); Valdivia (hourly; 11hr).

TERMINAL DE BUSES ALAMEDA

Just east of Terminal de Buses Santiago, Terminal de Buses Alameda is used by Tur Bus (☏ 2 2822 7500, ⓦ turbus.cl) and Pullman Bus, Chile's largest and most comprehensive bus companies, travelling to a wide variety of destinations in all directions.

Destinations Antofagasta (hourly; 19hr); La Serena (every 30min–1hr; 6hr 30min); Valparaíso (every 15min; 1hr 30min–1hr 45min); Viña del Mar (every 15min; 1hr 30min–1hr 45min).

TERMINAL SAN BORJA

San Borja is at the back of a shopping mall behind the Estación Central (from the metro, follow the signs carefully to exit at the terminal). This is the main departure point for buses to the north of Chile. There are several regional buses, as well, and some services to the coastal resorts. Bus companies going north include Elqui Bus (☏ 2 2778 7045), Pullman Bus and Tas Choapa. Tur Bus also runs services to the Litoral.

Destinations Antofagasta (hourly; 19hr); Arica (hourly; 30hr); Calama (hourly; 22hr); Iquique (hourly; 24hr); La Serena (hourly; 6hr 30min).

TERMINAL LOS HÉROES

Terminal Los Héroes is located on Tucapel Jiménez, just north of the Plaza de Los Héroes, near the metro stop of the same name. It hosts a mixture of northbound and southbound services and buses to destinations in Argentina. The terminal is used by companies including Buses Ahumada (☏ 2 2696 9798, ⓦ busesahumada.cl), Cruz del Sur (☏ 2 2696 9324, ⓦ webcds.cl), Libac (☏ 2 2698 5974), Pullman del Sur (☏ 2 2673 1967, ⓦ pdelsur. cl) and Tas Choapa.

Destinations Bariloche (several daily; 16hr); Buenos Aires (several daily; 22hr); Mendoza (several daily; 7hr).

BY TRAIN

The only train services are between Santiago and destinations in the Central Valley to the south, with all trains departing from the Estación Central, next to the metro stop of the same name. For train information, call ☏ 600 585 5000 or check ⓦ efe.cl.

Destinations Chillán (3 daily; 5hr 30min); Curicó (3 daily; 2hr 45min); Rancagua (10 daily; 1hr 30min); San Fernando (6 daily; 2hr); Talca (3 daily; 3hr 30min).

GETTING AROUND

You'll probably spend most time in the city centre, which is entirely walkable, but for journeys further afield public transport on the **Transantiago** network of metro trains and buses is inexpensive, safe and abundant. You can plan your journey via the Spanish-only website ⓦ www.transantiago.cl. Paying for journeys – for both the metro and bus network – you have to use a **Tarjeta Bip! magnetic-stripcard** (CH$1550), which you load up with credit at machines or ticket windows. **Fares** are the same regardless of the length of your journey, but vary according to time of day (CH$610–740); you are permitted up to two transfers between modes of transport.

BY METRO

Santiago's spotless metro system (most lines Mon–Fri 6.30am–11pm; Sat, Sun & public holidays 8.30am–10.30pm; ☏ 600 600 9292, ⓦ metro.cl) is modern and efficient, though packed solid at rush hour. The system is being constantly expanded and currently boasts six lines. Many stations are decorated with huge murals, and often offer free wi-fi.

CROSSING INTO ARGENTINA

The international highway that connects Santiago with **Mendoza**, capital of Argentina's wine-growing region, is probably the most popular overland route between the two cross-Andes neighbours. It's a spectacular journey – six or seven hours, although a busy border crossing can add more time onto that – and you should certainly drive it by day if possible in order to see the scenery. **Buses** regularly make the trip in both directions; from Santiago, most leave the Los Héroes terminal.

The **border crossing** is around 155km from Santiago, 7km past the Portillo turn off; basic food and drink and money exchange is available on both sides, but be prepared for long queues at passport control and customs, especially at holiday times. On the Argentine side, the **Alta Montaña** route, with fantastic views of Aconcagua, snakes 210km past mountain villages, sulphur springs and small ski resorts and on into Mendoza.

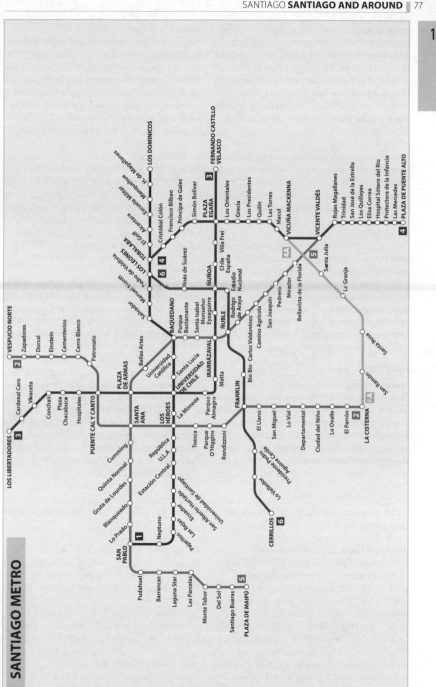

SANTIAGO METRO

1

METRO LINES

Line #1 is the most useful, running east–west under the Alameda and Av Providencia. Line #5 runs parallel to it for part of its length, stopping at the Plaza de Armas and Bellavista. The new Line #3 cuts through the centre north to south before veering east. The other lines mostly serve residential *barrios*, while large chunks of the city, including Vitacura and the airport, are off the network completely.

BY BUS

Buses often involve a long wait but are useful for reaching destinations off the metro, or going east or west along the Alameda – as a general rule, buses displaying "Estación Central" will take you west, while those displaying "Providencia" or "Apoquindo" are going east.

BY TAXI

Santiago has more taxis than New York, and in the centre you'll have no trouble flagging one down. Taxis are black with yellow roofs and have a small light in the top right-hand corner of the windscreen that's lit to show the cab is available. If you're going somewhere out of the way, don't expect the driver to know it; it's best to check where it is beforehand. Radiotaxis (such as Metropolitana on ☎ 2 2506 6595) are more expensive but a bit less of a lottery and can be booked beforehand.

FARES

Fares are relatively low and displayed on the window – black and yellow cabs charge CH$130 for every 200m, while radiotaxis start at CH$2000 and then quote according to the destination; you're not expected to tip. Drivers are allowed to charge more at night, so try to verbally confirm an estimate to your location. Scams such as drivers taking extra-long routes, and rip-offs on large bills, do occasionally happen. Be firm and pay with small notes.

BY COLECTIVO

Santiago's *colectivos* (shared taxis) look like ordinary taxis except they're black all over and cram in as many as four passengers at a time. They travel along fixed routes, mostly from the centre out to the suburbs; a sign on the roof indicates the destination. Plaza Baquedano (usually called Plaza Italia) is the starting point for many *colectivo* routes. Prices vary along the route, but *colectivos* generally cost CH$550–650.

BY BIKE

The city authorities are expanding the network of cycle lanes in Santiago, with a 5.6km stretch of road from Quinta Normal to Parque Forestal through the centre closed to cars every Sun morning. La Bicicleta Verde, Loreto 6 (see below), rents good quality bikes (with helmets) from US$10 for half a day and also offers tours on two wheels.

INFORMATION

Sernatur Sernatur has an office in Providencia at at Av Providencia 1550 (Jan & Feb daily 9am–9pm; March–Dec Mon–Fri 9am–6pm, Sat 9am–2pm; ☎ 2 2731 8336, ⓦ sernatur.cl), and a much smaller kiosk at the airport. It has free booklets on Santiago's attractions, maps and free wi-fi, and some of the staff speak English; the website includes hotel and restaurant listings.

Municipal tourist office The city authorities have their own tourist office (Mon–Fri 9am–6pm, Sat & Sun 10am–4pm; ☎ 2 2713 6745, ⓔ turismo@munistgo.cl) in the Municipilidad on the Plaza de Armas, offering what's-on information as well as free, Spanish-language walking tours (daily 10am).

Conaf There's a Conaf office south of downtown at Paseo Bulnes 265 (Mon–Thurs 9.30am–5.30pm, Fri 9.30am–4.30pm; ☎ 2 2663 0125, ⓦ conaf.cl).

ACTIVITIES AND TOURS

Several excellent travel agencies in Santiago offer an eclectic range of tours of the city, the surrounding area, Chile and South America as a whole.

Andina del Sud Av El Golf 99, 2nd floor ☎ 2 2388 0101, ⓦ andinadelsud.com. This agency is good for booking inexpensive domestic and international flights, and also offers holidays and guided trips throughout Chile and neighbouring countries aimed at younger travellers. Four-night Easter Island trip around US$600.

Chile Running Tours ☎ 09 9330 6804, ⓦ chilerunningtours.com. These guided running tours (from CH$36,000; up to 10km) are an excellent way to get a feel for Santiago in a short space of time and keep fit. As well as several routes in the city (of varying levels), they also offer "running and wine tours" in the Casablanca Valley (you do the tastings at the end).

La Bicicleta Verde Loreto 6 ☎ 2 2570 9338, ⓦ labicicletaverde.com. This well-run company offers excellent cycling trips, including visits to the Maipo Valley vineyards (CH$35,000) and nighttime city tours (CH$25,000).

Slow Travel ☎ 09 9919 8471, ⓦ slowtravel.cl Flexible, personalized wine, food and nature tours in Chile and Argentina. The culinary tour of Santiago, which takes in the Central and La Vega markets, and finishes with a cookery lesson, is highly recommended.

Turistik Plaza de Armas in the same building as the municipal tourist office ☎ 2 2820 1000, ⓦ viajesturistik.com. The ubiquitous Turistik runs bright red buses on a hop-on, hop-off route around Santiago (daily 9.30am–6pm, every 30min; CH$30,000 for the day), as well as a range of tours to nearby wineries and ski resorts, also starting around CH$30,000.

Upscape Tegualda 1352, Providencia ☎2 2244 2750, ⓦupscapetravel.com. A well-respected, comprehensive agency offering upscale cycle, wine and city tours, skiing trips and holidays throughout Chile and South America. Prices start at US$400.

ACCOMMODATION

There's plenty of **accommodation** to suit most budgets, though really inexpensive places are scarce. Most of the city's low-cost rooms are small, simple and sparsely furnished, often without a window but usually fairly clean; the many hostels with dorms make a good alternative. There are numerous good mid-range hotels and B&Bs, plus several luxurious top-end options. Apartment rentals are also popular, such as the excellent selection offered by Oasis (ⓦoasiscollections. com/santiago). Prices don't fluctuate much, though a few hotels charge more between November and February. All prices include **breakfast**.

PLAZA DE ARMAS TO THE ALAMEDA

Andes Hostel Monjitas 506 ☎2 2632 9990; map p.60. Funky hostel with tidy four- and six-bed dorms, swish marble bathrooms, a roof terrace and a bar area with big-screen TV and a pool table. There are also private rooms and – in a nearby building – apartments that sleep three or four. Cheaper if booked via an online agent. Dorms CH$13,000, doubles CH$48,000, apartments CH$50,000

París 813 París 813 ☎2 2664 0921, ⓦhotelparis813. com; map p.60. Decent low-cost hotel offering a range of slightly old-fashioned rooms, with TVs and private bathrooms; the older ones sometimes lack outside windows so unless pesos are really tight, opt for one in the newer annexe. CH$28,000

Plaza de Armas Compañía 960, apartment 607 ☎2 2671 4436, ⓦplazadearmashostel.com; map p.60. This gem of a hostel, on the sixth floor of a building hidden within an alleyway filled with fast-food joints, has a prime location on the Plaza de Armas. There are bright dorms, colourful if compact private rooms, ample communal space and a terrace with fine views. Dorms CH$8,000, doubles with shared bathroom CH$15,000, doubles with private bathroom CH$26,000

Plaza San Francisco Alameda 816 ☎2 2360 4444, ⓦplazasanfrancisco.cl; map p.60. This is the most luxurious downtown top-end hotel choice: the en suites are large and handsome with tubs and easy chairs. There's also an indoor pool, mini art gallery and quality restaurant. Good online deals. US$190

Vegas Londres 49 ☎2 2632 2514, ⓦhotelvegas.net; map p.60. A national monument, in the quiet París-Londres neighbourhood, this hotel is great value, with spacious en suites, friendly service and thoughtful touches including secondhand novels to read and a collection of umbrellas for use on rainy days. Apartments with small kitchens also available. Doubles CH$38,000, apartments CH$52,000

BARRIO LASTARRIA

Although this lively neighbourhood is focused more on restaurants and bars than hotels, there are a handful of choices and the location is excellent – easy walking distance from the old centre and Bellavista, and a bit smarter than both.

★ **Luciano K** Merced 84 ☎2 2620 0900, ⓦlucianokhotel.com; map p.60. Wedged between Parque Forestal and the Alameda, this smart boutique hotel with 1920s Art Deco features, such as the original mosaic tiles, was the tallest building in Chile when built in the 1920s and the first to have a lift, which is still in use. There is a snazzy resto-bar on the roof terrace. US$140

Montecarlo Victoria Subercaseaux 209 ☎2 2639 2945, ⓦhotelmontecarlo.cl; map p.60. Location is the USP here: the hotel overlooks Cerro Santa Lucia, and the Alameda is a couple of blocks away. The building has an unusual modernist shape, and the small rooms could do with a freshen up, but overall it's a decent choice. CH$48,000

★ **Río Amazonas** Vicuña Mackenna 47 ☎2 2635 1631, ⓦhostalrioamazonas.cl; map p.60. Travellers of all ages flock to this charming *hostal*, next to the Argentine embassy. Each room has a private bathroom (and often a bath), colourful decor, phone, TV and plenty of space. The communal areas are attractive, and light meals are available. CH$58,000

The Singular Merced 294 ☎2 2306 8821, ⓦthesingular.com; map p.60. Well located in Lastarria, this elegant five-star is an excellent choice. Highlights include spacious and stylish en suites, a rooftop bar and swimming pool, well-equipped spa, fine restaurant and attentive service. It has an equally impressive sister hotel in Puerto Natales (see page 396). US$310

THE WESTERN NEIGHBOURHOODS

Bohemian Barrio Brasil, north of the Alameda, is a popular choice thanks to its supply of cool cafés, restaurants and bars.

★ **Happy House** Moneda 1829, Barrio Brasil ☎2 2688 4849, ⓦhappyhousehostel.cl; map p.58. This restored early twentieth-century townhouse is a cut above most other hostels, with beautiful, airy rooms (shared or en suite) that put many mid-range hotels to shame, as well as

1

a bar, terrace and pool table. Dorms CH$13,000, doubles CH$34,000

Princesa Insolente Moneda, Barrio Brasil 2350 ☎2 2671 6551, ⓦprincesainsolentehostel.cl; map p.58. This popular and sociable hostel has clean and economical private rooms, three- to ten-bed dorms, a TV lounge and a patio. The cheerful staff members host regular barbecues. Dorms CH$8000, doubles CH$30,000

BARRIO BELLAVISTA

The Aubrey Constitución 317 ☎2 2940 2800, ⓦtheaubrey.com; map p.72. Nestling beside Cerro San Cristóbal, with Bellavista's restaurants and bars just a stone's throw away, *The Aubrey* is based in two beautifully restored 1920s mansions, and boasts some of Santiago's most stylish en suites: swish bathrooms, Tom Dixon lamps and MP3 docks are just a few of the features. The hotel also has a pool, piano lounge and a fine restaurant. US$240

Casa Mosaico Loreto 109 ☎2 2671 2008, ⓦcasamosaicohostel.cl; map p.60. Just a few blocks from the nightlife action but quiet enough for a good night's sleep, this gaily painted hostel offers a range of six- or eight-bed dorms, plus en-suite singles and doubles. Activities include barbecues and dance classes. Dorms CH$10,000, doubles CH$30,000

PROVIDENCIA

As the glitzy commercial heart of Santiago, Providencia, well served by metro line #1 is worth considering as a base. It has a number of pricey hotels, as well as a range of B&Bs and small mid-range hotels.

L'Ambassade Av Suiza 2084 ☎2 2761 9711, ⓦambassade.cl; map p.58. Run by a very welcoming Franco/Chilean family, this intimate and peaceful boutique B&B has tasteful en-suite doubles, an artwork-filled lounge, a small outdoor pool and a sauna. Super online discounts and an excellent breakfast. CH$40,000

Chilhotel Cirujano Guzmán 103 ☎2 2264 0643, ⓦchilhotel.cl; map p.58. This small hotel, on a quiet street in central Providencia, is a good choice. The rooms are comfortable and good value, though the decor is a bit

twee; all come with private bathrooms, TVs and fridges. CH$46,000

Hotel Orly Pedro de Valdivia 27 ☎2 2630 3000, ⓦorlyhotel.com; map p.58. Welcoming and cosy hotel in the heart of Providencia. The immaculate en suites have wood fittings, colourful throws, mini fridges and TVs; they can range quite considerably in size, however, so ask to see a few. The apartments, which sleep up to four, are good value. Doubles CH$93,000, apartments CH$85,000

Le Rêve Orrego Luco 23 ☎2 2757 6000, ⓦlerevehotel. cl; map p.58. An excellent addition to Santiago's luxury accommodation options, *Le Rêve* is a welcoming boutique hotel with plenty of French touches in both the architecture and the furnishings. The en suites are elegant though overpriced, and service is welcoming and efficient. US$250

★ **Vilafranca** Pérez Valenzuela 1650 ☎2 2235 1413, ⓦvilafranca.cl; map p.58. A charming eight-room B&B in an ivy-clad 1940s-era home on a peaceful street: each room is unique and supremely tasteful, service is personalized, black-and-white photos of historic Santiago cover the walls and there's a sunny patio area. CH$50,000

LAS CONDES

Las Condes – and, in particular, Sanhattan – is Santiago's burgeoning luxury hotel neighbourhood, with large shopping centres and art galleries nearby. The metro goes as far as Los Dominicos while a taxi to the centre runs to about CH$6000–10,000.

Ritz-Carlton El Alcalde 15 ☎2 2470 8500, ⓦritzcarlton. com; map p.58. One of Santiago's top five-stars, Sanhattan's *Ritz-Carlton* has classically styled en suites, attentive but not overbearing service, excellent restaurants and bars, and a fifteenth-floor swimming pool, gym and spa sheltered from the elements by a glass dome. US$379

The W Isidora Goyenechea 3000 ☎2 2770 0000, ⓦstarwoodhotels.com; map p.58. In an eye-catching skyscraper, *The W* is a glamorous, achingly hip hotel. Highlights include the über-modern en suites with floor-to-ceiling windows, and the rooftop (21st-floor) pool and bar with superlative views. Service, however, can be inconsistent. US$309

EATING

Santiago has a wide range of **places to eat**, from humble *picadas* serving traditional favourites to slick modern restaurants offering cuisines such as Japanese, Southeast Asian, Spanish, Peruvian, French and Italian. Some are modestly priced but most are fairly expensive, although at lunchtime many offer a good-value fixed-price *menú del día* or *menú ejecutivo*. In most places there's no need to **book**. The city also features innumerable fast food joints and (generally) unappealing *fuentes de soda*.

CAFÉS AND CHEAP EATS

Santiago is not a café city, but a number of places cater to the great tradition of *onces* (afternoon tea). There are also some decent ice-cream parlours and innumerable joints specializing in *empanadas*.

PLAZA DE ARMAS TO THE ALAMEDA

Blue Jar Almirante Amanda Labarca 102 ☎2 6155 4650, ⓦbluejar.cl; map p.60. Just around the corner from La Moneda, this is where government officials from the nearby ministry buildings come to gossip about politics and sip excellent coffees and cocktails. Meals also available (set lunch CH$10,000). Mon–Fri 8am–9pm.

Café Caribe Ahumada 120 ☎2 2695 7081, ⓦcafecaribe.cl; map p.60. It's a curiosity, at least: one of the city's traditional *cafés con piernas* ("cafés with legs", staffed by scantily clad women), where (mostly) male members of Chile's ageing business class stand around for what seems like hours, ogling the waitresses and talking on their mobile phones. It's not an exclusively male haunt, by any means, and the coffee (from CH$1400) is not at all bad. Mon–Fri 8am–9pm.

Café Colonia Mac Iver 161 ☎2 26397256, ⓦcafecolonia. cl; map p.60. At this cute little café, which has been going for more than fifty years, matronly waitresses serve the best cakes, tarts, *küchen* and strudel (all from CH$1500/slice) in Santiago. Mon–Fri 8am–9pm, Sat & Sun 10am–8pm.

Café Haiti Ahumada 140 ☎2 2562 2698, ⓦcafehaiti. cl; map p.60. One of the city's famous, timewarp *cafés con piernas* (see above); dodgy gender politics aside, the coffee (from CH$1400) is not to be sniffed at. There are many branches around town. Mon–Fri 8am–9pm.

El Rápido Bandera 347 ☎2 2672 2375; map p.60. For decades, *El Rápido* has lived up to its name, with a brisk turnover in excellent *empanadas* (from CH$1100) with a range of fillings such as cheese, chicken or seafood. Mon–Fri 9am–9pm, Sat 9am–3.30pm.

BARRIO LASTARRIA

Bonbon Oriental Merced 355 ☎2 2639 1069; map p.60. Photos of regular customers cover the walls of this tiny Middle Eastern café, which serves cardamom-scented Arabic coffee (CH$1800), falafel sandwiches and sticky-sweet baklavas; there's also a sister joint a few doors down. Daily 9am–9pm.

Café del Opera Merced 391 ☎2 2664 3048; map p.60. This slick *heladería* (ice-cream parlour) has a great range of flavours including the wonderful *maracujá* (passion fruit), served in cones, cups or in sundaes (from CH$4000), as well as coffee, sandwiches and snacks. Mon–Fri 9am–9pm, Sat & Sun 10.30am–10pm.

Emporio La Rosa Merced 291 ☎2 2638 0502, ⓦemporiolarosa.com; map p.60. Popular with students, this ice-cream parlour has delicious, inventive flavours, such as green tea with mango, and banana with palm honey (from CH$2100), as well as breakfast and snacks. There are several other branches. Mon–Thurs 8am–9pm, Fri 8am–10pm, Sat 9am–10pm, Sun 9am–9pm.

LAS CONDES

Cafe Melba Don Carlos 2898 ☎2 2232 4546, ⓦcafemelba.cl; map p.58. Next to the British embassy and run by New Zealanders, this is a favourite expat hangout. Brunch (from around CH$6000), with options such as eggs Benedict or eggs and bacon, as well as fine

coffee, is a Sun ritual for many. Mon–Fri 7.30am–7pm, Sat & Sun 8am–3.30pm.

RESTAURANTS

Most of Santiago's restaurants are concentrated along the Alameda, around Plaza de Armas, or in Barrio Lastarria, Bellavista, Barrio Brasil, Providencia and Las Condes, where Isidora Goyenechea is lined with options. There are also some imaginative places springing up around Plaza Ñuñoa in the southeast part of town, and in pricey Vitacura. A memorable place for lunch is the Mercado Central (see page 70), whose central hall is lined with seafood restaurants (*marisquerías*). Alternatively follow the locals to the cheaper joints across the river in the Feria Municipal La Vega.

PLAZA DE ARMAS TO THE ALAMEDA

El Ají Seco San Antonio 530 ☎2 2638 8818, ⓦelajiseco. cl; map p.60. A hectic Peruvian joint serving sizeable portions of *ceviche*, fried chicken, seafood and *lomo saltado* (a heaped plate of beef, onions, chips and rice); Inca Cola and Cusqueña beer are also available. Mains CH$5000–10,000; set lunch CH$5500. There are a dozen or so related branches. Mon–Thurs noon–11.30pm, Fri & Sat noon–12.30am, Sun noon–11pm.

Bar de la Unión Nueva York 11 ☎2 2696 1821; map p.60. Old wooden floors, shelves of dusty wine bottles and animated, garrulous old men make this an atmospheric place to pop in for a cheap glass of wine or a leisurely meal. Set lunch CH$3950, mains CH$7000–8000. Mon–Fri 10am–10.30pm, Sat 10am–5pm.

Bar Nacional Paseo Huérfanos 1151 ☎2 2696 5986, ⓦbarnacional.cl; map p.60. This unpretentious stalwart of the Santiago dining scene serves hearty Chilean staples with the minimum of fuss. There's another branch at Bandera 317 and two in the suburbs. Mains CH$7000–14,000. Mon–Sat 8am–11pm.

Confitería Torres Alameda 1570 ☎2 2688 0751, ⓦconfiteriatorres.cl; map p.60. Open since 1879, this is one of Santiago's oldest restaurants. While the food is a little overpriced (most mains from CH$10,000), the wood-panelled walls, old mirrors and sagging chairs provide a fabulous atmosphere. The classic Chilean *barros luco* beef and cheese sandwich was supposedly invented here. There are two other branches, including one in Las Condes. Mon–Sat 9am–midnight.

El Naturista Moneda 846 ☎2 2390 5940, ⓦelnaturista. cl; map p.60. The original pioneer of vegetarian food in Santiago, this large, inexpensive restaurant attracts a huge, frenetic crowd at lunchtime. Dishes (around CH$4000–5000) include potato and onion soufflé and quinoa risotto. There are a couple of other branches around town. Mon–Fri 8.30am–9pm, Sat 9am–4pm.

Quijote Nueva York 52 ☎2 2243 7715, ⓦquijoterestaurant.cl; map p.60. Another restaurant,

1

TOP 5 PLACES TO EAT TRADITIONAL CHILEAN FOOD

El Caramaño See below
Fuente Alemana See below
Galindo See page 84
El Hoyo See below
Liguria See page 84

a bit more refined than most, offering a good-value three-course lunch for CH$6990. The international menu includes items like the delicious rustic octopus with unagui sauce (CH$9990). Mon–Fri 8.30am–8.30pm.

★ **Ramen Kintaro** Monjitas 460 ⓦkintaro.cl; map p.60. This clean, modern Japanese joint has reinvented itself as a ramen house, with meal deals for around CH$6000–7000. Sit at the counter and watch the chefs at work. Mon–Fri 12.30–3pm & 7.30–11pm, Sat 7.30–11.30pm.

THE WESTERN NEIGHBOURHOODS

Interesting, offbeat cafés, restaurants and bars are springing up all the time in Barrio Brasil, with seafood a particular speciality. Reservations at weekends are recommended for all the establishments listed below.

★ **El Hoyo** San Vicente 375, just south of Estación Central ☎2 2689 0339, ⓦelhoyo.cl; map p.58. The much-missed travelling gastronome Anthony Bourdain said the best food he ate in Chile was at El Hoyo, and the hearty, pork-focused dishes (CH$5600–10,000) don't disappoint. Specialities include *pernil* (leg of pork) and *arrollado* (rolled pork). The restaurant is also the originator of the *terremoto* (earthquake), an earth-tremblingly potent mix of young white *pipeño* wine, pisco and pineapple ice cream. Mon–Fri 11am–11pm, Sat 11am–9pm.

Ocean Pacific's Ricardo Cumming 221, Barrio Brasil ☎9 6831 0750, ⓦoceanpacifics.cl; map p.58. Worth going for the kitsch nautical interior decor alone. Every patch of wall is covered with whale bones, ships' instruments and the like, the staff dress as sailors and the food is – of course – seafood orientated, with an enormous menu that is nearly as dizzying as the decor. Mains around CH$7000–9000. There is a smaller branch in Vitacura at Padre Hurtado 1480. Mon–Thurs noon–11.30pm, Fri & Sat noon–12.30am, Sun noon–11pm.

Ostras Azocar General Bulnes 37, Barrio Brasil ☎2 2681 6109, ⓦostrasazocar.cl; map p.58. This seafood restaurant has been serving king crab, lobster, squid and more since 1945. The house speciality is baked razor clams in cheese sauce. Sadly the waiting staff can be a bit slack. Mains CH$8000–15,000. Mon–Thurs 12.30–4.30pm & 7.30–11.30pm, Fri & Sat 12.30–11.30pm, Sun 12.30–5.30pm.

★ **Las Vacas Gordas** Cienfuegos 280, Barrio Brasil ☎2 2697 1066; map p.58. This superior steakhouse serves

top-quality meat (CH$8000–14,000) – try the melt-in-the-mouth wagyu beef or the flavoursome *entrecôte*, as well as *ceviche* and other seafood. Service is sharp, and the large, airy dining room has a pleasantly relaxed ambience. Mon–Sat 12.30pm–12.30am, Sun 12.30–5pm.

BARRIO LASTARRIA AND AROUND

Reservations are recommended here in the evenings, as many of the restaurants have fewer than ten tables. Parking is easy, and the *barrio* is very close to the Universidad Católica metro stop. This neighbourhood is generally safe, but Cerro Santa Lucia park should be avoided at night.

BocaNariz Jose V. Lastarria 276 ☎2 2638 9893, ⓦbocanariz.cl; map p.60. With more than three hundred wine labels in its cellar, this restaurant seeks to introduce you to new tipples and the ideal food to pair with it. Its most popular wine tasting options are the *vuelos* of three glasses, each a different blend. Mains include short ribs with mash (CH$11,500). Mon–Wed noon–midnight, Thurs–Sat noon–12.30am, Sun 7–11pm.

Fuente Alemana Alameda 58 ☎2 2639 3231, ⓦfalemana.cl; map p.60. This fun Santiago institution feels a bit like a Germanic take on an American-style diner. Grab a seat at the counter, order a draught beer and watch your vast *lomito* beef sandwich (CH$3500), *churrasco* or other artery-clogging meal being prepared before you. Mon–Sat 10am–10.30pm.

Japón Baron Pierre de Coubertin 39 ☎2 2222 4517, ⓦrestaurantjapon.cl; map p.60. Tucked away on a quiet side street south of the Alameda is Santiago's oldest and best Japanese restaurant. The sushi is outstanding, making full use of Chile's wonderful range of seafood. Mains CH$4000–20,000. Mon–Sat noon–11.15pm.

Squadritto Rosal 332 ☎2 2632 2121, ⓦsquadrittoristorante.cl; map p.60. This long-running Genoese Italian restaurant serves superb, if rather pricey, pizzas, pastas and other traditional dishes – the risottos are a particular highlight. Staff are welcoming, though the atmosphere is somewhat formal. Mains CH$8000–10,000. Mon–Sat 1–4pm & 7pm–midnight, Sun 1–4pm.

BELLAVISTA

Bellavista – particularly Calle Constitución, which runs parallel with the area's main drag, Pio Nono – is at the heart of Santiago's eating-out scene, with a wide range of excellent, and often innovative, restaurants.

El Caramaño Purísima 257 ☎2 2737 7043; map p.72. Graffiti-covered walls, soft live guitar music, amiable waiters, excellent, wallet-friendly Chilean food including *pastel de choclo*, and frequent free aperitifs make this restaurant a standout. Mains CH$5000–8000. Mon–Sat 1pm–midnight.

★ **Ciudad Vieja** Constitución 92 ☎2 2248 9412, ⓦciudadvieja.cl; map p.72. This cool *sanguchería*

MERCADO CENTRAL

1

turns sandwich-making into an art form: varieties (around CH$5000) include teriyaki chicken, suckling pig, fried *merluza* (hake) and the *chivito*, Uruguay's take on the steak sandwich. Deliciously salty French fries come on the side, and there's an extensive range of artisanal beers, too. Tues 12.30pm–1am, Wed 12.30pm–1.30am, Thurs 12.30pm–2am, Fri & Sat 12.30pm–2.30am, Sun 1–5pm.

Étniko Constitución 172 at Lopez de Bello ⊤2 2732 0119; map p.72. The blue-neon-lit, Japanese-inspired interior attracts a cool 20s–30s crowd drawn by more than forty types of sushi and sashimi, plus numerous other Southeast Asian dishes, and excellent *ceviche*. It turns into a bar-club (with a focus on house/electro) later on – try the knockout sake-based cocktails. You have to ring the doorbell to enter. Mains from CH$7000. Mon–Thurs 8pm–midnight, Fri & Sat 8pm–2am.

Galindo Dardignac 098 ⊤2 2777 0116, Ⓦgalindo.cl; map p.72. Classic Bellavista hangout, busy at all hours for hearty dishes including beef casserole and *longaniza* (spicy sausage) and chips. During the summer the tables spill out onto the street. Mains CH$5000–8500. Mon–Sat 10am–2am.

★ **El Toro** Loreto 33 ⊤2 2761 5954, Ⓦfacebook.com/eltororestoran; map p.60. An effortlessly trendy restaurant with an appealingly whimsical air – pots of crayons are left on each table so that you can doodle while you wait for your food – and an array of tempting dishes such as shrimp crêpes. Mains CH$5000–10,000. Mon–Sat 1–4pm & 7pm–midnight.

PROVIDENCIA AND ÑUÑOA

Conveniently located on metro line 1, Providencia offers many lunch and dinner options. Nearby, though less accessible, Ñuñoa has trendier restaurants, often with good music thrown in.

Barandiaran Manuel Montt 315, Providencia ⊤2 2236 6854, Ⓦbarandiaran.cl; map p.58. Some of the best Peruvian food in Santiago is served here: *ceviche*, sea bass and the more leftfield choice of Patagonian lamb in a coriander sauce are all on offer. There are also branches in Patio Bellavista and Plaza Ñuñoa. Mains CH$7000–11,000. Tues–Thurs 1–4pm & 8pm–midnight, Fri & Sat 1–4pm & 8pm–1am, Sun 1–4pm.

★ **Le Flaubert** Orrego Luco 125, Providencia ⊤2 2231 9424, Ⓦleflaubert.cl; map p.58. This exemplary Chilean/French bistro and *salon de thé* has an ever-changing menu marked up on chalkboards. Dishes (around CH$9000) could include country pâté, *coq au vin* and *tarte tatin*. There are also thirty different varieties of tea, and home-made cheeses and preserves for sale, too. Tea with cakes and sandwiches CH$6200. Mon–Fri 10.45am–11.45pm, Sat 12.30–11.45pm, Sun 12.30–5pm.

El Huerto Orrego Luco 54, Providencia ⊤2 2231 4443, Ⓦelhuerto.cl; map p.58. The best vegetarian restaurant in Santiago, with a mouthwatering range of inventive, seasonal dishes (CH$7000–8000); asparagus and ricotta strudel, *paneer tikka masala* and vegetable quesadillas all feature. The freshly squeezed juices and artisan beers are also great. Mon–Wed 12.15–11pm, Thurs–Sat 12.15–11.30pm, Sun 12.30–4.30pm.

Las Lanzas Humberto Trucco 25, Plaza Ñuñoa ⊤2 2225 5589; map p.58. This traditional bar-restaurant, with tables spilling onto the pavement, is *the* classic drinking spot in Ñuñoa. It also offers a range of meat and fish dishes at amazingly low prices (mains CH$3000–5000). Mon–Thurs noon–1am, Fri & Sat noon–3am.

Liguria Av Providencia 1373, Providencia ⊤2 2235 7914, Ⓦliguria.cl; map p.58. Portraits, film posters, flower designs and football pennants adorn the walls of this legendary Santiago restaurant-bar, which has outdoor tables, a bar, main dining area and several back rooms, so you can normally find a seat. Dishes include pot roast, pork ribs in mustard sauce and sea bass with capers. There are two other branches, but this one is the best. Mains CH$8000–9000. Mon–Sat 11am–2am.

Santo Remedio Roman Diaz 152, Providencia ⊤2 2235 0984, Ⓦsantoremedio.cl; map p.58. The idiosyncratic decor has a surreal edge – including high-backed wooden chairs and a zebra print sofa – and the food is billed as "an aphrodisiacal experience", with pastas, Thai curries, steaks and seafood all on the menu. It's also good for drinks and *the* place for a Sun night out. Mains and set lunches CH$5700–7900. Mon–Fri 1–3.30pm & 6.30pm–late, Sat & Sun 9pm–late.

LAS CONDES AND VITACURA

As you'd expect in these exclusive neighbourhoods, restaurants are often more about money than taste, but those reviewed here are well worth the extra outlay.

Amicci Apoquindo 7741, Las Condes ⊤2 2934 3722, Ⓦamicci.cl; map p.58. A short walk from Los Dominicos craft market (see page 87), this restaurant combines attentive service, a creative cocktail menu (from CH$3900) and refined Italian cuisine, including a particularly memorable seafood risotto (CH$8900). Mon–Sat 12.30–3.30pm & 7.30–11.30pm, Sun 12.30–3.30pm.

Boragó Nueva Costanera 3467, Vitacura ⊤2 2953 8893, Ⓦborago.cl; map p.58. Considered to be one of Latin America's best restaurants, *Boragó* employs a tasting menu (CH$43,000–65,000) to present its innovative take on Chilean traditional cuisine. The dishes vary according to the season and whim of the chef, but include such delights as *machas* marinated in garlic, or parma violet ice cream. Reserve ahead. Mon–Sat 8–11pm.

★ **Fuente Las Cabras** Thayer Ojeda 0166, Las Condes ⊤2 2232 9671, Ⓦfuentelascabras.cl; map p.58. Simple, traditional restaurant with pavement seating, serving daily specials such as spicy chicken for CH$7000–

10,000, plus a range of wine and cocktails. Mon–Sat 9am–11pm, Sun 10am–8pm.

Nolita Isidora Goyenechea 3456, Las Condes ☎ 2 2232 6114, ⓦ nolita.cl; map p.58. Self-consciously aping the style of the eponymous New York district, *Nolita* produces top-quality, artfully presented Italian cuisine (mains CH$8000–12,000); the seafood dishes, pastas, burgers and desserts are all outstanding. Mon–Thurs 1–3.30pm & 8–11pm, Fri & Sat 1–3.30pm & 8pm–midnight, Sun 1–3.30pm.

Tanta Boulevard Parque Arauco local 371, Las Condes ☎ 2 2364 1368, ⓦ tantaperu.com; map p.58. By far the best restaurant in the popular Parque Arauco shopping complex, this branch of a bright and breezy Peruvian chain does large portions of very tasty Peruvian food, including *tacu tacu*, *lomo saltado* and, of course, huge pisco sours.

Tanta is also found in the other main malls (see page 87). Daily 11am–9pm.

Tiramisú Isidora Goyenechea 3141, Las Condes ☎ 2 2519 4900, ⓦ tiramisu.cl; map p.58. Long-running Italian restaurant with a vast array of thin-crust pizzas (CH$6500–13,800), pastas, salads and desserts, all at reasonable prices considering the area. Daily 12.45–4pm & 7pm–midnight.

Zanzibar Monseñor Escriva de Balaguer 6400, inside the Borde del Río complex, Vitacura ☎ 2 2218 0120, ⓦ zanzibar.cl; map p.58. One of Santiago's most beautiful restaurants, with a host of Moroccan-style dining rooms, including a rooftop tented lounge. The global menu has an eclectic range of dishes including lamb *tagine* and conger eel with a black olive crust. Mains CH$10,5000–16,900. Mon–Sat 6pm–midnight, Sun 6–10pm.

DRINKING

Santiago's **bars** range from dusty, mahogany-panelled corner spots full of ancient regulars to ultra-trendy spaces. **Lastarria** has a number of cool, idiosyncratic bars and there are also plenty of options in grungier **Bellavista**. **Providencia** sports a number of bar-restaurants, but the dozens of dispiriting American-style bars, particularly around the junction of Suecia and Holley, are best avoided.

THE WESTERN NEIGHBOURHOODS

The Clinic Av Brasil 258, Brasil ☎ 2 2697 2578, ⓦ cerveceriatheclinic.cl; map p.60. Run by the people behind satirical magazine *The Clinic*, this restaurant-bar maintains an appealingly irreverent air with its cartoon menus. There are also inexpensive snacks and meals (CH$4000–10,000), plus branches in Plaza Ñuñoa and other cities. Daily 12.30pm–2am.

BARRIO LASTARRIA

Bar Don Rodrigo Victoria Subercaseaux 353 ☎ 2 2639 6261, ⓦ forestahotel.cl; map p.60. Officially a hotel bar, attached to the *Hotel Floresta*, this place channels the 1950s, with an old-school bar area and live piano. The drinks aren't quite at 1950s prices, but are pretty cheap nonetheless (from CH$2700 for a cocktail); be careful, they pack a punch. Mon–Sat 7pm–2am.

Catedral Miguel de la Barra 407 ☎ 2 2664 3048, ⓦ operacatedral.cl; map p.60. This second-floor bar is a swish, modern space with a roof terrace ideal for a summer evening. There's a good menu of drinks (from CH$3000), and a small selection of dishes (around CH$10,000) such as fried tilapia if you get peckish. Mon–Thurs 12.30pm–3am, Fri & Sat 12.30pm–5am.

★ **Culto** Estados Unidos 246 ☎ 2 2632 3585, ⓦ cultobar.cl; map p.60. Laidback rock bar that specializes in theme days dedicated to bands from Pink Floyd to The Verve. Decent range of cocktails starting at CH$2700 and snacks from CH$4500. Mon–Thurs 5pm–1am, Fri & Sat 5pm–2am, Sun 5pm–midnight.

BELLAVISTA

Bar Dos Gardenias Antonia López de Bello 199 ☎ 9 7757 2887, ⓦ bardosgardenias.cl; map p.72. A chilled-out and welcoming Cuban bar, with a faded red and yellow exterior, the obligatory Che picture, live Latin folk and rock and refreshing drinks (a mojito will set you back CH$3500). It's especially lively on Fri and Sat nights. Mon & Tues 7pm–1am, Wed 7pm–2.30am, Thurs–Sat 7pm–3.30am.

La Casa en el Aire Antonia López de Bello 125 ☎ 2 2735 6680, ⓦ lacasaenelaire.cl; map p.72. Named after Neruda's poem *Voy a hacerte una casa en el aire* ("I will build you a house in the air"), this bar-café is one of the nicest places in Bellavista to enjoy a drink and live folk music, with occasional poetry recitals thrown in. There's a much less atmospheric branch in Patio Bellavista. Daily 8pm–2/3am.

Ky Av Peru 631 ☎ 2 2777 7245, ⓦ restobarky.cl; map p.58. From the outside this old house appears to have been abandoned, but once inside you find a beautifully renovated resto-bar kitted out with an eclectic array of knick-knacks. Great for a late-night drink or a Southeast Asian meal (from CH$8000). Tues–Sat 8pm–2am.

LAS CONDES

Flannery's Tobalaba 379 ☎ 2 2303 0192, ⓦ flannerys. cl; map p.58. The inevitable Irish pub, but a good choice for a night out in the Sanhattan area – large and busy, with a loyal local clientele and good number of expats, who come to sup Guinness and English ale, watch the football or rugby and eat Irish stew or fish and chips (CH$6800). Mon–Wed noon–1.30am, Thurs & Fri noon–2.30am, Sat 6pm–2.30am, Sun 6pm–12.30am.

1

NIGHTLIFE

Santiago is not a 24/7 party town, but Thursday, Friday and Saturday nights are lively, and the **club scene** is constantly evolving, while **live music** – from folk to heavy metal – is popular. Dance festival **Creamfields** (Ⓦ creamfields.cl) and rock festival **Lollapalooza** (Ⓦ lollapalooza.cl) have run Chilean editions in recent years (in November and March respectively). You'll find venues everywhere from the historic centre to bohemian Ñuñoa, in bars, jazz clubs and concert venues. **Bellavista**, in particular, has many resto-bars with live music, as well as a number of (generally unappealing) clubs on Pío Nono; this area can be a bit unsafe at night, so take care.

La Batuta Jorge Washington 52, Plaza Ñuñoa ☏ 2 2724 4037, Ⓦ batuta.cl; map p.58. There's a wonderful grungy atmosphere at this dark, packed club just off Plaza Ñuñoa, which hosts rock bands, hip-hop groups and heavy metal outfits. Wed & Thurs 10pm–2am, Fri & Sat 10pm–4.30am

Blondie Alameda 2879, Estación Central, Ⓜ ULA ☏ 2 2681 7793, Ⓦ blondie.cl; map p.58. A popular student hangout with loud – and often live – music, including techno, dance, electro and indie, plus plenty of dancing. Thurs–Sat midnight–4/5am; occasional events on other nights too.

Club de Jazz Av Ossa 123, Mall Plaza Egaña, La Reina, Ⓜ Plaza Egaña ☏ 2 2830 6208, Ⓦ clubdejazz.cl; map p.58. Founded in 1943 and still going strong, *Club de Jazz* has an invariably excellent line-up of Chilean and international jazz musicians. Tues–Sat 10.30pm–late.

Club La Feria Constitución 275, Bellavista ☏ 2 2735 8433, Ⓦ clublaferia.cl; map p.72. The best place in Santiago for electro, *Club La Feria* – which has been running since 1996 – hosts an illustrious cast of Chilean and international DJs. Wed–Sat 10pm–4/5am. ·

La Maestra Vida Pío Nono 380, Bellavista ☏ 2 2777 5325, Ⓦ maestravida.cl; map p.72. One of Santiago's oldest *salsatecas* and popular with dancers of all ages, giving it a friendly vibe – there's no need to feel shy about practising your steps here. It also runs salsa classes. Tues–Fri 11pm–late, Sat midnight–late, Sun 10.30pm–late.

Teatro Caupolicán San Diego 850, San Diego, Ⓜ Parque Almagro Ⓦ teatrocaupolican.cl; map p.58. Long-running live music venue near Parque O'Higgins, used by popular international, Latin American and local musicians. Check the website to see listings (*cartelera*). Days and times vary.

LGBT NIGHTLIFE

Santiago is the only city in Chile with anything resembling an organized LGBT community. The scene centres around Bombero Nuñez and adjacent streets in **Bellavista**, and consists of a small collection of bars, restaurants, discos and saunas. Local LGBT rights organization **Movilh** (Ⓦ movilh.cl) holds an annual pride march and cinema festival.

Bokhara Pío Nono 430, Bellavista; map p.72. A legendary, multistorey club with a mixed gay and lesbian crowd, and shows featuring drag artists and Brazilian dance troupes. The queues to get in, however, can be long. Daily 10pm–4/5am.

Dionisio Bombero Nuñez 111, Bellavista ☏ 2 2737 1782, Ⓦ facebook/dionisio.divas.5; map p.60. Popular nightclub for dancing, which also hosts a host of the city's most famous drag artists. Wed–Sun 11pm–5am.

Farinelli Bombero Nuñez 68, Bellavista ☏ 2 2732 8966; map p.60. Bar with nightly shows, many of them

hilarious comic drag acts requiring a decent level of Spanish to be fully appreciated. Tues–Thurs 7pm–3.30am, Fri & Sat 7pm–4.30am, Sun 7pm–2am.

Fausto Av Santa Maria 832, Providencia ☏ 9 9479 7857, Ⓦ fausto.cl; map p.58. Lively disco featuring live shows and a variety of musical styles. Free entry before midnight. Wed–Sun 11.30pm–late.

XLimon Dardignac 142, Bellavista ☏ 9 5236 7363, Ⓦ facebook.com/XLimonSantiago; map p.60. A favourite with the young crowd, this is one of the few dance clubs open nightly. They offer a cheap *vaso* with free refills. Mon–Thurs & Sun 11pm–4am, Fri & Sat 11pm–5am.

ENTERTAINMENT

Santiago is, unsurprisingly, the best place in Chile to enjoy the **arts**. The Friday newspapers include comprehensive entertainment **listings**, and you can also check listings for the bigger events and buy tickets at Ticketek Chile (Ⓦ ticketek. cl). The **website** Ⓦ santiagochile.com also has what's-on listings. Unless stated otherwise, the venues below are in the **central area** between Plaza de Armas and the Alameda.

CINEMA

There are plenty of cinemas in Santiago, though the choice of movies in the larger venues tends to be limited to the latest Hollywood blockbusters; note that those with family appeal are usually dubbed into Spanish. Huérfanos is the main cinema street in the historic centre. Tickets start at around CH$4000.

Centro Arte Alameda Alameda 139 ☎2 2664 8821, ⓦcentroartealameda.cl. Comfy cinema with a regularly changing and wide-ranging choice of foreign films.

Cine Arte Normandie Tarapacá 1181 ☎2 2697 2979, ⓦnormandie.cl. Cinema with a reputation for showing obscure contemporary European films.

Cine Hoyts Moneda 835 ☎600 500 0400, ⓦcinehoyts.cl. In a convenient location in the historic centre of Santiago, this cinema has six screens.

Cinemark Theatres Av Kennedy 9001, Mall Alto Las Condes ☎600 586 0058, ⓦcinemark.cl. Modern multiplex offering Hollywood's latest flicks.

Extensión Cultural de la Universidad Católica Alameda 390 ☎2 2354 6516, ⓦextension.uc.cl. Especially good for older films, often presented as part of themed programmes. Many free showings for students with ID.

M100 Centro Cultural Matucana 100, near Parque Quinta Normal ☎2 2682 4502, ⓦm100.cl. Regular film seasons, sometimes in English, plus art exhibitions and concerts.

THEATRE, CLASSICAL MUSIC, DANCE AND OPERA

The best time to experience Chilean theatre is in Jan, when Santiago hosts Santiago a Mil (ⓦsantiagoamil.cl), an enormous international festival of theatre (plus dance and other arts). During the rest of the year, many theatres are only open Thurs to Sat. Ticket prices are usually reasonable, from around CH$4000–5000.

Centro Cultural Mori Constitución 183, Bellavista ☎2 2777 5046, ⓦcentromori.cl. A cutting-edge theatre, dance and arts venue.

Centro Gabriela Mistral Alameda 227, Lastarria ☎2 2566 5500, ⓦgam.cl. You shouldn't miss Santiago's most exciting cultural offering – a huge weathered steel edifice on the Alameda (see page 64). GAM has a wide-ranging programme of contemporary theatre, dance, music, art and cinema.

Teatro Bellavista Dardignac 110, Bellavista ☎2 2735 2395, ⓦteatrobellavista.cl. This long-established and reliable theatre usually stages modern foreign plays, often comedies.

Teatro Municipal Agustinas 749, downtown ☎2 2463 1000, ⓦmunicipal.cl. Santiago's most prestigious performing arts venue, offering a menu of classical concerts, ballet and opera in a splendid old building (see page 63).

Teatro San Ginés Mallinkrodt 112, Bellavista ☎2 2738 2159, ⓦteatrosangines.cl. Top Chilean productions are staged here, as are fine children's shows on weekend afternoons.

Teatro UC Jorge Washington 26, Ñuñoa ☎2 2205 5652, ⓦteatrouc.uc.cl. This university-run venue offers classic shows and adaptations of international works.

SHOPPING

Chileans love to go **shopping** and the capital has a number of modern, American-style **shopping centres** packed with imported brands from the US and elsewhere. The historic centre is perhaps of more interest to visitors, with its small, old-fashioned shops and a warren of arcades (*galerías*) that seem to lurk behind every other doorway.

BOOKS AND CDS

Funtracks Av Providencia 2124, Providencia ☎2 2335 0392, ⓦfuntracks.cl; map p.58. Sells a mix of vinyl, CDs and DVDs, including plenty of Chilean and other Latin music CDs. Mon–Fri 10am–9pm, Sat & Sun 10am–8pm.

Librería Inglesa Huérfanos 669, local 11, downtown ☎2 2632 5153, ⓦlibreriainglesa.cl; map p.60. Fairly good, expensive choice of Penguin paperbacks and other English-language books. Mon–Fri 10.10am–7.30pm, Sat 10.30am–1.50pm.

SANTIAGO MARKETS

The city's **markets** offer some great shopping: **Feria Santa Lucía** (daily 11am–9pm) sells crafts, clothes and lapis lazuli; the enormous and very lively **Persa Bio Bio** (Sat & Sun 9am–around 2pm) runs the length of Franklin and Bío Bío, and at the junction with Victor Manual has a great flea market, with lots of antiques stalls; the excellent **Pueblito de los Dominicos** (daily: summer 10.30am–8pm; rest of year 10am–7pm) has more than two hundred stalls selling knitwear, ceramics, glass objects, books, and antiques (see page 74); **Antiguedades Parque Los Reyes** (Brasil 1157; daily 10am–around 2pm) is a great place to browse for antique furniture, musical instruments, books and bric-à-brac. Also don't miss the stalls at the **Mercado Central** (see page 70) and the **Feria Municipal La Vega** (see page 70), which are great places to explore and grab a bite to eat. In **Bellavista** head to Avenida Bellavista, between Puente Pío Nono and Puente del Arzobispo, where a string of workshops and salesrooms sell jewellery and other objects made of lapis lazuli.

POTTERY IN POMAIRE

Some 50km southwest of Santiago, the dusty, quaint village of **POMAIRE** was one of the *pueblos de indios* created by the Spanish in the eighteenth century in an attempt to control the native population. Its inhabitants quickly developed a reputation for their **pottery** and the village streets (particularly the main street, San Antonio) are packed with dozens of workshops selling a vast range of pots, bowls and kitchenware, many of them made from the characteristic attractive but brittle coffee-coloured *greda* clay. Simple cafés line the streets, some specializing in giant 1.5kg *empanadas*. To get to Pomaire by **public transport**, take a Melipilla bus from Terminal San Borja and ask to be set off at the side road to Pomaire (regular; 1hr–1hr 30min from Santiago). From here, it's a 30min walk, or an inexpensive *colectivo* or **taxi** ride, into the village.

La Tienda Nacional Merced 369, Lastarria ☎2 2638 4706, ⓦlatiendanacional.cl; map p.60. As the name suggests, this shop specializes in all things Chilean, with an emphasis on music and film, although it sells all sorts of knick-knacks. A good place to find something different to take home, from a Chilean folk CD to a rainbow-coloured anti-dictatorship NO mug. Mon–Sat 11am–8.30pm.

SHOPPING CENTRES

Alto Las Condes Av Kennedy 9001, Las Condes ☎2 2299 6965, ⓦaltolascondes.cl; map p.58. Huge, modern shopping centre with more than two hundred shops, a food court and bowling alley. Daily 10am–10pm.

Costanera Center Andrés Bello 2425, Providencia ☎2 2916 9200, ⓦcostaneracenter.cl; map p.58. One of Latin America's largest shopping centres, at the base of one of its tallest skyscrapers (see page 74). The six floors of retail are rather bland, even by shopping centre standards, though it does have the virtue of being close to a metro station (Tobalaba). Daily 10am–10pm.

Mall Sport Av Las Condes 13451, La Dehesa ☎2 2429 3030, ⓦmallsport.cl; map p.58. On the main route up to the ski resorts at Farellones, this shopping centre is dedicated, as its name suggests, to sports. As well as a plethora of stores selling trekking, skiing and gym gear, it has a climbing wall, artificial wave for surf lessons, and a winter ice rink. Daily 10am–9pm.

Parque Arauco Av Kennedy 5413, Las Condes ☎2 2299 0629, ⓦparquearauco.cl; map p.58. The best mall in town, with some unexpectedly good restaurants,

cinemas and a theatre. Take a taxi or walk from Estación Militar metro; the Turistik bus (see page 78) also stops here. Daily 11am–9pm.

FOOD AND DRINK

Larbos Estado 26, downtown ☎2 2639 3434, ⓦlarbos. cl; map p.60. A lovely, old-fashioned shop selling fine wines, spirits (such as pisco) and fancy foodstuffs including chocolates. Mon–Sat 10am–8pm, Sun 10am–5pm.

Wain Nueva Costanera 3955, Vitacura ☎2 2953 6290, ⓦwain.cl; map p.58. Well-informed staff guide you through an extensive range of quality wine from across Chile; the shop also produces its own wine magazine. Mon–Sat 10am–6pm.

MOUNTAIN CLIMBING AND OUTDOOR EQUIPMENT

As well as the places listed below, Mall Sport (see above) has a wide range of stores selling outdoor clothing and equipment, although not usually at the cheapest prices.

La Cumbre Av Apoquindo 5220, Las Condes ☎2 2220 9907, ⓦlacumbreonline.cl; map p.58. Run by friendly staff, this shop has world-class boots, eyewear and climbing accessories as well as a small library of books about exploring the Andes. Mon–Fri 11am–8pm, Sat 11am–4pm.

Tatoo Los Leones 81, Providencia ☎2 2946 0008, ⓦtatoo.ws; map p.58. Hiking, climbing and camping equipment at competitive prices. Mon–Fri 10.30am–8pm, Sat 10.30am–7pm.

DIRECTORY

Embassies Argentina, Miraflores 285 (☎2 2582 2606); Australia, Isidora Goyenechea 3621 (☎2 2550 3500); Bolivia, Av Santa Maria 2796 (☎2 2232 8180); Brazil, Alonso Ovalle 1665 (☎2 2698 2486); Canada, 12th floor, World Trade Centre, Nueva Tajamar 481 (☎2 2652 3800); France, Condell 65 (☎2 2470 8000); Germany, Las Hualtatas 5677 (☎2 2463 2500); Israel, San Sebastián 2812 (☎2 2750 0500); Netherlands, Apoquindo 3500 (☎2 2756 9200); New Zealand, Isidora Goyenechea 3000, 12th floor (☎2 2616 3000); Peru, Av Andrés Bello 1751 (☎2 2339 2600); South Africa, Av 11 de Septiembre 2353 (☎2 2820 0300); UK, Av El Bosque Norte 0125 (☎2 2370 4100); US, Av Andrés Bello 2800 (☎2 2330 3000).

Emergencies Ambulance ☎131; fire department (*bomberos*) ☎132; police (*carabineros*) ☎133.

Hospitals Clínica Alemana, Vitacura 5951, Vitacura (☎2 2210 1111, ⓦalemana.cl); Clínica Las Condes, Estoril 450, Las Condes (☎2 2210 4000, ⓦclinicalascondes.cl); Clínica Indisa, Av Santa María 1810, Providencia (☎2 2362 5555, ⓦindisa.cl).

WINE TOURS NEAR SANTIAGO

Santiago is within easy reach of some of Chile's oldest **wineries**, several of which offer tours and tastings. Those by the Río Maipo, in particular, are beautifully located, with large swaths of emerald-green vines framed by the snowcapped cordillera and bright-blue skies. Harvesting takes place in **March**, and if you visit then you'll see the grapes being sorted and pressed. If you want to visit a vineyard you should book at least a day beforehand. We've listed some relatively easily reached wineries below, which are accessible by public transport. All tours include free tastings.

Concha y Toro Virginia Subercaseaux 210, Pirque ☎2 2476 5269, ⊛conchaytoro.com. This handsome vineyard, behind the famous Casillero del Diablo wine brand, was founded in 1883 by Don Melchor Concha y Toro. It is now the largest wine producer in Latin America and one of the world's leading brands. English-language tours CH$16,000; premium tasting tours CH$25,000. It's a short taxi ride from Ⓜ Las Mercedes. Daily regularly 10am–4pm; premium tours 4pm.

Cousiño Macul 7100 Av Quilin ☎2 2351 4135, ⊛cousinomacul.com. The main estate and park of Chile's oldest winery (dating from 1550) make a nice quick trip from central Santiago. Bilingual tours CH$14,000 or CH$24,000 for premium tasting. From Ⓜ Quilin take a taxi or walk 30min east along Av Quilin. Mon–Fri 11am, 12.15pm, 3pm & 4.15pm, Sat 11am & 12.15pm.

Santa Rita Padre Hurtado 695, Alto Jahuel ☎2 2362 2520, ⊛www.santarita.com. Santa Rita and sister vineyard Carmen are the home of Carmenere, where the signature Chilean grape, thought extinct, was rediscovered in the 1990s by a visiting French oenologist. As well as tours and tastings, the site has the anthropological Museo Andino, an elegant restaurant and a beautifully located hotel (doubles US$480) in the old family hacienda. Tours from CH$12,000. Take the train to Buin, from where you can catch a bus or taxi, or join the Turistik tour (spage 78).Tues–Sun several tours daily.

Uncorked ☎2 2981 6242, ⊛uncorked.cl. Maria and José run premium wine tours, all in English, to boutique wineries in and around Santiago (US$195 for day tour with three visits and tastings, all transfers and lunch included). They also run cooking classes that are packed with info on Chilean cuisine, and come with the odd pisco sour (half-day US$95).

Undurraga Old road to Melipilla Km 34 ☎2 2372 2900, ⊛undurraga.cl. Still run by the Undurraga family, this vineyard was established in 1885, complete with mansion and park. It's now a large, modern winery, and you're likely to be shown around by someone who's directly involved in the wine-making process. Bilingual tours CH$10,000. Take the bus to Talagante from Terminal San Borja (every 15min; 30min), and ask to be dropped off at the vineyard. Mon–Fri 10.15am, noon, 2pm & 3.30pm, Sat & Sun 10.15am, noon & 3.30pm.

Language courses BridgeChile, Los Leones 439, Providencia (☎2 2233 4356, ⊛bridgechile.com); Centro Chileno Canadiense, Office 601, Luis Thayer Ojeda 191, Providencia (☎2 2334 1090, ⊛canadiense.cl); Natalislang, Arturo Bürhle 47, Providencia (⊛natalislang.com).

Maps Topographical maps on all parts of Chile are available at the Instituto Geográfico Militar, Calle Dieciocho 369, near Toesca metro (☎2 4210 9463, ⊛igm.cl). For tourist and walking maps, go to Sernatur (see page 78).

Newspapers There are numerous newspaper kiosks around town; those at the corner of Huérfanos and Ahumada sell a reasonable range of foreign newspapers, including *Die Welt*, the *Financial Times* and *The New York Times*, and magazines.

Pharmacies Farmacias Ahumada (☎600 222 4000, ⊛farmaciasahumada.cl) has a number of 24hr branches, including Huérfanos 896, and El Bosque 164, Providencia; they'll deliver for a small charge.

Cajón del Maipo

The **CAJÓN DEL MAIPO** is a beautiful river valley carved out of the Andes by the Río Maipo. Served by a good paved road and punctuated by a string of hamlets offering tourist facilities, it's one of the most popular weekend escapes from the capital. The potential for outdoor adventures is enormous, with organized **hiking**, **rafting** and **mountain biking** trips all on offer.

Start at the mouth of the *cajón*, just 25km southeast of Santiago, at **Las Vizcachas**. Here the scenery is lush and gentle, and as you climb into the valley you'll pass vineyards (see above), orchards, roadside stalls selling locally produced fruit, and signs advertising home-made *küchen* (cake), *miel* (honey), *pan amasado* (fresh oven-baked bread) and *chicha* (cider).

Note that there are **no banks** or ATMs in the Cajón del Maipo, so bring cash.

San José de Maipo

Twenty-five kilometres on from Las Vizcachas is the administrative centre of the valley, **SAN JOSÉ DE MAIPO**. It's quite attractive, with single-storey adobe houses and an old, colonial church. The town is also the last place along the road where you can fill up with **petrol**.

San Alfonso

Some 15km beyond San José is **SAN ALFONSO** (1100m altitude), a lovely place if you just want to unwind for a few hours in beautiful mountain scenery. Former nineteenth-century horse ranch *Cascada de las Animas* (see page 91) offers **horseriding**, **kayaking** and **whitewater rafting** as well as a good ninety-minute guided walk up to a 20m **waterfall** (the **Cascada de las Animas**) on the other side of the river. You can also arrange similar trips through Altué Expediciones in Santiago (☎2 2333 1390, ⊛altue.com).

San Gabriel and El Volcán

By the time you reach **SAN GABRIEL**, 50km from the start of the valley road at Las Vizcachas, you are entering increasingly rugged Andes scenery. This uninteresting village marks the end of the asphalt road, which continues as a very poor dirt track for another 20km to Lo Valdés. To carry on, you have to go through a *carabineros* (police) checkpoint, so make sure you've got all your driving documents and passport with you. Unless you're in a 4WD you should expect to go *very* slowly from this point onwards. The village of **EL VOLCÁN**, at Km 56, was practically wiped out by a landslide some years ago. By now the scenery is really dramatic as you snake between 4000m mountains coloured with jagged mineral-patterns of violet, cream and blue.

Baños Morales and Baños de Colina

The village of **BAÑOS MORALES**, the site of an uninviting thermal pool about 12 km from El Volcán, is the closest base to the beautiful, jagged-peaked **Monumento**

HIKING IN THE MONUMENTO NACIONAL EL MORADO

A path from the bus stop in Baños Morales crosses a bridge and leads to the Conaf hut at the entrance to **Monumento Nacional El Morado** (daily: Jan–April & Oct–Dec 8.30am–6pm; May–Sept 8.30am–1pm; CH$5000; ☎2 2328 0339). Stop here to pick up the latest hiking and climbing information, as landslides, snowmelts and the glaciers change the terrain from year to year. The park's single 8km trail follows the Río Morales through a narrow valley that ends at the glacier that feeds the river. Towering above the glacier, and visible from almost all points along the trail, is the magnificent silhouette of El Mirador del Morado (4320m) and, just behind, El Morado itself (5060m).

Apart from the first half-hour, the path is fairly level and not hard going, though you may find yourself feeling breathless as you gradually climb in altitude. About 5km beyond the Conaf hut – after roughly two to three hours of hiking – you reach a small **lake**, Laguna de Morado, where there is free camping, a toilet and water pump. Once past the lake, the path is less defined, but it's easy enough to pick your way through the stones to the black, slimy-looking **glacier** 3km beyond, at an altitude of 2500m. Don't enter the tempting ice caves – they are unstable. This is a good place for day-trekkers to turn around and head back.

Nacional El Morado (see page 90). From here the road deteriorates into an even poorer track, but continues for another 11km to **Baños de Colina**, a series of natural thermal pools carved into the mountainside; for all their remoteness they can get horribly crowded in summer weekends, but otherwise are blissfully empty. This is also the embarkation point for multi-day **horse treks** into the Andes. Up to week-long excursions often leave in packed caravans that snake into the mountains. For less arduous trips, ask around about the many locals who rent out horses by the hour or afternoon.

ARRIVAL AND DEPARTURE CAJÓN DEL MAIPO

By bus Getting to Cajón del Maipo is easy from Santiago: the #72 bus to San José de Maipo (every 10–20min; 1hr 30min) runs from Av Concha y Toro, outside Las Mercedes metro station. There are less frequent services from Santiago to Baños Morales (#72 bus 7.30am from Bellavista La Florida metro station, daily Jan & Feb; weekends only mid-Sept to Dec; 2hr 30min) and El Volcán (several daily; 2hr). Shared taxis and minibuses connect

San José de Maipo with San Alfonso and other places in the *cajón*.

By car For private vehicles the road from Santiago is fine until San Gabriel, where it may be filled with rocks and landslides. Weekend traffic can be horrendous, with 2–3hr backups. To avoid the traffic, make sure you enter the *cajón* well before 10am and leave before 3pm (or, if necessary, late at night).

ACCOMMODATION AND EATING

★ **Cascada de las Animas** By the river, San Alfonso ☏ 2 2861 1303, ⓦ cascadadelasanimas.cl. Set in a park, this highly recommended lodge has a wide range of accommodation including camping spots, cosy rooms in a renovated 1930s building, and lovely wooden cabins, as well as a fabulous outdoor pool, a restaurant overlooking the steep river gorge and a good bar. An extensive range of activities includes trekking, horseriding, rafting and ziplining. Camping CH$12,000, doubles CH$54,000, cabins CH$94,000

Refugio Lo Valdés About 1km beyond the fork to Baños Morales, Lo Valdés ☏ 09 230 5930,

ⓦ refugiolovaldes.com. This atmospheric alpine-style mountain refuge, dating back to 1932, has comfortable dorm-style accommodation, plus a restaurant-bar. Numerous activities – such as horseriding, trekking and mountain biking – are on offer. CH$25,000

Residencial España Camino al Volcán 31443, San Alfonso ☏ 2 2861 1543. There are just five rooms at this simple B&B; all are clean, homely and share bathrooms. Rates include breakfast, and there's an excellent attached Spanish restaurant that serves – among other dishes – a very tasty paella. Daily noon–7pm. CH$27,000

Los Andes and around

There's nothing wildly exciting about **LOS ANDES**, 80km north of Santiago, but this old colonial town, with its narrow streets and lively main square, makes a convenient base for day-trips to the ski resort of **Portillo** (see page 92). On the international road to Mendoza, Argentina, the town is set in the beautiful Aconcagua Valley; the first ridge rises to 3500m and then soars to 6959m Aconcagua, the highest peak outside the Himalayas, just across the border in Argentina. The surrounding region is fertile, and as you approach Los Andes from Santiago you'll pass vineyards and numerous peach and lemon orchards.

Museo Arqueológico

Av Santa Teresa 398 • Tues–Sun 10am–6pm • CH$1000 • ☏ 34 242 0115

The **Museo Arqueológico**, based in a lovely old house, has an impressive collection of pre-Columbian pottery, petroglyphs and skulls, and an astonishing mummy from the Atacama Desert, as well as more recent exhibits that date from the Independence period.

SKIING NEAR SANTIAGO

Santiago is close to some of the best **skiing** in South America. **Sunshine** is abundant and queues for lifts are practically nonexistent during weekdays. The **season** normally lasts from mid-June to early October, with snow virtually guaranteed from mid-July to the first week in September.

Sitting high in the Andes at the foot of Cerro Colorado, a 90min drive along a snaking road (Camino a Farellones) from Santiago, **Farellones** is a straggling collection of hotels and apartments that serves the triple Tres Valles resorts of **El Colorado** (4km north), **La Parva** (2km further on) and **Valle Nevado** (a winding 14km east). All three resorts are connected by pistes and can theoretically be skied in the same day if the runs are open. Alternatively, a 2hr drive from Santiago on the better-condition international road (Autopista Los Libertadores and R-57) takes you to posh **Portillo**, close to the Argentine border.

TRANSPORT AND EQUIPMENT RENTAL

The least expensive way to go skiing is to stay in Santiago and visit the slopes for the day. A number of **minibus** companies offer daily services to the resorts, including Ski Total, Apoquindo 4900 (📞 2 2246 0156, 🌐 skitotal.cl). Buses leave 8am–8.30am daily for El Colorado, La Parva (return ticket to either CH$15,000) and Valle Nevado (CH$18,000), and at the same times on Wednesdays and Saturdays to Portillo (CH$28,000); buses return from the resorts at 5pm. Ski/snowboard equipment rental starts around CH$23,000 for the full kit.

If you intend to drive up yourself, note that traffic is only allowed up the road to Farellones until noon, and back down to Santiago from 2pm onwards; tyre chains are often required but seldom used; they can be rented on the way up.

Each resort has its own **lift ticket** costing around CH$46,000 per day in high season and CH$33,000 in low.

THE RESORTS

All of the resorts have ski schools, English-speaking instructors, and equipment rental outlets.

El Colorado 🌐 elcolorado.cl. Linked to Farellones by ski lift (when there is enough snow), as well as by road, El Colorado has fifteen lifts and 22 runs. The busiest resort, it is particularly good for beginners, with a wide range of blue and green runs. The resort's base is known as Villa El Colorado, and includes several apart-hotels, restaurants and pubs.

La Parva 🌐 laparva.cl. La Parva has mostly red runs, huge areas of backcountry skiing and a classy feel. The skiing here is often excellent, with some very long intermediate cruising runs and a vertical drop of nearly 1000m. The resort has thirty pistes and fourteen lifts, but limited accommodation facilities.

Portillo 🌐 skiportillo.com. Portillo is a sophisticated place in a beautiful lake setting, with no condominiums and just one hotel – the restored 1940s-vintage *Hotel Portillo* (see below). The ski-runs are world-class, and it's best known for its endless off-piste options; it's therefore well suited to advanced skiers. There are twelve lifts, plus extensive snow-making equipment. Portillo is avidly kid-friendly and its ski school is routinely ranked one of the world's best.

Cerro de la Virgen

If you're feeling energetic, climb **Cerro de la Virgen**, the hill rising behind the town. It takes about an hour to reach the top following the path from the picnic site on Independencia. The views are wonderful, especially just before sunset when the whole valley is bathed in a clear, golden light.

Santuario de Santa Teresa de los Andes

About 10km southwest of Los Andes • Daily 9am–6.30pm • Free • 📞 34 240 1900, 🌐 santuarioteresadelosandes.cl

The **Santuario de Santa Teresa de los Andes** is a huge, modern church built in 1987 to house the remains of **Santa Teresa**, who became Chile's first saint when she was canonized in 1993. Her shrine attracts thousands of pilgrims each year, especially on July 13, her feast day.

Valle Nevado Ⓦvallenevado.com. On the whole, it's worth the short extra journey from Farellones to reach Valle Nevado, which often has better snow than El Colorado, a wider range of pistes among its 27 runs, and more modern lifts, including a gondola. It also has first-class hotels and some good restaurants and is the clear favourite for snowboarders.

ACCOMMODATION

Alongside the hotels listed below, you can also rent an **apartment** – this is often a more economical option, particularly if you negotiate with private owners. Chilean Ski (Ⓦchileanski. com) has a selection. The accommodation is aimed chiefly at foreign visitors and rates quoted in US dollars; there is often a minimum stay of up to a week in high season.

Condominio Nueva La Parva La Parva, Tres Valles Ⓣ2 2964 2100, Ⓦlaparva.cl. The only commercial place to stay in La Parva with a range of apartments – each featuring a kitchen – sleeping four to eight. Four-person apartment US$880

Hotel Portillo Portillo Ⓣ2 2361 7000, Ⓦskiportillo. com. The only hotel in Portillo, perched by the shores of the Laguna del Inca, offers the hippest ski scene in South America. There is a wide range of (very expensive) accommodation options, from simple bunks in the *Inca Lodge* to suites with stunning views. Rates include full board and ski lift pass; there is a minimum stay of three nights during ski season. The hotel also opens in the summer as a base for walks around the lake or stopover on the route to/from Argentina (when rates start at around US$70/person/night). *Inca Lodge* US$179, doubles US$281

Hotel Posada de Farellones El Colorado, Tres Valles Ⓣ2 2248 7672, Ⓦskifarellones.com. The best place to stay near El Colorado, this hotel has smart en suites, a jacuzzi and a good restaurant. Prices include half board and transport to the slopes. US$250

Hotel Valle Nevado Valle Nevado, Tres Valles Ⓣ2 2477 7701, Ⓦvallenevado.com. This hotel has classy en suites with panoramic mountain views, a gym and spa, and an excellent restaurant. You have direct "ski-in, ski-out" access to the slopes, and heli-skiing is also on offer. Rates include half board and ski lift pass. US$380

Lodge Andes Camino La Capilla 662, Farellones, Tres Valles Ⓣ2 2264 9899, Ⓦlodgeandes.cl. A sociable lodge with simple private rooms and shared bathrooms, as well as four-, six- and eight-bed dorms (including a women-only one) with bunk beds and lockers; all rooms and dorms have central heating. There is also a decent restaurant and bar, a pool table, multilingual staff and a lounge with a TV and a log fire. Rates include half board. Dorms CH$30,000, doubles CH$90,000

BACKCOUNTRY SKIING

There are some great **backcountry options** for skiers who want to escape the resorts. **Ski Arpa**, near the city of **San Esteban**, a 2hr drive from Santiago, offers cat skiing (off-trail skiing accessed via a snowcat vehicle, rather than a ski lift) and snowboarding in two beautiful valleys, el Arpa and la Honda, which lie to the west of Argentina's Cerro Aconcagua, the highest mountain in the Andes. Note there is no equipment rental available. A full day here (featuring four runs with a guide) costs around US$400. Santiago Adventures (Ⓣ2 2244 2750, Ⓦsantiagoadventures.com) can organize transport and accommodation nearby; the company also offers (pricey) heli-skiing trips.

ARRIVAL AND DEPARTURE   LOS ANDES AND AROUND

By bus Frequent buses (1hr 20min) depart from Terminal Los Héroes in Santiago, dropping you at the bus station on Membrillar, one block east of the main square; most of them stop at the Santuario de Santa Teresa en route.

ACCOMMODATION AND EATING

Casa Vieja Maipu 151 Ⓣ34 246 0367. Classic *parrilla* style restaurant, with occasional live music, brisk service and plates piled high with beef. Fish dishes such as corvina in seafood sauce (CH$13,000) are also available, but most people share the two-person *parrillada*, or mixed barbecue (CH$28,000). Mon–Sat 1pm–midnight, Sun 1–6pm.

Hotel Plaza Manuel Rodriguez 368 Ⓣ34 240 2157, Ⓦhotelplazalosandes.cl. If you want to stay the night, *Hotel Plaza* is a decent choice. The rooms – which have private bathrooms and TVs – are comfortable, if nothing to write home about. There's also a good restaurant. CH$55,000

Inca Hoteles Av Argentina Oriente 11 Ⓣ34 234 5500, Ⓦincahoteles.cl. Situated near the Cerro de la Virgen, this is the best place to stay in town, with pleasant rooms, good breakfasts and an outdoor pool in summer. US$125

Valparaíso, Viña and the Central Coast

VALPARAÍSO

Valparaíso, Viña and the central coast

Of Chile's 4000km-plus coastline, the brief central strip between Rocas de Santo Domingo and Los Vilos is the most visited and developed. Known as the Litoral Central, this 250km stretch boasts bay after bay lined with gorgeous beaches and coastal resorts. Valparaíso (or "Valpo" for short) and Viña del Mar (or "Viña") sit next to each other near the middle of the strip. They may be geographical neighbours, but they are poles apart in appearance, atmosphere and outlook.

Viña is Chile's largest beach resort and one of its ritziest. With its high-rises, casino and seafront restaurants, as well as the beaches and clubs in nearby **Reñaca**, Viña typifies modern hedonism. **Valparaíso**, on the other hand, has far more personality, with ramshackle, colourful houses spilling chaotically down the hills to the sea, and plenty in the way of history and culture (though no decent beaches).

Closest to Santiago, via the "Autopista del Sol" (Ruta 78), are the resorts **south of Valparaíso**, which are busy and developed. Further south, among an almost uninterrupted string of small, unappealing resorts, it's still possible to find places with charm and soul, especially where Pablo Neruda found them, at **Isla Negra** – though it, too, is fast being swallowed up by development.

Heading **north of Viña** you leave most of the concrete behind at **Concón**, and from **Horcón** up, the coast begins to look more rugged. Thing feels distinctly wild and windswept by the time you reach **Maitencillo**, where sandstone cliffs tower above a huge, white beach. The stretch from here to **Papudo** is easily the most beautiful of the region. Not even the new villas and second-home complexes that have sprung up in these parts have managed to spoil **Zapallar**, the most architecturally graceful of the resorts, or Papudo, a small town dramatically hemmed in by steep hills. Two more resorts lie further north: **Los Vilos** and **Pichidangui**.

Inland and a world away from the coastal glitz, **Parque Nacional la Campana** offers excellent hiking.

Valparaíso

Valparaíso es un montón, un racimo de casas locas [Valparaíso is a heap, a bunch of crazy houses]

Pablo Neruda

Spread across an amphitheatre of hills encircling a wide bay, **VALPARAÍSO** is the most intriguing and distinctive city in Chile. Its most striking feature is the array of houses – a mad, colourful tangle tumbling down the hills to a narrow shelf of land below. Few roads make it up these gradients and most people get up and down on the city's *ascensores*, ancient-looking funicular lifts that slowly haul you up to incredible viewpoints.

The eastern end of town near the bus station is of limited interest; instead head west to the **old town**, which stretches along a narrow strip of land between Plaza Victoria and Plaza Wheelwright (also known as Plaza Aduana), at the city's historic core. The

When to visit the central coast p.99
Valparaíso's antiquated lifts p.104

Pablo Neruda p.111
Casablanca Valley Wine Route p.115

CASA MUSEO ISLA NEGRA

Highlights

❶ Historic Valparaíso Chile's most remarkable city, set on a series of undulating hills above a huge bay, is a historical treasure trove, with antique funiculars, a grand but crumbling downtown, and some wonderfully restored mansions. See page 96

❷ Eating and drinking in Valparaíso Valpo is home to some of Chile's most inventive chefs who have created a refreshingly diverse dining scene, with a set of excellent bars to boot. See pages 107 and 108

❸ Casa Museo Isla Negra Pablo Neruda set up home in Isla Negra village and wrote many of his Nobel Prize-winning poems while gazing out at his favourite beach. His house is now an enchanting museum. See page 110

❹ Viña del Mar Away from the touristy gloss, Viña del Mar has a collection of beautiful palaces, verdant parks and gardens, and interesting museums. See page 110

❺ Casablanca Valley The vineyards in this area are famed for their production of quality white wines, and can be visited on a variety of tours, independently by car, or by bus. See page 115

❻ Zapallar Soothingly empty beaches, opulent holiday homes and excellent, super-fresh seafood make this eternally fashionable coastal resort one of the region's gems. See page 116

❼ Parque Nacional la Campana Follow in the footsteps of Charles Darwin and hike through this easily accessible national park. See page 118

HIGHLIGHTS ARE MARKED ON THE MAP ON PAGE 100

VALPARAÍSO, VIÑA & THE CENTRAL COAST

HIGHLIGHTS
1. Historic Valparaíso
2. Eating and drinking in Valparaíso
3. Casa Museo Isla Negra
4. Viña del Mar
5. Casablanca Valley
6. Zapallar
7. Parque Nacional la Campana

ARGENTINA

PACIFIC OCEAN

N

Combarbalá

Huentelauquén

5

Los Vilos

Pichidangui

Los Molles

Petorca

Cabildo

La Ligua

Papudo

Zapallar **6**

Cachagua

Playa Aguas Blancas

Horcón

Maitencillo

5

La Calera

San Felipe

Quintero

Ritoque

Quillota

Cerro La Campana (1880m)

Llaillay

Los Andes

Portillo

Río Blanco

Túnel Chacabuco

Reñaca

Concón

4

7 PARQUE NACIONAL LA CAMPANA

Viña del Mar

Limache

Olmué

Cerro El Plomo (6050m)

Valparaíso **1 2**

Quilpué

Villa Alemana

Laguna Verde

La Parva

Colina

El Colorado

Quintay

68

5

Casablanca

Aeropuerto Arturo Merino Benítez

Quilicura

Farallones

Valle Nevado

Tunquén

Curacaví

Pudahuel

Las Condes

Algarrobo

El Quisco

3

Isla Negra

Las Cruces

El Tabo

Túnel Zapata

68

Maipú

SANTIAGO

Cartagena

San Antonio

Rocas de Santo Domingo

Pomaire

El Monte

Peñaflor

Talagante

San Bernardo

La Obra

Río Tupungato

Puente Alto

San José de Maipo

El Melocotón

San Alfonso

Melipilla

78

Isla de Maipo

5

Paine

PARQUE NACIONAL RÍO CLARILLO

San Gabriel

Río Colorado

Río Blanco

0 ——————— 40
kilometres

WHEN TO VISIT THE CENTRAL COAST

Most Chileans take their annual holiday in February, when all the resort towns are unbearably crowded. They also get busy on December and January weekends. November and March are probably the **best months** to visit, as the weather is usually agreeable and the beaches virtually deserted, especially midweek. Even in summer, however, the coast is prone to **fog** or cloudy weather, and temperatures in Valpo can be considerably lower than in Santiago.

From April to October **accommodation rates** in Viña drop, and even in November, December and March you should be able to negotiate a midweek discount; rates in Valpo are pretty stable throughout the year, save at New Year when they double or triple. At this time of year some, not all, beaches are safe for **swimming**, but stay out of the water if a red flag is displayed; you might also be put off by the frigid **Humboldt current**, which leaves the water chilly even in the height of summer.

2

port district, with its British-style banks, atmospheric bars and old-fashioned shops, is the most idiosyncratic part of the city and should not be missed. Unfortunately, you'll also have to contend with a certain amount of noise, shabbiness and crime. However, just go up two or three **ascensores**, check out the enchanting **cerros Alegre** and **Concepción,** and sample the views by night, when the city's flickering lights are reflected in the ocean – and you're sure to fall under Valparaíso's spell.

Brief history

The bay was chosen as the site of the new colony's port as early as 1542, when Pedro de Valdivia decided it would "serve the trade of these lands and of Santiago". Growth was slow, however, owing to trading restrictions, but when Latin American trade was liberalized in the 1820s, after independence, Valparaíso started to come into its own. On the shipping route from Europe to America's Pacific Coast, it became the main port of call and resupply centre for ships after they crossed the Straits of Magellan. As Chile's own foreign trade expanded with the silver and copper booms of the 1830s, the port became ever more active, but it was the government's innovative creation of public warehouses that really launched Valparaíso into its economic ascent.

Progress and setbacks

Foreign businessmen, particularly British ones, flocked to the city where they ran **trading empires** built on copper, silver and nitrate. By the late nineteenth century Valparaíso had become Chile's foremost financial and commercial centre. Even as it prospered, however, the city continued to be dogged by the kind of violent setbacks that had punctuated its history, from pirates and buccaneers to earthquakes and fires. On March 31, 1866, following Chile's entanglement in a dispute between Spain and Peru, the Spanish admiralty bombarded Valparaíso, wreaking devastation. It took a long time to rebuild the city, but worse was to come. On August 16, 1906, a colossal **earthquake** practically razed the city, killing more than two thousand people. The disaster took a heavy toll and Valparaíso never really recovered. Eight years later, the opening of the **Panama Canal** signalled the city's inexorable decline.

Valpo today

Valparaíso still has a rundown, moth-eaten air. Crime and poverty remain, the sex trade continues, and at night parts of the city are dangerous. That said, it's still a vital **working port**, and the seat of Congress. The port underwent a mini-economic boom in the early years of the new millennium, though the benefits for the residents, known as *porteños*, have been uneven. As the regional capital, Valparaíso also has its share of galleries and museums, but the chief attractions lie in its crumbling, romantic atmosphere and stunning setting.

2

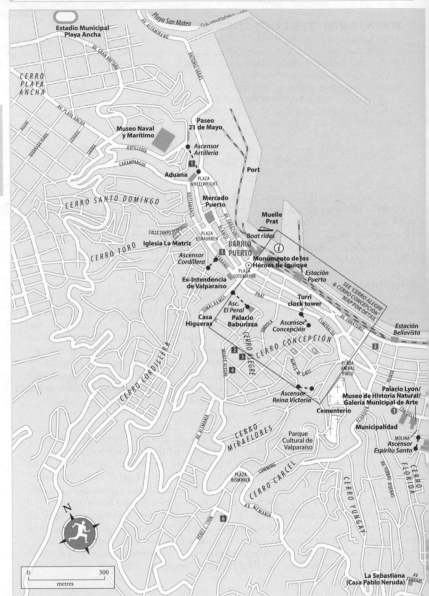

In April 2014, a devastating **fire** broke out in the southeastern side of the city, killing fifteen people and destroying around three thousand homes. Three years later, another blaze injured nineteen and wiped out more than a hundred homes. Despite these blows, Valpo's profile has risen in recent years, accompanied by increasing **gentrification** on the more touristy *cerros*, with many locals selling up or forced out by rising rents and property prices.

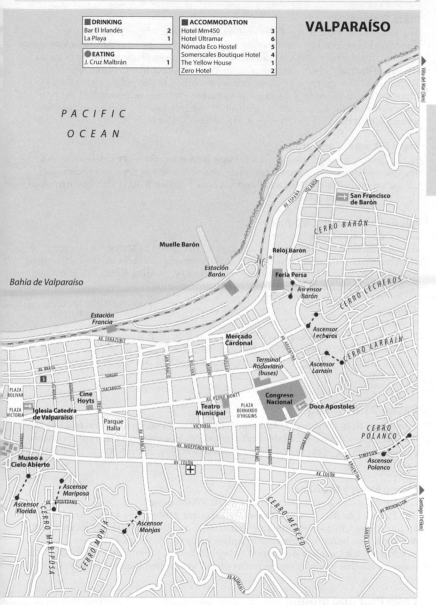

VALPARAÍSO

■ DRINKING	
Bar El Irlandés	2
La Playa	1

● EATING	
J. Cruz Malbrán	1

■ ACCOMMODATION	
Hotel Mm450	3
Hotel Ultramar	6
Nómada Eco Hostel	5
Somerscales Boutique Hotel	4
The Yellow House	1
Zero Hotel	2

Barrio Puerto

At the heart of Porteño history and identity, the **Barrio Puerto**, the port neighbourhood, is a good place to start exploring. However, you should keep a close eye on your belongings as pickpockets and thieves are rife during the day; at night the area is unsafe.

Plaza Sotomayor

The focal point of the Barrio Puerto is **Plaza Sotomayor**, a large public square dominated at one end by the imposing grey facade of the **ex-Intendencia de Valparaíso** (now occupied by the navy). At the other end is the triumphant **Monumento de los Héroes de Iquique**, where statues of Arturo Prat and other heroes of the War of the Pacific tower above a crypt housing their tombs (open to the public each May 21). Opposite the monument is the gateway to **Muelle Prat**, the only stretch of the port open to the public. Geared almost exclusively towards tourists, it's the embarkation point for **boat rides** around the bay (CH$3000; 30–45min).

Plaza Echaurren and around

In the lower town, on Calle Serrano, is **Plaza Echaurren**, the city's oldest square and very picturesque save for the wine-swilling characters who occupy its benches. Just off the square is the iron **Mercado Puerto**, a once bustling market that has been closed since the 2010 earthquake.

Iglesia La Matriz and around

Santo Domingo s/n • No fixed opening times • Free

A couple of blocks east of the Mercado Puerto, the **Iglesia La Matriz** – a graceful, Neoclassical church with a seventeenth-century carving of Christ inside – sits at the foot of Cerro Santo Domingo surrounded by narrow, twisting streets full of colour, activity and a slightly menacing feel.

Aduana

Plaza Wheelwright

If you walk along Calle Serrano (which becomes Bustamante) you reach Plaza Wheelwright (also known as Plaza Aduana), which is flanked by the large, colonial-looking **Aduana** building. The structure dates from 1854 and remains a working customs house.

Paseo 21 de Mayo

A few steps from the Aduana, **Ascensor Artillería** takes you up to the **Paseo 21 de Mayo** on Cerro Playa Ancha. Of all the city's viewpoints, this provides the most spectacular panorama, taking in the bay of Valparaíso and sweeping 20km north to the Punta de Concón.

Museo Naval y Marítimo

Paseo 21 de Mayo 45 • Tues–Sun 10am–5.30pm • CH$1000 • ☎ 32 243 7651, ⓦ museonaval.cl

The Paseo 21 de Mayo curves around the luxuriant gardens of a former naval school, an impressive whitewashed building that now houses the well-laid-out **Museo Naval y Marítimo**. The beautifully presented displays bring to life some of the central figures in Chile's history, such as Ambrosio O'Higgins, Lord Cochrane and Arturo Prat. The museum also has a display on the rescue of the 33 San José miners (see page 157).

Calle Prat and around

Valparaíso's **city centre** is formed by a narrow strip stretching from Plaza Sotomayor in the west to Plaza Victoria in the east. Almost completely devastated by the 1906 earthquake, it has evolved into a mixture of ugly, modern blocks and elegant buildings left over from the early twentieth century.

Calle Prat, which runs east from Plaza Sotomayor, has some good examples – take a look inside the **Banco Santander**, opposite the Turri clock tower, originally the Banco de Londres and dripping with bronze and marble brought over from England. Next door, **Ascensor Concepción** (or Ascensor Turri) provides access to Cerro Concepción, a lovely residential area once the preserve of British businessmen. Further east, **Plaza Aníbal Pinto** is a pretty cobbled square overlooked by some of the city's oldest restaurants and bars, including *El Cinzano* (see page 108).

Cerro Cárcel

From Plaza Aníbal Pinto, you can climb up Calle Cumming to **Cerro Cárcel**, where you'll find a collection of **cemeteries**; the names on the graves – Clampitt, Laussen, Van Buren, Matthews, Rivera, to name just a few – reflect the diversity of the city's early settlers.

Museo de Historia Natural

Condell 1546 • Tues–Sat 10am–6pm, Sun 10am–2pm • Free • ☎ 32 254 4840, ⓦ mhnv.cl

Southeast from Plaza Aníbal Pinto, the main drag continues along Calle Condell, where the **Palacio Lyon**, a splendid 1881 mansion (one of the few to survive the 1906 earthquake), now houses the **Museo de Historia Natural**. You'll find a mix of archeological and anthropological exhibits from across the country (and beyond), as well as the stuffed animals and birds that populate so many of Chile's museums. The **Galería Municipal de Arte**, in the cellars, occasionally stages temporary art exhibitions.

Iglesia Catedral de Valparaíso

Plaza Victoria; administrative office on Chacabuco at the north side of the building • Mon–Fri 10am–1pm & 4–6.30pm; to visit, ask at the administrative office

Calle Condell ends at **Plaza Victoria**, a large tree-filled square where most of Valparaíso seems to come to chat and sit in the sunshine. It's flanked, on its eastern side, by the **Iglesia Catedral de Valparaíso**, whose simply decorated interior includes a delicate ivory carving of Christ and, most intriguingly, a marble urn (in the crypt) containing the heart of Chilean statesman Diego Portales.

Museo a Cielo Abierto

Open access

From Plaza Victoria, calles Molina and Edwards lead up to the **Museo a Cielo Abierto**, a circuit of narrow streets and passageways painted with seventeen colourful, bold, abstract murals by students and leading local artists; most memorable are the enormous paintings by Roberto Matta. Keep your wits about you here.

La Sebastiana (Casa Pablo Neruda)

Av Ferrari 692 • Tues–Sun: Jan & Feb 10am–7pm; March–Dec 10.10am–6pm • CH$7000, including audio tour • ☎ 2 2777 8741, ⓦ fundacionneruda.org • Bus "O" (officially the #612) from Av Argentina or, if you're on cerros Alegre or Concepción and don't fancy the 25min walk, Plaza San Luis at the top of Templeman; stay on the bus for the whole route for a low-cost city tour

Of the three Pablo Neruda homes open to the public – the others being La Chascona (see page 71) and Isla Negra (see page 110) – **La Sebastiana** offers the most informal look at the poet, who moved here in 1961 with Matilde Urrutia, his third wife. Perched high on the aptly named Bellavista hill, giving dramatic views over the bay, it was his *casa en el aire* (house in the air). After the 1973 coup it was repeatedly vandalized by the military but has been meticulously restored by the Fundación Neruda, which opened it as a museum in 1992. Its narrow, sinuous passages and bright colours seem to mirror the spirit of Valparaíso, and the bizarre objects brought here by the poet are astonishing, from the embalmed Venezuelan Coro-Coro bird hanging

2

VALPARAÍSO'S ANTIQUATED LIFTS

Most of Valparaíso's fifteen **ascensores**, or funicular "lifts", were built between 1883 and 1916 to provide a link between the lower town and the new residential quarters spreading up the hillsides. Today appearances suggest that they've scarcely been modernized. However, despite their rickety frames and alarming noises they've so far proved safe and reliable. What's more, nearly all drop off passengers at a panoramic viewpoint. They generally operate every few minutes from 7am to 11pm, cost around CH$100–300 one-way, and are periodically closed for repair. Here are a few of the best, from east to west:

Ascensor Polanco The most picturesque *ascensor*, and the only one that's totally vertical, Polanco is on Calle Simpson, off Av Argentina (opposite Independencia). It's approached via a cavernous, underground tunnel and rises 80m through a yellow wooden tower to a balcony that gives some of the best views in the city. A narrow bridge connects the tower to Cerro Polanco, with its flaking, pastel houses in varying states of repair. The *cerro* is known for its graffiti, but take care as the area is decidedly sketchy.

Ascensor Concepción (also known as Ascensor Turri) Hidden in a small passage opposite the Turri clock tower, at the corner of Prat and Almirante Carreño, this was the first *ascensor* to be built, in 1883, and

was originally powered by steam. It takes you up to the beautiful residential area of Cerro Concepción, well worth a visit (see below).**Ascensor El Peral** Just off Plaza Sotomayor, this *ascensor* leads to one of the most romantic corners of the city: Paseo Yugoslavo (see below). It's worth walking from here to Ascensor Concepción.

Ascensor Artillería Always busy with tourists, but highly recommended for the stunning vistas at the top, from the Paseo 21 de Mayo. It was built in 1893 to transport cadets to and from the naval school at the top of the hill, now the site of the Museo Naval y Marítimo (see page 102).

from the ceiling of the dining room to the wooden horse in the living room, taken from a merry-go-round in Paris.

Cerros Alegre and Concepción

The hilltop residential quarter spread over **cerros Alegre** and **Concepción** is a rambling maze of steep streets and small alleys lined with elegant, brightly painted houses and aristocratic mansions clinging precipitously to the hillside. It grew up as the enclave of Valparaíso's immigrant businessmen, particularly the British, who left street names like Leighton, Templeman and Atkinson, and the Germans, whose influence can be seen in the many half-timbered, shuttered houses.

There are two points of access from the lower town; **Ascensor Concepción** (see above), near the Turri clock tower on Calle Prat, takes you up to **Paseo Gervasoni** on Cerro Concepción, while **Ascensor El Peral** (see above), next to the Tribunales de Justicia just off Plaza Sotomayor, ascends to Cerro Alegre's **Paseo Yugoslavo**, one of the most attractive and peaceful parts of the city. A good way to explore the area is to walk between the two *ascensores*: we have marked a **walking tour** on the Cerro Alegre & Cerro Concepción map (see page 105).

Museo de Bellas Artes de Valparaíso

Paseo Yugoslavo 176 • Jan–March Tues–Sat 10.30am–7pm, Sun 10.30am–2pm & 2.30–7pm; April–Dec Tues–Sat 10.30am–6pm, Sun 10.30am–2pm & 2.30–6pm • CH$2000 • ☎ 32 225 2332, ⓦ museobaburizza.cl

An extravagant, four-storey mansion behind Paseo Yugoslavo, **Palacio Baburizza** was built in 1916 for a wealthy Italian family and later purchased by a Yugoslavian nitrate baron. Today it houses the **Museo de Bellas Artes de Valparaíso**, displaying a collection of nineteenth- and twentieth-century Chilean and European art. It's worth a look for the evocative paintings of an earlier Valparaíso by artists such as Juan Mauricio Rugendas, Alfred Helsby, Thomas Somerscales and, notably, Juan Francisco González.

CERRO ALEGRE & CERRO CONCEPCIÓN

---- Walking Tour

ACCOMMODATION			EATING					DRINKING & NIGHTLIFE			
Casa Aventura	5	Hotel Da Vinci	2	Allegretto	4	Emporio La Rosa	2	El Bar Inglés	6	El Internado	5
Casa Higueras	7	Hotel Ibis	1	Amor Porteño	7	Le Filou de Montpellier	6	El Cinzano	3	La Piedra Feliz	1
Hostal Jacaranda	6	Palacio Astoreca	3	Ápice	9	Foto Café	1	Fauna	4		
Hostel Voyage	4			Cafe del Pintor	5	Pasta e Vino	3				
						Vinilo	8				

Casa Mirador de Lukas

Paseo Gervasoni 448 • Tues–Sun 11am–2pm & 2.45–6pm • CH$1500 • ☎ 32 222 1344, ⓦ www.lukas.cl

Casa Mirador de Lukas, near the Ascensor Concepción, pays homage to *El Mercurio*'s great satirical cartoonist, Lukas, who captured the spirit of his country in the sharply hilarious drawings he produced for the newspaper between 1958 and 1988. There's also an appealing café. The museum was closed at the time of research for a revamp, so the opening times/entry fee are subject to change.

Paseo Atkinson

Don't miss **Paseo Atkinson**, an esplanade affording great panoramas and lined with pretty houses whose tiny front gardens and window boxes recall their original British owners. From here you can see the tall tower of the **Lutheran church** (open for services 1st and 3rd Sat of month 7pm, Sun 11am) a distinctive, green-walled structure built in 1897; a block or so northwest you'll find the towerless **St Paul's Anglican Church** (1858; English-language service Sun 10.30am) whose solemn interior contains a huge organ donated by Queen Victoria in 1903.

Congreso Nacional

The first thing that hits you as you emerge from the bus station is the imposing **Congreso Nacional**, described by Simon Collier and William Sater in their *History of Chile* as "half neo-Babylonian, half post-modernist atrocity". It was one of Pinochet's projects, but the dictator relinquished power before it was completed. Its working life began on March 11, 1990, when Patricio Aylwin was sworn in as president and Congress resumed its activities after a sixteen-year absence – away from the capital for the first time.

ARRIVAL AND DEPARTURE VALPARAÍSO

By bus The Terminal Rodoviario (☎ 32 293 9646) is on the eastern end of Pedro Montt, opposite the Congreso Nacional; it's a 20min walk to the old town centre. Buses run up and down the coast from here, including with Sol de Pacifico (☎ 32 228 1026), Pullman Bus (☎ 32 225 3125, ⊛ www.pullman.cl) and Mirasol (☎ 32 223 5985). To get to Viña del Mar, pick up one of the frequent *micros* on Pedro Montt; they take about 15 min, twice that time in bad traffic; the train is much more convenient. Plenty of

micros and *colectivos* also go to the centre from outside the bus station.

Destinations Isla Negra (every 15min; 1hr 30min); La Serena (hourly–every 2hr; 6hr); Santiago (every 15min; 1hr 30min–1hr 45min).

By train The Metro (⊛ metro-valparaiso.cl) departs for Viña del Mar from several stations in Valpo (every 5–20min). Buy a plastic charge card (CH$1450) first, and then top it up with credit before travelling.

GETTING AROUND

By micro and colectivo Countless *micros* run through the city: those displaying "Aduana" on the window take you west through the centre, past the port, while those marked "P. Montt" take you back to the bus station. Some bus routes take you to the upper town, and you can catch *colectivos* at Plazuela Ecuador, at the bottom of Calle Ecuador.

On foot To climb to the upper town, it's easiest to use the *ascensores* (see page 104).

By taxi Taxis are numerous; there are stands at the bottom of most of the *cerros*.

INFORMATION AND TOURS

Tourist office Muelle Prat, by the port (Mon–Fri 9am–2pm & 3–6pm, Sat 9am–2pm & 3–5pm; ☎ 32 223 6264, ⊛ sernatur.cl). Note that (despite an old sign) there is no official tourist office at the bus station, which is filled with accommodation touts offering partial (at best) information.

City tours One of the best operators is Ruta Valparaíso (☎ 32 259 2520, ⊛ rutavalparaiso.cl). Half-day city tours

cost from CH$25,000 (full-day tours from CH$35,000); it also offers excursions throughout the region. A good alternative for city tours is Tours for Tips (⊛ tours4tips. com), which leave from Plaza Sotomayor daily at 10am and 3pm and follow several routes.

Wine tours Wine Tours Valparaíso (☎ 09 8428 3502, ⊛ winetoursvalparaiso.cl) organizes wine tasting trips in the Casablanca Valley (see page 115) and beyond.

ACCOMMODATION

Valparaíso has a good range of accommodation. There are hotels in the lower sections of town, but you won't get the full Valpo experience unless you head up to one of the **cerros**. Many places will pick you up from the bus station if you call ahead.

HOTELS AND B&BS

Casa Higueras Higuera 133, Cerro Alegre ☎ 32 249 7900, ⊛ hotelcasahigueras.cl; map p.105. One of the city's best top-end hotels, with stately 1930s-style en suites, a pool and huge jacuzzi with exquisite vistas, plus the classy (and, considering the quality, reasonably priced) *Montealegre* restaurant. US$320

Hotel Da Vinci Urriola 426, Cerro Alegre ☎ 32 317 4494, ⊛ hoteldavincivalparaiso.cl; map p.105. As the name suggests, there's an arty feel to this mid-range hotel, whose en suites, some split-level, are set around a light-filled central atrium, with photos and paintings covering the walls. Good value. CH$69,000

Hotel Ibis Errazuriz 811 ☎ 32 280 2300, ⊛ ibis.com; map p.105. In a downtown location, overlooking the port, this modern, mid-range hotel has a distinctive, multicoloured exterior, spick-and-span en-suite rooms

(many with wonderful sea views), efficient staff and an in-house restaurant-bar. CH$41,000

Hotel Mm450 Tomás Lautaro Rosas 450, Cerro Alegre ☎ 32 222 9919, ✉ admm450@gmail.com; map p.100. A delightful boutique hotel that has quickly earned a high reputation. It offers large, light-filled en suites, charming staff and an attractive garden terrace. There's also a good seafood restaurant on site. CH$85,000

Hotel Ultramar Tomás Pérez 173, Cerro Cárcel ☎ 32 221 0000, ⊛ hotelultramar.com; map p.100. Striped, spotted and checked decor – fortunately not all together – give this modern hotel, a refurbished 1907 Italianate townhouse, a unique feel. It's worth paying a little extra for a view. US$91

Palacio Astoreca Montealegre 149, Cerro Alegre ☎ 32 327 7700, ⊛ hotelpalacioastoreca.com; map p.105. Just steps from Paseo Yugoslavo, this gorgeously restored mansion is one of Valpo's top luxury hotels. Chic en suites, many with stunning views, smart service, a spa and heated indoor pool, plus the excellent *Alegre* restaurant and a piano bar, make this a great choice. US$321

Somerscales Boutique Hotel San Enrique 446, Cerro Alegre ☎32 233 1006, ⓦhotelsomerscales.cl; map p.100. Each of the en suites at this beautifully restored home of renowned local painter Thomas Somerscales is fitted out with period furniture and artwork, as well as modern comforts. Stunning views, a roof terrace and a large stained-glass window make this one of the most memorable hotels in town. US$160

The Yellow House Capitán Muñoz Gamero 91, Cerro Artillería ☎32 233 9435, ⓦtheyellowhouse.cl; map p.100. Even by Valpo's high standards, the views from this renovated 200-year-old building, a welcoming B&B, are spectacular. Most of the rooms at are en suite, and there's a comfortable apartment with a kitchenette. Book exchange, and a range of tours available. Doubles CH$29,000, apartments CH$45,000

Zero Hotel Tomás Lautaro Rosas 343, Cerro Alegre ☎32 211 3113, ⓦzerohotel.cl; map p.100. This attractive boutique hotel, in a lovely, pale blue townhouse, offers elegant, uncluttered en suites (the pricier ones have sea views), terraces and a glass-enclosed "winter garden", while nice touches include an honesty bar. US$210

HOSTELS

Casa Aventura Pasaje Gálvez 11, Cerro Alegre ☎32 275 5963, ⓦcasaventura.cl; map p.105. Well-established, friendly place with spotless dorms and private rooms (including good-value singles for CH$20,000), a sunny lounge and a communal kitchen. A reliable budget choice. Dorms CH$11,500, doubles CH$29,000

Hostal Jacaranda Urriola 636, Cerro Alegre ☎32 324 5077, ⓦhostaljacaranda.blogspot.co.uk; map p.105. Friendly, no-frills hostel for travellers on a really tight budget. It's split over two sites, within easy walking distance of the city's best restaurants and bars. No breakfast. Dorms CH$8000, doubles CH$23,500

Hostel Voyage Leighton 229, Cerro Alegre ☎32 324 5241, ⓦhostelvoyage.com; map p.105. Beautifully decorated in and out with amazing street art, this hostel has a chilled atmosphere, ample kitchen and nice courtyard area, where they screen movies on a whitewashed wall. Dorms CH$8500, doubles CH$26,000

Nómada Eco Hostel Brasil 1822 ☎32 327 3081, ⓦnomadaecohostel.cl; map p.100. If you're not set on staying on one of the cerros, this downtown hostel is a great choice. The cheerful five- to ten bed dorms and private rooms boast wooden floors, and there's plenty of artwork dotted around. It aims to be the first carbon-neutral hostel in Valpo. Dorms CH$11,000, doubles CH$33,000

EATING

Valparaíso has some of Chile's best and most inventive **restaurants**; cerros Concepción and Alegre, in particular, are filled with great places to eat (and drink).

CAFÉS AND CHEAP EATS

Amor Porteño Almirante Montt 418, Cerro Concepción ☎32 221 6253, ⓦfacebook.com/AmorPortenoValparaiso; map p.105. Charming ice-cream parlour/cafe, with a tiny dining area decorated with flowery murals and vintage mirrors. As well as real Argentine-style *helado* (from CH$1750), you can tuck into *churros* and *medialunas* (sweet, doughy croissants), and enjoy good coffee. Tues–Thurs & Sun 10.30am–9pm, Fri & Sat 10.30am–10pm.

Emporio La Rosa Plaza Aníbal Pinto 1189 ☎09 7516 4920, ⓦemporiolarosa.cl; map p.105. Pink-shirted waiting staff serve *onces* (CH$6900–8100), breakfasts, light meals and huge coffees at this cheerful café. Best of all, though, are the ice cream sundaes (CH$3900–4200): flavours include lemon, mint and basil. Mon–Fri 8.30am–9.30pm, Sat 9am–9.30pm, Sun 11am–9.30pm.

Foto Café Av Esmeralda 1111 ☎32 223 1515, ⓦfotocafe.cl; map p.105. Something of a curiosity, combining a photography business with a classy café. There's a good value three-course set lunch (around CH$8000), plenty of options for *onces*, coffee and alcoholic drinks (the latter best enjoyed in the cosy upstairs nook,

accessed via a spiral staircase). Mon–Fri 9.30am–7.30pm, Sat 10am–2pm.

RESTAURANTS

Allegretto Pilcomayo 259, Cerro Concepción ☎32 296 8839, ⓦallegretto.cl; map p.105. British-/Chilean-run restaurant with colourful decor, black-and-white photos, local draft beer on tap and live football on TV. The menu features thin-crust pizzas (CH$5800–9200), risottos, gnocchi and ravioli, and there's a good weekday lunch special (CH$5900). The owners also run a B&B. Mon–Thurs 1–3.30pm & 7–11pm, Fri 1–3.30pm & 7.30pm–1am, Sat 1–4.30pm & 7.30pm–1am, Sun 1–4.30pm & 7–11pm.

Ápice Montt 462, Cerro Concepción ☎32 208 9737, ⓦrestaurantapice.cl; map p.105. This slick restaurant with a pared-down dining room and a chef with a "philosophy" may not be to everyone's taste, but the inventive, artfully presented food is undeniably good – think local *pescado de roca* with mustard, truffle oil and dauphinoise potatoes, and chocolate fondant (mains CH$12,600–13,200). Book ahead. Mon & Thurs–Sun 8–10pm.

Cafe del Pintor Urriola 652, Cerro Alegre ☎32 228 7208; map p.105. With a bohemian atmosphere, and murals by a local artist on the walls, this café-restaurant offers an economical three-course set dinner (CH$8500) and a particularly good *chupe de mariscos* (seafood stew). Daily noon–10.30pm.

★ **Le Filou de Montpellier** Almirante Montt 382, Cerro Concepción ☏32 222 4663, ⊛facebook.com/lefiloudemontpellier; map p.105. A delightful little piece of France in Valpo: postcards of Montpellier and paintings by local artists decorate the place, while the set lunch (CH$8900) may include French onion soup, moules mariniere and peach melba. Tues–Thurs 1–5pm, Fri 1–9pm, Sat 1–10.30pm, Sun 1–6.30pm.

★ **J. Cruz Malbrán** Condell 1466, up alley next to the Municipalidad ☏32 221 1225, ⊛jcruz.cl; map p.100. Billing itself as a restaurant and museum in one, and accessed via a heavily graffitied alleyway, this extraordinary place is packed with china, old clocks, musical instruments, crucifixes and other kitsch trinkets. It also claims to have invented the *chorrillana* (a vast plate of steak strips, onions, eggs and French fries; CH$7500), which is not to be missed. Mon–Thurs noon–2am, Fri & Sat noon–4.30am, Sun 1pm–2am.

Pasta e Vino Papudo 427, Cerro Concepción ☏32 249 6187, ⊛pastaevinoristorante.cl; map p.105. One of Valpo's finest restaurants, providing an inventive and ambitious take on Italian cuisine – pistachio gnocchi with shredded lamb sauce or clam ravioli, for example. Reservations vital at weekends. Mains CH$11,000–18,000. Tues–Sat 1–3.30pm & 7–11pm.

Vinilo Almirante Montt 448, Cerro Concepción ☏32 223 0665, ⊛facebook.com/vinilovalpo; map p.105. Intimate bistro with a bizarre mix of abstract and children's artwork, a stack of vintage vinyl and a select menu of contemporary Chilean dishes (CH$9000–14,000) such as ossobucco. There's regular live music, and the owners also run a speakeasy-style pisco bar a few doors up. Mon–Thurs 9am–1.30am, Fri & Sat 9am–3.30am, Sun 10am–1.30am.

DRINKING AND NIGHTLIFE

Valpo has an excellent **bar scene**, especially on Thursday, Friday and Saturday nights. The speciality is its old-fashioned, charming bar-restaurants serving *comida típica* and putting on live *bolero*, *tango* or *música folklórica*. There's also a range of younger, hipper bars, many with live music and dancing. Take care after dark, especially anywhere near the port area.

★ **El Bar Inglés** Cochrane 851 (rear entrance at Blanco 870) ☏32 223 2874, ⊛baringles.cl; map p.105. This atmospheric bar, dating back to the early 1990s, closed briefly in 2017 due to financial difficulties, but is now back up and running under new owners. The new decor blends British kitsch with Santiago Wanderers pennants, model shops and the like. Beer from CH$2500. Mon–Fri 1–9pm.

Bar El Irlandés Blanco 1279 ☏32 346 9757, ⊛facebook.com/barelirlandes.valparaiso; map p.100. This Irish-run joint has an authentic pub feel, with a long bar to prop yourself up at, an excellent range of imported and local beers and a friendly, relaxed atmosphere. Tues & Wed 5pm–1.30am, Thurs 6.30pm–3am, Fri 4pm–3.30am, Sat 4pm–4.30am.

El Cinzano Plaza Aníbal Pinto 1182 ☏32 221 3043, ⊛barcinzano.cl; map p.105. One of the oldest restaurant-bars in the city, decked out with nautical knick-knacks and offering a fantastic atmosphere, especially on Thurs, Fri and Sat nights when it fills with locals and ageing crooners singing sentimental ballads. Beer from CH$1800; set lunch CH$5500. Mon–Wed 10am–1am, Thurs 10am–2am, Fri & Sat 10.30am–4.30am.

Fauna Dimalow 166, Cerro Alegre ☏32 327 0719, ⊛faunahotel.cl; map p.105. The terrace at this restaurant-bar has panoramic views of Valpo's *cerros* and bay, making it an ideal spot for a sundowner, especially given the range of craft beers (from CH$3000) and the good food. Daily 12.30–10.30pm.

El Internado Paseo Dimalow 167, Cerro Alegre ☏32 335 4153, ⊛elinternado.cl; map p.105. This restaurant-bar-cultural venue offers expansive views from its terraces, well-mixed cocktails, film screenings, a games room, live music and DJs, and even its own radio station. Decent food, too. Mon–Thurs & Sun noon–12.30am, Fri & Sat noon–1.30am.

La Piedra Feliz Errázuriz 1054, near the junction with Blanco ☏32 225 6788, ⊛lapiedrafeliz.cl; map p.105. Mellow place with creaky wooden floors and live music – including jazz, *bolero*, rock and disco – every night, as well as regular art exhibitions, salsa classes and poetry readings. Entry around CH$10,000 (including a drink). Tues–Sat 9pm–late.

La Playa Serrano 567 ☏32 259 4262; map p.100. The old sea dogs that once frequented La Playa have mostly departed, but it's still a characterful spot for a drink (from CH$2000); the food, though, is decidedly average. There's frequently live music in the evenings. Mon–Wed 10am–10.30pm, Thurs–Sat 10am–late.

ENTERTAINMENT

Valpo is *the* place to go in Chile to ring in the **New Year**, with huge parties and fireworks extravaganzas; be sure to arrive by noon on the 30th or you'll get stuck in horrible traffic.

Parque Cultural de Valparaíso Castro s/n ☎ 32 235 9400, ⓦ parquecultural.cl. Midway up Cerro Cárcel is Parque Cultural de Valparaíso, a former prison that has been transformed into a vibrant cultural hub. As well as hosting artists' workshops, the complex stages a wide range of –

generally free – cultural events including exhibitions, film screenings, concerts and theatrical performances.
Teatro Municipal Uruguay 410 ☎ 32 225 7480. The city's main theatre hosts regular plays, music and dance performances.

DIRECTORY

Hospital Public hospital Carlos Van Buren, Colón and San Ignacio (☎ 32 236 4000, ⓦ hospitalcarlosvanburen.cl); private clinic Clínica Valparaíso, Av Brasil 2350 (☎ 600 411 2000, ⓦ clinicavalparaiso.cl).

Markets One of Chile's best antique/flea markets is held every Sat and Sun at Plaza Bernardo O'Higgins, though prices are high.

South of Valparaíso

The resorts **south of Valparaíso** are among the busiest and most developed in the region. Most sit on overcrowded beaches, are overrun with ugly apartment blocks and are jam packed with noisy vacationers. However, a few places in the area are well worth a visit: peaceful **Quintay**, the **vineyards** of the **Casablanca Valley** and – most notably – the village of **Isla Negra**, site of Pablo Neruda's extraordinary house and now a museum.

Quintay

Buses depart from the corner of 12 de Febrero and Rawson in Valparaíso (4–5 Mon–Fri, fewer at weekends; 1hr); there are also frequent *colectivos* from the rank on 12 de Febrero

Secluded and relatively untouched by tourism, the village of **QUINTAY** makes an ideal day-trip from Valparaíso. It has a scenic cove and a series of small beaches, backed by pine and eucalyptus trees, cacti and wild flowers. There are a few fish restaurants, a former whaling station and a lighthouse.

Casa Museo Isla Negra

Poeta Neruda s/n, Isla Negra • Tues–Sun: Jan & Feb 10am–7pm; March–Dec 10am–6pm • CH$7000, including audio tour; the museum has limited capacity for visitors, so it's best to arrive in the morning • ☎ 2 2777 8741, ⓦ fundacionneruda.org • Pullman (ⓦ pullman.cl) and Tur Bus (ⓦ turbus.cl) run from Santiago's Terminal Alameda (every 30min; 2hr); there are also services from Valparaíso (every 15min; 1hr 30min)

From 1939, poet **Pablo Neruda** (see page 111) spent forty years of his life, on and off, in the village of Isla Negra, enlarging his house and filling it with the strange and beautiful objects he gathered from far-flung corners of the world. The Fundación Neruda, acting on the wishes of the poet's widow, Matilde Urrutia, transferred Neruda's and Matilde's graves to its garden and runs the house as the **Casa Museo Isla Negra**. Inside, the winding passages and odd-shaped rooms are crammed full of fascinating exotic objects including ships' figureheads, Hindu carvings, African and Japanese masks, ships in bottles, seashells, butterflies, Victorian postcards and a good deal more.

Viña del Mar

Just a fifteen-minute bus or train ride takes you from the colourful *cerros* and chaotic alleys of Valparaíso to the tree-lined avenues and ostentatious high-rises of **VIÑA DEL MAR**, Chile's biggest and best-known beach resort. In many ways, it's indistinguishable from beach resorts elsewhere in the world, with oceanfront condos, bars, restaurants and a casino.

Lurking in the older corners of town, however, are extravagant **palaces**, elegant **villas** and sumptuous gardens. Many date from the late nineteenth century when Viña del

PABLO NERUDA

The village of **Isla Negra** was put on the map when **Pablo Neruda** moved into a half-built house on the beach in 1939. Born **Neftalí Reyes** in 1904, this son of a local railwayman made his name in the world of poetry as a teenager under the pseudonym Pablo Neruda. He published his first collection, *Crepusculario*, in 1923 and success came quickly. The following year came a slim volume of sensual, tormented verses, *Veinte Poemas de Amor y una Canción Desesperada* (Twenty Love Poems and a Song of Despair), and he suddenly found himself, aged 20, with one of the fastest-growing readerships on the continent.

RANGOON AND BEYOND

Despite this success, Neruda still needed to fund his writing, and so, aged 24, he began his career as **Chilean consul** in Rangoon, the first of many posts. It seems ironic that this most Chilean of poets should have spent so much of his adult life far from his native land. His years in Rangoon, Colombo, Jakarta and Singapore were often intensely lonely, but also coloured with vivid episodes and sexual adventures. The most dramatic of these was his love affair in Rangoon with **Josie Bliss**. Described by Neruda as his "Burmese panther", she was a jealous and possessive lover who would sometimes terrorize him with her silver dagger. When he was transferred to Ceylon (now Sri Lanka), he left without telling her, but she turned up on his doorstep several months later. Neruda's outright rejection of her was to haunt him for many years, and Bliss makes several appearances in his poems.

POLITICIZATION AND EXILE

During his time in Asia, Neruda's poetry was inward-looking, reflecting his dislocation and solitude. His posts in Barcelona (1934) and Madrid (1935–36), however, marked a major turning-point: with the outbreak of the **Spanish Civil War**, and the assassination of his friend, Federico García Lorca, Neruda became increasingly politicized. He provided Spanish refugees with a safe passage to Chile, and sought to give his poetry a meaningful "place in man's struggle", with *España en el Corazón*. On returning to Chile he joined the Communist Party, and was **elected as a senator**. This landed him in serious trouble when new president González Videla, who had previously enlisted Neruda's help, switched sides from left to right, and outlawed communism. When Neruda publicly attacked him, the president issued an arrest warrant, and he was forced into hiding. In 1949 the poet was smuggled across the Andes, and spent the next three years in exile.

MATILDE URRUTIA

It was during his **exile** that Neruda met the woman who was to inspire some of his most beautiful poetry: Matilde Urrutia, whom he later married. Neruda had been married twice before: first, briefly, to a Dutch woman he'd met in Rangoon; and then for eighteen years to the Argentinian painter, Delia del Carril. The poet's writings scarcely mention his first wife, nor their daughter – his only child – who died when she was 8, but Delia is described as "sweetest of consorts, thread of steel and honey". It was so as not to hurt Delia that *Los Versos del Capitán* – passionate love poems written for Matilde – was published anonymously.

THE RETURN HOME

Nonetheless, when the order for his arrest was revoked in 1955, three years after his return to Santiago, Neruda divorced Delia and moved into **La Chascona**, in Santiago, and then to **Isla Negra** with Matilde. From then on, Neruda devoted himself to politics and poetry almost in equal measure. In 1970, Salvador Allende, whose campaign Neruda had tirelessly participated in, was elected president. The following year, Neruda was awarded the Nobel Prize for Literature. His happiness was short-lived, however. Diagnosed with cancer, the poet was unable to withstand the shock brought on by the 1973 military coup, which left his dear friend Allende dead. Less than two weeks later, on September 23, Neruda died in Santiago.

Mar – then a large hacienda – was subdivided into plots that were sold or rented to the wealthy families of Valparaíso and Santiago who came to spend their summers. The city also has **beautiful botanical gardens** and an intriguing **museum**.

Plaza Vergara

Viña's centre is marked by the large, green **Plaza Vergara**, full of tall, stately trees and surrounded by some fine, early twentieth-century buildings including the Neoclassical **Teatro Municipal**, the stately **Hotel O'Higgins** and the Italian Renaissance-style **Club de Viña**, an old-school gentlemen's club.

Avenida Valparaíso

Avenida Valparaíso, Viña's main commercial street, borders the south side of Plaza Vergara. Much of the shopping activity occurs in the five blocks between the plaza and Calle Ecuador. There's also a good **feria artesanal** in Pasaje Cousiño, a narrow passage off the south side of the avenue, just west of Plaza Vergara.

Quinta Vergara

Off Errázuriz • Daily: summer 7am–7pm; rest of year 7am–6pm • Free

The exceptionally beautiful **Quinta Vergara** park, filled with exotic, subtropical trees and surrounded by wooded hills, sits two blocks south of Plaza Vergara, across the railway tracks. The amphitheatre hosts the hyped **Festival Internacional de la Canción** (International Music Festival) every February.

Museo de Bellas Artes

Quinta Vergara

In the centre of Quinta Vergara sits **Palacio Vergara**, a dazzling, whitewashed Venetian-style palace built in 1906. Now home to the **Museo de Bellas Artes**, which has a collection of Chilean and European paintings, it has been closed for restoration for several years.

Museo Palacio Rioja

Quillota 214 • Tues–Sun 9.30am–1.30pm & 3–5.30pm • Free • ☎ 32 218 4690, ⓦ facebook.com/palaciorioja

The restored **Museo Palacio Rioja**, built in the style of an eighteenth-century French chateau and surrounded by a sumptuous park, is all that remains of the once extensive vineyards that gave the town its name. Situated just north of the Estero Marga Marga, it was built in 1906 for Don Fernando Rioja Medel, a Spanish millionaire who owned the Banco Español. The perfectly preserved ground floor provides a fascinating close-up view of early twentieth-century luxury and hosts concerts, film screenings and cultural events.

Palacio Carrasco

Libertad 250

The **Palacio Carrasco**, an elegant, three-storey building designed in a French Neoclassical style, now functions as the city's cultural centre, hosting regular exhibitions of work by Chilean and international artists. The palacio has been closed for several years for restoration.

Museo Francisco Fonck

4 Norte 784 • Mon 10am–2pm & 3–6pm, Tues–Sat 10am–6pm, Sun 10am–2pm • CH$2700 • ☎ 32 268 6753, ⓦ museofonck.cl

The excellent **Museo Francisco Fonck** has one of Chile's most important **Easter Island collections**, plus fascinating pre-Hispanic exhibits. One of the museum's best pieces stands by the entrance in the garden: a giant stone *moai*, one of just six that exist outside Easter Island. Inside, the three rooms dedicated to Easter Island include wooden and stone carvings of those long, stylized faces, as well as jewellery, weapons and ceremonial objects.

Castillo Wulff

Av Marina 37 • Tues–Sun 9.30am–1.30pm & 3–5.30pm • Free

In a prime waterfront location, the neo-Gothic **Castillo Wulff** was built in 1906 for a local nitrate and coal baron. Formerly a museum, it is now an exhibition space, and is well worth a quick look: check out the glass-floored passage through which you can gaze at the waves breaking below.

The beaches

Take any of the Reñaca or Concón buses from Puente Libertad (the bridge just north of Plaza Vergara), and get off at 10 or 12 Norte for Playas Acapulco and El Sol, or ask the driver to let you off on the coast road for the beaches further north

Viña's most central beach is the sheltered, sandy **Playa Caleta Abarca** at the eastern end of Calle Viana. Just off the beach, at the foot of Cerro Castillo, is the **Reloj de Flores**, a large clock composed of colourful plants and mechanical dials.

Just beyond Castillo Wulff is the **Estero Marga Marga** – follow it inland a couple of blocks to reach the bridge that crosses it. On the other side is the **Casino Municipal** and the coast road, **Avenida Perú**. A pedestrian promenade runs alongside the ocean but there's no sand here, just a stretch of rocks.

A few blocks north, Avenida Perú swerves inland to make way for the long unbroken strip of sand stretching for more than 3km towards Reñaca (see page 116). Though effectively a single beach, the different sections each have their own name: just north of Avenida Perú is the 200m-long **Playa Acapulco**, which is very popular but a bit hemmed in, followed by **Playa El Sol** and **Playa Los Marineros**, where it's often too rough for swimming. Finally, **Playa Larga** has restaurants and showers – it's very crowded in the summer.

Jardín Botánico Nacional

6km east of Viña • Daily 9am–7pm • CH$2000 • ☎ 32 267 5091, ⓦ jbn.cl • Bus #20, eastbound, from Calle Bohn (10min)

Set in a sheltered valley and surrounded by sun-baked hills, the **Jardín Botánico Nacional** contains three thousand plant species from Latin America, Europe and Asia. The gardens are a great place to unwind, but if you fancy a bit of action, it is also possible to go zip lining (closed at time of research).

2

ARRIVAL AND DEPARTURE

By bus The bus terminal is at the eastern end of Av Valparaíso. To go down the coast, your best bet is to catch a bus from Valparaíso (see page 106), reached by any *micro* (every 10min) marked "Puerto" or "Aduana" from Plaza Vergara or Arlegui; alternatively take the Metro (see page 106). Buses/*micros* up the coast don't stop at the bus terminal, but at Libertad (just north of Puente Libertad). Destinations Cachagua (hourly; 1hr 30min); Concón (every 15min; 15min); Horcón (hourly; 1hr); La Ligua (hourly;

VIÑA DEL MAR

2hr); Maitencillo (hourly; 1hr 20min); Papudo (1–3 daily; 1hr 45min); Reñaca (every 15min; 25min); Santiago (every 15min; 1hr 30min–1hr 45min); Zapallar (hourly; 1hr 30min).
By train The Metro (ⓦ metro-valparaiso.cl) departs for Valparaíso from the centrally located Miramar and Viña del Mar stations (every 5–20min). Buy a plastic charge card (CH$1450) and top it up before travelling.

INFORMATION AND TOURS

Tourist office The main office is off the northeast corner of Plaza Vergara, next to *Hotel O'Higgins* (Mon–Fri 9am–9pm, Sat 10am–9pm, Sun 10am–8pm; ☎ 32 218 5710, ⓦ visitevinadelmar.cl). There's a smaller booth at the bus station (daily 9am–6pm; ☎ 32 275 2000).

Walking tours Tours 4 Tips (☎ 2 2570 9338, ⓦ tours4tips.com) runs daily English- and Spanish-language walking tours, departing from the Reloj de Flores at 10am and 3pm (free, but tips expected).

ACCOMMODATION

Viña has numerous places to stay, but most are **overpriced** and only a few offer sea views. Book well in advance during the high season or national holidays; at other times prices drop.

Casa Olga 18 de Septiembre 31 ☎ 32 318 2972, ⓦ casa-olga.com; map p.112. Based in a handsome 1930s townhouse, this charming B&B is one of the best-value options in town, with a handful of spick-and-span en-suite rooms, some with sea views. It's in the residential Recreo neighbourhood, a 20min walk from the Reloj de Flores. CH$40,000
Hotel Agora 5 1/2 Poniente 253 ☎ 32 269 4669, ⓦ hotelagora.cl; map p.112. Appealing Art Deco-style hotel that feels like it's been transplanted from 1970s Miami. Located on a quiet side street, it has pastel-shaded en suites with fridges and TVs, and a stylish yellow-and-white tiled lobby. CH$70,000
Hotel Monterilla 2 Norte 65 ☎ 32 297 6950, ⓦ monterilla.cl; map p.112. The en suites at this small, family-run hotel are comfortable and well appointed, if

not the most stylish. Staff are friendly and professional, and the location convenient for Viña's bars and restaurants. CH$75,000
My Father's House Gregorio Marañón 1210 ☎ 32 261 6136, ⓦ myfathershouse.cl; map p.112. Spacious, quiet single, double and triple rooms (with shared or private bathrooms), swimming pool and gracious owners. The only drawback is that it's about 2km from the centre of town; catch *colectivo* #31, #82 or #131. US$62
Street Garden Hostel 3 Poniente 379 ☎ 32 320 0208, ⓦ streetgardenhostel.cl; map p.112. Hostels open and close remarkably frequently in Viña: this is one of the current popular spots, with a lively (and noisy) atmosphere, four- to eight-bed dorms, basic private rooms and a handy central location. Dorms CH$10,000, doubles CH$30,000

EATING

Cevasco Av Valparaíso 688–700 ☎ 32 271 4256, ⓦ cevasco.cl; map p.112. Bustling *fuente de soda*, split between two locations, either side of an arcade, serving tasty – if decidedly unhealthy – hot dogs, burgers and *barros lucos* (CH$1750–4750) to a steady stream of locals. Two other branches. Mon–Sat 8.30am–11pm, Sun 12.30–9.30pm.

★ **Divino Pecado** San Martín 180 ☎ 32 297 5790; map p.112. Classy Italian offering mouthwatering fish, seafood and pasta dishes (mains CH$10,300–12,500) such as tuna carpaccio and scallops *au gratin*. Reservations are necessary at weekends. Mon–Thurs 12.30–3pm & 8–11pm, Fri 12.30–3pm & 8pm–midnight, Sat 12.30–4pm & 8pm–midnight, Sun 12.30–4pm & 8–11pm.

CASABLANCA VALLEY WINE ROUTE

The **Casablanca Valley**, famed for its excellent white wines, is accessed via Ruta 68, which connects Valparaíso and Viña with Santiago. **Ruta del Vino Valle de Casablanca** (☎ 32 274 3755, ⊛ rutadelvinodecasablanca.cl), Oscar Bonilla 56, in Casablanca, organizes tours (from CH$33,000) of the wineries, as do operators in Valparaíso (see page 106) and Santiago (see page 78). You can also visit the vineyards independently; having your own car makes things a lot easier, but it is also possible to access some using the frequent Valparaíso/Viña–Santiago buses.

2

Donde Willy 6 Norte 353 ☎ 32 342 1261; map p.112. Tucked away down a narrow alleyway, this little restaurant specializes in Chilean classics like *pastel de jaiba* (crab pie) and *caldo de congrio* (conger eel soup). Mains CH$4900–9000. Daily noon–12.30pm.

Entre Masas 5 Norte 235 ☎ 32 297 9919; map p.112. Excellent little bakery, specializing in *empanadas* (CH$1500–2500): the 49 varieties include crab and cheese, spinach and ricotta, and chicken, bacon and mushroom. There's another branch in Reñaca (Av Central 75). Daily 10am–10pm.

La Flor de Chile 8 Norte 601 ☎ 32 268 9554, ⊛ laflordechile.cl; map p.112. Atmospheric restaurant dating back to 1930 and with a Spanish-influenced menu – try one of the hearty tortilla omelettes or share a *tabla* (platters of cheeses, cured meats and olives). Mains CH$5000–10,000. Mon–Sat 11am–midnight.

Panzoni Paseo Cousiño 12B ☎ 32 271 4134; map p.112. This charming Italian joint has a handful of tables, great service and inexpensive pastas and salads. You may have to queue at lunchtime, but it's worth the wait (mains CH$5000–8000). Mon–Sat noon–4pm & 8pm–midnight.

The Tea Pot 5 Norte 475 ☎ 32 268 7671; map p.112. Kitsch wood-panelling gives this café the feel of a Patagonian cabin. The menu features around fifty types of tea – from matcha to Earl Grey (from CH$1300) – plus breakfast options, cakes, sandwiches and *onces*. Summer Mon–Sat 10am–10pm, Sun 4.30–9pm; rest of year Mon–Sat 10am–9pm.

DRINKING AND NIGHTLIFE

Nightlife tends to be seasonal, reaching a heady peak in January and February when everyone flocks to the bars and clubs of **Reñaca**. In summer, micros run to and from Reñaca right through the night. In winter, the partying dies out, and the focus shifts back to Viña.

Café Journal Agua Santa and Alvarez ☎ 32 266 6654, ⊛ facebook.com/cafejournal1999; map p.112. This is a pub-club, rather than a café, and proximity to Viña's university ensures a healthy crowd of student drinkers, with pitchers of beer setting them up for a night dancing and carousing. It's busy throughout the week until the early hours, often featuring live music and/or DJs. Drinks CH$1500–4000. Mon–Wed noon–3.30am, Thurs 11.30am–3.30am, Fri & Sat 11.30am–4.30am, Sun 8pm–3.30am.

ENTERTAINMENT

Cine Arte Plaza Vergara (through passage off west side of square) ☎ 32 288 2798, ⊛ cinearte.cl. Excellent little arts cinema, especially worth a visit during the Festival Internacional de Cine Viña del Mar (⊛ cinevina. cl) in Nov/Dec.

Teatro Municipal Plaza Vergara ☎ 32 268 1739. The grand Neoclassical Teatro Municipal, which dates back to the 1920s, puts on theatrical performances, classical music concerts and dance shows.

North of Viña

North of Viña, **Reñaca** and neighbouring **Concón** are easy to get to, though **Cachagua** and **Zapallar** are the most exclusive resorts. Beyond here, the coast road meanders to the small fishing village of **Papudo**, about 75km from Viña, inland to the farming town of **La Ligua** and back coastwards again to the family resort of **Los Vilos**. The northern coast road is far quieter than its southern counterpart, and very beautiful in parts.

Reñaca

Lively, developed **REÑACA**, 6km north of central Viña, is a 1.5km stretch of coast lined with bars, restaurants and apartment blocks. The beaches are among the cleanest (and busiest) in the country, and the resort is particularly popular with Chile and Argentina's beautiful young things. Reñaca's **clubs** are pricey but remain lively throughout the summer. Accommodation is generally overpriced; you're better off staying in Viña.

Concón

CONCÓN, 10km north of Reñaca, is a strange sort of place: part concrete terraced apartment blocks, part elegant villas with flower-filled gardens and part rundown, working-class fishing village, with six beaches spread out along the bay. When the wind is blowing south, nasty fumes drift over from the nearby oil refinery.

The most interesting bit of town is **La Boca**, the ramshackle commercial centre at the mouth of the Río Aconcagua. The *caleta* here is now a bustling fish quay, lined with **marisquerías** (seafood restaurants).

The most popular beaches are **Playa Amarilla** and **Playa Negra**, south of La Boca. More attractive, and quieter, is **Playa Ritoque**, a few kilometres north of town.

Horcón

The charming – if slightly tatty – fishing village of **HORCÓN**, about 30km north of Concón, is a chaotic tumble of houses straggling down the hill to a rocky bay. (En route, you'll pass Quintero, a scruffy town with filthy beaches.) In the summer, Horcón is taken over by artisans on the beaches and unfeasible numbers of young Chileans; this is the hippy alternative to Reñaca.

The **beach** in front of the village is crowded and uninviting, but a short walk up the main street and then along Avenida Cau-Cau takes you down a steep, rickety staircase to the remote **Playa Cau-Cau**, a pleasantly sheltered beach surrounded by wooded hills, though a hideous condo mars the beauty of the area. An hour's walk along the beach north towards Maitencillo takes you to Playa Luna, a nudist beach.

Maitencillo

Stretching 4km along one main street, **MAITENCILLO** is little more than a long, narrow strip of holiday homes, *cabañas* and hotels along the shoreline. The chief reason for coming here is to enjoy **Playa Aguas Blancas**, a superb white-sand beach sweeping 5km south of the village, backed by steep sandstone cliffs and good for surfing. Maitencillo is also a popular spot for paragliding.

Cachagua

CACHAGUA, just north of Maitencillo, with a stunning expanse of pale sand curling round the bay, backed by gentle hills, is synonymous with Chile's upper crust. It is blessed by a relative lack of holiday homes on the land off the beach, which instead is home to a golf course. Ask for directions to the long staircase from Avenida del Mar down to **Playa Las Cujas**, a tiny, spectacular and often empty beach. Just off the coast, Isla de los Pingüinos is a **penguin sanctuary** to which local fishermen sometimes offer boat rides; canoe tours are also available.

Zapallar

The classiest and most attractive of the resorts, **ZAPALLAR** is a sheltered, horseshoe bay backed by wooded hills where luxurious holiday homes and handsome old mansions nestle between the pine trees. Apart from the beach, you can also stroll along the coastal path around the bay, or walk up Avenida Zapallar, admiring the early twentieth-century townhouses, manicured gardens and a pretty stone church. More strenuous possibilities include renting a sea-kayak, climbing the 692m **Cerro Higuera** or following the coastal path back to Maitencillo.

Papudo

The development in **PAPUDO**, just 10km around the headland, hasn't been as graceful as in Zapallar, and several ugly buildings mar the seafront. However, the steep hills looming dramatically behind the town are undeniably beautiful, and the place has a friendly, local atmosphere. The best beach in the area is the dully named **Playa Grande**.

La Ligua

The chief appeal of **LA LIGUA**, a bustling agricultural town, is its setting, enfolded by undulating hills that take on a rich honey glow in the early evening sunlight. It is also known for its confectionery. There's a small museum and an artisan market in the main square. La Ligua was once notorious as the home of one of Chile's darkest figures: Catalina de los Ríos y Lisperguer. Born in 1604, La Quintrala, as she was known, murdered more than forty people in a brutal lifetime, including her father, a Knight of the Order of St John (after first seducing him), and numerous slaves. She evaded justice, dying before she could be put on trial.

Pichidangui

North of the Papudo–La Ligua crossroads, the Panamericana follows the coast for some 200km before dipping inland again, towards Ovalle (see page 125). This stretch of highway takes you past a succession of gorgeous, white-sand **beaches** dotted with villages and resorts. Set 4km back from the Panamericana, 50km beyond the Papudo–La Ligua interchange, is **PICHIDANGUI**, with a lovely beach: 7km of white, powdery sand and little beachfront development.

Los Vilos

Legend has it that **LOS VILOS**, 30km north of Pichidangui, takes its name from the Hispanic corruption of "Lord Willow", a British pirate shipwrecked on the coast who decided to stay. The town later became notorious for highway robberies. Today it is a great place to spend a couple of days by the sea without paying over the odds. The town's chief attraction is its long golden **beach**, but there's also a **fish market** and **Isla de los Lobos**, a seal colony 5km south.

ARRIVAL AND DEPARTURE · NORTH OF VIÑA

By bus Cachagua, Concón, Horcón, La Ligua, Maitencillo, Reñaca and Zapallar are all served by regular buses to and from Viña del Mar, while Papudo has a twice-daily service. From Santiago there are also buses to La Ligua and buses (hourly; 3hr 15min) to Los Vilos from the Terminal de Buses Santiago and the Terminal San Borja. Daily buses head to

Pichidangui (2hr 30min) from the capital's Terminal de Buses Santiago (Condor Bus; ☎ 2 2779 3721, ⓦ www. condorbus.cl) and from Valparaíso (Buses La Porteña, which leave from the company's office at Molina 366; ☎ 32 221 6568).

ACCOMMODATION AND EATING

Cabañas Hermansen Av del Mar 592, Maitencillo ☎ 32 277 1028, ⓦ hermansen.cl. A 5min drive north of Aguas Blancas, this lodge has great views of the beach,

rustic *cabañas* (sleeping up to six) with cute wooden picnic tables, bike rental and switched-on staff. The attached *La Canasta* is the best restaurant-bar in the area. **CH$82,000**

2

★ **El Chiringuito** Southern tip of the bay, Zapallar ☎ 33 274 1024. It's worth visiting Zapallar just to eat at this legendary seafood restaurant, down by the *caleta*, though bring a full wallet (mains CH$10,000–18,000) – the scallops, in particular, are divine. Summer Mon–Thurs 12.30–6pm, Fri & Sat 12.30–6pm & 8pm–1am; autumn and winter often weekends only.

Hotel Isla Seca Northern end of the bay, Zapallar ☎ 33 274 1224, ⓦ hotelislaseca.cl. This swanky hotel offers sizeable, classically styled rooms with balconies; those with sea views cost significantly more than those without. There's an excellent restaurant. US$180

La Rosa Náutica El Dorado 120, Pichidangui ☎ 53 253 1133, ⓦ rosanautica.cl. A mixture of standard hotel rooms and more atmospheric wooden *cabañas* sleeping up to six; both are simple but comfortable. There's a pool and a restaurant. Doubles CH$52,000, *cabañas* CH$62,000

Parque Nacional La Campana

Cordillera de la Costa • Daily 9am–5.30pm • CH$4000 • ⓦ www.conaf.cl/parques/parque-nacional-la-campana

Set in the dry, dusty mountains of the coastal range, **Parque Nacional La Campana** is a wonderful place to hike and offers some of the best views in Chile. From the 1880m-high summit of Cerro La Campana you can see the Andes on one side and the Pacific Ocean on the other – in the words of Charles Darwin, who climbed it in 1834, Chile is seen "as in a map". There's also a profusion of **Chilean palms**; this native tree was all but wiped out in the nineteenth century, and the Palmar de Ocoa, a grove in the north of the park, is one of just two remaining places in the country where you can find wild specimens. You can also spot eagles, giant hummingbirds and, if you're lucky, mountain cats and foxes.

The park, about 60km east of Valparaíso and 110km northwest of Santiago, is divided into three "sectors" – Granizo, Cajón Grande and Ocoa – each with its own entrance. **Sector Granizo** and **Sector Cajón Grande** are in the south, near the village of **Olmué**; head here if you want to follow Darwin's footsteps and climb **Cerro La Campana**. These sectors could be seen on a day-trip from Valparaíso, Viña or Santiago, although if you have the time it is better to spend a night or two in Olmué. The less accessible and less visited **Sector Ocoa**, on the northern side of the park, can also be reached on a day-trip from Valparaíso, Viña or, at a push, Santiago; if you want to stay the night, you'll need to camp.

ARRIVAL AND DEPARTURE

PARQUE NACIONAL LA CAMPANA

SECTOR GRANIZO AND SECTOR CAJÓN GRANDE

By bus Aim for the gateway village of Olmué: Ciferal Express runs buses from Playa Ancha in Valparaíso (every 2hr; 1hr); Pullman runs from Santiago's San Borja and Alameda terminals (hourly; 1hr 30min–2hr). From Olmué it's a further 9km to the park; regular buses (every 15min) run from the main square to Granizo; the last bus stop is a 15min walk from the Conaf hut in Sector Granizo, and a 40min walk from Sector Cajón Grande.

By car The best route from Valparaíso is via Viña del Mar, Quilpué, Villa Alemana and Limache. If you're coming from Santiago, take the RN-5 north, then follow the signs for Tiltil, from where the road takes the zigzagging and very scenic route from Cuesta La Dormida to Olmué.

SECTOR OCOA

By bus Sector Ocoa is approached on a gravel road branching south from the Panamericana about halfway between Llay-Llay and Hijuelas; coming from Llay-Llay, it's the left turn just before the bridge across the Río Aconcagua. Any northbound bus along the Panamericana will drop you at the turn-off, but from here it's a 12km hike to the park entrance.

ACCOMMODATION

Olmué has a good choice of **places to stay**. It is also possible to camp in the park itself – ask at the Conaf hut at the entrance.

Centro Turístico La Campana Blanca Encalada 4651 ☎ 33 244 1722, ⓦ campana.cl. The friendly *La Campana* has the feel of a motel: pink buildings house clean, slightly gaudy but good-value rooms and cabins sleeping up to six. There's also a restaurant, garden, and pool. Doubles CH$44,000, cabins CH$65,000

Hostería El Copihué Portales 2203 ☎ 33 244 1544, ⓦ copihue.cl. The top place to stay in town, with comfortable en suites, a good restaurant, a nice pool, spa, jacuzzi, beautiful gardens and a good restaurant. CH$96,000

2

El Norte Chico

GOAT-HERDING, SOUTHERN ATACAMA

El Norte Chico

A land of rolling, sun-baked hills streaked with sudden river valleys that cut across the earth in a flash of green, the Norte Chico, or "Little North", of Chile is what geographers call a "transitional zone". Its semi-arid scrubland and sparse vegetation mark the transformation from the country's fertile heartland to the barren deserts bordering Peru and Bolivia. Starting around the Río Aconcagua, just north of Santiago, it stretches all the way to Taltal, and the southernmost reaches of the Atacama, more than 800km north.

A series of **rivers** flow through the Norte Chico region from the Andes to the coast, allowing the surrounding land to be irrigated and cultivated. The result is spectacular: lush, vibrant green terraces laden with olives, apricots and vines snake between the brown, parched walls of the valleys, forming a sensational visual contrast. The most famous product of these valleys is **pisco**, the pale, aromatic brandy distilled from sun-dried grapes and treasured by Chileans as their national drink.

The largest population centre – and one of the country's most fashionable seaside resorts – is **La Serena**, its pleasing, colonial-style architecture and lively atmosphere making it one of the few northern cities worth visiting for its own sake. The town, along with the nearby **Coquimbo**, and the market town of **Ovalle** to the south, were hit hard by an 8.4 earthquake on September 15 2015, but there are few signs left of the destruction today. La Serena in particular makes an ideal base for exploring the beautiful **Elqui Valley**, immortalized in the verses of the Nobel laureate Gabriela Mistral, and home to luxuriant vines and idyllic riverside hamlets. Just down the coast from La Serena lies the **Parque Nacional Bosque de Fray Jorge**, with a microclimate that supports a small, damp cloudforest. Another botanical wonder is the famous *desierto florido* or **flowering desert**. Occasionally, after heavy winter rains, the normally dry earth sprouts vast expanses of vibrantly coloured flowers. This rare, unpredictable phenomenon is centred on **Vallenar**.

Skies that are guaranteed cloudless almost year-round and low levels of air pollution have made the region the obvious choice for some of the world's major **astronomical observatories**. They range from the state-of-the art facility at dazzling-white **Tololo** to the modest yet easily accessible municipal installation at **Mamalluca**, near the picturesque village of **Vicuña**, where you don't have to be an expert reserving months in advance to look through the telescope.

The Norte Chico also boasts a string of superb **beaches**, some totally deserted and many of them tantalizingly visible from the Panamericana as you enter the region, just north of Santiago. **Bahía Inglesa** is famous for its turquoise waters, though increasingly prolific algae is turning the bay greener.

Copiapó, the region's northernmost major city, serves as a useful springboard for excursions into the nearby **desert** or, further afield, up into the high cordillera.

FERIA MODELO DE OVALLE

Highlights

❶ Feria Modelo de Ovalle Wander this food market and fill your bags with plump olives, giant pumpkins, ripe tomatoes and very smelly cheeses. See page 126

❷ La Serena Chile's second-oldest city offers long beaches, beautiful churches and a lively ambience. See page 133

❸ Horseriding in the Elqui Valley Pretend you're in the Wild West as you trek through Chile's untrammelled northern plains. See page 140

❹ Planta Capel Sample the fiery, fruity brandy – Chile's national drink – straight from the barrel

at the Elqui Valley's largest distillery. See page 142

❺ Stargazing Observe the unbelievably limpid night skies at impressive observatories, from Del Pangue to Mamalluca. See page 143

❻ Desierto florido If you're lucky enough to be in the right place at the right time, you can watch the desert around Vallenar burst into bloom. See page 152

❼ Parque Nacional Nevado de Tres Cruces One of the country's least-known national parks, with emerald-green lakes, snowcapped volcanoes and plentiful wildlife. See page 156

HIGHLIGHTS ARE MARKED ON THE MAP ON PAGE 124

0   40
kilometres

N

PACIFIC
OCEAN

Taital

PARQUE NACIONAL
PAN DE AZÚCAR

Caleta Pan de Azúcar

Chañaral

El Salvador

Diego de
Almagro

Portrerillos

Caldera

Bahía Inglesa

Aeropuerto
Chamonate

SALAR DE
MARICUNGA
Laguna
Santa Rosa

Paso de
San Francisco

Laguna
Verde

Puerto Viejo

Copiapó

Tierra Amarilla

Nantoco

Volcán Copiapó
(6080m)

Mina Marte

PARQUE NACIONAL
NEVADO DE TRES CRUCES

Tres
Cruces
(6753m)

Ojos del
Salado
(6893m)

⑦

Bahía Salada

Laguna del
Negro
Francisco

Carrizal Bajo

⑥

Juntas

PARQUE NACIONAL
LLANOS DE CHALLE

Huasco

R. Huasco

Vallenar

Santa Juana
dam

Alto del Carmen

El Tránsito

Domeyko

San Félix

ARGENTINA

Isla Chañaral

RESERVA
NACIONAL
PINGÜINO DE
HUMBOLDT

Isla Damas

Isla Choros

Cerro las Campanas

Cerro la Silla

Pinto

La Higuera

Mamalluca
Observatory

La Serena

②

Aeropuerto
La Florida

⑤

R. Elqui

Vicuña

Montegrande

Guayacán

La Herradura

Coquimbo

Cerro
Tololo

④

Del Pangue
Observatory

Pisco Elqui

③

Cancana
Observatory

Guanaquero

Andacollo

Río Cochiguaz

Tongoy

Pichasca

PARQUE
NACIONAL
BOSQUE DE
FRAY JORGE

Ovalle

①

Monte Patria

Termas
de Socas

Valle del
Encanto

Caleta Teniente

HIGHLIGHTS

① Feria Modelo de Ovalle

② La Serena

③ Horseriding in the Elqui Valley

④ Planta Capel

⑤ Stargazing

⑥ Desierto florido

⑦ Parque Nacional Nevado de Tres Cruces

EL NORTE CHICO

Here the **Parque Nacional Nevado de Tres Cruces**, the **Volcán Ojos del Salado** and **Laguna Verde** present some of Chile's most magnificent yet least-visited landscapes: snow-topped volcanoes, bleached-white salt flats and azure lakes. A few hours to the north, near the towering cliffs and empty beaches of **Parque Nacional Pan de Azúcar**, a small island is home to colonies of seals, countless pelicans and thousands of penguins.

Note that whereas the Norte Grande, Chile's northernmost region, can be visited year-round, the Norte Chico is at its best in **summer** (Oct–March) when the valleys are at their greenest, the coast is likelier to be free of fog and the ocean and sky are pure blue. On the downside, the beach resorts can be horribly overcrowded and overpriced in the high season, especially in January.

Brief history

Mining has shaped the region's growth, giving birth to towns, ports, railways and roads, and drawing large numbers of settlers to seek their fortune here. **Gold** was mined first by the Incas for ritual offerings, and then intensively, to exhaustion, by the Spaniards until the end of the eighteenth century. Next came the great nineteenth-century **silver** bonanza, when a series of dramatic silver strikes – some of them accidental – set a frenzy of mining and prospecting in motion, propelling the region into its heyday. Further riches and glory came when the discovery of huge **copper** deposits turned it into the world's largest copper producer from the 1840s to 1870s. Mining is still the most important industry, its presence most visible up in the cordillera, where huge mining trucks hurtle around the mountain roads, enveloped in dust clouds.

Ovalle

Almost 380km north of Santiago – some 140km beyond Los Vilos – a lone sign points to the little-visited market town of **OVALLE**. The birthplace of one of Chile's outstanding contemporary writers, Luis Sepúlveda, it is also a good base for exploring the dramatic **Hurtado Valley** or the deeply rural **Limarí Valley**, where a few low-key attractions include the Monumento Natural Pichasca, the Termas de Socos hot springs and the petroglyphs at the Valle del Encanto.

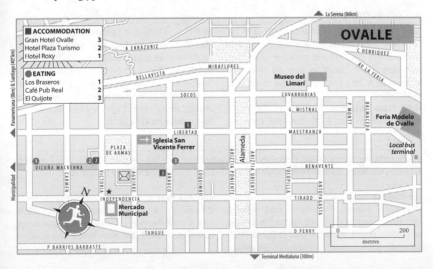

Plaza de Armas

The **Plaza de Armas**, with expansive lawns, nineteenth-century Phoenix palms and rows of jacaranda, marks Ovalle's centre. Dominating the east side of the square is the white-and-mustard **Iglesia San Vicente Ferrer**, a large, colonial-style church dating to 1849, with thick adobe walls and a diminutive tower. From the plaza, a pedestrian mall leads three blocks east along Vicuña Mackenna.

Museo del Limarí

Covarrubias and Antofagasta • Tues–Fri 10am–6pm, Sat & Sun 10am–2pm • Free • ☎ 53 243 3680, ⓦ musellimari.cl

Ovalle's excellent **Museo del Limarí** stands on the northeast edge of town in the grand old building that once housed the train station. The museum's collection of beautifully restored **Diaguita pottery** is shown to great effect in modern cases. Famed for its exquisite geometric designs painted in black, white and red onto terracotta surfaces, the pottery was produced by the Diaguita people who inhabited this part of Chile from 1000 AD until the Inca invasions in the sixteenth century.

Feria Modelo de Ovalle

Av la Feria and Benavente • Mon–Sat 6.30am–6pm, Sun 6am–2.30pm

About ten blocks east of the plaza, you'll find a huge, ramshackle iron hangar that houses the colourful **Feria Modelo de Ovalle**, the largest fresh-produce market in the north of Chile and definitely worth a visit; you can pick up fantastic home-made cheeses (including some alarmingly pungent goat cheeses) as well as delicious dried figs and a range of fresh fruit and vegetables.

ARRIVAL AND INFORMATION   OVALLE

By bus The bus terminal, known as Medialuna, is at Ariztía Oriente 769 (☎ 53 262 6612). Rural buses leave from the Feria Modelo and outside the Mercado Municipal at Victoria and Independencia.
Destinations Antofagasta (25 daily; 14hr); Arica (6 daily; 24hr); Calama (15 daily; 17hr); Chañaral (10 daily; 9hr); Copiapó (10 daily; 7hr); La Serena (every 15min; 1hr 20min); Los Vilos (10 daily; 2hr 30min); Santiago (18 daily; 6hr); Vallenar (20 daily; 4hr 30min).

Information There is no tourist office but the website Turismo Región de Coquimbo (ⓦ turismoregiondecoquimbo.cl) is a relatively useful source of information on the town and surrounding area.

ACCOMMODATION

Gran Hotel Ovalle Vicuña Mackenna 210 ☎ 53 262 1084, ⓦ granhotelovalle.cl; map p.125. Operating for more than sixty years, this solid mid-range option offers serviceable doubles – some are nicer and pricier than others, so ask to see a few – with artwork on the walls. CH$42,500

Hotel Plaza Turismo Victoria 295 ☎ 53 262 1970, ⓦ plazaturismo.cl; map p.125. This hotel occupies a handsome old building in a prime location in front of the Plaza de Armas. Inside things aren't quite so impressive, but the rooms are spacious and well kept. CH$64,000

Hotel Roxy Libertad 155 ☎ 53 262 0080, ✉ hotelroxy@hotmail.com; map p.125. For an economical option, try the *Hotel Roxy*, which has comfortable if dated rooms arranged around a large, brightly painted patio filled with flowers and chairs. CH$24,000

EATING

Ovalle's **restaurants** tend to limit themselves to the standard dishes you find everywhere else in Chile – which is frustrating, considering this is the fresh-produce capital of the North. However, you will find a few worthwhile spots.

Los Braseros Vicuña Mackenna 595 ☎ 53 262 4917; map p.125. Delicious, if unoriginal, food, including juicy *parrillas* (around CH$19,000 for two) in pleasant surroundings marred only by the giant TV screen. Mon–Sat 11am–4pm & 7.30pm–midnight, Sun 10am–4pm.

Café Pub Real Vicuña Mackenna 419 ☎ 53 262 2860, ⓦ facebook.com/cafepubreal; map p.125. If you're in need of real coffee (around CH$1500–2000), head to this appropriately named café, which morphs later on into a

pub and live music venue. Café Mon–Sat 9am–8.30pm; pub Tues–Sat 9pm–late.
El Quijote Arauco 294 ☎ 53 262 0501, ⍟ bit.ly/2CC9r45; map p.125. An intimate, bohemian restaurant-bar,

with political graffiti and poetry on the walls, and an inexpensive menu (CH$2000–5000) featuring simple staples such as *cazuela* and *lomo*. Mon–Sat 11.30am–4pm & 8pm–4am.

Around Ovalle

If you have your own car, you can take the scenic road northeast of Ovalle – an alternative route to Vicuña and the Elqui Valley (see page 140) – which winds slowly up into the mountains, passing ancient petrified wood stumps at **Pichasca** and the delightful oasis village of **Hurtado**, the main settlement along the dramatic but seldom visited **Hurtado Valley**. If you head west, you'll find a concentration of rock carvings in the **Valle del Encanto**, a hot springs resort at the **Termas de Socos** and the impressive cloudforest reserve of **Parque Nacional Bosque de Fray Jorge**.

Monumento Natural Pichasca

About 48km northeast of Ovalle • April–Nov Wed–Sun 9am–4.30pm; Dec–March daily 9am–5.30pm • CH$6000 • ☎ 53 262 0058, ⍟ www.conaf.cl • On market days (Mon–Sat 6.30am–6pm, Sun 6am–2.30pm) it's possible to get to the turn-off to San Pedro de Pichasca on a rickety bus from Ovalle's Feria Modelo (see page 126), but this involves walking 3km from the main road to the site entrance, and then a further 2km to the cave and fossil remains

Northeast of Ovalle, a first-rate, paved road climbs through the fertile Hurtado Valley, skirting – 12km out of town – the deep-blue expanse of water formed by the Recoleta Dam, one of three that irrigate the Limarí Valley. About 50km up the road, beyond a string of tiny villages, a side road to San Pedro Norte dips down across the river leading, just beyond the village, to the Conaf-run **Monumento Natural Pichasca**, the site of a seventy-million-year-old petrified wood. As you arrive at the parking area, two paths diverge: the right-hand path leads north to a hillside scattered with stumps of **fossilized tree trunks**, some of them imprinted with the shape of leaves; the left-hand, or southern, path leads down to an enormous **cave** formed by an 80m gash in the hillside topped by a massive overhanging rock. Archeological discoveries inside the cave point to human habitation some ten thousand years ago.

Hurtado

Around 30km northeast of Pichasca, set at an altitude of around 1200m amid dramatic mountain scenery, is the traditional oasis village of **HURTADO** with just four hundred inhabitants. The main draw, a few kilometres outside the village, is *Hacienda Los Andes*.

ARRIVAL AND ACCOMMODATION   HURTADO

By bus Hurtado-bound buses leave from Ovalle's Feria Modelo (3–4 daily; 3hr).

Hacienda Los Andes Casilla 98, Río Hurtado ☎ 53 269 1822, ⍟ haciendalosandes.com. A Mexican-style ranch run by German expats, with spacious rooms enjoying mesmerizing views across the verdant valley.

Excellent meals are served and they have their own private observatory. The main focus is equestrian, and they offer horseback adventures (from CH$60,000/person), with all meals and transfers to and from Vicuña or Ovalle included. Camping CH$5000, doubles CH$66,000

Valle del Encanto

19km southwest of Ovalle • Daily 8am–4.30pm • CH$500 • Take any westbound bus and asked to be dropped off at the highway turn-off and then walk the heavily potholed dirt road that leads 5km south of Ruta 45 into the ravine

The dry, dusty **Valle del Encanto** boasts one of Chile's densest collections of **petroglyphs** – images engraved on the surface of rocks – carved mainly by people of the El Molle

3

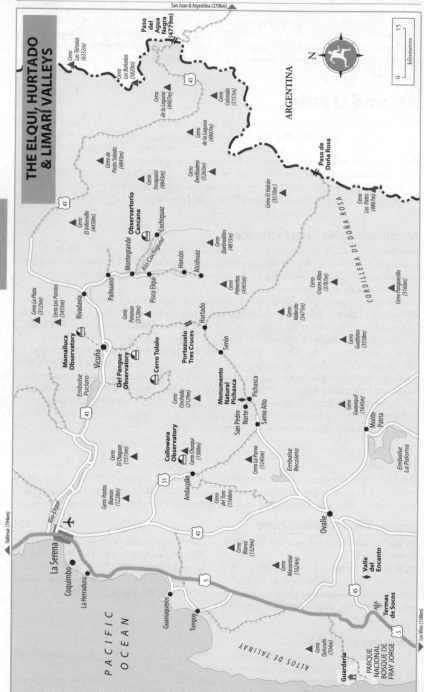

San Juan & Argentina (270km)

THE ELQUI, HURTADO & LIMARÍ VALLEYS

N

0   15
kilometres

ARGENTINA

Paso del Agua Negra (4779m)

Cerro Los Tórtolos (6332m)

Cerro Los Baños (5820m)

Cerro de la Laguna (4907m)

41

Cerro Colorado (5151m)

Cerro de la Laguna (4907m)

Paso de Doña Rosa

Cerro de Pasto Solado (4843m)

Cerro Incaguasi (4843m)

Cerro Desfiladero (5263m)

Cerro Los Patos (4867m)

Cerro El Volcán (3510m)

Cerro El Infiernillo (4450m)

41

Montegrande

Observatorio Cancana

Cochiguaz

Río Cochiguaz

Horcón

Altohuaz

Cerro Quebrositos (4815m)

CORDILLERA DE DOÑA ROSA

Cerro Cruces Altas (3787m)

Cerro Panguecillo (3160m)

Rivadavia

Paihuano

Pisco Elqui

Cerro La Plata (3125m)

Cerro Los Porotos (3455m)

Cerro Paranoa (3120m)

Hurtado

Cerro Patrentios (4365m)

Cerro Vallecito (3471m)

Cerro Guatitatos (3550m)

Mamalluca Observatory

Vicuña

Embalse Puclaro

41

Del Pangue Observatory

Cerro Tololo

Portezuelo Tres Cruces

Serón

Cerro Cinchado (2129m)

Monumento Natural Pichasca

Pichasca

Samo Alto

San Pedro Norte

Cerro Guayaquil (1645m)

Monte Patria

Collowara Observatory

Cerro El Chaguar (1515m)

Cerro Chanral (1300m)

Cerro La Parva (1245m)

Embalse Recoleta

Embalse La Paloma

Andacollo

Cerro Pastos Blancos (1228m)

51

Cerro del Toro (1568m)

Ovalle

Río Elqui

43

Cerro Blanco (1329m)

Cerro Manantial (1024m)

Valle del Encanto

45

Termas de Socos

La Serena

Coquimbo

La Herradura

Guanaqueros

Tongoy

5

5

Los Vilos (338km)

PACIFIC OCEAN

Vallenar (194km)

ALTOS DE TALINAY

Cerro Quiscudo (704m)

Guardería

PARQUE NACIONAL BOSQUE DE FRAY JORGE

culture (see page 465) between 100 and 600 AD. Most of the images are geometric motifs or stylized human outlines, including faces with large, wide eyes and elaborate headdresses. A few are very striking, while others are faint and difficult to make out; the best time to visit is between 2 and 3pm, when the outlines are at their sharpest, unobscured by shadows. Go prepared with a picnic.

Termas de Socos

Panamericana Norte km 370, 35km southwest of Ovalle • Baths CH$4500 (or free for hotel guests); pool reserved for guests of the hotel (see below) • ☎ 53 198 2505, ⓦ termasocos.cl • Twice daily bus services from Ovalle (30min) and La Serena (1hr 30min)

The thermal baths complex of **Termas de Socos** lies 2km down a track. It is notable for its 22°C (72°F) outdoor pool, surrounded by palm and eucalyptus trees, wicker armchairs and huge potted ferns, as well as cubicles containing private bathtubs where you can soak in warm spring water, supposedly rich in medicinal properties.

ACCOMMODATION	TERMAS DE SOCOS

Hotel Termas Socos Panamericana Norte km 370 ☎ 53 198 2505, Santiago ☎ 2 2236 3336, ⓦ termasocos.cl. This studiously rustic hotel offers comfortable rooms and easy access to the hot springs. In addition to the B&B rates listed here, there are excellent package deals that include three meals in the restaurant. **CH$67,600**

Parque Nacional Bosque de Fray Jorge

Panamericana RN-5, Autopista del Elqui • April–Nov Thurs–Sun 9am–4.30pm; Dec–March daily 9am–4pm • CH$6000 • ☎ 09 9346 2706, ⓦ www.conaf.cl • No public transport to the park; for taxis try Tacso in Ovalle (☎ 53 263 0989), or El Faro in La Serena (☎ 51 222 5060) or take a tour from La Serena (see page 133); if driving, allow about 1hr 30min from Ovalle, and 2hr from La Serena – the park is reached by a dirt road that branches west from the Panamericana 14km north of the junction with Ruta 45 to Ovalle; from the turn-off, it's 27km to the park entrance, where you pay your fee and register

A UNESCO World Biosphere Reserve since 1977, **Parque Nacional Bosque de Fray Jorge** sits on the Altos de Talinay, a range of steep coastal hills plunging into the Pacific some 80km west of Ovalle and 110km south of La Serena. It extends across 100 square kilometres, but its focal point, and what visitors come to see, is the small **cloudforest** perched on the highest part of the sierra, about 600m above sea level.

The extraordinary thing about this forest is how sharply it contrasts with its surroundings, indeed with everywhere else in the area. Its existence is the result of **camanchaca**, the thick coastal fog that rises from the ocean and condenses as it meets the land, supporting a cover of dense vegetation – fern, bracken and myrtle trees – normally found only in southern Chile. Close to the parking area, a 1km path dotted with information panels guides you through a poorly labelled range of plants and trees, and leads to the **forest** proper, where a slippery, wooden boardwalk takes you through tall trees dripping with moisture. The whole trail takes less than half an hour to walk. Three kilometres beyond the Conaf control there's a **picnic and barbecue** area, but note that camping is not allowed in the park.

Andacollo and around

Enfolded by rolling, sun-bleached hills midway between Ovalle and La Serena, **ANDACOLLO** is a tidy little town of small adobe houses grouped around a long main street. It lies along a side road which branches northeast from the Ruta 43, the most direct, scenic route between Ovalle and La Serena. An important gold- and copper-mining centre ever since the Inca mined its hills in the sixteenth century, Andacollo is best known as the home of the **Virgen de Andacollo**, a small wooden carving that draws more than one hundred thousand pilgrims to the town each year between

December 23 and 26 for the **Fiesta Grande de la Virgen**, four days of music and riotous dancing performed by costumed groups from all over Chile. Andacollo is also home to one of the country's newest **observatories**.

Basílica

Plaza Pedro Nolasco Videla • Daily 9am–6.30pm • Free, but donation expected

Andacolla has two temples erected in honour of the Virgin. Largest and grandest is the **Basílica**, which towers over Plaza Pedro Nolasco Videla, the main square, in breathtaking contrast to the small, simple scale of the rest of the town. Built from 1873 to 1893, almost entirely of wood in a Roman-Byzantine style, its pale, cream-coloured walls are topped by two colossal 50m towers and a stunning 45m dome. Inside, sunlight floods through the dome, falling onto huge wooden pillars painted to look like marble.

Templo Antiguo

Plaza Pedro Nolasco Videla • **Templo** Daily 9am–9pm • Free • **Museo del Peregrino** Mon–Fri 10am–1pm & 3–7pm, Sat & Sun 10am–7pm • Free, but donation expected

On the other side of the square from the Basílica stands the smaller, stone-built **Templo Antiguo**, dating from 1789 and restored in 2016. This is where the image of the Virgin de Andacollo (see above) stands for most of the year, perched on the main altar, awaiting the great festival when it's transported to the Basílica to receive pilgrims' petitions and prayers. Devotees of the Virgin have left an astonishing quantity of gifts here over the years, all displayed in the crypt of the Templo Antiguo as part of the **Museo del Peregrino**.

Collowara Observatory

7km northeast of Andacollo; ticket office Urmeneta 599 • Daily 9am–1pm & 2.30–8pm; tours (2hr) summer 9.30pm, 11pm & 12.30am, winter 7pm, 8.30pm & 10pm • CH$4500 • ☎ 51 243 1419, ⓦ collowara.cl • There is no organized transport to the observatory but a return taxi costs around CH$20,000; ask the driver to pick you up when the tour ends

For a celestial experience, the **Collowara Observatory** (named after the Aymara term for "land of the stars") lies near Andacollo, atop the 1300m Cerro Churqui. Built specifically for public use, like the observatory run by the Municipalidad of Vicuña (see page 143), this one also features a top-quality Smith-Cassegrain telescope. The **evening tours** start with a high-tech audiovisual talk (in Spanish and English) about the galaxy and other astronomical matters, followed by the opportunity to observe the heavens through one of the telescopes – unless, of course, you're unlucky enough to be here on a cloudy night. Reserve in advance.

ARRIVAL AND INFORMATION · ANDACOLLO

By bus/colectivo You can reach Andacollo by bus (every 2hr) or *colectivo* from La Serena (1hr) or Coquimbo (1hr 20min).

Tourist office Urmeneta 599 (Mon–Fri 9am–1.30pm & 2.30–5.30pm; ☎ 51 254 6494, ⓦ andacollochile.cl).

ACCOMMODATION AND EATING

Hostal Arcón de Oro Alfonso 652 ☎ 09 7750 9575, ⓦ hostalarcondeoro.cl. This family-run hotel has spick-and-span rooms with TVs and private bathrooms. There's even a special deal for wedding night guests, should the urge strike to tie the knot. **CH$42,000**

Sol de Andacollo Chepiquilla 90 ☎ 09 8815 8723. Come to *Sol de Andacollo* to feast on typical Chilean dishes cooked in solar-powered ovens (mains around CH$6000). It's worth the 10min walk out of town. Daily noon–5pm.

Coquimbo and the coast

West of Ovalle, the Panamericana turns towards the ocean and skirts a string of small resorts that provide a calmer and more attractive beach setting than the built-up coast at La Serena. Spread over a rocky peninsula studded with colourful houses, the busy port of **COQUIMBO** was established during colonial times to serve neighbouring La Serena and became Chile's main copper exporter during the nineteenth century. Despite its impressive setting, the town has a slightly rough-edged, down-at-heel air, but is useful as an inexpensive base from which to enjoy La Serena's beaches, or for visiting the nearby resorts of **Guanaqueros** – a fishing village 37km south with a sweeping beach – and **Tongoy**, 13km further south. A few blocks north of Coquimbo's main street, Avenida Costanera runs along the shore, past the large **port**, the **terminal pesquero**, and along to the lively **fish market**. This area makes for a pleasant oceanside stroll, accompanied by the strong whiff of fish.

Cruz del Tercer Milenio

3

Juan Pablo II s/n · Daily 8.30am–9pm · CH$2000 · ☎ 51 232 0125, ⓦ cruzdeltercermilenio.cl

From Coquimbo's main street, Aldunate, several stairways lead up to lookout points with sweeping views down to the port and across the bay; if you can't face the climb, take any *micro* marked "**Parte Alta**". The peak is crowned with a 93m-high, concrete Cruz del Tercer Milenio ("Third Millennium Cross"), ablaze at night, and claims to be the only major spiritual monument in the world built at the turn of the millennium (that's probably just as well, if they all looked like this one). The only conceivably redeeming feature is that you can enjoy superb panoramic views of the coast from up here. There is a religious museum on site and an elevator that whisks you up to the arms of the cross.

Mezquito Centro Mohammed VI

Los Granados 500, Cerro Dominante · April–Nov Mon–Fri 9am–12.30pm & 2.30–5pm; Dec–March daily 9am–12.30pm & 2.30–6.30pm · ☎ 51 231 0440, ⓦ centromohammed6.cl

A gift from the king of Morocco, the hilltop **Mezquito Centro Mohammed VI**, completed in 2007, is a replica of the Mezquita Kutubia in Marrakech. The mosque provides a curious religious counterbalance, competing for attention (and panoramic vistas) with the Cruz del Tercer Milenio. It also functions as a cultural centre and library, annd you can marvel at the ornate tile work inside.

Barrio Inglés

North of the central **Plaza de Armas**, and mostly on Aldunate, you'll find the **Barrio Inglés**, a district housing the city's finest properties, many carved in wood by English craftsmen during the prosperous mining era. The restored buildings are beautifully lit at night and often resurrected as bars, restaurants or arts venues; the **Centro Cultural Palace** at Alduante and Benevente is one such restored endeavour. Halfway along Aldunate is the pretty **Plaza Gabriela Mistral**, with its colourful artisan markets (Mon–Fri 11am–8pm).

Domo Cultura Ánimas

Plaza Gabriela Mistral · Mon–Fri 9am–5pm · Free · ☎ 51 231 7006

In the middle of Plaza Gabriela Mistral is the **Domo Cultura Ánimas**, a small archeological museum exhibiting a pre-Columbian sacrificial graveyard dating from between 900 and 1100AD, with the skeletal remains of humans and llamas.

By bus Coquimbo's busy bus terminal is on the main road into town, at Varela and Garriga. Nearly all the main north–south intercity buses stop here, as do local buses to coastal resorts including Tongoy (every 30min; 40min) and Guanaqueros (every 30min; 30min). Buses to La Serena (every 10min; 25min) can be picked up from the corner of Melgarejo and Alcalde.

By colectivo You can also reach the resorts, and Guayacán and La Herradura, by *colectivo* – they pick up behind the bus terminal and throughout the centre of town.

ACCOMMODATION

Hostal Nomade Regimiento Coquimbo 5 ☎51 275 1161, ⓦhostalnomadecoquimbo.cl. There's a haunted mansion feel to this rambling old HI-affiliated hostel in the building that once housed the French Consulate. Spacious, if austere, dorms are complemented by superb views over the bay, kitchen and large common area. Dorms CH$13,000, doubles CH$30,000

Hotel Iberia Lastra 400 ☎51 231 2141. Located just off Aldunate in Barrio Inglés, *Hotel Iberia* offers reasonable, sizeable rooms – with either shared or private bathrooms – in an attractive old building. Aim for a room with a balcony. CH$25,000

Hotel Lig Aldunate 1577 ☎51 231 1171, ⓔhotellig@ gmail.com. A satisfactory option just two blocks from the bus terminal, with 24 bright and comfortable rooms with TVs and private parking. CH$27,000

EATING AND DRINKING

For simple, cheap seafood lunches, go to the little **marisquerías** by the fish market; some have lovely water views. Plenty of lively **bars** are clustered around Barrio Inglés, often changing hands and names.

Dolce Gelato Aldunate 862 ☎51 232 6185. If the ice-cream stand out front doesn't tempt you in, then live music wafting from the terrace will. Filling and reasonably priced Italian food includes seafood lasagne. Ice cream from CH$1700. Mon–Fri 10am–11pm, Sat 11am–11pm.

Pub Blue Moon Sierra 351 ☎9 9820 0105. Decent mixology, mainly pisco based, and live music ensure Coquimbo's youth frequents this popular joint. Drinks from CH$2500. Daily 9pm–5am.

Guayacán

The southern shore of the peninsula, known as **Guayacán** – accessible by *colectivo* from Coquimbo – has a sandy beach, dominated at one end by a huge mechanized port used for exporting iron. While you're here, take a look at the tall steeple of the nearby **Iglesia de Guayacán**, a prefabricated steel church designed and built in 1888 by Alexandre Gustave Eiffel, of the tower fame, and the **British cemetery**, built in 1860 at the behest of the British Admiralty and full of the graves of young sailors etched with heart-rending inscriptions like "died falling from aloft" (if the gates are locked, ask in the caretaker's house).

La Herradura

Guayacán's beach curves south to that of **La Herradura**, which although long, golden and sandy is marred by its proximity to the Panamericana. That said, the night-time views across the bay to the tip of Coquimbo are superb, and if you want to spend a night or two at the seaside, La Herradura makes a convenient, cheaper alternative to La Serena's Avenida del Mar.

ARRIVAL AND DEPARTURE LA HERRADURA

By colectivo La Herradura is accessible by *colectivo* from Coquimbo.

ACCOMMODATION AND EATING

Bucanero Av La Marina 201 ☎51 265 5153. Perched on a jetty projecting into the ocean, this is one of La Herradura's poshest restaurants, offering good but overpriced seafood (mains around CH$9000–12,000) and great views across to Coquimbo (best at night). Daily noon–7pm.

Cabañas Bucanero Av La Marina 201 ☎ 51 226 5153. There are terrific views of the bay from these eleven fully equipped *cabañas* set around an inviting pool. Each has two bathrooms, a kitchen and TV. CH$50,000

Hotel La Herradura Av La Marina 200 ☎ 51 265 1647. Just off the beach, this family-friendly hotel offers decent rooms, with cable TV, at reasonable prices. No credit cards. CH$33,000

Tongoy

Some 30km south of Coquimbo, and 5km west of the Panamericana along a toll-paying side road, lies **TONGOY**, a popular family resort spread over a hilly peninsula. It has two attractive sandy **beaches**, the Playa Socos, north of the peninsula, and the enormous Playa Grande, stretching 14km south. While there are plenty of hotels, *cabañas* and restaurants, development has been low-key, and the place remains relatively unspoiled.

ARRIVAL AND DEPARTURE

TONGOY

By bus Regular services run from Coquimbo to Tongoy (every 30min; 40min), which can also be accessed from La Serena (hourly; 1hr) using Buses Serena Mar (☎ 51 232 3422) and Sol de Elqui (☎ 51 221 5946).

By colectivo Tongoy is also accessible by *colectivo* from Coquimbo.

ACCOMMODATION

Cabañas Tongoy Urmeneta Norte 237 ☎ 09 9956 2401, ⌨ cabañastongoy.cl. These rustic, wooden A-framed huts, close to the water's edge, come with kitchenettes and small gardens. There are also play areas for children, and private parking. CH70,000
Camping Ripipal Av Playa Grande ☎ 51 239 1192, ⌨ campingripipal.cl. On the beach 2km from the centre of town, this quiet, year-round campsite has good facilities:

showers, drinking water, washing machines, a shop, a children's play area and games room. CH$5000
Hotel Panorámico Av Mirador 745 ☎ 51 239 1944, ⌨ hotelpanoramico.cl. Set right on the water, this small, mid-range hotel has decent rooms and is crammed with 1950s items including a great TV set and a stand-up hairdryer. Marine spa treatments are on offer (CH$20,000). CH$45,000

EATING

La Picá del Veguita Av Playa Grande 3 ☎ 51 239 1475. A seaside restaurant with amicable service, a well-positioned terrace and giant portions of simple yet

honest food. Grilled fish and chips CH$7000. Mon–Thurs 10.30am–9.30pm, Fri & Sat 10.30am–10pm.

La Serena

Sitting by the mouth of the Río Elqui, 11km north of Coquimbo and 88km north of Ovalle, **LA SERENA** is for many visitors their first taste of northern Chile, after whizzing straight up from Santiago by road or air. Situated 2km inland from the northern sweep of the Bahía de Coquimbo, the **city centre** is an attractive mix of pale colonial-style houses, carefully restored churches and bustling crowds. Aside from the noteworthy **Museo Arqueológico**, La Serena's main appeal lies in just strolling the streets and squares, admiring the grand old houses, browsing the numerous craft markets, wandering in and out of its many stone churches and hanging out in the leafy, central **Plaza de Armas**.

In warmer months, hordes of Chilean tourists head for the 6km **beach**, just 3km away along **Avenida del Mar** – a rather charmless esplanade lined with oceanfront aparthotels and *cabañas* that are gloomily empty out of season. La Serena is also surrounded by some rewarding places to visit: the fine beaches at Tongoy (see above) and, above all, the glorious **Elqui Valley** (see page 140).

3

Brief history

La Serena is Chile's second-oldest city, with a history chequered by violence and drama. Founded by Pedro de Valdivia in 1544 as a staging post on the way to Peru, it got off to an unpromising start when it was completely destroyed in an **attack by native groups** four years later. Undeterred, Valdivia founded the city in a new location the following year, but La Serena continued to lead a precarious existence, subjected to frequent and often violent raids by pirates, many of them British.

Happier times arrived in the nineteenth century, when the discovery of large silver deposits at Arqueros, just north of La Serena, marked the beginning of the region's great **silver boom**. These heady days saw the erection of some of the city's finest mansions and churches, as the mining magnates competed in their efforts to dazzle with their wealth.

In the 1940s, **Gabriel González Videla**, president of Chile and a local Serenense, instituted his "**Plan Serena**", through which the city developed its signature architectural style. One key element of Videla's urban remodelling scheme was the vigorous promotion of the Spanish colonial style, with facades restored or rebuilt on existing structures and strict stylistic controls imposed on new ones. Unimaginative and inflexible though some claimed these measures to be, the results are undeniably

3

DOWNTOWN LA SERENA

Vallenas (196km) & Copiapó (337km)

Río Elqui

0   100
metres

ACCOMMODATION
Aji Verde Hostel	2
Hostal El Punto	8
Hostal Family Home	9
Hostal Maria Casa	10
Hotel del Cid	1
Hotel Francisco de Aguirre	4
Hotel Londres	3
Hotel Pacífico	5
El Huerto	7
Mar de Ensueño	6

DRINKING & NIGHTLIFE
| La Biblioteca | 2 |
| Café Centenario | 1 |

EATING
La Casa del Guatón	1
Daniella II	4
Govinda's	2
La Mia Pizza	3

Iglesia Santa Inés

ALMAGRO

ALMAGRO

COLÓN

COLÓN

CIENFUEGOS

RENGIFO

BRASIL

Buses to Valle Elqui

ZORRILLA

Museo Histórico Casa Gabriel González Videla

BRASIL

BALMACEDA

O'HIGGINS

La Recova

CANTOURNET

VICUÑA

PRAT

Cambios Afex

Iglesia San Agustín

GANDARILLAS

Plaza de Armas

Iglesia Catedral

LOS CARRERA

Scotiabank

Museo Arqueológico

CORDOVEZ

MATTA

Teatro Centenario

Parque Japonés Kokoro No Niwa

Iglesia Santo Domingo

Iglesia de San Francisco/ Museo de Arte Religioso

LAS CASAS

AV JUAN BOHON (PANAMERICANA)

DE LA BARRA

CIENFUEGOS

VICUÑA

LAUTARO

PABLO MUÑOZ

Colectivos to Elqui Valley Ovalle and Andacollo

DOMEYKO

BENAVENTE

INFANTE

FRANCISCO DE AGUIRRE

COLO COLO

Talinay Chile

N

Buses to Elqui Valley (100m) & Aeropuerto La Florida (5km)

9, 6, 7 & Avenida del Mar

JUAN DE DIOS PEÑI

Eco Turismo

JUAN DE DIOS PEÑI

P PABLO MUÑOZ

ANFIÓN MUÑOZ

9, 10, Cinemark Mall Plaza (100m) & Bus terminal (500m)

LA SERENA'S CHURCHES

Including Iglesia Catedral and Iglesia Santo Domingo on the Plaza de Armas, a remarkable 29 **churches** dot La Serena, lending an almost fairy-tale look to the city. This proliferation of places of worship dates from the earliest days of the city, when all the religious orders established bases to provide shelter for their clergy's frequent journeys between Santiago and Lima (the viceregal capital). Nearly all the churches are built of stone, which is unusual for Chile, and all are in mint condition.

Standing at the corner of Balmaceda and de la Barra, **Iglesia de San Francisco** (closed Mon) is one of La Serena's oldest churches, though the date of its construction is unknown, as the city archives were burnt in the pirate Sharp's raid of 1680. Its huge walls are 1m thick, covered in a stone facade carved in fanciful Baroque designs. Inside, the **Museo de Arte Religioso** (Tues & Thurs 10am–12.30pm; donation welcome) contains a small but impressive collection of religious sculpture and paintings from the colonial period.

Beautiful for its very plainness, the 1755 **Iglesia San Agustín**, on the corner of Cienfuegos and Cantournet, was originally the Jesuit church but was taken over by the Augustinians after the Jesuits were expelled from Chile in 1767. Its honey-toned stone walls were badly damaged in the 1975 earthquake, but have been skilfully restored. On the northern edge of town, overlooking the banks of the Río Elqui, the seventeenth-century **Iglesia Santa Inés** was constructed on the site of a rudimentary chapel erected by the first colonists and its thick white adobe walls recall the Andean churches of the northern altiplano.

pleasing, and La Serena boasts an architectural harmony and beauty noticeably lacking in most Chilean cities.

Iglesia Catedral

East side of Plaza de Armas • Mon–Fri 9.30am–1pm & 3.30–7pm • Free

Grand and dominating, the pale walls of the **Iglesia Catedral** date from 1844, when the previous church on the site was finally pulled down because of the damage wrought by the 1796 earthquake. Inside, among its more curious features are the wooden pillars disguised to look like stone. Just off the opposite side of the square, on Cordovez, the pretty **Iglesia Santo Domingo** was first built in 1673 and then again in 1755, after it was sacked by the pirate Sharp.

Museo Histórico Casa Gabriel González Videla

Southwest corner of the Plaza de Armas • Mon–Fri 10am–6pm, Sat 10am–1pm • Free • ☎ 51 220 6797, ⊕ museohistoricolaserena.cl

This two-storey adobe house was, from 1927 to 1977, home to Chile's erstwhile president, Gabriel González Videla, best known for outlawing the Communist party after using its support to gain power in 1946. Inside, the small **Museo Histórico Casa Gabriel González Videla** has an eclectic display of photos, objects, documents and paintings relating to the president's life and works, along with a section on regional history; the occasional temporary art exhibitions are often better than the permanent display.

Museo Arqueológico

Corner of Cordovez and Cienfuegos • Tues–Fri 9.30am–5.50pm, Sat 10am–1pm & 4–7pm, Sun 10am–1pm • Free • ☎ 51 222 4492

Entered through an imposing nineteenth-century portico, La Serena's **Museo Arqueológico** – overhauled substantially in 2017 – boasts two outstanding treasures, though most of the displays could do with improving. The first of these is its large collection of **Diaguita pottery**, considered to be among the most beautiful pre-Columbian ceramics in South America. The terracotta pieces, dating from around 1000 to 1500 AD, are covered in intricate geometric designs painted in black and

3

OBSERVATORIES IN THE LA SERENA REGION

Thanks to the exceptional transparency of its skies, northern Chile is home to the largest concentration of astronomical **observatories** in the world. The region around La Serena, in particular, has been chosen by a number of international astronomical research institutions as the site of their telescopes, housed in white, futuristic domes that loom over the valleys from their hilltop locations. Among the research organizations that own the observatories are North American and European groups that need a base in the southern hemisphere (about a third of the sky seen here is never visible in the northern hemisphere).

Some observatories offer guided tours, including the impressive **Cerro Tololo Inter-American Observatory**, whose 4m telescope was the strongest in the southern hemisphere until it was overtaken by Cerro Paranal's Very Large Telescope, the most powerful in the world, located near Antofagasta (see page 169). All the tours listed below take place during the day and are free of charge but are strictly no-touching; a more hands-on night-time experience is provided by the small but user-friendly observatory on **Cerro Mamalluca** (see page 143), 9km north of Vicuña, the newer Del Pangue observatory 17km south of Vicuña (see page 143) and the **Collowara** observatory outside Andacollo (see page 130).

Las Campanas 155km northeast of La Serena ☎51 220 7301, ⊛lco.cl. The Carnegie Institute's observatory contains four telescopes, with two 6.5m telescopes under construction as part of its Magellan Project. Contact the offices in La Serena to make reservations; they're next to Cerro Tololo's offices on Colina El Pino. Sat 2.30–5.30pm.

Tololo 88km east of La Serena, reached by a side road branching south of the Elqui Valley road ☎51 220 5200, ⊛www.ctio.noao.edu. Tours need to be booked several days in advance; you'll need to collect your visitor's permit from the observatory's offices in La Serena (up the hill behind the university, at Colina El Pino) the day before the tour. Sat 9.15am–noon & 1.15–4pm.

La Silla 150km northeast of La Serena, reached by a side road branching east from the Panamericana ☎51 227 2601, ⊛eso.org. The site of the European Southern Observatory's fourteen telescopes, including two 3.6m optical reflectors. Book in advance through the observatory's Santiago offices or the La Serena office near the airport at Panorámica 4461. Jan–May & Aug–Dec Sat 2–4pm.

white and, in the later phases, red. Starting with simple bowls and dishes made for domestic use, the Diaguita went on to produce elaborately shaped ceremonial pots and jars, often in the form of humans or animals, or sometimes both, such as the famous *jarros patos*, or "duck jars", moulded in the form of a duck's body with a human head.

The moai

The museum's other gem is the giant stone statue, or **moai**, from Easter Island, "donated" to La Serena at the behest of President González Videla in 1952. Until the mid 1990s, it stood in a park on Avenida Colo Colo, covered in graffiti and urinated on by drunks. Then, as part of an exhibition of Easter Island art in 1996, it travelled to Barcelona, where it was accidentally decapitated. Tragedy turned to good fortune, however, when the insurance money paid for plastic surgery as well a brand-new *sala* to be built for the statue in the archeological museum.

La Recova

Corner of Cienfuegos and Cantournet • Daily 10am–7pm

Of La Serena's numerous **craft markets**, the biggest and best is the bustling **La Recova**, occupying two large patios inside an arcaded building opposite the Iglesia San Agustín. The quality of the merchandise is decent, and goods include finely worked objects in *combabalita* (a locally mined marble), lapis lazuli jewellery, alpaca sweaters and candied papaya.

Parque Japonés Kokoro No Niwa

Pedro Pablo Muñoz and Eduardo de la Barra • Tues–Sun 10am–6pm • CH$1000

Backing onto the Panamericana, two blocks west of the Plaza de Armas, the **Parque Japonés Kokoro No Niwa**, whose Japanese name means "Garden of the Heart", is an oasis of perfectly manicured lawns, ponds awash with water lilies, ice-white geese and little Japanese bridges and pagodas. Unfortunately, the sense of peace and tranquillity it creates is undermined by the din of the highway.

Avenida del Mar

No bus or colectivo service along Av del Mar; take a micro headed for Coquimbo from almost any street corner (if in doubt, go to Av Francisco de Aguirre) and get off on the Panamericana at Cuatro Esquinas or Peñuelas (6km from the city), both a short walk from the beach

Stretching 6km round the rim of a wide, horseshoe bay 2km west of the city, **Avenida del Mar** is a staid collection of glitzy hotels, tourist complexes and *cabañas* that bulge with visitors for two months of the year and are otherwise empty. In January and February hundreds of cars inch their way up and down the avenue, bumper to bumper, and mostly Chilean tourists pile onto the sandy beaches, which are clean but spoiled by the horrific high-rise backdrop.

ARRIVAL AND DEPARTURE
LA SERENA

By plane Aeropuerto La Florida (☎51 227 0191), 5km east of the city, is served by taxis (CH$5000) and shared transfers (CH$3000), as well as *micros*. Airlines incude LATAM, Balmaceda 406 (☎600 526 2000, ⓦlatam.com) and Sky Airline, Eduardo de la Barra 495 (☎51 221 8372, ⓦwww.skyairline.com).

Destinations Antofagasta (2 daily; 1hr 25min); Santiago (6 daily; 1hr).

By bus Intercity buses operate from La Serena's large bus terminal on El Santo, a 15min walk southwest of the central plaza. There's no direct bus from the terminal into town, but there are plenty of taxis, charging about CH$3000. Buses for the Elqui Valley depart every 30min and also stop southeast of the centre at the Plaza de Abastos, on Calle Esmeralda (just south of Colo Colo). To get to Tongoy, take a Serenamar or Sol de Elqui bus from the terminal.

Destinations Andacollo (every 2hr; 1hr); Antofagasta (20 daily; 12hr); Arica (5 daily; 24hr); Calama (11 daily; 15hr); Chañaral (11 daily; 7hr); Copiapó (every 30min–1hr;

5hr); Horcón (3 daily; 2hr 45min); Iquique (8 daily; 18hr); Montegrande (every 30min–1hr; 1hr 50min); Ovalle (every 15min; 1hr 20min); Pisco Elqui (every 30min; 2hr); Santiago (every 30min; 7hr); Vallenar (every 30min–1hr; 2hr 45min); Tongoy (hourly; 1hr); Valparaíso (6 daily; 5hr); Vicuña (every 30min–1hr; 1hr).

By micro The coastal resorts of Tongoy and La Herradura are more easily reached from Coquimbo – to get there, take a *micro* (marked "Coquimbo Directo 1") from Av Francisco de Aguirre or calles Brasil, Infante or Matta. Alternatively, you can flag down a *micro* from the Panamericana, a 5min walk west.

By colectivo Two *colectivo* services (look for the yellow taxis) from La Serena operate from Calle Domeyko one block south of Iglesia San Francisco: Anserco, at no. 530 (☎51 221 7567), goes to Andacollo, Vicuña and Ovalle; Tasco, at no. 575 (☎51 222 4517), goes to Vicuña, Montegrande and Pisco Elqui. The service is slightly more expensive than the bus.

GETTING AROUND

Car rental In addition to the airport, there are many outlets on Av Francisco de Aguirre, including Avis at no. 063 (☎51 254 5300, ⓦavis.cl); Budget at no. 015 (☎51 221 8272, ⓦbudget.cl); Econorent at no. 0135 (☎51 222

0113, ⓦeconorent.cl); and Hertz at no. 0225 (☎51 222 6171, ⓦhertz.cl).

Taxis 24hr radio taxis (☎51 221 2122).

INFORMATION AND TOURS

Tourist office There is a helpful and friendly Sernatur office on the west side of the Plaza de Armas at Matta 461 (Jan, Feb & Dec daily 9am–8pm; March–Nov Mon–Fri 9am–6pm, Sat 10am–4pm; ☎51 222 5199).

Tours The two most popular day tours from La Serena are to the Elqui Valley (also easily reached on public transport)

and to the cloudforest reserve at Parque Nacional Bosque de Fray Jorge (see page 129), about 2hr south of the city and not served by public transport. Other favourite destinations include night tours to the Cerro Mamalluca observatory near Vicuña (see page 143); the ancient petroglyph site of the Valle del Encanto, near Ovalle (see page 127); Monumento Natural Pichasca, where you'll find the remains of a "fossilized wood" (see page 127); and the Reserva Nacional Pinguino de Humboldt, a penguin and dolphin sanctuary 120km north of La Serena that is not served by public transport (see page 150). Most tours cost from CH$20,000–30,000/person. Try Eco Turismo, Andres Bello 937 (☎ 51 221 8970, ⓦ ecoturismolaserena.cl) or Ovi Travel, Vicuña 628 (☎ 51 234 0540, ⓦ ovitravel.cl).

ACCOMMODATION

You'll find a large choice of **budget** accommodation and mid- to upscale options in the centre, while **Avenida del Mar**, 3km from town, is lined with overpriced beachside *cabañas* and hotels.

HOTELS

Hostal Family Home Av El Santo 1056 ☎ 51 221 2099, ⓦ familyhome.cl; map p.134. Good-value hostel that lives up to its name and is conveniently located close to the bus terminal (albeit on a busy road), with singles, doubles and triples (some en suite), plus use of a kitchen. CH$28,000

Hotel del Cid O'Higgins 138 ☎ 51 221 2692, ⓦ hoteldelcid.cl; map p.134. Beyond the drab exterior is a charming hotel run by a welcoming Scottish/Chilean couple, with a selection of spotless and comfortable rooms set around a flower-filled terrace. Secure parking. CH$52,000

Hotel Francisco de Aguirre Cordovez 210 ☎ 51 222 2991, ⓦ hotelfranciscodeaguirre.com; map p.134. One of La Serena's smartest hotels, a few steps away from the plaza, *Francisco de Aguirre* has somewhat overpriced but spacious rooms in a handsome old three-storey building, as well as a restaurant with toothsome food. CH$90,000

Hotel Londres Cordovez 550 ☎ 51 221 9066, ⓦ hotellondres.cl; map p.134. This central hotel has clean and tidy rooms, some with private bathrooms and others with just a washbasin. Parking CH$2000. CH$30,000

Hotel Pacífico Av de la Barra 252 ☎ 51 222 5674, ⓦ hotelpacifico.cl; map p.134. Located three blocks from the Plaza de Armas, this long-standing, rambling hotel offers basic but clean and comfortable rooms (with shared or private bathrooms) and a friendly welcome. Good-value singles, too. CH$30,000

Mar de Ensueño Av del Mar 900 ☎ 51 222 2381, ⓦ hotelmarensueno.com; map p.134. If you're in La Serena in summer with the kids in tow, this beachside complex with ocean-facing rooms and fully equipped *cabañas* is a good bet. Facilities include a swimming pool, gym, bicycles for guest use and a games room. Doubles CH$95,000, *cabañas* CH$209,000

HOSTELS

Ají Verde Hostel Vicuña 415 ☎ 51 248 9016, ⓦ ajiverdehostel.cl; map p.134. A fun atmosphere pervades this central, HI-affiliated hostel with young staff, a roof terrace, kitchen and plenty of common areas for connecting with fellow travellers. A good fall-back if *Hostal El Punto* (see below) is full. Dorms CH$9000, doubles CH$33,000

★ **Hostal El Punto** Andres Bello 979 ☎ 51 222 8474, ⓦ hostalelpunto.cl; map p.134. Charming, German-run hostel with spacious, impeccably clean rooms (some with private bath) and one dorm. Mosaic-tiled courtyards, a restaurant and big breakfasts with home-made jam and goat's cheese ensure this place books up fast. There's also parking and a kitchen. Dorms CH$10,000, doubles CH$21,000

Hostal Maria Casa Las Rojas 18 ☎ 51 222 9282, ⓦ hostalmariacasa.cl; map p.134. This friendly, family-run option is situated a block from the bus terminal with dorms and basic rooms off a lovely garden. There's a communal kitchen, book exchange and bikes to rent. Dorms CH$12,000, doubles CH$25,000

CAMPSITE

El Huerto Parcela 66, Peñuelas ☎ 51 231 2531, ⓦ turismoelhuerto.cl; map p.134. Lovely, grassy campsite down at the quieter end of the beach, halfway between La Serena and Coquimbo. Good facilities and lots of shade. Buses between La Serena and Coquimbo stop nearby. CH$25,000

EATING

The restaurants on **Avenida del Mar** are overpriced but have fine sea views, while those downtown are better value yet unexceptional. The **La Recova market** has dozens of good-value *marisquerías* (seafood restaurants) on the upper gallery of the handicrafts market, making it a perfect place for lunch. For the freshest **seafood** around, head to the Sector de Pescadores at Playa Peñuelas, 6km along the coast between La Serena and Coquimbo.

La Casa del Guatón Brasil 750 ☎ 51 221 1519; map p.134. Lively, friendly and intimate, this colonial-style restaurant serves the best *parrilladas* (from CH$19,000) in La Serena, as well as more unusual dishes such as fried conger eel and Chiloé-style shellfish (mains CH$6000–11,000). Mon–Sat 12.30pm–12.30am, Sun 1–6pm.

3

Daniella II Av Francisco de Aguirre 335 ☎ 51 222 7537; map p.134. Typical Chilean restaurant with friendly service and a traditional menu (set price CH$3000) of local fish and meat dishes like *pastel de jaiba* (a crab and corn pie) and *lomo a lo pobre* (steak with chips, onions and fried egg). Daily 10am–6pm.

Govinda's Lautaro 841 ☎ 51 222 4289; map p.134. A lunchtime vegetarian spot run by Hare Krishnas, serving wholegrain bread, fresh and healthy Italian- and Indian-inspired dishes (around CH$3000–6000) and fragrant teas. Yoga and cookery classes are available. Mon–Fri 1–3pm.

La Mia Pizza Av del Mar 2100 ☎ 51 221 2232; map p.134. Locals pile into this beachside restaurant for its crisp, thin-crust pizzas loaded with fresh toppings (from CH$5000). The pastas, steaks and fish dishes are also recommended. Mon–Sat 12.30pm–midnight, Sun 12.30–4.30pm.

DRINKING AND NIGHTLIFE

The best **nightlife** is concentrated on O'Higgins between avenidas Francisco de Aguirre and de la Barra, where there are many student bars. The pubs and discos by the beach are more seasonal, reaching their heady zenith in January and February.

La Biblioteca O'Higgins and Av Francisco de Aguirre ☎ 09 8139 0449; map p.134. "The Library" is anything but: students congregate around small wooden tables, feeding the jukebox while downing *terremoto* cocktails (sweet white wine, pineapple ice cream and Amaretto). Drinks from CH$2000. Daily 2.30pm–3am.

Café Centenario Cordovez 391; map p.134. Lavazza coffee (CH$1500–3000), regional wines and local beer are served in this chic corner spot on the southeast corner of Plaza de Armas. Try the house speciality, *café camanchaca* – a mix of pisco, espresso and milk. Mon–Fri 8am–8pm.

ENTERTAINMENT

Cinemark Mall Plaza Av Albert Solari 1400 ☎ 51 247 0310, ⓦ cinemark.cl. This six-screen cinema near the bus terminal shows blockbuster films and also hosts themed festivals.

Teatro Centenario Cordoves 391 ☎ 51 221 2659, ⓦ teatrocentenario.blogspot.com. One of the best jazz venues in Chile, located in a remodelled theatre in the city's old cinema. Local and international acts perform to a head-nodding, wine-sipping crowd. Jan, Feb & Dec Sat 7/8pm–late; March–Nov every second Sat 7/8pm–late.

Elqui Valley

Quiet, rural and extremely beautiful, the **Elqui Valley** unfolds east from La Serena and into the Andes. Irrigated by canals fed by the Puclara and La Laguna dams, the valley floor is given over entirely to cultivation – of papayas, custard apples (*chirimoyas*), oranges, avocados and, most famously, the vast expanses of grape vines grown to produce **pisco**. It's the fluorescent green of these Muscat vines that makes the valley so stunning, forming a spectacular contrast with the charred, brown hills that rise on either side.

Some 60km east of La Serena, appealing little **Vicuña** is the main town and transport hub of the valley. East from here, the valley gets higher and narrower and is dotted with tiny villages like **Montegrande** and the odd pisco distillery. **Pisco Elqui**, 105km east of La Serena, is a pretty village that makes a great place to unwind for a few days. If you really want to get away from it all, head for one of the rustic *cabañas* dotted along the banks of the **Río Cochiguaz**, which forks east of the main valley at Montegrande, or delve beyond Pisco Elqui into the farthest reaches of the Elqui Valley itself. Buses and a paved road will get you all the way to **Horcón** but not to the farthest village of all, **Alcohuaz**.

GETTING AROUND
ELQUI VALLEY

By bus Many tour companies in La Serena offer day-trips to the Elqui Valley, but it's hardly worth taking a tour, as public transport up and down the valley is so frequent and cheap. If you're here in Jan or Feb, it might be worth investing in a 24hr day pass (available at the bus station), so that you can hop on and off any bus plying the valley as many times as you choose. The two main bus companies are Sol de Elqui (☎ 51 221 5946) and Via Elqui (☎ 51 221 1707).

Vicuña

An hour by bus inland from La Serena, **VICUÑA** is a neat and tidy agricultural town ringed by mountains and laid out around a large, luxuriantly landscaped square. It's a pleasant, easy-going place with a few low-key attractions, a good choice of places to stay and eat, a couple of **pisco distilleries** just outside town and two visitor-friendly **observatories** on its doorstep. If you're looking to stretch your legs, you can get panoramic views of the town and entire Elqui Valley from the top of **Cerro de la Virgen**, a thirty-minute walk northeast of the centre.

Plaza de Armas

Life revolves firmly around the central **Plaza de Armas**, which has at its centre a huge stone replica of the **death mask** of Nobel Prize-winning poet **Gabriela Mistral**, the Elqui Valley's most famous daughter. On the square's northwest corner stands the **Iglesia de la Inmaculada Concepción**, topped by an impressive wooden tower built in 1909 – take a look inside at its vaulted polychrome ceiling, painted with delicate religious images and supported by immense wooden columns. Right next door, the eccentric **Torre Bauer** is a bright red, mock-medieval tower prefabricated in Germany in 1905 and brought to Vicuña on the instructions of the town's German-born mayor, Adolfo Bauer.

Museo Entomológico

Chacabuco 334, on the south side of the Plaza de Armas • Mon–Fri 10.30am–1.30pm & 3.30–7pm, Sat & Sun 10.30am–7pm • Free • ☎ 09 9323 7177

The **Museo Entomológico** hoards a fascinating collection of creepy-crawlies from Chile, the Amazon, Africa and Asia, including hairy spiders and vicious-looking millipedes, plus exotic butterflies and shells. Hopefully this is the closest you'll get to two of Chile's deadliest critters: the *araña del rincón* (recluse spider) and the blood-sucking *vinchuca*, which spreads Chagas disease.

Museo Gabriela Mistral

Calle Gabriela Mistral 759 • Museum Jan & Feb Mon–Fri 10am–7pm, Sat & Sun 10.30am–8pm; March–Dec Mon–Fri 10am–5.45pm, Sat 10.30am–6pm, Sun 10am–1pm; Children's Library Mon–Fri 10am–5.45pm • Free • ☎ 51 241 1233, ⓦ mgmistral.cl

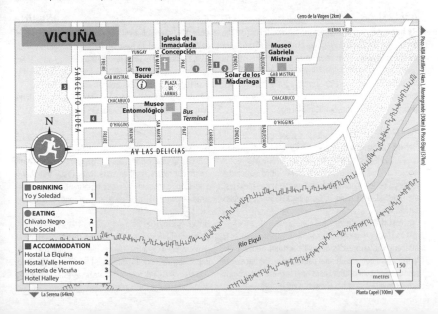

Four blocks east of the square, the **Museo Gabriela Mistral** displays photos, prizes, articles and personal objects bequeathed to the city by the poet, along with panels giving an account of her life and works. The museum itself is a striking building, taking its inspiration from the natural elements of Mistral's beloved Elqui Valley – stone, light, water and mountains. Also on the grounds is a **children's library** housing a four-thousand-strong collection of books. Next door stands the modest house where Mistral was born in 1889.

Solar de los Madariaga

Calle Gabriela Mistral 683 • Daily 11am–12.30pm & 4–6pm • ☎ 51 241 1220 • CH$1500

A few steps from the Museo Gabriela Mistral is the **Solar de los Madariaga**, a 140-year old colonial-style adobe house that has been preserved and turned into a museum, displaying a modest collection of nineteenth-century furniture and clothes.

Planta Capel

Camino Peralillo, 2km southeast of Vicuña • Guided tours (various lengths) every 30min 10am–4.30pm • CH$4000–15,000 • ☎ 51 255 4337, ⓦ piscocapel.cl

Just out of town, across the bridge by the filling station, you'll find the **Planta Capel**, the largest **pisco distillery** in the Elqui Valley. It offers a range of guided tours in English and Spanish, with tastings, visits to the small onsite museum and (of course) the chance to buy bottles and souvenirs at the end.

Pisco ABA distillery

Ruta 41 Km 66, 8km east of Vicuña • Tours (45min) spring & summer daily 10am–7pm, though sometimes closes early; call ahead • Free • ☎ 51 241 1039, ⓦ piscoaba.cl

A family-owned boutique distillery in the village of El Arenal, the **Pisco ABA distillery** is a short drive from Vicuña. It produces around sixty thousand bottles a year, including the ABA and Fuegos piscos as well as a creamy mango sour cocktail. Tours include tastings, a glimpse of its bucolic 148-acre farm where Muscat grapes are hand-picked, and a visit to production facilities, where distillation takes place in huge copper stills. Call ahead for a tour in English (also free).

ARRIVAL AND INFORMATION

VICUÑA

By bus Buses drop passengers off at the terminal on the corner of O'Higgins and Prat, one block south of the Plaza de Armas. Santiago services are operated by Expreso Norte (☎ 51 254 6890) and Pullman Buses (☎ 51 241 1466). Destinations La Serena (every 30min–1hr; 1hr); Montegrande (every 30min–1hr; 50min), Pisco Elqui (every 30min–1hr; 1hr); Santiago (4 daily; 7hr).

Colectivos Taxi *colectivos* leave from the bus terminal for La Serena and while their set fares are marginally more than the bus, the journey takes less time. They also service the immediate area, and for local journeys you'll need to negotiate a price with the driver.

Tourist office Northwest corner of the plaza, beneath the Torre Bauer (daily 9am–5.30pm; ☎ 51 267 0308).

ACCOMMODATION

Hostal La Elquina O'Higgins 65 ☎ 51 241 1317; map p.141. Dowdy rooms with and without private bathrooms are set around a breezy, central flower-filled patio; the garden is perfect for camping. Kitchen access and breakfast are included, as is parking. Camping CH$5000, doubles CH$25,000,

★ **Hostal Valle Hermoso** Gabriela Mistral 706 ☎ 51 241 1206, ⓦ hostalvallehermoso.com; map p.141. Motherly Cecilia presides over this restored century-old house with a gorgeous central patio. Minimalist but sweet rooms have comfortable beds and private bathrooms complete with piping-hot showers. CH$36,000

Hostería de Vicuña Sargento Aldea 101 ☎ 51 241 1301, ⓦ hosteriavicuna.cl; map p.141. Slightly overpriced rooms – all en suite, with TVs – but there's a fabulous pool and a decent restaurant, which serves unadventurous if good-quality meat and fish dishes. CH$50,000

Hotel Halley Gabriela Mistral 542 ☎ 51 241 2070, ⓦ turismohalley.cl; map p.141. This central hotel comes recommended, offering large, albeit somewhat dark, impeccably decorated rooms in a colonial-style building. There are pleasant communal areas, a restaurant and a swimming pool in the garden. CH$39,000

EATING

Chivato Negro Gabriela Mistral 565 ☎09 7862 9430, ⍟cafeovejanegra.com; map p.141. Located in a 1920s-built heritage property in the Mistraliano neighbourhood, this literary-themed café offers abundant sandwiches, veggie quiches and salads. Three-course lunch CH$4900. Daily 9am–10pm.

Club Social Gabriel Mistral 445 ☎51 241 1853; map p.141. The atmosphere is always convivial inside this grand, sprawling colonial building, popular for its typical Chilean dishes (mains CH$5500–10,000), seafood pancakes and gut-busting *parrilladas* to share between two (or more). Mon–Sat 10am–midnight.

DRINKING

Keep an eye out for beers from the award-winning Elqui Valley brewery, **Guayacán**.

Yo y Soledad Carrera 320 ☎51 241 9002; map p.141. If you're returning from an observatory tour and have the late-night munchies, you'll find this lively bar-restaurant

(drinks from CH$2000) at your service. Mon–Thurs noon–1am, Fri–Sun 11am–3am.

Cerro Mamalluca observatory

3

9km northeast of Vicuña; office Gabriela Mistral 260, Vicuña • Office Mon–Fri 9am–last tour; tours (2hr) May–Sept 6.30pm & 8.30pm; Oct–April 8.30pm, 10.30pm & 12.30am • CH$7000 • ☎51 267 0331 • Assemble 30min before your slot at the office, from where transport is provided (CH$3000 return); reservations essential; if you have your own transport you must still report to the office, to confirm and pay, and to follow the minibus in a convoy

The **Cerro Mamalluca observatory**, built specifically for public use, is run by the Municipalidad de Vicuña and features a 30cm Smith-Cassegrain telescope donated by the Cerro Tololo team. The **evening tours** start with a high-tech audiovisual talk on the history of the universe, and end with the chance to look through the telescope. If you're lucky, you might see a dazzling display of stars, planets, galaxies, nebulas and clusters, including Jupiter, Saturn's rings, the Orion nebula, the Andromeda galaxy and Sirius. These tours are aimed at beginners, but with a few weeks' notice serious astronomers can arrange in-depth, small-group sessions.

Del Pangue Observatory

17km south of Vicuña; office San Martín 233, Vicuña • Office daily 10am–7pm; tours (2hr) Jan & Feb 9pm & 11pm; June–Aug 6pm; rest of year 8pm; no tours five days around the full moon; tour times often change depending on planet positions; group tours are limited to ten people • CH$24,000 • ☎51 241 2584, ⍟observatoriodelpangue.blogspot.com • Assemble 30min before the tour at the Vicuña office, from where you must take the transport provided (free); private vehicles are not allowed

With a spectacular mountaintop setting not far from the Tololo scientific observatory, **Del Pangue Observatory** offers an intimate and personalized star-gazing experience specifically designed for amateur astronomers. Tours are conducted by bona fide astronomers, and Del Pangue's state-of-the-art 63cm Obsession telescope is light years ahead of other public observatories. Two telescopes and a variety of adjustable eyepieces ensure you get a stunning view of the moon's craters, distant galaxies and blazing stars.

English-, Spanish- and French-speaking astronomers deliver sophisticated yet down-to-earth celestial commentary and can also answer questions on life, the universe and everything in between. Wear warm clothes; it gets cold.

Montegrande

The picturesque village of **MONTEGRANDE**, 34km east of Vicuña (if you're driving, take the right turn for Paihuano at Rivadavia), features a pretty church whose late-nineteenth-century wooden belfry looms over a surprisingly large square. The childhood home of **Gabriela Mistral** (see page 144), Montegrande assiduously devotes itself to preserving her memory: her profile has been outlined in white stones on the valley wall opposite the plaza, and the school where she lived with, and was taught by,

3

GABRIELA MISTRAL

Possibly even more than its pisco (see page 145), the Elqui Valley's greatest source of pride is **Gabriela Mistral**, born in Vicuña in 1889 and, in 1945, the first Latin American to be awarded the **Nobel Prize for Literature**. A schoolmistress, a confirmed spinster and a deeply religious woman, Mistral wrote poetry with an aching sensitivity, and her much romanticized life was punctuated with tragedy.

Lucila Godoy de Alcayaga, as she was christened, was just 3 years old when her father abandoned the family, the first of several losses in her life. Her older sister, Emiliana, supported her and her mother, and for the next eight years the three of them lived in the schoolhouse in the village of **Montegrande**, where Emiliana worked as a teacher. At the age of 14, she started work herself as an assistant schoolteacher, near La Serena, where she took her first steps into the world of literature, publishing several pieces in the local newspaper under the pseudonyms "Alguien" ("Someone"), "Soledad" ("Solitude") and "Alma" ("Soul"). When she was 20, railway worker Romelio Ureta, who for three years had been asking her to marry him, committed suicide; a card bearing her name was found in his pocket.

Although his love for her was unrequited, the intense grief caused by Ureta's suicide was to inform much of Mistral's intensely morbid poetry, to which she devoted her time with increasing dedication while supporting herself with a series of teaching posts. In 1914 she won first prize in an important national poetry competition with *Los Sonetos de la Muerte* (Sonnets of Death), and in 1922 *Desolación* (Desolation), her first collection of verse, was published, followed a few years later by a second collection, *Ternura* (Tenderness). Her work received international acclaim, and the Chilean Government offered Gabriela Mistral a position in the **consular service**, allowing her to concentrate almost exclusively on her poetry. As consul, she spent many years abroad but her poems continued to look back to Chile, particularly her beloved **Elqui Valley**, which she described as "a cry of nature rising amid the opaque mountains and intense blue sky". Her most frequently recurring themes, however, were her love of children and her perceived sorrow at her childlessness.

Gabriela Mistral was however a surrogate mother for her adored nephew, **Juan Miguel** or "Yin Yin", who had been placed in her care when he was just 9 months old. Once again, though, tragedy struck: at the age of 17, Yin Yin committed suicide in Brazil, where Gabriela was serving as consul. She never recovered from that and her Nobel Prize, awarded two years later, was little consolation. Mistral outlived her nephew by twelve years, and in 1957, aged 67, she died in New York of cancer of the pancreas, leaving the proceeds of all her works published in South America to the children of Montegrande.

her sister, has been turned into a **museum** (Mon–Fri 9am–6pm; CH$1500), displaying her furniture and belongings. You'll find it opposite El Mesón del Praile on the main road. Just south of the village, Mistral's **tomb** rests on a hillside, opposite the turn-off for Cochiguaz.

One kilometre before the village is the **Cavas del Valle organic winery**, run by a retired couple who offer free 45-minute tours and tastings (daily: summer 10am–8pm; rest of year 10am–7pm; ☎09 6842 5592, ⓦcavasdelvalle.cl).

ARRIVAL AND DEPARTURE   MONTEGRANDE

By bus Buses stop in the village. Three buses weekly (Mon, Wed & Fri) go along the Río Cochiguaz.

Destinations Pisco Elqui (every 30min–1hr; 10min); Vicuña (every 30min–1hr; 50min).

ACCOMMODATION AND EATING

El Galpón La Jarilla ☎51 198 2554, ⓦhotelgalpon. cl. Halfway between Montegrande and Pisco Elqui, in a wonderful quiet location with mountain views, is one of the area's best places to stay. Stylishly built, it is owned by a friendly Chilean who lived for many years in the USA. Each room has a huge bathroom, TV and a minibar; two- and five-person *cabañas* are also available. The well-kept

grounds have an eye-catching swimming pool. Doubles **CH$55,000**, *cabañas* **CH$60,000**

El Mesón del Fraile Calle Principal s/n ☎51 245 1232. Beckoning opposite the museum, this restaurant has tables on a wide, breezy balcony and serves delectable stone-oven pizzas and the regional goat speciality, *cabrito al jugo*. Mains around CH$7000–10,000. Tues–Sun noon–9pm.

Las Pléyades Calle Principal s/n ☏ 09 8520 6983, ⓦ elquihotelpleyades.cl. The only hotel in Montegrande itself, set in an old mansion. Its five rustic yet chic rooms have artistic touches and come with private bathroom, swimming pool and access to a river beach. **CH$60,000**

Pisco Elqui and around

PISCO ELQUI was known as La Unión until 1939, when Gabriel González Videla – later President of Chile – cunningly renamed it to thwart Peru's efforts to gain exclusive rights to the name "Pisco". An idyllic village, increasingly popular with backpackers and independent travellers, it boasts a beautiful square filled with lush palm trees and flowers, overlooked by a colourful church with a tall, wooden tower. Locals sell home-made jam and jewellery in the square, and its abundant shade provides a welcome relief from the sun.

Pueblo Artesanal de Horcón

Horcón • Tues–Sun noon–6.30pm

Beyond Pisco Elqui, the narrow road leads through increasingly unspoiled countryside and ever deeper into the valley. After 10km you'll pass by a large craft market known as the **Pueblo Artesanal de Horcón**, which lies just before the sleepy village of the same name (the end of the road for four buses daily from La Serena). Here you can browse

---

PISCO

Pisco has been enjoyed by Chileans for more than four centuries, but it wasn't until the 1930s that it was organized into an effective commercial industry, starting with the official creation of a pisco *denominación de origen*. Shortly afterwards, a large number of growers, who'd always been at the mercy of the private distilleries for the price they got for their grapes, joined together to form **cooperatives** to produce their own pisco. The largest were the tongue-twisting *Sociedad Cooperativa Control Pisquero de Elqui y Vitivinículo de Norte Ltda* (known as "Pisco Control") and the *Cooperativa Agrícola y Pisquera del Elqui Ltda* (known as "Pisco Capel"), today the two most important producers in Chile, accounting for more than ninety percent of all pisco.

The basic **distillation technique** has been used since colonial times: in short, the fermented wine is boiled in copper stills at 90°C, releasing vapours that are condensed, then kept in oak vats for three to six months. The alcohol – of 55° to 65° – is then diluted with water, according to the type of pisco it's being sold as: 30° or 32° for *Selección*; 35° for *Reservado*; 40° for *Especial*; and 43°, 46° and 50° for *Gran Pisco*. It's most commonly consumed as a tangy, refreshing aperitif known as **Pisco Sour**, an ice-cold mix of pisco, lemon juice and sugar – sometimes with whisked egg-white for a frothy head and angostura bitters for an extra zing.

Note that the **Peruvians** also produce pisco and consider their own to be the only authentic sort, maintaining that the Chilean stuff is nothing short of counterfeit. The Chileans, of course, pass this off as jealousy, insisting their pisco is superior (it is certainly grapier) and proudly claiming pisco is a Chilean, not Peruvian, drink. Whoever produced it first, there's no denying that the pisco lovingly distilled in the Elqui Valley is delicious, drunk neat or in a cocktail. A visit to one of the region's distilleries is not to be missed – if only for the free tasting at the end.

PISCO DISTILLERY TOURS

On the south side of the Plaza de Armas, the **Pisco Mistral** is Chile's oldest pisco distillery, which today (and now considerably modernized) produces the famous Tres Erres brand. Hour-long **guided tours** explore the old part of the plant, with tastings and a pisco sour at the end; the restaurant was revamped in 2017 (O'Higgins s/n; tours daily, hourly 11am–5pm, in English at 3pm; CH$6000; ☏ 51 245 1358, ⓦ piscomistral.cl). You can also take a thirty-minute tour of the 150-year-old private distillery at **Los Nichos**, 4km beyond Pisco Elqui on the road to Horcón (tours daily: April–Nov 11am–6pm; Dec–March 11am–7pm; CH$1000; ☏ 51 245 1085, ⓦ fundolosnichos.cl).

CROSSING INTO ARGENTINA ON RUTA 41

After Rivadavia – where the right fork leads to Pisco Elqui – **Ruta 41** from La Serena follows first the Río Turbio and then the Río de la Laguna all the way to the Paso del Agua Negra (4779m) and the **Argentine border**, nearly 170km away. Only partly tarmacked, often narrow and hemmed in by imposing mountains, many of them over 4000m high, this **road** (Oct/Nov–April only) is one of the most dramatic linking the two countries. Seventy-five kilometres on from Rivadavia you'll come to the **Complejo Aduanero Junta del Toro**, the Chilean customs post (Jan–April, Nov & Dec daily 7am–5pm; ☎51 265 1184). The Argentine border lies some 95km from the customs post. On the other side of the frontier, the RN 150 winds down to the easygoing market town of **Rodeo** and hits the adobe-built town of Jachal, from where RN-40 strikes south to the laidback provincial capital of San Juan, nearly 270km on from the border post.

among the many craft and food stalls, or just enjoy a fresh juice and a massage by the river.

ARRIVAL AND DEPARTURE

By bus Buses stop by the plaza and also go up into the village to calle Prat. Three buses weekly (Mon, Wed & Fri) go along the Río Cochiguaz.
Destinations Montegrande (every 30min–1hr; 10min); Vicuña (every 20–30min; 50min).

PISCO ELQUI AND AROUND

By jeep Jeep Tours La Serena (☎09 9454 6000, ⓦ jeeptour-laserena.cl) offers day-tours and transfers (Nov–April; CH$95,000/person) to San Juan in Argentina.

INFORMATION AND TOURS

Tourist information There is a small tourist office in the square (daily 9am–5pm); ⓦ piscoelqui.com is also a useful source of information.
Tours Turismo Migrantes (☎51 245 1917, ⓦ turismomigrantes.cl) on O'Higgins, and El Quijote

(☎09 9782 5369) on Manuel Rodríguez, offer horseriding, trekking, cycling and observatory excursions, as well as day-trips to remote thermal springs near the Argentinian border.

ACCOMMODATION

Elquimista Aurora de Chile s/n ☎51 245 1185, ⓦ elquimista.cl. Enjoy the silence and dazzling views from your own *cabaña* perched on a hillside about 1km from town. *Cabañas* are kitted out with antique Asian furniture and quality mattresses. English spoken. CH$50,000
★ **Hostal Triskel** Baquedano s/n ☎09 9419 8680, ⓦ hostaltriskel.cl. Genial owner Yayo is a wealth of local information and offers simple yet cosy rooms with shared bathrooms in a stylishly rustic setting with a peaceful, labyrinthine garden. Dorms CH$15,000, doubles CH$30,000
★ **Misterios de Elqui** Prat s/n ☎51 245 1126, ⓦ misteriosdeelqui.cl. For a real treat, stay 800m out of town on the road to Alcohuaz. Design-mag-style *cabañas* with fabulous views are spaced comfortably apart among

landscaped gardens leading down to a stunning swimming pool. Golfers can practise on the putting green. CH$80,000
Refugio del Angel El Condor s/n ☎51 245 1292, ⓦ campingrefugiodelangel.cl. Less than 1km southeast of the plaza, this pretty riverside campsite has a world away from the village. Rustic wooden bridges lead to shady camping spots, with picnic tables and hot showers. The cute "teahouse" provides breakfast, drinks and snacks. CH$10,000
★ **El Tesoro de Elqui** Prat s/n ☎51 245 1069, ⓦ tesoro-elqui.cl. The friendly German owners offer attractive, spotless adobe-style *cabañas* with hammocks slung on the verandas, amid fragrant gardens, vine-covered terraces and a gorgeous pool. There is one dorm and the café is one of the best in town. Dorms CH$16,000, *cabañas* CH$57,000

EATING

★ **El Durmiente Elquino** Los Carrera s/n ☎09 8906 2754. Pebble floors, local artwork and mellow music set the scene for dining on Chilean staples (CH$5000 upwards)

as well as pork ribs and nutritious quinoa salads. Local wines and pisco cocktails fuel the late-night revelry. Daily noon–1am.

★ **Miraflores** Road to Horcón ☎51 228 5901, ⓦhaciendamiraflores.cl. Not to be missed, this wonderful restaurant is a family-run place a couple of kilometres along the road that goes out of town towards Alcohuaz. Here you can feast on excellent roast meats (CH$8000–11,000), including suckling pig and *bife de chorizo* cooked up on the *parrillada*, while savouring mesmerizing views down the valley. Tues–Sun 1–6pm.

Misterios de Elqui Prat s/n ☎51 245 1126, ⓦmisteriosdeelqui.cl. This tastefully decorated restaurant offers the most romantic setting in town: a wide wooden balcony with sweeping views down the valley. A gourmet chef prepares delicious food (dishes around CH$8000–10,000), such as prawn crêpes. Wed–Sun 12.30–3pm & 8–10pm.

El Tesoro de Elqui Prat s/n ☎51 245 1069, ⓦtesoroelqui.cl. Stylish café food, from sandwiches to waffles and *küchen* cake made with local berries (CH$3000–7000). Also smoothies, real coffee and to-die-for papaya ice cream. Daily 11am–8pm.

Alcohuaz

Some 15km beyond Pisco Elqui is the tiny community of **ALCOHUAZ**. Apart from a handsome terracotta-hued **church** (in sharp contrast to Horcón's, which is sky blue), this remote settlement has little to offer in the way of standard attractions.

Colmenares Alcohuaz

No fixed opening hours, so phone or email ahead of your visit • ☎09 9003 5297, ✉nelsoncorreacl@yahoo.com

Alcohuaz is home to a popular curiosity, the **bee-cure centre** known as **Colmenares Alcohuaz**, or "Alcohuaz Hives". People come from throughout the country to treat all kinds of ills by means of apitherapy (bee stings) – after being tested for allergies, of course. You can also buy a variety of excellent bee products such as honey, royal jelly, propolis and creams to treat skin ailments.

ARRIVAL AND DEPARTURE · ALCOHUAZ

By bus Though there are two buses daily to Horcón, 8km beyond Pisco Elqui (and not to be confused with its more popular coastal namesake), there is no public transport along the final 7km rough stretch to Alcohuaz.

Bike tours Tour companies in Pisco Elqui offer half-day bicycle excursions, dropping you off in Alcohuaz by minibus and letting you ride back.

Hitchhiking Hitchhiking is common.

ACCOMMODATION

La Casona Distante ☎09 9226 5440, ⓦcasonadistante.cl. "The secluded ranch" is a 75-year-old adobe house offering verdant grounds, stunning valley views from the charming rooms and a swimming pool. Meals, massage, bike rental and horseriding trips can all be arranged. CH$86,000

Refugios La Frontera ☎09 9279 8109, ⓦrefugioslafrontera.cl. These seven *cabañas* (sleeping two to eight) boast a magical setting by the river willows. Onsite is a swimming pool, a restaurant where you can sample the region's tasty river prawns and an observatory. CH$75,000

Along the Río Cochiguaz

Back in Montegrande, a rough, unpaved road branches off the main route, dips down the valley and follows the northern bank of the **Río Cochiguaz**, a tributary of the Elqui. Rustic *cabañas* dot the riverbank; many offer holistic therapies and meditation classes. The small community of **Cochiguaz**, 11km along the valley, was founded in the 1960s by a group of hippies in the belief that the Age of Aquarius had shifted the earth's magnetic centre from the Himalayas to the Elqui Valley. But don't let this put you off – the multicoloured highland scenery is fabulous and the remoteness and tranquillity of the valley irresistible.

Cancana observatory

11km southwest of Montegrande • Tours (2hr) summer 10pm & midnight; rest of year 7pm & 9pm • CH$7500 • ☎09 9047 3859, ⓦcancana.cl

In keeping with the valley's reputation for UFO sightings and celestial activity, the new **Cancana observatory** at Cochiguaz offers nightly opportunities to stargaze, using two 35cm Meade telescopes; most people visit on a tour from Pisco Elqui.

ARRIVAL AND DEPARTURE

By bus Public transport between Montegrande and Cochiguaz is limited to three weekly buses (Mon, Wed & Fri; 30min), leaving Pisco Elqui early in the morning, before

ALONG THE RÍO COCHIGUAZ

following the Río Cochiguaz and then turning back and heading on to La Serena.

Hitchhiking Hitchhiking is common along the bus route.

ACCOMMODATION

El Alma Zen 11km southwest of Montegrande ☎09 9047 3861. Spa therapies and river swimming meet poolside posing at this hotel across from the Cancana observatory. The two-storey *cabañas* by the pool are nice but uninspiring; for something more back-to-nature, try the riverside domes with shared bathroom. Domes **CH$25,000**, *cabañas* **CH$45,000**

Camping Cochiguaz 18km southwest of Montegrande ☎51 245 1154, ⓦcampingcochiguaz.blogspot.com. At the end of the road from Montegrande, this riverside

campsite is as far as you can get from civilization without forfeiting hot showers or picnic tables. Staff can arrange horseriding trips. **CH$7000**

Spa Cochiguaz Parcela 8B, El Pangue, 11.5km from Montegrande ☎09 8501 2680, ⓦspacochiguaz.cl. This wellness complex offers rudimentary rooms as well as much nicer cabins with indigenous wall hangings. If you're not into meditation or spa therapies, there's a fine pool to splash about in. The vegetarian restaurant is open to the public and serves three top-notch meals a day. **CH$50,000**

Vallenar and around

North of La Serena, the Panamericana turns inland and heads via a couple of winding passes towards the busy but somewhat run-down little town of **VALLENAR**, 190km up the road. The town, a service centre for local mining and agricultural industries, was founded in 1789 by Governor Ambrosio O'Higgins, who named the city after his native Ballinagh in Ireland. It makes a convenient base for an excursion east into the fertile **upper Huasco Valley** or northwest towards the coast and, in the spring, the wild flowers of the **Parque Nacional Llanos de Challe**.

The self-appointed "*capital del desierto florido*", Vallenar is indeed the best base for forays into the **flowering desert** (see page 152), if you're here at the right time. The **Museo del Huasco** at Prat 1542 (Mon–Fri 9am–1pm & 4–6pm; CH$1000) has some moderately diverting displays on indigenous cultures and photos of the nearby flowering desert.

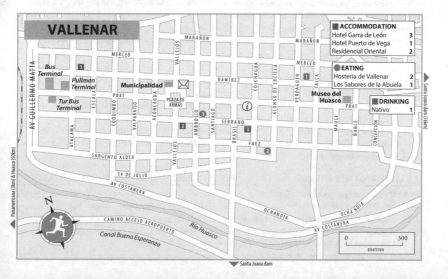

ARRIVAL AND INFORMATION   VALLENAR

By bus Vallenar's main bus terminal is on the corner of Prat and Av Guillermo Matta, six blocks west of the main square. Destinations Antofagasta (10 daily; 9hr); Calama (10 daily; 11hr); Caldera (10 daily; 3hr); Chañaral (10 daily; 4hr); Copiapó (every 30min–1hr; 2hr); Iquique (2 daily; 14hr); La Serena (every 30min–1hr; 2hr 45min); Santiago (26 daily; 9hr 30min).

Tourist office Staff at the small tourist office at Prat 1094 (Mon–Fri 8.30am–6pm; ☏ 51 275 6417, ✉ turimovallenar@ gmail.com) can advise on tour guides and car rentals.

ACCOMMODATION

Hotel Garra de León Serrano 1052 ☏ 51 242 8800, ✉ reservas@hotelgarradeleon.cl; map p.149. A 5min stroll from the Plaza de Armas, the solid, mid-range *Hotel Garra de León* has comfortable and spacious rooms (with a/c, TVs and pristine attached bathrooms), as well as friendly service. **CH$65,000**

Hotel Puerto de Vega Ramírez 201 ☏ 51 261 3870, ⓦ puertodevega.cl; map p.149. A boutique-style hotel near the bus terminal, with beautifully decorated rooms and suites, covered parking, a small swimming pool in a tidy garden, afternoon tea and huge, delicious breakfasts. Doubles **CH$114,000**, suites **CH$147,000**

Residencial Oriental Serrano 720 ☏ 51 234 9926, ✉ reservasoriental@gmail.com; map p.149. If pesos are tight, *Residencial Oriental* is decent for a night. Revamped in 2017, rooms, some with private bathrooms, are set around a quiet patio. The hot water is erratic. **CH$25,000**

EATING

Hostería de Vallenar Alonso de Ercilla 848 ☏ 51 261 4379, ⓦ hotelesatacama.cl; map p.149. This surprisingly good restaurant, attached to a *hostería*, offers well-cooked Chilean cuisine with imaginative sauces. Seafood mains cost around CH$10,000. Daily 12.30–3pm & 7.30–11pm.

Los Sabores de la Abuela Serrano 802 ☏ 51 260 1963; map p.149. A second-storey restaurant decked in *huaso* garb where the focus is on Chilean meat and fish staples (mains around CH$8000–10,000). Two should share the abundant *parrillada* meat fest for CH$29,000. Mon–Sat 12.30–4pm & 8pm–late, Sun 12.30–4pm.

DRINKING

Nativo Ramirez 1387 ☏ 51 261 8308; map p.149. With its loud music and rock art-inspired walls, this is a good spot to sink a beer over a plate of *picadillos*. Pizzas and seafood mains (including ceviche) are made to be shared – and portions are generous (mains from CH$7000). There are also plenty of salad options. Mon–Sat 1pm–3am.

Reserva Nacional Pingüino de Humboldt

129km northwest of La Serena and 126km southwest of Vallenar • Jan–March & Dec daily 9am–5.30pm • CH$2500 • ☏ 51 261 1555 or ☏ 09 9544 3052, ⓦ www.conaf.cl

Bottle-nosed dolphins, colonies of Humboldt penguins, sea lions and otters frolic in the two-thousand-acre-plus **Reserva Nacional Pingüino de Humboldt**. The reserve comprises three main islands: Choros, Damas and Chañaral, the first two best visited from La Serena. Travelling 87km north of La Serena, a dirt road heads 42km west to Punta de Choros, from where you can sail along the east coast of Isla Choros and go ashore on Isla Damas, the only island where it's possible to disembark. A rough 22km coastal road links Punta de Choros with Caleta Chañaral, the jumping-off point for the furthest and most wildlife-rich island, Isla Chañaral. It's more common, however, to visit **Isla Chañaral** from Vallenar: 50km south of town is a turn-off opposite Domeyko and the 76km dirt track leads to Caleta Chañaral. Plenty of tour operators in La Serena and Vallenar offer day-trips.

ARRIVAL AND DEPARTURE   RESERVA NACIONAL PINGÜINO DE HUMBOLDT

By boat Boats can be rented (CH$8000/person) at Punta de Chorros. The tour company ExploraSub (☏ 09 9402 4947, ⓦ explorasub.cl) runs diving, kayaking and boat trips to Isla Chañaral.

By bus and boat From Vallenar, buses leave for Caleta Chañaral every Fri at 3pm (also Wed Jan–March) and return Sun at 5pm with Buses Alvarez (☏ 09 7618 4389). From Caleta Chañaral you can take boat trips (around CH$80,000/boat; La Marianela is a reliable local guide (☏ 09 6813 8411) who circumnavigates the island and offers accommodation.

ACCOMMODATION

Several people on Isla Chañaral rent out simple **rooms** in their homes (around CH$20,000 a double). **Camping** is permitted on Isla Damas.

The Upper Huasco Valley

From Vallenar, a paved road follows the Río Huasco through a deep, attractive valley that climbs towards the mountains. The road weaves back and forth across the river, taking you through dry, mauve-coloured hills and green orchards and vineyards. About 20km from Vallenar, you pass the enormous **Santa Juana dam**, which after a season of heavy rainfall overflows into a magnificent waterfall that can be viewed close-up from an observation deck.

Alto del Carmen

Thirty-eight kilometres from Vallenar, the valley forks at the confluence of the El Carmen and El Tránsito rivers. The right-hand road takes you up the **El Carmen Valley** where, just beyond the fork, you'll find **Alto del Carmen**, a pretty village that produces one of the best-known brands of pisco in Chile; book ahead to visit the **Planta Pisquera Alto del Carmen** for a free thirty-minute tour and tastings (Mon–Fri 11am–5pm, Sat 9am–noon; ☎ 51 261 6035).

San Félix

A further 26km up the road from Alto del Carmen, **San Félix** has a beautiful setting and a hundred-year-old **pisco plant** that produces high-quality, traditionally made pisco called Horcón Quemado. You can try – and buy – the pisco in their shop (daily 8am–5pm; ☎ 51 261 0985).

ARRIVAL AND DEPARTURE	**UPPER HUASCO VALLEY**
By bus Buses Pallauta (☎ 51 261 2117) leave from the corner of Marañon and Alonso de Ercilla in Vallenar.	Destinations Alto del Carmen (5 daily; 1hr); San Félix (5 daily; 1hr 30min).

ACCOMMODATION

Complejo Turístico y Deportivo Portezuelo Sector La Falda s/n, Alto del Carmen ☎ 09 9548 3571, ⓦ hospedajeportezuelo.cl. A relaxed and leafy spot by the river, with fifty camping sites, 14 *cabañas*, and natural swimming pools (open to non-guests for a small fee). Horseriding and other activities can be arranged. Camping CH$12,000, *cabañas* CH$25,000

Hospedaje y Restaurante El Churcal Hijuela 75, 1km south of San Félix ☎ 09 7684 4222, ⓦ elchurcal. cl. A range of rooms (all with private bathrooms and TVs; breakfast costs extra) at this eco-minded place with solar-powered showers and plenty of fruit trees. The restaurant offers a lunch menu. CH$25,000

Parque Nacional Llanos de Challe

77km northwest of Vallenar • Jan & Feb 8.30am–8pm; March–Dec 8.30am–5.30pm • CH$3000 • ☎ 52 261 1555, ⓦ www.conaf.cl

---

THE PRICE OF GOLD

A massive threat currently hangs over the Upper Huasco valley: locals fear water shortages and contamination of the pristine Río Huasco from a massive **gold-mining project** by Canadian giant Barrick Gold. The company is currently exploring the Pascua Lama deposits straddling the Argentinian border, believed to be the world's largest untapped gold deposit, and environmental groups claim the company's activities have already had a detrimental effect on glaciers. In 2013 the project was "temporarily suspended", and Barrick remains embroiled in a legal battle with Chile's environmental agencies.

3

THE FLOWERING DESERT

For most of the year, as you travel up the Panamericana between Vallenar and Copiapó you'll cross a seemingly endless, semi-desert plain, stretching for nearly 100km, sparsely covered with low shrubs and *copao* cacti. But take the same journey in spring, and in place of the parched, brown earth, you'll find green grass dotted with beautiful flowers. If you're really lucky and you know where to go after a particularly wet winter, you'll happen upon fluorescent carpets of multicoloured flowers, stretching into the horizon.

This extraordinarily dramatic transformation is known as the **desierto florido**, or "flowering desert"; it occurs when unusually heavy rainfall (normally very light in this region) causes dormant bulbs and seeds, hidden beneath the earth, to sprout into sudden bloom, mostly from early September to late October. In the central strip, crossed by the highway, the flowers tend to appear in huge single blocks of colour (*praderas*), formed chiefly by the purple *pata de guanaco* ("guanaco's hoof"), the yellow *corona de fraile* ("monk's halo") and the blue *suspiro de campo* ("field's sigh"). The tiny forget-me-not-like *azulillo* also creates delicate blankets of baby blue.

On the banks of the *quebradas*, or ravines, that snake across the land from the cordillera to the ocean, many different varieties of flowers are mixed together, producing a kaleidoscope of contrasting colours known as *jardines*. These may include the yellow or orange lily-like *añañuca* and the speckled white, pink, red or yellow *alstroemeria*, a popular plant with florists also known as the "Peruvian lily". West, towards the coast, you'll also find large crimson swaths of the endangered *garra de león* ("lion's claw"), particularly in the **Parque Nacional Llanos de Challe**, near Carrizal Bajo, created especially to protect them. Of course, removing any plant, whole or in part, is strictly forbidden by law.

There's no predicting the *desierto florido*, which is relatively rare – the frequency and intensity varies enormously, but the general phenomenon seems to occur every four to five years, although this has been more frequent in recent years. The best **guide** in Vallenar, and a veritable gold-mine of information about the dozens of flower varieties, is Roberto Alegría (☏ 51 261 3908, ✉ desiertoflorido2010@hotmail.cl).

If you have the good luck to be around while the desert's in bloom, head for the **Parque Nacional Llanos de Challe**, for the full impact. This 450-square-kilometre swath of coastal plain has been singled out for national park status because of the abundance of **garra de león** – an exquisite, deep-red flower in danger of extinction – that grows here during the years of the *desierto florido*. The park is crossed by an 82km dirt road branching west from the Panamericana, 17km north of Vallenar, and terminating at **Carrizal Bajo**, a once-important mining port now home to a tiny fishing community.

ARRIVAL AND INFORMATION

By bus Buses Carmelita (☏ 51 261 3037) leave from Vallenar's bus terminal for Carrizal Bajo (3 weekly; around 2hr).

By 4WD If you have a 4WD, a tent and a taste for wilderness, follow the very rough track north of Carrizal Bajo up to Puerto Viejo, near Caldera and Copiapó. The deserted beaches along this stretch, particularly the northern half, are breathtaking, with white sands and clear, turquoise waters.

Conaf The Conaf information office is 11km north of Carrizal Bajo at the pretty, white-sand Playa Blanca (Jan & Feb 8.30am–8pm; March–Dec 8.30am–5.30pm; ☏ 52 261 1555).

ACCOMMODATION

Camping Playa Blanca 11km north of Carrizal Bajo. There is a beachside campsite near the Conaf office, with solar-powered hot showers (for which there is a small extra charge), barbecues, picnic tables and drinking water. CH$5000

Copiapó

Overlooked by arid, rippling mountains, the prosperous city of **COPIAPÓ** sits in the flat basin of the **Río Copiapó**, some 60km from the coast and 145km north of Vallenar. To the east is the most northerly of Chile's "transverse valleys" and beyond it the transformation from semi-desert to serious desert is complete, and the bare, barren Atacama stretches a staggering 1000km north towards the Peruvian border. Just to the north of the city, Arabian-style dunes await exploration. There isn't a great deal to do here, however, and Copiapó's main use to travellers is as a springboard for **excursions** into the surrounding region (see page 155).

Brief history

When **Diego de Almagro** made his long trek south from Cuzco in 1536, following the Inca Royal Road down the spine of the Andes, it was into this valley that he descended, recuperating from the gruelling journey at the *tambo*, or resting place, where Copiapó now stands. The valley had been occupied and cultivated by the **Diaguita** people starting around 1000 AD and was then inhabited, beginning around 1470, by the **Inca**, who mined gold and copper here. Although Spanish *encomenderos* (see page 470) occupied the valley from the beginning of the conquest, it wasn't until 1744 that the city of Copiapó was founded, initially as "San Francisco de la Selva". A series of random **silver strikes** in the nineteenth century, most notably at Chañarcillo, threw the region into a frenzied boom.

Following a period of decline at the beginning of the twentieth century, Copiapó is once more at the centre of a rich **mining industry**, revolving around copper, iron and gold. The city shot to international notoriety in October 2010, when 33 workers from the nearby San José mine were rescued after 69 days trapped underground (see page 157).

COPIAPÓ

Plaza Prat

A lively, busy city, Copiapó has a fairly compact downtown composed of typical adobe houses, some churches and the odd mansion, with the large, tree-filled **Plaza Prat** at its centre. The square is lined with 84 towering old pepper trees planted in 1880. On its southwest corner stands the mid-nineteenth-century **Iglesia Catedral**, designed by the English architect William Rogers, sporting a Neoclassical three-door portico and topped by an unusual, tiered wooden steeple.

Museo Mineralógico

Corner of Colipí and Rodriguez • Mon–Fri 10am–1pm & 3.30–7pm, Sat 10am–1pm • CH$600

Just off the northeast corner of Plaza Prat, the University of Atacama's **Museo Mineralógico** displays a glittering collection of more than two thousand mineral samples from around the world, including huge chunks of malachite, amethyst, quartz, marble and onyx; it's a pity that the museum is so poorly presented, with virtually no explanations or guides of any kind.

Museo Regional de Atacama

Corner of Atacama and Rancagua • Tues–Fri 9am–5.45pm, Sat 10am–12.45pm & 3–5.45pm, Sun 10am–12.45pm • Tues–Sat CH$600; Sun free • ☎ 52 221 2313, ⓦ museodeatacama.cl

The **Museo Regional de Atacama** repays a visit, not least for its display on the trapped miners of the San José mine (see page 157), which includes their fateful hand-written note: "We are fine in the shelter – the 33." The handsome mansion that houses the museum, the **Casa Matta**, was built in the 1840s for one of Copiapó's wealthy mining barons. The other well-presented displays cover the exploration of the desert, the development of mining, the War of the Pacific, pre-Columbian peoples of the region and the Inca road system.

Plazoleta Juan Godoy

Towering over the tiny **Plazoleta Juan Godoy**, site of a busy Friday market selling fresh produce and household items, the imposing, red-walled 1872 **Iglesia San Francisco** sits one block south and west of the regional museum. The square's centre is marked by a statue of a rough-clad miner, tools in hand – none other than **Juan Godoy**, the goatherd who accidentally discovered the enormous silver deposits of nearby Chañarcillo in 1832, and who is now honoured in Copiapó as a local legend.

ARRIVAL AND DEPARTURE   **COPIAPÓ**

BY PLANE

Airport The Desierto de Atacama international airport (☎ 52 252 5104) is just over 50km northwest of the city, at Chamonate, and is actually closer to Caldera. Both the Manuel Flores Salinas minibus and Casther bus meet arriving planes and travel into town; a taxi costs around CH$30,000.

Airlines LATAM, Colipí and Los Carrera (☎ 52 221 3512); Sky Airlines, Mall Plaza Real (☎ 52 221 4640).

Destinations Note that some of these routes require stopovers, which the travel times listed here take into account: Calama (1–2 daily; 1hr 10min–4hr); Santiago (5–7 daily; 1hr 20min).

BY BUS

Bus terminal Copiapó's main bus terminal is at Chañarcillo 655, two blocks south of Plaza Prat. Across the road, also on Chañarcillo, is the Tur Bus terminal, while one block south, at Freire and Colipí, sits the Pullman Bus terminal.

Bus companies Intercity services are offered by all the main companies, including Flota Barrios (☎ 52 221 3645), Pullman Bus (☎ 52 221 2977), Expreso Norte (☎ 52 223 1176) and Tur Bus (☎ 52 223 8612). For Caldera and Bahía Inglesa, Casther (☎ 52 221 8889), Expreso Caldera (☎ 09 6155 8048) and Trans Puma (☎ 52 223 5841) run a frequent service from the small bus station on the corner of Esperanza and Chacabuco, opposite the Líder Hypermarket (you can also catch a Casther transfer to the airport here). Alternately you can catch one of the yellow *colectivos* that wait on the same corner opposite Líder.

Destinations Antofagasta (15 daily; 7hr); Arica (11 daily; 17hr); Calama (15 daily; 10hr); Caldera (every 30min; 1hr); Chañaral (10 daily; 2hr); Iquique (12 daily; 13hr); La Serena (every 30min–1hr; 5hr); Ovalle (6 daily; 7hr); Santiago (22 daily; 12hr); Vallenar (every 30min–1hr; 2hr); Valparaíso (6 daily; 12hr).

GETTING AROUND AND INFORMATION

Car rental Rodaggio, Colipí 127 (☎52 221 2153, ⊚rodaggio.cl), rents good-value 4WD jeeps. Other firms include Europcar at the airport (☎51 250 8880, ⊚europcar.cl) and Salfa Rent at Ramón Freire 330 (☎52 220 0400, ⊚salfa.cl). Hertz is on the opposite side of the highway at Copayapú 173 (☎52 221 3522, ⊚hertz.cl).

Tourist office Los Carrera 691 on Plaza Prat (Mon–Fri 8.30am–6pm; ☎52 221 2838).

Conaf Juan Martínez 56 (Mon–Thurs 8.30am–5.30pm & Fri 8.30am–4pm; ☎52 221 3404). Provides information on protected areas in the region, including Pan de Azúcar and Nevado de Tres Cruces national parks; it's also a good source of information on road conditions in the altiplano.

Camping gear *Bencina blanca* (white gas) and butane gas are available at Ferretería El Herrerito, Atacama 699. Dolomiti, Maipú 400 (☎52 253 5443 5451, ⊚dolomiti.cl), has a range of Camping Gaz appliances and other outdoor stuff.

ACTIVITIES AND TOURS

The main full-day destinations are located east into the cordillera, taking in Parque Nacional Nevado de Tres Cruces (see page 156) and sometimes Laguna Verde (see page 157) and Ojos del Salado (see page 158); and north to Parque Nacional Pan de Azúcar (see page 162). Half-day trips go north into the Atacama dunes, west to the beaches around Bahía Inglesa (see page 161), or east up the Río Copiapó Valley (see page 156). Ask at Sernatur (⊚sernatur.cl) for a list of guides.

Atacama Chile Los Carrera 525 ☎56 221 1191, ⊚atacamachile.cl. This agency runs a range of trips, including to Parque Nacional Nevado de Tres Cruces, Pan de Azúcar and Llanos de Challe.

Aventurismo ☎09 9599 2184, ⊚aventurismo.cl. Maximiliano Martínez has been taking tourists up to Ojos del Salado (eight-day trips from US$1800/person), Laguna Verde and around for longer than anyone else in the business. Note there is no physical office; contact them direct.

ACCOMMODATION

★ **Hotel La Casona** O'Higgins 150 ☎52 221 7277, ⊚lacasonahotel.cl; map p.153. This small, charming and impeccably decorated hotel provides attractive en suites, pleasant garden, and an English-speaking owner. **CH$45,000**

Hotel Chagall O'Higgins 760 ☎52 235 2900, ⊚chagall.cl; map p.153. The large, upscale *Hotel Chagall* has comfortable, fully fitted en suites (though they are a little short on character), a good restaurant and bar, outdoor pool, gym and private parking. **CH$79,000**

Hotel Montecatini Infante 766 ☎52 221 1363, ⊚hotelmontecatini.cl; map p.153. Bright, spacious rooms that fall into two classes: smart, newer *ejecutivo* and older but cheaper *turista*, all of which have private bathrooms. There's also a tiny pool, and parking facilities. **CH$41,000**

Hotel Palace Atacama 741 ☎52 233 6427, ⊚hotelpalacecopiapo.cl; map p.153. Copious wood-panelling gives *Hotel Palace* a vaguely 70s feel. The carpeted rooms are comfortable enough, though overpriced (try bargaining the price down): all have private bathrooms and TVs. **CH$38,000**

Residencial Benbow Rodriguez 541 ☎52 221 7634; map p.153. If you're on a tight budget, this is an acceptable option. Rooms are cramped, but perfectly fine; most have shared bathrooms but you can pay CH$6000 more for an en suite. Breakfast costs CH$3500. **CH$22,000**

EATING

Café Colombia Colipi 484 ☎52 223 7288; map p.153. Located right on the plaza, with a shady open-air seating area, *Café Colombia* is a good place for a coffee (CH$1000–3000), snack or treat: the menu ranges from sandwiches and pizzas to cakes and ice-cream sundaes. Mon–Sat 8am–10pm.

Don Elías Los Carrera 421 ☎52 236 4146; map p.153. For a cheap and cheerful meal, the least insalubrious option in town is this great-value diner with bargain set lunches, fish and meat dishes (from CH$4000) that keep the locals piling in. Mon–Sat 10am–9pm.

Flor de la Canela Chacabuco 710 ☎ 52 221 9570; map p.153. This cheerful Peruvian joint offers a change from the Copiapó norm, with tasty dishes such as ceviche and *lomo saltado* (stir-fried strips of beef with tomatoes, onions, chips and rice), as well as a killer (Peruvian-style) pisco sour. Mains CH$8300–14,900. Mon–Sat noon–4pm & 7pm–midnight, Sun noon–11pm.

Legado O'Higgins 12 ☎ 52 252 3895; map p.153. One of Copiapó's top restaurants, the intimate and friendly *Legado* offers pricey, good-quality meat and fish dinners (most mains around CH$10,000). The star dish is the Wagyu beef steak. Mon–Sat 7pm–midnight.

NIGHTLIFE

Orum Discoteque Los Carrera 2440 ☎ 52 223 4100, ⓦ antaycasinohotel.cl; map p.153. This sleek club inside the *Antay Casino & Hotel* is one of the hottest spots in town. Weekends are all about retro and pop standards, while weeknights mix things up with salsa and karaoke. Wed & Thurs 9pm–2am, Fri & Sat 9pm–late.

Around Copiapó

The region around Copiapó features some of Chile's most striking and varied landscapes. To the east, the **Río Copiapó Valley** offers the extraordinary spectacle of emerald-green vines growing in desert-dry hills, while high up in the Andes, you'll ascend a world of salt flats, volcanoes and lakes, encompassed by the **Parque Nacional Nevado de Tres Cruces**, the **Volcán Ojos del Salado** and the blue-green **Laguna Verde**. To the west, **Bahía Inglesa**, near the port of **Caldera**, could be a little chunk of the Mediterranean, with its pristine sands and odd-shaped rocks rising out of the sea. Further south, reached only in a 4WD, the coast is lined with wild, deserted **beaches** lapped by turquoise waters.

Río Copiapó Valley

Despite an acute shortage of rainfall, the **Río Copiapó Valley** is one of the most important grape-growing areas of Chile. This is thanks mainly to new irrigation techniques that have been developed over the past two decades tapping into the valley's abundance of underground flowing water. While the Copiapó Valley is not quite as pastoral or picturesque as the Elqui Valley, its cultivated areas provide, more than anywhere else in the north, the most stunning contrast between deep-green produce and parched, dry earth – from September to May, in particular, it really is a sight to behold.

Museo Minero de Tierra Amarilla

Tierra Amarilla, 16km southeast of Copiapó • Mon–Fri 8am–5pm, Sat 2–6pm • Free • ☎ 52 232 9136, ⓦ museominerodetierraamarilla.cl

Aside from the Río Copiapó Valley's scenery, the excellent **Museo Minero de Tierra Amarilla** in the town of Tierra Amarilla is worth a visit; it is set inside a restored nineteenth-century house and provides an overview of mining in the Atacama region.

GETTING AROUND
RÍO COPIAPÓ VALLEY

By bus From Copiapó, Casther, Expreso Caldera and Trans Puma have several daily services up the Copiapó River Valley. Buses go as far as Manflas, 150km southeast (the last 12km of the journey is along an unpaved road).

Parque Nacional Nevado de Tres Cruces

Around 95km east of Copiapó • Summer daily 9.30am–5pm; rest of year call ahead to check whether the park is open • CH$5000 • ☎ 52 221 3404, ⓦ www.conaf.cl

East of Copiapó, the Andes divide into two separate ranges – the Cordillera de Domeyko and the Cordillera de Claudio Gay – joined by a high basin, or plateau, that stretches all the way north to Bolivia. The waters trapped in this basin form vast salt

THE RESCUE OF LOS 33

On August 5, 2010, a boulder collapsed inside the **San José copper and gold mine**, 32km northeast of Copiapó, trapping 33 workers some 700m below the desert. That may well have been the end of the story – the miners consigned to statistics in Chile's notoriously dangerous mining industry – but for a fortuitous combination of **determined families**, a captivated media and a president in dire need of a ratings boost. In the aftermath of the accident, relatives of the trapped miners set up camp outside the pithead and refused to budge, urging the company to continue their search effort.

LIMELIGHT IN THE DARKNESS

The families kept up the pressure via the national media, compelling the then new right-wing president **Sebastián Piñera** – perceived to be out of touch with the working class and reeling from a ratings blow following his handling of February's earthquake and tsunami – to get involved. On day 17 of the search operation, just as hope was fading, rescue workers struck media gold – a handwritten note attached to their drillhead which read: "We are fine in the shelter – the 33." The miners' relatives were euphoric, the president triumphant and the international media dispatched to "Camp Hope" to cover the miracle (and soap opera) unfolding in the Chilean desert.

Food, medicine, pornography and video cameras were sent down a narrow communications shaft to the desperate men. What happened next was beamed around the world: one miner proposed a church marriage to his partner; a two-timer was exposed when his wife *and* mistress turned up at Camp Hope to lend support; a musical miner kept his colleagues entertained with Elvis impersonations; and another lay in the hot, dark tunnel while above ground his wife gave birth to his daughter, named, appropriately, Esperanza (Hope).

SAVED

Just after midnight on **October 13**, 69 days after the miners were buried alive (the longest underground entrapment in history), state-of-the-art rescue capsules hauled the first of "Los 33" to freedom, to an estimated global TV audience of 1.5 billion people. In the aftermath of the rescue, the miners enjoyed a flurry of media attention, flown around the world and paraded as heroes. Most, however, chose to remain tight-lipped about what really went on in that subterranean hell, and as well as struggling with post-traumatic stress, the majority now lives quiet, unassuming lives in Copiapó.

flats and lakes towered over by enormous, snow-capped volcanoes, and wild vicuña and guanaco roam the sparsely vegetated hills. This is a truly awe-inspiring landscape, conveying an acute sense of wilderness and space. The **Parque Nacional Nevado de Tres Cruces** takes in a dazzling white salt flat, the **Salar de Maricunga**; two beautiful lakes, the **Laguna Santa Rosa** and **Laguna del Negro Francisco**; and the 6753m volcano **Tres Cruces**.

A 4WD is required to take on the very bumpy road up to Parque Nacional Nevado de Tres Cruces takes you through a brief stretch of desert before twisting up narrow canyons flanked by mineral-stained rocks. As you climb higher, the colours of the scoured, bare mountains become increasingly vibrant, ranging from oranges and golds to greens and violets. Some 165km from Copiapó, at an altitude of around 3700m, the road (following the signs to Mina Marta) reaches the first sector of the park, skirting the pale-blue **Laguna Santa Rosa**, home to dozens of pink flamingos.

Immediately adjacent, the gleaming white **Salar de Maricunga** is Chile's most southerly salt flat, covering an area of more than eighty square kilometres. A two- to three-hour drive south from here, past Mina Marta, the park's second sector is based around the large, deep-blue **Laguna del Negro Francisco**, some 4200m above sea level and home to abundant birdlife, including wild ducks and flamingos. Towering over the lake, the 6080m **Volcán Copiapó** was the site of an Inca sacrificial altar.

Laguna Verde

Close to but not part of the park, by the border with Argentina, the stunning, blue-green **Laguna Verde** lies at the foot of the highest active volcano in the world,

3

VOLCÁN OJOS DEL SALADO: CLIMBING PAPERWORK

As **Volcán Ojos del Salado** sits on the border with Argentina, climbers need to present written permission from the Dirección de Fronteras y Límites (DIFROL; ✉ infodifrol@minrel. gov.cl) plus a *permiso regional*, obtained from the tourist office, to the *carabineros* before climbing up. If you need to arrange transport to the base, or a guide for the ascent, contact Aventurismo or Sernatur in Copiapó (see page 155).

the **Volcán Ojos del Salado**. The first, sudden sight of **Laguna Verde** is stupendous. The intense colour of its waters – green or turquoise, depending on the time of day – almost leaps out at you from the muted browns and ochres of the surrounding landscape. The lake lies at an altitude of 4500m, about 250km from Copiapó on the international road to Argentina (follow the signs to Paso San Francisco or Tinogasta). At the western end of the lake, a small shack contains a fabulous **hot-spring bath**, where you can soak and take blissful refuge from the biting wind outdoors. The best place to camp is just outside the bath, where a stone wall offers some protection from the wind, and hot streams provide useful washing-up water. At the lake's eastern end there's a *carabineros* checkpoint, where you should make yourself known if you plan to camp.

Volcán Ojos del Salado

Laguna Verde is surrounded by huge volcanoes: Mulas Muertas, Incahuasi and the monumental **Ojos del Salado**. At 6893m, this is the highest peak in Chile and the highest active volcano in the world; its last two eruptions were in 1937 and 1956. A popular **climb** (Oct–March), the volcano ascent takes up to twelve days and is not technically difficult, apart from the last 50m that border the crater. The base of the volcano is a 12km walk from the abandoned *carabineros* checkpoint on the main road, and there are two *refugios* on the way up, one at 5100m (four beds, with latrines) and another at 5750m (twelve beds with kitchen and lounge). Temperatures are low at all times of year, so take plenty of warm gear.

ARRIVAL AND INFORMATION

By car From Copiapó, it's about a 3hr drive to Laguna Santa Rosa, and a 6hr drive to Laguna Verde. There's no public transport to this area – for information on tours, see page 155.

Conaf In summer (Jan–March & Dec), Conaf has its two park headquarters at Laguna Santa Rosa and about 4km from Laguna del Negro Francisco (both 8.30am–6pm; ☎ 52

PARQUE NACIONAL NEVADO DE TRES CRUCES

221 3404); the *guardaparques* are very friendly and take visitors on educational excursions to the lake and around, but if you want to stay over check with Conaf in Copiapó first. Park fees are not enforced through the rest of the year but there are *guardaparques* at the Chilean immigration post at Complejo Fronterizo Maricunga, 100km west of the Argentinian border.

ACCOMMODATION

Hotel Refugio Guanaco Laguna Santa Rosa Western shore of the lake ☎ 09 5401 3069. Private bathrooms, a kitchen and dining room are the draw at this pricey refuge – you also get great views of the lake backed by the snow-capped Volcán Tres Cruces. This team also run *Refugio Flamenco*, 1km *south*, which costs half the price and offers camping for CH$15,000. <u>CH$40,000</u>

Refugio Laguna del Negro Francisco 4km south of the lake ☎ 52 221 3404. This large, comfortable *refugio* sleeps up to fifteen people and has bunk beds, electricity, hot showers and a kitchen. It is necessary to bring your own food and drinking water. <u>CH$12,000</u>

Caldera

Just over 70km northwest of Copiapó, **CALDERA** is a small, easygoing seaside town with a smattering of nineteenth-century buildings, a beach, a pier and a few good fish restaurants. Chosen as the terminus of Chile's first railway by mining and railway

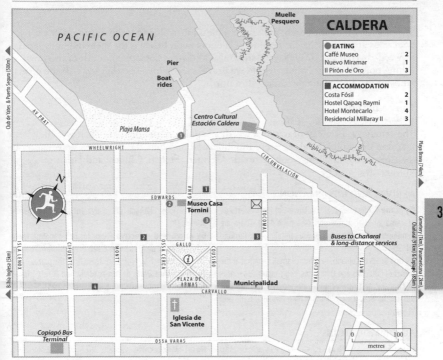

pioneer William Wheelwright, it became the country's second-largest port in the last decades of the nineteenth century, when it exported all the silver extracted in the region's dramatic silver boom.

Caldera's two ports are still busy – one exporting table grapes, the other exporting copper – but they don't totally dominate the bay, which remains fairly attractive. The town's principal landmarks are the Gothic-towered **Iglesia de San Vicente** on the main square, built by English carpenters in 1862, and the former **train station** at the pier, dating from 1851. It's also a good base to reach some of the area's more attractive **beaches**, including Bahía Inglesa and Playa Brava.

Centro Cultural Estación Caldera

Wheelwright s/n • **Museo Paleontológico** Tues–Sun 10am–2pm & 4–7pm • CH$600 • ☎ 52 231 6891

The former train station has been converted into the **Centro Cultural Estación Caldera**, which hosts community events and houses the fascinating little **Museo Paleontológico**, with its collection of fossils, rocks and locally unearthed artefacts.

Museo Casa Tornini

Gana 210 • Guided tours (50min) daily: Jan & Feb noon & 8pm; March–Dec 11.30am & 4.30pm • CH$2500 • ☎ 52 231 7930, ⓦ casatornini.cl

Now the **Museo Casa Tornini**, this handsome, ochre-coloured and well-preserved house, which dates back to 1890, was the residence of a wealthy Italian family, the Torninis. Guided tours provide a snapshot of Caldera's nineteenth-century heyday. There are also temporary art exhibitions, and the owners run the nearby *Caffè Museo* (see page 160).

The pier and beaches

The **pier**, down by the beach, makes for a pleasant stroll and is the starting point for **boat rides** around the bay in summer. Caldera's main **beach** is the sheltered, mid-sized, seaweed-covered and dirty **Playa Mansa** (also known as **Copiapina**), south of the small fishing port. The large, windswept **Playa Brava**, meanwhile, stretches towards the desert sands of the Norte Grande some 74km north.

The cemetery

Av Diego de Almeyda s/n • Daily 8am–7pm • Free

The **cemetery**, 1km east of town, is worth a wander; dating from 1876, it was the first non-denominational cemetery in Chile, and harbours the weathered graves and mausoleums of English, Welsh, Scottish, German, French, Chinese and Japanese immigrants.

ARRIVAL AND INFORMATION

CALDERA

By plane Caldera lies 20km northwest of the Desierto de Atacama international airport (see page 154). There are minibus transfers into town, or you can take a taxi (around CH$20,000).

By bus Buses to Copiapó leave from a small terminal at the corner of Cifuentes and Ossa Varas. Long-distance services to Chañaral and further north are provided by Pullman Bus and Tur Bus, from Caldera's main terminal at Gallo and Vallejos.

Destinations Chañaral (12 daily; 1hr); Copiapó (every 30min; 1hr).

By micro and colectivo *Micros* for Bahía Inglesa leave from the Plaza de Armas (Jan & Feb every 15min). The rest of the year, black taxi *colectivos* leave from the plaza.

Tourist office Plaza de Armas (daily: Jan & Feb 10am–1am; March–Dec 9am–2pm & 4–7pm; ☎52 253 5761).

ACCOMMODATION

Costa Fósil Gallo 560 ☎52 231 6451, ⓦjandy.cl; map p.159. Three levels of bright and spotless rooms, some with (partial) ocean views, sit around a tranquil, flower-filled patio. An information board, a massive map of the region and friendly staff ensure guests feel right at home. **CH$46,000**

Hostel Qapaq Raymi Edwards 420 ☎09 7386 3041, ⓔhostel.qapaqraymi@gmail.com; map p.159. Friendly young owners run this hostel three blocks from the main square, with an array of rooms. Beds are comfy, the vibe relaxed and the spacious patio and bar make up for a cramped shared kitchen. Dorms **CH$10,000**, doubles **CH$30,000**

Hotel Montecarlo Carvallo 627 ☎52 231 5388, ⓦhotel-montecarlo.cl; map p.159. Reasonable, though overpriced, mid-range hotel, with a faded yellow exterior, a lush courtyard garden, straightforward rooms with colourful bedspreads, clean attached bathrooms, TVs and safes. **CH$45,000**

Residencial Millaray II Cousiño 177 ☎52 231 5528, ⓔrubenhmarre@yahoo.es; map p.159. Just a block away from the central plaza, this is a relatively decent budget choice in town (not a contested title, it must be said), with simple rooms. Breakfast costs extra. **CH$25,000**

EATING

Fresh seafood is sold at Caldera's **muelle pesquera** (fishing jetty) where a handful of outdoor **restaurants** hustle up fish dishes, paella and piping hot octopus *empanadas*.

Caffè Museo Edwards 479 ☎09 7986 6167; map p.159. Under the same management as Museo Casa Tornini, this cute café is good spot for breakfast or *onces*, with a concise menu featuring coffees (CH$1000–2600), sandwiches and cakes. While you're waiting, check out the old newspaper front pages on the walls. Mon–Fri 9am–1.30pm & 4.30–8.30pm, Sat & Sun 10.30am–2pm & 5–9pm.

Nuevo Miramar Gana 090 ☎52 231 5381; map p.159. The location of this seafood restaurant couldn't be better, right on the beach, with wonderful views of

the bay. For a romantic evening, order a plate of oysters, prawn omelette or crab gratin (mains CH$6000–10,000) and watch the lights flicker on the water. Mon–Sat noon–4pm & 7pm–midnight, Sun noon–8pm.

Il Pirón di Oro Cousiño 218 ☎52 231 5790; map p.159. In a town that prides itself on its fish and shellfish, this no-frills restaurant with lime-green tablecloths is arguably the best, serving imaginatively prepared dishes (around CH$6000–9000), including exquisite crab pie. Daily 11am–4pm & 7–10pm.

Bahía Inglesa and around

The **beaches** of **Bahía Inglesa** are probably the most photographed in Chile, adorning wall calendars up and down the country. More than their white, powdery sands – which, after all, you can find the length of Chile's coast – it's the exquisite clarity of the turquoise sea and the curious rock formations that rise out of it which set these beaches apart.

Northern beaches

Several beaches are strung along the bay to the **north of Caldera**, separated by rocky outcrops: the long Playa Machas is the southernmost beach, followed by Playa La Piscina, then by Playa El Chuncho and finally Playa Blanca. Surprisingly, this resort area has not been swamped by the kind of ugly, large-scale construction that mars Viña del Mar and La Serena, and **Bahía Inglesa** remains a fairly compact collection of *cabañas* and a few hotels. While the place gets hideously crowded in the height of summer, at most other times it's peaceful and relaxing.

Southern beaches

South of Bahía Inglesa, beyond the little fishing village of Puerto Viejo that marks the end of the paved road, the coast is studded with a string of **superb beaches** lapped with crystal-clear water and backed by immense sand dunes. The scenery is particularly striking around **Bahía Salada**, a deserted bay indented with tiny coves some 130km south of Bahía Inglesa. You might be able to find a tour operator that arranges excursions to these beaches, but if you really want to appreciate the solitude and wilderness of this stretch of coast, you're better off renting a jeep and doing it yourself.

ARRIVAL AND DEPARTURE   BAHÍA INGLESA

By colectivo You can visit Bahía Inglesa for the day from Caldera, just 5km away; plenty of taxi *colectivos* leaving from Caldera's plaza connect the two resorts, and also Copiapó. The best place to catch a *colectivo* back to Caldera is on the corner by *Rocas de Bahía*.

ACCOMMODATION

The problem with staying here is that **accommodation** tends to be ridiculously overpriced, but you should be able to bargain the rates down outside summer. Caldera is close enough, however.

Camping Bahía Inglesa Playa Las Machas ☎52 231 5424. A large, expensive campsite just off Playa Las Machas and overlooking Bahía Inglesa, with hot showers, picnic tables and a swimming pool. There are also *cabañas* which sleep up to four people, the cheapest with shared bathroom. Camping CH$26,000, *cabañas* CH$40,000

Coral de Bahía El Morro 559 ☎09 8434 7749, ⓦcoraldebahia.cl. Long-standing, popular hotel with an extensive selection of rooms, from simple en-suite doubles (the cheapest don't have sea views) to big apartments sleeping up to eight people. There's also a good restaurant. Doubles CH$55,000, apartments US$150

Domo Bahía Inglesa El Morro 610 ☎09 8162 8642, ⓦfacebook.com/domobahia. At the end of the promenade, these three futuristic mini-dome *cabañas*, with huge beds and private bathrooms, are quite the novelty. Staff can arrange tours to remote beaches as well as the Parque Nacional Pan de Azúcar. CH$90,000

Los Jardines de Bahía Inglesa Copiapó 100 ☎52 231 5359, ⓦjardinesbahia.cl. A few blocks back from the beachfront, these smart *cabañas* sleep up to six people. There's a good-sized pool, a table tennis table and a decent Italian restaurant. CH$90,000

EATING AND DRINKING

El Domo El Morro 610 ☎09 5678 3197 8642. Sitting in front of its namesake hotel (see above) this tent-like cupola is the place to try satisfying dishes like mixed seafood ceviche (CH$10,000). It's also a great spot to just linger over a real coffee (CH$2000–3000) or nurse a drink while taking in the ocean vista. Mon–Sat noon–midnight, Sun noon–5pm.

El Plateao El Morro 756 ☎09 6677 5174. The most sophisticated restaurant in town, with deckchairs on a terrace opposite the seafront. *El Plateao* serves international cuisine including flavoursome Thai and Indian curries (most mains around CH$8000–10,000). Daily 1–3pm & 5pm–midnight.

Chañaral

Sitting by a wide, white bay and the Panamericana, **CHAÑARAL**, 167km north of Copiapó, is a rather sorry-looking town of houses staggered up a hillside, with more than its fair share of stray dogs. Originally a small *caleta* used for shipping out the produce of an inland desert oasis, it still serves chiefly as an export centre, these days for the giant El Salvador copper mine, 130km east in the cordillera. Despite efforts to clean it up, Chañaral's huge beach remains contaminated by the toxic wastes deposited by the mine. You can visit the **Parque Nacional Pan de Azúcar** from Chañaral, which sits 30km up the coast, although it is preferable to visit as a day-trip from Copiapó.

ARRIVAL AND DEPARTURE   CHAÑARAL

By bus Many north–south buses make a stop in the town; those that don't will drop you off if you ask.

Destinations Antofagasta (11 daily; 5hr); Arica (6 daily; 15hr); Calama (11 daily; 8hr); Copiapó (12 daily; 1hr);

Iquique (9 daily; 11hr); La Serena (12 daily; 7hr); Mejillones (4 daily; 6hr); Ovalle (11 daily; 9hr); Santiago (11 daily; 14hr); Taltal (2 daily; 2hr 30min); Tocopilla (7 daily; 8hr); Vallenar (12 daily; 4hr).

ACCOMMODATION AND EATING

Alicanto Panamericana Norte 49 ☎ 52 248 1168. Take in ocean views as you make your way through fresh seafood hauled in by local fisherman at the adjacent cove. Mains around CH$8000. Daily 9.30am–5pm.

Hotel Aqualuna Merino Jarpa 521 ☎ 52 248 9607, ⓦ aqualunahotel.cl. For a central option, this simple, ten-room hotel pulls out all the stops: comfy mattresses,

TVs and private parking. It also has a few apartments for four people. Doubles CH$40,000, apartments CH$48,000

Hotel Jiménez Merino Jarpa 551 ☎ 52 248 0328, ⓦ hoteljimenez.cl. A budget choice with a prime position on the main street close to the Pullman Bus stop, with basic but clean and bright rooms, some with private bath, and all with cable TV. Breakfast costs extra. CH$28,000

Parque Nacional Pan de Azúcar

Daily 8.30am–12.30pm & 2–6pm • CH$5000 • ☎ 52 221 3404, ⓦ www.conaf.cl

Home to two dozen varieties of cactus, guanacos and foxes, and countless birds, **Parque Nacional Pan de Azúcar** is a 40km strip of desert containing the most stunning coastal scenery in the north of Chile. Steep hills and cliffs rise abruptly from the shore, which is lined with a series of pristine white-sand beaches. Though bare and stark, these hills make an unforgettable sight as they catch the late afternoon sun, when the whole coastline is bathed in rich shades of gold, pink and yellow. The only inhabited part of the park is **Caleta Pan de Azúcar**, 30km north of Chañaral, where you'll find a cluster of twenty or so fishermen's shacks as well as the Conaf information centre and a campsite (see page 163).

Isla Pan de Azúcar

Opposite the village, 2km off the shore, the **Isla Pan de Azúcar** is a small island sheltering a huge collection of marine wildlife, including seals, sea otters, plovers, cormorants, pelicans and more than three thousand Humboldt penguins; you can (and should) take a boat trip out to get a close look at the wildlife. The island's distinctive conical silhouette gives the park its name "sugarloaf".

Mirador Pan de Azúcar

For fabulous panoramic views up and down the coast, head to **Mirador Pan de Azúcar**, a well-signposted lookout point 10km north of the village; the different varieties of cactus are fascinating and you may have the place all to yourself – unless you're joined by a curious grey fox or guanaco.

Las Lomitas

More difficult to reach, and less rewarding, **Las Lomitas** is a 700m-high clifftop about 30km north of the village; it's almost permanently shrouded in mist and is the site of a large black net, or "fog catcher", that condenses fog into water and collects it below.

ARRIVAL AND INFORMATION

By car There are two access roads to the park, both branching off the Panamericana: approaching from the south, the turn-off is at the north end of Chañaral, just past the cemetery; approaching from the north, take the turn-off at Las Bombas, 45km north of Chañaral. Both roads are bumpy but passable in a car.

By taxi There are no public buses to the park. Taxis from Chañaral cost around CH$25,000 each way – worth it for a group. Alternatively, take a day-trip tour from Copiapó.

PARQUE NACIONAL PAN DE AZÚCAR

Conaf Near the village (daily 8.30am–12.30pm & 2–6pm). Offers maps, leaflets and souvenirs. This is where you pay your park fee.

Tours Several tour operators in Copiapó (see page 155) offer day-trips to the park. Boat trips to the Isla Pan de Azúcar depart from the *caleta* and cost around CH$5000/person (minimum fifteen people). It takes about 90min to do the circuit; the best times are around 7–8am and 6pm, when the penguins come out to eat. Ask in the village for Segundo Lizana, Manuel Carasco or Alex Guerra, all of whom offer the same trip at the standard price.

ACCOMMODATION AND EATING

Rough camping is not allowed in the park, but there are a number of authorized **camping** areas.

Camping Los Pingüinos Just north of the Caleta Pan de Azúcar ☎ 52 248 1209. If you've got your own camping gear, this campsite has decent facilities, including bathrooms (CH$1000 extra for shower), drinking water, picnic tables, rubbish collection and first-aid supplies. CH$5000

Pan de Azúcar Lodge Playa Piqueros, south of Caleta Pan de Azúcar ☎ 09 9280 3483, ⊛ pandeazucarlodge. cl. The national park's best camping facilities, with barbecues and picnic tables, as well as a handful of fully equipped solar-powered *cabañas* sleeping up to eight people. Camping CH$5000, *cabañas* CH$40,000

El Norte Grande

VICUÑAS NEAR PUTRE

El Norte Grande

"El Norte Grande" occupies almost a quarter of Chile's mainland territory but contains barely five percent of its population. Its most outstanding feature is the Atacama Desert; the driest desert in the world, it contains areas where no rainfall has been recorded – ever. Its landscape is typically made up of rock and gravel spread over a wide plain, alleviated only by crinkly mountains. To the west, the plain is lined by a range of coastal hills that drop abruptly to a shelf of land where most of the region's towns and cities are scattered. To the east, the desert climbs towards the altiplano: a high, windswept plateau composed of lakes and salt flats ringed with snowcapped volcanoes.

Formidable and desolate as it is, the region contains a wealth of superb attractions, and, for many visitors, constitutes the highlight of a trip to Chile – particularly for European travellers, who will find nothing remotely like it back home. The Pacific seaboard is lined by vast tracts of stunning **coastal scenery**, while inland the **desert pampa** itself impresses not only with its otherworldly geography, but also with fascinating testimonies left by humankind. One of these is the trail of decaying nitrate **ghost towns**, including **Humberstone** and **Santa Laura**, easily reached from Iquique. Another is the existence of immense images known as **geoglyphs** left by indigenous peoples on the hillsides and ravines of the desert – you'll find impressive examples at **Cerro Pintados**, south of Iquique, **Cerro Unitas**, east of Huara, and **Tiliviche**, between Huara and Arica.

As you journey towards and up into the cordillera, you'll come across attractive **oasis villages**, some – such as **Pica** and **Mamiña** – with **hot springs**. Up in the Andes, the altiplano is undoubtedly one of the country's highlights, with its dazzling **lakes**, **salt flats and volcanoes**, its abundance of **wildlife** and its tiny, whitewashed villages inhabited by native Aymara. The main altiplano touring base – and, indeed, one of the most popular destinations in the whole country, for Chileans and foreigners alike – is **San Pedro de Atacama**, a pleasant oasis 315km northeast of Antofagasta, where numerous operators offer excursions to the famous **El Tatio geysers** and the haunting moonscapes of the **Valle de la Luna**.

Further north, the stretch of altiplano within reach of Iquique and Arica boasts wild vicuña and spectacular scenery, preserved in **Parque Nacional Lauca** and several adjoining parks and reserves. Some towns and cities of the Far North, mainly **Antofagasta** and **Calama**, tend to be dreary and uninviting, but serve as unavoidable departure points for excursions into the hinterland. Bear in mind also the **Bolivian Winter**, when sporadic heavy rains between December and February in the altiplano can wash roads away and seriously disrupt communications and access.

FLAMINGOS IN THE SALAR DE ATACAMA

Highlights

❶ Valle de la Luna Watch the setting sun heighten the textures and deepen the colours of the valley's sweeping dunes and undulating rock formations. See page 183

❷ Salar de Atacama Explore the vast salt flats of the Atacama Desert, the driest place on Earth – parts of it never, ever see rain. See page 183

❸ El Tatio geysers At 4300m, pools of boiling water send clouds of steam into the air at the crack of dawn. See page 184

❹ Iquique's beaches and mountains The city has made a name for itself as a surfers' haven and is also one of the best places to paraglide in

the world. See page 185

❺ Cerro Pintados geoglyphs Discover these mysterious, indigenous images, the largest collection of geoglyphs in South America. See page 194

❻ Isluga and Lauca parks Trek through a landscape of mineral baths, cobalt lakes, sparkling salt flats and spongy bogs at dizzying altitudes. See pages 197 and 209

❼ Altiplano wildlife Thousands of llamas and alpacas, vicuñas and vizcachas, flamingos and condors – a photographer's dream. See page 209

HIGHLIGHTS ARE MARKED ON THE MAP ON PAGE 168

EL NORTE GRANDE

HIGHLIGHTS

1. Valle de la Luna
2. Salar de Atacama
3. El Tatio geysers
4. Iquique's beaches and mountains
5. Cerro Pintados geoglyphs
6. Isluga and Lauca parks
7. Altiplano wildlife

N

PERU

Tacna

Museo
Arqueológico
AZAPA VALLEY

Arica

San Miguel
de Azapa

Visviri

PARQUE
NACIONAL
LAUCA

Putre

Parinacota

Socoroma

Tambo Quemado

RESERVA
NATURAL
LAS VICUÑAS

SALAR DE
SURIRE

Enquelga

Islunga

Colchane

SALAR DE
COLPASA

BOLIVIA

Pisagua

Hacienda
de Tiliviche

PARQUE
NACIONAL
VOLCAN ISLUGA

Chusmisa

Huara

Cerro Unitas

Mamiña

SALAR DE UYUNI

Iquique

Humberstone
Pozo Almonte

La Tirana

Pica

Matilla

Cerro
Pintados

RESERVA
NACIONAL
PAMPA DEL
TAMARUGAL

Ollagüe

PACIFIC
OCEAN

Tocopilla

Chug Chug
Geoglyphs

Chuquicamata

Caspana

RESERVA
NACIONAL
EDUARDO
AVAROA

Maria Elena

Calama

Chiu
Chiu

Ayquina

Gatico

Pedro de
Valdivia

El Tatio

Cobija

Mejillones

NITRATE
PAMPA

Chacabuco

Baquedano

San Pedro
de Atacama

Valle de la Luna

Toconao

Museo de la
Biodiversidad

Antofagasta

SALAR DE
ATACAMA

Camar

ALMA
Observatory

Socaire

Peine

Cerro Paranal

ARGENTINA

0 — 80
kilometres

Taital

Brief history

It seems almost inconceivable that such a hostile land can support life, but for thousands of years El Norte Grande has been home to indigenous peoples who've wrested a living either from the sea or from the fertile oases that nestle in the Andean foothills. The excessive dryness of the climate has left countless relics of these people almost perfectly intact – most remarkably the **Chinchorro mummies** (see page 208), buried on the desert coast near Arica some seven thousand years ago. It wasn't until the nineteenth century that Chile's more recent inhabitants – along with British and German businesses – turned their attention to the Atacama, when it became apparent that the desert was rich in **nitrates** that could be exported at great commercial value. So lucrative was this burgeoning industry that Chile was prepared to go to war over it, for most of the region at that time in fact belonged to Bolivia and Peru. The **War of the Pacific**, waged against Bolivia and Peru between 1878 and 1883, acquired for Chile the desired prize, and the desert pampas went on to yield enormous revenues for the next three decades.

With the German invention of synthetic nitrates at the end of World War I, Chile's industry entered a rapid decline, but a financial crisis was averted when new mining techniques enabled low-grade **copper**, of which there are huge quantities in the region, to be profitably extracted. Today, copper continues to play a crucial role in the economy, with Chile the world's leading supplier. The country is also the second highest producer of **lithium**, another element in abundance in the desert.

GETTING AROUND   EL NORTE GRANDE

Many of the region's attractions can be reached by **public transport**, though in order to explore the region in depth you'll need to book some **tours** or, better still, rent a **4WD** vehicle. Whatever your mode of transport, don't underestimate the **distances** involved in getting to most points of interest, particularly in the altiplano. It makes sense to isolate a few chosen highlights rather than try to see everything, which would be both time-consuming and costly.

Antofagasta and around

A Bolivian town until 1879, when it was annexed by Chile in the War of the Pacific, **ANTOFAGASTA** is one of the country's largest and most rapidly growing cities. Many tourists bypass this decidedly lacklustre desert port altogether, and with good reason. Overpriced and unattractive, the regional capital holds little of cultural or aesthetic interest, but is a major transport hub and one of Chile's most prosperous cities, serving as an export centre for the region's great mines, most notably Chuquicamata (see page 175). Sitting on a flat shelf between the ocean and the hills, Antofagasta has a compact downtown core, made up of dingy, traffic-choked streets that sport a few handsome but run-down old public buildings, and a modern stretch along the coastal avenue. The area around Latorre and Condell, between Bolivar and Riquelme streets, is best avoided after 9.30pm – Antofagasta has a prostitution problem.

A couple of blocks northeast of the central square – **Plaza Colón** – along Bolívar, you'll find the magnificently restored nineteenth-century **offices and railway terminus** of the former Antofagasta and Bolivia Railway Company, complete with polished wooden verandas and dark-green stucco walls (albeit with no public access). Further north still, and an easy stop-off if you're heading out to the airport, is **La Portada**, an iconic natural arch of rock looming out of the sea.

South of the city centre the busy coastal avenue runs past a couple of tiny, coarse-sand **beaches**, first at the Balneario Municipal, then, much further south, at the Playa Huascar, the latter only suitable for sunbathing – take *micro* #103 from Washington, near the square. In this direction lies one of the city's most curious sights, the **Ruinas de Huanchaca**, vestiges of a disused silver refinery, as well as the **Museo Desierto de Atacama**, which shares the same site.

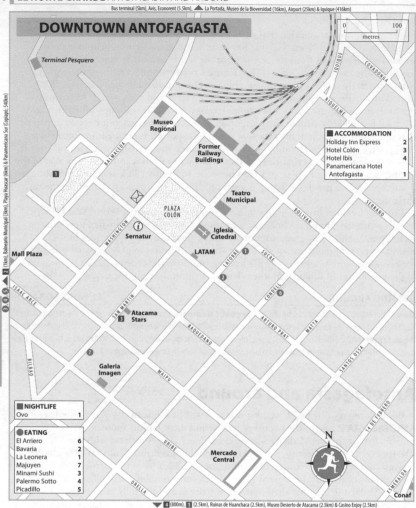

Bus terminal (5km), Avis, Econorent (5.5km), ▲ La Portada, Museo de la Bioversidad (16km), Airport (25km) & Iquique (416km)

DOWNTOWN ANTOFAGASTA

0   100
metres

Terminal Pesquero

Museo Regional

Former Railway Buildings

Teatro Municipal

PLAZA COLÓN

Iglesia Catedral

Sernatur

LATAM

Mall Plaza

Atacama Stars

Galeria Imagen

ACCOMMODATION

Holiday Inn Express	2
Hotel Colón	3
Hotel Ibis	4
Panamericana Hotel Antofagasta	1

NIGHTLIFE

| Ovo | 1 |

EATING

El Arriero	6
Bavaria	2
La Leonera	1
Majuyen	7
Minami Sushi	3
Palermo Sotto	4
Picadillo	5

Mercado Central

N

Conaf

BALMACEDA · WASHINGTON · SAN MARTIN · BILBAO · ISAAC ARCE · LATORRE · SUCRE · CONDELL · MATTA · BOLIVAR · SERRANO · IQUIQUE · COVADONGA · RIQUELME · ARTURO PRAT · BAQUEDANO · MAIPU · URIBE · ORELLA · SANTOS OSSA · 21 DE FEBRERO · ESMERALDA

(1km), Balneario Municipal (3km), Playa Huascar (6km) & Panamericana Sur (Copiapó, 540km)

Panamericana Norte (Calama, 217km)

4 (800m), 1 (2.5km), Ruinas de Huanchaca (2.5km), Museo Desierto de Atacama (2.5km) & Casino Enjoy (2.5km)

If you have time to kill or if deserted nitrate-era ghost towns and different types of rock formations are your thing, you may want to dedicate a day or afternoon to exploring the area surrounding the city. Highlights include the cliff formations of **La Portada** (a natural arch, now a symbol of the region), a couple of **observatories** and the **Chug Chug geolyphs**.

Plaza Colón

In Antofagasta's centre sprawls the large, green **Plaza Colón**, dominated by a tall clock tower whose face is supposedly a replica of London's Big Ben – one of many tangible signs of the role played by the British in Antofagasta's commercial development. The city's administrative and public buildings, including the Neo-Gothic **Iglesia Catedral**, built between 1906 and 1917, surround the square.

Museo Regional

Bolívar 188 • Tues–Fri 9am–5pm, Sat & Sun 11am–2pm • Free • ☎ 55 222 7016, ⊕ museodeantofagasta.cl

The 1866 customs house (or Ex-Aduana as it is now called) is the oldest building in the city, and within it sits the **Museo Regional**. The museum houses an impressive mineral display downstairs and, upstairs, a collection of clothes, furniture and toys.

Ruinas de Huanchaca and the Museo Desierto de Atacama

Av Angamos 01606, 3km south of the centre by the Universidad del Norte • **Ruinas de Huanchaca** No fixed opening hours • Free • **Museo Desierto de Atacama** Tues–Sun 10am–1pm & 2.30–7pm • CH$2000 • ☎ 55 241 7860, ⊕ ruinasdehuanchaca.cl • Bus #303 from Plaza Colón; several southbound micros also make the journey

These remains of an old Bolivian silver refinery sit on a hilltop a short distance inland, yet still within the city. The **Ruinas de Huanchaca** were built to process the silver brought down from the Potosí mine (at that time the most important silver mine in South America), before being shipped out of Antofagasta. Looking at the square and circular walls of the complex from below, you'd be forgiven for thinking they were ruins of a pre-Columbian fortress. You are not allowd to climb up into the ruins.

On the same site is the impressive modern **Museo Desierto de Atacama**. A must for aspiring geographers and geologists, this modern museum is divided into several parts. These include a "rock garden", exhibiting rocks and minerals indigenous to northern Chile; rooms named "the creation of space" dedicated to explaining how the desert and altiplano were formed; an exhibition on "the miner", looking at the history of mining in this part of Chile; and a room financed by the European Southern Observatory exploring astrology in the Atacama Desert. There's also a space dedicated to temporary exhibitions. Audio tours (included in the entry fee) are available in Spanish and English.

ARRIVAL AND GETTING AROUND

By plane Aeropuerto Cerro Moreno, 25km north of the city, right on the Tropic of Capricorn, is served by LATAM flights (Prat 445; ☎ 55 226 5151). Regular *colectivos* and infrequent *micros* head to the centre or you can take a minibus directly to your accommodation (they await every arrival).
Destinations Iquique (1–2 daily; 55min); La Serena (1–3 daily; 1hr 20min); Santiago (13–20 daily; 1hr 50min–3hr).
By bus The main Terminal Carlos Oviedo Cavada is on Pedro A. Cerda 5750, about a 15min drive from the centre – a cab will set you back approximately CH$7000. A much cheaper option is to take local bus #103 or #111 from outside the terminal to the centre.

ANTOFAGASTA

Destinations Arica (hourly–every 3hr; 10hr); Calama (hourly; 3hr); Caldera (hourly; 6hr); Chañaral (hourly; 5hr); Chuquicamata (5 daily; 3hr); Copiapó (houry–every 2hr; 7hr); La Serena (every 30min–1hr; 12hr); Mejillones (every 30min; 40min); San Pedro de Atacama (4–6 daily; 4hr 30min); Santiago (hourly; 20hr).
Car rental Avis, airport & Baquedano 364 (☎ 55 256 3140, ⊕ avis.cl); Budget, airport (☎ 55 256 3143, ⊕ budget.cl); Econorent, airport & Pedro Aguirre Cerda 6100 (☎ 55 259 4177, ⊕ econorent.cl).

INFORMATION AND TOURS

Tourist office Prat 384 (Mon–Thurs 8.30am–5.30pm, Fri 8.30am–4.30pm; ☎ 55 245 1818, ⊖ infoantofagasta@sernatur.cl). For tourist information on the city of Antofagasta, head to the ground floor of the Intendencia at the corner of the central plaza.
Conaf Av Argentina 2510 (Mon–Fri 9am–1pm & 2.30–5.30pm; ☎ 55 238 3320). Details on the protected areas

around San Pedro de Atacama, which lies within this region.
Travel agencies A number of travel agencies in the centre offer a variety of tours around the city and surrounding region – try Atacama Stars, San Martín 2326, local 9 (☎ 55 243 8875, ⊕ atacamastars.com).

ACCOMMODATION

You'll find an abundance of **accommodation** in Antofagasta, ranging from cheaper, old-fashioned places downtown to the more expensive business-oriented hotels on the coastal avenue, which is well connected by local transport; the latter offer cheaper rates at weekends.

4

Holiday Inn Express Av Grecia 1490 ☎ 800 028 5880 or ☎ 55 222 8888, ⓦ hilatam.com/cl; map p.170. Modern, super-clean US chain hotel around 2km southwest of the main plaza, with pool and parking – a good place to pamper yourself if the desert is getting to you. **CH$50,000**

Hotel Colón San Martín 2434 ☎ 55 226 1851, ⓔ colonantofagasta@gmail.com; map p.170. Decent option with clean, fairly comfortable and light en-suite rooms with TVs. Those facing the road can be rather noisy. The restaurant next door, owned by the same people, serves good-value home-cooked meals. **CH$35,000**

Hotel Ibis Av Jose Miguel Carrera 1627 ☎ 55 245 8200, ⓦ ibis.com; map p.170. This mid-range hotel, around 1.5km southwest of the main plaza, is a reassuring choice: staff are professional, the en suites are comfortable and well equipped (some even have sea views), there's a good restaurant and the rates represent good value. **CH$39,900**

Panamericana Hotel Antofagasta Balmaceda 2575 ☎ 55 222 8811, ⓦ panamericanahoteles.cl; map p.170. Large, venerable national chain hotel overlooking the ocean, with well-furnished rooms. The on-site restaurant's outdoor terrace is one of the most pleasant lunch spots in the city – *menú del día* CH$15,500. **CH$48,000**

EATING

Antofagasta's **restaurants** tend to be busy and lively, with a couple of classy establishments standing out among the grill houses and pizzerias. On the coast just west of the town centre is the **Mall Plaza**, Balmaceda 2355, home to several newer eating establishments. At the corner of Ossa and Maipú, the huge, pink-and-cream **Mercado Central** sells fresh food and *artesanía*.

★ **El Arriero** Condell 2644 ☎ 55 226 4371, ⓦ arrieroafta.cl; map p.170. There is sometimes live jazz at this inviting spot. Try the excellent-value *parrilladas* (CH$10,900 for one person, CH$18,200 for two) or go for the good-value lunch menu (CH$4900). The attached *Fuente Alemana* is even cheaper. Mon–Sat 11.30am–4pm & 7.30pm–midnight, Sun 11.30am–4pm.

Bavaria Latorre 2624 ☎ 55 228 3821, ⓦ bavaria.cl; map p.170. The same pine decor, the same grilled meat, the same indifferent service you find in every other branch of the *Bavaria* chain in the country. At least you know what you're getting – and the German-style food's not bad, after all, nor is it particularly expensive (a hearty *parrillada* for two costs CH$29,000). Daily noon–midnight.

La Leonera Latorre 2670 ☎ 55 225 1436; map p.170. Perhaps the best cheap eats in town – no-frills *La Leonera* has been a locals' favourite for years, offering brisk service and a good-value lunch menu (CH$3500). Expect the likes of fried fish, *empanadas* and stews. Mon–Sat 9am–1am.

Majuyen San Martín 2326 ☎ 55 282 8318, ⓦ majuyen. jimdo.com; map p.170. Set back from the road in the Patio Alcántara, this tiny Japanese/Peruvian joint has a handful of tables and a delivery service. Tasty sushi, sashimi and *ceviche* (CH$4000–8000) are the order of the day here. Daily 1–4pm & 7–11pm.

Minami Sushi Av Grecia 1748 ☎ 55 298 3957, ⓦ minamisushi.cl; map p.170. This lively spot with loud music has sea views and great deals on sushi (thirty pieces for CH$7990), as well as a full bar. Mon–Sat 12.30–11pm, Sun 3–11pm.

Palermo Sotto General Velasquez 855 ☎ 55 231 9906; map p.170. Bright Italian café-cum-restaurant not far up from the seafront, with sidewalk seating. Pizzas from CH$10,000 and a good fixed lunch for CH$5000. Daily 11am–10pm.

★ **Picadillo** Av Grecia 1000 ☎ 55 224 7503; map p.170. Popular restaurant offering the likes of beef carpaccio marinated in ginger for starters and delicious, unusual sushi, plus inventive desserts (most mains CH$7000–12,000); the music and service are faultless. Reservations recommended at weekends. Mon–Fri 12.30–3.30pm & 7.30pm–1am, Sat 8pm–2am.

NIGHTLIFE

The **nightlife** scene, thanks mainly to the number of university students around town, is surprisingly vibrant, with limited options near the city centre – those right in the centre tend to be very sleazy – and most dance clubs located down at **Playa Huáscar**, way south of town (take a taxi and pick one that appeals).

Ovo Av Angamos 1455 ☎ 55 265 3000, ⓦ enjoy.cl; map p.170. Within the new *Enjoy* casino, right opposite the Ruinas de Huanchaca (see page 171), this popular disco is the most accessible dance venue from the centre, if not the hippest spot around. Fri & Sat midnight–late.

La Portada and Museo de la Biodiversidad

16km north of Antofagasta along the coast road • **La Portada** Open access • Free • **Museo de la Bioversidad** Tues–Sun 10am–6pm • Free • *Micro* #15 from the Terminal Pesquero; if you're driving, follow the coast road north and take the turn-off to Juan López, from where La Portada is well signed

A huge eroded arch looming out of the ocean, **La Portada** was declared a national monument in 1990, and has become something of a regional symbol, with its picture gracing postcards and calendars all over Chile. Makeshift signs quite rightly warn you not to approach the crumbling cliffs or descend the rickety steps to the unsafe beach, while the nearby bar-restaurant and shops are often closed, even in high season, lending the place a sadly abandoned air. The **Museo de la Biodiversidad** on the site is dedicated to the flora and fauna of northern Chile's coastal region.

Cerro Paranal Observatory

Cerro Paranal, 120km south of Anto • Tours Sat 10am & 2pm; you'll need to register well in advance • Free • ☎ 55 243 5000, ⓦ eso.org/paranal • Head south from Antofagasta on the Panamericana (Ruta 5); the unpaved turn-off 24km south of the Mina Escondida crossroads leads due south over a mountain pass to the observatory; observatry trips are included on some tours from Antofagasta (see page 171)

A little under two hours south of Antofagasta, perched on **Cerro Paranal** at 2644m above sea level, is the **Cerro Paranal Observatory**, run by the ESO. While you have to be a recognized researcher to stand any chance of looking through its **Very Large Telescope** (VLT), one of the world's strongest, you can visit on weekly tours the dazzling site, set among suitably lunar, and even Mars-like, landscapes of reddish rock. In fact, NASA tested the Mars Pathfinder rover in the nearby Atacama Desert (and parts of the James Bond movie *Quantum of Solace* were filmed here).

The VLT – strictly speaking a set of four 8.2m telescopes, each weighing 430 tonnes, whose combined might enables observers to see objects as small as humans on the Moon – is housed in a futuristic-looking set of four trapezoidal cylinders, dramatically located on the barren Cerro Paranal, which averages 330 clear nights a year. A luxurious 120-room residence (for scientists only), complete with a cafeteria and an indoor garden (both open to the public), stands nearby. Take warm clothing, as it is very cold inside the observatory.

The nitrate pampa

Northeast of Antofagasta, the vast *pampa salitrera*, or **Nitrate Pampa**, pans across the desert towards the cordillera – it's not the prettiest landscape in the world, a mass of scruffy plains that look as though they have been ploughed, fertilized and then left for fallow. Between 1890 and 1925 there were more than eighty *oficinas* here, extracting the nitrate ore and sending it down to the ports by railroad. Some of them are still standing, abandoned and in ruins, including Chacabuco, crumbling in the desert heat.

Two highways cross the pampa: the Panamericana, heading due north to Iquique, and Ruta 25, branching off northeast to the mining city of Calama. The former skirts **María Elena**, home to the last remaining nitrate *oficina* (or plant), and a place that can be reached on public transport. Although you can find basic accommodation if you look hard enough (there are two hotels), you may as well forge on if you can; it's a desperately soulless place to spend the night.

Chug Chug geoglyphs

The Panamericana is crossed by a lateral road, Ruta 24, 107km north of the Carmen Alto junction. This is connected to Tocopilla, 60km west, and Chuquicamata, 66km east. Just short of 50km along the road for Chuquicamata, a sign points north to the **Chug Chug Geoglyphs**, reached by a 13km dirt road that's just about passable in a car. These consist of some three hundred images spread over several hills, many of them clearly visible from below, including circles, zoomorphic figures, human faces and geometric designs. It's an impressive site, and certainly deserves a visit if you're driving in the area.

Calama and around

Sitting on the banks of the Río Loa, at an altitude of 2250m, **CALAMA** is an ugly, bland town, whose chief role is as a service centre and residential base for **Chuquicamata**, the massive copper mine 16km north (see page 175). It's best avoided if possible, especially as it is quite a hot spot for petty crime, but many visitors end up spending a night here on their way to or from **San Pedro de Atacama**, the famous oasis village and tourist centre 100km east.

Brief history
Calama began life as a **tambo**, or resting place, at the intersection of two Inca roads – one running down the Andes, the other connecting the altiplano with the Pacific – and both Diego de Almagro and Pedro de Valdivia visited on their journeys into Chile. It was never heavily populated by pre-Hispanic peoples, who preferred nearby Chiu Chiu, with its less saline water supply. The town took on a new prominence, however, as an important stop on the **Oruro–Antofagasta railway** in the late nineteenth century, and its future was sealed with the creation of the **Chuquicamata copper mine** in 1911. Today its busy streets are built around a surprisingly small and laidback central core.

Parque El Loa
Av O'Higgins s/n • Park daily 10am–8pm; museum daily 10am–noon & 3–6.30pm • Free

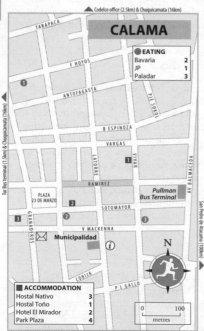

About 2km south of the centre of town is the **Parque El Loa**, a good spot for a picnic. One of the star attractions is the **archeological museum**, which holds displays on pre-Columbian history. The other famous landmark is a mini-reconstruction of the famous Chiu Chiu church.

ARRIVAL AND DEPARTURE CALAMA AND AROUND

By plane Aeropuerto El Loa is 5km south of the centre – the only way into town from here is by taxi (around CH$6500).
Destinations Copiapo (4 weekly; 1hr 10min); Iquique (4 weekly; 45min); La Serena (5 weekly; 1hr 35min); Santiago (12–18 daily; 2hr).

By bus Arriving by bus you'll be dropped at your bus company's office, generally near the city centre; there's no single terminal, and the Tur Bus terminal is inconveniently situated nearly 2km north of town. Hail down *colectivo* (shared taxi) #5 or #11 right outside the latter to get to the centre, or take a taxi (around CH$4000). Some buses to Argentina and Bolivia also originate here (see page 178).
Destinations Antofagasta (hourly–every 2hr; 3hr); Arica (5–6 daily; 10hr); Chañaral (10–12 daily; 8hr); Chuquicamata (every 30min; 30min); Copiapó (hourly;

10hr); Iquique (5–6 daily; 6hr); La Serena (10 daily; 12hr 30min–15hr); San Pedro de Atacama (every 30min–1hr; 1hr 30min); Santiago (hourly; 22hr 30min); Uyuni (Bolivia; 1 daily; 8–9hr).

GETTING AROUND AND INFORMATION

Car rental Avis (☎ 55 279 3968, ✺ avis.cl) and Hertz (☎ 55 231 5762, ✺ hertz.cl) both have offices at the airport.

Tourist office Latorre 1689, near the corner of Vicuña Mackenna (Mon–Fri 8am–1pm & 2–6pm; ☎ 55 253 1707). Offers maps and other basic information, but not much else.

ACCOMMODATION

Calama has a wide range of **accommodation**, but many places are overpriced owing to the mining clientele, and many can get fully booked during the San Pedro tourist seasons. Beware of overbooking and always call or send an email to confirm if possible.

Hostal Nativo Sotomayor 2215 ☎ 55 231 0377, ✺ nativo.cl; map p.174. This centrally located, family-run hotel offers friendly service and plain, immaculately clean rooms with TV; those with private bathrooms cost CH$10,000 more. They also offer inexpensive car rental and have an on-site restaurant. **CH$33,000**

Hostal Toño Vivar 1970 ☎ 55 234 1185, ✉ david6013@ live.com; map p.174. A short walk from Plaza 23 de Mayo, this *residencial* is a decent, pretty quiet budget choice which has been going for years, offering very simple rooms, some with private bathrooms. **CH$20,000**

Hotel El Mirador Sotomayor 2064 ☎ 55 234 0329, ✺ hotelmirador.cl; map p.174. A smart, small hotel with spacious rooms – including one with a Victorian cast-iron bath – and attractive furnishings, set in a colonial-style house that dates from the nineteenth century. There's a spacious lounge and café-bar. **CH$57,000**

Park Plaza José Lira 1392 ☎ 55 271 5800, ✺ parkcalama.cl; map p.174. Popular with business travellers, the *Park Plaza* boasts elegant decor, a good restaurant (try the weekday lunch buffet; CH$16,500) and an attractive swimming pool – a godsend in the sweltering summer months. **US$119**

EATING

Bavaria Sotomayor 2095 ☎ 55 234 1496, ✺ bavaria.cl; map p.174. *Bavaria*, on the plaza, is part of a well-known nationwide chain offering decent if very predictable mid-priced meat dishes (CH$5000–11,000) and sandwiches. The lunchtime *menú ejectivo* costs just CH$4500. Daily: café 8am–midnight; restaurant noon–4.30pm & 7.30pm–midnight.

JP Felix Hoyos 2127 ☎ 55 231 2559; map p.174. The friendly and unpretentious *JP* – just a short walk from the

plaza –serves tasty fish and seafood (CH$6000–14,000) such as *sopa de mariscos* and *pescado frito*. Tues–Sat noon–3.30pm & 8–11.30pm, Sun noon–3.30pm.

Paladar Vivar 1797 ☎ 55 292 6554; map p.174. The swish *Paladar* has an imaginative menu compared with other Calama eating options (mains CH$7000–15,000), offering sharing platters and international cuisine with a French twist, plus a great Chilean wine list. Mon–Sat 12.30pm–1.30am.

Chuquicamata

16km north of Calama • Official guided tours (by minibus, Jan & Feb departing Calama Mon–Fri 1.30pm & 3.30pm; March–Dec 1.30pm only; 1hr 30min) must be booked in advance from Codelco's Calama office on Av Granadero and Av Central (☎ 55 232 2122), or through Calama's tourist information office (see above) • Free, but donations to a children's charity supported by the mine are welcomed

One of the world's largest open-pit copper mines, **Chuquicamata** produces 600,000 tonnes per year – outstripped only by Mina Escondida, 200km southeast of Antofagasta, whose capacity exceeds 800,000 tonnes. Carved out of the ground like a giant, sunken amphitheatre, the massive mine dwarfs everything within it, making the huge trucks carrying the ore up from the crater floor – whose wheels alone are an incredible 4m high – look like tiny, crawling ants. Its size is the result of some ninety years of excavation, and its reserves are predicted to last at least until the middle of this century.

Along with all of Chile's large-scale copper mines, or "*grandes minerías*" as they're called, Chuquicamata belongs to Codelco, the government-owned copper corporation. Codelco also used to maintain an adjacent company town, complete with its own school, hospital, cinema and football stadium, but the nine thousand workers and their families who lived there have now been moved to Calama, making way for further excavation.

Tours take place almost entirely on a bus, though you're allowed to get out at the viewpoint looking down to the pit – wear sensible shoes and clothing that covers most of your body. The rest of the tour takes you round the machinery yards and buildings of the plant, which you see from the outside only.

San Pedro de Atacama

The little oasis village of **SAN PEDRO DE ATACAMA**, 100km southeast of Calama, with its narrow dirt streets and attractive adobe houses, is *the* tourism centre of Chile. Sitting at an altitude of 2400m between the desert and the altiplano, or *puna* (the high basin connecting the two branches of the cordillera), this has been an important settlement since pre-Hispanic times, originally as a major stop on the trading route connecting the llama herders of these highlands with the fishing communities of the Pacific. Later, during the nitrate era, it was the main rest stop on the cattle trail from Salta in Argentina to the nitrate *oficinas*, where the cattle were driven to supply the workers with fresh meat.

The large numbers of Chilean tourists and hordes of gringos here can come as quite a shock if you have arrived from more remote parts of northern Chile, and San Pedro has recently begun to lose some of its charm. The predilection for the almost uniform "native-style" design, involving lots of adobe walls, thatched roofs and faux

SAN PEDRO DE ATACAMA

ACCOMMODATION
Alto Atacama	2
Awasi	3
Camping Los Perales	11
Casa de Don Tomás	14
La Casa de Mireya	4
Hostal Mama Tierra	7
Hostal Pangea	5
Hostal Sonchek	6
Hostal Takha-Takha	10
Hostelling International	8
Hotel Altiplánico	1
Hotel Cumbres San Pedro de Atacama	12
Puritama Hostal	9
Tierra Atacama	13

DRINKING
Chela Cabur	1

EATING
Adobe	10
Babalu	6/7
Blanco	12
La Casona	11
Las Delicias de Carmen	2
Paatcha	5
Peregrino	1
Pizzeria El Charrúa	3
Salon de Té O2	8
Tierra Todo Natural	9
El Toconar	4

ALMA OBSERVATORY

The **Atacama Large Millimeter Array** (ALMA; Ⓦ almaobservatory.org), a joint North American, East Asian, European and Chilean venture, started scientific observations in 2011 and is the largest, most powerful astronomical project in existence. Positioned at a staggering 5000m above sea level at a site east of San Pedro de Atacama called the Chajnantor plateau, this is the highest astronomical observatory of its kind on the planet. The ALMA uses state of the art technology, initially comprising 66 giant high-precision antennae working together at millimetre and submillimetre wavelengths. These can be moved up to 16km across the desert, but act as a single giant telescope. ALMA's slogan – "in search of our cosmic origins" – gives an exciting sense of what this project is really about.

For the first time in history, astronomers will be able to study new stars being born, watch planetary systems and galaxies with unprecedented clarity and, in time, be able to answer big questions about the origins of life itself.

rock paintings, can seem a little forced at times. Mercifully, however, there's a local ordinance that nobody can build above two storeys, meaning that only the trees are visible from afar, enhancing the oasis impression. The main street, **Caracoles**, is where you'll find the main concentration eating places and services, although accommodation is spread out more widely. There's a **swimming pool** (open year round; free) at Pozo Tres, a 3km walk east of the archeological museum along the Paso de Jama.

If you time your visit for the villages **saint's day** on June 29, you will witness a fine celebration, alive with exuberant dancing and feasting.

Iglesia de San Pedro

Plaza • Daily except Wed 10am–9pm; Mass Mon–Sat 7.30pm, Sun noon

The focus of San Pedro is the little **plaza** at its centre, dotted with pepper trees and wooden benches. On its western side stands the squat coffee-coloured **Iglesia de San Pedro**, one of the largest Andean churches in the region. It's actually San Pedro's second church, built in 1744, just over one hundred years after the original church was erected near the present site of the archeological museum. The bell tower was added towards the end of the nineteenth century, and the thick adobe walls surrounding the church rebuilt in 1978. Inside, **religious icons** look down from the brightly painted altar, among them a stern-looking St Peter, the village's patron saint. Overhead, the sloping roof is made of rough-hewn planks of cactus wood and gnarled rafters of reddish algarrobo timber, bound together with leather straps.

Casa Incaica

Opposite the Iglesia de San Pedro, on the other side of the square at Toconao 421b, sits San Pedro's oldest building, the lopsided **Casa Incaica**, now a souvenir store. The house dates from the earliest days of the colony (a plaque outside claims it is the former home of Spanish conquistador Pedro de Valdivia), though its roof seems to be in imminent danger of collapse. A narrow alley full of **artesanía** stalls, where you can buy alpaca knitwear and other souvenirs, leads off the northern side of the square.

Museo Arqueológico Gustavo Le Paige

Gustavo Le Paige 380

Unfortunately, the excellent **Museo Arqueológico Gustavo Le Paige**, just off the northeast corner of the square, is closed for reconstruction until at least the end of 2020. Named after the Belgian missionary-cum-archeologist who founded it in 1957,

CROSSING INTO ARGENTINA AND BOLIVIA

Although not the most commonly used border crossing between the two countries, the bus ride between San Pedro de Atacama and **Jujuy** or **Salta** in Argentina is certainly a spectacular one, climbing up gradually into the Andes before a sharper descent on the eastern flank. Pullman offers a regular service, usually departing San Pedro at 9.30am on Wednesday, Friday and Sunday, with other companies sometimes operating the same route. The bus actually originates in Calama and can be boarded there a couple of hours earlier.

There is also a daily bus connection to Uyuni in Bolivia from Calama with Atacama 2000, departing at 6am, although many people prefer to take a three-day tour from San Pedro in a 4WD, so that they can really experience the salt flats (see page 179).

the museum houses more than 380,000 artefacts gathered from the region around San Pedro, of which the best examples are displayed in eight "naves" arranged around a central hall. Charting the development, step by step, of local pre-Columbian peoples, the displays range from Neolithic tools to sophisticated ceramics, taking in delicately carved wooden tablets and tubes used for inhaling hallucinogenic substances, and a number of gold cups with engraved faces used by village elders during religious ceremonies.

4

Museo del Meteorito

Tocopilla 101 • Tues–Sun 10am–1pm & 3–7pm • CH$3500 • T 9 8360 3086, W museodelmeteorito.cl

A good way to complement some local star-gazing with a hands-on experience is to handle some of the 77 meteorites on display at the **Museo del Meteorito**, which is housed in several geodesic domes on the north side of the village. There are also numerous educational interactive displays and audio guides in English included in the entry fee.

ARRIVAL AND INFORMATION — SAN PEDRO DE ATACAMA

By bus Several bus companies have regular services from Calama to San Pedro; they all arrive at, and depart from, the new bus terminal on Tumiza, a 10min walk southeast of the plaza. You usually have to change at Calama (often with a delay) for major destinations, including Iquique, Arica and Santiago. For more details on buses to Argentina, see page 178.

Destinations Antofagasta (5–6 daily; 5hr); Arica (3 nightly; 12–13hr); Calama (every 30min–1hr; 1hr 30min); Iquique (1 nightly; 7hr); Salta and Jujuy (Argentina; 3–5 weekly; 10–12hr).

Tourist office On the main plaza at Toconao and Gustavo Le Paige (Mon, Tues, Thurs & Fri 9.15am–8.15pm, Wed 9.15am–6pm, Sat & Sun 10am–8.15pm; T 55 285 1420, W sernatur.cl). This helpful office hands out regional maps and lists of tour companies.

Website Check W sanpedroatacama.com for information and links.

GETTING AROUND

By bike Many places rent bikes in San Pedro, notably along Caracoles: most charge around CH$4000/half-day or CH$7000/day; try to get an emergency bike-repair kit too.

By taxi The taxi situation in San Pedro is complicated – you must call ahead, so ask your hotel to arrange this for you.

Car rental Europcar, Calama 479 (T 09 7388 9848, W europcar.cl).

ACCOMMODATION

There are loads of places offering **rooms** in San Pedro, including numerous backpacker hostels, some mid-range options and an increasing number of classy places; prices tend to be higher across the range than elsewhere in the region. A wonderful alternative for visitors on a smaller budget is provided by a scheme of *albergues turísticos*, rural guesthouses in the nearby villages of Peine and Socaire. For details and bookings contact the tourist office. You'll also find a few **campsites** not far from the village centre; the best is listed below.

TOURS FROM SAN PEDRO

San Pedro has a high concentration of **tour operators** offering excursions into the surrounding altiplano, all broadly similar and all at pretty much the same price. This can, of course, be a curse as well as a blessing, for it increases tourist traffic in the region to the point where it can be difficult to visit the awe-inspiring landscape of the *puna* in the kind of silence and isolation in which it really ought to be experienced. Some of the tours are responsibly managed but many are not; the astounding environmental damage of late has finally, if belatedly, forced local communities (but not the national authorities) to take action; they now charge entrance fees to each site and do their best to clean up after visits. The **tourist office** (see page 178) keeps volumes of complaints registered by tourists (usually concerning reliability of vehicles or lack of professionalism) and they are worth consulting to find out which operators to avoid.

Tours usually take place in minibuses, though smaller groups may travel in jeeps. Competition keeps prices relatively low – you can expect to pay from around CH$15,000 to visit the Valle de la Luna, CH$25,000 for a tour to the Tatio geysers, and around CH$45,000 for a full-day tour of the local lakes and oases (excluding entrance fees); three- to four-day tours (around US$200–250) that finish in Bolivia and take in the spectacular Salar de Uyuni are also popular. Don't necessarily choose the cheapest tour, as some companies cram passengers in and offer below-par services, so it is often worth paying a bit more. Talk to other travellers and visit several companies or their websites to get a feel for how they operate. If you don't speak Spanish, check that they can offer guides who speak your language (French, German and English are the most common languages on offer).

TOUR OPERATORS

★ **Cosmo Andino** Caracoles s/n ☎ 55 285 1069, ⓦ cosmoandino.cl. Well-established and respected company offering interesting variations on the most popular tours, as well as off-the-beaten track expeditions. Choose to explore the countryside on foot, or go on a 4WD tour across the mountains. Highly recommended.

Rancho Cactus Tocanao 568 ☎ 9 6671 0028, ⓦ rancho-cactus.cl. For an alternative San Pedro experience, try the horse treks (from CH$22,000) run by Rancho Cactus. Treks last from 2hr to three days and are led by guides passionate about both the region and the horses. English and French spoken.

Sandboard San Pedro Caracoles 362H ☎ 55 298 3669, ⓦ sandboardsanpedro.com. Run by an amiable bunch of hipsters, this is the only dedicated sandboarding operation. Trips of 3–4hr to the Death or Mars valleys leave at 9am and 4pm (CH$20,000). They also rent bikes.

★ **Space Obs** Caracoles 166 ☎ 55 256 6278, ⓦ spaceobs.com. Excellent, highly memorable tours (in English, French and Spanish; CH$25,000/2hr 30min) of Northern Chile's night sky led by enthusiastic and personable astronomers. Book in advance and check which night is in your preferred language.

Vulcano Expediciones Caracoles 317 ☎ 9 5363 6648, ⓦ vulcanochile.com. This is the best operator for mountain and volcano ascents (from CH$60,000), trekking and bike tours. They also offer fun horseriding tours around San Pedro and even adventurous four-day treks into Bolivia.

4

HOTELS

Alto Atacama Camino Pukará s/n, Suchor, Ayllú de Quitor, 3.5km northwest of San Pedro 4 ☎ 2 2912 3910, ⓦ altoatacama.com; map p.176. This tranquil top-end hotel has super-stylish en suites (all with private terraces), plus no fewer than six pools, a well-equipped spa and a highly rated restaurant. Rates include full board, daily excursions and transfers. <u>US$1540</u>

★ **Awasi** Tocopilla 4 ☎ 55 285 1460, ⓦ awasiatacama. com; map p.176. This special place is exclusive, without being stuffy. The ten rooms each come with a guide and vehicle for guests to tailor the shape of their stay. The staff are young and friendly, the food outstanding and comfort paramount. Relax and be spoiled. Three-night minimum; rates include full board, activities and transfers. <u>US$900</u>

Casa de Don Tomás Tocopilla s/n ☎ 55 285 1055, ⓦ dontomas.cl; map p.176. Located away from the buzz of central San Pedro, 300m south of the crossroads with Caracoles, this rustic, well-established hotel has spacious rooms, a pool, good breakfasts and a friendly welcome. <u>US$159</u>

La Casa de Mireya Domingo Atienza 404A ☎ 55 285 1036, ⓦ hostalcasamireya.cl; map p.176. Neat family-run *hostal*, with squat but spacious rooms, each with a private bathroom and decked out in attractive wooden fittings and furniture. CH$50,000

Hostal Takha-Takha Caracoles 101a ☎ 55 285 1038, ⊛ takhatakha.cl; map p.176. Small but tidy and quiet rooms giving onto a large garden. There's a lovely small pool and you can also camp here. Also some good-value, basic singles. Camping CH$13,000, doubles CH$41,000

Hotel Altiplánico Domingo Atienza 282 ☎ 55 285 1212, ⊛ altiplanico.cl; map p.176. Located in a calm spot 250m from the centre, on the way to the Pukará de Quitor, this gorgeous hotel complex is built in typical San Pedro adobe style, with fantastic views, tasteful decor, comfortable en-suite rooms, a swimming pool, a café-bar and bicycle rental. Good online deals. US$162

Hotel Cumbres San Pedro de Atacama Av de Chilcas s/n ☎ 55 285 2136, ⊛ cumbressanpedro.com; map p.176. Located outside the village, and formerly known as *Hotel Kunza*, this mega-stylish boutique hotel is decorated in gorgeous Atacama chic. Panoramic views of the snowcapped Andes from each private adobe-style hut are a highlight, as is the spa and wonderful restaurant. US$409

Puritama Hostal Caracoles 113 ☎ 55 285 1540, ⊛ hostalpuritama.cl; map p.176. Imaginatively decorated rooms (some with shared bathrooms) of various sizes right in the heart of the village. Shared kitchen; breakfast not included. CH$37,000

★ **Tierra Atacama** Calle Séquitor s/n ☎ 55 255 5977, ⊛ tierrahotels.com; map p.176. Superb boutique hotel and spa, with a vast open-plan dining area, bar and reception, a pool, jacuzzi and extremely luxurious rooms. The staff are very friendly and professional. B&B rates (quoted here) are available but most guests choose the all-inclusive plan (two-night minimum from US$1400/ person), which offers full board, unlmited drinks and a range of excursions. US$590

HOSTELS

Hostal Mama Tierra Pachamama 615 ☎ 55 285 1418, ⊛ hostalmamatierra.cl; map p.176. Popular with backpackers and a 10min walk from the centre, this tidy hostel offers dorms, singles and doubles with private or shared bathrooms. Extras include laundry service, and the congenial hostess can help organize volcano climbs in the area. Dorms CH$16,000, doubles CH$42,000

★ **Hostal Pangea** Calama 375 ☎ 55 320 5080, ⊛ hostalpangea.cl; map p.176. An excellent, sociable hostel in a converted traditional building just minutes from the centre, with six- to ten-bed dorms and a range of rooms with shared or private bathrooms. Facilities include games, a shared kitchen and a nice leafy courtyard. Dorms CH$12,000, doubles CH$30,000

Hostal Sonchek Gustavo Le Paige 198 ☎ 55 285 1112, ⊛ hostalsonchek.cl; map p.176. Great-value hostel run by a personable and eco-conscious Slovenian/Chilean couple (recycling system and solar panel in place) and their cats. Rooms are cosy (those with private bathrooms are particularly attractive) and there's a small communal kitchen and garden. No breakfast. Dorms CH$16,000, doubles CH$27,000

Hostelling International Caracoles 360 ☎ 55 256 4683, ⊛ hostellingsanpedro.cl; map p.176. San Pedro's official YHI-affiliated hostel is rather cramped but offers some of the best prices in town, along with the chance to mix with other travellers. As well as six-bed dorms, there are a few private rooms, some en suite. Dorms CH$8000, doubles CH$16,000

CAMPSITE

Camping Los Perales Tocopilla 481 ☎ 55 285 1114; map p.176. The best campsite in San Pedro, a few minutes' walk south of Caracoles, with lots of trees, hot water, a climbing wall and an outdoor kitchen. CH$6000

EATING

Thanks to the steady flow of young travellers passing through town, San Pedro boasts a lively **restaurant scene**, centred on Caracoles. Just about every restaurant offers a fixed-price evening meal, usually including a vegetarian option; despite fierce competition, though, prices are notably higher than in other parts of the country. For cheaper set meals, try one of the handful of restaurants at the top end of Licancabur or near the bus station. While most restaurants serve **alcohol**, note that with one exception at least a small snack must be ordered with a drink.

CAFÉS

Babalu Caracoles 160 & 419; map p.176. The two branches of this tiny *heladería* offer home-made ice creams (from CH$1900) that quench the thirst. Daily-changing flavours include pisco sour, *chirimoya* and lip-smackingly good fruits of the forest. Both branches daily 10am–8pm.

Peregrino Le Paige 348 ☎ 09 8885 8197; map p.176. Occupying a prime spot overlooking the plaza, this café is a good option for coffees and teas (CH$1500–3000), as

well as reasonably priced (for San Pedro at least) snacks and light meals – think pancakes, quesadillas, omelettes, salads and sandwiches (CH$2500–6000). Daily 9am– 9pm.

Salon de Té 02 Caracoles 295B; map p.176. This unpretentious café, right in the centre of town, serves up good-value, hearty breakfasts (from CH$2450), tasty quiches (often available as part of a meal deal) and home-made cakes, as well as the usual range of snacks and hot drinks. Colourful interior and larger, shady courtyard. Daily 8am–10pm.

RESTAURANTS

Adobe Caracoles 211 ☎ 55 285 1132; map p.176. Bustling outdoor restaurant with a roaring fire lit every night, serving the usual Chilean dishes (mains CH$7000–12,000). Try the *carne a lo pobre* (beef with chips, fried egg and fried onion). Uncomfortable benches, and perhaps not the best value in town, but a warm atmosphere nevertheless. Live music every night from 9pm. Daily 11am–1am.

★ **Blanco** Caracoles 195 ☎ 55 285 1164; map p.176. Conceived in white minimalist-chic adobe, this stylish joint certainly stands out from the crowd. Select, sophisticated menu – try the caramelized salmon or the Thai chicken soup (mains CH$8000–13,000) – and great beers, wines and cocktails (from CH$3000). Daily 6pm–12.30am.

La Casona Caracoles 195A ☎ 55 285 1337; map p.176. Busy restaurant with an elegant dining room (mains CH$7000–11,000; *menú del día* CH$8500) inside a large, colonial-style house. The fire-lit bar out the back, complete with a mini Virgin Mary shrine, is a great spot for after-dinner drinks (beer from CH$3000). Daily 9am–midnight.

★ **Las Delicias de Carmen** Calama 370B ☎ 09 9758 9291; map p.176. Relocated off the main drag, but owner Carmen still serves up heapings of of hearty, home-cooked food (mains CH$9000–15,000, set menu

with wine CH$9000). Try the freshly baked *empanadas* and sweeter treats such as the lemon meringue pie. Daily 8am–10.30pm.

Paatcha Caracoles 218 ☎ 9 8515 6317; map p.176. This compact, simply decorated restaurant is rightly popular for its cosy atmosphere, excellent food and rock soundtrack. The three-course menu costs CH$8000, while mains such as "grunting pork ribs", "restless *guanaco*" and "happy chicken" go for CH$7000–12,000. Daily 10am–11pm.

Pizzeria El Charrúa Tocopilla 442 ☎ 55 285 1443; map p.176. The wonderful aroma wafting out of this intimate pizzeria entices hungry punters inside. It may only have four tables but it serves the best thin-crust pizza (from CH$5000) in town, plus exciting salads. No alcohol on sale – opt for a fresh fruit juice instead. Daily 11am–11pm.

Tierra Todo Natural Caracoles 271 ☎ 55 285 1585; map p.176. Friendly restaurant specializing in wholesome home-made food (mains CH$5500–12,000; set menu CH$8500), including wholemeal bread, pizzas, *empanadas*, fish, fantastic salads and pancakes – a good choice for vegetarians. There are also delicious but expensive fruit juices. Daily 8.30am–12.30am.

El Toconar Caracoles 330 ☎ 9 6657 1985; map p.176. Huge, partly covered outdoor restaurant serving meals (CH$10,000–15,000) such as *lomo Andino* or *parilladas* for two at CH$30,000. There's a proper stage where live bands play nightly. Daily noon–12.30am.

DRINKING

★ **Chela Cabur** Caracoles 211 ☎ 55 285 1576; map p.176. The name says it all: *Chela Cabur* translates as "mountain of beer" in Kunza-Chilean. Owned by a Finnish beer aficionado, this laidback bar (beer CH$2500–3500)

– kitted out with wooden benches and music posters on the walls – is extremely popular as the only place where you can drink without ordering food. Mon–Thurs & Sun noon–1am, Fri & Sat noon–2am.

Around San Pedro

The spectacular landscape around San Pedro includes vast, desolate plains cradling numerous **volcanoes** of the most delicate colours imaginable, and beautiful **lakes** speckled pink with flamingos. You'll also find the largest **salt flat** in Chile, the **Salar de Atacama**, a whole field full of fuming **geysers** at El Tatio, a scattering of fertile **oasis villages** and several fascinating **pre-Columbian ruins**.

The otherworldliness of this region is reflected in the poetic names of its geographical features – **Valle de la Luna** (Valley of the Moon), Llano de la Paciencia (Plain of Patience), Garganta del Diablo (Devil's Throat) and Valle de la Muerte (Valley of Death), to mention but a few. You might prefer to explore these marvels by yourself (there's no public transport, so you'd have to rent a 4WD), but numerous companies in San Pedro trip over themselves to take you on guided tours, often a more convenient option (see page 179). There is a fee to pay at each of the park entrances, though with the exception of the **Puritama thermal baths** (controversially owned by the luxury *Hotel Explora*), these go straight back to the local community and help maintain the parks.

4

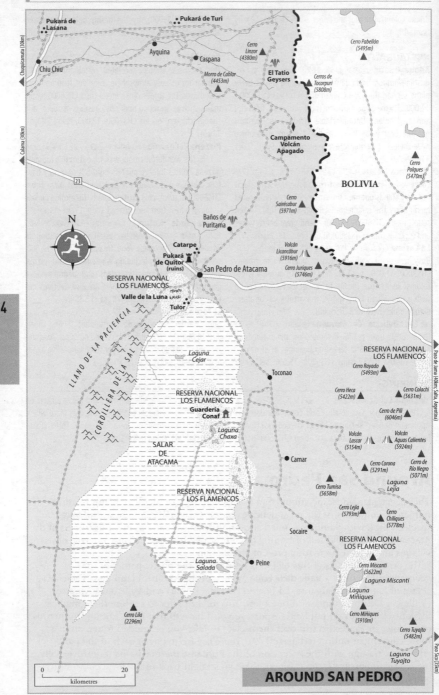

Chuquicamata (30km)

Calama (30km)

Pukará de Lasana

Chiu Chiu

Pukará de Turi

Ayquina

Caspana

Cerro Linzor (4380m)

Cerro Pabellón (5495m)

Morro de Cablor (4453m)

El Tatio Geysers

Cerros de Tocorpuri (5808m)

Cerro Polques (5470m)

23

Campamento Volcán Apagado

BOLIVIA

Cerro Sairécabur (5971m)

N

Baños de Puritama

Catarpe

Pukará de Quitor (ruins)

San Pedro de Atacama

Volcán Licancábur (5916m)

Cerro Juriques (5746m)

RESERVA NACIONAL LOS FLAMENCOS

Valle de la Luna

Tulor

LLANO DE LA PACIENCIA

CORDILLERA DE LA SAL

Laguna Cejar

Toconao

RESERVA NACIONAL LOS FLAMENCOS

Paso de Jama (40km; Salta, Argentina)

Cerro Rayado (5493m)

Cerro Heca (5422m)

Cerro Colachi (5631m)

RESERVA NACIONAL LOS FLAMENCOS

Cerro de Pili (6046m)

Guardería Conaf

Laguna Chaxa

Volcán Lascar (5154m)

Volcán Aguas Calientes (5924m)

SALAR DE ATACAMA

Camar

Cerro Corona (5291m)

Cerro de Río Negro (5071m)

RESERVA NACIONAL LOS FLAMENCOS

Cerro Tumisa (5658m)

Laguna Lejía

Cerro Lejía (5793m)

Cerro Chiliques (5778m)

Socaire

RESERVA NACIONAL LOS FLAMENCOS

Laguna Salada

Peine

Cerro Miscanti (5622m)

Laguna Miscanti

Laguna Miñiques

Cerro Lila (2296m)

Cerro Miñiques (5910m)

Cerro Tuyajto (5482m)

Laguna Tuyajto

Paso Sico (135km)

0   20
kilometres

AROUND SAN PEDRO

Pukará de Quitor

3km north of San Pedro • Daily 8.30am–7pm • CH$3000

Just 3km north of San Pedro (head up Calle Tocopilla then follow the river), the **Pukará de Quitor** is a ruined twelfth-century fortress built into a steep hillside on the west bank of the Río San Pedro. It has been partially restored and you can make out the defence wall encircling a group of stone buildings huddled inside. According to Spanish chronicles, this *pukará* was stormed and taken by Francisco de Aguirre and thirty men as part of Pedro de Valdivia's conquest in 1540. Another 4km up the road you'll find the ruins of what used to be an Inca administrative centre at **Catarpe**, but there's little to see in comparison with the ruins of Quitor.

Valle de la Luna

16km west of San Pedro on the old road to Calama • Summer 8.30am–7.30pm; winter 8.30am–5.30pm • Morning CH$2500, afternoon CH$3000

The **Valle de la Luna**, or Valley of the Moon, really lives up to its name, presenting a dramatic lunar landscape of wind-eroded hills surrounding a crust-like valley floor, once the bottom of a lake. An immense sand dune sweeps across the valley, easy enough to climb and a great place to sit and survey the scenery.

The valley is at its best at sunset, when it's transformed into a spellbinding palette of golds and reds, but you'll have to share this view with a multitude of fellow visitors, as all San Pedro tour operators offer daily sunset trips. A more memorable (but more demanding) experience would be to get up before daybreak and cycle here for sunrise; you can rent a bike in San Pedro (see page 178). Camping is not permitted.

Tulor

9km southwest of San Pedro • Daily: summer 9am–7pm; rest of year 8.30am–5.30pm • CH$3000

The site of the earliest example of settled habitation in the region, **Tulor** dates from around 800 BC. It was discovered only in the mid-twentieth century by Padre Le Paige, founder of the Museo Arqueológico in San Pedro. Today, the uppermost parts of the walls are exposed, protruding from the earth, while the rest remains buried under the sand. Two reconstructions of these igloo-like houses stand alongside the site.

Salar de Atacama

10km south of San Pedro • Daily: summer 8am–8pm; rest of year 8am–6pm • Free access but entry fee to lake areas CH$2500

The northern edge of this 3000-square-kilometre basin, covered by a vast crust of saline minerals, lies some 10km south of San Pedro. The largest salt flat in Chile, **Salar de Atacama** is formed by waters flowing down from the Andes which, unable to escape from the basin, are forced to evaporate, leaving salt deposits on the earth. It's not a dazzling white like the Salar de Surire (see page 213), or Bolivia's Salar de Uyuni, but it's fascinating all the same – especially when you get out and take a close look at the crust, which looks like coffee-coloured coral reef, or ice shards, and cracks when you walk on it. Some parts of the *salar* have been closed off by private companies for lithium extraction. It also contains several small lakes, including **Laguna Chaxa**, home to dozens of flamingos and a visitor centre, and the beautiful **Laguna Salada**, whose waters are covered with floating plates of salt.

Many tour companies also take you for a float in the saline waters of **Laguna Cejar**, 19km from San Pedro. This emerald green lagoon contains even more salt than the Dead Sea. Your guide will warn you to wear shoes when walking on the banks, as very sharp salt crests can cut your feet. Remember to bring bottles of water to wash the salt off afterwards.

4

The southern oases

Heading south from San Pedro, on the eastern side of the Salar de Atacama, you enter a region of beautiful lakes and tiny oasis villages. The first oasis, 38km south, is **TOCONAO**, whose softwater stream enters the village through the **Quebrada de Jérez** (daily 8am–8pm; CH$1500), a steep, narrow gorge with figs and quinces growing on its southern banks. Though not as pretty as some of the other villages, Toconao does possess a handsome whitewashed bell tower dating to 1750 and set apart from the main church.

Some 35km further south you reach **CAMAR**, a tiny hamlet with just sixty inhabitants, set amid lush green terraces. **SOCAIRE**, 15km beyond, is less picturesque, save for its little church set by a field of sunflowers. **PEINE**, off a track branching west from the "main road" between Camar and Socaire, has a mid-eighteenth-century church and a large swimming pool, invariably full of squealing children. It is possible to **stay** in Peine and Socaire under the **rural guesthouse scheme** run from San Pedro, for details of which consult the San Pedro tourist office (see page 178).

The lakes

One of the most stunning lakes in the region, **Laguna Miscanti** (near Socaire, 4350m above sea level; CH$3000), boasts brilliant blue waters. Adjacent lies the much smaller **Laguna Miñeques**, whose waters are a deep, dark blue; both lakes are protected areas, part of the Reserva Nacional Los Flamencos. Further south, pastel-coloured **Laguna Tuyajto** is home to dozens of flamingos and is set against a fabulous backdrop of mineral-streaked mountains, while **Laguna Lejía**, further north, is filled with emerald-green waters tinged white with salt deposits floating on the surface; it, too, is home to large numbers of flamingos.

El Tatio geysers and Termas de Puritama

El Tatio geysers 95km north of San Pedro • CH$10,000 • **Termas de Puritama** 35km northeast of San Pedro • Daily 9.30am–5.15pm • All day CH$15,000, after 2pm CH$9000

A trip to the **El Tatio geysers** is quite an ordeal: first, you drag yourself out of bed in the dead of night; then you stand shivering in the street while you wait for your tour company to come and pick you up between 4am and 5am; and finally, you embark on a three-hour journey on a rough, bumpy road. Added to this is the somewhat surreal experience of finding yourself in a pre-dawn rush hour, part of a caravan of minibuses following each other's lights across the desert.

But hardly anyone who makes the trip regrets it. At 4300m above sea level, these geysers form the highest **geothermal** field in the world. It's essentially a large, flat field containing countless blowholes full of bubbling water that, between around 6am and 8am, send billowing clouds of steam high into the air (strictly speaking, though, geysers spurt water, not steam). At the same time, the spray forms pools of water on the ground, streaked with silver reflections as they catch the first rays of the sun. It's a magnificent spectacle. Take great care, however, when walking around the field; the crust of earth is very thin in some parts, and serious accidents can happen.

You should also remember that it will be freezing cold when you arrive, though once the sun's out the place warms up quite quickly. There's also a **swimming pool** near the geysers, visited by most tour companies, so bring your swimming gear.

On the way back from trips to the El Tatio geysers, some tour companies also pay a visit to the **Termas de Puritama**, a rocky pool filled with warm thermal water, 60km south of the geysers and run by a local community but owned and maintained by San Pedro's *Hotel Explora*.

Iquique

Dramatically situated at the foot of the 800m coastal cordillera, with an enormous sand dune looming precariously above one of its *barrios*, **IQUIQUE**, 390km north of Calama, is a sprawling, busy and surprisingly cosmopolitan city that is fast gaining a reputation as one of the world's finest spots for **paragliding**. Predictably cloudless skies and winds that come in off the Pacific and rise up the dunes create near-perfect conditions; you'll see many enthusiasts swooping down to the **beaches**, silhouetted by dawn or dusky sunsets. Iquique rivals Arica as the best place to base yourself for a tour of the extreme northern tip of the country. From here, you can easily arrange excursions into the interior, whose attractions include the famous nitrate ghost towns of **Humberstone** and **Santa Laura** (both UNESCO World Heritage sites) , the beautiful hot-spring oases of **Pica** and **Matilla**, and the stunning altiplano scenery of **Parque Nacional Volcán Isluga**.

Iquique falls into two quite distinct areas: **downtown**, lined with shops, services and old historic buildings, and the modern stretch along the **oceanfront**, given over almost entirely to tourism. Iquique's **Zona Franca**, or "Zofri" duty-free zone, is just north of the centre, in an industrial area.

Brief history

Iquique started out as a small settlement of indigenous fishing communities, and during the colonial period became a base for extracting guano deposits from the coast. It continued to grow with the opening of a nearby silver mine in 1730, but it wasn't until the great nineteenth-century nitrate boom that it really took off as a city.

Following its transferral to Chilean hands during the War of the Pacific (1878–83), Iquique became the **nitrate capital** of Chile – where the largest quantities of ore were shipped from, and where the wealthy nitrate barons based themselves, building opulent mansions all over the rapidly expanding city. By the end of the nineteenth century, Iquique was the wealthiest and most hedonistic city in Chile – it was said that more champagne was consumed here, per head, than in any other city in the world.

With the abrupt end of the nitrate era after World War I, Iquique's boom was over, and the grand mansions were left to fade and crumble as the industrialists headed back to Santiago. **Fishing** stepped in to fill the economic gap and over the years Iquique transformed itself into the world's leading exporter of fishmeal, though copper subsequently took over as the city's main industry.

4

Downtown Iquique

Downtown Iquique's central square, **Plaza Prat**, and main avenue, **Calle Baquedano**, conserve some splendid buildings from the nitrate era, which, along with the city's beaches, are for many people a good enough reason to visit. Seizing upon this, the authorities have invested in an ambitious restoration scheme aimed at enhancing the beauty of this historic part of the city.

Plaza Prat

The focus of town is the large, partly pedestrianized **Plaza Prat**, dominated by the gleaming white **Teatro Municipal**, whose magnificent facade features Corinthian columns and statues representing the four seasons. It was built in 1889 as an opera house and showcased some of the most distinguished divas of its time. At the time of writing productions had been suspended and the entire building was undergoing extensive renovations.

Opposite the theatre, in the centre of the square, the **Torre Reloj** is a tall white clock tower with Moorish arches, adopted by Iquique as the city's symbol. On the

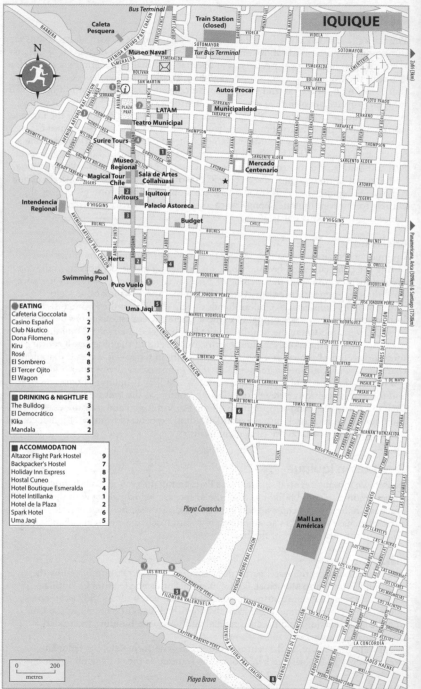

IQUIQUE

Zofri (3km) ▶

Panamericana, Arica (309km) & Santiago (1759km) ▶

◉ EATING
Cafeteria Cioccolata	1
Casino Español	2
Club Náutico	7
Dona Filomena	9
Kiru	6
Rosé	4
El Sombrero	8
El Tercer Ojito	5
El Wagon	3

■ DRINKING & NIGHTLIFE
The Bulldog	3
El Democrático	1
Kika	4
Mandala	2

■ ACCOMMODATION
Altazor Flight Park Hostel	9
Backpacker's Hostel	7
Holiday Inn Express	8
Hostal Cuneo	3
Hotel Boutique Esmeralda	4
Hotel Intillanka	1
Hotel de la Plaza	2
Spark Hotel	6
Uma Jaqi	5

0   200
metres

4, 9 (6km), Altazor (6km), Airport (40km) & Antofagasta (416km) ▼

PARAGLIDING PARADISE

Iquique is one of the best places on Earth to **paraglide**, thanks to the unique geography of the city; the mountain range and air current that comes all the way from the Antarctic create the perfect conditions for flying. Plus, you'll regularly hear paragliding instructors proudly boast about the fact you can fly 365 days a year in Iquique – it hardly ever rains and temperatures hover between 16 and 25°C year round. Tandem flights lasting approximately 45 minutes usually leave from Alto Hospicio and land on either Playa Cavancha or Playa Brava (equipment, pick-up and drop-off are included). If you've time to spare and you're really serious about flying, you might consider enrolling on a two-week course, at the end of which you'll receive a licence which allows you to brave the Iquique skies on your own, without an instructor. Be sure to book in advance.

The pros at **Puro Vuelo** (Baquedano 1440; ☏ 57 231 1127, ⊛ purovuelo.cl) come highly recommended. A tandem flight will set you back CH$45,000 and includes a set of photos of you flying, which you can download from their website afterwards. **Altazor** (☏ 09 9886 2362, ⊛ altazor.cl), based in the *Altazor Flight Park Hostel*, also has a good reputation.

northeast corner of the square, the **Casino Español** – formerly a gentlemen's club, now a restaurant (see page 190) – features an extravagant interior with oil paintings depicting scenes from *Don Quijote*; it's definitely worth a visit.

Calle Baquedano

Leading south from Plaza Prat, **Calle Baquedano** is lined with an extraordinary collection of late nineteenth-century timber houses, all with porches, balconies and fine wooden balustrades, and many undergoing loving restoration. This is the showcase of Iquique's nitrate architecture and has been designated a national monument. The street is pedestrianized from the plaza all the way down to the seafront, using noble materials such as fine stone for the paving and polished timber for the sidewalks. There are often bric-a-brac stalls at the Plaza Prat end, and an old tram sometimes trundles up and down the road.

Three buildings are open to the public: the **Sala de Artes Collahuasi** at no. 930 (Mon–Fri 10am–2pm & 3.30–7pm, Sat 10am–2pm; free), an impeccably restored building used for temporary art exhibitions, usually of outstanding quality; the **Museo Regional** at no. 951 (Tues–Sat 9am–5.30pm; free), which houses an eclectic collection of pre-Columbian and natural history artefacts, including deformed skulls and a pickled two-headed shark; and the **Palacio Astoreca** (entrance on O'Higgins; Mon–Fri 10am–1pm & 4–7pm, Sat 11am–2pm; free), a glorious, though deteriorating, mansion featuring a massive wood-panelled entrance hall with a painted glass Art Nouveau ceiling.

The harbour

A short walk north from Plaza Prat at Esmeralda 250 is the **Museo Naval** (Tues–Fri 10am–1pm & 4–7pm; free), which displays letters, maps and photos relating to Arturo Prat, hero of the War of the Pacific (see page 474). If this whets your appetite, head to the **Museo Corbeta Esmeralda**, Prat s/n (obligatory Spanish-only guided tours Jan & Feb daily 10am–12.15pm & 2–5pm, March–Dec Tues–Sun 10am–12.15pm & 2–5pm; CH$3500; ☏ 57 253 0812, ⊛ museoesmeralda.cl), a full-scale model of the *Esmeralda*, a corvette captained by Prat during the war. From the **Caleta Pesquera**, or fishermen's wharfs, the huge, yawning pelicans strutting around the pier make compelling viewing. You can take **boat tours** around the harbour which leave from Muelle Pasajero (CH$3500), worth it for the views onto the steep desert mountains, rising like huge slabs of chocolate cake behind the city.

The beaches

Two beaches lie within striking distance of the city centre: **Playa Cavancha**, the nearest, most popular, and more sheltered; and **Playa Brava**, larger, less crowded and more windswept, which is only suitable for sunbathing due to a strong current and crashing waves rendering it dangerous for swimming (although you do see adrenaline junkies surfing at either end of the beach). You can walk to Playa Cavancha, which begins at the southern end of Amunategui, but there are plenty of local buses or *colectivos* constantly travelling between the plaza and the beach; many continue to Playa Brava, as well, for a slightly higher fare. Further south, between Playa Brava and the airport, there's a series of attractive sandy beaches including **Playa Blanca**, 13km south of the centre, **Playa Lobito**, at Km 22, and the fishing cove of **Los Verdes**, at Km 24. You can get to these on the airport bus or by *colectivo* (see below).

The Zofri

About 3km north of the centre • Mon–Sat 11am–9pm • Take any *colectivo* marked "Zofri" heading north out of town – the east side of the Plaza or Calle Amunategui are both good bets for catching one

located in a large industrial compound, the duty-free shopping complex known as the **Zofri** is widely touted as one of the great attractions of the north. Thousands of Chileans flock here from up and down the country to spend their money at what turns out, at close quarters, to be a big, ugly mall crammed full of small shops selling mainly electronic items includig cameras, watches and domestic gadgets, but also perfumes and food. There's a curious mixture of the upmarket and the tacky, with the latter tending to dominate. The building itself is shabby and old-fashioned, and the bargains aren't really good enough to deserve a special trip.

ARRIVAL AND DEPARTURE

IQUIQUE

By plane Diego Aracena airport, which sees services from LATAM (Tarapacá 465; ☎ 57 242 7600) and Sky Airline (airport; ☎ 7 242 4139), is a whacking 40km south of the city. You can get to the centre by transfer (☎ 57 231 0800; CH$5500), regular taxi (CH$8000 shared, CH$17,000 private) or *colectivo*.

Destinations Antofagasta (1–2 daily; 45min); Arica (1 daily; 40min); Santiago (13–18 daily; 2hr 10min).

By bus Iquique's main bus terminal is in a rather run-down quarter at the northern end of Patricio Lynch, several blocks from the centre – best take a taxi to the centre, or wait for a *colectivo*. Tur Bus, however, has its own terminal (also known as Terminal Esmeralda) in a beautifully converted town house, proudly sporting a dazzling 1917 vintage black Ford, in a more agreeable area at the corner of Ramírez and Esmeralda. To save yourself from trekking to the terminals to buy a ticket in advance, you can purchase (and compare prices) at the bus company stands opposite the Mercado Centenario on Barros Arana. A taxi into the centre from either costs CH$3000–4000.

Destinations Antofagasta (every 30min–1hr; 6hr); Arica (every 30min; 5hr); Calama (5–6 daily; 6hr); Caldera (12 daily; 12hr); Chañaral (12 daily; 11hr); Copiapó (12 daily; 13hr); La Serena (8–10 daily; 18hr); La Tirana (8 daily; 1hr 40min); Mamiña (2 daily; 2hr 30min); Mejillones (3 daily; 5hr); Oruro (Bolivia; 1 daily; 12–13hr); Pica (6 daily; 2hr); Santiago (hourly; 25hr).

GETTING AROUND AND INFORMATION

Car rental Autos Procar, Serrano 796 (☎ 57 247 0668); Budget, Bulnes 542 (☎ 57 241 6332, ⌨ budget.cl); Hertz, Aníbal Pinto 1303 (☎ 57 251 0432, ⌨ hertz.cl).

By taxi Except for fares from the bus terminal and airport, nearly all Iquique's taxis function like *colectivos*, with fixed, low prices (from CH$600) but flexible routes. This is very handy for shuttling to and from the beach, or even going from your hotel to a restaurant. Find out from Sernatur (see below) or your hotel what the going rate is, and confirm this with the taxi driver before you get in. Recommended companies include Taxi Aeropuerto Plaza Prat (☎ 57 241 3368) and Playa Brava Radio Taxi (☎ 57 244 3460).

Tourist office Aníbal Pinto 436 (Mon–Fri 9am–5pm, Sat & Sun 10am–2pm; ☎ 57 241 9241, ⌨ sernatur.cl).

ACTIVITIES AND TOURS

A number of Iquique **tour companies** offer one-day circular tours – from around CH$20,000/person – taking in the nitrate ghost towns of Humberstone and Santa Laura (see page 192); the geoglyphs of Pintados (see page 194); the

DRIVING ACROSS THE ALTIPLANO

With the proposed **Ruta Altiplánica de Integración** – a paved highway stretching 1500km across the altiplano, from San Pedro de Atacama in Chile to Cusco, Peru – still not having come to fruition, crossing the altiplano's pothole-riddled dirt tracks by jeep remains the road adventure of a lifetime and should be enjoyed to the full before the arrival of tarmac and increased traffic. Probably the best starting point is **Iquique** (the ascent in altitude is more gradual in this direction), heading into the cordillera as far as Parque Nacional Volcán Isluga, continuing north across the altiplano to Parque Nacional Lauca, and finally descending in Arica. It's a **700km journey**, and takes about four days at an easy pace.

If you do the trip, remember that there's no petrol station once you're off the Panamericana, which means taking it all with you in jerry cans (*bidones*, available in most ironmongers). Always take far, far more than you think you need. Another essential precaution is to take two spare tyres, not just one. There's more on 4WD driving in Basics (see page 29).

oases villages of Matilla and Pica, with a plunge in Pica's hot springs (see page 194); and the basilica and nitrate museum of La Tirana. Day-trips to the Parque Nacional Volcán Isluga (see page 197) cost around CH$40,000. Longer tours include the memorable loop up into the cordillera, north across the altiplano and down into Arica; these excursions take in Parque Nacional Volcán Isluga, the Salar de Surire (see page 213) and Parque Nacional Lauca (see page 209). The tour entails two or three overnight stays, with prices starting around CH$300,000/person (see page 205).

Avitours Patricio Lynch 563 ☎ 9 7861 6806, ⓦ avitours. cl. Avitours offers an extensive range of trips across northern Chile, including a three-day excursion to Arica via Lauca and Isluga national parks, and a day-trip to the hot springs of Mamiña (see page 196).
Iquitour Patricio Lynch 563 ☎ 57 242 8772, ⓦ iquitour. cl. This travel agency is useful for flight and hotel bookings, as well as multi-day tours throughout Chile (and South America).
Magical Tour Chile Baquedano 997 ☎ 57 221 7290, ⓦ magicaltour.cl. A good all-rounder, Magical Tour Chile offers city and cycling tours, day-trips to the ghost towns

of Humberstone and Santa Laura, and multi-day tours to destinations like Parque Nacional Volcán Isluga.
Surire Tours Baquedano 170 ☎ 57 244 5440 ⓦ suriretours.cl. Specializes in multi-day, group tours in northern Chile (and beyond), including to Humberstone and Santa Laura, Pica and Matilla, and the Atacama Desert.
Uma Jaqi Obispo Labbé 1591 ☎ 09 8771 5768, ⓦ umajaqi.cl. Based in the hostel of the same name (see below), Uma Jaqi offers private and group surfing lessons, organizes surf-themed trips in northern Chile and Peru, and rents out boards.

ACCOMMODATION

Iquique is a popular holiday resort and offers an abundance of **accommodation**. Both in the centre and by the beaches, always ask what the "best price" is, as many places will give discounts when pushed. One thing to bear in mind is that, owing to the region's severe water shortage, supplies are occasionally cut in the busy summer months, sometimes without warning.

DOWNTOWN IQUIQUE
Hostal Cuneo Baquedano 1175 ☎ 57 242 8654, ⓔ hostalcuneo@hotmail.com; map p.186. With a good location in an old timber building (painted a striking turquoise) on the historic stretch of Calle Baquedano, this hospitable, homely and good-value *hostal* has small and neat if slightly dark rooms off a leafy patio. <u>CH$20,000</u>
Hotel Boutique Esmeralda Obispo Labbé 1386 ☎ 57 221 6996, ⓦ esmeraldahotel.cl; map p.186. Solid, mid-range hotel in a modern building a 10–15min walk from the plaza. All of the spotless rooms are en suite and have TVs and phones, and staff are friendly and helpful. <u>CH$50,000</u>

Hotel Intillanka Obispo Labbé 825 ☎ 57 231 1105, ⓦ inti-llanka.cl; map p.186. Friendly and efficiently run hotel offering spacious, light rooms with fans rather than a/c, and private bathrooms. The place could do with a revamp, but it's very clean. <u>CH$43,000</u>
Hotel de la Plaza Baquedano 1025 ☎ 57 241 7172; map p.186. An airy and light Georgian building on the main stretch with pictures of old Iquique adorning the walls and some racially dubious statues in the lobby. A leafy staircase leads up to pleasant, clean rooms, and there's a restaurant and bar. <u>CH$35,000</u>
Uma Jaqi Obispo Labbé 1591 ☎ 09 8771 5768, ⓦ umajaqi.cl; map p.186. This slightly ramshackle but

friendly hostel has dorms of various sizes, plus doubles and triples, some with private bathrooms. There's a small bar and cushioned chillout zone on the roof terrace. Dorms CH$7500, doubles CH$25,000

THE BEACHES AND AROUND

Altazor Flight Park Hostel Via 6, Manzana Am Sitio 3, Bajo Molle, about a 15min bus ride from town ☎ 57 238 0110, ⓦ altazor.cl; map p.186. Built almost entirely of ship containers, the rooms at this international paragliding centre are surprisingly inviting, with shared kitchen and chilled-out communal areas. There are also smarter apartments, and camping spots. Check their website for directions. Camping CH$5000, doubles CH$19,000, apartments CH$32,000

★ **Backpacker's Hostel** Amunategui 2075 ☎ 57 232 0223, ⓦ hosteliquique.cl; map p.186. Solid HI-affiliated hostel (discount for HI members) offering weekly barbecues, surfboard and wetsuit rental, and clean dorms, rooms and facilities. The huge kitchen is a big plus point, as is the leafy outdoor space, in-house bar and restaurant, and location right next to the beach. Dorms CH$9000, doubles CH$27,000

Holiday Inn Express 11 de Septiembre 1690 ☎ 57 243 3300, ⓦ ihg.com; map p.186. You know what you're getting at this impersonal but immaculate US chain hotel, with a pool, a/c and spacious rooms with ocean views (though only from those at the front of the hotel). Discounts available Fri–Sun. CH$66,000

Spark Hotel Amunategui 2034 ☎ 57 241 0000, ⓦ sparkhoteles.cl; map p.186. This super-slick hotel has a rather formal feel to it, and is popular with business guests and couples on a romantic break. There's a lovely outdoor pool on the ground floor as well as what is probably the best sushi restaurant in town. Top-floor rooms have amazing views of the beach and city. CH$75,000

EATING

While there's a reasonable choice of **restaurants** in the centre, it's worth coming out to have at least one evening meal by the beach, to see the ocean lit up with coloured lights projected from the promenade. Almost all restaurants serve a good value *menú del día* at lunchtime. For a quick, cheap eat, the lively **Mercado Centenario** on Barros Arana between Latorre and Sargento Aldea is popular for fish lunch specials, though hygiene standards are dubious. Most bars in Iquique double up as restaurants, so it's perfectly fine to go to a restaurant just for drinks, and vice versa.

CAFÉS AND CHEAP EATS

Cafeteria Cioccolata Av Aníbal Pinto 487 ☎ 57 253 2290; map p.186. This sweet, old-fashioned tearoom opposite the tourist office serves up good coffee (CH$1500–3300) and obscenely huge slices of cake, waffles and pancakes. The lemon yellow interior is filled with businessmen and ladies who lunch (*menú del día* CH$4900). There are other branches on Arturo Prat and the Zofri. Mon–Fri 8.45am–10pm, Sat 11am–10pm.

Dona Filomena Filomena Valenzuela 298 ☎ 57 231 1235; map p.186. Very reliable *empanada*, beer and pizza joint, popular with a youngish crowd. Main dishes from CH$5000, *ceviche* CH$9000. Simple wooden decor and attractive outside seating. Also does delivery. Mon–Sat 12.30pm–12.30am.

RESTAURANTS

DOWNTOWN IQUIQUE

Casino Español Plaza Prat 584 ☎ 57 276 0630, ⓦ casinoespanoliquique.cl; map p.186. Huge, fabulous dining room decorated like a mock Moorish palace, complete with beautiful tiles and suits of armour, inside a startling blue and white building. The Spanish food is unexceptional, and a little overpriced (mains CH$8000–15,000), but this is a must-visit. Mon, Sat & Sun noon–3.30pm, Tues–Fri noon–3.30pm & 8–10.30pm.

Rosé Baquedano 764 ☎ 57 234 0361; map p.186. The cutest and most reasonably priced of the restaurants along the pedestrianzed strip, with iron tables set out on the patio. *Parilladas* for two cost CH$18,000, a wide range of other meals CH$4500–12,000. Daily 11am–11pm.

★ **El Tercer Ojito** Patricio Lynch 1420A ☎ 57 242 6517, ⓦ eltercerojito.cl; map p.186. This peaceful garden oasis is the mellowest place to spend a shady afternoon or candlelit evening. A healthy menu (mains CH$5500–12,000) darts from Chilean seafood to Thai curries via salads, pasta and various veggie options, showcasing the best ingredients the region has to offer. Service is impeccable. Be sure to leave room for pudding; the home-made *kulfi* (Indian ice cream) is superb. Tues–Sat 12.30–5pm & 7.30pm–1am, Sun 12.30–5pm.

El Wagon Thompson 85 ☎ 57 234 1428; map p.186. Nitrate-era paraphernalia lines the walls of this warm and friendly restaurant. Take your pick from an extensive menu of imaginative fish and seafood dishes (CH$8000–12,000): the spicy *pescado a la Huara-Huara* is particularly good. There's also a great choice of wines and live music at weekends. Mon–Sat 1–4pm & 8pm–2am, Sun 1–4pm.

THE BEACHES

Club Náutico Los Rieles 110 ☎ 57 243 2951; map p.186. This is a first-rate, reasonably priced restaurant that's been going strong for years, with great views from

its outdoor terrace, especially at night. Mains such as *ceviche* and fish from CH$8000. Daily noon–3pm & 7pm–midnight.

★ **Kiru** Amunategui 1912 ☎57 276 0795, ⓦkiru.cl; map p.186. Peruvian restaurant that feels sophisticated and exclusive – there's no sign at the door; just follow the palm-fringed corridor and chill-out music. The chef rustles up fantastic fusion dishes and memorable *ceviche*, plus there are plenty of wines and cocktails. Starters CH$8000–10,000, *asado de tiro* CH$15,800. Mon–Sat 1–3.30pm & 8pm–12.30am, Sun 1–4pm.

El Sombrero Los Rieles 704 ☎57 236 3900, ⓦterrado.cl; map p.186. Part of the *Hotel Terrado Suites*, this rather formal, expensive restaurant only does a lavish buffet for CH$24,800 a head. The floor-to-ceiling windows give great bay views. Daily 1–3.30pm & 8–11.30pm.

DRINKING AND NIGHTLIFE

You'll find several **nightclubs** that get very crowded in summer and maintain a gentle buzz during low season. They are nearly all down on the Costanera Sur. Otherwise, much of Iquique's nightlife is concentrated around **Playa Brava**.

The Bulldog Valenzuela 230 ☎9 4263 7465; map p.186. Modern bar with big screens showing Premier League football and other sports by day and a decent sound system for the nights. Tasty bar meals available from CH$6000 and a well-stocked bar serving fine pisco sours and other drinks. Mon–Wed & Sun 11am–2am, Thurs–Sat 11am–4am.

El Democrático Obispo Labbé 466 ☎57 276 6875, ⓦbardemocratico.cl; map p.186. If it's the true essence of Chile you're after, this scruffy 80-year-old local, with huge dried fish hanging from the walls, fits the bill. On weekdays it's filled with drunk fishermen, but at the weekend, young locals and live bands join the party. Don't come to eat, unless it's a boiled egg you're after, but do try the Chilean beers (from CH$1500) and, if you're brave, an old-school Chilean cocktail, "El Terremoto", made from pineapple ice cream, sweet white wine, whisky and grenadine. Don't dress up! Daily 11.30am–late.

Kika Playa Brava ☎9 7979 1740, ⓦfacebook.com/kikaclubiquique; map p.186. One of the city's most happening dance clubs, with plenty of space both in the chilled interior and steamier outdoor area. Daily 11pm–4am.

Mandala Hernan Baquedano 1334 ☎09 6473 5400, ⓦfacebook.com/MandalaClubIquique; map p.186. This stylish hangout has benefited from the creative flair of its architect-cum-artist-cum-chef and owner, Rodrigo. Attractive recycled lampshades adorn the place, and there's an airy patio with sofas – perfect on a balmy summer's night. Great cocktails go for CH$7000–10,000 and there's a sushi bar on the roof terrace. DJs on weekends. Mon–Thurs noon–4pm & 7pm–1am, Fri & Sat noon–4pm & 7pm–3am.

Inland from Iquique

Iquique lies within easy reach of many inland sights. Just half an hour away, **Humberstone** and **Santa Laura** are perhaps the most haunting of all the nitrate ghost towns. South of here, close to the Panamericana, **Cerro Pintados** features a dense collection of geoglyphs, among the most impressive in Chile. East of Pintados sits the pretty oasis village of **Pica**, with a lovely thermal pool, while **Mamiña**, further north, is the Norte Grande's hot-springs town *par excellence*. You can also visit **La Tirana**, an important pilgrimage centre, famous for its colourful festival in July. Public transport around this area is sporadic but manageable.

Humberstone

45km inland from Iquique • Daily: Jan–March 9am–7pm; April–Dec 9am–6pm • CH$3000 (includes entry to Santa Laura)

The best-preserved ghost town in Chile, **HUMBERSTONE** is a nitrate *oficina* that was abandoned in 1960 and today appeals especially to lovers of industrial architecture. It sits some 45km inland from Iquique, by Ruta 16 just before it meets the Panamericana. The town began life in 1862 as Oficina La Palma, but was renamed in 1925 in honour of James "Santiago" Humberstone, an important nitrate entrepreneur famous for introducing the "Shanks" ore-refining system to the industry. In its time it was one of the busiest *oficinas* on the pampas; today it is an eerie, empty ghost town, slowly crumbling beneath the desert sun.

What sets Humberstone apart from the other ghost towns is that just about all of it is still standing – from the white, terraced workers' houses (now in total disrepair) and the plaza with its bandstand, to the theatre, church and company store. The **theatre**, in particular, is highly evocative, with its rows of dusty seats staring at the stage. You should also seek out the **hotel**, and walk through to the back where you'll find a huge, empty **swimming pool** with a diving board – curiously the pool is made from the sections of a ship's iron hull. Located a short distance from the town are the sheds and workshops, with old tools and bits of machinery lying around, and invoices and order forms littering the floors.

Many of the homes have been revamped to show what life was like in the 1930s – the room with old toys is particularly evocative.

Santa Laura

At **SANTA LAURA**, about 2km down the road and clearly visible from Humberstone, you'll see only a couple of remaining houses (one of which has been turned into a

---

THE NITRATE BOOM

Looking around the desert pampa, it's hard to believe that this scorched, lifeless wasteland was once so highly prized that a war was fought over it – and still more difficult to imagine it alive with smoking chimneys, grinding machinery, offices, houses and a massive workforce. But little more than a century ago, the Far North of Chile was the scene of a thriving industry built on its vast **nitrate deposits**, heavily in demand in Europe and North America as a fertilizer. Nitrates were first exploited in the Atacama Desert in the 1860s, when the region belonged to Bolivia (around Antofagasta) and Peru (around Iquique and Arica). From the early stages, however, the Chilean presence was very strong, both in terms of capital and labour.

THE WAR OF THE PACIFIC

When in 1878 the Bolivian government violated an official agreement by raising export taxes on nitrate (hitting Chilean shareholders, including several prominent politicians), Chile protested by sending troops into Antofagasta. Two weeks later, Chile and Bolivia were at war, with Peru joining in (on the Bolivian side) within a couple of months. **The War of the Pacific** (see page 474) went on for five years, and resulted in Chile taking over all of the nitrate grounds.

THE BOOM YEARS

With the return of political stability after the war, the nitrate industry began to boom in earnest, bringing in enormous export revenues for Chile, and a trail of processing plants, known as **oficinas**, sprang up all over the pampa. Each *oficina* sat in the centre of its prescribed land, from where the raw nitrate ore was blasted using gunpowder. The chunks of ore, known as *caliche*, were then boiled in large copper vats, releasing a nitrate solution which was crystallized in the sun before being sent down to the ports to be shipped abroad. The plants themselves were grimy, noisy places. It was a hard life for the labourers, who worked long hours in dangerous conditions, and were housed in squalid shacks, often without running water and sewerage. The (mostly British) managers, meanwhile, lived in grand residences, dined on imported delicacies and enjoyed a whirl of elegant social activities. Nitrate provided more than half of the Chilean government's revenues until 1920, by which time the boom was over and the industry in decline.

THE BEGINNING OF THE END

It was **World War I** that dealt the first serious blow to the nitrate companies, when the suspension of sales to Germany – Chile's major European buyer – forced almost half the *oficinas* to close down. The final death knell was sounded when Germany, forced to seek alternative fertilizers, developed cheap synthetic nitrates which quickly displaced Chile's natural nitrates from their dominant role in the world market. Most of what was left of the industry was killed off by the **World Depression** in the 1930s, and today just one *oficina* – **María Elena** – remains in operation.

4

small museum), but the processing plant is amazing, seeming to loom into the air like a rusty old dinosaur. As you walk around the site, listening to the endless clanging of machinery banging in the wind, the sense of abandonment is nigh-on overwhelming.

Reserva Nacional Pampa del Tamarugal

About 20km south of the junction between Ruta 16 and the Panamericana, the latter passes through the **Reserva Nacional Pampa del Tamarugal**, an extensive plantation of wispy, bush-like *tamarugo* trees. These are native to the region and especially adapted to saline soils, with roots that are long enough to tap underground water supplies. There's a Conaf-run **campsite** here, exactly 24km south of Pozo Almonte, on the west side of the Panamericana. While the *tamarugos* aren't really interesting enough to merit a special trip, you can take a look at them on your way to the far more impressive **Cerro Pintados**, with the largest collection of **geoglyphs** in South America, situated within the reserve's boundaries.

Cerro Pintados geoglyphs

45km south of Pozo Almonte, 5km west of the Panamericana on a gravel road that branches off the highway, almost opposite the turn-off to Pica • Tues–Sun 9.30am–6.30pm • CH$4000 (payable at the Conaf control point 2km along the access road) • ☎ 57 275 1055, ⓦ conaf. cl • *Colectivos* leave from the stand outside Iquique's Mercado Centenario, or you visit on a tour (see page 188)

Extending 4km along a hillside, the **Cerro Pintados geoglyphs** site features approximately four hundred images (not all of them visible from the ground) of animals, birds, humans and geometric patterns, etched on the surface or formed by a mosaic of little stones around the year 1000 AD. The felines, birds, snakes and flocks of llamas and vicuñas scratched into the rock are thought to have been indicators for livestock farmers. The circles, squares, dotted lines and human figures are more enigmatic, however, and may have had something to do with rituals, perhaps even sacrifices. Note that it's probably not a good idea to hitch and then try walking to the site from the Panamericana, owing to the relentless heat and lack of shade.

Pica and Matilla

As you cross the vast, desert pampa, the neighbouring oases of **Pica** and **Matilla** first appear as an improbable green smudge on the hazy horizon. As you get nearer, it becomes apparent that this is not a mirage and you are, indeed, approaching cultivated fields and trees. It's a remarkable sight, and anyone who has not seen a desert oasis should make a special effort to visit.

Pica

By far the larger of the two oases, **PICA** is a sleepy little town overflowing with lemon and lime trees, bougainvilleas and jasmine. It's the largest supplier of fruits to Iquique – *limas de Pica* are famous throughout the country – and one of the treats of visiting is drinking the delicious *jugos naturales* – orange, mango, pear, guava and grapefruit juices – freshly squeezed in front of you in the little streetside kiosks. The tidy plaza, by the entrance to town, is overlooked by a beautiful, pale-coloured **church** dedicated to St Andrew. It has a grand Neoclassical facade and was built in 1880.

Cocha Resbaladero

General Ibáñez s/n • Daily 8am–8pm • CH$3000

Pica's real selling point is the **Cocha Resbaladero**, a gorgeous **hot-springs pool** carved into a rocky hollow with two caves at one end. It's quite a walk from the main part of town, but there are several places to stay up here if you want to be close to the waters. To enjoy the waters in peace, arrive early before the buses of day-trippers start arriving at noon.

ARRIVAL AND INFORMATION   PICA

By bus There are regular buses from Iquique for Pica (6 daily; 2hr).

Tourist office Balmaceda 299 (Mon–Fri 8.30am–1.30pm & 3–6pm, Sat & Sun 10.30am–1.30pm & 3–6.30pm;

☎ 57 274 1310). The town's friendly Oficina de Turismo sits opposite the Municipalidad building just beyond the main square on the way to the hot springs.

ACCOMMODATION AND EATING

Hostal Los Emilios Lord Cochrane 213 ☎ 57 274 1126. The nicest place to stay in the centre, *Hotel Los Emilios* offers comfortable rooms with private bathrooms and TVs in a handsome old house with a plunge pool in the back garden. CH$28,000

Los Naranjos Barbosa 200. For something a bit different, this homely little place has a hearty menu of tasty Andean

specialities (CH$5000–10,000) such as llama stew with quinoa. Mon–Sat 12.30–3pm & 8.30–11pm, Sun 12.30–3pm.

Refugio Sombra Verde La Banda ☎ 09 8403 2348. A 10min walk from the centre, signposted off Balmaceda, is this excellent campsite, offering great facilities and plenty of trees for shade. Bring your own camping equipment. CH$5000

Matilla

The tiny, pretty village of **MATILLA**, about 5km southwest of Pica, has a beautiful church, albeit more humble than Pica's. You'll also see an eighteenth-century wine press, just off the plaza, originally used by the Spaniards; the roots of grapevines were brought over by the conquistadors.

Santuario de la Tirana

La Tirana, around 20km northwest of Pica • All buses between Iquique and Pica make a stop in La Tirana

Driving back to the Panamericana from Pica, if you take the right-hand (northbound) road, rather than the left-hand one, you'll pass through the little town of La Tirana, 10km before you get back to the highway. It's a rather cheerless place, made up of dusty streets and neglected adobe houses, which makes it all the more surprising when you come upon the immense, paved square stretching out before the imposing **Santuario de la Tirana**. This curious church, at once grand and shabby, is made of wood covered in cream-coloured corrugated iron. It's the home of the Virgen del Carmen, a polychrome carving that is the object of a fervent cult of devotion.

4

The fiesta

Every year, from July 12 to 18, up to eighty thousand pilgrims come to honour the Virgin and take part in the riotous **fiesta** in which dozens of masked, costumed dancers perform *bailes religiosos*. These dances have their roots in pre-Spanish, pre-Christian times, with an exuberant, carnival feel wholly out of keeping with traditional Catholic celebrations. If you're not around to see them in action, you should at least visit the small **museum** in a wing of the church where many of the costumes and masks are displayed (no fixed hours; try asking the caretaker to let you in if it's shut).

Mamiña

A paved road branches east from the Panamericana at Pozo Almonte and climbs gently through the desert to **MAMIÑA**, 125km – a two-and-a-half-hour drive – northeast of Iquique. First impressions are not encouraging; huddled on a hillside overlooking a valley, its narrow streets and crumbling stone houses seem to belong to a forgotten town, left to the mercy of the heat and dust. Continue down the valley, however, and its charms become more apparent as you come upon the fertile terraces emerald with alfalfa, and the little stream running through the gorge (*quebrada*).

THE LEGEND OF LA TIRANA

La Tirana is named after an Inca princess whose story is vividly recorded in twelve large panels inside the town's church. It all began in 1535 when **Diego de Almagro** marched south from Cuzco to conquer Chile. He took with him some five hundred Spaniards and ten thousand locals, including Huillac Huma, high priest of the cult of the Sun God, who was accompanied by his beautiful 23-year-old daughter, **la ñusta** (the princess). Unknown to Almagro, the party also included a number of **Wilkas**, or high-ranking warriors from the Inca Royal Army. When the party reached Atacama la Grande, the high priest slipped away from the group and fled to Charcas, where he planned to stir up rebellion against the Spaniards.

Later, the princess followed her father's lead and she too escaped – with a hundred Wilkas and followers – and fled to the *tamarugo* forests of the pampa. She organized her followers into a fierce army that, for the next four years, waged a relentless war against their oppressors. Her mission was clear: death to all Spaniards, and to every indigenous person who had been baptized by them. Before long, this indomitable woman became known far and wide as La Tirana del Tamarugal – the **Tyrant of the Tamarugal**.

STAR-CROSSED LOVERS

One day, in 1544, La Tirana's army returned to their leader with a prisoner – a certain **Don Vasco de Almeyda**, one of the Portuguese miners established in Huantajaya. According to the legend, "*Mirarle y enamorarse fue una sola cosa*", simply to look at him was to fall in love with him. La Tirana, hitherto immovable, fell passionately in love with the foreigner. But according to everything she stood and fought for, he must be sentenced to death. In desperation, she consulted the stars and her tribe's gods, and claimed that they had ordered her to keep him alive until four moons had passed.

For the next four months, a tender love grew between La Tirana and her prisoner. The princess neglected her people and her duties, arousing the suspicion of the Wilkas. As the fourth month was coming to an end, La Tirana asked her loved one if they would be reunited for eternity in heaven if she too were a Christian. On his affirmative reply, she begged him to baptize her. Almeyda began to do so, but before he could finish, the couple were showered with arrows from the bows of the betrayed Wilkas. As she lay dying in the wood, the princess cried, "I am dying happy, sure as I am that my immortal soul will ascend to God's throne. All I ask is that after my death, you will bury me next to my lover and place a cross over our grave."

A TOWN IS BORN

Ten years later, when Padre Antonio Rondon arrived in these parts to evangelize to native communities, it was with astonishment and joy that he discovered a simple cross in a clearing of the wood. The priest erected a humble chapel on the site, later replaced by a larger building that became, in time, the centre of worship in a town that took its name from the beautiful princess who had died there.

The hot springs

The real lure of Mamiña, though, is the **hot springs** for which the town is famous throughout Chile; the delicious bottled mineral water from here is on sale in the region only, as production is small. Unlike Pica, Mamiña doesn't have just one hot spring, but many, and their waters are piped into every house in the village.

Furthermore, these waters are not merely hot, but are reputed to cure all manner of afflictions, from eczema and psoriasis to respiratory problems and anxiety. Indeed, the town is named in honour of an Inca princess whose blindness was reputedly cured here. Whatever their medicinal value, there's no doubt that the waters are supremely relaxing to bathe in. This you can do in any of the village's hotels or *residenciales*, usually in your own private *tina*, or bathtub.

Baños Ipla
Daily 8am–1.30pm & 3–9pm • CH$2500

There are also a number of public springs, including the **Baños Ipla**, down in the valley, whose four unattractive *tinas* are filled with hot sulphurous water (45°C) bubbling up from underground. Nearby, the **Vertiente del Radium** is a little fountain whose radioactive waters are supposed to cure eye infections and, according to legend, once restored the sight of an Inca princess.

Barros Chino

Daily 9am–4pm • CH$2500

A short walk from the Vertiente del Radium, behind the water-bottling plant, you'll find the mud baths of **Barros Chino** where you can plaster yourself in mud (don't let the caretaker do it for you), lie on a wooden rack while it dries, then wash it off in a small thermal pool.

ARRIVAL AND DEPARTURE   MAMIÑA

By bus Buses leave from outside the market in Iquique (2 daily; 2hr 30min).

ACCOMMODATION

Accommodation is centred in two quite separate areas, one on the ridge overlooking the valley, and the other down in the valley, by the Baños Ipla. Many are run on a **full-board basis**. You can **camp** for free by the pool on the track out to Cerro del Inca, about a 30min walk from the Ipla baths.

Hotel Kusitambu Sulumpa s/n ☎57 257 4644, ⓦhotelkusitambu.cl. Meaning "place of rest" in Aymara, the *Hotel Kusitambu* has basic rooms, all with private bathrooms, and two *cabañas* with thermal water in the bathrooms, but sadly no pool – though there is a games room. Breakfast costs extra. Popular with miners. CH$28,000

Hotel Termas la Coruña Santa Rosa 687 ☎57 257 3664, ⓦtermaslacoruña.cl. With unbeatable views of the Mamiña Valley, and just 100m from the plaza, this strategically located hotel has an outdoor hot spring pool, tennis court and games room. Rooms are simple but clean; there are also smarter *cabañas* sleeping up to four people. Doubles CH$25,000, *cabañas* CH$45,000

Parque Nacional Volcán Isluga

At the one-horse town of **Huara**, 33km up the Panamericana from the turn-off to Iquique, a good road branches east into the desert, then climbs high into the mountains, continuing all the way to Oruro in Bolivia. It's paved as far as **Colchane**, on the Chilean side of the border, but the main appeal lies in getting off the tarmac once you're up into the cordillera and heading for the deserted wilderness in and around **Parque Nacional Volcán Isluga.** Here you'll find a remote, isolated landscape of wide plains, dramatic, snowcapped volcanoes (one of which is the park's namesake) and semi-abandoned villages, home to indigenous Aymara herding communities that have been a part of this windswept land for thousands of years.

Unlike Parque Nacional Lauca, further north, this region hasn't yet been "discovered", and it's unlikely you'll come across many other tourists. There are a number of attractions on the way up, as well, in particular the weird desert geoglyph known as the **Gigante de Atacama**, in the pampa, and the frozen geysers of **Puchuldiza**, on the lower slopes of the Andes.

Enquelga

Parque Nacional Volcán Isluga's administrative centre is in **ENQUELGA**, a dusty, tumbledown hamlet – 3850m above sea level – home to a small Aymara community. Many of its inhabitants, particularly the women, still dress in traditional, brightly coloured clothes, and live from tending llamas and cultivating potatoes and barley.

4

Aguas Calientes

Two kilometres on from Enquelga, **Aguas Calientes** is a long, spring-fed pool
containing warm (but not hot) waters, set in an idyllic location with terrific views of
Volcán Isluga. The pool is surrounded by pea-green *bofedal* – a spongy grass, typical of
the altiplano – and drains into a little stream, crossed every morning and evening by
herds of llamas driven to and from the sierra by Aymara shepherdesses. There's a stone
changing-hut next to it, and a few **camping** spaces and picnic areas, protected from the
evening wind by thick stone walls.

Isluga

Six kilometres east of Enquelga, still within the park's boundaries, **ISLUGA** is composed
of a hundred or so stone and adobe houses huddled around a beautiful **church**. Built in
the seventeenth century (it's not known when, exactly), it's a humble little construction
of thick, whitewashed adobe that flashes like snow in the constant glare of the sun.
The main building, containing a single nave, is enclosed by a low wall trimmed with
delicate arches; just outside the wall sits the two-tier bell tower with steps leading up to

THE AYMARA OF CHILE

The **Aymara** people are the second-largest indigenous linguistic group of South America (after the Quechua). The culture flourished around **Lake Titicaca** and spread throughout the high-plain region, known as the altiplano, of what is now Bolivia, Peru and Chile. Today there are around three million Aymara scattered through these three countries, with the Chilean Aymara forming the smallest group, totalling some forty thousand people. Following the big migrations from the highlands to the coast that took place in the 1960s, most of the Aymara people of Chile now live and work in the coastal cities of **Arica** and **Iquique**. At least thirteen thousand Aymara, however, remain in the altiplano of northern Chile, where their lifestyle is still firmly rooted in the traditions of the past thousand years. The main economic activities are llama and sheep herding and the cultivation of crops such as potatoes and barley.

Traditionally, the Aymara live in **small communities**, called *ayllu*, based on extended family kinship. Their houses are made of stone and mud with rough thatched roofs, and most villages have a square and a small whitewashed church with a separate bell tower – often dating from the seventeenth century when **Spanish missionaries** evangelized the region.

RELIGIOUS BELIEFS

Nowadays many of the smaller villages, such as Isluga (see page 198), are left abandoned for most of the year, the houses securely locked up while their owners make their living down in the city or in the larger cordillera towns like **Putre**. Known as "ceremonial villages" they're shaken from their slumber and burst into life when people return for important religious festivals or funerals. Andean **fiestas** are based on a fascinating blend of Catholic and indigenous rites. At the centre of Aymara culture is respect for the life-giving **Mother Earth**, known as *pachamama*, and traditional ceremonies – involving singing and dancing – are still carried out in some communities at sowing and harvest time.

The Aymara also believe that the tallest mountains looming over their villages contain spirits, or *mallku*, that guard over them, protecting their animals and crops. Once a year, on **May 3** – Cruz de Mayo – the most traditional communities climb up the sacred mountains, where a village elder speaks to the *mallku*, which appears in the form of a condor. Today's young Aymara go to local state schools and speak Spanish as their main language, and while traditional lifestyles continue in the altiplano, it's with increasingly closer links with mainstream Chilean life.

the top, where you can sit and survey the scenery or watch the hummingbirds that fly in and out.

The church, along with the entire village, remains locked up and abandoned for most of the year – Isluga is a "**ceremonial village**", whose inhabitants come back only for festivals, important religious ceremonies and funerals; the principal **fiestas** are held on February 2 and 3, March 10, Easter week, and December 8, 12 and 21 to 25.

Colchane

Ten kilometres from Isluga, at the end of the paved road from Huara, at 3730m above sea level, **COLCHANE** is a small, grim border town of grid-laid streets and truckers' canteens. Most days, the only reason you might want to come here is for **accommodation** or to cross over into **Bolivia** (see page 178). Twice a month, however, on alternate Saturdays, Colchane takes on a bit of life and colour as the neighbouring altiplano villagers bring their fresh produce, weavings and knitwear to sell at the **market**.

Cariquima

Charming **CARIQUIMA**, just 17km south of Colchane, has picturesque, cleanly swept streets and an old altiplano-style church with a painted interior. Seek out the **crafts cooperative**, housed in a beautifully decorated building along one of the village's few streets, and where you'll find high-quality woollens for sale. Cariquima sits in the lee of the dramatic Nevado Cariquima, while, 5km to the north is the minute hamlet of **Ancovinto**. There you'll see a forest of giant cacti that sway in the breeze and enjoy fantastic views across the altiplano to Bolivia and the Salar de Coipasa.

ARRIVAL AND DEPARTURE

By vehicle There's no public transport around this region, so you must either rent a 4WD (see page 188) or take an organized tour from Iquique (see page 189). For

PARQUE NACIONAL VOLCÁN ISLUGA

information on crossing the border into Bolivia, see page 178.

ACCOMMODATION

Camino del Inca Teniente Gonzalez s/n, Colchane ☎ 09 8446 3586. Given the lack of other accommodation options, it's fortunate that this family-run budget hotel is a solid option. It has very basic but clean rooms with shared bathrooms and hot water. **CH$20,000**

Conaf refugio Enquelga. This Conaf-run *refugio* can provide accommodation for up to five people; it's supposed to be open year-round, but sometimes isn't. Call Arica's Conaf office (see page 205) to reserve a bed in advance. Dorms **CH$5500**

Pisagua

Most people whizz up the Panamericana between Iquique and Arica in about four hours without stopping, but some 80km north of the turn-off to Iquique, a poorly paved side road leads 52km west down to **PISAGUA** – a crumbling, evocative nitrate port that makes an interesting option for a night's stopover. The final stretch down to the port is very steep, giving dramatic views down to the little toy town cowering by the ocean, the only sign of life on this barren desert coast.

Pisagua is a funny sort of place, part scruffy, ramshackle fishing town, part fascinating relic of the past. It was one of the busiest and wealthiest ports of the nitrate era, and is still dotted with many grand nineteenth-century buildings, some of them restored and repainted, others decaying at the same slow pace as the rest of the town (which has only about 150 inhabitants today). Most striking of all is the handsome, white-and-blue timber **clock tower**, built in 1887 and still standing watch from the hillside.

The old theatre

The **old theatre**, a fine wooden building erected on the main square in 1892, with a typical nineteenth-century facade featuring tall wooden pillars, a balcony and a balustrade, is Pisagua's main monument to the nitrate era. You can borrow the key from the *carabineros* station at the far end of town, and wander inside to take a look at the large, empty stage, the rows of polished wooden seats and the high ceiling, lavishly painted with cherubs dancing on clouds. The ghostliness of the place is made all the more intense by the monotonous sound of the waves crashing against the building's rear wall, which plunges directly down to the sea.

PINOCHET'S LEGACY IN PISAGUA

At the far end of town, next to the carabineros station, Pisagua's more recent history is the subject of a haunting **mural** dedicated to the memory of those executed here during the military dictatorship, when the village was used as a concentration camp. A couple of kilometres north, on the edge of the cemetery, the former site of the mass graves is marked by an open pit bearing a simple cross, a scattering of wreaths and a block of stone inscribed with a single line by Pablo Neruda: "Even though a thousand years shall pass, this site will never be cleansed of the blood of those who fell here."

ARRIVAL AND DEPARTURE

By bus There is only one bus a day, which leaves Iquique at 7pm and returns from Pisagua at 7am, so to have a full day there you need to stay two nights.

ACCOMMODATION

Hostal La Roca Manuel Rodriguez 20 ☎ 57 273 1502. Lovely modern-rustic, family-run hotel with big clean rooms, all boasting private bathrooms with hot water. Ask for a room with sea view. Friendly owner Sra Catherine will make you feel right at home. **CH$27,000**

Hacienda de Tiliviche

Ten kilometres north of the turn-off for Pisagua, just before the bridge across the Quebrada de Tiliviche, a short track branches left (west) to the **HACIENDA DE TILIVICHE**. At the end of the track you'll find the old *casa patronal*, a charmingly dilapidated house overlooking a yard full of clucking chickens and lethargic dogs. It was built in 1855 for a British nitrate family and remained in British hands until very recently; the current owners have vague plans to renovate it and turn it into a hotel.

The British Cemetery

Set within the grounds of Hacienda de Tiliviche, on the other side of the stream, stands a nostalgic testimony to the nitrate era: the old **British Cemetery**, enclosed by tall iron railings and a huge, rusty gate – you can borrow the key from the hacienda caretaker. Inside, about a hundred lonely graves stand in the shade of a few *tamarugo* trees at the foot of the desolate mountain that rises over the *quebrada*. This stark desert setting is strikingly at odds with the very English inscriptions on the tombstones ("Thy will be done" and the like). The graves read like a who's who of the erstwhile British business community, including people like Herbert Harrison, the manager of the Tarapacá Waterworks Company and, most famously, **James Humberstone**, the manager of several nitrate *oficinas*.

The geoglyphs

The southern wall of Tiliviche's *quebrada* also features some of the most impressive **geoglyphs** in Chile. They're best viewed from the lay-by just off the Panamericana, a few hundred metres up from the bridge on the northern side of the *quebrada*. From this vantage point, you can see the images in all their splendour – a large crowd of llamas covering the hillside. All of the llamas are moving in the same direction, towards the sea, and it's thought that the drawings were designed to guide caravans descending from the mountains on their journey towards the coast.

Arica

ARICA likes to call itself "*la ciudad de la eterna primavera*" – "city of everlasting spring". Chile's northernmost city, just 16km south of the Peruvian border, is certainly blessed with a mild climate, which, along with its sandy **beaches**, makes it a popular holiday resort for Chileans and Bolivians. Although a lingering sea fog can dampen spirits, in the winter especially, just head a few kilometres inland and you'll usually find blue skies.

The city's compact, tidy centre sits proudly at the foot of the Morro cliff, the site of a major Chilean victory in the War of the Pacific (and cherished as a symbol of national glory). It was this war that delivered Arica, formerly Peruvian, into Chilean hands, in 1883, and while the city is emphatically Chilean today, there's no denying the strong presence of *mestizo* and Quechua-speaking Peruvians on the streets, trading their fresh produce and *artesanía*. This, added to its role as Bolivia's main export centre, makes Arica more colourful, ethnically diverse and vibrant than most northern Chilean cities, even if parts of it look somewhat impoverished.

The liveliest streets are pedestrianized **Calles 21 de Mayo** and **Bolognesi**, the latter clogged with **artesanía stalls**, while by the port you'll see the smelly but colourful **terminal pesquero**, where inquisitive pelicans wander around the fish stalls. Though far from beautiful, Arica does boast a couple of fine pieces of nineteenth-century architecture, pretty squares filled

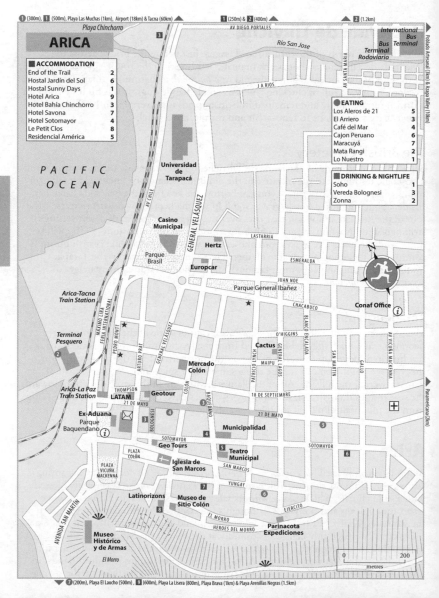

ARICA

■ ACCOMMODATION

End of the Trail	2
Hostal Jardín del Sol	6
Hostal Sunny Days	1
Hotel Arica	9
Hotel Bahía Chinchorro	3
Hotel Savona	7
Hotel Sotomayor	4
Le Petit Clos	8
Residencial América	5

● EATING

Los Aleros de 21	5
El Arriero	3
Café del Mar	4
Cajon Peruano	6
Maracuyá	7
Mata Rangi	2
Lo Nuestro	1

■ DRINKING & NIGHTLIFE

Soho	1
Vereda Bolognesi	3
Zonna	2

with flowers and palm trees, and a young, lively atmosphere. It's a pleasant enough place to spend a couple of days – or longer, if you feel like kicking back on the beach.

Iglesia de San Marcos

Plaza Colón • Daily 9am–2pm & 6–8pm • Free

In the centre you'll find the small, tree-filled **Plaza Colón**, dominated by the **Iglesia de San Marcos**, a pretty white church with a high, Gothic spire and many tall, arched windows. Designed by Gustave Eiffel, this curious church, made entirely of iron, was prefabricated in France before being erected in Arica in 1876, when the city still belonged to Peru. The riveting key used to assemble the structure was kept in a display case inside the church, but when Chilean troops attacked, it was thrown into the sea to prevent the invaders from dismantling the building and stealing it as a war trophy. Instead, they took the whole city.

El Morro

Arica's most visible feature is the 139m-high cliff to the south known as **El Morro**, which signals the end of the coastal cordillera. Steps starting at the southern end of Calle Colón lead you to the top, where sweeping, panoramic views (especially impressive at night) and the very nationalistic **Museo Histórico y de Armas** await. This cappuccino-coloured cliff is *the* source of pride for Arica's citizens, heightened by a big sign saying "*Arica siempre Arica, mayor es mi lealtad*" (roughly translated as "Arica, forever Arica, my loyalty will always be to you"). It's also an important national landmark, given its historical significance as the place where Chile won a crucial 1880 battle against Peru during the War of the Pacific.

At the top, along with the museum, is a statue of Christ with his arms outstretched – a symbol of peace between the two once-enemy nations. It's a pleasant ten- to fifteen-minute hike up Calle Colón, but you can get a taxi to take you and wait for you while you explore and admire the wonderful view of the city and beaches, before dropping you off in town afterwards.

Museo Histórico y de Armas

El Morro • Jan & Feb Tues–Sun 10am–8pm; March–Dec Tues–Sun 9am–7pm • CH$1000

Built on top of a former Peruvian fortification, the **Museo Histórico y de Armas** is owned by the army, rather than the government, and has clearly had more money spent on it than most Chilean museums. The exhibits – primarily nineteenth-century guns and military uniforms – are very well displayed, but the theme is rather chauvinistic in tone, the main thrust being the superiority of the Chileans and the inferiority of the Peruvians in the Battle of the Morro, when Chilean forces stormed and took possession of the hilltop defence post.

Museo de Sitio Colón

Colón 10 • Tues–Sun 10am–6pm • CH$2000

The **Museo de Sitio Colón** has a rather curious history: while carrying out construction work for a new hotel back in 2004, the builders came across some very old human remains. Plans for the new hotel stopped and the University of Tarapacá was called in and it soon became apparent that the site was a 4000-year-old funerary space for the Chinchorro people. Because of the extremely fragile nature of these age-old human remains, transportation was out of the question and a museum on the site was opened to exhibit the 48 **Chinchorro mummies** (see page 208) found, left in their resting places under plate glass that you can walk over. Labels are only in Spanish but audio guides in English are included in the entry.

Ex-Aduana

Parque Baquedano • Mon–Fri 8.30am–7pm • Free

The 1874 **Ex-Aduana** (customs house) is another Eiffel-designed building with an attractive stone facade of pink and white horizontal stripes. Also known as the "*casa de la cultura*", these days it's used as a cultural centre and puts on regular photographic and art exhibitions. Its pleasant location on a little square full of palm trees and shady benches, flanked to the south by the coastal avenue, adds to its charm.

The beaches

Arica is a major destination for serious **surfers**, who travel far and wide to test out the famous waves. The city holds a couple of important international surfing competitions every year, though sunbathers and swimmers will also appreciate Arica's **beaches**; although not as attractive as Iquique's sandy shores, the water is slightly warmer. The closest beach to the centre is the popular **Playa El Laucho**, a curved, sandy cove about a fifteen-minute walk down Avenida San Martín, south of El Morro. You can also get *micros* down the avenue, which continue to several other beaches, including **Playa La Lisera** and **Playa Brava**, both attractive, and the usually deserted **Playa Arenillas Negras**, a wide expanse of dark sand backed by low sand dunes, with a fish-processing factory at its southern end.

Northern beaches

Starting less than 2km north of the centre, **Playa Chinchorro** is a large, clean beach with activities such as a small zip line. To get there, take bus #12 or #14; both will drop you off one block from the beach. Just further north, its extension **Playa Las Machas** is quieter but more exposed to the wind, and popular with surfers. The only beaches suitable for swimmers are Playa Lisera, Playa Laucho and Playa Chinchorro – these all have lifeguards during the summer months.

Poblado Artesanal

On your way out towards the Azapa Valley, on Calle Hualles, just south of the river, the **Poblado Artesanal** is a replica of an altiplano village, where twelve white houses serve as workshops for artisans selling handicrafts ranging from ceramics and glass to knitwear and leather items; its hours of operation are erratic.

ARRIVAL AND DEPARTURE ARICA

By plane Arica's Chacalluta airport, served by LATAM (Arturo Prat 391; ☎ 58 225 2650) and Sky Airline (airport; ☎ 58 229 0768) lies 18km north of the city and is connected to the centre by reasonably priced airport taxis (around CH$8000) or minibus transfers (CH$4000).

Destinations Iquique (1 daily; 40min); Santiago (8–10 daily; 2hr 30min).

By bus Coming in by bus, you'll arrive at Arica's Terminal Rodoviario, which uniquely charges a CH$200 platform fee for all domestic departures, which you pay at a separate booth. The fee is CH$350 for departures to Tacna in Peru

from the adjacent international terminal (see page 206). Both terminals lie 2km northeast of the centre on Av Diego Portales, but you can easily catch a *colectivo* or *micro* into the centre along intersecting Av Santa Maria.

Destinations Antofagasta (houry–every 3hr; 10hr); Calama (5–6 daily; 10hr); Chañaral (7 daily; 15hr); Copiapó (hourly–every 2hr; 17hr); Iquique (every 30min; 5hr); La Paz (Bolivia; 4–6 daily; 8–9hr); Putre (1 daily; 3hr); San Pedro de Atacama (3 nightly; 14hr); Santiago (10 daily; 29hr); Tacna (Peru; every 10–15min; 2–3hr); Vallenar (10 daily; 20hr).

GETTING AROUND

By colectivo The colour and number on top of the taxi *colectivo* denotes which direction it´s heading. To avoid confusion, it´s best to take a local bus or private taxi from the bus station when you first arrive, until you figure out the number system.

Private taxis Radiotaxi Chacalluta, Patricio Lynch 371 (☎ 58 225 4812); Radio Taxi ☎ 58 225 7000.

Car rental Europcar, Colón 996 (☎ 58 225 8911); Cactus, General Lagos 666 (☎ 58 225 8353); Hertz, Baquedano 999 (☎ 58 223 1487).

4

TOURS FROM ARICA

Three or four companies in Arica regularly offer **tours** up to **Parque Nacional Lauca** (see page 209). The problem is that the most commonly available tour takes place in a single day, which means rushing from sea level to up to 4500m and down again in a short space of time – really not a good idea, and likely to cause those prone to altitude sickness some ill effects, ranging from tiredness and mild headaches to acute dizziness and nausea. In very rare cases the effects can be more serious, and you should always check that the company carries a supply of oxygen and has a staff member trained to deal with emergencies.

Altitude aside, the amount of time you spend inside a minibus is very tiring, which can spoil your experience of what is one of the most beautiful parts of Chile. Therefore it's really worth paying extra and taking a tour that includes at least one overnight stop in the town of **Putre** (see page 208); better still is one continuing south to the **Salar de Surire** (see page 213) and **Parque Nacional Isluga** (see page 197). However, it's worth noting that the availability of these longer tours can be frustratingly scarce during the quieter, low-season months. One-day trips usually cost around CH$30,000 per person, while you can expect to pay from CH$100,000 for a one-night tour, overnighting in Putre, and from around CH$250,000 for a two-night tour, sleeping in Putre and Colchane.

TOUR OPERATORS

Geotour Bolognesi 421 ☎ 58 225 3927, ⓦ geotour. cl. Slick, professional but fairly impersonal company offering mostly one-day tours around Arica, as well as trips further afield to Lauca, Matilla and Pica. There are two other branches in San Pedro de Atacama and Iquique.

★ **Latinorizons** Colón 7 ☎ 58 225 0007, ⓦ latinorizons.com. Friendly and extremely reliable Belgian-run company offering a wide range of altiplano tours, including overnight, with a more adventurous feel than most of the others on offer. French and English spoken. Charlie, the very knowledgeable owner, also owns the *hostal* next to their office (see page 206).

Parinacota Expediciones Héroes del Morro 632 ☎ 58 223 3305, ⓦ parinacotaexpediciones.cl. Well-established company offering several options for visiting Parque Nacional Lauca and around, including the usual day-trip, an overnight stop in Putre and a two-night tour taking in the Salar de Surire.

INFORMATION

Tourist office San Marcos 101 (Jan, Feb & Dec Mon–Fri 9am–7pm; March–Nov Mon–Fri 9am–6pm; ☎ 58 225 4506, ⓦ sernatur.cl).
Conaf Vicuña Mackenna 820 (Mon–Fri 8.30am–5.30pm; ☎ 58 225 0750, ⓦ conaf.cl). The regional Conaf office has basic maps and information on Parque Nacional Lauca and adjoining protected areas. You can also reserve beds at the Conaf *refugio* in the Reserva Nacional las Vicuñas (see page 212).

ACCOMMODATION

Unlike Iquique, Arica has very little seafront **accommodation** and most places to stay are situated in and around the town's centre. Here, there's no shortage of *residenciales*, ranging from the dirt-cheap to the polished and comfortable. The hostels are conveniently located between the bus terminal and Playa Chinchorro.

HOTELS

Hostal Jardín del Sol Sotomayor 848 ☎ 58 223 2795, ⓦ hostaljardindelsol.cl; map p.202. Small, tidy rooms with private bathrooms off a flower-filled courtyard with tables, chairs and loungers. Good value for money and very friendly too, a great place to mix with like-minded travellers. CH$36,500
Hotel Arica Av San Martín 599 ☎ 58 225 4540, ⓦ panamericanahoteles.cl; map p.202. High-end but rather dated and overpriced hotel overlooking the ocean, with pleasant rooms and *cabañas*, plus a pool, tennis courts and mini golf, as well as a mediocre restaurant. Doubles US$103, *cabañas* US$115

Hotel Bahía Chinchorro Av Luis Beretta Porcel 2031 ☎ 58 226 5270, ✉ bahia_arica@latinmail.com; map p.202. A 20min walk from the centre, this place has direct access to Playa Chinchorro. The simple and rather shabby rooms – with attached bathrooms, a/c and TVs – are all glass-fronted, giving them superb ocean views. CH$35,000
Hotel Savona Yungay 380 ☎ 58 223 1000, ⓦ hotelsavona.cl; map p.202. Low-rise, 1970s-style

4

CROSSING INTO BOLIVIA AND PERU

There are two main routes from the far north of Chile across the Andes into **Bolivia**. The more southerly of the two is from **Iquique** to **Oruro** (for connections to Cochabamba or La Paz), served by a daily Jet Nort bus that usually departs at 6pm and takes 10–12hr. Far more frequently travelled is the busy road between **Arica** and **La Paz**, which has several daily buses operated by different companies. The journey of just under 500km takes 8–9hr, depending how long you have to wait at the border, and has the added bonus of going right through Parque Nacional Lauca (see page 209).

One of the busiest and easiest border crossings in all South America is the one on the Panamericana between **Arica** and **Tacna** in **Peru**, which lie less than 60km apart. Departing from Arica, you first pay the CH$350 terminal fee at the international terminal and then choose between the continuous stream buses and *colectivos* that ply between the cities as soon as they are full. The journey can take little over an hour or well over two, depending how many vehicles coincide at the efficient border post.

hotel built around a bright patio garden with a swimming pool. Rather tasteless yet comfortable rooms have small private bathrooms and TVs. Bikes are available for rent. CH$49,000

Hotel Sotomayor Sotomayor 367 ☎58 258 5761, ⓦhotelsotomayor.cl; map p.202. This dazzlingly multicoloured building features clean, airy yet somewhat dated rooms (disappointing after the beautiful old Spanish tiles in the lobby) with private bath and parking. CH$38,000

★ **Le Petit Clos** Colón 9 ☎58 232 3746, ⓦlepetitclos. cl; map p.202. This elegantly converted old house is now the delightful *hostal* belonging to the owner of Latinorizons (see page 205). Some of the compact but comfortable rooms have private baths and there are great views of the ocean and nearby El Morro from the roof terrace. CH$27,000

Residencial América Sotomayor 430 ☎58 225 4148, ⓦresidencialamerica.com; map p.202. Right in the heart of the city, opposite the town hall, this *residencial*

offers good-value budget rooms with an encouraging aroma of furniture polish. Some rooms have private bathrooms. CH$28,000

HOSTELS

End of the Trail Esteban Alvarado 117 ☎58 231 4316, ⓦendofthetrail-arica.cl; map p.202. The congenial American owner runs this hostel, which has comfortable, quiet rooms around an indoor courtyard, amazing showers and a specially designed roof that keeps the house cool. To get here from the bus station, walk two blocks west on Diego Portales, then four blocks north on Pedro de Valdivia. Dorms CH$11,000, doubles CH$26,000

★ **Hostal Sunny Days** Tomas Aravena 161 ☎58 224 1038, ⓦsunny-days-arica.cl; map p.202. Extremely friendly and knowledgeable Kiwi/Chilean hosts preside over travellers of all ages in this custom-built hostel. An excellent breakfast, spacious kitchen and lounge facilities and a relaxed communal atmosphere all add to its appeal. Dorms CH$11,000, doubles CH$26,000

EATING

Los Aleros de 21 21 de Mayo 736 ☎58 225 4641; map p.202. Traditional Chilean restaurant serving pricey, excellent steaks, seafood and other meat dishes (mains around CH$11,000–14,000). Great quality and service – it's a favourite among locals, and deservedly so. Mon–Sat noon–4pm & 8pm–midnight, Sun noon–4pm.

El Arriero 21 de Mayo 385 ☎58 223 2636, ⓦrestaurantelarriero.cl; map p.202. Recommended grill house serving tasty fillet steaks and other meat dishes (from CH$9000); there is often live folk music at the weekends. Book ahead, as it gets busy. Mon–Sat noon–4pm & 7–11pm.

Café del Mar 21 de Mayo 260 ☎58 223 1936, ⓦcafedelmararica.cl; map p.202. This café on the main pedestrian strip is popular with Arica's residents,

both young and old, thanks to its colourful decor, outside seating and tasty menu, which includes big salads, sandwiches, pizzas and, best of all, delicious crêpes (from CH$2000). *Menú del día* CH$4700. Mon–Sat 9.30am–midnight.

Cajon Peruano Yungay 570 ☎9 8226 5195; map p.202. This long rectangular dining hall serves set lunches for CH$4000 and mains, including *chicharron*, for CH$4000–7000. In the evening it becomes a club mainly for Peruvian expats. Mon–Sat noon–5pm.

★ **Maracuyá** Av San Martín 0321, Playa La Lisera ☎58 222 7600, ⓦrestaurantmaracuya.cl; map p.202. Dramatically sited as it is, right over the ocean's edge, this smart restaurant (one of Arica's best) offers boldly prepared fish and seafood (dishes around CH$9000–15,000) amid a spectacle of breaking waves.

Mon–Sat noon–3.40pm & 8.15pm–12.30am, Sun noon–5pm.

Mata Rangi Terminal Pesquero ☏ 9 5422 1507; map p.202. Tucked inside the fishermen's harbour, a rustic inexpensive place serving unfussy fish and seafood lunches (CH$6000–8000) – sit by the window and you may even spot a pelican or sea lion. Daily 12.30–5pm.

Lo Nuestro Raul Pey 2492 ☏ 58 223 0796; map p.202. Fine buffet restaurant behind Playa Chinchorro, where you can help yourself to as much tenderly grilled meat and food from the salad bar as you like. The price (lunch CH$9400, dinner CH$11,500) includes two desserts and a glass of wine. Tues–Sat 1–3pm & 9pm–midnight, Sun 1–3.30pm.

DRINKING AND NIGHTLIFE

Soho Buenos Aires 209, Playa Chinchorro ☏ 09 8905 1806, ⓦ facebook.com/sohoclubarica; map p.202. A stone's throw from Chinchorro beach, this nightclub is attached to *Pub Capitán Drake* and often has live music and several DJs. Entry is often free before 1.30am. Daily midnight till late.

Vereda Bolognesi Bolognesi 340 ☏ 58 223 1273; map p.202. By night, from about 8pm, this smart little shopping gallery in town turns into a buzzing patio bar

zone – several resto-bars compete with their happy hours so it´s easy to get a good cocktail at a decent price. Mon–Sat 10am–11pm.

Zonna Av Argentina 2787 ☏ 58 222 1509, ⓦ zonna.cl; map p.202. *Zonna*, the biggest, best-known and most popular nightclub in Arica, is really a collection of venues each playing different types of music ranging from salsa to 1980s hits. Ask about the weekly drink promotion. Thurs–Sun midnight till late.

Azapa Valley

Avenida Diego Portales extends out of Arica's city centre into the green **Azapa Valley**. The far western end of the valley is, to all intents and purposes, a suburb of Arica, crammed as it is with condos and villas, some of which have been converted into trendy discos, along with a couple of good restaurants. The highlight of a trip to the Azapa Valley is the **Museo Archeológico**, which houses a collection of the world's most ancient **mummies**. This museum is among Chile's best and is definitely worth the trip. If you're booked on a multi-day tour of the Altiplano, it's very likely this will be a stop-off.

4

Museo Arqueológico

Km 12, Azapa Valley • Daily: Jan & Feb 10am–7pm; March–Dec 10am–6pm • CH$2500 • ☏ 58 220 5551, ⓦ masma.uta.cl

Twelve kilometres along the road from Arica's Poblado Artesanal, the outstanding **Museo Arqueológico**, part of the University of Tarapacá, houses an excellent collection of regional pre-Columbian artefacts, including a collection of extraordinary **Chinchorro mummies** (see page 208) buried more than four thousand years ago. Other exhibits include finely decorated Tiwanaku ceramics, ancient Andean musical instruments and snuff trays, and many beautifully embroidered tapestries – look out for the one in Case 11, decorated with images of smiling women – and displays on contemporary Aymara culture.

All the pieces are extremely well presented, and there are unusually explanatory leaflets available in several languages, including English, French and German.

San Miguel de Azapa

In the village of **SAN MIGUEL DE AZAPA**, around 10km south of Arica, the only place of interest is the fabulously multicoloured desert **cemetery**, which climbs like a mini-Valparaíso for the deceased towards a dune-like cliff. The colour comes from the artificial flowers laid on the graves. By the entrance sits the morbidly named **restaurant** *La Picá del Muertito* (the "Little Dead Man's Snack-Bar"), famous for miles around for its first-rate *pastel de choclo*, a sugar-glazed corn-bake containing meat, egg and olives.

4

CHINCHORRO MUMMIES

In 1983, while laying a new pipeline near the foot of El Morro, the Arica water company came across a hoard of withered corpses buried a couple of metres beneath the sand. Work immediately ceased and archeologists from the University of Tarapacá were rushed in to assess the scene, which turned out to be 7000-year-old burial site containing 96 bodies – the largest and best-preserved find, to date, of **Chinchorro mummies**.

The ancient practice of mummification in this region – the oldest known in the world – was first identified in 1917 when a series of highly unusual human remains were discovered. Further excavations revealed similar findings spread along the coast, concentrated between Arica and Camerones, 65km south, and it became apparent that they were relics of an ancient society that archeologists have named the Chinchorro culture. Modern radiocarbon dating has established that the practice was well under way by 5000 BC – more than two millennia before the Egyptians began practising mummification.

ORIGINS OF THE CHINCHORRO

No one knows exactly where the Chinchorro people came from; some archeologists speculate that they moved down from the north, others that they came from the Andean highlands. What's clear, however, is that by 7000 BC scattered groups of people – possibly extended families – were spread along the coast of Chile's **far north**, where they lived on the abundant crabs, clams, mussels, seaweed, pelicans, sea lions and other marine life of the region, supplementing their diet with guanaco and wild berries.

THE MUMMIFICATION PROCESS

The great simplicity of their hunter-gatherer lifestyle makes the sophisticated techniques they developed to **preserve the dead** all the more extraordinary. The practice involved removing the brain through a hole at the base of the skull, and removing all internal organs, which were probably discarded. After this, the cavities were dried with hot stones or fire and then refilled with straw and ashes. The bones of the arms and legs were replaced with sticks bound into place with reeds, and the skeleton was given extra padding before the body was stitched up. The face was then coated in paste, which dried into a hard mask with a sculpted nose and incisions marking the eyes and mouth. The finishing touch was provided by a wig made of human hair, which was attached to the skull.

The Chinchorro culture performed this elaborate process for more than three thousand years until, for unknown reasons, the practice died out around 1500 BC, and the era of the oldest known form of artificial mummification came to an end.

Alto Ramírez

The Azapa Valley is home to several **geoglyphs**. The most impressive example is **Alto Ramírez**, a large, stylized human figure surrounded by geometric shapes; you can see it, at a distance, from the main road on the way to the archeological museum (ask your *colectivo* driver to point it out to you) or take a detour to get a closer look.

ARRIVAL AND DEPARTURE   AZAPA VALLEY

By colectivo Colectivos for the Azapa Valley, including the Museo Arqueológico and the nearby geoglyphs, leave from the corner of Lynch and Chacabuco in Arica's centre and cost CH$1200.

Putre

The sleepy little mountain town of **PUTRE**, surrounded by a patchwork of green fields and Inca terraces, lies 150km northeeast of Arica at a height of 3500m. It's a popular overnight stop en route to the higher altitudes of **Parque Nacional Lauca** – climbers, in particular, like to spend a few days walking in the hills here before attempting the volcanoes in the park. Putre's rustic houses are clustered around a large, tiered and nicely landscaped square, overlooked by the Municipalidad.

The church

Off the northeast corner of the square you'll find the **church**, built in 1670 after an earthquake destroyed the original, which, according to old Spanish chronicles, was clad in gold and silver. The current building, heavily restored in 1871, is considerably more modest, consisting of a small stone chapel and a whitewashed, straw-roofed bell tower.

The village observes the **Feast of the Assumption**, August 15, with a week-long celebration that features much singing and dancing; accommodation is hard to find during this time.

ARRIVAL AND INFORMATION
PUTRE

By bus Buses La Paloma, Germán Riesco 2071 (☎ 58 222 2710), has a daily bus to Putre from Arica at 1.30pm (3hr).

Tourist office Arturo Prat s/n (Mon–Fri 9am–6pm; ☎ 58 225 2803).

ACTIVITIES AND TOURS

Alto Andino Nature Tours Baquedano 299 ☎ 58 230 0013, ✉ altoandino@yahoo.com. Run by an Alaskan naturalist who offers wildlife-viewing excursions, specializing in ornithology and marine mammals in Parque Nacional Lauca and coastal areas; phone or email for more details. She also has a few simple, inexpensive rooms to rent.

Alvaro Mamani ☎ 9 9763 9318 ✉ amamaniguia@ gmail.com. Leading informative trips into the altiplano, Alvaro Mamani is a very personable Aymara guide.
Tour Andino Baquedano 340 ☎ 9 9011 0702, ⊛ tourandino.com. A wide range of treks and tours in the cordillera and up into the high Andes.

ACCOMMODATION

4

La Chakana Viña Andrea s/n ☎ 9 9745 9519, ⊛ la-chakana.com. On the western edge of town, about a 15min walk from the plaza, the large detached huts here stand on spacious grounds and are simply but pleasantly furnished. Breakfast is taken in the owner's dining room. CH$35,000
★ **Hostal Pachamama** Centro s/n ☎ 9 6353 5187, ⊛ panchamamahosteltours.cl. By far the most backpacker-friendly place in Putre, with colourful but cramped four-bed dorms, doubles with shared bathrooms and one spacious en-suite cabin. Large kitchen and lounge. Dorms CH$15,000, doubles CH$25,000, cabin CH$60,000

Hotel Kukuli Baquedano 301 ☎ 09 9161 4709. Run by the very friendly Libertad, this hotel has comfortable en-suite rooms in a modern-ish building. An on-site restaurant, hearty breakfasts and parking are plus points. CH$30,000
Terrace Lodge 5km east of Putre ☎ 58 258 4275, ⊛ terracelodge.com. This charming thatched guesthouse boasts a tranquil location outside town, comfortable en suites, helpful staff and a range of tour options. It's a popular choice so book ahead – two-night minimum. CH$39,000

EATING

Café Putre Latorre 400 ☎ 9 9890 7291. Cute little place that does a fine *menú del día* for CH$5000 and mains such as chicken or stew for similar prices. Daily 10am–10pm.
★ **Canta Verdi** Arturo Perez Canto 339 ☎ 9 9890 7291. This welcoming place at the top of the square, decorated in warm earth colours, serves great alpaca steaks (CH$7500)

and other local staples. Best wi-fi in town, too. Daily noon–3pm & 6–11pm.
Rosamel Latorre 400C ☎ 9 4164 2843. Simple L-shaped restaurant on the square, serving good set menus made up of local dishes such as stews, spicy meat dishes and *papas rellenas* at affordable prices (CH$4500–6000). Daily 5.30am–10pm.

Parque Nacional Lauca

A few hours east of Putre, up in the cordillera, **Parque Nacional Lauca** has become one of the most popular attractions in the north of Chile. It's on the main route to La Paz in Bolivia, so the road is wide and well paved all the way there; most of Arica's tour operators (see page 205) will get you there if you don't have your own transport.

PARQUE NACIONAL LAUCA AND RESERVA NACIONAL LAS VICUÑAS

Las Cuevas

A 4400m-high mountain pass signals the boundary of Parque Nacional Lauca. Up here the air is thin and cold, and the road is flanked by light-green *bofedal* (highland pasture) where herds of wild vicuña come to feed in the mornings. Ten kilometres into the park, you reach **Las Cuevas**, a good place to observe the comical antics of the vizcachas, cuddly chinchilla-like rodents with curly tails and a spring-like leap.

Parinacota

From Las Cuevas the road continues through a wide, green plain filled with grazing llamas and alpacas. Some 19km on from Las Cuevas, it passes the turn-off for **PARINACOTA** (the name means "flamingo lake" in Aymara), site of the park's headquarters and an idyllic *pueblo altiplánico* in its own right, composed of fifty or so crumbling, whitewashed houses huddled around a beautiful little **church**. Opposite the church, in the plaza, local women sell alpaca knitwear and other **artesanía**. Many of the village houses are under lock and key for much of the year, their owners returning only for important fiestas and funerals.

The church

Built in 1789, Parinacota's **church** is one of Chile's most assiduously maintained Andean churches, sporting brilliant white walls and a bright-blue wooden door,

PARINACOTA'S WANDERING TABLE

Among the oddities of Parinacota's venerable church is a **magical "walking" table** that's kept chained to the wall, for fear it will wander off in the night. According to local legend, the table can predict death and, if left unchained, stops outside the home of the next villager to die.

trimmed with yellow and green. Like most churches of the altiplano, it has thick stone and adobe walls and a sloping straw roof, and is enclosed within a little white wall incorporating the bell tower into one of its corners. It's usually open in the morning (if not, you can borrow the key from the caretaker – ask at the *artesanía* stalls). Inside, you'll find a series of faded, centuries-old friezes depicting the Stations of the Cross and vivid scenes of sinners suffering in hell. There's also an unusual collection of skulls belonging to former priests.

Lagunas de Cotacotani

A collection of small, interconnected lakes lying in a dark lava field, filled with exquisite jade-green water, the **Lagunas de Cotacotani** lie about 8km east of Parinacota, clearly visible from the paved highway to Bolivia. The lakes were formed by volcanic eruptions and are surrounded by fine dust and cinder cones, further adding to their lunar appearance. The waters are filtered down from Lago Chungará and then continue to the *bofedal de Parinacota*, which is the source of the Río Lauca. On closer inspection the lakes aren't as lifeless as they first appear; many wild Andean geese flock here, while plentiful herds of alpaca graze the soggy marshland. This area is definitely worth exploring as a day hike from Parinacota, but if you are pressed for time take a good look from the *mirador* on the highway, marked by a giant multicoloured *zampoña* (Andean panpipes).

Lago Chungará

Eighteen kilometres southeast of Parinacota, at an altitude of 4515m, you'll see **Lago Chungará**, a wide blue lake spectacularly positioned at the foot of a snowcapped volcano that rises over its rim like a giant Christmas pudding covered in cream. This is 6330m-high **Volcán Parinacota**, one of the highest peaks in Chile and the park's most challenging climb (see page 212). When the lake is mill-pond calm – in other words when there is no wind – the reflection of the volcano is the most memorable view in the entire region. On the southern shore, right by the highway, you'll find a small stone **Conaf refugio**. If open, this is unquestionably the best place to stay in the park, allowing you to observe the changing colours of the lake and volcano at different times of day, from the transparent pinks of early morning to the deep blues and gleaming whites of the afternoon.

ARRIVAL AND INFORMATION | PARQUE NACIONAL LAUCA

By bus You can reach Parinacota, where the park's headquarters are located, by bus from Arica with Buses La Paloma, Germán Riesco 2071 (Tues & Fri 11.30am; 4hr; ☏ 58 222 2710, ⊛ translapaloma.cl).

By car Take the CH-11 motorway from Arica for approximately 145km.

Conaf The Conaf administration centre (☏ 58 258 5704), housed in a large, chalet-style building at Parinacota, makes a valiant attempt at informing the public about the park and its wildlife, though opening times are erratic.

ACCOMMODATION

Hostal y Restorante Uta Kala de Don Leo Parinacota s/n ☏ 58 226 1526, ✉ leonel_parinacota@hotmail.com. This is the only place open to stay in the whole national park at the time of writing. Thankfully it's a good one, with comfy beds, hot water, heating, meals and splendid views onto fields of grazing llama. Meals available. Dorms CH$12,000

WALKS AND CLIMBS IN PARQUE NACIONAL LAUCA

Parque Nacional Lauca doesn't offer a great many hiking possibilities, and most people are content to just admire the scenery and the wildlife. There are, however, at least three half-day or day **walks**, and many more possibilities for **climbing**. Remember to respect the altitude, and to allow yourself more time to cover distances that you could walk quite easily at lower elevations. You must get authorization from DIFROL (governmental borders organization) if you are planning on climbing any of the mountains or volcanoes in the region. Fill in the authorization form on their website (⊕ difrol.cl) at least two days before climbing, or else ask Putre's municipalidad to do it for you.

Cerro Choquelimpie No technical experience or equipment is necessary to climb this 5288m peak, reached in about four hours from the refugio at Lago Chungará. From the top, you get views down to the gold mine behind the mountain, and on to Lago Chungará and Volcán Parinacota.

Cerro Guane Guane A slow but straightforward climb up this 5096m peak is rewarded by panoramic views over the park. It's suitable for any fit person used to hill-climbing and takes around four hours to the top from the Conaf centre at Parinacota, and two to three hours back down.

Lago Chungará to Parinacota (or reverse) This 18km walk from the refugio at Lago Chungará to Parinacota takes about six hours. Follow the paved highway as far as the *mirador de Lagunas Cotacotani*, then climb down to the lakes, from where a jeep track continues to Parinacota.

Parinacota to Lagunas de Cotacotani A rewarding, not-too-difficult walk, taking about three hours (one way) from Parinacota; ask the Conaf *guardaparque* to point you in the direction of the jeep track you need to follow.

Sendero de excursión de Parinacota An easy, 6km circular walk, marked by blue stones starting behind the Conaf centre, taking you past the *bofedal de Parinacota*, where you can observe numerous grazing alpaca. Good views onto surrounding mountains. Allow two to three hours.

Volcán Parinacota Suitable only for experienced climbers carrying crampons and ropes (though it's not always necessary to use them). Allow two days to get up and down from the base camp (a day's hike from Parinacota), including one night camping on the volcano. Avoid this climb between mid-December and February, because of the weather conditions. Volcan Parinacota's brother volcano, Pomerape, is just across the border and makes an equally interesting climb.

Reserva Nacional las Vicuñas

Directly south of Parque Nacional Lauca, the **Reserva Nacional las Vicuñas** stretches more than 100km south across spectacular altiplano wilderness filled with wild vicuña, green *bofedales*, abandoned Aymara villages, groves of *queñoa* – spindly, rickety-looking trees belonging to a species that miraculously defies the treeline – and sweeping vistas of volcanoes. The reserve's administrative centre is about a ninety-minute drive from Putre, in **Guallatire** (4428m altitude), a pretty hamlet with a traditional seventeenth-century Andean church. There's also an obligatory *carabineros* checkpoint here, and a Conaf *refugio*. Looming over the village, snowcapped **Volcán Guallatire** puffs wispy plumes of smoke from its 6060m peak, while a grassy-banked stream snakes at its foot.

ARRIVAL AND DEPARTURE
RESERVA NACIONAL LAS VICUÑAS

By organized tour and 4WD There's no public transport, so you need to rent a high-clearance 4WD vehicle or take an organized tour; try one of the travel agencies in Putre (see page 208). Note that the drive into the reserve involves fording several streams, which are usually very low but can swell dangerously with heavy summer rains – check with Conaf in Arica before setting out.

ACCOMMODATION

Conaf refugio Guallatire s/n ☏9 8784 4017, @ olgasanchezcalle@gmail.com. One of the few Conaf *refugios* in the region still open, with adequate dorm accommodation. <u>CH$15,000</u>

Salar de Surire

Following the road soutgh of Guallatire, you'll be rewarded, about 40km on, with sudden, dramatic views of the **Salar de Surire**, a dazzling white salt flat containing several lakes with nesting colonies of three species of flamingo. Originally part of Parque Nacional Lauca, its status was changed to that of national monument in 1983 to allow borax to be mined from its surface. The mining is still going on today, and you can see the mine's enormous trucks driving over the *salar*, dwarfed by its massive dimensions but a nuisance nonetheless.

Polloquere

Sixteen kilometres on from the Salar de Surire, skirting the southern edge of the salt flat, **Polloquere** (also known as Aguas Calientes) is the site of several pale-blue pools filled with hot thermal water and with a muddy bottom reminiscent of the Dead Sea, an absolutely stunning place to take a bath, despite the lack of facilities – though be sure to get here in the morning, before the bone-chilling afternoon wind picks up. There are a couple of picnic areas and **camping** spaces here, too, but it's a treacherously exposed site.

ARRIVAL AND DEPARTURE   SALAR DE SURIRE

By 4WD There is no public transport, and although it is sometimes possible to get a ride from the trucks that carry minerals to and fro, it's best to rent your own 4WD vehicle or take a tour (see page 189).

4

The Central Valley

SALTO DEL LAJA

5 The Central Valley

Extending south from Santiago as far as the Río Bio Bío, Chile's Central Valley is a long, narrow plain hemmed in by the Andes to the east and the coastal range to the west, with lateral river valleys running between the two. This is the most fertile land in Chile, and the immense orchards, vineyards and pastures that cover the valley floor form a dazzling patchwork of greenery. Even in urban zones, country ways hold sway, and the Central Valley is perhaps the only part of the country where it is not uncommon to see horse-drawn carts plodding down the Panamericana Highway.

While the main artery of the Panamericana – Ruta 5 – runs all the way south from Santiago, through Rancagua to Los Angeles and beyond, the kernel of the Central Valley lies between the capital and the city of **Chillán**, some 400km south – a region where, during the colonial era, the vast private estates known as **estancias**, or haciendas, were established. The people have held on to many of their rural traditions and the cult of the *huaso*, or cowboy, is as strong as ever, as can be witnessed at the frequent **rodeos** held in stadiums known as *medialunas*.

Further south again, the busy city of **Concepción** guards the mouth of the **Bio Bío**, the mighty river that for more than three hundred years was the boundary between conquered, colonial Chile and unconquered **Mapuche territory**, whose occupants withstood domination until 1883. Traces of the frontier still linger, visible in the ruins of colonial Spanish forts, the proliferation of Mapuche place names and the tin-roof pioneer architecture. Beyond the Bio Bío, towards the Lake District, the gently sloping plains give way to verdant native forests and remote Andean lakes.

Many visitors bypass the Central Valley altogether, whizzing south towards the more dramatic landscapes of the Lake District and beyond. Certainly, the agricultural towns dotted along the highway – **Rancagua**, **San Fernando**, **Curicó**, **Talca** and **Los Angeles** – are, on the whole, rather dull, although they make useful stopovers on the long hike between Patagonia and the capital. Stray a few kilometres off the Panamericana and you'll catch a glimpse of an older Chile abounding with pastoral charms. Chief among these are the region's small, **colonial villages**, with their colourful adobe houses topped by overhanging clay-tiled roofs. Among the prettiest examples are **Vichuquén**, west of Curicó, and **Villa Alegre**, south of Talca in the Maule Valley, where you can also visit a trail of lush, emerald **vineyards**. Wine is also the main draw in attractive **Santa Cruz**, a popular weekend destination from Santiago from where you can gaze out over vineyards as you sip vintages on your hotel veranda.

Away from the valley floor, you'll find attractions of a very different nature. To the west, up in the coastal hills, a couple of lakes offer great **watersports** facilities, notably **Lago Rapel**, while further west a number of inviting **beaches** and cheerful seaside towns are scattered down the coast, among them the popular surfer hangout of **Pichilemu**. East of the valley, the dry, dusty slopes of the Andes offer excellent **horseriding** and **hiking** opportunities, particularly along the trails of protected areas such as **Reserva Nacional Altos del Lircay**, near Talca. After a strenuous day in the mountains, you can

MAKING WINE, SANTA CRUZ

Highlights

❶ Santa Cruz Visit the exceptional museum in this pretty wine valley town, then taste your way through some of the world's best red wines on the "Ruta del Vino". See page 225

❷ Pichilemu Relax or hit the waves at this inexpensive haven for surfing and other watersports. See page 228

❸ Parque Nacional Radal Siete Tazas This stunning park features lush forests, abundant waterfalls and natural swimming pools. See page 232

❹ Reserva Nacional Altos del Lircay Hiking trails, spectacular views and relatively easy access make this one of Chile's few Andean parks perfect for camping trips. See page 236

❺ Nevados de Chillán Legendary hot springs on the side of a volcano; in the winter, the skiing is excellent; during the rest of the year you can hike, bike and embark on horse treks. See page 244

❻ Salto del Laja Marvel at these thundering waterfalls, an ideal journey break just a stone's throw from the main highway. See page 252

HIGHLIGHTS ARE MARKED ON THE MAP ON PAGE 218

THE CENTRAL VALLEY

N

PACIFIC OCEAN

ARGENTINA

SANTIAGO
Rocas de Santo Domingo
Melipilla
Navidad
Río Rapel
Chapa Verde ski centre
Sewell
Rancagua
El Teniente Mine
El Manzano
Río Pangal
Machali
Lago Rapel
Termas de Cauquenes
Rengo
Pichilemu
RESERVA NACIONAL RÍO LOS CIPRESES
San José del Carmen del Huique Museum
Santa Cruz
San Fernando
RESERVA NACIONAL LAGUNA TORCA
Río Tinguiririca
Llico
Termas del Flaco
Lago Vichuquén
Vichuquén
Hualañe
Curicó
Molino
Río Mataquito
Constitución
Viña Via Wines
San Rafael
Río Maule
Talca
Vilches Alto
PARQUE NACIONAL RADAL SIETE TAZAS
Viña Balduzzi
Villa Cultural Huilquilemu
RESERVA NACIONAL FEDERICO ALBERT
Viña Gillmore
San Javier
San Clemente
Chanco
Armerillo
RESERVA NACIONAL ALTOS DEL LIRCAY
Pelluhue
Villa Alegre
Colbún
TRICAHUE PARQUE
Curanipe
Lago Colbún
Caverna de Brujas
Cauquenes
Linares
Buchupureo
Paso Pehuenche
Iglesia de Piedra
Laguna del Maule
Cobquecura
Playa Rinconada
Parral
Santuario Cuna de Prat
Ninhue
Playa Purda
Playa Cocholgue
Dichato
Río Itata
Chillán
Playa El Morro
Tomé
PARQUE DE AGUAS NEVADOS
Talcahuano
Lirquen
Concepción
Valle Las Trancas
Nevados de Chillán
Isla Santa María
Valle Hermoso
Coronel
Arauco
Lota
PARQUE NACIONAL LAGUNA DEL LAJA
Playa Millaneco
Río Laja
Salto del Laja
Laguna del Laja
Lebu
Antuco
Río Bíobío
El Alamo
El Abanico
Los Angeles
Volcán Antuco (2985m)
Playa Millaneco
Paso Pichachén
Cañete
Mulchén
Lago Lanalhue
Río Bíobío
PARQUE NACIONAL NAHUELBUTA
Angol
Contulmo
Ercilla
CORDILLERA DE NAHUELBUTA
Victoria
Termas de Tolhuaca
Curacautín
Longuimay

0   40
kilometres

HIGHLIGHTS

1. Santa Cruz
2. Pichilemu
3. Parque Nacional Radal Siete Tazas
4. Parque Nacional Altos del Lircay
5. Nevados de Chillán
6. Salto del Laja

relax in one of the many **hot springs** in the area, including the **Nevados de Chillán** at the base of a booming ski resort.

The amount of annual **rainfall** picks up steadily as you head south; by the time you reach the Bío Bío there is a significant amount of rain every month. While winter is never too cold, most visitors come here between October and March.

GETTING AROUND   THE CENTRAL VALLEY

By bus Getting down the Central Valley by public transport is easy, with hundreds of buses ploughing down the Panamericana. Branching off into the cordillera and to the coast normally requires catching a "rural bus" from one of the cities dotted down the highway, though some of the more remote places can only be reached with your own transport.

By train A more leisurely and scenic option is the train from Santiago, which stops at Rancagua, San Fernando, Curicó, Talca and Chillán.

Rapel Valley

Zipping down the Panamericana from Santiago, you can be in the **Rapel Valley**, centred around the agricultural town of **Rancagua**, in about an hour. With a little more time and your own transport, however, the old road from Santiago (via Alto Jahuel, running east along the highway) is more appealing, winding its way past estates of vines, fruit trees and old haciendas, half-hidden behind their great adobe walls. The best place in the country to see Chile's traditional **rodeo**, the Rapel Valley is also home to the 40km long **Lago Rapel**, the largest artificial lake in Chile, the copper mining town of **Sewell**, close to a small **ski centre**, and the rarely visited **Reserva Nacional Río de los Cipreses**.

Rancagua and around

RANCAGUA presents a picture that is to repeat itself in most of the Central Valley towns – a large, well-tended central plaza; single-storey adobe houses; a few colonial buildings, which were damaged in the 2010 earthquake but to a greater or lesser extent are being restored; sprawling, faceless outskirts. Once in town, you'll find little to hold

---

RODEOS

The Central Valley is the birthplace and heartland of Chilean **rodeo**, whose season kicks off on Independence Day, September 18. Over the following six months, regional competitions eliminate all but the finest horses and *huasos* in the country, who go on to take part in the national championships in Rancagua (Chile's rodeo capital) on the first weekend in April. Rodeos are performed in *medialunas* ("half moons"), circular arenas divided by a curved wall, forming a crescent-shaped stadium and a smaller oval pen called an *apiñadero*. In Rancagua it is on the northern edge of town (on the corner of Av España and Germán Ibarra). The participants are **huasos** – cowboys, or horsemen – who cut a dashing figure with their bright, finely woven ponchos, broad-rimmed hats, carved wooden stirrups and shining silver spurs. The horses they ride in the rodeo are specially bred and trained *corraleros* that are far too valuable for day-to-day work.

A rodeo begins with an inspection of the horses and their riders by the judges, who award points for appearance. This is followed by individual displays of horsemanship that make ordinary dressage look tame. In the main part of a rodeo, pairs of *huasos* have to drive a young cow, or *novillo*, around the edge of the arena and pin it up against a padded section of the wall. This isn't a popular sport with everyone – local animal rights groups campaign against it, arguing that it leads to injuries to both horses and cows. The rodeos are in any case as much about eating and drinking as anything else, and the canteen and foodstalls by a *medialuna* are a good place to sample **regional food**, gourmet wine and the sweet fruity alcohol known as *chicha*. Rodeo events are spread over the course of a weekend and end with music and dancing. This is where you can see the **cueca** (see page 38) being danced at its flirtatious best. For the dates of official rodeos, contact the **Federación del Rodeo Chileno** in Santiago (☎ 2 2420 2553) or visit ⓦ fenaro.cl.

your interest for more than a few hours – unless your arrival coincides with a **rodeo** (see page 219) – but Rancagua makes a useful jumping-off point for attractions in the Rapel Valley. The town is also home to the **Centro Cultural y Spiritual Gaudí de Triana**, at Riesco 344 (Mon–Fri 9.30am–1.30pm; ⓦgaudichile.cl), centring on a chapel that is the only structure designed by Catalan architect Antoni Gaudí to have been built outside of his homeland.

Plaza de los Héroes and around

Unusually, Rancagua's square is known not as the Plaza de Armas, but as the **Plaza de los Héroes**. The name honours the patriot soldiers, headed by Bernardo O'Higgins, who defended the city against Royalist forces in 1814, only to be crushed in what has gone down in Chilean history as the "Disaster of Rancagua" (see page 473). In the centre of the square, a rearing equestrian statue celebrates O'Higgins' triumphant return to the city, four years after he had left it in ruins, to present it with a coat of arms depicting a phoenix rising from the ashes. The square's other major monument is the towering, pink-walled **Iglesia Catedral**. One block north of the square, at the corner of Cuevas and Estado, the **Iglesia de la Merced** was used as O'Higgins' headquarters. You can still see where the 2010 earthquake split it nearly in two; the congregation now uses a marquee erected next door.

Museo Regional Rancagua

Paseo Estado 685 & 682 • Tues–Fri 10am–6pm, Sat & Sun 9am–1pm • Free • ☎ 72 222 1524, ⓦ museorancagua.cl

Most of Rancagua's historic buildings are found along **Paseo Estado**, a pedestrianized street that runs from the Plaza de los Héroes to Avenida Millán. Two splendid eighteenth-century houses opposite each other on the Paseo are home to the **Museo Regional Rancagua**, with exhibits on local history, crafts and mining.

Casa de Cultura
Cachapoal 90 • Daily 10am–7pm • ☎ 72 222 6076, ⓦ rancaguacultura.cl/casa-de-la-cultura

Across Avenida Millán, beyond the regional museum, another eighteenth-century building, now the municipal **Casa de Cultura**, hosts local art exhibitions. This is a fine example of rural colonial architecture, its thick foundations made of river boulders mortared with mud.

ARRIVAL AND DEPARTURE   RANCAGUA

By bus The main terminal for long-distance services, known as Terminal O'Higgins, is at O'Higgins 0480 (☎ 72 222 5425, ⓦ terminalohiggins.cl). The regional bus terminal, called Rodoviario, is at Salinas 1165, north of the train station (☎ 72 223 6938).
Destinations Chillán (8 daily; 4hr); Concepción (16 daily; 5hr); Curicó (every 30min; 1hr 45min); Lago Rapel–El Manzano (every 20min; 2hr); Los Angeles (5 daily; 5hr); Pichilemu (every 30min; 3hr 30min); Puerto Montt (8 daily; 11hr); San Fernando (every 15min; 50min); Santa Cruz (every 15min; 2hr); Santiago (every 10min; 1hr–1hr 30min); Talca (every 30min; 2hr); Temuco (10 daily; 7hr).
By train The train station is at the corner of Estación and Carrera Pinto (☎ 600 585 5000).
Destinations Chillán (2 daily; 3hr 40min); Curicó (2 daily; 1hr 5min); San Fernando (6 daily; 30min); Santiago (9 daily; 1hr 30 min); Talca (2 daily; 1hr 50min).

INFORMATION AND TOURS

Conaf Cuevas 480 (Mon–Fri 8.30am–5.30pm; ☎ 72 220 4610, ✉ rancagua.oirs@conaf.cl).
Tourist office Germán Riesco 277 (Mon–Thurs 8.30am–5.30pm, Fri 8.30am–4.30pm; ☎ 72 223 0413, ✉ inforancagua@sernatur.cl).
Tours Turismo Dakota, Mujica 605 (☎ 72 222 8166, ⓦ turismodakota.cl), can arrange local tours, treks and horseriding.

ACCOMMODATION

Hotel Turismo Santiago Brasil 1036 ☎ 72 223 0860, ⓦ hotelsantiago.cl; map p.220. Squarely aimed at the business traveller market, with comfortable but antiseptic en suites, this 64-room hotel boasts an outdoor pool and a restaurant. **CH$60,000**

EATING

Reina Victoria Paseo Independencia 667 ☎ 72 223 9827; map p.220. For something sweet, join the steady stream of shoppers and schoolchildren at this bustling café for coffee, cakes, biscuits and huge tubs of ice cream. Savoury offerings include the ubiquitous *completo* (hot dog with all the trimmings; CH$2000). Daily 7.30am–10.30pm.

El Viejo Rancagua Estado 607 ☎ 72 222 7715; map p.220. Crammed with historic photos and memorabilia, this ramshackle restaurant does a cheap lunch menu (CH$3000) and on Fri and Sat nights transforms into an atmospheric bar, with live tango, bolero and folkloric music. Mon–Fri 12.30–3.30pm & 7.30pm–4am, Sat 7.30pm–4am.

Chapa Verde ski centre
53km east of Rancagua • July–Sept • Lift tickets CH$17,000; equipment rental CH$15,000 • ☎ 72 221 7651, ⓦ chapaverde.cl • Codelco's own bus service, Buses El Teniente, runs from the Club de Ski ticket office in Rancagua, Miguel Ramírez 655, next to the Lider Vecino supermarket (daily 8.30am–9.30am, return trip 4.30pm; CH$14,000; times are prone to change so it is worth confirming with the ski centre) – you can also drive up in your own vehicle (4WD is advisable) as long as you call for a permit beforehand

A few kilometres north of the El Teniente mine, and ranging from 2300m to 3100m, is the Codelco-owned **Chapa Verde ski centre**, initially built for the company's miners but now open to the public between July and September. There is no accommodation, but check with the Club de Ski ticket office in Rancagua for information on private homes for rent nearby.

5

Sewell and El Teniente

60km east of Rancagua · Various tours of Sewell with VTS leave from Rancagua and Santiago · From CH$41,000/person · ☎ 72 295 2692, ⓦ vts.cl or ⓦ www.sewell.cl

Sewell is an abandoned company mining town, staggered in dramatic tiers up the mountainside by **El Teniente**, the largest **underground copper mine** in the world. Local legend has it that the name of the mine – "the lieutenant" – refers to a disgraced Spanish officer who, while heading to Argentina to escape his creditors, discovered enormous copper deposits, thus making a fortune and saving himself from bankruptcy. Today the mine, not currently open to visitors, belongs to Codelco, the government-owned copper corporation (see page 63), which also owns the famous Chuquicamata mine in northern Chile. You aren't allowed to just turn up and visit Sewell, a UNESCO Heritage Site, but VTS-run **tours** include the photogenic brightly coloured housing, the old church and theatre and a copper-mining museum.

Reserva Nacional Río de Los Cipreses

Machali, Cachapoal province, 56km south of Sewell · Daily 8.30am–5pm · CH$5000 · ☎ 72 229 7505 · There's no direct public transport to the reserve, but you can take a bus from Rancagua to Coya (1hr) from where taxis can drive you the 12km to the reserve entrance (CH$10,000)

A little-visited gem, the **Reserva Nacional Río de Los Cipreses** encompasses 36 square kilometres of protected land stretched along the narrow canyon of the Río de los Cipreses, with altitudes ranging from 900m to 4900m. It's a great spot for multi-day **hiking** or **horseriding**, and you may spot foxes, eagles, condors and rare burrowing parrots.

Sector El Ranchillo

At the entrance to the reserve, a Conaf office provides maps and a diorama of the park. Ask about the trails that offer a look at the parakeets nesting in the cliffs. From the office, a jeep track leads 6km to **Sector El Ranchillo**, a camping and picnic area with a swimming pool. This is the end of the track, and vehicles must be parked.

Sector Maitenes

From the camping and picnic area, take the left fork just before El Ranchillo, continue past a second gate (locked) and after another 6km you'll reach **Sector Maitenes**, with a few camping spots and running water. Beyond, a trail follows the river along the canyon, passing through forests and with occasional views of high Andean peaks including Cerro El Indio and Cerro El Cotón. Lateral ravines regularly branch out from the river, leading to waterfalls, lakes and "hanging" valleys carved out of the hills by glaciers. These aren't signed, however, so unless you're with an *arriero* (horseman), stick to the main path.

Sector Urriola

Twenty kilometres beyond Sector Maitenes, you reach **Sector Urriola**, where there's a rustic *refugio* (1500m) and a few camping areas; count on taking around six or seven hours to get here on foot from Maitenes, and about four or five hours on horseback. Beyond Urriola, the path continues for a further 10km or so, giving great views onto the 4900m-high Volcán Palomo. To hire a horse, ask around at the community of Chacayes at the park's entrance.

Lago Rapel

The 40km-long artificial **Lago Rapel** nestles in the low coastal hills 114km southwest of Rancagua. Most of the action is centred around the main town of **El Manzano**, on the lake's eastern shore. The main attraction is the excellent **watersports**, with speedboats, windsurfers and jet skis available for rent from several hotels and campsites.

ARRIVAL AND DEPARTURE
LAGO RAPEL

By bus Galbus (☎72 223 0640, ⍵galbus.cl) runs buses to El Manzano from Rancagua's regional terminal (every 20min; 2hr 30min) as does Sextur (☎72 223 1342; 4 daily; 2hr 30min).

ACCOMMODATION

Camping Bosque Hermoso Along the lakeshore in El Manzano ☎09 9902 0269. Fully equipped campsite with a swimming pool and restaurant. Two-person tents CH$20,000, five-person tents CH$27,500
Camping Náutico Rapel Lago Rapel ☎2 2862 6300, ⍵campingnauticorapel.cl. Campers have access to a pool and volleyball court as well as a wharf that's ideal for a spot of lake fishing. Per pitch CH$40,000
Jardín del Lago 10km north of El Manzano ☎09 9743 4420, ⍵jardindellago.cl. Smart, self-contained, apartment-style cabin accommodation sleeping up to nine people. There are also jet skis, canoes and row boats for rent. CH$76,500

Colchagua Valley

The 120km-long valley of the Río Tinguiririca is known locally as the **Colchagua Valley** after the province through which it runs. This is serious fruit-production territory, as signalled by the numerous fruit stalls and large Del Monte factories that line the highway on the approach to San Fernando. Some 41km west of San Fernando is **Santa Cruz**, one of the best places to stay in the region, and a starting point for the **Ruta del Vino del Valle de Colchagua**. Further east, high in the cordillera, the **Termas del Flaco** is an inexpensive option for soaking in hot springs, while if you continue to the coast, you'll get to the hip, budget seaside town of **Pichilemu**, which is popular with surfers. Note that the main highway connecting San Fernando and Pichilemu, **Ruta 90**, is still often referred to by its old name the I-50, and also sometimes denominated the "Carretera del Vino".

San Fernando

Surrounded by low, rippling hills that are washed golden in the sunlight, **SAN FERNANDO**, some 55km south of Rancagua, is a busy little agricultural town that, as the area's hub, makes a useful stop-off. Though it is less beguiling than the smaller Santa Cruz (see page 225), once you get out of town and into the vineyards there are some appealing places to stay and eat. The main commercial artery is Manuel Rodríguez; here, on the corner with Valdivia, stands the huge nineteenth-century **Iglesia de San Francisco**, a Neo-Gothic church with a 32m-high tower, which took

> ### AFTERSHOCKS
>
> Central Chile was devastated by one of the most powerful **earthquakes** in recorded history when an 8.8-magnitude earthquake struck off its coast on February 27, 2010, triggering a powerful Pacific-wide **tsunami**. The earthquake cost 521 lives, injured twelve thousand people and left more than 800,000 people homeless. **Concepción**, 115km southeast of the epicentre, was hardest hit, with looting and violence bringing further chaos to the city. The cities of Curicó, Talca and Chillán also suffered severe damage, while the tsunami washed away parts of the coastal towns of Constitución, Talcahuano, Pichilemu and Iloca. The cities of Valparaíso and Santiago sustained some, albeit comparatively small, damage.
>
> Roads and bridges were repaired soon after the earthquake, and in the ensuing months and years the region has picked itself up and rebuilt with heroic determination. Note however that many of the region's century-old adobe homes and haciendas, particularly those in the Colchagua Valley, were lost forever.

5

quite a blow in the 2010 earthquake. The verdant Plaza de Armas is surrounded by handsome colonial buildings, with the cavernous nineteenth-century **Parroquia San Fernando Rey** church on its southeastern corner.

Casa Patronal de Lircunlauta

Jiménez 1595 • Mon–Fri 9am–1pm & 3–6pm, Sat & Sun 3–6pm • CH$200 • ☎ 72 258 3438

The **Casa Patronal de Lircunlauta** is the oldest building in San Fernando. It was originally the homestead of the eighteenth-century Hacienda Lircunlauta, whose owner donated 450 "blocks" of land to San Fernando when the town was founded in 1742. The museum closed after the 2010 earthquake, reopening seven years later, and houses an exhibit on the Uruguayan rugby team whose plane crashed into the Andes some 55km east of San Fernando in October 1972, their plight made famous by the book and film *Alive*.

ARRIVAL AND TOURS   SAN FERNANDO

By bus The main bus terminal (☎ 72 271 3912) is on Av Manso de Velasco and Rancagua.

Destinations Angol (1 daily; 7hr); Chillán (6 daily; 3hr); Concepción (4 daily; 4hr 30min); Curicó (every 30min; 50min); Los Angeles (9 daily; 4hr 30min); Pichilemu (every 30min; 2hr 50min); Puerto Montt (5 daily; 12hr); Rancagua (every 15min; 50min); Santa Cruz (every 15min; 50min); Santiago (every 15min; 2hr); Talca (9 daily; 1hr 30min); Temuco (11 daily; 7hr); Termas del Flaco (Jan –Easter & Dec 2 daily; 2hr 30min); Valdivia (4 daily; 9hr).

By train The train station is three blocks south of the bus terminal at Quechereguas s/n (☎ 600 585 5000).

Destinations Chillán (2 daily; 3hr 10min); Curicó (2 daily; 30min); Rancagua (2 daily; 30min); Santiago (5 daily; 1hr 30min); Talca (2 daily; 1hr 20min).

Tours Andes Adventures (☎ 09 9630 1152, ⊛ andesadventures.cl) offers fishing, trekking and horseriding trips in the Colchagua Valley as well as overnight excursions into the high Andes.

ACCOMMODATION

While hotel options are uninspiring in San Fernando itself, travellers with their own transport can soak up the Colchagua Valley's verdant charms at one of the rustic **guesthouses** on the town's doorstep.

★ **Mapuyampay Hostal Gastronómico** Parcela 2, Huemul, 45km southeast of San Fernando ☎ 09 9327 2589, ⊛ mapuyampay.cl. The rural retreat and cooking school of Ruth Van Waerebeek, the Belgian-born executive chef of Concha y Toro winery near Santiago, is a real foodie find. Spacious guest rooms are set within landscaped gardens and tastefully accented with tribal furnishings. Gourmet meals are prepared by Ruth and her husband Vicente, using ingredients plucked straight from the garden. Meals and cooking classes cost extra (CH$30,000). Open Oct–April; over-14s only. **CH$98,000**

Posada Curali Curali 130 ☎ 72 271 3445, ⊛ posadacurali.cl. A decent budget option in town. The

eight musty, canary-yellow rooms have immense en suites and are set around a pretty, vine-covered patio. Staff are warm and welcoming. **CH$49,000**

★ **Tumuñan Lodge** Las Peñas, 27km southeast of San Fernando ☎ 09 9630 1152, ⊛ tumunanlodge.com. A destination in itself, this British-/Chilean-run lodge in the foothills of the Andes is surrounded by dazzling scenery, with a series of trails leading into the mountains. There are just four luxurious en-suite rooms, and guests can socialize, wine in hand, by the cosy fireplace. There's also attentive service, an inviting pool, a wood-fired hot tub, sumptuous home-cooked meals and the opportunity to go on guided fly-fishing, horseriding and hiking trips. **CH$79,000**

EATING AND DRINKING

Arenpastycaf Chillán 557 ☎ 72 271 5314, ⊛ arenpastycaf.cl. An international menu and good buffet lunches (CH$5000) keep punters pouring into this bright and breezy café-bar-restaurant. One glimpse of the drinks menu and you'll want to make a night of it. Mon–Sat 10am–11.30pm.

Café Roma Manuel Rodríguez 815 ☎ 72 237 3588. With its welcoming red-brick interior and a TV tuned to *telenovelas*, this café is a good spot for a light meal, ice cream, cake or coffee. Lunches (from CH$4500) are more

substantial, with meat, fish and pasta dishes on offer. Daily 8am–10.30pm.

★ **Casa Silva** Polo Club House, Casa Lotel A Angostura, 7km north of San Fernando ☎ 09 6847 5786, ⊛ casasilva.cl. This winery restaurant is one of the Central Valley's top dining experiences: feast on imaginative tapas and top-quality beef (mains around CH$13,000) while overlooking lush vineyards and manicured polo fields. Daily 12.30–3.30pm & 7.30–11.30pm.

Termas del Flaco

78km east of San Fernando • Jan–Easter & Dec daily 6am–11pm • CH$2000 • Buses Amistad (☎ 72 238 4188) provides transport to the *termas*, with two daily afternoon departures from San Fernando and one daily from Santiago

Sitting high in the cordillera 1700m above sea level, the **Termas del Flaco** are among the cheapest and consequently most visited thermal baths in the Central Valley. They're reached by a serpentine dirt road that follows the Río Tinguiririca through a beautiful gorge, so narrow in parts that traffic is able to travel in just one direction at a time. Bizarrely, vehicles are only allowed up late in the day, after 4pm (Mon–Sat), while traffic travels down in the morning until 2pm (Mon–Sat); Sunday is the opposite way round (up until noon, down from 2pm). Given the awkwardness of these hours, you'll need to stay at the baths overnight if you visit during the week.

The thermal baths

The wild beauty of the cordillera and the feeling of remoteness and solitude are, upon arriving, suddenly interrupted by the appearance of numerous shack-like, tin-roofed houses – almost all of them *residenciales*, with little to distinguish one place from the next, and most operating on a full-board basis – crowded around the **thermal baths**. Nor are the actual baths themselves particularly attractive, consisting of several rectangular concrete open-air pools. The waters, however – which reach up to 57°C (135°F) in some pools – are bliss. If you manage to get here midweek, when there are usually no crowds (except during high season, Jan and Feb), you can lie back, close your eyes and simply relax without another soul around.

Around the termas

You'll find several short treks **around the termas**, including one that leads to a set of dinosaur footprints preserved in the rock. Many local guides offer horseriding trips in the summer, including Eugenio Mancilla (☎09 8987 4453).

ACCOMMODATION   **TERMAS DEL FLACO**

Hotel Cabaña Las Vegas Ruta I 45, 1km west of baths ☎72 222 2478, ⓦvegasdelflaco.cl. Guests at these comfortable and roomy wooden *cabañas* have access to a large dining room with floor-to-ceiling windows looking down to the valley and the hotel's own small thermal pool. Rates include all meals; minibus transfer from Santiago or Rancagua is CH$15,000. **CH$130,000**

Posada Amistad Camino Las Pozas s/n ☎72 281 7227, ⊙turismo.willy@hotmail.com. Roll straight off the bus and into these small, basic rooms set around a garden patio. The *posada* enjoys a prime position overlooking the baths. Closed March–Oct; full board. **CH$60,000**

Santa Cruz and around

The paved Ruta 90 running through the Colchagua Valley to the coast takes you past a trail of **wineries** (see page 227). The small, well-preserved town of **SANTA CRUZ**, 40km west of San Fernando, sits in the heart of this renowned wine-making district and boasts the **Museo de Colchagua**, one of the best museums in the country, as well as a clutch of fantastic places to stay, eat and drink the local produce.

Museo de Colchagua

Errázuriz 145 • Daily 10am–7pm • CH$7000 • ☎72 282 1050, ⓦmuseocolchagua.cl

The private **Museo de Colchagua** is housed in a splendid, plum-coloured colonial hacienda. Owned by international arms dealer Carlos Cardoen (the so-called "king of cluster bombs"), it has a well-designed, extensive and eclectic collection, which includes fossils, a huge amount of amber, pre-Columbian pottery and jewellery, relics from the War of the Pacific and memorabilia from the Chilean independence movement. Among the most evocative exhibits are the beautiful old saddles, carved wooden stirrups and silver spurs in the *huaso* display, as well as the multimedia exhibit

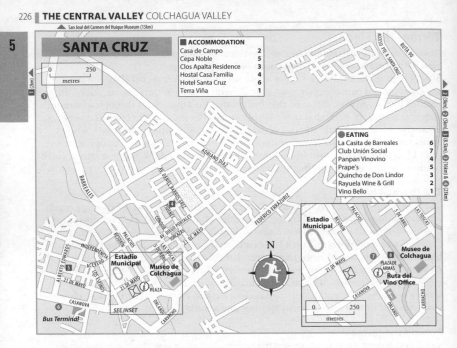

on the 2010 rescue of "Los 33" (see page 157), complete with a reconstruction of their "refugio".

San José del Carmen del Huique Museum

Ruta 90 Km 56 • Wed–Sun 9am–noon & 2–5pm, Tues 2–5pm by reservation only • CH$3000 • ☎ 09 7331105, ⦾ www.museoelhuique.cl • Yellow taxi *colectivos* depart from in front of Santa Cruz's bus terminal for the 30min journey to the museum

Twenty-four kilometres beyond Santa Cruz, along the road towards the coast, and 6km beyond the Los Errázuriz bridge, sits the superb **San José del Carmen del Huique Museum**. One of the Central Valley's loveliest haciendas, its history dates from the seventeenth-century colonial period, but the current *casa patronal* was built in the early years of independence, in 1829. Standing alongside, and entered through a huge doorway, is the **chapel**, sporting a 23m-high bell tower.

ARRIVAL AND INFORMATION
SANTA CRUZ AND AROUND

By bus The bus terminal is at Casanova 478 (☎72 282 2191).
Destinations Pichilemu (every 30min; 1hr 50min); Rancagua (every 15min; 2hr); San Fernando (every 15min; 50min); Santiago (every 15min; 3hr).

Tourist office In the municipal building at Plaza de Armas 242 (Mon–Fri 8.30am–4pm; ☎72 297 8904).

ACCOMMODATION

★**Casa de Campo** Los Pidenes, Ruta 90 Km 40 ☎09 4496 9340, ⦾hotelcasadecampo.cl; map above. Wonderful family-run hotel just outside town, with comfortable rural-chic rooms and cosy shared living spaces. The best rooms are in the main house, with balconies or verandas overlooking the extensive gardens, vineyards and open air pool. CH$95,000

Cepa Noble Alberto Edwards 205 ☎72 282 1644, ⦾hostalcepanoble.cl; map above. The eleven modern rooms at this welcoming B&B in the town centre all have incredibly comfy beds; there's also a small pool, a good breakfast and bicycles for rent. CH$60,000
Clos Apalta Residence Ruta 90 Km 36, Cunaquito ☎72 295 3360, ⦾en.lapostollewines.com; map above. Four enchanting, luxurious cabins nestled in the forested

RUTA DEL VINO VALLE DE COLCHAGUA

The Valle de Colchagua lies in the middle of one of Chile's finest wine-making districts. Eight wineries in the area have formed an itinerary called the **Ruta del Vino**. Tours (half-day/two wineries CH$66,000, full-day/three wineries CH$99,000) run daily and include multilingual guides and the chance to sample wines at each winery. Reservations must be made at least 24 hours in advance via Ruta del Vino (Plaza de Armas 298, Santa Cruz; T 72 282 3199, E reservas@rutadelvino.cl, W rutadelvino.cl). The agency can also arrange accommodation and transfers from Santiago. Tours run year round but the best time to go is in late March, during harvest. The following are some of the best wineries to visit.

Viña Casa Silva Casa Lotel A Angostura, 7km north of San Fernando T 72 291 3117, W casasilva.cl. Founded in 1892, this picturesque vineyard has classic wine-tasting facilities and a top-notch restaurant (see page 224). Hour-long tours cost around CH$20,000. Five tours daily.

Viña Clos Apalta Ruta 90 Km 36, Cunaquito T 72 295 3339, W en.lapostollewines.com. The titular tipple produced at Lapostolle's gravity-fed winery is organic and biodynamic. There are standard 1hr tasting tours of the 445-acre estate (CH$20,000) as well as private visits (CH$35,000). Accommodation at *Clos Apalta Residence* is also available (see page 226). Standard tasting tours 10.30am, 12.30pm, 4pm & 5.30pm.

Viña Laura Hartwig Camino Barreales s/n T 72 282 3179, W laurahartwig.cl. On the outskirts of Santa Cruz, this compact winery has 198 acres of vines dating from 1979. As well as tasting tours (CH$12,000–16,000), the winery has the excellent hotel *Terra Viña* (see below) and restaurant *Vino Bello* (see page 228). Tasting tours daily 9.30am–7pm.

Viña Montes Parcela 15, Millahue de Apalta T 72 281 7815, W monteswines.com. A tractor ride through the picturesque 23-year-old vineyard is included in the tours of Monte's Apalta estate, 43km northeast of Santa Cruz. As well as standard 1hr tours (CH$7000–30,000), they offer guided nature hikes and a lunch option (CH$30,000). Standard tours daily 11am, 12.30pm, 3.30pm & 5.30pm

Viña MontGras Camino Isla de Yáquil s/n, Palmilla T 72 282 2845, W www.montgras.cl. This 494-acre *bodega* 12km west of Santa Cruz produces, among others, the once rare and now classic Chilean Carmenère wine. The vineyard tours (from CH$12,000) are packed with interesting information about Chilean wine, and include atasting. Three or four tours daily.

Viña Viu Manent Ruta 90 Km 37, Santa Cruz T 72 284 8751, W viumanent.cl. Just 7km east of Santa Cruz, this is one of the most visited vineyards in the area. A trip to the third-generation, family-owned winery includes a vintage carriage ride through the 370-acre estate and a comprehensive tasting (CH$13,000). There's also a nice on-site wine and crafts store and gourmet restaurant, *Rayuela* (see page 228). Four tours daily.

hillside above the Clos Apalta vineyards (see page 227); rates include breakfast and activities. US$900

Hostal Casa Familia Los Pidenes 421 T 72 282 5766, W hostalcasafamilia.cl; map p.226. This hostel is located on a quiet residential street northeast of the plaza, with neat but unremarkable rooms. The friendly owners serve a good breakfast with fruit and eggs. CH$48,000

Hotel Santa Cruz Plaza de Armas 286 T 72 220 9600, W www.hotelsantacruzplaza.cl; map p.226. On the edge of the Plaza de Armas sits this impressive hotel owned by Carlos Cardoen (see page 225) with a large and somewhat incongruous casino attached to it. There are two swimming pools, a spa and a good restaurant. US$400

Terra Viña Camino Los Boldos s/n T 72 282 1284, W terravina.cl; map p.226. Part of the Laura Hartwig winery (see above), each oak-floored room here has a balcony overlooking the vineyards, and there's a pool for use in summer. US$160

EATING

You're spoiled for dining options in Santa Cruz and in the surrounding area, where many **vineyards** have their own restaurants.

La Casita de Barreales Rafael Casanova 570 T 72 282 4468, W lacasitadebarreales.cl; map p.226. If you're looking for spice in your life, head to this popular Peruvian restaurant. Seafood-centric dishes such aas *ceviche mixto* (CH$8000) are balanced by carb-and-*carne* classics including *lomo saltado* (beef strips with fries, rice and vegetables) for CH$9000. Tues–Sun 1–3.30pm & 8–11.30pm.

Club Unión Social Plaza de Armas 178 T 72 282 2529; map p.226. Chilean staples (around CH$9000) and more adventurous dishes such as eel omelette are served

5

beneath a relaxing vine-covered terrace. Mon–Sat noon–11pm, Sun noon–4pm.

★ **Panpan Vinovino** Ruta 90 Km 31 ☎09 9519 3823; map p.226. Dine among antique cartwheels and furniture (some of which is for sale) in this cute restaurant housed in an old hacienda bakery. Dishes include steak with red wine sauce and pork marinated in chardonnay and rosemary. Mains around CH$7500. Mon–Thurs & Sun 1–3pm, Fri & Sat 1–3pm & 8–11pm.

Prape's Errázuriz 319 ☎72 282 1158, ⓦsushisprapes.cl; map p.226. This sushi bar has pretty authentic food, including California rolls (from CH$3800), teriyaki salmon and tempura ice cream. It's also a fine spot for an evening cocktail. Mon–Sat noon–3pm & 6pm–midnight.

Quincho de Don Lindor Ruta 90 Km 25 ☎72 285 8409; map p.226. Near Santa Cruz's neighbouring village, Nancagua, this picturesque country *parrilla* (barbecue restaurant) has outdoor tables and attentive but not formal service. The pisco sours and *empanadas* are especially tasty. Mains around CH$5000. Mon & Sun 11am–5pm, Tues–Sat 10am–midnight.

Rayuela Wine & Grill Ruta 90 Km 37 ☎2 2840 3180; map p.226. Dine among the vines at the Viu Manent wineyard (see page 227), just outside Santa Cruz. The wines are matched to the food – try oysters (CH$8000) with the sauvignon blanc, or lamb cutlets (CH$13,000) with the malbec. Mon–Sat noon–4.30pm.

★ **Vino Bello** Camino Los Boldos s/n ☎72 282 2755; map p.226. Attached to the Laura Hartwig winery (see page 227), this is one of the most atmospheric places to eat in the area, serving Italian dishes such as gnocchi and *ossobuco cannelloni* (CH$10,000) on a candlelit terrace looking out over the vines. Mon–Sat 11.30am–11.30pm, Sun 11.30am–3.30pm.

Pichilemu

The bustling surfer town of **PICHILEMU** lies 87km west of Santa Cruz. Built around a wide, sandy bay at the foot of a steep hill, the town dates from the second half of the nineteenth century, when Agustín Ross Edwards set out to create a European-style seaside resort. Today Pichilemu wears the charming, melancholy air of a faded Victorian seaside town. From the seafront, a broad flight of steps sweep up the hillside to the splendid **Parque Ross**, planted with century-old Phoenix palms and extravagant topiary.

On the edge of the park, jutting out over the hillside, the grand old **casino** – Chile's first but now functioning as a cultural centre – is perhaps the most evocative of Ross's legacies. In contrast, Pichilemu's central streets are crammed with snack bars and *schoperías* (cafés serving beers) catering to the crowds of young surfers who come to ride the waves – among the best in all Chile.

ARRIVAL AND INFORMATION   PICHILEMU

By bus Arriving in town by bus, you'll be dropped a couple of blocks north of the main street, Ortúzar, or at the terminal at the corner of Millaco and Los Alerces. Services are provided by Pullman del Sur and Buses Nilahue.

Destinations Rancagua (every 30min; 3hr 30min); San Fernando (every 30min; 2hr 50min); Santiago (12 daily; 3hr 30min).
Tourist office Gaete 365, inside the town hall (Mon–Fri 8am–1pm, 2pm–5.20pm; ☎72 297 6530).

SURFING IN PICHILEMU

The most challenging surf is at Punta de Lobos, 6km south of Pichilemu town, where the **national surfing championships** are held in September. Look out for the sea lions in the beach's peculiar escarpments. Closer to town, surfers wade into the chilly sea (the ocean temperature rarely rises above 14°C) at La Puntilla, which juts out at the western end of the calmer main beach, Playa Las Terrazas. Just south of here lies Playa Infiernillo, with a faster wave for more experienced surfers.

SURF SCHOOLS

Lobillos del Pacífico Av Costanera 720 ☎09 6915 4409, ⊜lobosdelpacifico@hotmail.com. 2hr classes (CH$18,000) and full-day surfboard and wetsuit rental (CH$8000).

Manzana 54 Av Costanera s/n ☎09 9574 5984, ⓦmanzana54.cl. Classes of surfing (from CH$18,000) and paddle boarding (CH$20,000), as well as occasional day-trips to beaches down the coast.

ACCOMMODATION

Pichilemu has a good selection of budget and mid-price options. Most of the town's accommodation caters to **surfers**, spreading out of town along the beachfront Costanera. Book ahead at busy times, as many of the places to stay have a two-night minimum or more at weekends and during holidays.

Cabañas Buena Vista Cerro La Cruz ☎ 72 284 2488, ⓦ cabanasbuenavista.com. This ecofriendly resort has fully equipped cabins and the English-speaking staff can help organize a range of activities including Spanish, surfing and kayaking classes. CH$35,000

Camping La Caletilla Doctor Eugenio Suárez 905 ☎ 72 284 1010, ⓦ campingpichilemu.cl. The delightful owner lavishes campers with every modern comfort: electricity, hot showers, barbecues and bike rental. And wait till you see the ocean views. CH$7000

Hotel Alaia Camino a Punta Lobos 681 ☎ 09 5701 5971, ⓦ hotelalaia.com. Splash out on this stunning boutique lodge in Punta de Lobos, where every room overlooks the ocean and pro surfers come to kick back. Surfing classes are included in the package, and the à la carte breakfasts will set you up for a day in the waves. CH$175,000

Natural Surf Lodge Comercio 2980 ☎ 09 9001 0179, ⓦ naturalsurflodge.cl. This beautifully designed lodge at Punta del Lobos is a favourite with interior design magazines, incorporating lots of natural materials including wood and stone. Staff can help organize surfing lessons and excursions to find the best waves. CH$51,000

★ **Pichilemu Surf Hostal** Eugenia Diaz Lira 167 ☎ 09 9270 9555, ⓦ surfhostal.cl. Stylish private rooms with ocean views and heaters? Check. Chic restaurant right on the beach? You bet. Free bike rental? They've got it. Surf school? Of course. Beachfront hot tubs? Absolutely. What this Dutch-owned boutique hostel-cum-B&B doesn't have is not worth mentioning. Dorms CH$13,000, doubles CH$45,000

EATING

La Casa de las Empanadas Anibal Pinto 268. Even the street dogs drooling outside know that *empanadas* don't come better than this: here they are huge, deep-fried and prepared while you wait. With 36 varieties to choose from, at CH$1500 each, you know you are on to a winner. Daily 11am–11pm.

Entre Mar Costanera 902, Infiernillo ☎ 72 284 1898. A friendly and casual spot serving an abundance of fish and mariscos, this oceanfront restaurant is popular with locals for its seafood mains (CH$10,000). Daily 1–5pm & 8pm–midnight.

La Gloria JJ Prieto 980 ☎ 72 284 1052. Ten blocks south of the seafront, this popular restaurant is worth the walk for its excellent and inexpensive seafood, which includes tasty *machas a la parmesana* (scallop gratin; CH$8000) and dressed crab. Daily noon–10pm.

NIGHTLIFE

Waitara Av Costanera 1039 ☎ 09 9799 8731. The party starts late at this massive beachside club, where reggaeton and drum'n'bass dominate the dance floor. The terrace, meanwhile, is a breezy place to sink a beer. Entry free before 1am, CH$10,000 after. Fri & Sat 10pm–5am.

Mataquito Valley

The Teno and Lontué rivers converge to form the broad Río Mataquito, which meanders west through Chilean wine country towards the Pacific. The town of **Curicó** (54km south of San Fernando) sits in the **Mataquito Valley** and makes a convenient place to break your journey or to visit the **wineries** (see page 231), **Lago Vichuquén**, near the coast, and the **Siete Tazas** waterfalls, southeast towards the mountains.

Curicó

Bustling little **CURICÓ**, founded in 1743, is the only town of any significance in the Mataquito Valley. An agro-industrial centre servicing the surrounding **vineyards**, it has little to hold your interest for more than a few hours, but is the gateway for excursions into the surrounding area. Note that on the third weekend in March, a **wine harvest festival** (*vendimia*) takes place in Curicó's Plaza de Armas, a celebration of the grape harvest that includes dances and beauty pageants.

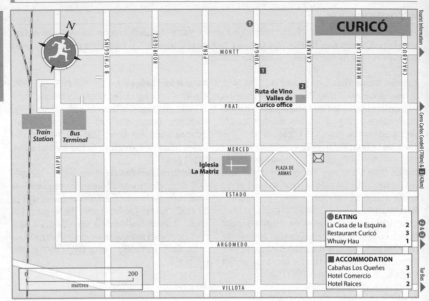

Plaza de Armas

Curicó is built around the **Plaza de Armas**, one of the most beautiful central **plazas** in Chile, luxuriantly planted with sixty giant Canary Island palms. Standing in their shade, on the northern side of the square, is a highly ornate, dark-green wrought-iron **bandstand**, constructed in 1904, while close by an elaborate fountain features a cast-iron replica of *The Three Graces*. In contrast to these rather fanciful civic commissions, the memorial to **Toqui Lautaro** – the Mapuche chief at whose hands Spanish conquistador Pedro de Valdivia came to a grisly end – is a raw and powerful work, carved out of an ancient tree trunk.

Standing on the northwest corner of the square, the **Iglesia La Matriz** makes for a curious sight, its grand Neoclassical facade giving way to a spacious and modern brick interior.

Cerro Carlos Condell

You can climb **Cerro Carlos Condell**, the little hill on the eastern edge of town, and survey the scene from its 99m-high summit or take a dip in its public **swimming pool** (Jan, Feb & Dec daily 10am–8pm; free).

ARRIVAL AND DEPARTURE   CURICÓ

By bus Curicó's main bus terminal (☎75 255 8118) is at Maipú and Prat, about four blocks west and one block north of the Plaza de Armas. Tur Bus (☎75 231 2115), for long-distance services, is inconveniently located a good 20min walk southeast of the plaza at Manso de Velasco and Castellón, while Línea Azul (☎75 222 7017) is half a block north of Tur Bus on Manso de Velasco.

Destinations Chillán (16 daily; 2hr 50min); Puerto Montt (2 daily; 11hr 30min); San Fernando (every 30min; 50min); Santiago (every 30min; 2hr 30min); Talca (every 15min; 1hr 15min); Vichuquén (2 daily; 2hr 30min).

By train The station (☎600 585 5000) is at Maipú 697, opposite the bus terminal.

Destinations Chillán (2 daily; 2hr 35min); Rancagua (2 daily; 1hr 5min); San Fernando (2 daily; 30min); Santiago (3 daily; 2hr); Talca (2 daily; 50min).

> ### WINE TOURS AROUND CURICÓ
>
> From Curicó, it's worth making the easy excursion 5km south to the **Miguel Torres winery** (daily 10am–5pm; ☎ 75 256 4121, ⊛ migueltorres.cl; 45min tours with tastings from CH$7000), owned by the innovative Spanish vintner who revolutionized Chile's wine industry in the 1980s. There's an excellent restaurant, too (see below; CH$33,000 for tour with lunch and wine). To get here, take a bus heading to Molina (every 10min) and ask to be let off outside the *bodega*, which is right next to the Panamericana.
>
> Other wine tours are arranged by **Ruta del Vino Valles de Curicó**, Prat 301-A, Curicó (Mon–Fri 9am–2pm & 3.30–7.30pm; ☎ 75 232 8972, ⊛ rutadelvinocurico.cl). Prices start from CH$87,000, including lunch and transport and a visit to two wineries.

ACCOMMODATION

Cabañas Los Queñes Camino Los Queñes Km 36, 40km east of Curicó ☎ 09 9513 3193, ⊛ cabanaslosquenes.cl; map p.230. This American-/Chilean-run lodge offers a comfortable way to experience the great outdoors, with a restaurant, bar, pool and hot tub. Rafting, kayaking and other outdoor activities are organized. Direct Buses San Cristobal leave from the bus station (5 daily; 1hr; ☎ 75 232 1512). CH$60,000

Hotel Comercio Yungay 730 ☎ 75 255 6000, ⊛ hotelescurico.cl; map p.230. The attractive "superior class" rooms with flatscreen TVs are the main draw at this classic mid-range town hotel, although the standard en suites are also decent. CH$62,000

Hotel Raices Carmen 727 ☎ 75 254 3440, ⊛ hotelraices.cl; map p.230. The best place to stay and eat in town is this slick modern hotel with cream and white en suites, as well as a large lounge area complete with palm-fringed garden, giant fireplace, bar, café and restaurant. CH$85,000

EATING

La Casa de la Esquina Isabel la Católica 392 ☎ 75 231 0767; map p.230. Spanish bullfighting posters adorn the walls, but the menu is a journey through the entire Mediterranean, from Greek salad to pasta to seafood paella (mains around CH$6000). Mon–Sat 1–3pm & 8–11pm.

Restaurant Curicó Miguel Torres winery, 5km south of Curicó ☎ 75 256 4110, ⊛ migueltorres.cl; map p.230. The superb restaurant of this excellent winery serves gourmet dishes. You'll spend CH$33,000 for a winery tour with lunch and wine; at dinner, expect rabbit tortellini or sustainable fish, with dishes always focusing on regional ingredients (mains CH$1200). Mon & Thurs–Sun 12.30–4pm, Fri 8.30–11pm.

Whuay Hau Yungay 853 ☎ 75 232 6526; map p.230. This restaurant serves reliable Cantonese dishes – fried rice, noodles and stir fries (CH$3000) – in a formal dining room with mini chandeliers. Daily noon–8pm.

Vichuquén and around

West of Curicó, a scenic road follows the northern bank of the Río Mataquito through the fertile river valley. Eighty-five kilometres along the road, just beyond Hualañé village, take the right fork and follow the signs for a further 25km along a dirt road to tiny **VICHUQUÉN**, one of the best-preserved villages in the Central Valley. Most of the brightly painted adobe houses date from the mid-nineteenth century, but Vichuquén's history goes back much further: there was a settlement here long before the arrival of the Spaniards, and it was chosen by the Inca as a site for one of their *mitimaes* (agricultural colonies populated by Quechua farmers brought down from Peru). You'll find relics of the Inca occupation – and a 3000-year-old mummy – in the **Museo Vichuquén**, on Calle Rodríguez 332 (Tues–Sun 10.30am–1.30pm & 4–8pm; CH$1500).

Llico

Some 20km northwest of Vichuquén, **LLICO** is a rugged little seaside town perched on the edge of an exposed sandy beach whose turbulent waves attract many **surfers** – in January and February numerous surf tournaments bring a buzz to this usually quiet stretch.

5

Lago Vichuquén

Four kilometres beyond Vichuquén you'll reach the southern tip of **Lago Vichuquén**, a long, narrow lake enclosed by deep-green, pine-covered hills. Considerably more upmarket than Lago Rapel, this is a popular holiday destination with Santiago's upper crust, whose beautiful villas line the lakeshore.

Reserva Nacional Laguna Torca

Llico, Vichuquén • Daily: April–Nov 8.30am–6pm; Dec–March 8.30am–8pm • CH$5000 • ☎ 71 220 9510, 🅦 lagunatorca.cl

The **Reserva Nacional Laguna Torca** is a marshy man-made lake a couple of kilometres outside of Llico across the rickety Puente de Llico, preserved as a breeding sanctuary for 106 species of birds, including hundreds of black-necked swans. Conaf runs a small campsite near the Puente de Llico, nestled in a eucalyptus grove.

ARRIVAL AND INFORMATION

By bus There are daily buses to Vichuquén from Curicó (2hr 30min), and several daily to Llico (2hr 30min), with Buses Diaz (☎ 75 231 1905) and Buses Bravo (☎ 75 231 2193); the Llico services pass by the Conaf office at Laguna Torca.

VICHUQUÉN AND AROUND

Tourist information There's a Conaf office just beyond the Puente de Llico bridge, hiding behind the large house with the veranda.

ACCOMMODATION

Camping Vichuquén Camino El Mirador s/n, Bahia El Durazno, Lago Vichuquén ☎ 75 240 0062, 🅦 campingvichuquen.cl. This family-friendly campsite rents out boats and kayaks and also organizes biking and hiking excursions, and night-time activities. It has a laundry, bakery and mini-market. Prices are much lower outside Jan & Feb. Closed April–Oct. **CH$14,500**

Marina Vichuquén Southern shore of Lago Vichuquén, in the village of Aquelarre ☎ 09 9334 1468, 🅦 marinavichuquen.cl. You'll find good food and accommodation at this hotel, with smart, spacious rooms with lots of natural light, as well as excellent watersports facilities and horseriding (all available for non-guests, too). **CH$99,000**

Parque Nacional Radal Siete Tazas

55km east of Molina • Daily: April–Nov 8.30am–5.30pm; Dec–March 8.30am–8pm • CH$5000 • ☎ 71 222 9517

Of all the natural phenomena in Chile, the **Siete Tazas**, 71km southeast of Curicó, must be one of the most extraordinary. In the depths of the native forest, a crystal-clear mountain river drops down a series of seven waterfalls, each of which has carved a sparkling *taza* ("teacup") out of the rock. The falls are inside **Parque Nacional Radal Siete Tazas**, reached by a poor dirt road from the village of **MOLINA**, 18km south of Curicó and 55km from the park – be sure to fill up with petrol there. Popular with locals on summer weekends but mostly ignored by foreign visitors, this park is almost empty much of the time. Also within the reserve are forests, several hiking trails and the **Velo de Novia** ("Bride's Veil"), a 50m waterfall spilling out of a narrow gorge. For keen hikers, it's also possible to trek from Siete Tazas to Reserva Nacional Altos del Lircay (see page 236), but you'll need to hire the services of a local guide.

ARRIVAL AND INFORMATION

By bus You can get to Siete Tazas on public transport (summer only) from Molina (8 daily; 2hr 30min) or Curicó (1 daily; 3hr).

Tours Local agencies can be reluctant to run tours to the park because of the bad road, but you may be able to pick up a tour from Talca (see page 234).

PARQUE NACIONAL RADAL SIETE TAZAS

Information Conaf has a small hut on the road towards the Siete Tazas, but for more information you need to go to the administrative office at the Parque Inglés sector of the park, 9km further east (daily: Jan, Feb & Dec 8.30am–8pm; March–Nov 8.30am–5.30pm).

ACCOMMODATION AND EATING

Camping Rocas Basálticas Parque Inglés ☎71 222 8029. Conaf runs this popular campsite, without electricity but with hot showers. **CH$3000**

Hostería Flor de Canela Parque Inglés ☎75 249 1613. This guesthouse near the administrative office offers adequate but small and draughty rooms with either private or shared facilities, as well as a simple restaurant. **CH$28,000**

Valle de Las Catas Halfway between Parque Inglés and the Siete Tazas, close to the Puente de Frutillar ☎09 9168 7820, ⓦwww.sietetazas.cl. For swimming, horse rides and accommodation ranging from camping to cabins (for up to six people), try this private ranch inside the park. Camping **CH$6000**, cabins **CH$48,000**

Maule Valley

The **Maule Valley**, some 70km south of the Mataquito, is formed by the **Río Maule**, which flows into the sea almost 75km west of its principal town of Talca at the industrial port of **Constitución**. South of here, a coast road leads to a string of seaside villages, including surfer hangout **Buchupureo**. To the east of Talca, meanwhile, the river has been dammed, resulting in Lago Colbún. Further east, high in the cordillera, the **Reserva Nacional Altos del Lircay** provides some of the region's best hiking trails, through dramatic mountain scenery.

The area is sprinkled with hot springs and has historically been known for its proliferation of **vineyards**, many of them conveniently located between the town of **Villa Alegre** and village of **San Javier** on a route (see below) served by plenty of local buses from Talca. Note that forest fires in summer 2017 devastated one hundred of these wineries, some of which lost century-old vineyards.

Talca

TALCA is mainly used as a jumping-off point for several rewarding excursions spread along the Maule Valley. The city boasts its fair share of services and commercial activity, mostly centred on the main shopping street, **1 Sur**, with a pedestrianized section between 3 Oriente and 6 Oriente. Away from the frantic bustle of this thoroughfare, however, the rest of Talca seems to move at a snail's pace, not least the tranquil **Plaza de Armas**, shaded by graceful bougainvilleas, jacarandas and magnolias. Half-hidden beneath their foliage is a handsome 1904 iron bandstand.

RUTA DEL VINO VALLE DEL MAULE

The **Ruta del Vino Valle del Maule** includes six wineries that are open to the public. All are easy to visit on day-trips from Talca, either by taxi or by using public transport down the Panamericana, into Villa Alegre, up to San Javier and back to Talca; they do not have set opening hours but are open to visitors according to demand and should be contacted in advance unless otherwise indicated. Visits can be arranged independently or through the **Ruta agency** (Corral Victoria, Camino a San Clemente Km 10; ⓦvalledelmaule.cl).

Viña Balduzzi Balmaceda 1189, San Javier ☎73 232 2138, ⓦbalduzziwines.cl. One of the best wineries to visit on your own, as you can drop in without a reservation for a 45min guided tour (CH$4500) of its *bodegas*. With 200 acres of vineyards and beautiful grounds featuring an old *casa patronal*, a chapel and a *parque centenario* full of 100-year-old trees, this is a very picturesque example of a Central Valley winery. Mon–Sat 9am–6pm.

Viña Gillmore Camino Constitución Km 20, San Javier ☎73 197 5539, ⓦtabonko.cl. This family-run winery is one of the oldest vineyards in Chile. Also known as Tabontinaja or Tabonko, it has a good set-up for tourists, with tours (45min; CH$6000) examining the ecology of its vineyards as well as a small hotel and spa offering wine-based therapies.

Viña Via Wines Fundo La Esperanza s/n, San Rafael ☎2 2355 9900, ⓦviawines.com. North of Talca, covering 1300 acres, this is the flagship vineyard for the Oveja Negra (Black Sheep) brand. Two-hour tours start from CH$15,000 for a minimum of two people.

5

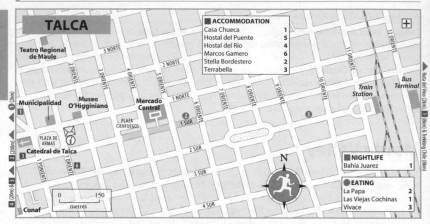

Catedral de Talca

Northwest corner of Plaza de Armas • Mon–Sat 11.30am–12.30pm, Sun 10am–12.30pm • Free

The Neo-Gothic **Catedral de Talca**, built in 1954, and restored in 2011 following earthquake damage, is pale grey with a long, thin spire and series of turrets running along each side. It's worth popping inside to look at the delicately coloured stained-glass Belgian windows and the sombre main altar.

Museo O'Higginiano

1 Norte 875 and 2 Oriente • Closed for repairs at time of writing • ⓦ museodetalca.cl

The **Museo O'Higginiano** occupies a handsome colonial house that hosted some of the most important developments of Chile's independence movement. It was here that Bernardo O'Higgins, future "Liberator" of Chile, lived as a child; where the Carrera brothers established the first Junta de Gobierno in 1813; and where in 1818, O'Higgins signed the country's declaration of independence. The earthquake of 2010 badly damaged the museum, and it has yet to re-open.

ARRIVAL AND DEPARTURE   TALCA

By bus Most buses pull in at the terminal (☎71 231 0815) on 2 Sur and 12 Oriente 938, eleven blocks east of the Plaza de Armas. To get into the centre, take any *colectivo* or *micro* along 2 Sur (and to get back, along 1 Norte).

Destinations Chanco (3 daily; 3hr); Chillán (8 daily; 2hr 30min); Concepción (hourly; 3hr 30min); Constitución (summer every 30min; winter 7 daily; 2hr 20min); Curanipe (summer 8 daily; winter 4 daily; 2hr 45min); Los Angeles (10 daily; 3hr 45min); Pelluhue (summer 8 daily; winter 4 daily; 2hr 30min); Puerto Montt (8 daily; 8hr 30min); Rancagua

(every 30min; 2hr); San Fernando (every 30min; 1hr 30min); San Javier (every 20min; 30min); Santiago (every 20min; 3hr 30min); Temuco (12 daily; 5hr 30min); Vilches Alto (summer 9 daily; winter 4 daily; 2hr); Villa Alegre (every 30min; 1hr).

By train The train station (☎600 585 5000) is at 11 Oriente 1150.

Destinations Chillán (2 daily; 1hr 45min); Constitución (2 daily; 3hr 30 min); Curicó (2 daily; 45min); Rancagua (2 daily; 1hr 50min); San Fernando (2 daily; 1hr 20min); Santiago (4 daily; 2hr 45min).

INFORMATION

Conaf 2 Poniente and 3 Sur (Mon–Thurs 8.30am–3pm; ☎71 222 8029).

Tourist office 1 Oriente 1150 (Mon–Thurs 8.30am–5.30pm, Fri 8.30am–4.30pm, Sat 9.30am–1pm; ☎71 223 3669, ⓔ infomaule@sernatur.cl).

ACTIVITIES AND TOURS

Costa y Cumbre Tours ☎09 9943 5766, ⓦ costaycumbretours.cl. Coastal and mountain tours,

Including multi-day trekking trips and day excursions to Radal Tazas.

Maule Sorprendente ☎09 6668 8640, ⓦ maulesorprendente.cl. This company runs day-trips to the coast, including to the Sahara-like Dunas de Putú sand dunes.

Trekking Chile Viña Andrea s/n, Casilla 143 ☎71 197 0097, ⓦ trekkingchile.com. A great general adventure tour operator, offering treks, snowshoeing, horseriding and kayaking. The company is run by the owners of *Casa Chueca* (see below).

ACCOMMODATION

★ **Casa Chueca** 4km down the road to Las Rastras ☎71 197 0096 or ☎09 9419 0625, ⓦ trekkingchile. com; map p.234. This German-/Austrian-run guesthouse/ hostel is well worth the detour. Surrounded by banana and palm trees, the "Crooked House" offers an abundance of services, amenities and tours, including a pool and intensive Spanish lessons. To get here, phone ahead and then catch the Taxutal "A" bus on 13 Oriente to the *El Toro Bayo* restaurant, an old colonial building at the end of the route, where you'll be picked up. The knowledgeable owners, who also run the tour company Trekking Chile (see above) and sell hand-drawn maps of the local area, also have a refuge in the beautiful Melado Valley. Closed June–Aug. Dorms CH$15,000, doubles CH$48,000

Hostal del Puente 1 Sur 407 ☎71 2220930; map p.234. In a quiet spot next to the river, this place has en-suite rooms set around a patio and attractive gardens – but it is somewhat overpriced in terms of service and breakfast. CH$32,000

Hostal del Río 1 Sur 411 ☎71 251 0218, ⓦ hostaldelrio. cl; map p.234. Next door to the *Hostal del Puente*, this is a reasonable budget choice. The small rooms are set around a large car park and have modern private baths and cable TV. CH$26,500

Marcos Gamero 1 Oriente 1070 ☎71 222 3388, ⓦ marcosgamero.cl; map p.234. While the en suites are fairly standard for this price range, the eclectic collection of aged record players, etchings and old irons strewn about the place give it a certain charm. CH$54,000

Stella Bordestero 4 Poniente 1183 ☎71 223 6545, ⓦ turismostella.cl; map p.234. This excellent-value, tranquil complex has eight timber cabins set in landscaped gardens with a jellybean-shaped pool. CH$45,000

Terrabella 1 Sur 641 ☎71 222 6555, ⓔ terrabella@ hotel.tie.cl; map p.234. Just half a block from the plaza. The best rooms overlook a serene leafy garden with a sparkling swimming pool; there's also a restaurant, computers for guest use and friendly staff. CH$69,000

EATING

The cheapest lunchtime menus are at the small canteens inside the **Mercado Municipal** (enter via 1 Norte).

La Papa 1 Sur 1271 ☎71 261 3784; map p.234. Ladies who *once* (do afternoon tea), and a few men too, catch up over cinnamon rolls (CH$700) and coffee at this popular café. Daily 8.30am–9pm.

Las Viejas Cochinas Rivera Poniente s/n, 2km west of the plaza ☎71 222 1749, ⓦ lasviejascochinas.cl; map p.234. This barnyard-sized restaurant by the River Claro has become a Talca institution on the strength of one dish:

pollo mariscal (chicken in a seafood and brandy sauce; CH$4000). Be prepared for long waits at weekends. Daily noon–1am.

Vivace 2 Sur 1659 ☎71 223 2350; map p.234. Delicious home-made pastas (around CH$7500) and grilled meats go down a treat with something from the classy, Maule Valley-centric wine list. Mon–Sat 11.30am–3.30pm & 7pm–midnight, Sun 11.30am–3.30pm.

NIGHTLIFE

Bahía Juarez 1 Poniente 1267 ☎71 268 6373, ⓦ bahiajuarez.cl; map p.234. You'll find plenty of nocturnal action at this restaurant, pub, karaoke bar,

nightclub and lounge complex. There are food and drink discounts before 10pm (go for the fajitas and tequila cocktails). Mon–Fri 6.30pm–late, Sat 7.30pm–late.

ENTERTAINMENT

Teatro Regional de Maule 1 Oriente 1484 ☎71 234 0591, ⓦ teatroregional.cl. A meeting point for Talquino culture vultures, this modern theatre boasts a steady

and varied programme of live music, theatre, dance and children's shows.

Villa Cultural Huilquilemu

Camino San Clemente Km 7 · Closed at the time of writing

Ten kilometres along the paved San Clemente Highway, also known as Ruta 115, that heads east out of Talca towards the Argentine border, is **Villa Cultural Huilquilemu**. A

5

casa patronal (homestead) built in 1850, it formerly functioned as a museum dedicated to religious art, but was damaged in the 2010 earthquake; it remains unclear when it will reopen.

Reserva Nacional Altos del Lircay

Vilches Alto • Daily: Jan, Feb & Dec 8.30am–7pm; March–Nov 8.30am–5.30pm • CH$5000

The paved Ruta 115 winds up and east through the mountains, eventually leading to the **Argentine border crossing**, Paso Pehuenche (daily 8am–6pm, sometimes closed in winter due to snow). Some 30km on from Villa Huilquilemu a left fork onto a poor dirt road leads 27km to the mountain village of **Vilches Alto** and from here to the entrance of the **Reserva Nacional Altos del Lircay**, 2km beyond. This is an extremely beautiful part of the central cordillera, with a covering of ancient native forests and fantastic views onto surrounding mountain peaks and volcanoes streaked with snow. The road is difficult to pass in winter months, so the best time to visit is between October and May. Close to the entrance, an **information centre** has displays on the park's flora and fauna and the area's indigenous inhabitants, whose traces survive in the **piedras tacitas** (bowls used for grinding corn) carved out of a flat rock face a few hundred metres away along a signed path. As well as a number of shorter **treks**, there is a popular five- to eight-day "condor circuit" that begins in Vilches and takes in several hot springs and waterfalls, as well as awesome mountain landscapes; contact Franz at the *Casa Chueca* in Talca (see page 235) for more information.

The trail to Enladrillado

Of the various **trails** inside the reserve, the most-trodden is to a hilltop platform at 2300m known as **Enladrillado**. From the reserve entrance, follow the steep track up the hillside for about 2.5km, then follow the signed turn-off, from where it's a stiff uphill walk of about five hours; count on an eight-hour round-trip. The views from the top are exhilarating, down to the canopy of native *coigües* and *lenga* forests covering the valley beneath, and across to the towering **Volcán Descabezado** and surrounding peaks. Up here you'll also find areas of exposed volcanic rock resembling giant crazy paving, giving the spot its name, which translates roughly as "brick paving".

The trail to Laguna del Alto

The hike from *Camping Antahuara* (see page 237) to **Laguna del Alto**, a lagoon inside a volcanic crater, is an eight-hour round trip, with great lookout spots along the way. If you want to explore further, try it on **horseback**: in Vilches Alto, contact don Toño (☎09 7772 4473).

ARRIVAL AND INFORMATION	RERSERVA NACIONAL ALTOS DEL LIRCAY
By bus Buses Vilches (☎71 220 3992, ⊛vilchesalto.com) runs regular daily buses to Vilches Alto from Talca.	**Tourist information** The staff at *Refugio Don Galo* (see below) can help organize trips, including overnight stays, and have lots of information on hikes and excursions.

LIGHTS IN THE SKY

The area around San Clemente and the Reserva Nacional Altos del Lircay has garnered a reputation in recent years as a focus of **UFOs**, with a high number of sightings of various kinds of lights in the sky. Some even believe that the Enladrillado platform in Altos del Lircay (see above) is a landing-pad for extraterrestrial craft. Whether aliens travel billions of kilometres across interstellar space to visit Colbún, or whether the lights have a more prosaic explanation linked to the hydroelectric project or seismic activity, or indeed whether it is all a figment of the tourist board's imagination, is for you to decide.

ACCOMMODATION AND EATING

There is one official **campsite** in the park. Note that because of wildfire dangers, no campfires are permitted. You will find several places to stay and eat in **Vilches Alto**, 2km west of the reserve.

Camping Antahuara 500m from Conaf office inside the reserve ☎71 222 8029. Hot showers, well-maintained toilets and electricity ensure campers live it up at this Conaf-run campsite in the forest. CH$3000
Refugio Don Galo Hijuela R, Vilches Alto ☎71 251 9553. Located just before the park entrance, this place offers basic but decent digs, a restaurant and owners brimming with local information. They can organize guided horseriding, trekking and rappelling excursions. CH$35,000

Lago Colbún and around

Chile's largest artificial reservoir, **Lago Colbún**, was created between 1980 and 1985 when the Río Maule was dammed as part of a huge hydroelectricity project, and it wasn't long before its shores, framed by undulating hills, were dotted with holiday chalets, wooden cabins and mini-markets. The town of **Colbún** is not actually on the lake, but just west of it. The lake's southern shore, where there are several campsites, can be a pain to reach – though two bridges span the lake, access to them is often barred by the hydroelectricity company, which means going back to the Panamericana and driving instead along the southern bank of the Río Maule.

ARRIVAL AND DEPARTURE

LAGO COLBÚN AND AROUND

By bus From Talca there are services with Interbus (☎71 261 3140) from the main terminal (10 daily; 1hr 10min).

By car There are various approaches to Lago Colbún, stretching 40km from east to west. From Talca, drive east and carefully follow signs to stay on the Ruta 115, which skirts the northern shore of the lake.

ACCOMMODATION

Cabañas Lago Colbún Ribera Norte ☎09 9895 6401, ⓦlodgecolbun.com. Set on the lake with head-on views of the Andes, these sheltered, fully equipped cabins in the woods sleep up to six people. There's a swimming pool and kayaks for rent. CH$50,000
Complejo Turístico Valshi Paso Pehuenche Km 58 ☎09 9221 8793, ⓦvalshi.cl. A relaxing complex with swimming pool (day pass for non-guests CH$3000), ping-pong tables and cabins that sleep up to ten people. Reiki and reflexology treatments offered. Campers are accommodated, too. Camping CH$4000, cabins CH$30,000
Lodge Colbún Camino Colbún Alto Km 10.5 ☎09 4023 0650, ⓦecoturismolagocolbun.cl. There are stunning lake views from the cabins, glamping tents and rooms at this ecofriendly lodge, where the owner whips up home-cooked meals. Horseriding, kayaking and trekking excursions are offered, or you can simply chill out at the private beach or stargaze while melting in the wood-fired hot tub. Camping/pitch CH$115,000, cabins CH$105,000
Termas de Panimávida Catedral s/n, 5km south of Colbún ☎73 221 1743, ⓦtermasdepanimavida.cl. A thermal bath complex popular with elderly visitors, in a nineteenth-century hacienda-style building built around numerous courtyards and patios. The gardens are immaculate but the rambling old building has rather gone to seed. It is, however, full of character, especially the distinctly Victorian-looking wing housing the long row of cubicles where guests soak in the thermal waters (not especially hot at 33°C/91°F), mud baths and steam rooms. Non-guests can visit for the day (CH$30,000). Full board. CH$160,000

Tricahue Parque

Around 25km east of Lago Colbún, at the confluence of the Maule and Armerillo rivers, is the village of **Armerillo**, close to the little-visited and remote **Tricahue Parque**, filled with tree-covered mountains, lakes and featuring the 2000m Picudo peak. A great way to explore the area is by staying at *Refugio Tricahue* (see page 238).

5

By bus Interbus runs services from Talca (6 daily; 1hr 30min).

ACCOMMODATION

Refugio Tricahue 1km southeast of Armerillo ⓦ refugio-tricahue.cl. This peaceful twelve-bed hostel has a Finnish sauna and pool, and the welcoming Belgian owner organizes fishing trips, walks, bike tours, swimming in thermal pools and, in the winter, snowshoe hikes. The best rooms have private bathrooms and a glass roof. Dorms CH$8000, doubles CH$30,000

San Javier and around

Twenty kilometres south of Talca is a massive iron bridge over the Río Maule, followed by the turn-off to **SAN JAVIER**, a bustling little town sitting in the heart of the Maule Valley's wine country. Its main interest lies in its proximity to two dozen local **vineyards** (see page 233) spread between and around San Javier and the village of **Villa Alegre**, 9km south. You approach Villa Alegre through a stunning avenue of trees whose branches meet overhead to form a dense green canopy. A stroll down the village's main street, lined with fragrant orange trees, takes you past grand *casas patronales* in luxuriant grounds.

ACCOMMODATION

Hotel Colonial Maule Cancha de Carreras s/n, Villa Alegre ☎ 73 238 1214, ⓦ hotelcolonialmaule.cl. For a peaceful place to stay in Villa Alegre, try this attractive old house with landscaped gardens, a swimming pool and restaurant. CH$45,000

Residencial Narvaez Cancha de Carreras 2365, San Javier ☎ 73 232 1203, ⓦ residencialnarvaez.cl. A good budget option in San Javier, this central hotel includes parking, cable TV and a restaurant. The cheapest rooms have shared bathroom. CH$15,000

Constitución and the coastal road

At the mouth of the Río Maule is the busy port of **CONSTITUCIÓN**. While it's now a popular holiday resort, the occasional foul stench of the local cellulose plant makes it unlikely you'll want to stay too long. This area was severely hit by the 2010 earthquake, and by the follow-up tsunami that also washed away parts of Talcahuano, Pichilemu and Iloca – the subsequent clean-up job and reconstruction mean there are few signs of the destruction now. Apart from the weird rock formations on the town's grey sand beaches, there is little to see, but it's a possible base for the 60km stretch of quiet beaches and small fishing towns to the south.

ARRIVAL AND DEPARTURE

By bus From Talca, Constitución is served by several buses daily with Buses Altos Cumbres, Contimar and Pullman. Buses pull in opposite the train station on the riverside, a few blocks northeast of the plaza.

By train One daily train runs to Talca at 7.30pm: sit on the left side of the train for the best views.

ACCOMMODATION

Alonso de Ercilla Colo Colo 334 ☎ 41 291 1301, ⓦ hotelalonsodeercilla.cl. This modern hotel with warm wooden touches and friendly staff is a good mid-range choice. It's just one block from the main plaza. CH$55,000

Chanco and around

From Constitución, a paved road follows the coast to the little seaside resort of **Curanipe**, 80km south. You pass extensive pine plantations bordered by grey, empty beaches and sand dunes before reaching **CHANCO**, a tiny village populated by ageing farmers who transport their wheat, beans and potatoes to market on creaky, ox-drawn

5

carts. Much of the village's colonial architecture was destroyed in the 2010 earthquake and tsunami.

Reserva Nacional Federico Albert
Chanco, Maule • Daily 8.30am–5.30pm • CH$5000 • ☎ 73 255 1004

On the northern edge of Chanco, the **Reserva Nacional Federico Albert** is a dense pine and eucalyptus forest planted in the late nineteenth century in an attempt to hold back the advance of the coastal sand dunes – which by then had already usurped much valuable farmland. A 3km **path** skirts the edge of the reserve, leading to an enormous sandy **beach** with small kiosks, picnic tables and running water.

ARRIVAL AND DEPARTURE   CHANCO

By bus Pullman del Sur goes to Chanco from Talca (3 daily; 3hr); Buses Amigo runs here from Constitución (6 daily; 1hr 30min).

ACCOMMODATION

Camping Reserva Nacional Federico Albert 300m from the reserve entrance ☎ 73 255 1004. This attractive camping area inside the wooded reserve has hot showers, drinking water and electricity. Per pitch <u>CH$3,000</u>

Hostal Mohor Av Fuentealba 135 ☎ 09 7355 1026, ✉ hostal.mohor@gmail.com. A rudimentary but clean hotel; all rooms have cable TV but only some have private bathroom. <u>CH$20,000</u>

Pelluhue and Curanipe

The summer seaside resort and popular surfing destination of **PELLUHUE** (11km south of Chanco) is a haphazard collection of houses strung around a long, curving black-sand beach. Though it's popular with backpackers and has cheap accommodation, the town has an untidy, slightly ramshackle feel that doesn't encourage you to stay long; unless you're here to surf, you'd be better off 7km south in the prettier village of **CURANIPE**. With a backdrop of rolling hills, wheat fields and meadows, Curanipe's dark-sand **beach**, with colourful wooden fishing boats, is a lovely place to hang out, though that's just about all there is do here. Bring enough cash with you, as there are no ATMs in these parts. Another 35km south of Curanipe, the mostly paved road arrives at the isolated surfer hangout of Buchupureo (see page 243).

ARRIVAL AND DEPARTURE   PELLUHUE AND CURANIPE

By bus Interbus (☎ 71 261 3140) runs regular services from Talca to Pelluhue and Curanipe. Pullman del Sur has four daily services from Santiago to Curanipe via Talca. If you're coming from Constitución, change buses in Chanco.

ACCOMMODATION

Cabañas Campomar Camino Pelluhue, Curanipe Km 3 ☎ 73 254 1000, ⓦ cabanascampomar.cl. About 3km south of Curanipe, near the top of a steep hill, these log cabins sleep between foir and six people and have great ocean views. There is a pool, children's playground and parking. <u>CH$52,000</u>

Hotel de Piedra Condell 1606, Pelluhue ☎ 09 6206 3889, ⓦ hoteldepiedra.cl. Set on the seafront between Pelluhue and Curanipe, this eighteenth-century stone house has comfortable rooms, a saltwater pool and a restaurant. Half board. <u>CH$78,000</u>

Itata Valley

Lush and very beautiful, the broad **Itata Valley** begins at the small city of **Chillán** just off the main RN5, and stretches northwest to a string of tranquil coastal towns, including the idyllic surfing village of **Buchupureo**. En route is the **naval museum** in the village of Ninhue.

Chillán

Lively **CHILLÁN** is famous as the birthplace of Bernardo O'Higgins, the founding father of the republic. It's a useful stopover on the Panamericana, with a **market** and fascinating **Mexican murals** to while away an hour or two. As a result of periodic earthquakes and regular Mapuche attacks, Chillán has repeatedly been rebuilt since being founded in 1550. Most of the architecture you seee today dates from just after the 1939 earthquake.

Plaza Bernardo O'Higgins

Chillán's main square, **Plaza Bernardo O'Higgins** is dominated by a giant, 36m concrete cross commemorating the thirty thousand inhabitants who died in the 1939 earthquake, and the futuristic, earthquake-resistant **cathedral**, built between 1941 and 1961 in the form of a tunnel of nine tall arches.

Escuela México

O'Higgins 250 • Mon–Fri 10am–1pm & 3–6.30pm • Donation requested

The **Escuela México**, a school built with money donated by the Mexican government following the 1939 disaster, looks out over leafy **Plaza de los Héroes de Iquique**. On Pablo Neruda's initiative, two renowned Mexican artists, David Alfaro Siqueiros and Xavier Guerrero, decorated the school's main staircase and library with fabulous murals depicting pivotal figures in Mexican and Chilean history. The Mexican images, entitled *Muerte al Invasor*, feature lots of barely clothed indigenous heroes and evil-looking, heavily armed Europeans engaged in various acts of cruelty. The Chilean tableau is even more gruesome, dominated by the lacerated, bleeding body of the Mapuche leader Galvarino, and his bloodthirsty Spanish captors.

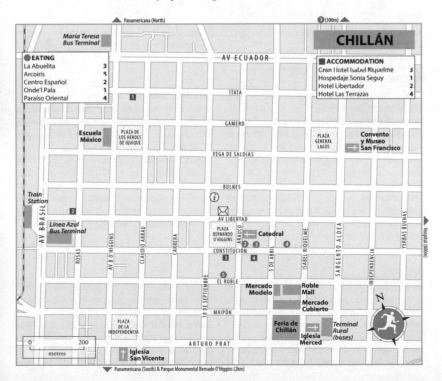

5

Feria de Chillán

Maipón and 5 de Abril • Mon–Sat 8am–8pm, Sun 8am–2pm

Filling Plaza de la Merced, the **Feria de Chillán** is an exuberant open-air market that sells fresh produce and *artesanía* ranging from knitwear and leather items to jewellery, paintings and secondhand books. The market is especially lively on Saturdays, when it bulges out of the square and spreads into the surrounding streets.

Parque Monumental Bernardo O'Higgins

O'Higgins and Parra • Daily 8.30am–8pm • Free • #1 bus from downtown Chillán

The **Parque Monumental Bernardo O'Higgins**, a twenty-minute bus ride southwest of town along Avenida O'Higgins, is a handsomely landscaped park featuring a 60m wall covered with a badly faded mosaic depicting the life of the city's most famous son. In a small chapel nearby, O'Higgins' mother, Isabel Riquelme, and his sister, Rosita, are both buried, not far from the site where Bernardo was born.

ARRIVAL AND DEPARTURE   CHILLÁN

By bus Most long-distance buses use the Terminal María Teresa at O'Higgins 010 (☎ 42 227 2149), on the northern edge of town. Línea Azul has its own terminal at Brasil and Constitución 01, four blocks west of Plaza Bernardo O'Higgins (☎ 42 222 1014). Local and regional buses operate out of the Terminal Rural, Maipón 890, a few blocks southeast of the main plaza (☎ 42 222 3606). Destinations Concepción (every 30min; 1hr 30min); Curicó (8 daily; 2hr 30min); Los Angeles (every 30min; 1hr

30min); Puerto Montt (8 daily; 9hr); Rancagua (8 daily; 4hr); San Fernando (5 daily; 3hr); Santiago (every 30min; 5hr); Talca (hourly; 2hr); Temuco (13 daily; 4hr).
By train The station is at Av Brasil and Av Libertad (☎ 600 585 5000), five blocks west of Plaza Bernardo O'Higgins. Destinations Curicó (2 daily; 2hr 30min); Rancagua (2 daily; 3hr 35min); San Fernando (2 daily; 3hr); Santiago (2 daily; 4hr 30min); Talca (2 daily; 1hr 45min).

INFORMATION AND GETTING AROUND

Car rental Larrañaga, 18 de Septiembre 870 (☎ 42 221 0112, ⟨w⟩ larranaga.cl).

Tourist office 18 de Septiembre 455 (Mon–Fri 9am–2pm & 3–6pm, Sat 10am–2pm; ☎ 42 222 3272, ⟨e⟩ infochillan@ sernatur.cl).

ACCOMMODATION

Gran Hotel Isabel Riquelme Constitución 576 ☎ 42 243 4400, ⟨w⟩ hotelisabelriquelme.cl; map p.241. This salmon-coloured hotel gazes proudly over Plaza O'Higgins. While it is undoubtedly the grandest place in town, the en suites are a little unexciting and overpriced. Its excellent restaurant serves innovative Chilean food and is a popular local haunt. **CH$94,000**
Hospedaje Sonia Seguy Itata 288 ☎ 42 221 4879, ⟨w⟩ hospedajesonia.cl; map p.241. Slightly ramshackle and chaotic but very friendly digs at rock-bottom prices. Most rooms have TVs, the shared facilities are clean and home-cooked meals are on offer for CH$2000. Solo travellers may have to share rooms at busy times. **CH$7000**

Hotel Libertador Libertad 85 ☎ 42 222 3255, ⟨w⟩ hlbo. cl; map p.241. Located half a block from the train station. Rooms on the second floor are the best, but all have big bathrooms, cable TV and paintings of European cities. **CH$45,000**
Hotel Las Terrazas Constitución 664 ☎ 42 243 7000, ⟨w⟩ lasterrazas.cl; map p.241. Excellent hotel split between two buildings that face each other across the street. The airy whitewashed rooms have swish facilities and modern art on the walls, while a relaxed ambience permeates the whole place. **CH$51,000**

EATING

La Abuelita Constitución 635 ☎ 42 223 1450; map p.241. This attractive *pastelería* with wood furnishings is the best place in Chillán for cakes (around CH$1500) and coffee. Daily 9am–9pm.
Arcoiris El Roble 525 ☎ 42 222 7549; map p.241. A rainbow sign guides diners into this bohemian, largely vegetarian, restaurant, which has a lunchtime buffet

(CH$3500) and fresh juices. A small selection of meat dishes kindly caters to carnivores. Mon–Sat 8.30am– 4pm.
Centro Español Arauco 555 ☎ 42 232 0705; map p.241. Penguin-suited waiters at this Spanish/Chilean restaurant serve paella with prawns, mussels, scallops, salmon, chorizo, pork ribs and chicken; the huge one-

person portion (CH$6000) is easily enough for two. Mon–Sat noon–4pm & 7–11.30pm, Sun noon–3.30pm. **Onde'l Pala** Flores Millan 31 ☎ 42 232 0705; map p.241. Well-priced Chilean cuisine, numerous beers on tap and plenty of local colour can be found at this classic canteen. Live folk music brings weekends to life; a small

cover fee (CH$1000–2500) is often charged. Mon–Fri 9am–10pm. **Paraíso Oriental** Constitución 715 ☎ 42 221 2296; map p.241. This popular Chinese restaurant is good for generous portions of fried rice and noodles (around CH$6000), either to eat in or take away. Daily 11.30am–midnight.

DIRECTORY

Banks and exchange There are several ATMs on Arauco and Constitución. Note that there is no ATM in the Valle de Aguas Calientes and ski resorts (see page 244); you will need to withdraw enough cash beforehand here.

Hospital Herminda Martín, Argentina and Francisco Ramírez (☎ 42 221 2345).

Santuario Cuna de Prat

Hacienda San Agustín de Puñal, just outside the village of Ninhue, 50km northwest of Chillán • Tues–Sun 10am–6pm • CH$1000

Naval enthusiasts will not be let down by the colonial **Hacienda San Agustín de Puñal**. Arturo Prat was born here in 1848, and the area is now a shrine to the naval hero who died in 1879 in the Battle of Iquique while trying to capture the Peruvian ironclad gunship *Huáscar* (see page 247), armed only with a sword.

Inside the hacienda is a museum devoted to the hero, the **Santuario Cuna de Prat**. While the national obsession with the young officer – a thousand Chilean plazas and streets are named after him – continues to mystify outsiders, the museum's collection of polished, lovingly cared-for naval memorabilia and colonial furniture are worth a visit in their own right, and the building they're housed in, with its large interior patio and elegant verandas, is a beautiful example of colonial rural architecture.

Buchupureo and around

The pristine surfer's paradise of **BUCHUPUREO** lies 120km northwest of Chillán and 132km north of Concepción. Word has spread in recent years, and a clutch of hotels and restaurants have been added to the sleepy fisherman's village on the sweeping, dark-sand Playa La Boca, with a verdant backdrop of thick pine forests and a stable microclimate ideal for growing papaya. At dawn and dusk, crab fishermen use oxen to haul in their colourful boats, while **surfers** hit the left point break to ride long, fast, tubular waves that reach up to 6m. Surf lessons can be arranged with Olas Altas in Sector La Boca (☎ 09 7938 7352).

While only hardy types in wetsuits brave the chilly sea, a slow-flowing freshwater river runs parallel to Buchupureo's Playa La Boca, with temperatures that, in summer, are ideal for splashing about in. Horseriding is also popular along the beach, and hotels in the area can arrange excursions with local guides.

Around Buchupureo

If the surf's not up you can explore the attractions around Buchupureo, in particular the string of **beaches** up and down the coast, such as **Playa Rinconada**, which lies 16km to the south. Some 13km south of Buchupureo is the livelier, but far less pretty town of **Cobquecura**, home to an offshore colony of sea lions; 5km north of Cobquecura you will find the awe-inspiring **Iglesia de Piedra**, a series of lofty caves with passages leading down to the ocean.

ARRIVAL AND DEPARTURE

BUCHUPUREO

By bus From Chillán, Buses Petoch services leave from the Terminal Rural (7 daily; 2hr 45min). From Concepción, Magabus (☎ 41 221 5147) leaves from Serrano and

Las Heras (4 daily; 3hr 30min). In summer, at least one bus daily plies the coastal route south of Curanipe to Buchupureo and Cobquecura.

5

ACCOMMODATION AND EATING

★ **La Joya del Mar** Playa La Boca ☎ 42 197 1733, ⓦ lajoyadelmar.com. Luxurious villas perched on the hillside have wide picture windows, immense bathtubs and balconies with breathtaking ocean views. There's also an infinity pool, jacuzzi and top-notch restaurant run by the Californian owners (mains around CH$8000). Surfing lessons, mountain biking and wine tours can be arranged. US$145

Los Maquis Camino Buchupureo Km 9.7 ☎ 09 8900 1815, ⓦ losmaquishotel.com. A stylish bed and breakfast with riverside hot tubs, run by a friendly Chilean/Australian couple. Breakfast is served in bed, guests can use the kitchen and transfers from Concepción airport are offered. CH$45,000

El Puerto Playa La Boca ☎ 09 9161 2315, ⓔ elpuertobuchupureo@gmail.com. Check the surf without leaving your bed at these excellent-value timber cabins, some with kitchenettes. The owner has two friendly dogs and takes good care of guests. The restaurant, which serves flavourful, simple seafood dishes (mains CH$4000–7000) is a popular local haunt. Two-night minimum stay at weekends. CH$35,000

Nevados de Chillán

Ski season runs June–Oct • Ski pass CH$37,000/day • ⓦ nevadosdechillan.com

The most famous and developed mountain resort south of Santiago is the **NEVADOS DE CHILLÁN**, an all-season tourist complex which includes one of the largest ski resorts in Chile, 80km east of Chillán, nestled at the foot of the 3122m **Volcán Chillán**. Formerly known as the Termas de Chillán, it possesses a clutch of year-round open-air **thermal pool complexes** surrounded by glorious alpine scenery. The resort's **skiing** facilities include eleven lifts and 29 runs, one of which, at almost 13km, is the longest in South America. Though primarily set up as a winter destination, the resort and facilities in the surrounding area stay open in summer, when possible activities include hiking, horseriding and mountain biking. Note that there is no ATM in the Valle de Aguas Calientes; withdraw **cash** beforehand in Chillán.

Valle de Aguas Calientes

An ideal one-day hike or horseriding trip from Nevados de Chillán is to the **Valle de Aguas Calientes**, where natural hot springs flow at the confluence of three rivers. The resort lies 8km uphill from the sprawling village of **Valle Las Trancas**.

Parque de Aguas Nevados and around

Base of Nevados de Chillán ski resort • Parque de Aguas Nevados pools daily 9am–10pm; Valle Hermoso pools daily 8.30am–5pm • Parque de Aguas Nevados pools CH$7000; Valle Hermoso pools CH$8000

At the base of the ski resort is the delightful, well-maintained **Parque de Aguas Nevados** with four hot sulphur pools of varying temperatures, a swim-up bar and water slide. Trails also lead from the complex to a Turkish steamroom (CH$6000) and natural mud bath. Some 2km downhill the more rustic **Valle Hermoso** has three outdoor pools, while the two resort hotels *Hotel Nevados* and *Gran Hotel Termas de Chillán* allow visitors access to their spas with a day pass (see page 245).

ARRIVAL AND TOURS

By car The vast majority of people who visit do so by private transport; a 4WD is recommended in winter.

By bus Buses Nilahue runs from Santiago to Valle Las Trancas (1 daily; 7hr). Alternatively, Rem Bus (☎ 42 222 9377) goes from Chillán to Valle Las Trancas (11 daily; 1hr 50min). Buses do not usually ply the 8km stretch to the ski resort from Valle Las Trancas. Private transfers cost from CH$15,000 one-way and can be organized by your hotel.

Hitchhiking Hitching from Chillán to the ski resorts is common and easy in the winter.

Tours Good treks, snowshoe walks, and year-round volcano hikes can be organized with Tierra Verde (☎ 09 8500 2514, ⓦ verdetour.com). If you book a tour make sure it includes transfers.

ACCOMMODATION

There are three large, expensive **resort hotels** near the slopes. As you move downhill towards the village of **Valle Las Trancas**, where most people stay, a glut of cheaper cabins, lodges, hostels and restaurants lines the road. Rates vary dramatically throughout the year, with July being the most expensive month.

Alto Nevados Nevados de Chillán resort ☎ 42 220 6105, ⓦ nevadosdechillan.com. Owned by the same company that controls the ski centre, this large hotel is right by the slopes, allowing for ski in/ski out, with its own spa and restaurant (winter only). Its older sister hotel *Hotel Nevados*, a little further down the valley, is open year round but badly in need of sprucing up. Day pass to *Hotel Nevados* spa with lunch CH$40,000. US$400

Cabañas Los Andes Camino Termas de Chillán Km 70.4 ☎ 09 9951 5238, ⓦ cabanaslosandes.com. British-/ Brazilian-run cabins set in undulating, forested surrounds. In winter, the large café and bar is a good après-ski hangout and in summer the owners offer guided hiking excursions. CH$70,000

Chil'In Hostal Camino Termas de Chillán Km 72.5 ☎ 42 224 7075, ⓦ chil-in.com. A large French-run hostel with clean dorms and doubles, all with shared bathrooms. A crackling fireplace warms up the living room in winter. Sound insulation is poor, however, so earplugs are essential. There's a restaurant, too (see below). Dorms CH$25,000, doubles CH$35,000

★ **Ecobox Andino** Camino Shangri-La Km 0.2, Valle Las Trancas ☎ 42 242 3134, ⓦ ecoboxandino.cl. Four

impeccably styled cabins made from recycled shipping containers are linked by raised wooden platforms and set within a magical *ñirres* forest. Plenty of natural light streams through the picture windows, which look onto snowcapped mountains, and the pool and hot tub are pure Zen. CH$70,000

Gran Hotel Termas de Chillán Nevados de Chillán resort ☎ 2 2233 1313 in Santiago, ☎ 42 243 4200 in Chillan, ⓦ termaschillan.cl. This imposing, five-star hotel is starting to show its age a little but has spacious en suites in soothing colours, heated pools, a restaurant, a bar and a casino. The state-of-the-art spa centre offers hot mud baths, facials, hydro-massages and a range of other treatments. A day pass with lunch and pool access is CH$37,000. Full board. US$800

M.I. Lodge Camino a Shangri-La s/n ☎ 09 9321 7997, ⓦ milodge.com. With its own observatory, swimming pool, spa and exquisite French restaurant, the "Mission Impossible" lodge brings everything but the mountain right to your doorstep. Rooms are comfortable if small, with head-on volcano views, and the lodge's zip-line canopy adventure park is a 30min walk away. Rates are half board. CH$120,000

EATING AND DRINKING

Chil'In Restaurant Camino Termas de Chillán Km 72.5 ☎ 42 224 7075, ⓦ chil-in.com. On the same site as *Chil'In Hostal* (see above), this restaurant can get you through the day, with hearty breakfasts, good-value set lunches with a French touch (CH$10,000), and the best pizzas in the valley. Daily noon–1pm.

Parador, Jamón, Pan y Vino Camino Termas de Chillán Km 74 ☎ 42 243 2100. The longest-running restaurant in the valley serves typical food in a setting that

oozes old-world charm. Quell your hunger with the *Olla Parador* (CH$18,000), a hearty, meaty stew which feeds two or three people. Daily 12.30–9.30pm.

Snow Pub Camino Termas de Chillán Km 71.5 ☎ 42 221 3910. For après-ski action, look no further than this popular pub where the music is loud, the beer is cheap (CH$2000), and by 2am, the dance floor is packed. Jan & Feb Mon–Wed & Sun 11.30am–11.30pm, Thurs–Sat 11.30am–4.30am; June–Oct daily 11.30am–late.

Bio Bío Valley

South of Chillán and the Itata Valley, Chile is intersected by the great **Río Bio Bío**, generally considered the southern limit of the Central Valley. One of Chile's longest rivers, it cuts a 380km diagonal slash across the country, emptying into the ocean by the coastal city of **Concepción**, over 200km north of its source in the Andean mountains. For more than three hundred years the Bio Bío was simply "La Frontera", forming the border beyond which Spanish colonization was unable to spread, fiercely repulsed by the native **Mapuche** population.

Today, the **Bio Bío Valley** still feels like a border zone between the tranquil pastures and meadows of central Chile and the lakes and volcanoes of the south. While the valley floor is still covered in the characteristic blanket of cultivation, dotted with typical Central Valley towns such as **Los Angeles** and **Angol**, the landscape on either

5

side is clearly different. To the west, the **coastal range** – little more than gentle hills further north – takes on the abrupt outlines of real mountains, densely covered with the commercial pine forests' neat rows of trees and, further south, there are hints of the dramatic scenery to come in the Lake District, with native araucaria trees in their hundreds within **Parque Nacional Nahuelbuta**.

Cut off by these mountains, the towns strung down the coast road south of Concepción – such as **Lota**, **Arauco**, **Lebu** and **Cañete** – feel like isolated outposts. To the east, the Andes take on a different appearance, too: wetter and greener, with beautiful wilderness areas including the **Parque Nacional Laguna del Laja**.

Concepción

CONCEPCIÓN is the region's administrative capital and economic powerhouse, sitting at the mouth of the Bio Bío. Chile's second-largest city, it has a much more provincial feel than Santiago, and with a population of around a quarter of a million it hardly seems more than a large town. Surrounded by some of Chile's ugliest industrial suburbs, Concepción's centre is a spread of dreary, anonymous buildings. This lack of civic splendour reflects the long series of catastrophes that have punctuated the city's growth – from the incessant Mapuche raids during its days as a Spanish garrison, guarding La Frontera, to the devastating earthquakes that have razed it to the ground dozens of times since its founding in 1551. It does, however, have the energy and buzz of a thriving commercial centre, and the large number of **university** students gives the place a young, lively feel and excellent nightlife.

Plaza de la Independencia

Concepción's focal point is the busy **Plaza de la Independencia**, where Bernardo O'Higgins read the Chilean declaration of independence in January 1818. In the centre, a classical column rises above the main fountain, atop which stands a gold-painted statue of the Greek goddess Ceres, symbolizing the region's agricultural wealth. On the western side of the plaza rises the Romanesque–Byzantine **Catedral**

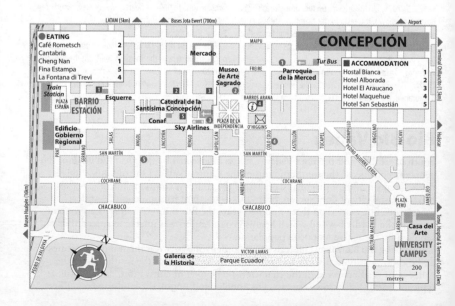

de la Santísima Concepción, built between 1940 and 1950 and adorned with faded mosaics.

Adjacent to the cathedral at Caupolicán 441 is the **Museo de Arte Sagrado** (Mon–Fri 11am–1.30pm & 2.15–6pm, Sat 11am–3pm; free), featuring colonial artwork, marble statues, gold-embroidered vestments and a replica of the Turin Shroud.

Galería de la Historia
Parque Ecuador • Tues–Fri 10am–1.30pm & 3–6.30pm, Sat & Sun 10am–2pm & 3–7pm • Free • ☎ 41 285 3756, ⓦ www.ghconcepcion.cl

For an in-depth introduction to Concepción, the **Galería de la Historia** at the southern end of Lincoyán has a series of impressive dioramas, from pre-Columbian times through the Conquest and to the modern day; most come with sound effects and narration in Spanish.

Casa del Arte
Larenas and Chacabuco • Tues–Fri 10am–6pm, Sat 10am–5pm, Sun 11am–2pm • Free • ☎ 41 220 3835

The **Universidad de Concepción**, set in splendid, landscaped gardens surrounded by thickly wooded hills, is one of Chile's most renowned universities and houses one of the country's largest national art collections in the **Casa del Arte**. The bulk of the collection consists of nineteenth-century landscapes and portraits by Chilean artists, but the showpiece is the magnificent mural in the entrance hall, *Presencia de América Latina*, painted by the Mexican artist Jorge González Camarena in 1964. Dominating the mural is the giant visage of an *indígena*, representing all the indigenous peoples of the continent, while the many faces of different nationalities superimposed on it indicate the intrusion of outside cultures and fusion of races that characterize Latin America.

Edificio Gobierno Regional
Arturo Prat 525 • Daily 9am–6pm • Free

The **Edificio Gobierno Regional** (local government building) was formerly a railway station and houses a massive mural, though it's not as impressive as the one in the Casa del Arte. More than 6m long and 4m tall, the *Historia de Concepción*, painted by Chilean artist Gregorio de la Fuente, was installed in 1964.

Museo Hualpén
Western end of the Bío Bío estuary • Tues–Sun 9am–6pm • Free; CH$2000 for parking • ☎ 41 242 6399 • A 25min taxi ride from Concepción's centre

A large park with several kilometres of footpaths and an extensive collection of native and exotic trees surrounds the **Museo Hualpén**. A traditional single-storey hacienda houses an eclectic collection of souvenirs from every corner of the globe, picked up by the millionaire industrialist Pedro del Río during three world trips taken in the nineteenth century.

Huáscar
Talcahuano, 16km northeast of Concepción • Tues–Sun 9.30am–noon & 2–4.30pm • CH$2500 • ☎ 41 274 5715, ⓦ huascar.cl • White buses marked "Base Naval" go from along O'Higgins right to the entrance of the base

The industrial city and naval base of **Talcahuano** is where the historic ironclad gunship **Huáscar** is moored. You need to ask the guard for permission to visit the ship at the entrance of the base. The *Huáscar* was built for the Peruvian navy at Birkenhead in 1866 and controlled the naval engagements during the War of the Pacific until 1879, when it was trapped off Cape Angamos, near Antofagasta, and forced to surrender. Kept in an immaculate state of preservation, the *Huáscar* is one of only two vessels of its type still afloat today.

ARRIVAL AND DEPARTURE

By plane Aeropuerto Carriel Sur (✆ 41 273 2000, ⓦ carrielsur.cl) is 5km northwest of the city. Several minibus companies offer inexpensive door-to-door transfers to the airport, including Transfer Service (✆ 09 8267 7607); a taxi into town will set you back around CH$10,000. LATAM has an office at Mall Plaza Trebol, Alessandri 3177 (✆ 600 526 2000); Sky Airlines is at O'Higgins 537 (✆ 600 600 2828).
Destinations Puerto Montt (1 weekly; 1hr 10min); Santiago (8–12 daily; 1hr 10 min); Temuco (1 weekly; 45min).

By bus Most buses arrive at Terminal Collao, northeast of the centre at Tegualda 860, just off the Autopista General Bonilla (✆ 41 274 9000); plenty of minibuses and taxis will take you into town. If you arrive with Tur Bus or Línea Azul, you may be dropped at the smaller Terminal Chillancito, also called Terminal Henríquez, at Henríquez 2565. There

are direct buses to most towns and cities between Santiago and Puerto Montt, most leaving from Terminal Collao. Tur Bus, whose downtown office is Tucapel 530 (✆ 41 223 3924), leaves from both Terminal Collao and Terminal Chillancito. If you're heading up the coast to Tomé, take a taxi *colectivo* from Chacabuco. The coastal route south of Concepción to Cañete, Arauco, Lebu and Contulmo is served by Buses Jota Ewert (✆ 41 285 1618).
Destinations Cañete (hourly; 3hr); Chillán (every 30min; 1hr 30min); Contulmo (4 daily; 4hr); Lebu (hourly; 3hr); Los Angeles (every 30min; 2hr); Puerto Montt (20 daily; 10hr); Santiago (every 30min; 6hr); Talca (hourly; 3hr 30min); Temuco (hourly; 4hr); Tomé (every 15min; 40min); Valdivia (11 daily; 6hr 40min).

INFORMATION AND GETTING AROUND

Conaf Lincoyán 471 (Mon–Thurs 8.30am–5.30pm, Fri 8.30am–4.30pm; ✆ 41 262 4000).
Tourist office The friendly Sernatur office is on the plaza at Aníbal Pinto 460 (Mon–Fri 9am–6pm; ✆ 41 274 1337, ✉ infobiobio@sernatur.cl).

Hospital San Martín and Lautaro (✆ 41 272 2500).
Car rental For car rental head to Avis (✆ 41 288 7420) or Budget (✆ 600 441 0000). Both have booths at the airport and an office downtown at Prat 750.

TOURS

Tours Concepción is not a tourist destination and there is little in the way of organized tours, but if you can get a group

together then Esquerre at Barros Arana 185 (✆ 41 274 9990) can organize city tours and visits to the nearby area.

ACCOMMODATION

Hostal Bianca Salas 643-C ✆ 41 293 0718, ⓦ hostalbianca.cl; map p.246. While service can be dour, this is a solid budget option, with small but bright rooms and a useful common area where you can prepare your own food. **CH$30,000**
Hotel Alborada Barros Arana 457 ✆ 41 291 1121, ⓦ hotelalborada.cl; map p.246. Modern hotel with a reflective glass exterior, plant-filled walkway and smart, if rather bland, rooms. **CH$56,000**
Hotel El Araucano Caupolicán 521 ✆ 41 274 0600, ⓦ hotelaraucano.cl; map p.246. A stellar – and reasonably priced – hotel boasting en suites with

flatscreen TVs and tubs. There also an indoor pool, a sauna and a good restaurant with a terrace overlooking the plaza. **CH$59,000**
Hotel Maquehue Barros Arana 786 ✆ 41 221 0261, ⓦ hotelmaquehue.cl; map p.246. This place offers very good value, with fresh, modern, brightly patterned rooms, some of which command fine city views. **CH$30,000**
Hotel San Sebastián Rengo 463 ✆ 41 295 6719, ⓦ hotelsansebastian.cl; map p.246. Rooms at this small, amiable budget hotel are a little old-fashioned, if spotless, and have cable TV; some have private bathrooms. Parking offered. **CH$32,000**

EATING

Concepción has a good range of **restaurants** and boasts the liveliest nightlife in the Central Valley, fuelled by the large student population. The **Barrio Estación** and **Plaza Perú** is buzzing at night, particularly on Calle Prat and Plaza España, revolving mainly around a string of small restaurants that double up as bars on the weekend evenings. You can also enjoy inexpensive meals at one of the dozens of little *picadas* in the **Mercado Central**, on the corner of Freire and Caupolicán, or at the student haunts close to the university campus.

Café Rometsch Barros Arana 685 ✆ 41 274 7040, ⓦ portalrometsch.cl; map p.246. Cavity-inducing ice-cream sundaes, cakes and crêpes (around CH$3500) are available at this long-standing café, which is decorated with city sketches. Mon–Fri 8.30am–8.30pm, Sat 9am–7pm.

Cantabria Caupolicán 415 ✆ 41 252 2693; map p.246. Prices are a little steep here on account of the prime people-watching location, but the good coffee and decadent cakes (CH$3000) make it eminently worthwhile. Mon–Sat 8am–10pm.

Cheng Nan Freire 877 ☏ 41 252 0202; map p.246. An inexpensive self-service vegetarian joint with wholesome, mainly Chinese, dishes, a few pastas and salads. The food is freshest at lunchtime (lunchtime menu CH$4000). Mon–Sat 9.30am–6pm.

Fina Estampa Angol 298 ☏ 41 222 1708; map p.246. Waiters in red shirts and large white kerchiefs around their necks serve delicious Peruvian food (CH$6000–10,000) including *ceviche* and *lomo saltado* (a popular dish of stir-fried steak strips with tomato, onion, chips and rice). Tues–Sat 12.30pm–midnight, Sun 12.30–4pm, Mon 12.30–4pm & 7.30pm–midnight.

La Fontana di Trevi Colo-Colo 336 ☏ 41 279 0300; map p.246. Chequered tablecloths and a display of dozens of wine bottles form the backdrop for a standard but tasty Italian meal of pizza and pasta (CH$5000–10,000). Mon–Sat noon–4pm & 6.30–10.30pm, Sun 12.30–4.30pm.

North of Concepción

North of Concepción, a series of small towns and golden, sandy **beaches** stretches up the coastline as far as the mouth of the Río Itata, 60km beyond. Heading up the road, 12km out of the city centre, you pass through the suburb of **Penco**, where the remains of a Spanish fort, **Fuerte La Planchada**, recall the area's turbulent history.

A couple of gentle hills separate Penco from **Lirquén**, a small industrial harbour used for exporting timber. Its beach is nothing special, but the nearby tangle of narrow streets known as the **Barrio Chino** is full of first-class, excellent-value **seafood restaurants**, famous throughout the region for their clam dishes and *paila marina* (seafood stew). Beyond Lirquén, the road runs inland for 30km; the only way to get to the ocean is by paying to access **Punta de Parra** (see page 250; per vehicle Mon–Fri CH$5000, Sat & Sun CH$7000).

Tomé and around

Some 28km out of Concepción, the thriving timber centre, textile town and port of **TOMÉ** is squeezed into a small flat-bottomed valley, its suburbs pushed up the slopes of surrounding hills. Hidden from the drab town by a rocky point is the long, white-sand **Playa El Morro**. The beach, while very attractive, gets dreadfully crowded on summer weekends; a quieter alternative is **Playa Cocholgue**, a fine white beach studded with rocky outcrops, reached by taking the 4km side road off the main coast road as you head out of Tomé.

Dichato and around

Eight kilometres north of Tomé, **DICHATO** is the most popular beach resort along this part of the coast, with a handful of **accommodation** options spread along the crescent-shaped, coastal avenue, Pedro Aguirre Cerda. About 4km north, the road turns to dirt and passes through dense forests with tracks leading off to a series of isolated, yellow-sand **beaches**, pounded by strong waves. Among the most beautiful of these are **Playa Purda**, 8km north of Dichato, and tiny **Playa Merquiche**, a further 2km north.

ARRIVAL AND DEPARTURE   **NORTH OF CONCEPCIÓN**

By bus Regular buses ply the coast road, heading up from Chacabuco street in Concepción, passing through Tomé (40min) and on to Dichato.

ACCOMMODATION

Cabañas Broadway Av Werner 1210, Playa El Morro, Tomé ☏ 41 265 8475. For your own private beach pad, you could do worse than move into one of these ten fully equipped cabins, which sleep up to four people. __CH$45,000__

El Encanto 4km north of Dichato, towards the Río Itata ☏ 09 9440 0578, ⓦturismoencanto.com. This restful campsite, with electricity and hot showers, also has a handful of cabins with kitchens that sleep up to six people. Camping __CH$7000__, cabins __CH$70,000__

5

Hotel Althome Sotomayor 669, Playa El Morro, Tomé ☎09 7926 4170, ✉althome.hotel@gmail.com. This serviceable hotel has no-frills rooms, some with ocean views, and all with private bathrooms. Parking is included. CH$32,000

Punta de Parra Camino a Tomé Km 19, Tomé ☎09 7669 1019, ⓦpuntadeparra.com. Situated between Lirquén and Tomé. Check in to stay in the cabins, close to the powdery white sands, or pay the fee for a day pass (see page 249). There's a restaurant, infinity pool and a beautiful coastal walk along the old rail tracks to several even more secluded beaches. CH$80,000

The southern coast road and beyond

South of Concepción, a road skirts the ocean, passing through the towns of Coronel, **Lota** and Arauco. This area was deserted until the mid-nineteenth century, when the enormous submarine coal seam – the **Costa del Carbón** – was discovered running off the coast. About 150km south of Concepción, **Lebu** has great beaches, while nearby **Cañete**'s Mapuche Museum is worth a visit en route to pretty **Lago Lanalhue**, 51km from Lebu.

Lota

Squeezed into a small valley on the edge of the sea, the soot-streaked town of **LOTA**, 43km south of Concepción along Ruta 160 , was the site of Chile's first and largest **coal mine**, opened by industrialist Matías Cousiño in 1849. Production finally ceased in 1997, and today the ex-colliery is turning its attention to tourism, with hotels, swimming pools and a casino. The town centre, in the lower part of town known as Lota Bajo, does not inspire enthusiasm. Spread up the hillside west of the centre is **Lota Alto**, containing the former miners' residences, as well as the impressive **Iglesia San Matías**, where the coal baron lies buried.

Mina Chiflón del Diablo

La Conchilla • Daily tours (45min) hourly 9.30am–6pm • CH$7500 • ☎41 287 0934, ⓦlotasorprendente.cl

You can visit **Mina Chiflón del Diablo**, the coal mine, on hourly **tours** guided by ex-miners, which take you down the 820m shaft. By the mine entrance is the Pueblito Minero (CH$800), a recreation of miners' houses that were constructed for the film set of the Chilean movie *Sub Terra*.

Parque Isidora Cousiño

El Parque • Daily 9.30am–6pm • Park CH$2500; museum CH$1000 • ☎41 287 0934, ⓦlotasorprendente.cl

On a headland to the west of town lies **Parque Isidora Cousiño**, a formal garden laid out by an English landscape gardener in 1862 under the direction of Cousiño's wife, *doña* Isidora Goyenechea. The park also has colonial homes, a museum containing a motley collection of photographs and colonial possessions, and actors who dress and speak like characters from the nineteenth century.

ARRIVAL AND DEPARTURE   LOTA

By bus Buses J. Ewert, Expresos del Carbón and Los Alces travel from Concepción to Lota (every 15min; 1 hr 30min). Ask to be let off in Lota Alto.

Isla Santa María

From Lota's pier you can take a two-hour boat ride to **Isla Santa María**, a small, lush island with steep cliffs, rolling hills and a population of about three thousand farmers and fishermen. The island's mild climate and fertile soil have supported small Mapuche communities for hundreds of years. There are secluded bays scattered around the island, with good beaches, sea lion colonies and excellent fishing opportunities.

ARRIVAL AND DEPARTURE

By boat The boat schedule (leaves Lota Sun noon, Tues 11am, Wed, Thurs & Fri 11am; returns Mon 8am, Tues 3pm, Thurs 8am & Fri 3pm; CH$5000 return; ☏41 288

ISLA SANTA MARÍA

9175, ⓦ navierasantamaria.cl) leaves you with the option of a half-day trip on Tues or Fri; otherwise you will have to spend the night on the island.

ACCOMMODATION AND EATING

There are no hotels as such, but some of the fishermen rent out **spare rooms** for around CH$18,000 per night per person, with meals included.

Lebu

Seventy-six kilometres south of Lota, a 31km side road shoots off the highway to the small coastal town of **LEBU**, one of the few places still mining coal in this region. It has huge, unspoiled **beaches**, including **Playa Millaneco**, 3km north, where you'll find several massive caves overgrown with ferns and lichen. Lebu's only other attraction is its pair of bronze cannons on display in the plaza, which were cast in Lima in 1772 and bear the Spanish coat of arms.

ARRIVAL AND DEPARTURE

LEBU

By bus Regular Buses J. Ewert and Línea Azul services run from Concepción to Lebu (hourly; 3hr).

ACCOMMODATION AND EATING

Plaza Lebu Saavedra 691 ☏41 251 2227, ⓦ hotelboutiqueplazalebu.cl. A well-maintained hotel on the plaza with ten comfortable rooms with private bath and cable TV. The hotel's restaurant often serves the local speciality – king crab. **CH$45,000**

Cañete

CAÑETE is a busy agricultural town perched on a small rise above a bend in the Río Tucapel, 16km south of the Lebu turn-off. Just off the northern end of the main street, commanding fine views over the river valley, the historic **Fort Tucapel** was founded by Spanish conquistador Pedro de Valdivia in 1552 and is the site of his gruesome death at the hands of the Mapuche chief Lautaro two years later.

Mapuche Museum

Camino Contulmo s/n • Jan & Feb Tues–Fri 9.30am–5.30pm, Sat & Sun 11am–5.30pm; March–Dec Tues–Fri 9.30am–5.30pm, Sat & Sun 1–5.30pm • Free • ☏ 41 261 1093, ⓦ www.museomapuchecanete.cl

Just south of Cañete, 1km down the highway, the **Mapuche Museum** houses a fine collection of indigenous artefacts, including textiles, silver jewellery, musical instruments and weapons. Perhaps the most striking exhibit is the *ruca* in the museum's garden – a traditional Mapuche dwelling made of wood and straw.

ARRIVAL AND DEPARTURE

CAÑETE

By bus Buses J. Ewert runs numerous services from Concepción to Cañete (hourly; 3hr).

By car From Cañete, a dirt road climbs 46km to Parque Nacional Nahuelbuta (see page 255), while the highway curves south through a lower pass in the Cordillera de Nahuelbuta.

ACCOMMODATION AND EATING

Club Social de Cañete Condel 283 ☏41 261 1653. The best place to eat in town is this plaza-side restaurant in an unprepossessing building. It specializes in well-cooked meat and fish dishes, including wild boar and sea bass (mains CH$6000–9000) while desserts include the exotic potato and hazelnut ice cream. Mon–Sat noon–midnight.

Nahuelbuta Villagrán 644 ☏41 261 1593, ⓦ hotelnahuelbuta.cl. The pleasant rooms have cable TV and a private bath while the adjacent café (daily until 11.30pm) offers a wide selection of meals from sandwiches to lasagne (CH$5000). **CH$30,000**

5

Lago Lanalhue

Ten kilometres out of Cañete, the road reaches the northern shore of **Lago Lanalhue**, nestled among dense pine forests on the western slopes of the coastal range. Its waters are crystal clear and warmer than the Pacific, and its heavily indented shores form numerous peninsulas and bays, some of them containing fine white sand. You can buy basic provisions in the village of **Contulmo**, about 5km along the highway; while you're there, carry on a couple of kilometres around the south shore of the lake to visit the **Molino Grollmus** (officially Jan–April Mon–Sat 10–11am & 6–7pm but in reality, opening hours are more sporadic; free), an early twentieth-century wooden mill whose gardens contain an impressive collection of *copihues* (Chile's national flower). Some 44km east of Contulmo, the highway forks, with one branch heading to the town of Angol (see page 254), and the other continuing south to the Panamericana.

ARRIVAL AND DEPARTURE
LAGO LANALHUE

By bus Buses J. Ewert has services from Concepción to Contulmo (4 daily; 4hr).

ACCOMMODATION

Terrazas del Lanalhue Camino Cañete Km 9.5 ☎ 09 9499 5330, ⓦ terrazasdelanalhue.cl. On the northern side of the lake, 2km from Peleco, these cosy, fully equipped cabins have TV, space for up to five people and direct wharf access. <u>CH$35,000</u>

Salto del Laja

From Concepción, the southern coastal route makes an appealing diversion but if you're in a hurry, take the direct 85km trunk road back to the Panamericana. Some 50km south from there, the first major town you reach is **Los Angeles** (see page 253); halfway along this route, the Panamericana crosses the Río Laja. Just off the highway is the **Salto del Laja**, which ranks among the most impressive waterfalls in Chile, cascading almost 50m from two crescent-shaped cliffs down to a rocky canyon. It's a popular stop-off for Chileans, who come here to take a dip and picnic during the summer. You'll need to pick your way through a veritable village of stalls selling cheap snacks, toys and so on to get to the falls.

ARRIVAL AND DEPARTURE
SALTO DEL LAJA

By bus If you are relying on public transport, your best bet is to visit the Salto del Laja on a short trip from Los Angeles (see page 253) – take one of the frequent Jota Be bus services, which run in both directions (hourly; 30min).

By car The Salto del Laja makes a good break on the long drive from Santiago, but beware of old maps that show the highway cruising by the falls. To actually get to the Salto del Laja, you'll need to follow the turn-off signs for the "Salto". From the parking areas, short paths lead you to a closer viewpoint.

ACCOMMODATION

Los Manantiales Panamericana Sur Km 480 ☎ 43 231 4275, ⓦ losmanantiales.saltosdellaja.com. This large 1970s-style complex includes hotel rooms, fully serviced cabins (for up to six people) and a campsite. There are three natural pools and the restaurant (daily 12.30–3pm; CH$5800 set lunch) has views over the waterfalls. Camping/pitch <u>CH$2500</u>, doubles <u>CH$35,000</u>, cabins <u>CH$55,000</u>

El Rincón Panamericana Sur Km 494, El Olivo ☎ 09 9441 5019, ⓦ elrinconchile.cl. This German-run guesthouse has average doubles (some with private bathrooms) in lovely surroundings. It also offers home-cooked meals and hearty breakfasts with muesli, fruit and yoghurt. <u>CH$48,000</u>

Salto del Laja Panamericana Sur Km 485 ☎ 43 232 1706, ⓦ saltodellaja.cl. This hotel is located on an island with sixty acres of parkland. It boasts swish suites, waterfall views, a restaurant and access to delightful swimming holes. <u>CH$86,000</u>

Los Angeles

5

LOS ANGELES is an easy-going agricultural town, pleasant enough but without any great attractions. At the north end of Colón, eight blocks from the orderly Plaza de Armas, is the colonial **Parroquia Perpetuo Socorro**, a church whose handsome colonnaded cloisters enclose a flower-filled garden. Otherwise, the town is really just a stop-off on the Panamericana or jumping-off point for the **Parque Nacional Laguna del Laja** (see below).

ARRIVAL AND DEPARTURE

LOS ANGELES

By bus The long-distance bus terminal is on Av Sor Vicenta 2051 (☎ 43 236 3035, ⓦ rodoviariolosangeles.cl), on the outskirts of town. The local terminal is at Villagrán 501 (☎ 43 231 5128).

Destinations Angol (every 30min; 1hr); Chillán (every 30min; 1hr 30min); Concepción (every 30min; 2hr); El Abanico (every 30min; 1hr 30min); Puerto Montt (hourly; 8hr); Rancagua (5 daily; 6hr 15min); Talca (6 daily; 3hr 45 min); Temuco (every 45min; 2hr 30min).

INFORMATION AND TOURS

Tourist office Colón 185 (Mon–Sat 10am–7pm; ☎ 43 240 9447).
Conaf Manso de Velasco 275 (Mon–Fri 8.30am–2.30pm; ☎ 43 321 1086). Conaf also has a hut at the Laguna del Laja park entrance.

Tours Harold Wicki (☎ 09 9720 4393, ⓔ aventurakumbre@gmail.com) offers guided tours of the National Park (English spoken). Turismo Curalemu (ⓦ curalemu.cl) owns some *cabañas* near Antuco, close to the park entrance, and can also organize guided treks in the park.

ACCOMMODATION AND EATING

Four Points by Sheraton Colo Colo 565 ☎ 43 240 6400, ⓦ fourpointsbysheraton.com. The new *Four Points by Sheraton* tower is the smartest hotel in town, with the usual comfortable rooms, as well as a great pool and jacuzzi complex and a decent restaurant. CH$60,000
Gran Hotel Muso Valdivia 222 ☎ 43 231 3183, ⓦ hotelmuso.cl. Even if you're not a fan of 1980s architecture and decor, then you'll at least appreciate the plaza-side location of this five-storey hotel. Rooms are bright and clean; try to get one with plaza views. CH$51,000

Hotel Oceano Colo Colo 327 ☎ 43 234 2432, ⓦ hoteloceano.cl. A good central budget option, with helpful staff and eleven neat, sunny rooms with a/c and clean private bathrooms. Breakfast and parking included. CH$48,000
Puerto Maddero Las Industrias 8325 ☎ 43 229 8149. Bar-restaurant offering good-value all-you-can-eat buffets with barbecue (CH$8000) as well as a standard menu. Tues–Sat 8–11.30pm, Sat & Sun 1pm–1.30am.

Parque Nacional Laguna del Laja

93km east of Los Angeles • Daily: Jan–April & Dec 8.30am–8pm; May–Nov 8.30am–6.30pm • CH$3000 • ☎ 43 232 1086

Set in an otherworldly volcanic landscape of lava flows and honeycombed rock, the **Parque Nacional Laguna del Laja** takes its name from the great green lake formed by the 1752 eruption of **Volcán Antuco** (2985m). The road from Los Angeles, 93km away, is paved most of the way; the last 6km is gravel but in decent condition. The park boundary is 4km east of the village of **El Abanico**. You pay your fee and can pick up advice and maps at a Conaf information hut a further 4km east.

Hike to the summit

From the Conaf hut, an easy path leads a couple of kilometres to a pair of large, thundering waterfalls, **Salto Las Chilcas** and **Salto del Torbellino**, fed by underground channels from the lake, which emerge here to form the source of the Río Laja. Hikes to the summit of Volcán Antuco are not particularly difficult, but allow four to five hours for the trip up and three hours for the hike down. Wear strong boots, as the volcanic rocks will shred light footwear.

5

The road east

The road through the park continues east from the information centre towards the lake, passing the mini single-lift **ski centre**, **Centro de Esquí Volcán Antuco** (5km along the road; July–Aug/Sept; CH$15,000; ☎42 232 2651, ⓦskiantuco.cl), which has a small restaurant. The road then skirts along the southern shore of the lake for 22km, continuing to the Argentine **border** at **Paso Pichachén** (daily 8am–8pm; ☎02948 421131, ⓔesc30-chosmalal@gendarmeria.gob.ar). Few vehicles make it along here, so the road serves as an excellent walking trail through the sterile landscape, with changing views of the lake and of the mountains of **Sierra Velluda** to the southwest, which are studded with hanging glaciers. Around 4km east of the ski resort you'll come to a haunting memorial to 45 young soldiers who were killed in the May 2005 "Tragedy of Antuco"; the ill-equipped conscripts died of hypothermia and exposure after being sent on a march around the volcano in a snowstorm.

ARRIVAL AND DEPARTURE   **PARQUE NACIONAL LAGUNA DEL LAJA**

By bus From Los Angeles' local terminal Buses Elper (☎43 236 2785) and Expresos Volcán run services to El Abanico (every 30min; 1hr 30min).

ACCOMMODATION

Survivo 1km from park entrance ☎09 9507 2559, ⓦparqueantuco.cl. A secluded camping area and four spacious cabins by the banks of the Río Laja. There is also a café. Open year-round. Camping/pitch CH$5000, cabins CH$45,000

Angol

Sixty-four kilometres southwest of Los Angeles, **ANGOL** is the final major town before Temuco, the gateway to the Lake District, and serves as a useful base for visiting the nearby **Parque Nacional Nahuelbuta**. In the centre of the town's attractive Plaza de Armas a large, rectangular pool is guarded by four finely carved – and comically stereotypical – marble statues of women representing the continents of Asia, Africa, Europe and the Americas.

Museo Dillman Bullock

Camino Angol Km 5 · Daily 9.30am–1pm & 3–6.30pm · CH$1000 · ☎45 271 1142 · Regular *colectivos* from the Plaza de Armas

Located within an agricultural college in the suburbs, **Museo Dillman Bullock** has beautifully landscaped gardens and an assortment of archeological finds including pre-Columbian funeral urns, a moth-eaten mummy, Mapuche artefacts and malformed foetuses.

ARRIVAL AND INFORMATION   **ANGOL**

By bus Angol's long-distance bus terminal is at Oscar Bonilla 428, seven blocks from the Plaza.

Tourist office Plaza de Armas (Jan & Feb Mon–Fri 8.30am–8pm, Sat & Sun 10am–1pm & 4–8pm; March–Dec Mon–Fri 8.30am–5.30pm; ☎45 2990840). **Conaf** Prat 191 (☎45 271 1870).

ACCOMMODATION

Duhatao Prat 420 ☎45 2714320, ⓦhotelduhatao.cl. This sleek boutique hotel has stylish rooms decorated with ethnic and recycled furnishings, and a restaurant and bar serving international cuisine. CH$59,500

Parque Nacional Nahuelbuta

35km west of Angol • Daily 8.30am–6pm • CH$4000 •
Ⓦ parquenahuelbuta.cl

From Angol, a hard-going stony road
(difficult to pass after rain) climbs
35km west to the entrance of **Parque
Nacional Nahuelbuta**, spread over
the highest part of the Cordillera de
Nahuelbuta. The park was created in
1939 to protect the last remaining
araucaria (monkey puzzle) trees in the
coastal mountains, after the surrounding
native forest had been wiped out and
replaced with thousands of radiata pines
for the pulp and paper industry. Today
it's a 68-square-kilometre enclave of
mixed evergreen and deciduous forest,
providing the coastal cordillera's only
major refuge for wildlife such as foxes,
pumas and *pudús* (pygmy deer).

You're unlikely to catch sight of any
of these shy animals, although if you
look up among the tree trunks you may

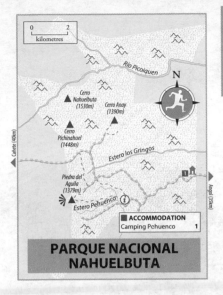

PARQUE NACIONAL NAHUELBUTA

■ ACCOMMODATION
Camping Pehuenco 1

well see large black woodpeckers hammering away. Of the park's trees, star billing goes
to the towering araucarias, with their thick umbrellas of curved, overlapping branches
covered in stiff pine needles. Some of these trees are more than 40m high, and the most
mature specimens in the park are more than a thousand years old.

ARRIVAL AND INFORMATION

By bus In the summer Buses Angol and Buses Nahuelbuta
come from Angol's rural terminal and stop at El Cruce, from
where it is a 1hr walk west to the entrance. The park is open
all year but expect snow and 4WD conditions in winter
(June–Sept).

PARQUE NACIONAL NAHUELBUTA

Tourist information You can discover more about the
park's flora and fauna from the park ranger at Centro de
Informaciones, 5km east along the road from the entrance
(daily 8am–1pm & 2–8pm).

ACCOMMODATION

Camping Pehuenco 5km from the entrance on the
Angol side ☎2 2840 6845; map p.255. Beside the
information centre and park headquarters, *Camping*

Pehuenco has eleven sites with picnic tables and cold
showers. Camping/pitch <u>CH$15,000</u>

TREKS IN PARQUE NACIONAL NAHUELBUTA

From the Centro de Informaciones (see page 255) there are main two treks: an interesting,
700m interpretative loop through the forest and an easy one-hour, 4km hike (look out for the
giant araucaria about a 5min walk along the path, estimated to be 1800 years old) up to the
Piedra del Aguila. This craggy rock offers superb views that on clear days take in the whole
width of Chile, from the Andes to the Pacific. At a slightly lower, flatter rock a few metres west,
you can enjoy even better views onto the smoking volcanoes of the northern Lake District.
To get here by car, take the road through the park to the signed car park, from where it's a
twenty-minute walk up to the viewpoint past a series of information panels on the trees.

There's another rewarding trek up the gentle slopes of **Cerro Anay**, 4km north of the
information centre, reached by a jeep track followed by a short path. Its 1390m peak is the
best place to take in the whole of the park.

The Lake District

ARUACARIA FOREST, PARQUE NACIONAL CONGUILLÍO

The Lake District

The Lake District, which stretches 339km from near Temuco in the north to Puerto Montt in the south, is a region of lush farmland, dense forest, snowcapped volcanoes and deep, clear lakes, hidden for the most part in the mountains. Until the 1880s, when small farm settlements arrived, the entire region was blanketed in thick forests: to the north, the high, spindly araucaria; on the coast, dense *selva valdiviana*; and to the very south, 2000-year-old *alerces*. These forests were inhabited by the Mapuche (literally "people of the land"), who fought off the Inca and resisted Spanish attempts at colonization for 350 years before finally falling to the Chilean Army in the 1880s.

In the century since the subjugation of the Mapuche, German, Austrian and Swiss settlers have transformed this region into some of the finest **dairy farmland** in Chile, and the extent of German influence is evident in architectural and culinary form, particularly in **Valdivia**, **Puerto Varas** and **Frutillar**. Indigenous culture survives as well: the **Mapuche** heritage is a badge of honour in today's Chile, and at least half a million of the region's population claim this ancestry, many of whom reside on the extensive indigenous *reducciones* (reservations) throughout the Lake District.

The real action lies in the region's many **national parks** and around the adventure sports capitals of **Pucón** and **Puerto Varas**, where the options abound for hiking, volcano-climbing, rafting, kayaking, horseriding and soaking in the many thermal springs. In the winter, **skiing** down volcanoes draws an adventurous crowd.

Temuco and around

Founded in 1881, **TEMUCO**, 677km south of Santiago, is a busy working city with a rich **Mapuche heritage**, particularly evident in the **Museo Regional de la Araucanía** – one of the region's highlights – and around the colourful **markets**. The town is also the birthplace of **Pablo Neruda**, Chile's beloved Nobel laureate poet, but is mainly used by visitors as a transport hub or a possible base for exploring the nearby Conguillío (see page 265) and Tolhuaca (see page 263) national parks.

Mercado Modelo

Portales between Bulnes and Aldunate • Summer Mon–Sat 8am–8pm, Sun 8am–3pm; rest of year Mon–Sat 8am–5pm

While Temuco's original **Mercado Modelo** burned down recently, the craft stalls selling silver Mapuche jewellery, baskets, belts, handbags, musical instruments, woven ponchos and more have moved into a new site across the street.

Highlights

❶ Mapuche museums View the most impressive collections of Mapuche silver jewellery and other artefacts at the excellent Museo Regional de La Araucanía and Museo de Volcanes. See pages 261 and 283

❷ Parque Nacional Conguillío Hiking is spectacular in this Andean park, where old lava flows mix with ancient araucaria forests. See page 265

❸ Villarrica Become a musher for a day with Chile's only husky dog operator, or join a week-long dog-sledding expedition across the Andes. See page 269

❹ Pucón The Lake District's adventure tourism

capital, where you can climb smoking Volcán Villarrica, raft the rapids of the Trancura or hike in the nearby nature reserves. See page 270

❺ Valdivia Visit old Spanish forts, drink some of Chile's best beer and go sea-lion-spotting at the lively waterfront market. See page 284

❻ Lago Llanquihue Spectacular waterfalls, one of the region's more challenging volcano climbs, whitewater rafting and some of the best food in the region. See page 294

❼ Cochamó Valley A top spot for hiking or horse-trekking into the oldest forests of the Americas, sometimes called "Chile's Yosemite", and for rock climbing around La Junta. See page 304

HIGHLIGHTS ARE MARKED ON THE MAP ON PAGE 260

THE LAKE DISTRICT

HIGHLIGHTS
1. Mapuche museums
2. Parque Nacional Conguillío
3. Villarrica
4. Pucón
5. Valdivia
6. Lago Llanquihue
7. Cochamó Valley

PACIFIC OCEAN

N

ARGENTINA

0   40
kilometres

Feria Libre

Two blocks of Av Pinto between Lautaro and Av Balmaceda • Daily: summer 8.30am–6pm; rest of year 8.30am–5pm

Near the old railway station, the **Feria Libre** is Chile's liveliest and most colourful fruit and vegetable market, pungent with fish and spices from the *merkén* (smoked chilli powder) stalls. This is a good place to savour typical **local food**, such as *cazuela*, in one of the numerous hole-in-the-wall eateries, and one of the few places you'll see *piñones* (araucaria tree nuts, traditionally boiled and eaten by the Mapuche) for sale.

Museo Regional de la Araucanía

Av Alemania 84, around 1km west of the centre • Mon–Fri 9.30am–5.30pm, Sat 11am–5pm, Sun 11am–2pm • Mon–Sat CH$600, Sun free • ⓦ museoregionalaraucania.cl • A 10min walk west of the centre along Av Alemania; you can also take bus #1, #7 or #9

One of Temuco's biggest attractions is the **Museo Regional de la Araucanía**. Housed in a fine 1920s-vintage building, its beautifully presented exhibits chart the history and migration of the Araucanían people and the Spanish conquest and subsequent European settlement of the Lake District. Spotlights in the large basement subtly illuminate displays of asymmetric *metawe* pottery, funerary urns, sceptre-like half-moon-shaped sacred stones of power, household objects, woven belts and Spanish weaponry. Highlights include an enormous seventeenth-century *wuampo* (hollow log canoe), traditional weavings, *kollong kollong* (crude wooden ceremonial masks) and *kultrung* (ceremonial drums), but the star of the show is the **Mapuche jewellery**; the Mapuche learned silverwork from the Spanish and some fine examples, including heavy silver *collares*, passed on from mother to daughter, are on display. Temporary exhibits present various aspects of Mapuche culture, from woodwork to pottery to weaving.

Museo Nacional Ferroviario Pablo Neruda

Barros Arana 565, 2km east of town • Tues–Fri 9am–6pm, Sat & Sun 10am–6pm • CH$1000 • ⓦ museoferroviariotemuco.cl • A taxi from the centre costs CH$1000

The railway arrived in Chile in 1851, the father of Chilean poet Pablo Neruda was a railway man, and Neruda himself immortalized the iron leviathans in his work. A treat for train buffs and poetry fans alike, the **Museo Nacional Ferroviario Pablo Neruda** brings all this together, with a collection of vintage trains set in grounds dotted with snippets of Neruda's poetry and abstract sculpture. You can climb aboard some of the trains (CH$1000), while the visitor centre holds displays on the history of the railway in Chile.

ARRIVAL AND INFORMATION   TEMUCO

By plane Temuco airport (ⓦ aeropuertoaraucania.cl) is 17km from the city, served by LATAM (Bulnes 687; ☏ 600 526 2000, ⓦ latam.com) and Sky Airline (ⓦ skyairline.cl) flights to Santiago and Concepción, and connected to it by minibus transfers (CH$6000). In peak season, there are direct transfers to Pucón.
Destinations Puerto Montt (1–2 daily; 45min); Santiago via Concepción (6 daily; 2hr).
By bus With the exceptions of Buses JAC (Aldunate at Balmaceda; ☏ 45 223 1340, ⓦ jac.cl), most long-haul buses have ticket offices in the centre but depart from the long-distance Terminal Rodoviario Araucario (☏ 45 222 5005), inconveniently located out of the centre at Vicente Pérez Rosales 1609, and served by *colectivos* and bus #7 from the city centre. The Terminal de Buses Rurales on Pinto and Balmaceda (☏ 45 221 0494) runs services to

more local destinations. Buses JAC has frequent departures to all major destinations in the Lake District; based at the Terminal Rodoviario, Andesmar (☏ 45 225 8626, ⓦ andesmar.com) serves Bariloche and San Martín de Los Andes, Argentina, Igi Llaima, Miraflores 1535 (☏ 45 240 7777, ⓦ igillaima.cl), also serves San Martín de Los Andes; Tur Bus, General Lagos 576 (☏ 45 227 0458, ⓦ turbus.cl), and Pullman, Claro Solar 561 (☏ 45 221 2137, ⓦ pullman. cl), serve Santiago and all major destinations north of the Lake District; Cruz del Sur, Lagos at Claro Solar (☏ 45 273 0320 ⓦ busescruzdelsur.cl), covers the Lake District and Chiloé.
Destinations Bariloche, Argentina (daily 5.30am; 10hr 45min); Concepción (4 daily; 5hr); Melipeuco (6 daily; 2hr 30min); Osorno (every 30min; 4hr); Pucón (every 30min; 2hr); Puerto Varas (hourly; 5hr 15min); San Martín de Los

6

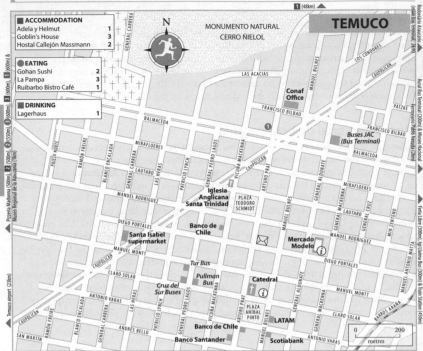

■ **ACCOMMODATION**
Adela y Helmut	1
Goblin's House	3
Hostal Callejón Massmann	2

● **EATING**
Gohan Sushi	2
La Pampa	3
Ruibarbo Bistro Café	1

■ **DRINKING**
Lagerhaus	1

Andes, Argentina (1–2 daily; 7hr); Santiago (every 30min; 9hr 30min); Valdivia (every 30min; 2hr 45min); Villarrica (every 30min; 1hr 30min).

Tourist office Bulnes 590 (Mon–Fri 9am–1pm & 2–5.30pm, Sat 10am–1pm; ☏ 45 240 6213, ⓦ sernatur. cl). Helpful, with maps of the city.

ACCOMMODATION

Adela y Helmut Km 5 N ☏ 09 8258 2230, ⓦ adelayhelmut.cl; map above. This small German/ Chilean-run farm comes warmly recommended by travellers. Stay either in a dorm or a fully equipped mini-apartment inside a large *cabaña*, feast on home-cooked *asado*, smoked trout or the ample breakfast (CH$4900) which includes eggs and honey from the property, or take part in one of the many tours of the Lake District organized by the helpful owners. To get here, take the frequent Nar Bus service from Temuco towards Cunco but alight at the Faja 16000 stop (call the owners before you leave Temuco). Dorms **CH$15,000**, apartments **CH$30,000**
Goblin's House Pirineos 841 ☏ 45 232 0044, ⓦ hotelgoblin.cl; map above. A block away from trendy

Av Alemania, the fourteen individually decorated doubles and twins at this hotel-cum-Irish-pub are all smart slate-grey linen, bold contemporary prints and powerful rain showers, each named after an Irish county (or symbol). Yet while the bar decor waxes nostalgic about Dublin, the only truly Irish thing on the menu is Guinness. **CH$50,000**
Hostal Callejón Massmann Callejón Massmann 350 ☏ 45 248 5955, ⓦ hostalcm.cl; map above. Down a quiet side street, within easy walking distance of Av Alemania's charms, this guesthouse has ten rooms, the austere black-and-white decor contrasting sharply with the bright modern art prints. The showers are poky but each room has a terrace. **CH$47,000**

EATING

West of the centre, **Av Alemania** is Temuco's main eating street.

Gohan Sushi España 390 ☏ 45 274 1110, ⓦ gohan.cl; map above. This sleek branch of the trendy sushi chain, just off Av Alemania, specializes in prawns done sixteen different

ways and imaginative sushi rolls, with fresh crab, tempura rice, scallops and razor clams featuring on the long list of options. Mains from CH$4500. Mon–Sat 12.30–3.30pm & 7–11pm.

★**La Pampa** Caupolicán 155 ☎45 232 9999, ⓦlapampa.cl; map p.262. The menu at this bustling Argentinian restaurant is the discerning carnivore's dream: aged rump steak, prime rib, bacon-wrapped sirloin medallion, sweetbreads, kidneys, slow-cooked ribs, bulls' testicles… Sure, you could come here for the salads, but why would you want to? Good wine list, too. Mains CH$6000–12,000. Mon–Sat noon–4pm & 7pm–midnight, Sun noon–4pm.

Ruibarbo Bistro Café Prat 20 ☎45 225 7115; map p.262. This cute little café serves good coffee, toasted cheese sandwiches and other breakfast items, and features a limited lunchtime menu of a starter, two mains and a dessert (CH$6500). You can expect the likes of spinach-stuffed crêpes, quiche, sushi, couscous and salad or whatever else takes the chef's global fancy on any given day; there will invariably be one vegetarian main. Mon–Fri 8am–6pm.

6

DRINKING

Lagerhaus Tizano 420–440 ☎45 273 1259, ⓦfacebook.com/lagerhaustemuco; map p.262. The pick of the craft beer bars off Av Alemana, with a menu

that reads as a Who's Who of Araucanía's breweries, with offerings from Valdivia, Pucón, Temuco, Osorno and more. Mon–Sat 6pm–late.

Parque Nacional Tolhuaca

120km northeast of Temuco • Daily 8.30am–6pm • CH$5000 • ⓦ conaf.cl/parques/parquet-nacional-tolhuaca

A pristine, forested landscape offering some very decent hiking, **Parque Nacional Tolhuaca** covers a long and relatively narrow strip of land stretching through the valley of the Río Malleco, hemmed in by steep, thickly wooded hills. Dominating the bottom of the valley is the wide and shallow **Laguna Malleco**, bordered by tall reeds rich in birdlife, while other attractions include waterfalls, small lakes and hundreds of araucaria trees.

There are two **approaches** to the park: one is along the 57km gravel road (via the village of Inspector Fernández) branching east from the Panamericana, 2km north of **Victoria**. This leads directly to the Conaf administration on the southeastern shore of Laguna Malleco, where you'll also find **camping** and picnic areas. From here, a footpath follows the northern shore of the lake for about 3km, through lush evergreen forest to the **Salto Malleco**, where the lake's waters spill down into the Río Malleco, forming a spectacular 50m waterfall. The other approach is from **Curacautín** via a 33km gravel road, which leads you straight to the Termas Malleco (see page 264).

Sendero Prados de Mesacura and Sendero Lagunillas

About halfway along the lake path, another trail branches north, climbing steeply up the hillside before forking in two. The left fork follows the 12km **Sendero Prados de Mesacura** across a gentle plain before climbing steeply again through dense forest. The right fork follows the **Sendero Lagunillas** (12km), climbing moderately to a group of small lakes near the summit of Cerro Amarillo, from where you get fabulous panoramic views onto the surrounding peaks, including the 2800m Volcán Tolhuaca. Both of these are full-day hikes.

PARQUE NACIONAL TOLHUACA

■ ACCOMMODATION	
Camping Laguna Malleco	1
Refugio Araucaria &	
Refugio Notro	2

N

Río Pichimalleco

(1290m)

(1792m)

Sendero Prados de Mesacura (1156m)

Sendero Lagunillas

(1355m)

Las Lagunillas

Laguna Verde

Sendero Laguna Verde (1606m)

Río Malleco

Salto del Malleco

Laguna Malleco

🏠 Conaf Ranger Station

0   4
kilometres

Termas Malleco

▼ Inspector Fernández (57km) & Victoria   Curacautín (33km) ▼

Sendero Laguna Verde

Following the flat path along the northern bank of the Río Malleco eastwards, after about 5km you'll reach the trailhead of the 8km **Sendero Laguna Verde**, which climbs up and around a steep hill to the small, emerald-green Laguna Verde, 1300m above sea level and surrounded by soaring peaks.

Termas Malleco

Daily 9am–6pm • CH$15,000 • ☎ 45 241 1111, ⓦ termasmalleco.cl

Nine kilometres east of the Conaf office (see page 265) or 33km north of Curacautín, **Termas Malleco** sit just outside the park's boundaries. The source of the *termas* is at the bottom of a narrow, rocky canyon, inside a large cave, where bubbling, sulphurous water seeps out of the rocks, and steam vents fill the cave with fumaroles. A little further down the canyon, where the thermal water has mixed with cold stream water, there are a couple of pools that are perfect for bathing.

The administration operates two **guesthouses**, and you can also visit the *termas* for the day. It can get very busy in January and February, especially at weekends.

ACCOMMODATION	PARQUE NACIONAL TOLHUACA
Camping Laguna Malleco Next to the Conaf administration by the lake; map p.263. Basic campsite with picnic areas, hot showers and a firepit by each site. <u>CH$16,000</u>	**Refugio Araucaria & Refugio Notro** Near the thermal pools ☎45 224 1111, ⓦtermasmalleco.cl; map p.263. The two lodge-like guesthouses have the same amenities – en-suite rooms with central heating

---

SKIING AND HIKING IN PARQUE NACIONAL CONGUILLÍO

The park splits neatly into two main sectors. The **western slopes** (Sector Los Paraguas) come into their own in winter, boasting a small ski centre, the **Centro de Esquí Las Araucarias** (☎45 227 4141, ⓦ skiaraucarias.cl), with breathtaking views, three drag lifts, a chair lift and three runs (day pass CH$27,000). In summer the focus shifts to the hiking action on the **eastern slopes**, which form the bulk of the park.

DAY HIKES

Visitors with sufficient experience, an ice axe and crampons can make the difficult **ascent of Volcán Llaima** (7hr), but you need permission from Conaf. Be prepared to deal with crevasses and fumaroles, and beware of sulphur fumes at the summit. The park also offers a good selection of hikes for all abilities. For incredible views of the Sierra Nevada range through araucaria forest, take the 7km (2hr 30min) trail from **Playa Linda**, at the east end of Lago Conguillío, to the base of the Sierra Nevada. The challenging **Travesía Río Blanco** (5km; 5hr), which crosses a small glacier before continuing into the Sierra Nevada proper, is recommended for very experienced trekkers only.

From the western shores of Laguna Verde, the 11km (5hr) **Sendero Pastos Blancos** runs to the Laguna Captrén, traversing spectacular scenery and rewarding you with panoramic views of Sierra Nevada, Lago Conguillío and the Truful-Truful Valley. From the Truful-Truful Conaf ranger station, you can take the **Sendero Subtramo Arpehue**, part of the Sendero de Chile, to Laguna Captrén, passing the Andrés Huenupi Mapuche community along the way.

SHORT TRAILS

The Truful-Truful ranger station is also the starting point for two **short nature trails**: the Cañadón Truful-Truful (900m; 30min) passes by colourful strata, exposed by the Río Truful-Truful's flow, while the Las Vertientes trail (800m; 45min) is characterized by the subterranean springs that rush out of the ground. The Laguna Captrén ranger station is the starting point for the **Sendero Los Carpinteros**, also part of the Sendero de Chile, a fairly easy 8km (5hr) return trip that starts from Lago Captrén, and loops around the lagoon before continuing to the administration centre and joining the El Contrabandista trail; the highlight is Araucaria Madre – an araucaria tree that's estimated to be 1500 years old.

generated by thermal water (no TV or wi-fi), though *Refugio Araucaria* is the larger of the two and some rooms have balconies. Guests have unlimited access to pool no.

2. Camping is permitted, with firepits, showers and pool access. Excellent restaurant. Camping CH$18,000, doubles CH$75,000

Parque Nacional Conguillío

120km east of Temuco · Jan–March & Oct–Dec · CH$6000 · ⓦ conaf.cl/parques/parque-nacional-conguillio

The grey peak of **Volcán Llaima** (3125m) looms over the horizon about 80km east of Temuco. Wrapped around its neck is **Parque Nacional Conguillío**, a 608 square km park that the volcano has been doing its best to destroy with belch after belch of black lava – Llaima is one of the three most active volcanoes on the continent; its last serious eruption was in 2008. The park's northern sector is lush, high forest, with steep cliffs covered in spindly armed araucaria trees often furred in lime-green moss. In the south, however, the volcano has wreaked havoc. The road from Temuco passes over a wide lava flow, consisting of either rolling plains of thin dust or walls of spiked, recently congealed rock.

The northern route into the park, through the village of **Curacautín** (84km from Temuco; see page 266), enters the park at sector Laguna Captrén; the paved southern road enters at sector Truful-Truful, via the compact village of **Melipeuco**. The latter makes a convenient base, with a couple of good accommodation options. From the west, a little-used dirt road runs from the village of **Cherquenco** to the **Centro de Esquí Las Araucarias**.

ARRIVAL AND INFORMATION

PARQUE NACIONAL CONGUILLÍO

By bus Nar Bus (☎ 45 240 7778, ⓦ narbus.cl) runs a service from Temuco to Melipeuco (Mon–Sat 8 daily, Sun 3; 1hr 45min) – the southern gateway to the eastern section of the park, 91km east of Temuco and 30km south of the park administration. From here, you'll have to hitch or take a taxi. There are frequent Buses Erbuc (☎ 45 223 3958) services daily from Temuco to Curacautín, the northern gateway to the park, 84km from Temuco and 30km from the administration (5 daily; 2hr). From Curacautín, Buses Curacautín Express (☎ 45 225 8125) run to the northern border of the park (Jan, Feb & Dec Mon–Fri daily; 1hr), from where it's a 12km hike to the *guardería* (ranger station) at Laguna Captrén.

By car The mostly unpaved road that bisects the park from Curacautín to Melipeuco is passable in a regular car (though only in Dec–Feb when there's little snow, and from north to south as there are steep and bumpy sections); a high-clearance vehicle is more comfortable. The minor dirt road connecting the Araucarias sector to the main road through the park is 4WD only.

Conaf Conaf's excellent Centro de Información Ambiental (Jan–March & Oct–Dec daily 9am–1pm & 3–6.30pm) sits near the wide Lago Conguillío, with displays on the park's geology, fauna and flora.

ACCOMMODATION

La Baita Conguillío 2.5km south of Laguna Verde, on the edge of a dense wood ☎ 45 258 1073, ⓦ labaitaconguillio.cl. Run by former singer Isabel, this complex consists of an attractive lodge (with hot tub) and six fully equipped, four- to six-person *cabañas*. It's also an activity centre, coordinating trekking and ecotourism in the summer, and skiing and snow-walking in the winter. *Cabañas* CH$75,000, doubles CH$90,000

Camping ☎ 45 229 8100. There are five campsites in all: two by the ranger stations inside the park, one along the south shore of Lago Conguillío and two along the El Contrabandista trail in the eastern section of the park, all run by concessionaires. Expect fire pits, toilets and cold water showers. Closed May–Oct. CH$6000

Hospedaje Icalma Cerda 729, Melipeuco ☎ 09 9280 8210, ⓦ melipeucohospedaje.cl. Run by a larger-than-life hostess who'll mother you to bits, this simple guesthouse has seven en-suite rooms with plenty of woollen blankets and a kitchen for guest use. Solo travellers pay half price. The hostess can help hikers arrange a lift into the park. CH$28,000

The road to Lonquimay

At **Lautaro**, 30km north of Temuco, a paved road branches east from the Panamericana to the small agricultural town of **LONQUIMAY**, 115km away, passing the entrance to the **Reserva Nacional Malalcahuello-Nalcas** en route and traversing **Curacautín**, the northern gateway to Parque Nacional Conguillío (see page 265). There's nothing especially appealing about Lonquimay itself, but the road there – running through a narrow valley overlooked by towering volcanoes – is spectacular, particularly the stretch across the **Paso de las Raíces**.

Curacautín and around

Some 54km beyond Lautaro, the road passes through the logging town of **CURACAUTÍN**, from where a 40km dirt road branches south to Lago Conguillío in Parque Nacional Conguillío. As the northern gateway to the park, Curacautín has several guesthouses.

ARRIVAL AND DEPARTURE   CURACAUTÍN

By bus Curacautín is served by buses from Concepción (2 daily; 5hr), Los Angeles (2 daily; 3hr) and Temuco (every 30min; 2hr). From the bus terminal, Buses Curacautín Express (☎ 45 225 8125) run to the northern border of Parque Nacional Conguillío (Mon–Fri; 1hr), from where it's a 12km hike to the *guardería* (ranger station) at Laguna Captrén.

ACCOMMODATION AND EATING

Fogón del Córdobes Yungay 215 ☎ 45 320 3653. The best restaurant in town (not that it's much of a horse race) is a good bet for simple dishes, such as grilled beef and salmon, German-style pork ribs and a filling mixed grill for two, involving a heap of chicken, pork chops and chorizo. Friendly service. Mains from CH$7000. Tues–Sun 12.30–10.30pm.

Hostal Epu Pewen Rodríguez 705 ☎ 45 288 1793, ✇ epupewen.cl. Appealing guesthouse run by a half-Mapuche couple, with an inviting common area complete with guitar for guest use. The owners run trekking ventures into the park and can arrange other outdoor activities. Dorms CH$12,000, doubles CH$29,000

Reserva Nacional Malalcahuello-Nalcas

30km west of Curacautín • CH$1000

Some 30km east of Curacautín, you'll pass the entrance to the **Reserva Nacional Malalcahuello-Nalcas**, with the administrative office just a few hundred metres from the road. The main attractions here are **hiking** and, from June to October, **skiing** at the Corralco ski resort (day pass CH$38,000; ✇ corralco.com), which has 28.5km of pistes on the side of the **Lonquimay Volcano**, with short ski runs for all abilities, four drag lifts and two chair lifts.

Hiking in the reserve

Hiking trips on the Lonquimay Volcano take about four hours up, one hour down; an ice axe and crampons are required. Ask for information at Conaf or the *Suizandina Lodge* (see page 267). Another popular walk is the 7.5km (5hr) **Sendero Piedra Santa**, a trail through different types of vegetation that illustrate the techniques used by Conaf to protect and manage native forest. The trail starts at the Conaf ranger station just off the main road in Malalcahuello and passes through quite separate areas of evergreen *tepa*, *rauli*, *coigüe*, *lenga* and the famous araucaria. Parts of the path give excellent views onto **Volcán Llaima** (3125m) and **Volcán Lonquimay** (2865m). The trail joins up with the two-hour (3.5km) **Sendero El Raleo**. The longest hikes in the park – a guide is recommended as the trails are not always easy to follow – are the 40km (two days one way) **Sendero Laguna Blanca**, which skirts the western side of the volcano, and the **Sendero Tolhuaca** (40km) trail that branches off from the former and follows the rivers Tolhuaca and Villucura, skirting the Cordón de la Mora before arriving at the hot springs inside Parque Nacional Tolhuaca (see page 263).

ARRIVAL AND DEPARTURE   RESERVA NACIONAL MALALCAHUELLO-NALCAS

By bus Buses Bío Bío and Erbuc run between Lonquimay and Curacautín (at least 1 hourly; fewer on weekends; 45min) passing the reserve. There are also buses from Temuco's Terminal de Buses Rurales to Lonquimay via Mellipeuco (5 daily; 2hr).

ACCOMMODATION

You can camp wild along the longer, remote trails; otherwise there are several great lodging options along the road to Lonquimay.

★**Andenrose** Camino Internacional Km 68.5 ☎ 09 9869 1700, ⊛ andenrose.com. Run by Hans the exuberant German, this Bavarian-style guesthouse is tucked away among the trees on the banks of the Cautín river. Featuring guest *cabañas* as well as cosy rooms with woollen throws, it's an ideal base for exploring the surrounding area. Hans is a wealth of local info, can cook meals on request for guests and can organize volcano ascents, mountain biking outings, kayaking and trips to the nearby hot springs. Doubles CH$53,000, *cabañas* CH$65,000

★**Ñamku Lodge** Ruta 89 Km 1 ☎ 09 6675 5738, ⊛ namkulodge.com. Run by Chilean-American Annette, this riverside lodge is a work of art. Spread across two buildings (that can be rented as a whole), it's all gorgeous wood-panelled rooms with woollen detail, petrified wood sinks, hanging bunks in the family room and swinging love seats in the common areas. Trails meander down to the river, and the lodge arranges numerous outdoor activities and cultural tours. Their links with the local Mapuche community are one of their strengths and the attached shop sells Mapuche wood carvings and woollen goodies of excellent quality; there's also a casual café next door. US$220

Suizandina Lodge Camino Internacional Km 83 ☎ 45 197 3725, ⊛ suizandina.com. This popular Swiss/Chilean guesthouse lies 30km east of Curacautín and offers guests a mix of spacious private rooms and dorms located in the main house and the adjoining guesthouse with guest kitchen. Camping is also possible. The restaurant features Swiss dishes such as raclette, there are home-made *kuchen* (cakes) for sale at reception and the owners organize all manner of outdoor adventures, from horseriding to mountainboarding. Camping CH$10,000, dorms CH$18,000, doubles CH$62,000

Termas Cañon del Blanco Ruta 929 ☎ 09 7668 4925, ⊛ canondelblanco.cl. Follow the gravel road south from *Andenrose* (see above) and you reach these idyllic hot springs (daily 11am–midnight; CH$12,000), with *tinas* (hot tubs) hidden amid thick vegetation. You can camp here (with hot spring access), come to the smoky *quincho* for meals or stay in the centrally heated hostel (which has down duvets on the beds). The owner arranges guided hikes and horseback treks onto his private land, and leads day treks into the Sierra Nevada and to nearby geysers, complete with overnight glamping options. Camping CH$35,000, dorms CH$35,000, doubles CH$80,000

EATING

La Esfera Camino Internacional Km 69.5 ☎ 45 289 7594, ⊛ vorticechile.com. Specializing in Andino-Peuenche fusion cuisine, this wooden dome restaurant – part of the *Vórtice EcoLodge* – is helmed by Pewenche chef Ariel Ñamcupil. A blend of indigenous and exotic ingredients is used to create such dishes as piñon ravioli, calamari rings with *merkén*-infused vegetables and slow-cooked lamb. Mains from CH$11,000. Daily 9am–11.30pm.

Restaurant MYA Rinconada 550A, Malalcahuello ☎ 09 8358 6322, ⊛ facebook.com/RestobarEntreCerros. Right in the heart of Malacahuello village, this little restaurant specializes in fish and seafood. Choose from beautifully presented grilled fish, *chupe de jaiba* (crab stew) and seafood *empanadas*. Three-course lunch/dinner CH$13,900; à la carte available. Daily 11am–10pm.

Paso de Las Raíces

A couple of kilometres further along the main road from the administration of the Reserva Nacional Malalcahuello-Nalcas, a paved road (signed Volcán Lonquimay) branches north, and then forks in two. The right fork leads 26km to the village of Lonquimay, across the **Paso De Las Raíces**, part of the volcanic chain that forms the highest peaks in this section of the Andes. This is a beautiful drive that switchbacks through lush araucaria forests, with birds of prey, such as buzzards, swooping around the tree branches.

The left fork leads 4km to the **Corralco ski centre** (see page 266). Near the ski lodge, an unpaved but easy-to-drive track skirts the desolate old lava slope up to a lookout point over **Cráter Navidad**, the gaping hole produced when the volcano last erupted, on Christmas Day 1988. En route you pass the trailhead for the moderately steep 1.8km slog up to the crater (2hr return).

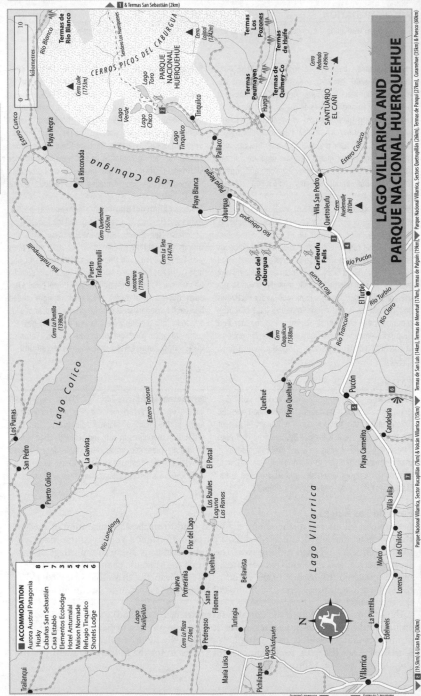

LAGO VILLARRICA AND
PARQUE NACIONAL HUERQUEHUE

Lago Villarrica and around

Lago Villarrica, tucked in the mountains some 86km to the southeast of Temuco, is Chile's most visited lake. The reason for its popularity is **Pucón**, a prime outdoor adventure centre. At the other end of the lake from Pucón is **Villarrica**, its more sedate counterpart.

The area around Lago Villarrica was first settled by the Spanish in the late sixteenth century, but they didn't have much time to enjoy their new territory: their towns were sacked by the Mapuche in 1602. Recolonization didn't take place until the Mapuche were subjugated 250 years later. With the arrival of the railroad from Santiago in 1933, the area became one of Chile's prime holiday destinations.

Villarrica and around

Sitting on the southwestern edge of the lake, with a beautiful view of the volcano, **VILLARRICA** has an attractive waterfront promenade and a couple of small, dark sand beaches, with killer views of **Volcán Villarrica** (see below) across the water. Mapuche culture is strong here, and visitors find it to be a more low-key destination than the ultra-touristy Pucón. The best time to immerse yourself in Mapuche culture is during the annual **Muestra Cultural Mapuche** in the second week of January, a festival featuring traditional crafts, food, music and dance.

Museo Histórico y Arqueológico

Pedro de Valdivia 1050 • Mon–Fri 9am–1pm & 2.30–6pm • Free; donations welcome

The municipal **Museo Histórico y Arqueológico**, on the main drag, offers a crash course in Mapuche culture. You can acquaint yourself with *ñillawaka* (food storage bags made from cow's udders), musical instruments such as the *trutruca* (bamboo-and-horn pipe), silver jewellery, passed on from mother to daughter, and traditional weaving: you can tell a Mapuche woman's marital and social status just by looking at her embroidered belt. Next to the craft market next door sits a thatched *ruca* (traditional dwelling). Inside you'll find carved wooden kitchen utensils, drums and a crudely carved *yuku* (similar to totem pole).

Feria Artesanal

Pedro de Valdivia at Julio Zegers • Mon–Fri 10am–6.30pm, Sat & Sun 11am–6pm • Free

The **Feria Artesanal** is made up of several Mapuche craft markets next to one another. While much of what's on offer is on the kitschy side, at the main Feria Wenteche Mapu you can also try Mapuche cooking and pick up quality weavings and attractive kitchen utensils carved from the native *rauli* wood.

ARRIVAL AND INFORMATION   VILLARRICA AND AROUND

By bus Long-distance buses each have their own terminal: Buses JAC, Bilbao 610 (☎45 241 1447) serve the greatest variety of destinations in the Lake District, while Tur Bus, Muñoz 657 (☎45 220 4102), and Pullman (☎45 241 4217), next door, run the most comfortable services to Santiago and Viña del Mar/Valparaíso. The central Terminal de Buses at Valdivia 621 hosts several smaller bus companies, including Igi Llaima (☎45 241 2733), and serves Junín de los Andes and San Martín de los Andes in Argentina, as well as running small Vipu-Ray shuttle buses to Pucón, and serving Coñaripe and Liquiñe via Coñaripe Bus. Buses San Martín (☎45 241 1584) serves Argentine destinations such as Bariloche and Junín de los Andes.

RECENT VOLCANIC ERUPTIONS

On March 3, 2015 **Volcán Villarrica** had its largest eruption in more than twenty years. People living within 10km of the volcano were evacuated and it was closed to climbers for a while. A month later, **Volcán Calbuco** erupted having lain dormant for more than forty years, forcing the evacuation of inhabitants within a 20km radius. Both are still smoking.

6

MUSHER FOR A DAY

No longer must you travel to Siberia or endure minus 35 degree temperatures in the frozen Arctic wastes to take part in dog-sledding expeditions. **Aurora Austral Patagonia Husky** (ⓦ novena-region.com), based near Villarrica, is home to a mix of Siberian and Alaskan huskies. While there are some husky-sledding opportunities near Ushuaia, Argentina (see page 428), Konrad is the only operator in South America who leads **multi-day husky-sledding expeditions** that allow you to drive your own sled. You can choose either a day-trip in the vicinity of Volcán Villarrica (around CH$80,000) or one of the multi-day expeditions – either to the Termas Geométricas hot springs or across the mountains into Argentina. Two-week expeditions with accommodation in cabins en route costs CH$2,400,000 per person.

The sledding **season** runs from June to October, August being an excellent time to visit. Visitors outside the snowy months can test the half-tricycle, half-chariot contraptions (CH$33,000/ person; two-person minimum) pulled by the huskies or go walking in the mountains with huskies (CH$38,000/half-day). Konrad also offers cottage accommodation (see below).

Destinations Pucón (every 10–20min; 45min); Puerto Montt (hourly; 5hr); San Martín de los Andes, Argentina (Mon–Sat daily 9am, Sun 11.30am; 4hr 30min); Santiago (6 daily; 9hr); Temuco (every 30min; 1hr 30min); Valdivia (6 daily; 2hr 30min).

Tourist office Pedro de Valdivia 1070 (Jan to mid-March & mid- to late Dec daily 9am–9pm; mid-March to mid-Dec Mon–Sat 9am–1pm & 2.30–6pm, Sun 9am–1pm & 2.30–4.30pm; ☎ 45 220 6619).

ACCOMMODATION

Aurora Austral Patagonia Husky 19.5km south of Villarrica, off S-239-T (contact for exact directions) ☎ 09 8901 4518, ⓦ novena-region.com; map p.268. Besides running husky tours (see above), Konrad rents out three beautiful cottages with skylights (two to six people) on his peaceful property, complete with wandering pet sheep, dogs and alpaca. CH$40,000

Hostería de la Colina Las Colinas 115 ☎ 45 241 1503, ⓦ hosteriadelacolina.com. This fabulous hilltop establishment is run with attention to detail by the Chilean owners. There are no TVs to detract from the tranquillity in

the homely, wood-panelled rooms or the garden suites, but there is a book exchange, library, hot tub and good on-site dining for guests. CH$85,000

Hotel Terraza Suite Zegers 351 ☎ 45 241 4508, ⓦ hotelterrazasuite.cl. Contemporary, slate-coloured boutique hotel with a lot going for it: an unobstructed view of the lake, a gorgeous little pool in a secluded garden and sixteen light, bright, carpeted rooms, their austere decor livened up with colourful Mapuche throws. The dining area hides behind a forest-like wooden stockade. CH$100,000

EATING AND DRINKING

Fuego Patagón Montt 40 ☎ 45 241 2207, ⓦ fuegopatagon.cl. From the glassed-over patio with faux-rustic decor to the expertly seared cuts of meat, this steakhouse means business. Your taste buds will thank you for the signature bacon-wrapped veal with quinoa and wild mushrooms, and the tender lamb in a garlicky *merkén* sauce. Mains from CH$9500. Mon–Sat 12.30–4pm & 7.30–11pm, Sun 1–5pm.

El Sabio Zegers 393 ☎ 45 241 9918, ⓦ elsabio.cl. Argentinian-run pizza joint specializing in wood-fired

pizzas; their *cuatro quesos* and pepperoni pizzas are difficult to fault and portions are ample. Pizzas CH$4900–12,800. Thurs–Sun 12.30–4pm & 6–10.30pm.

Travellers Letelier 753 ⓦ facebook.com/ travellersrestobar. This aptly named watering hole attracts global wanderers with its diverse culinary range that spans India, China, Thailand and Mexico. There are regional craft beers for lovers of hops, and the cocktails are among the best in the Lake District. Mains from CH$7500. Mon–Sat 9am–4am.

Pucón and around

On a clear day, you'll be greeted by the awe-inspiring sight of **Volcán Villarrica** (see page 269) smouldering in the distance long before the bus pulls into **PUCÓN**, 25km from Villarrica. This small mountain town has firmly established itself as a top **backpacker destination**. Each November to April season brings scores of outdoor lovers looking to ascend the volcano, ride the Río Trancura rapids or hike in the remote forested corners of the nearby Parque Nacional Huerquehue.

Evenings are generally spent eating, drinking and partying in the restaurants and bars, or soaking in one of the many surrounding thermal springs. The place gets particularly busy in January and February when the international travellers are joined by Chilean holidaymakers.

ARRIVAL AND DEPARTURE   PUCÓN AND AROUND

By plane While there are summer-only flights (Jan, Feb & Dec several weekly; 1hr 40min) to Pucón's tiny aerodrome from Santiago with LATAM and Sky Airline, the majority of visitors fly into Temuco's considerably larger airport (see page 261) and arrange transfers from there.

By bus JAC (Palguín 605; ☎ 45 244 3331, ⓦ busjac.cl), Tur Bus (O'Higgins 910; ☎ 45 244 3963, ⓦ turbus.cl) and Pullman (Palguín 555; ☎ 45 244 3498, ⓦ pullman.cl) each have their own purpose-built terminals. JAC serves destinations within the Lake District; Tur Bus and Pullman have overnight departures to Santiago. Buses Caburga leave for Parque Nacional Huerquehue from their own

little terminal opposite JAC, and Buses Curarrehue run to Curarrehue from the side of the Pullman bus station. At Palguín and Uruguay, the Agencia de Buses sells advance tickets for Igi Llaima (☎ 45 244 4762, ⓦ igillaima.cl) departures to Argentina's Junín de los Andes and San Martín de los Andes; buses stop in front of the ticket office.

Destinations Curarrehue (every 30min; 45min); Parque Nacional Huerquehue (3 daily; 45min); Puerto Montt (hourly; 6hr 15min); Puerto Varas (hourly; 5hr 45min); San Martín de Los Andes, Argentina (Mon–Sat daily 9.20am; 5hr); Santiago (2 daily; 10hr); Temuco (every 30min; 2hr); Valdivia (7 daily; 3hr 15min); Villarrica (every 30min; 45min).

GETTING AROUND

Bike rental Sierra Nevada, O'Higgins at Palguin (☎ 09 6173 0055, ⓦ sierranevadapucon.com) rents out decent mountain bikes (CH$8000/CH$14,000/half/whole day).

Car rental Pucón Rent a Car, Pedro de Valdivia at Arauco (☎ 09 8998 0294, ⓦ puconrentacar.cl) has the best rates.

INFORMATION

Tourist office O'Higgins 447 (daily: Jan, Feb & Dec 8.30am–10pm; March–Nov 8.30am–7pm; ☎ 45 229 3001, ⓦ informacionespucon.com).

Conaf Lincoyán 336 (Mon–Fri 8.30am–noon & 2–5pm; ☎ 45 244 3781). Rangers can advise as regards national park trail conditions.

HOT SPRINGS AROUND PUCÓN

Ample amounts of volcanic activity mean that there are more commercialized **hot springs** in the Pucón region than nera any other town in Chile. Getting to some of the *termas* without your own car is difficult, though various companies in town run **tours** (see page 272). The *termas* are mainly divided into two river valleys, the Río Liucura and the Río Trancura. Here are three of the best; some also offer accommodation.

Termas de Menetúe Camino Internacional Pucón–Curarrehue Km 30 ☎ 45 244 1877, ⓦ menetue.com. Set in beautiful gardens near the river, with naturally heated rock pools, spa, sauna and jacuzzi, a small restaurant and *cabañas*. The swimming pools are seasonal (Dec–April), while the termas (daily 9am–9pm; CH$20,000, CH$25,000 with transfer from Pucón) operate year-round. To get here, head out of Pucón towards Argentina on the international road for 27km then turn left across the Puente (bridge) San Luis and continue west for 5km. CH$85,000

Termas Peumayen Camino Pucón–Huife Km 28 ☎ 45 197 0060, ⓦ termaspeumayen.cl. This newcomer on the *termas* scene has established itself as

much for its beautiful riverside pools (daily 10am–8pm; CH$14,000) as for its appealing lodge with luxurious rooms and also for its superb French-Mapuche fusion restaurant, serving the likes of red quinoa tabuleh and honey-glazed veal. Restaurant Tues–Sat 1.30–4pm & 7.30–9pm. CH$82,000

Termas Los Pozones Camino Pucón–Huife Km 34 ☎ 45 244 3059, ⓦ termas.cl/pozones.html. The most rustic and natural of the hot springs in the area, these simple, shallow *termas* (daily 11am–3am; CH$9000) are dug out beside the river and dammed with stones, with basic wooden changing huts above them. Extremely popular with backpackers, and most tours from Pucón come here at night. There is a 3hr limit on visits.

6

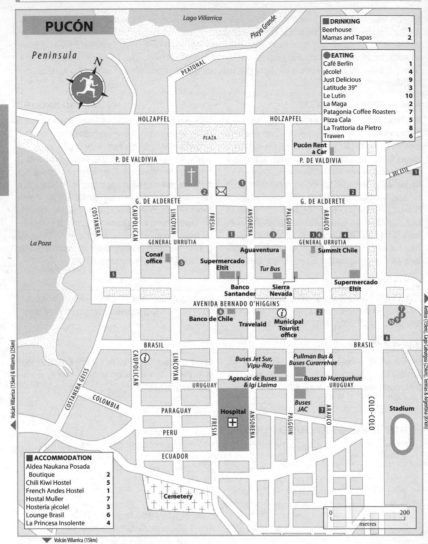

PUCÓN

Lago Villarrica

Playa Grande

Peninsula

N

PEATONAL

HOLZAPFEL

HOLZAPFEL

PLAZA

P. DE VALDIVIA

P. DE VALDIVIA

Pucón Rent a Car

J. DEL ESTE

G. DE ALDERETE

G. DE ALDERETE

COSTANERA

CAUPOLICAN

LINCOYAN

FRESIA

ANSORENA

PALGUIN

ARAUCO

GENERAL URRUTIA

GENERAL URRUTIA

La Poza

Conaf office

Aguaventura

Summit Chile

Supermercado Eltit

Tur Bus

Supermercado Eltit

Banco Santander

Sierra Nevada

AVENIDA BERNADO O'HIGGINS

Banco de Chile

Travelaid

Municipal Tourist office

BRASIL

BRASIL

CAUPOLICAN

LINCOYAN

COSTANERA GEISS

Buses Jet Sur, Vipu-Ray

Pullman Bus & Buses Curarrehue

COLOMBIA

Agencia de Buses & Igi Llaima

URUGUAY

Buses to Huerquehue

URUGUAY

PARAGUAY

FRESIA

Hospital

ANSORENA

Buses JAC

PALGUIN

ARAUCO

COLO-COLO

Stadium

PERU

ECUADOR

Cemetery

DRINKING
| Beerhouse | 1 |
| Mamas and Tapas | 2 |

EATING
Café Berlín	1
¡école!	4
Just Delicious	9
Latitude 39°	3
Le Lutin	10
La Maga	2
Patagonia Coffee Roasters	7
Pizza Cala	5
La Trattoria da Pietro	8
Trawen	6

ACCOMMODATION
Aldea Naukana Posada Boutique	2
Chili Kiwi Hostel	5
French Andes Hostel	1
Hostal Muller	7
Hostería ¡école!	3
Lounge Brasil	6
La Princesa Insolente	4

Volcán Villarrica (15km & Villarrica (25km)

Volcán Villarrica (15km)

Antilco (15km); Lago Caburga (25km); Termas & Argentina (67m)

0   200
metres

Travelaid Ansorena 425, Local 4 (Mon–Fri 10am–1.30pm & 3.30–7pm, Sat 10am–2pm; ⓦtravelaid.cl). Stocks detailed trekking maps and road maps of Chile, and rents GPS systems for trekking around Pucón. English and German spoken.

Hospital Hospital San Francisco, Uruguay 325 (☏45 244 1177).

ACTIVITIES AND TOURS

There are a multitude of tour companies in Pucón, mostly offering the same trips for similar prices. Most run tours of the area, which take in the **Ojos de Caburgua** waterfalls and any of the **thermal springs** at Huife, Palguín, Menetúe and Pozones (CH$20,000–25,000), as well as night-time visits to Termas Los Pozones and pricier outings to Termas Geométricas. Below are specialized operators who excel at one particular activity.

Aguaventura Palguín 336 ☎45 244 4246, ⓦaguaventura.com. Your best bet for whitewater rafting on the nearby Río Trancura, offering a popular class II–III run on the lower part of the river, with the more challenging class VI – Upper Trancura – run made up almost entirely of drop pools. Both of these trips are half-day excursions; you can combine the two. Prices for 2–3hr rafting range from CH$20,000 for the Lower Trancura to CH$28,000 for the Upper Trancura. Aguaventura also offers hydrospeeding (bodyboarding) down the Río Liucura rapids (no greater than class III); the half-day excursion, including 1hr in the river, costs CH$30,000. They also offer river kayaking instruction (CH$25,000) and ducky (mini-rafting) outings (CH$30,000).

Air Skydive ☎09 7477 3763, ⓦfacebook.com/ AirSkydive. Of the two skydiving operators in Pucón, this highly professional operator gets consistently stellar feedback. CH$180,000 for a 1hr tandem jump.

Antilco Camino a Currarehue Km 15 ☎09 9713 9758, ⓦantilco.com. Experienced and highly recommended operator organizing anything from half-day trips to a nine-day glacier and hot springs ride. English and German spoken. You can go for a full-day or half-day ride in the mountain wilderness of the Parque Nacional Villarrica, or even on a multi-day horseback expedition across the Andes into Argentina. Prices start at about CH$30,000/half-day, CH$50,000 for a full day.

Aurora Austral Patagonia Husky See page 270.

Elementos Camino a Caburgua Km 16 ☎45 244 1750, ⓦelementos-chile.com. Friendly German operator that offers plenty of tours focusing on Mapuche culture – from cooking with the Mapuche to homestays and multi-day, multi-activity options. Lafkenche cultural tour CH$95,500.

Summit Chile Urrutia 585 ☎45 244 3259, ⓦsummitchile.org. Bilingual, internationally qualified mountain guide Claudio leads small group treks (six maximum per group) in Villarrica National Park – from the standard ascent of Volcán Villarrica (CH$55,000) to the more technical two-day ascent of Volcán Lanín (CH$220,000) on the border with Argentina. Also half-/full-day (CH$28,000/ CH$38,000) rock climbing ventures, suitable for beginners and advanced climbers, and ski touring excursions.

ACCOMMODATION

HOTELS AND B&BS

Aldea Naukana Posada Boutique Alderete 656 ☎45 244 3508, ⓦaldeanaukana.com; map p.272. Bare volcanic stone, wood-panelled walls and a spiral staircase leading up to the suite with jacuzzi are just some of the features of this nine-room boutique lodge. The super-central location, range of alternative relaxation treatments and a via ferrata on their private reserve are additional boons. US$157

Casa Establo Camino Pucón–Villarica Km 6 ☎45 244 3084, ⓦcasaestablo.com; map p.268. With all ten rooms named after famous racehorses and the design of the boutique hotel mimicking some features of a traditional Chilean stable, this is an excellent mid-range choice a short drive from Pucón. There's an ooutdoor pool and sauna, and the spacious rooms overlook a tranquil wooded property. CH$70,000

Elementos EcoLodge Camino a Caburgua Km 16 ☎45 244 1750, ⓦelementos-chile.com; map p.268. This newly built lodge on a riverside property, with a friendly menagerie of dogs and cats, offers eight individually designed rooms, drawing on the elements and Mapuche culture for inspiration. German owner Sarina's tour agency has strong links with Mapuche communities all over the Lake District and offers multi-day cultural immersions, as well as outdoor adventures. CH$110,000

Hostal Muller Arauco 560 ☎45 244 1735, ⓦhostalmuller.cl; map p.272. In this homely, family-run guesthouse there are just six beautiful, wood-panelled rooms with sumptuous beds. The owners can advise on hiking in the area, you can relax by the volcanic stone fireplace in the lounge and there's kitchen access. US$70

Hostería ¡école! Urrutia 592 ☎45 244 1675, ⓦecole. cl; map p.272. Apart from some snug singles and doubles in the main building, one of the town's long-established guesthouses has added a clutch of new en suites in the tranquil garden out back, complete with colourful weavings. Add to that one of the town's best restaurants, plenty of info on outdoor activities in the area and a wonderfully central location, and it's easy to understand why this place is always full. CH$45,000

★ **Hotel Antumalal** Camino a Villarica Km 2 ☎45 244 1011, ⓦantumalal.com; map p.268. Built into a slope, this architectural gem was designed by a student of Frank Lloyd Wright and is the most atmospheric hotel in town (as testified to by Queen Elizabeth II, Buzz Aldrin and other famous guests). The warm decor, fireplaces and large panoramic windows drinking in views of Lago Villarrica add to the comfort of the rooms, while the spa features waterfalls, and the organic cuisine at the on-site restaurant is superb, as is the service. Doubles US$280, chalets US$425

★ **Maison Nomade** Camino a Caburgua Km 15 ☎09 8293 6367, ⓦnomadepucon.com; map p.268. On this tranquil plot of land with fantastic volcano views you'll find an attractive, ecofriendly guesthouse, next door to the house where the French/Chilean owners live with their two friendly dogs. There are just six beautifully designed rooms with colourful woollen hangings and state-of-the-art bathrooms, a fantastic breakfast with home-made bread and jams, a playground for the kids and even hammocks in

6

6

the tranquil grounds. It's signposted en route to Caburgua. **CH$85,000**

Shotels Lodge Camino al Volcán Km 4.2 ☎ 09 6802 9145, ⓦ bambulodge.com; map p.268. The seven exquisite rooms at this guesthouse on the road to the volcano offer tranquillity and a fantastic view of the forest and the lake beyond. All come with big double beds, superior linens and bathtubs, and the white of the walls contrasts with the colourful Moroccan rugs and woollen throws. Breakfast is good, and there's a guest kitchen. **CH$80,000**

HOSTELS

★ **Chili Kiwi Hostel** O'Higgins 20 ☎ 45 244 9540, ⓦ chilikiwihostel.wixsite.com; map p.272. Right on the lakefront, and run by affable Kiwi James, this is, hands down, Pucón's best backpacker hostel. Guests can bed down in snug dorms, the Harry Potter room, or else the treehouse rooms, converted vans or Hobbity Hollows in the garden for some privacy. The on-site bar serves excellent craft beer and gourmet dinners, the hostel employs its own mountain guides for the volcano trek and there's a daily talk on what backpackers can do around Pucón that's worth their time and money. Stellar. Dorms **CH$12,000**, doubles **CH$42,000**

★ **French Andes Hostel** Pasaje Tinquilco 3 ☎ 45 244 3324, ⓦ french-andes.com; map p.272. Run by charming Frenchman Vincent and catering to backpackers and budget travellers looking for a bit of privacy, this top-notch hostel accommodates its guests in Japanese-inspired capsule dorms and rooms, as well as regular doubles. Perks include rain showers, excellent kitchen facilities and a large garden for barbecues. Vincent also rents compact camper vans. Dorms **CH$10,000**, doubles **CH$20,000**

Lounge Brasil Colo-Colo 281 ☎ 45 244 4035, ⓦ cafeloungebrasil.com; map p.272. Not only is there an adorable wood-fire-heated café on the premises, but prices at this intimate, super-central guesthouse, run by a friendly Brazilian proprietress, are a steal for the six snug singles and doubles (all en suite). The vegetarian café serves local craft beers. **CH$40,000**

La Princesa Insolente Urrutia 660 ☎ 45 244 1492, ⓦ princesainsolentehostel.cl; map p.272. Run by energetic staff, this place ticks all the party hostel boxes: two cosy, fireplace-warmed common rooms, on-site bar and restaurant, hot tub in the hammock-festooned garden, guest kitchen and free breakfast, plus plenty of info on local attractions and occasional barbecues. Snug doubles and dorms come with brand-new beds and most have their own bathroom. Dorms **CH$10,000**, doubles **CH$30,000**

EATING

CAFÉS AND CHEAP EATS

Café Berlín Miguel Ansorena 160 ☎ 45 263 9849, ⓦ cafeberlinpucon.cl; map p.272. Bright lights, video footage of Berlin and black-and-white prints of the city's landmarks greet visitors to this uber-modern café. Come for good coffee, light and tasty cakes or chunky sandwiches. Cakes CH$2500. Daily 8.30am–midnight.

★ **Just Delicious** Colo Colo at O'Higgins ☎ 09 7430 0016; map p.272. Bringing Middle Eastern flavours to Araucania, this Israeli/Chilean-run hole-in-the-wall serves superb falafel and hummus, as well as quiche and vegetable soup. Mains CH$1500–5000. Mon–Sat noon–4pm & 6.30–9pm.

Le Lutin Colo-Colo at O'Higgins; map p.272. Located at the strip mall on the corner, this bakery is the place to come in Pucón for proper bread and humungous *pains au chocolat* (from CH$1000). Mon–Sat 10am–2pm & 4–8pm.

★ **Patagonia Coffee Roasters** Colo-Colo at O'Higgins ☎ 09 9644 4831; map p.272. The American owner of the best coffee shop in Pucón roasts his own beans and focuses on brews from all over the world that no other local café serves, including Sumatran and Ethiopian blends. Free wi-fi attracts laptop and iPad toters. Daily 10am–7.30pm, Sat 10am–4pm.

RESTAURANTS

¡école! Urrutia 592 ☎ 45 244 1675; map p.272. Tasty, inexpensive and imaginative vegetarian dishes served in a vine-covered courtyard or an attractive dining room. The vegetable lasagne is superb, as are the yellow veg curry with chutney and the home-made bread. Mains CH$4300–5400. Daily 8am–11pm.

★ **Latitude 39°** Urrutia 436 ☎ 09 7430 0016; map p.272. Run by friendly Californians, this is your (newly expanded) home from home for fish tacos, heaped breakfast burritos, imaginative burgers (the Buddha Burger with Asian slaw is a winner), and other Tex-Mexicana, accompanied by generous lemonades and regional Chilean beers. Mains from CH$5500. Mon–Sat noon–11pm.

La Maga Gerónimo de Alderate 264 ☎ 45 244 4277, ⓦ lamagapucon.cl; map p.272. In addition to filet mignon, sirloin and skirt steak, Pucón's best *parrilla* offers ample mixed grills involving *morcilla* and chorizo for two or more. Steaks CH$13,900–18,900. Daily noon–4pm & 7.30pm–midnight.

Pizza Cala Lincoyán 361 ☎ 45 246 3024, ⓦ pizzacala. cl; map p.272. Pucón's best pizzeria serves excellent thin-crust pizza with some exotic and welcome toppings, baked in a clay oven in front of you. Their barbecue chicken also gets rave reviews. Mains CH$6500–7800. Daily 12.30pm–midnight.

La Trattoria da Pietro O'Higgins at Colo Colo ☎ 45 244 9024; map p.272. Handmade saffron-infused spaghetti, filled paninis, proper tiramisu and other Italian dishes are served with aplomb at this welcoming, authentically Italian joint that hides in the strip mall at the edge of town. Mains from CH$8500. Tues–Sat 11am–10pm, Sun 11am–5.30pm.

★ **Trawen** O'Higgins 311 ☎ 45 244 2024, ⓦtrawen. cl; map p.272. This longstanding, offbeat restaurant tantalizes your tastebuds with imaginative, organic and internationally inspired dishes, such as goat's cheese gnocchi, bacon-wrapped venison with polenta, quinotto with trout and ample fresh fruit juices. It's a great spot for granola-rich breakfasts, too. Mains CH$5900–11,800. Daily 8am–11.30pm.

DRINKING

Beerhouse Urrutia 324 ⓦfacebook.com/ BeerHousePucon; map p.272. A classic rock soundtrack accompanies nightly sessions at this thimble-sized craft beer bar with a covered outdoor terrace. Regional brews are the stars, from Pucón's very own Alasse to Villarrica's Crater and Valdivia's Cuello Negro, with a supporting cast of beer cocktails and burgers. Daily 5.30pm–2am.

Mamas and Tapas O'Higgins 587 ☎ 45 244 9002; map p.272. A local institution of many years that entices a large clientele nightly with their excellent selection of beers (from CH$2500), and two-for-one cocktail specials from a long list. Mon–Thurs & Sun noon–2am, Fri & Sat noon–4am.

Ojos de Caburgua

20km northeast of Pucón • Jan–March & Oct–Dec • CH$4000 for motorists • Take the international road to Argentina, then follow signposted road for 17km or be dropped at the entrance by a Caburgua-bound bus

Thousands of years ago, an eruption blocked this southern end of the valley, drowning it. The water from **Lago Caburgua** now flows out through subterranean streams and porous rock until it reappears as the **Ojos de Caburgua** (Eyes of Caburgua): three extremely photogenic waterfalls in the forest plunging into a deep pool of crystal-clear water.

Parque Nacional Huerquehue

30km from Pucón • Officially open Jan–March but accessible at other times of year • CH$5000 • ⓦ conaf.cl/parques/parque-nacional-huerquehue

Rising up almost 2000m from the eastern shore of Lago Caburgua are the forest-clad hills and peaks that form the 125-square-kilometre **Parque Nacional Huerquehue**. Crowned by araucaria forests, the horseshoe-shaped **Cerros Picos de Caburgua** (Caburgua Mountains) enclose a dozen beautiful lakes of which the largest four – Tinquilco, Chico, Toro and Verde – are the most visited. At lower altitudes there are mixed forests of *coigüe* (southern beech) and the conifer *mañío*. The park is also home to more than eighty **bird** species, including the Magellanic woodpecker, as well as the little Darwin's frog.

ARRIVAL AND DEPARTURE   PARQUE NACIONAL HUERQUEHUE

By bus Buses Caburgua (☎ 09 9641 5761) runs services from Pucón to the Conaf *guardería* at the park entrance during peak season (3–4 daily, 8.30am–7.30pm; Jan & Feb last bus returns at 7.30pm; March–Dec last bus returns at 4.30pm; 45min).

ACCOMMODATION

As well as the options below, there's a basic Conaf-run **campsite** near the park entrance.

Cabañas San Sebastián Termas San Sebastián ☎ 09 9231 8329, ⓦtermassansebastian.cl; map p.268. Serene campsite and *cabañas* at the end of the Sendero Los Huerquenes; the rustic wood *cabañas* can accommodate up to seven people, and are all equipped with bathrooms and showers supplied by the hot springs (day use CH$7000). Camping **CH$10,000**, *cabañas* **CH$40,000**

Refugio Tinquilco Lago Tinquilco ☎ 09 9539 2728, ⓦtinquilco.cl; map p.268. Excellent, airy wooden guesthouse in a beautiful streamside location a 2km hike from the park entrance, with home-cooked meals (breakfast included), sauna, book exchange and an owner you'd want to share a bottle of wine with. Dorms **CH$16,000**, doubles **CH$34,900**

HIKING IN PARQUE NACIONAL HUERQUEHUE

From the park entrance, the short and pleasant **Sendero Ñirrico** leads down to Lago Tinquilco through dense bamboo groves before rejoining the main trail (800m; 30min). From Lago Tinquilco, there's a worthwhile two-hour hike up **Cerro Quinchol**, rewarding you with excellent views of Lago Caburgua beyond. A steep and challenging hike continues up **Cerro San Sebastián** where you'll find snow on the summit even in summer, and which affords great views (16km; 8–10hr return from Lago Tinquilco). The most popular hike is the moderately strenuous **Sendero Los Lagos** (9km), which climbs to a height of 1300m through dense forest to the beautiful Chico, Toro and Verde lakes from the *Refugio Tinquilco*; allow three hours one way, as the trail is steep in sections and can be muddy. About halfway up there's a picturesque detour to the thundering **Salto Nido del Aguila**, and several scenic viewpoints.

Beyond Lago Chico, the trail splits, the left fork leading to Lago Verde and the right to Lago Toro; the two join further up. If you wander off the main trail along the shores of Lago Verde or Lago Toro, you can often have the spot completely to yourself. You can take in the tiny Lago de los Patos and Lago Huerquehue (2hr) before rejoining the Los Lagos loop, or you can continue along the **Sendero Los Huerquenes** to **Termas de San Sebastián** (see below), a hot spring outside the park's northeastern boundaries, via the stunning Renahue viewpoint overlooking the lakes below. It's possible to hike to the *termas* in one day (23km from the park entrance; 8–9hr), since much of the Sendero Los Huerquenes is downhill, and you can either stay at the comfortable *Cabañas San Sebastián* (see page 276) before retracing your steps, or make advance arrangements for a ride out to the nearest town, also called Renahue, and from where you can catch a bus back to Pucón. You'll find the free Conaf map of the park useful; it's readily available at the Pucón Conaf office (see page 271).

Santuario El Cañi

Jan–March, Nov & Dec • CH$5000 • All buses from Pucón to Parque Huerquehue pass by the entrance

Some 21km east of Pucón, the near 990-acre **Santuario El Cañi**, comprising mixed araucaria forest, was created in 1991 when the small Fundación Lahuen, made up of concerned locals, fought off logging interests to preserve this beautiful piece of land. The main **hiking trail** (9km; allow 5-6hr return) runs steeply up through the forest from the park entrance, ascending to the attractive Laguna Negra, from which you get an all-encompassing view of the surrounding volcanoes on a clear day.

Curarrehue

Visitors interested in **Mapuche** culture will want to stop in the frontier town of **CURARREHUE**, 40km east of Pucón, where you'll find an appealing **museum** and a celebrated **restaurant**.

Aldea Intercultural Trawupeyüm

On the plaza behind the bright green Municipalidad buildings • Daily 10am–8pm • CH$2500

The **Aldea Intercultural Trawupeyüm** is housed inside a traditional Mapuche ruca. An enthusiastic guide is on hand to talk you through the exhibits, which include traditional musical instruments.

ARRIVAL AND DEPARTURE   CURARREHUE

By bus Buses Curarrehue services run from Pucón (every 30min; 45min).

EATING

★ **Cocina Mapuche Mapu Lyagl** Camino Internacional s/n, on the right-hand side around 500m before the entrance to town ☎ 09 8788 7188. The highlight of the Mapuche town of Curarrehue is a meal with celebrated Mapuche chef Anita Epulef at the helm. You may taste roasted *piñónes* (fruit of the araucaria tree), roasted cornbread, quinoa creations and more. Mains from CH$7500. Jan, Feb & Dec daily noon–3pm (call ahead to confirm).

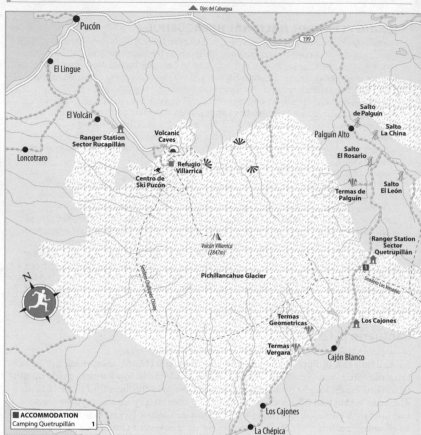

Parque Nacional Villarrica

15km south of Pucón · CH$5000 · ⓦ conaf.cl/parques/parque-nacional-villarrica

The centrepiece of the **Parque Nacional Villarrica** is, of course, **Volcán Villarrica**, in all its smoking, snowcapped glory (see page 269). Located just south of Pucón, the vast park divides into three sectors: **Rucapillán**, **Quetrupillán** and **Puesco**, and stretches 40km to the Argentine border (74km by road). It also contains two other volcanoes and is one of the few national parks in the Lake District in which you can camp wild and hike for long distances. If you plan on doing lengthy hikes, take the TrekkingChile (ⓦ trekkingchile.com) **map** of the national park, available in the town.

Sector Rucapillán

Sector Rucapillán, home to the magnificent **Volcán Villarrica** (2847m), presents a visual contradiction: below the tree line it's a lush forest; above, it's a black waste of lava, dotted with snow and encrusted with an icecap. The volcano forms the obvious focal point, standing sentinel over the park, and it's very active – there were sixteen recorded eruptions in the last hundred years, the most recent in 2015 (see page 269). A good 4km trail starts by the ski centre (see below), Los Cráteres, and runs to a lookout point (around 3hr return).

6

PARQUE NACIONAL VILLARRICA

Centro de Ski Pucón

12km southeast Pucón • Late June to mid-Oct 9am–5pm • Day ski pass CH$35,000

A good road branches off the Pucón–Villarrica road, running up the northern slopes of the volcano. After 7km you reach the **park entrance**, and almost halfway up is the **ski centre**. Skiing here is an experience, though the snow quality is not as consistent as at the resorts around Santiago or in Valle Nevado. While on good days the views are amazing, the nine ski lifts are affected when it's too windy.

The twenty runs are geared mostly towards beginners and intermediate skiers, though experienced boarders and skiers can have some fun off-piste. Boarders in particular can make use of the natural half-pipes created by the lava chutes. Agencies in Pucón rent cheaper skis and snowboards, and some run transport to the slopes in season.

VILLARRICA'S DEMONIC PEAKS

The area covered by **Parque Nacional Villarrica** was inhabited long before the arrival of the Spanish, and the **names of the peaks** reflect this: Volcán Villarrica's original Mapuche name, Rucapillán, means "house of the devil", because of its frequent eruptions, while Quetrupillán, the dormant volcano next door, means "mute devil". Another peak towards the border with Argentina is called Quinquili, or "devil's fang".

6

ACTIVITIES IN PARQUE NACIONAL VILLARRICA

Pretty much as soon as you arrive in Pucón, you'll realize that that town's main attraction is **Volcán Villarrica**, just begging to be climbed.

CLIMBING VOLCÁN VILLARRICA

Climbing Volcán Villarrica is a full-day excursion, usually leaving at around 7am, and prices are around CH$55,000. Climbing is not possible when the weather is bad, though some operators will still take customers up when it's cloudy, only to turn back halfway. The best of the volcano operators are Summit Chile (see page 273). The path leaves from the ski centre (see page 279); it's four hours up to a crater in which, if you're lucky and the gas clears, you'll see bubbling pits of molten rock. If it's not too windy, the chair lift (CH$10,000) trims an hour off the climb. While it doesn't demand technical climbing skills, you do need a hard hat, ice-axe, sturdy boots, gaiters, waterproof overtrousers and crampons – all provided by the tour agency you go with. The view from the top on a clear day is stupendous (though you won't linger for long because of the noxious fumes); this will be followed by a rollicking tobogganing down the side of the volcano along snow slides, using your ice-axe as a brake.

THE VILLARRICA TRAVERSE

Park Nacional Villarrica's best long-distance hike, the **Villarrica traverse** (72km; five days), starts at the ski centre and consists of three trails joined together. The first half comprises the moderately difficult **Sendero Challupen-Chinay** (28.5km; 14hr), which skirts around the southern side of Volcán Villarrica and ends at the Quetrupillán Conaf ranger post and the basic Chinay campsite, connected to the main road by a very rough 10km dirt track. From the ranger post, this dirt road continues on to Coñaripe (see page 281); you'll need a sturdy 4WD vehicle,

Sector Quetrupillán

Sector Quetrupillán, the middle section of the park, is dominated by the rarely visited majesty of Volcán Quetrupillán (2350m). It's a remote area of wilderness, tucked between two volcanoes and accessible only on foot or down a 35km dirt road that turns south from the Camino International 18km out of Pucón, climbing through native *coigüe* and araucaria forest. Here you can find the contemporary hotel at **Termas de Palguín**, with its all-curing waters, and also four splendid **waterfalls** – Palguín, La China, El León and Salto El Rosario – a little way off the main track.

Sector Puesco

East of Quetrupillán, close by the border with Argentina, the third part of the park, **Sector Puesco**, is a region of pine forests and craggy mountainsides. The Conaf station is at the Puesco frontier post. South of here, the tough **Sendero Momolluco** (22km; approx 8hr one way) leads southeast from the main road towards Volcán Lanín, before finishing at the remote Laguna Verde. From here, the **Sendero Lagos Andinos** (11km; 4hr 30min one way) loops back to the main road via Lagunas Huinfiuca, Plato and Escondida, ending at the east end of Lago Quilleihue, just across the main road. Make an easy day-walk of it by taking the Sendero Lagos Andinos partway from Lago Quilleihue.

ARRIVAL AND INFORMATION
PARQUE NACIONAL VILLARRICA

SECTOR RUCAPILLÁN

By organized tour There's no public transport to Sector Rucapillán, though there are dozens of tour buses. In the winter, most tour agencies will take you to the park for CH$10,000/person, leaving Pucón at 9.30am and returning at 4.30pm.

SECTORS QUETRUPILLÁN AND PUESCO

By bus For Sector Quetrupillán you can take a Curarrehue-bound bus from Pucón (hourly) along the international road, though the nearest you'll get will be the hamlet of Palguín Alto, 10km away down a dirt track. For Sector Puesco, get on an international bus heading to San Martín or Junín de los Andes in Argentina (several weekly) and

even in the summer. For the Sendero Challupen–Chinay section, you'll need to carry all your water with you as there are no streams to be relied on.

Sendero Los Venados heads southeast from the same ranger post, along the south side of Volcán Quetrupillán, passing the tranquil Laguna Azul – a haven for birds – before merging with the Sendero Las Avutardas (43.4km; three days), which finishes at the Argentina-bound road in the Puesco sector, around 2km south of the Conaf ranger post at Puesco. From here, you can hitch a lift to Curarrehue with the Chile-bound traffic. This section is crossed by numerous streams from which drinking water can be collected.

Many hikers choose to do the Chinay–Puesco section only, as it's more picturesque. From the Los Venados campsite, **Sendero Quetrupillán** ascends steeply to the eponymous volcano crater; allow 4hr return. Before you start out on any of the longer trails in the park, you must pay the park entry fee at the Conaf office in Pucón (see page 271) and inform them of your intended route/dates.

GUIDES AND PRICES

Conaf keeps a list of companies **authorized to guide** climbers up the volcano. A maximum of nine climbers are allowed with one guide. There is nothing to stop you from tackling the mountain without a guide, as long as you have proper equipment. Unless you're an experienced mountaineer, however, it's not advisable. Competition keeps prices down to a reasonable CH$55,000 or so, which includes transport and all necessary equipment. Most agencies start off at around 6.30am, though a couple leave at 4.30am to beat the crowds. Do not be tempted to go for the cheapest trip – cost is commensurate with safety, and companies offering much cheaper deals can sometimes do so by using inferior equipment and hiring inexperienced guides. We do not recommend Trancura or Politur due to their record of fatalities on the mountain. For recommended operators, see page 272.

ask to be dropped off; you should be able to get off at the Puesco customs post and Conaf station. Private transfers can be arranged in Pucón.

INFORMATION

Conaf Lincoyán 336, Pucón (Mon–Fri 8.30am–noon & 2–5pm; ☎ 45 244 3781). Rangers can advise on trail conditions and dish out rudimentary trail maps.

ACCOMMODATION

Wild **camping** is not allowed east of the Puesco border post. There are serviced campsites near the entrance to Rucapillán.

Camping Quetrupillán Near the Quetrupillán Conaf station; map p.278. The only campsite within the park: a remote site with simple pitches with fire pits and cold water showers. **CH$9000**

The Siete Lagos

Overshadowed by the popular resort of Pucón, the region known as **Siete Lagos** – Seven Lakes – is south of Villarrica. Six of the lakes are in Chile, one (Lago Lácar) in Argentina; all can be easily reached on a day-trip from Pucón or Villarrica.

The busiest lakes are the largest ones, the relatively warm **Lago Calafquén**, 30km south of Villarrica, and **Lago Panguipulli**, 17km further on. The next valley down contains the slightly smaller **Lago Riñihue**, hardly visited and perfect for nature lovers and fishermen. To the east of lagos Panguipulli and Riñihue, nestling deep in the pre-cordillera and surrounded by 2000m peaks, are the most remote of the Siete Lagos, **Lago Neltume** and **Lago Pirehueico**, near which you'll find some spectacular waterfalls, the region's best museum and its quirkiest hotels – all part of the private **Huilo Huilo reserve**.

Lago Calafquén and around

The most developed of the seven lakes, **Lago Calafquén** features a paved road for the 30km along its northern shore between the settlements of **Lican Ray** and **Coñaripe**, and a mostly paved road around the rest. To the east is tiny **Lago Pellaifa**, created by a 1960

6

SIETE LAGOS

EATING
Petermann Craft Brewery	2
Restaurante People	
Help People	1

ACCOMMODATION
| Montaña Mágica Lodge | 1 |

earthquake that altered the region's water flow. It's bordered by an international road to Argentina that passes a clutch of thermal springs around the mountain hamlet of **Liquiñe**.

Termas Geométricas

12km northeast of Coñaripe • Jan, Feb & late to end Dec daily 10am–11pm; March to late Dec shorter hours • CH$20,000–28,000 • 09 7477 1708, ☎ termasgeometricas.cl

The land around Coñaripe bubbles with numerous thermal springs, the most appealing of which is **Termas Geométricas**, with seventeen smart, slate-covered pools linked by a series of wooden walkways strung along 0.5km of lush mountain stream and peeping out of thickets of *nalca* (wild rhubarb). There's a decent restaurant. The road is good enough for city cars, and numerous companies in Pucón run trips (CH$35,000).

ARRIVAL AND DEPARTURE   LAGO CALAFQUÉN

By bus Lican Ray and Coñaripe are connected to Villarrica by hourly JAC services. There are also less frequent Pirehueico services (3–4 daily) from both Coñaripe and Liquiñe to Panguipulli.

Lago Panguipulli

Ten kilometres south of Lago Calafquén is the northern snout of long, thin **Lago Panguipulli**, a lake that stretches 26km southeast into the cordillera. On the lake's northwesternmost tip is the neat little town of **Panguipulli**, while a paved road skirts the eastern shore to the remote lagos **Neltume** and **Pirehueico**.

Panguipulli

The attractive village of **PANGUIPULLI**, bright with colourful roses, dark copper beech trees and manicured lawns, was founded in 1885 as a trading post for Pehuenche and Mapuche driven off the Argentine pampas. It grew beyond these humble origins in 1903 when a Capuchin mission was established here, and its church, **Iglesia de San Sebastián**, is an impressive twin-towered latticed confection of yellow, red, brown and white.

6

ARRIVAL AND INFORMATION   PANGUIPULLI

By bus The bus terminal is at Gabriela Mistral 1000. Buses Pirehueico (☎63 231 1497) serves Valdivia and Puerto Montt, while Buses Lafit (☎63 231 1647, ⓦbuseslafit.cl) runs to Puerto Fuy via Neltume.

Destinations Puerto Fuy via Neltume (Mon–Sat 10.40am, 5pm & 6.45pm, Sun 6.30pm & 7.30pm; 1hr 45min); Puerto Montt (3–4 daily; 3hr 30min); Valdivia (3-4 daily; 2hr 30min).
Tourist office Near the church, Plaza Arturo Prat (Jan & Feb daily 9am–8pm; March–Dec Mon–Sat 9am–5pm; ☎63 231 0435, ⓦsietelagos.cl).

EATING

Restaurante People Help People Martínez de Rozas 777 ☎63 231 0925 ⓦhotelescuela.cl; map p.282. Cheerful restaurant with smart service and imaginative dishes made with local ingredients. Try the trout *ceviche* or the baby ribs with red cabbage. Mains from CH$8600. Daily noon–3pm & 7–11pm.

Lago Neltume

The 38km road that skirts the eastern shore of Lago Panguipulli terminates at a T-junction. A good 16km gravel road heads east to the smallish **Lago Neltume**, passing through the village of Neltume and the **Reserva Huilo Huilo** en route to **Lago Pirehueico**. Before reaching Neltume, you pass a turnoff for the minor road that skirts the eastern shore of Lago Neltume before joining the Coñaripe–Liquiñe road; this eastern shore road is a narrow, gorgeous drive through the forest, possible in a regular car.

Salto del Huilo-Huilo

Daily 9am–8pm • CH$3000

Between Lago Neltume and the village of Neltume is the turnoff for the 37m waterfall, **Salto del Huilo-Huilo**, a powerful torrent forced through a 10m-wide green cleft in the rock, cascading into the swirling aquamarine pool below to deafening effect. It's a ten-minute walk through the woods to reach the viewpoint, and a further ten to reach the equally spectacular **Salto de Puma**.

Museo de Volcanes

Mon–Fri 8am–6pm, Sat & Sun 10am–6pm • CH$3000 • ⓦhuilohuilo.com

A turnoff from the Lago Neltume to Neltume village road, just before the *Montaña Mágica Lodge* hotel group (see page 284), leads to the architecturally striking **Museo de Volcanes**. The two floors showcase the most complete collection of **Mapuche** items

---

PUERTO PIREHUEICO: CROSSING THE ARGENTINE BORDER

From **Puerto Pirehueico**, it's 11km to the **Argentine border**, where there's a café and a customs post (8am–8pm year-round). There's no public transport from the border to San Martín de los Andes but, in peak season, TravelAid in Pucón (see page 272) offer a transfer-and-boat border crossing from Pucón to San Martín that takes in five Lake District lakes en route and culminates with the crossing of Lago Pirehueico.

in Chile, from the crescent stones of power and traditional musical instruments to the matchless collection of silver adornments – collars, pendants, necklaces passed from mother to daughter, spurs. Other exhibits focus on pre-Columbian pottery found near Arica and San Pedro and the geology of the region, with splendid examples of semi-precious stones.

Lago Pirehueico

Six kilometres beyond Lago Neltume lies **Lago Pirehueico**. Pirehueico means "worm of water" in the local Mapuche language, and there couldn't be a better name for this curving, twisting, snake-like lake, bordered by forest-clad mountains. It's crossed by a **ferry** from Puerto Fuy in the north to **Puerto Pirehueico** in the south. The crossing is beautiful and extremely worthwhile, whether as a day-trip or a one-way journey towards Argentina, not to mention far cheaper than the Puerto Varas–Bariloche crossing (see page 296).

ARRIVAL AND DEPARTURE   LAGO PIREHUEICO

By bus In summer there are buses between Panguipulli and Puerto Fuy (up to 7 daily).

By ferry Ferry Hua-Hum (w barcazahuahum.com) crosses Lago Pirehueico from Puerto Fuy in the north to Puerto

Pirehueico in the south (Jan to late March & mid-Dec to late Dec 5–6 daily 7am–7pm; April to mid-Dec 2–3 daily 9am–4pm; returning 2hr later; 1hr 30min; CH$990/CH$5480/CH$17,940/passenger/motorcycle/car).

ACCOMMODATION

Montaña Mágica Lodge Huilo Huilo reserve, Camino Internacional Panguipulli–Puerto Fuy Km 60 ☎63 267 2020, w huilohuilo.com; map p.282. This Tolkienesque creation, shaped like a grass-covered volcano with windows, encases uniquely shaped wood-panelled rooms and an entry hall with a stream running through it; if you are tall, get a room on one of the lower floors.

Wooden walkways connect the volcano to the beehive-meets-treehouse that is *Nothofagus Hotel* and the organic-spaceship-like *Reino Fungi* (all doubles cost the same). This trio of hotels – along with the new *Nawelpi* and *Marina del Fuy* lodges, also in the reserve – offers a bewildering array of tours and outdoor activities. US$267

EATING

Petermann Craft Brewery Camino Internacional Panguipulli–Puerto Fuy Km 60, w huilohuilo.com; map p.282. Across the road from the *Nothofagus Hotel*, this brewery-cum-pizzeria serves four palatable own

brews – a porter, amber ale, blond ale and lager – as well as thin and crispy pizzas, snacks and coffee. Daily noon–9pm.

Valdivia and around

Fifty kilometres west of the Panamericana lies the attractive city of **VALDIVIA**, one of Chile's oldest settlements, founded by Pedro de Valdivia as a supply halt on the route to Lima, six days' sail from the Magellan Strait. Post-independence there was a great influx of **German** settlers who founded shipyards, breweries and mills, leaving a lasting legacy. Today Valdivia is a vibrant, cosmopolitan university town, a mixture of the colonial and the contemporary, even though many of its old buildings are gone – lost to earthquakes, fires and floods throughout the last century.

Bierfest Kunstmann, at the end of January, celebrates the joys of locally produced craft beer, while on February 9 the city marks the founding of Valdivia, and between the second and third Saturday in February "Valdivia Week" sees the river light up with a **parade of boats** and a fireworks show.

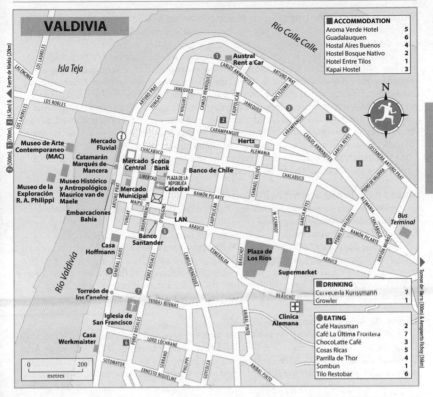

Map of Valdivia

ACCOMMODATION

Aroma Verde Hotel	5
Guadalauquen	6
Hostal Aires Buenos	4
Hostel Bosque Nativo	2
Hotel Entre Tilos	1
Kapai Hostel	3

DRINKING

Cervecería Kunstmann	2
Growler	1

EATING

Café Haussman	2
Café La Última Frontera	7
ChocoLatte Café	3
Cosas Ricas	5
Parrilla de Thor	4
Sombun	1
Tilo Restobar	6

The waterfront

Valdivia's social centre is not its plaza but its **waterfront**, where the Río Calle Calle and the Río Cau Cau meet the Río Valdivia. Just to the south of the Mercado Fluvial, touts offer ferry tours (see page 287).

Mercado Fluvial

Av Arturo Prat • Daily 8am–5pm

Valdivia's lively produce market, the **Mercado Fluvial**, sits on the riverfront, with fishermen expertly gutting the day's catch and throwing scraps to the clamouring seagulls, cormorants, pelicans and the gargantuan sea lions who wait right behind the fishmongers and treat the market as their local takeaway. Opposite, on the other side of the path, vendors sell all types of fruit, vegetables, strings of smoked shellfish and smoked salmon. Across the road, on the corner of Chacabuco and Pratt, the **Mercado Central** hosts inexpensive *marisquerías* (seafood restaurants).

Isla Teja

Opposite the town centre, across the Pedro de Valdivia bridge, **Isla Teja** is home to a trio of good **museums** and has beautiful views back across the river to the Mercado Fluvial.

6

Museo Histórico y Antropológico Maurice van de Maele

Jan & Feb daily 10am–8pm; March–Dec Tues–Sun 10am–1pm & 2–6pm • CH$1500 or CH$2500 for combined ticket with Museo de la Exploración R.A. Philippi • Ⓦ museosaustral.cl

Isla Teja's main attraction is the splendidly located **Museo Histórico y Antropológico Maurice van de Maele**, in an old colonial house surrounded by a veranda. Once owned by Karl Anwandter, founder of Chile's first brewery, it's still furnished with the trappings of nineteenth-century European society, including an ornate red-marble fireplace and a magic lantern. Also on display is an absorbing collection of old sepia prints, antique maps and household objects of the first German settlers, as well as the Anwandter and Haussmann family trees. Highlights include **Mapuche artefacts**, mainly splendid silverwork and textiles, a room of memorabilia pertaining to British-born Lord Cochrane, who played a decisive role in securing independence for Chile, and Chile's first piano, imported from Britain.

Museo de la Exploración R.A. Philippi

Jan & Feb daily 10am–8pm; March–Dec Tues–Sun 10am–6pm • CH$1500 or CH$2500 for combined ticket with Museo Histórico y Antropológico Maurice Van de Maele • Ⓦ museosaustral.cl

Dedicated to the groundbreaking German-born naturalist Rudolph Amadeus Philippi, the **Museo de la Exploración R.A. Philippi** is next door to the Museo Histórico y Antropológico, inside a Jugendstil building. Upstairs you'll find Philippi's study, complete with period furniture, numerous pickled denizens of the sea and a superb collection of photos of local wildlife, while the ground floor is occupied by larger fauna, colourful beetle and butterfly collections and local Mapuche crafts.

Museo de Arte Contemporáneo (MAC)

Jan & Feb daily 10am–2pm & 4–8pm; March–Dec Tues–Sun 10am–1pm & 3–7pm • Jan & Feb CH$1200; March–Dec free • Ⓦ mac.uchile.cl

Down by the water, housed in Valdivia's old Kunstmann brewery, is the **Museo de Arte Contemporáneo**, or **MAC**. MAC's changing exhibitions focus on contemporary art, installations, photography and graphic design by Chilean and international artists. Craft fairs featuring the best of the Lake District's woodwork, jewellery, art and more are held here, too.

ARRIVAL AND DEPARTURE | VALDIVIA

By plane Valdivia's Aeropuerto Pichoy (Ⓣ 63 227 2294 Ⓦ aeropuertovaldivia.com), 32km northeast of town, is served by LATAM (Maipú 271; Ⓦ latam.com) and Sky Airline (Ⓦ skyairline.cl). Transfer Aeropuerto Valdivia (Ⓣ 63 222 5533, Ⓦ transfervaldivia.cl; CH$5000/person) runs a door-to-door minibus service; a taxi should cost around CH$25,000.
Destinations Santiago (2 daily; 1hr 30min).

By bus Most long-distance buses travelling north–south along the Panamericana service the highly efficient bus terminal (Ⓣ 63 222 0498, Ⓦ terminalvaldivia.cl), on the corner of Anwandter and Muñoz, five blocks from the city centre; most bus company offices are here. Shared taxis to Niebla operate from the corner of Yungay and Chacabuco, and you can catch bus #20 along Independencia. Buses JAC

(Ⓣ 63 221 2925, Ⓦ jac.cl) has frequent departures to all major Lake District destinations; Pullman (Ⓣ 63 227 8576, Ⓦ pullman.cl) and Tur Bus (Ⓣ 63 221 3840, Ⓦ turbus.cl) serve the Lake District and all major destinations in central and northern Chile, while Cruz del Sur (Ⓣ 63 221 3840, Ⓦ busescruzdelsur.cl) heads to the island of Chiloé and Igi Llaima (Ⓣ 63 221 3542) and Andesmar (Ⓣ 63 222 4665, Ⓦ andesmar.com) cross the border to Argentina.
Destinations Ancud (4 daily; 5hr); Bariloche, Argentina (1 daily 8.15am; 8hr); Castro (4 daily; 7hr); Osorno (every 30min; 1hr 30min); Pucón (6 daily; 3hr 15min); Puerto Montt (every 30min; 3hr 45min); Puerto Varas (every 30min; 3hr); Santiago (hourly; 11hr); San Martín de Los Andes, Argentina (Wed, Fri & Sun 7.30am; 7hr 30min).

GETTING AROUND AND INFORMATION

Car rental Austral Rent a Car, Anwandter 288 (Ⓣ 63 221 2770, Ⓦ rentacaraustral.cl); Hertz, Av Alemania at Janequeo (Ⓣ 63 221 8316).
Tourist office Av Arturo Prat s/n (daily 9am–9pm; Ⓣ 63 223 9060, Ⓦ turismolosrios.cl). Very helpful Sernatur office

on the waterfront, with plenty of information on the region and maps of the city.
Hospital Clínica Alemana, Beaucheff 765 (Ⓣ 63 224 6201).

ACTIVITIES AND TOURS

Catamarán Marqués de Mancera Mercado Fluvial ☎63 224 9191, ⓦmarquesdemancera.cl. This catamaran runs a large loop behind Isla del Rey, with 35min stops at the Corral and Mancera forts (5hr; CH25,000–40,000, bilingual guide, lunch and *onces* included); tours depart at 1.30pm.

Embarcaciones Bahía Mercado Fluvial ☎63 237 8727. With four boats, Bahía specializes in 3hr tours of the Santuario de la Naturaleza Carlos Anwandter (see page 289), as well as cruises either to Isla Teja or Corral and Isla Mancera (CH$40,000; see page 288).

ACCOMMODATION

Aroma Verde Hotel Pedro de Valdivia 579 ☎63 223 0517, ⓦaromaverde.cl; map p.285. Just eight snug, wood-panelled rooms with all mod cons, creative use of recycled materials (such as old wood shingles, copper) and an excellent breakfast (including good coffee) distinguish this small boutique hotel. The staff are wonderfully helpful, too. CH$52,000

Guadalauquen Cochrane 173 ☎09 9843 6610, ⓦedificiogaudalauquen.cl; map p.285. A treat for independent travellers and excellent value for couples and families, these modern, fully equipped, spacious apartments are centrally located and can be rented overnight. CH$48,000

★ **Hostal Aires Buenos** García Reyes 550 ⓤ63 222 2202, ⓦairesbuenos.cl; map p.285. Central, American-owned hostel with serious eco credentials that engages its guests in its burgeoning permaculture project. Colourful, secure dorms and snug private rooms are popular with international backpackers, the communal spaces include a guest kitchen (they'll let you use herbs from their garden) and breakfast includes proper coffee and good bread. Dorms CH$12,000, doubles CH$32,000

Hostel Bosque Nativo Fresia 29 ☎63 243 3782, ⓦhostelnativo.cl; map p.285. This beautifully restored 1920s house offers cosy wood-panelled rooms, kitchen, lounge and rooftop terrace. There's just one dorm; the rest are private rooms, with solo travellers, couples and groups well-catered for. Profits go towards the preservation of native Chilean forest. Dorm CH$10,000, doubles CH$22,000

Hotel Entre Tilos Anwandter 624 ☎63 223 2359, ⓦhotelentretilos.com; map p.285. There are many reasons to like this new, three-storey boutique hotel: terraces on each storey, overlooking the river; the fourteen spacious, well-equipped rooms with excellent beds; the helpful staff; the extensive breakfast featuring home-made jams. No parking, though, and no lift. CH$75,000

Kapai Hostel Prat 737 ☎09 9207 2616; map p.285. The rooftop terrace overlooking the river is one of the boons at this new hostel, just a few minutes' walk from the bus terminal. The capsule-style dorms offer the most privacy (but the least fresh air); it's worth going for the four-bed dorm rather than the twelve-bedder. Bilingual owner Felipe is extremely helpful and the spacious kitchen and common area encourage lingering. Dorms CH$10,000, doubles CH$30,000

EATING

Café Haussman Av Los Robles 202 ☎63 222 2100, ⓦcafehaussman.cl; map p.285. This Isla Teja offshoot of the original, founded by Don Ricardo Haussmann in 1959 and harking back to Valdivia's German roots, serves its specialities of *crudos* (steak tartare) on toast (CH$1950), Kunstmann beers and excellent cakes (from CH$1700). Mon–Sat 8am–9pm.

★ **Café La Última Frontera** Pérez Rosales 787 ☎63 223 5264; map p.285. Everything about this café screams "bohemian", from the reggae on the stereo, mismatched colour scheme and photos of cats and tattoos gracing the walls to the grungy staff who serve you real coffee, sandwiches named after Etta James and Chairman Mao, and the selection of local microbrews. Mon–Sat 9am–2am.

ChocoLatte Café Anwandter 569 ☎63 229 0303; map p.285. Near the bus terminal and the river, this is the pick of Valdivia's cafés as far as good coffee is concerned. Wide assortment of interesting cupcakes and *kuchen* (cakes), too. Mon–Sat 9am–9pm.

Cosas Ricas Pérez Rosales 644 ☎63 222 0606; map p.285. This large, two-storey café serves locally roasted coffee and a good selection of Valdivian craft beers. Ample, creative breakfasts and wood-fired pizzas seal the deal. Lunch mains from CH$4000. Mon–Sat 9am–10pm.

Parrilla de Thor Prat 653 ☎63 227 0767; map p.285. This Argentinian steakhouse overlooking the river has a ski-lodgey feel and leisurely service, but serves satisfying slabs of grilled meats (sides cost extra). Mains from CH$9000. Daily noon–4pm & 8pm–midnight.

Sombun Andwandter 288 ☎09 7659 2055; map p.285. A first in the Lake District, this low-key little restaurant serves genuine Thai dishes such as *tom yum* (fragrant, spicy soup), *phad prik* (dry curry with meat), and *phad katit* (pork cooked in spiced coconut milk). The spice factor is toned down for local tastes, but genuine heat is provided on request. Mains CH$3500–5000. Daily 11am–midnight.

6

6

Tilo Restobar Yungay 745 ☎ 63 243 4594; map p.285. The large riverside terrace is ideal for lazy afternoon beers or (an extensive range of) cocktails, and the bistro serves terrific *ceviche*, palatable pizza and the likes of lamb and sage ravioli. Mains CH$7500–12,500. Mon–Fri 12.30–3pm & 6pm–midnight, Sat 7pm–midnight.

DRINKING

Cervecería Kunstmann 950 Ruta T-350 ☎ 63 229 2969, ⓦ cerveza-kunstmann.cl; map p.285. German-style beerhall serving monster portions of smoked meat, sauerkraut and potatoes to accompany its ten celebrated beers (from CH$2700). Tours of the celebrated brewery daily in peak season. To get here, take bus #20 bound for Niebla. Daily noon–midnight.

★ **Growler** Saelzer 1 ☎ 63 222 9545, ⓦ elgrowler. cl; map p.285. Not only is this Valdivia's premier craft beer brewery (with six own beers on tap and as many guest beers), it's also the nighttime gathering spot for locals and travellers alike. The Oregonian owner makes sure that the food doesn't let the side down either, from the delectable fish tacos and carpaccios to chunky sandwiches. Mains CH$6500–9000. Mon–Thurs noon–midnight, Fri & Sat noon–2am, Sun noon–11pm.

Niebla and around

At the mouth of the Río Valdivia, the village of **NIEBLA**, 18km west of Valdivia, is the base for boat trips to a number of interesting forts. Though the views from the ferry are sometimes obscured by the *niebla* (rolling fog) that lends the village its name, quite often you'll catch sight of sea lions and black-necked swans along the way.

Fuerte de Niebla

Niebla • Tues–Sun: Jan, Feb & Dec 10am–7pm; March–Nov 10am–5.30pm • Free • ⓦ museodeniebla.cl • Colectivos run regularly from Valdivia, leaving from Yungay near the Mercado Fluvial (CH$1200)

The **Fuerte de Niebla** (or Castillo de la Pura y Limpia Concepción de Montfort de Lemus) was built by the Spanish from 1667 to 1672 as part of an extensive line of defences of this key position in their empire. Today it houses a museum dedicated to the fortification of the Valdivia area, but more interesting are the old features: the powder room, double-walled and well below ground level, the crenellated curtain wall hacked out of the bare rock, and the twelve slightly rusting cannons.

Half the cannons are missing their cascabels; these are the original fort cannons which were defaced by the forces of Lord Thomas Cochrane (see page 473) when they overwhelmed the fort. Two of the original cannons now grace Santiago's Plaza de Armas.

Corral and around

The only way across the river from Niebla to Corral is on a 30min car ferry (daily every 30min–hourly 7am–midnight; adult CH$730, car CH$4620)

On the other side of the estuary from Niebla lies the little village of **CORRAL**; it was a thriving port until it was flattened by the 1960 tidal wave. Another Spanish fort, the somewhat dilapidated **Castillo de San Sebastián de la Cruz** (1645), with its 21 cannon – originally the most powerful of all the Spanish forts in the vicinity – is a short walk from the pier (daily 8.30am–7pm; CH$1700).

Castillo de San Pedro de Alcántara

Isla Mancera • Jan & Feb daily 10am–8pm; March–Dec Tues–Sun 10am–1pm & 2–6pm • Fort CH$700 • ⓦ museoaustral.cl • Five daily boats from Niebla (9.30am–6pm; CH$300)

Between Niebla and Corral sits the pretty **Isla Mancera**, with the most intact of the forts, **Castillo de San Pedro de Alcántara**, visible a little way up its forested side. The fort was built in 1645 and reinforced first in 1680 and later in 1762; its grounds house the atmospheric ruins of the San Francisco Convent and you can also descend into the dungeons. When the boat from Niebla drops you off, don't forget to ask to be picked up again.

Santuario de la Naturaleza Carlos Anwandter

Boat tours from Valdivia (see page 287)

After the 1960 earthquake, the 50km of low-lying land around the Río Cruces north of Valdivia was flooded, forming an extensive delta which has been protected as the UNESCO-listed **Santuario de la Naturaleza Carlos Anwandter**. This marsh now forms an important breeding ground and resting place for 119 species of birds, including the black-necked swan, black skimmer and the white-faced ibis.

Osorno

Despite being founded in one of the best defensive positions of all the Spaniards' frontier forts, **OSORNO** was regularly sacked by the Mapuche from 1553 until 1796. From tentative beginnings, it has grown into a thriving agricultural city mainly as a result of the industry of European settlers who felled the forests and began to develop the great dairy herds that form the backbone of the local economy today. The German heritage is evident in the row of **wooden houses** along Calle Mackenna, built between 1876 and 1923.

The transport hub for the southern Lake District and starting point for the region's main road into Argentina, Osorno is also the gateway for **Parque Nacional Puyehue**. It is also notable for its two contemporary **churches**: the **Catedral San Mateo** on the Plaza de Armas, and **Iglesia San Francisco** on Prat, three blocks east – controversial creations of concrete and lattice that divide opinion still.

Museo Municipal

Matta 809 • Mon–Fri 9.30am–6pm, Sat & Sun 2–6pm • Free

Osorno's one worthwhile attraction is the **Museo Municipal**, where displays run the gamut from prehistory (including a fine mummy from the Atacama Desert) to stones of power, ritual drums and heavy silver collars, found in the Mapuche room. Upstairs, walk through the history of the town and take a glimpse at its lively cultural life in the late nineteenth century.

ARRIVAL AND DEPARTURE

OSORNO

By plane Aeropuerto Carlos Hott Siebert, 7km east, is served by daily LATAM and Sky Airline flights from Santiago. Taxis to town cost around CH$8000 and any bus to Entre Lagos (CH$800) can drop you at the airport entrance. The LATAM office is at Ramírez 802 (ⓦlatam.com).

Destinations Santiago (2 daily; 2hr).

By bus Buses from Osorno serve all major destinations along the Carretera Austral from the central Terminal de Buses at Errázuriz 1400 (☎64 221 1120), while the Terminal de Buses Rurales, a block away at Mercado Municipal, Errázuriz 1300, serves Aguas Calientes with Expreso Lago Puyehue (☎64 224 3919) and Anticura with Buses Carlos (☎9 9408 8453). Bariloche, Argentina, is served by Igi Llaima (☎64 223 4371) and Cruz del Sur

(☎64 223 2777). There are also departures for Coyhaique (see page 362) with Queilen Bus (☎64 226 0025, ⓦqueilenbus.cl) and Buses Transaustral (☎64 223 3050) via Argentina. JAC (☎64 264 3114, ⓦjac.cl) serves all major Lake District destinations, as does Tur Bus (☎64 223 4170, ⓦturbus.cl), which also serves Santiago.

Destinations Aguas Calientes, Puyehue (hourly 8am–7pm; 1hr 30min); Anticura, Puyehue (daily 5pm; 1hr 30min); Bariloche, Argentina (5 daily; 5hr); Coyhaique (1 weekly; 20hr); Puerto Montt (every 30min; 1hr 30min); Puerto Octay (5 daily; 1hr); Puerto Varas (every 30min; 1hr); Santiago (hourly; 10hr); Temuco (every 30min; 3hr); Valdivia (every 30min; 1hr 30min).

INFORMATION

Tourist office O'Higgins 667 (Mon–Fri 9am–6pm; ☎64 223 4104). Sernatur's helpful information office in the

Gobernación building on the west side of the Plaza de Armas has good city maps and accommodation lists.

6

ACCOMMODATION

Hostal Vermont Toribio Medina 2020 ☎ 64 224 7030, ⓦ hostalvermont.cl. A proper backpacker hostel, run by a bilingual Chilean, with a set of simple rooms and a great upstairs outdoor terrace for socializing. It's around eight blocks southeast of the bus terminal. Dorms CH$12,500, doubles CH$30,500.

Hostel Chaman Angulo 556 ☎ 9 5410 1213, ⓦ hostelchaman.cl. Just around the corner from the main bus station, yet enjoying the tranquility of its leafy location, this guesthouse has a cluster of spotless rooms

(with skylights making up for the windows that don't open), a dorm and a guest kitchen. Dorms CH$12,500, doubles CH$22,500.

Santuario Patagonia Hotel Boutique Camino a Pilauco 546 ☎ 9 7568 4847, ⓦ santuariopatagonia.cl. Just four blocks from the city centre, this old world hotel presides over lush grounds. Each room is individually decked out with native woods and punchy wallpaper and there's an excellent (meat-heavy) restaurant next door. CH$93,000

EATING

By far the best place to find a cheap and filling meal is the **market** by the rural bus terminal.

★ **Panca Sabor Peruano** Rodríguez 1905 ☎ 64 223 2924, ⓦ panca.cl. Genuine Peruvian food in a cutting-edge setting is a welcome find. From the super-fresh *ceviche* and *jalea del mar* (battered fish), to the *arróz con mariscos* (seafood rice) and *ají de gallina* (chicken in a spicy yellow sauce), the flavours are hard to fault. Mains CH$7500–13,500. Mon–Fri & Sun 1–3pm & 8pm–midnight, Sat 1–3.30pm.

Parrilla El Galpón Cochrane 816 ☎ 64 223 9922, ⓦ hotelwaeger.cl. The steak list at Osorno's finest grill includes the signature Tomahawk and a supporting cast of filet mignons, sirloins and skirt steaks. The decor is rustic barn meets sleek bistro and there's a succinct wine list. Mains CH$10,000–18,500. Mon–Sat 12.30–3pm & 7.30–11.30pm.

Parque Nacional Puyehue and around

81km east of Osorno • CH$1500, payable only in the Anticura section of the park • ⓦ conaf.cl/parques/parquet-nacional-puyehue

Parque Nacional Puyehue is one of Chile's busiest national parks, largely because of the traffic on the international road that runs through its centre. It's part of a massive, 15,000-square-kilometre area of protected wilderness, bordering the Parque Nacional Vicente Pérez Rosales to the south, and some Argentine parks that stretch all the way to Parque Nacional Villarrica in the north. The land is high temperate rainforest spread over two volcanoes, Volcán Puyehue (2236m) to the north, and Volcán Casablanca (2240m), on the west slope of which is the Antillanca ski resort. The park is divided into three sectors: **Aguas Calientes**, where the *termas* are; **Antillanca**; and **Anticura**, straddling the international road near the Argentine border.

The 47km road that shoots east from Osorno to **Lago Puyehue** passes through the nondescript village of **Entre Lagos**. Around 30km beyond Entre Lagos, the road forks: the left-hand road heads on to the Anticura section of the national park and the Argentine border, while the right-hand one leads to the Aguas Calientes section and the Antillanca ski resort.

Note that **wild camping** is permitted in the national park.

Aguas Calientes

At **AGUAS CALIENTES** you'll find a Conaf Centro de Información Ambiental (see page 265) where there's a large, detailed **map of the park**, along with basic park maps. Aguas Calientes is also home to the most accessible of the Puyehue area's **hot springs** (ⓦ termasaguascalientes.cl), right at the park's entrance. There's a hot outdoor pool and a very hot indoor pool (daily 9am–7pm; day pass CH$23,000/CH$25,000 for outdoor pool only/both pools).

6

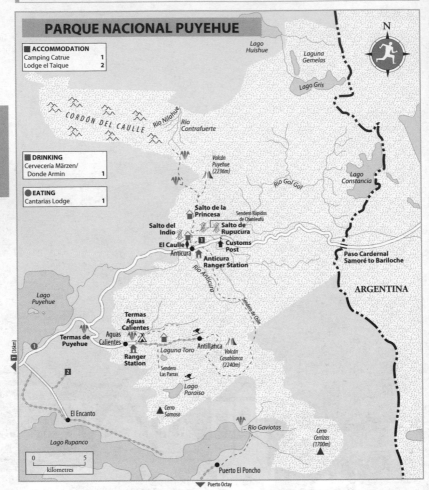

Walks in the area consist mainly of short, self-guided **nature trails**, such as the Sendero Rápidos del Chanleufú, a 1250m track alongside the river rapids. There are also a couple of **longer trails** (see page 293).

Antillanca

Ski season July & Aug • ☎ 64 261 2070, ⊛ skiantillanca.cl • Ski day-passes around CH\$32,000

The **ski centre** at **ANTILLANCA** lies 18km from Aguas Calientes by rather rough road, at the foot of the Volcán Casablanca (also known as Antillanca). The centre has three T-bar lifts, one chair lift and ski slopes with more than two dozen runs, including at least eight challenging off-piste slopes. In summer the ski runs turn into a mountain-biking park (CH\$5000 for 2hr rent), plus you can hike to the crater.

Trails from Antillanca

Several (free) **trails** begin at Antillanca, including the 3.7km **Cerro Volcán Casablanca**, which ascends the eponymous volcano, where you can peer into its crater (2hr one way); the challenging 50km **Anticura–Antillanca traverse** (see below); and the multi-day **Sendero de Gaviotas** that passes along the east shore of Lago Rupanco (where you can camp or stay in a basic guesthouse) before leading south to Laguna Los Quetros and beyond. Halfway between Aguas Calientes and Antillanca, the little-trodden **Lago Paraíso** trail branches off from the main road towards the pretty namesake lake (5km; 2hr one way), where there's a shelter and basic campsite; from here another 4.6km trail continues to the secluded **Lago El Palmar** (2hr one way). Finally, the steep swtichbacks of **Sendero Bertín** traverse the slopes of Volcán Antillanca before the trail descends to Aguas Calientes (20km; 6hr one way).

Anticura

ANTICURA lies 22km east of Aguas Calientes, just off the main Ruta 215 to Argentina. There's an information centre where you pay the CH$2000 **fee** to walk the short **trails** and arrange accommodation, and a Conaf ranger post across the road. The information centre has an exhibition on the 2011 eruption of Volcán Puyehue, complete with mind-blowing photographs.

Short trails

One of the prettiest of the short **hikes** is the 900m walk to El Salto del Indio, a thirty-minute loop through a forest of ancient *coigüe* to a pretty **waterfall** amid dense greenery. A slightly longer 1.2km walk leads to **Salto de la Princesa**, another waterfall. Across the road, from the Conaf side, a steep 1km track leads to the single gushing fall of **Salto de Pudú** (40min) while from the other side of the office, a moderate 1.2km ascent (40min) brings you to the **Miradór del Puma**, where you get a great view of Salto Anticura and the Volcán Puyehue beyond.

Sendero Pampa Frutilla

The 50km (two days) **Sendero Pampa Frutilla** trail leads from behind the Anticura Conaf office to Antillanca, forming part of the Sendero de Chile. The track is reasonably well maintained and signposted and runs through lush *ulmo*, *coigüe* and *lenga* forest, skirting the eastern flank of Volcán Casablanca and affording great views of the neighbouring volcanoes. The last part of the trail is a steep slog over volcanic slopes. Roughly halfway along, a 10km trail branches off east, taking you to two pretty little lagoons harbouring a wealth of waterfowl and a rudimentary shelter.

Volcán Puyehue trail

Another adventurous hike is the 32km return trail to **Volcán Puyehue** (2–3 days), which starts 2km west of Anticura, at the *El Caulle* restaurant (☎09 5008 6374, ⓦelcaulle. com; follow the signposts). The beginning of the trail crosses private land belonging to the restaurant owners; you have to pay a CH$10,000 entrance fee. This pays for trail maintenance and entitles you to use the basic *refugio*, which sleeps fourteen; it's a three-hour walk along the trail from the Conaf office. You can also stow any excess luggage at the restaurant and splurge on a grilled meat feast upon your return.

Shortly beyond the *refugio*, the trail forks. The right-hand route goes up the volcano; from the crater there are views over lagos Puyehue and Rupanco. The left-hand path skirts the crater, leading to a thermal spring next to an icy stream, half a day's walk from the *refugio*. You can mix the waters and bathe – an amazing experience at night, cooking yourself gently in the waters underneath the stars. For an extra treat, leave your gear in your tent and hike for another couple of hours along the ridge to another set of hot springs before returning for the night and descending the next day.

ARRIVAL AND INFORMATION

By bus Expreso Lago Puyehue runs several daily buses from Osorno to Aguas Calientes between 7am and 7pm. There is no public transport from Osorno to Antillanca, but private transfers can be arranged via the *Antillanca Hotel* (CH$70,000 for up to four people; CH$80,000 for up to ten people).

PARQUE NACIONAL PUYEHUE

By car Take Ruta 215 from the Panamericana towards the Argentinian border. The road to Antillanca is a somewhat bumpy and narrow gravel road.
Tourist information The Conaf office at Aguas Calientes (Mon–Fri 9am–1pm & 2–6pm) is the most helpful.

ACCOMMODATION

Camping Catrue Ruta 215 Km 90 ☎09 9104 8061, ⓦanticura.com; map p.292. Large, sheltered campsite in the Anticura section of the park, with electricity, hot showers and fire pits. There are also secluded, chalet-like *cabañas* for up to eight people and a café in the visitor centre serving local standards. Camping CH$7000, *cabañas* CH$45,000

★ **Lodge El Taique** Ruta 215 Km 76 ☎65 297 0980, ⓦlodgeeltaique.cl; map p.292. A tranquil woodland

location, beautiful lodge with eight luxurious rooms, two fully equipped *cabañas* with volcano views and hot tub access – this French-run retreat has a lot going for it. The owners are founts of local knowledge when it comes to trekking in the region, too. There's also an excellent on-site restaurant (open to non-guests), serving the likes of steak with quinoa, wild boar goulash and profiteroles. Doubles CH$78,000, *cabañas* CH$90,000

EATING

Cantarias Lodge Ruta 215 Km 63.5 ☎64 261 2320, ⓦcantarias.com; map p.292. This is a gorgeous, exclusive five-room boutique lodge popular with the flyfishing set. The spacious, stylish rooms (CH$260,000) can't be faulted, but are overpriced. It's well worth visiting

the restaurant, though, which is the best in the region, to sample the likes of duck confit with apple mash and grilled shrimp and vegetable risotto (mains CH$11,000–15,000). Daily noon–4pm & 7–10pm.

DRINKING

Cervecería Märzen/Donde Armin Ruta 215 Km 10 ☎09 8294 1818; map p.292. Fantastic German-owned microbrewery hidden behind trees en route from Osorno to Parque Nacional Puyehue. Sample the Bock, Doppeldock

and Märzen, accompanied by the likes of bratwurst and other meaty German goodies, in the attractive *biergarten*. Tues–Sat 1.30–11pm.

Lago Llanquihue and around

Located just off the Panamericana, **Lago Llanquihue** is an immense inland sea of 870 square kilometres, a backdrop for one of the icons of the Lake District, the Mount Fuji-like **Volcán Osorno** (2661m), in all its stunning, symmetrical perfection, surrounded by gently rolling pastures. The little towns and villages around Lago Llanquihue have a shared German heritage, but differ greatly in character. **Puerto Varas** is a bustling adventure tourism centre to rival Pucón, **Frutillar** is a summer holiday resort beloved by Chileans, and **Puerto Octay** is a neat little Bavarian-looking town. By the time you come to the village of **Ensenada**, on the far eastern shore of the lake, forest has overtaken dairy fields and the land begins to rise as you enter the foothills of the Andes. This forest extends to the border, and is protected by the **Parque Nacional Vicente Pérez Rosales**. The national park is a favourite scenic route into Argentina, taking in the magical green waters of **Lago Todos Los Santos**.

South of Ensenada the road winds its way down through isolated country to the placid calm of Chile's northernmost fjord, a branch of the **Estuario de Reloncaví**. Here you can horse-trek into South America's oldest rainforest – the famous *alerce* groves found in the valleys above the village of **Cochamó**.

Puerto Varas

Arguably the most appealing base along the shore of Lago Llanquihue, **PUERTO VARAS** is a spruce little town with wide streets, grassy lawns and exquisite views of two volcanoes, Osorno and Calbuco, particularly at sunset. Puerto Varas is a prime location for all manner of outdoor activities, with volcanoes, rivers and forests throwing down a gauntlet that few outdoor enthusiasts can refuse.

The town's German colonial architecture gives it a European feel, and notable early twentieth-century private residences include **Casa Kuschel**, on Klenner 299 (1910), Casona Alemana (1914) at Nuestra Señora del Carmen 788 and Casa Ángulo (1910) at Miraflores 96.

ARRIVAL AND DEPARTURE

PUERTO VARAS

By plane The nearest airport is near Puerto Montt, with flights to Santiago and Punta Arenas (see page 385) offered by LATAM (office at Av Gramado 560; ⓦlatam.com) and Sky Airline (ⓦskyairline.cl). Most lodgings can organize airport transfers (CH$18,000).

By bus All bus companies are scattered around the outskirts of Puerto Varas and no longer have offices in the centre. Tur Bus (☎65 223 3787, ⓦturbus.cl), Tas Choapa (☎65 223 3787, ⓦtaschoapa.cl) and JAC/Cóndor (☎65 238 3800, ⓦjac.cl) share a terminal at Del Salvador 1093; Cruz del Sur (☎65 223 6969, ⓦbusescruzdelsur.cl) is at San Francisco 1317; Pullman (☎65 223 4612, ⓦpullman.cl) is at San Francisco 1004 and Andesmar (☎65 223 4053, ⓦandesmar.com) is at San Francisco 1119. Tur Bus

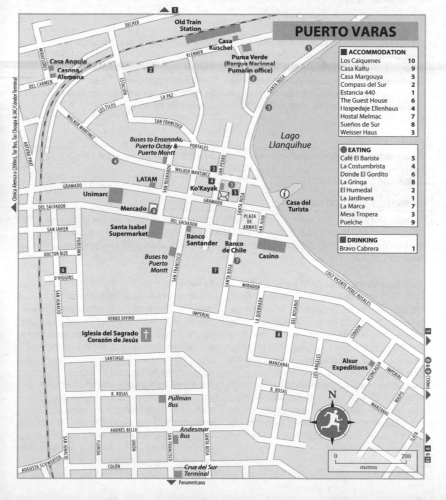

PUERTO VARAS

■ **ACCOMMODATION**
Los Caiquenes	10
Casa Kalfu	9
Casa Margouya	5
Compass del Sur	2
Estancia 440	1
The Guest House	6
Hospedaje Ellenhaus	4
Hostal Melmac	7
Sueños de Sur	8
Weisser Haus	3

● **EATING**
Café El Barista	5
La Costumbrista	4
Donde El Gordito	6
La Gringa	8
El Humedal	2
La Jardinera	1
La Marca	7
Mesa Tropera	3
Puelche	9

■ **DRINKING**
Bravo Cabrera	1

6

6

THE LAND-AND-LAKE CROSSING INTO ARGENTINA

If you're Argentina-bound, taking the **land-and-lake crossing** between Puerto Varas and San Carlos de Bariloche allows you to experience the beauty of Chile's **Parque Nacional Vicente Perez Rosales**, and is an excellent alternative to a long bus journey. The bus leaves at 8am, driving along the banks of Lago Llanquihue to **Petrohué**, where you baord the ferry that takes you across **Lago Todos Los Santos**, a spectacular expanse of clear blue-green. As you sail along the densely forested shores, skirting lovely Isla Margarita, the volcanoes Osorno (2661m) and Puntiagudo (2493m) loom to the north, with the majestic Tronador (3491m) to the east. You stop for lunch in Peulla, but since the only place to eat is a fairly pricey and mediocre restaurant at *Hotel Peulla*, it's worth packing a picnic lunch and going for a stroll to see the nearby waterfall instead. After going through **Chilean customs** at Peulla, you then cross the Argentine border at **Paso Pérez Rosales**, and get stamped in at tiny Puerto Frías. At this point you'll board the ferry again for the short crossing of Laguna Frías, then transfer by bus to your final nautical leg of the journey – a car ferry across the vast **Lago Nahuel Huapi**, arriving at your destination around 9pm. At US$280, crossing by lake is significantly pricier than a bus journey, but the scenery is worth it. Book this popular trip in advance with **Turistour** (☎65 243 7127, ✆turistour.cl).

and Pullman serve all major destinations between Puerto Montt and Santiago, while JAC covers the Lake District, Tas Choapa runs to Argentina and Cruz del Sur serves Chiloé. The efficient minibuses that connect Puerto Varas to Ensenada, Petrohué, Frutillar and Puerto Octay stop at a bus shelter at San Bernardo 240, while the Puerto Montt buses stop along San Francisco.

Destinations Ancud (8 daily; 2hr 30min); Castro (8 daily; 4hr); Ensenada (hourly; 1hr); Frutillar (4 daily; 40min); Puerto Montt (every 15min; 30min); Puerto Octay (2 daily; 1hr 15min); Santiago (6 daily; 16hr).
By boat There are daily boat crossings to Bariloche, Argentina (see above).

INFORMATION

Tourist office On the wharf, Piedraplén s/n, Muelle de Puerto Varas (Mon–Fri 9am–6.30pm, Sat & Sun 10am– 6.30pm; ☎65 223 7956, ✆puertovaras.org).

Hospital Clínica Alemana, Otto Bader 810 (☎65 258 2100).

ACTIVITIES AND TOURS

The **main tours** offered by the many companies in Puerto Varas are rafting on the Río Petrohué (grade 3 and 4; from CH$35,000/half-day); climbing Volcán Osorno (from CH$140,000); hiking in the Parque Nacional Vicente Pérez Rosales and Alerce Andino (day-trip around CH$35,000); and horseriding, generally on the slopes of Volcán Calbuco, through old *coigüe* forest (from CH$55,000/half-day).

Alsur Expeditions Aconcagua at Imperial ☎65 223 2300, ✆alsurexpeditions.com. As well as offering standard trips, Alsur specializes in multi-day sea-kayaking to the northern part of Parque Nacional Pumalín (see page 350), rafting trips on the Ríos Petrohué, Puelo and Futaleufú, and hiking in Parque Nacional Vicente Pérez Rosales and Parque Nacional Alerce Andino (see page 347).
Campo Aventura Around 4km south of Cochamó ☎09 9289 4314 or ☎09 9289 4318, ✆campo-aventura. com. This experienced American operator runs multi-day horseriding adventures in the Cochamó Valley (see page 304) and the Río Puelo Valley (see page 306), complete with stays at their two lodges.

Ko'Kayak San Pedro 311 ☎65 223 3004, ✆kokayak. cl. Excellent French-run multilingual rafting and kayaking specialists who run half- to four-day rafting trips in the Lake District, as well as one- or three-day sea kayaking trips, with more challenging twelve-day expeditions to the southern fjords. Adrenaline-filled options include rafting the Petrohué in smaller, four-person rafts and riding a whitewater kayak as a passenger.
Yak Expediciones ☎09 8332 0574 or ☎09 9299 6487, ✆yakexpediciones.cl. Long-standing operator running multi-day sea-kayaking adventures to the northern part of Parque Nacional Pumalín (see page 350), Chepu valley in Chiloé and the Reloncaví Fjord, as well as multi-day trekking and horseriding in Río Puelo Valley and day kayaking on Todos Los Santos (CH$72,000).

ACCOMMODATION

HOTELS, B&B AND LODGES

★ **Los Caiquenes** Ruta 225 Km 9.5 ☎ 09 8159 0489, ⓦ hotelloscaiquenes.cl; map p.295. In a beautiful setting on the shores of Lago Llanquihue, this wood-shingled boutique hotel oozes tranquillity. All centrally heated, cream-coloured rooms are decked out in native woods, with king-size beds and jacuzzis in the bathrooms. As for the food, the chef uses locally sourced ingredients to put together a creative menu that changes daily. **US$350**

Casa Kalfu Tronador 1134 ☎ 65 275 1261, ⓦ casakalfu. cl; map p.295. With a warm colour scheme and weavings on the walls by celebrated local artists, this rambling, blue-hued, 1940s German mansion attracts a lively European, Argentine and Brazilian clientele. The spacious, homely rooms are centrally heated and you can relax on the terrace overlooking the lake. **CH$86,000**

Estancia 440 Decher 440 ☎ 65 223 3921, ⓦ estancia440.cl; map p.295. Efforts have been made to give this boutique B&B an *estancia* look – from huge sepia prints of *huasos* (Patagonian cowboys) to woollen bedspreads and baskets of yarn. The bathrooms of the artfully rustic en suites thoughtfully come with heated floors and the breakfast is ample. **CH$71,000**

The Guest House O'Higgins 608 ☎ 65 223 1521, ⓦ theguesthouse.cl; map p.295. This characterful B&B is housed inside a beautifully restored 1926 mansion. There are eleven big, sunny rooms, bathrooms with actual tubs, a living room with a wonderful collection of art books and an extensive breakfast including home-made jams and granola. **CH$35,000**

Sueños de Sur Imperial 204 ☎ 65 271 1907, ⓦ suenosdesur.com; map p.295. With just four homely rooms, this cosy blue-shingled house is run by friendly *Santiagueños*. Cristina makes you feel welcome and her home-made breads and jams are a real breakfast treat. As for the rooms, great emphasis is placed on quality: good mattresses, powerful showers, superior linen and towels. **CH$65,000**

Weisser Haus Martínez 252 ☎ 65 234 6479, ⓦ weisserhaus.cl; map p.295. As central as you can get, this German mansion is a boutique hotel consisting of just ten rooms, with plenty of Mapuche carvings and antique Singer sewing machines scattered about. The well-appointed rooms are decked out in neutral colours and the staff are wonderfully attentive. **CH$78,000**

HOSTELS

Casa Margouya Santa Rosa 318 ☎ 65 223 7640, ⓦ margouya.com; map p.295. This ever-popular hostel has a great downtown location, a smattering of dorms and a snug double branching off from the lounge area. There's a good ratio of guests/bathroom and the owner can help organize all manner of outdoor adventures. Dorms **CH$10,000**, double **CH$22,000**

★ **Compass del Sur** Klenner 467 ☎ 65 223 2044, ⓦ compassdelsur.cl; map p.295. This lovely three-storey hostel is popular with international travellers of all ages, who come to appreciate the creaky wooden floors, snug attic rooms, powerful showers and communal vibe. The helpful staff or the friendly Chilean/Swedish owners can help you organize your stay. Dorms **CH$12,500**, doubles **CH$34,000**

Hospedaje Ellenhaus Walker Martínez 239 ☎ 65 223 3577, ⓦ ellenhaus.cl; map p.295. This super-central labyrinth of compact rooms is your best bet for a cheap swing-a-cat single (facilities shared) or double (some en suite). Wi-fi works everywhere. Breakfast CH$3500 extra. **CH$30,000**

Hostal Melmac Santa Rosa 608 ☎ 65 223 0863, ⓦ melmacpatagonia.com; map p.295. Up a steep staircase from the centre, this self-proclaimed "hostel from another world" features a snug three-bed dorm, two individually decorated doubles, a twin and plenty of *buena onda* (good vibes). The Argentinian/Colombian owner is good to share a beer with and he sometimes hosts barbecues in the garden. Dorms **CH$14,000**, doubles **CH$45,000**

EATING

CAFÉS AND CHEAP EATS

Café El Barista Walker Martínez 211 ☎ 65 223 3130, ⓦ elbarista.cl; map p.295. A great spot for people-watching, this trendy café serves some of the best coffee for miles around, with large slices of tasty *kuchen* and a good *menú del día* (CH$8500) that might involve vegetable risotto and palm heart salad. Becomes a happening bar in the evening. Daily 9am–late.

La Costumbrista Del Salvador 547 ☎ 09 6237 2801; map p.295. It's hard to beat this café for the sheer price/quality ratio. Frequently changing dishes on the succinct menu may include ossobuco, German-style pork chop, grilled hake and pasta of the day. The killer pisco sours are

the cherry on the cake. Mains from CH$5000. Mon–Sat 1–4pm & 7–9.30pm.

Donde El Gordito San Bernardo 560 ☎ 65 223 3425; map p.295. Busy little local institution inside the market, its walls and ceilings covered in knick-knacks, and serving large portions of inexpensive fish and seafood to hungry locals. Squid in *pil-pil* sauce, clams baked with parmesan, grilled fish – it's all fresh and fantastic. Anthony Bourdain ate here. Mains from CH$6500. Daily 11am–10pm.

★ **La Gringa** Imperial 605 ☎ 65 223 1980; map p.295. *La Gringa*'s expat owner hails from Seattle and has done her best to re-create her home town's perfect rainy

6

6

day café vibe, one that locals and travellers gravitate to. There are sticky, gooey cinnamon rolls and chocolate chip cookies to go with your coffee, and come noon the place fills up with ladies that lunch, with imaginative soups, salads and the likes of pulled pork sandwiches gracing the menu. *Menú del día* CH$9000. Mon–Sat 9am–8pm.

Puelche Imperial 695 ⓣ 09 4229 2499, ⓦ hotelpuelche.cl; map p.295. Inside the namesake hotel, this casual bistro, staffed by young, enthusiastic servers, is the place in Puerto Varas for vast, American-style burgers – with bacon, with barbecue sauce, with battered onion rings, and more. Wash them down with an immense mint lemonade. Burgers from CH$4500. Tues–Sun 12.30–4pm & 7.30–11pm.

RESTAURANTS

★ **El Humedal** Turismo 145 ⓣ 65 223 6382; map p.295. On a slight hillock overlooking the waterfront, this sleek bistro makes the most of local, seasonal ingredients to create internationally inspired dishes such as shiitake and prawn dim sum, seafood *ceviche* with *aji verde*, seafood-fried rice and abalone *empanadas*. Mains from CH$8200. Mon–Sat 12.30–11.30pm, Sun 12.30–4.30pm.

La Jardinera Blanco Encalada 1160 ⓣ 65 223 1684, ⓦ lajardinera.cl; map p.295. At the northern end of the *costanera*, this stylish restaurant offers an upscale take on Chilean standards with a twist. Expect the likes of grilled conger eel with seafood broth, polenta with mushroom ragout and slow-cooked lamb. Mains CH$8000–11,000. Mon–Sat 1–3.30pm & 8–11pm, Sun 1–3.30pm.

★ **La Marca** Santa Rosa 539 ⓣ 65 223 2026, ⓦ lamarca.cl; map p.295. With *gaucho* music on the stereo and cowboy paraphernalia on the wall, this is one of the best steakhouses in the Lake District. The *bife de chorizo* is mouthwateringly juicy and the menu features a few less common items, such as *criadillos* (bull's testicles). The wine list is succinct and well chosen. Mains from CH$10,000. Mon–Sat 12.30–11pm, Sun 1–4pm.

Mesa Tropera Santa Rosa 161 ⓣ 65 223 7973, ⓦ mesatropera.cl; map p.295. Jutting out over the lake, this long, wood-panelled pizzeria/beer bar is always hopping. Ironically, pizza is the least appealing of their offerings: go for the grilled octopus or the salmon tartar instead and wash it down with one of eight craft beers from Tropera's brewery in Coyhaique (see page 362). Mains from CH$6000. Mon–Sat 10am–2am.

DRINKING

★ **Bravo Cabrera** Vicente Pérez Rosales 1071 ⓣ 65 223 3441, ⓦ bravocabrera.cl; map p.295. This is still one of the "it" places and justifiably so: "BC" has an incomparable selection of around fifty beers, including many Chilean microbrews, as well as excellent wood-fired pizzas, *tablas* to share, and vast platters of slow-cooked ribs. Occasional DJs liven up this already lively lakefront joint. Mon–Thurs 7pm–2am, Fri & Sat 12.30pm–3am, Sun 12.30–6pm.

Frutillar

The Panamericana first approaches Lago Llanquihue at **Frutillar Alto**, 4km west of **Frutillar Bajo** – the two are collectively known as **FRUTILLAR**. The town's **beaches** get very crowded with locals in summer, as does the town in general, especially during the last week of January and the first week of February, when the town hosts **Semanas Musicales** (ⓦ semanasmusicales.cl), a **classical music festival**. Frutillar can easily be visited as a day-trip from Puerto Varas; accommodation tends to be expensive and catering to well-heeled older travellers.

Teatro del Lago Sur

Av Philippi 1000 • ⓦ teatrodellago.cl

A state-of-the-art music venue that would do any capital city proud, the cutting-edge, copper-roofed **Teatro del Lago Sur** rises above the waterfront, against a backdrop of volcanoes. Its 1178-seat concert hall and a smaller amphitheatre play host mostly to classical music performances and attract renowned orchestras and soloists from all over the world. There's an appealing café on the ground floor.

Museo Colonial Alemán de Frutillar

Pérez Rosales at Prat • Jan & Feb daily 9am–7.30pm; March–Dec 9am–5.30pm • CH$2500 • ⓦ museosaustral.cl

Besides an old water mill and several other traditional wooden buildings, the **Museo Colonial Alemán de Frutillar** features a wide variety of household objects used by the earliest German immigrants to the Lake District. Most interesting is a circular barn *campanario*; inside, pairs of horses were once tethered to the central pillar and driven round in circles, threshing sheaves of corn with their hoofs. Further up the hill is the **Casa del Herrero**, the blacksmith's house, and higher still the reconstruction of a typical early farmhouse, filled with period furniture and decorated with old family photos.

ARRIVAL AND INFORMATION · FRUTILLAR

By bus Frequent minibuses from Puerto Montt and Puerto Varas stop on the corner of Montt and Philippi in Frutillar Bajo. Other buses arrive in Frutillar Alto, connected to Frutillar Bajo by *colectivo* shuttle services (CH$600).

Tourist office Av Philippi at O'Higgins (daily 8.30am–1pm & 2–6.30pm; ⓦ frutillar.com).

ACCOMMODATION AND EATING

Duendes del Lago Av Philippi at O'Higgins. Spot this café by the giant garden gnomes parked outside (and inside). Excellent coffee, cakes and an assortment of paninis (from CH$3400) make this a popular gathering spot. Daily 9am–9pm.

Hotel Boutique Frau Holle Varas 54 ☎65 242 1345, ⓦ frauholle-frutillar.cl. This historic home-cum-boutique hotel offers top-notch service, refined rooms with thoroughly modern bathrooms and a central location. Dining at the on-site restaurant is worth every penny, too. <u>CH$75,000</u>

Se Cocina 2km south of Frutillar ☎09 8972 8195, ⓦ secocina.cl. Wood-shingled restaurant with a seasonally changing menu that relies on locally sourced produce; treat yourself to the likes of crab-filled semolina ravioli and chocolate crêpes flambéed in rum. There's also excellent beer produced on the premises. Mains from CH$10,500. Jan & Feb daily 12.30–4pm & 7.30pm–midnight; March–Dec Fri & Sun 12.30-4pm, Sat 12.30–4pm & 7.30pm–midnight.

Puerto Octay

PUERTO OCTAY, the first German settlement on Lago Llanquihue, lies 28km northeast of Frutillar on the shores of Lago Llanquihue. Dating to 1852, it's a friendly little place with a needle-steepled church and balconied houses with ornate eaves.

Museum "El Colono"

Independencia 591 · Daily 10am–1pm & 3–5pm · CH$1000

Exhibits at the small and well-organized **Museum "El Colono"**, which shares the 1920 Casa Niklitschek with the local library, span the history of the area from the earliest human settlement to the founding and growth of Puerto Octay. They includ bilingual (Spanish/English) accounts, old photographs and period objects – from stone arrowheads to nineteenth-century household pieces, agricultural machines and stills for making the sweet alcoholic *chicha* drink, a local speciality.

ARRIVAL AND DEPARTURE · PUERTO OCTAY

By bus Puerto Octay is served by Buses Via Octay (hourly) from Osorno and buses from Frutillar and Puerto Montt (up to 5 daily).

ACCOMMODATION AND EATING

Hostal Triwe Montt 475 ☎64 239 1359, ⓦ triwe.cl. As central as you can get, this appealing guesthouse, run by the effusive Claudia, welcomes cyclists and budget travellers. There's a clutch of light, bright rooms, all carpeted, with central heating and rain showers. Claudia cooks a mighty breakfast that includes home-made bread and jams. <u>CH$45,000</u>

Rancho Espantapájaros 6km from Puerto Octay towards Frutillar ☎65 233 0049, ⓦ espantapajaros. cl. Overlooking the lake, this family-run restaurant serves

a great all-you-can-eat barbecue buffet (CH$17,000). The spit-roasted goat is excellent, as is the *jabalí* (wild boar). Jan & Feb daily noon–10pm; March–Dec Mon–Fri & Sun noon–5.30pm, Sat noon–10pm.

★ **Zapato Amarillo** 2.4km north of town ☎65 221 0787, ⓦ zapatoamarillo.cl. This well-signposted backpacker and cyclist favourite consists of a homely main lodge with grass roof and an eight-bed dorm, kitchen and communal area in a separate building. A canoe, bike, sailing boat, climbing gear and a scooter are available to rent, and the breakfast spread is extensive. The owners speak German and English and can organize trekking excursions to Vicente Pérez Rosales National Park, to Volcán Osorno or around Lake Rupanco. Dorms **CH$14,000**, doubles **CH$36,000**

Ensenada

Near the turnoff to Volcán Osorno (see below) and clustered around the easternmost corner of the lake sits **ENSENADA**, a small village with a smattering of *hospedajes*, campsites and restaurants that stretch towards Puerto Varas.

ARRIVAL AND DEPARTURE   ENSENADA

By bus Frequent minibuses (Mon–Fri at least hourly; Sat & Sun fewer) run to Ensenada from Puerto Varas and Puerto Montt, most continuing on to Petrohué.

ACCOMMODATION

★ **Hamilton's Place** Off Ruta 225 Km 42 ☏ 09 8466 4146, ✉ hamiltonsplaceensenada@gmail.com; map p.301. The hospitable Brazilian owner/chef Eloa receives guests at this beautiful guesthouse in a tranquil location off a dirt side road, with excellent views of Calbuco and Osorno volcanoes. Wood-panelled rooms are decked out in neutral shades, with colourful woollen touches, and Eloa cooks hearty *feijoada* (pork and bean stew) and other Brazilian dishes for her guests on request. **CH$38,000**

★ **Hotel AWA** Ruta 225 Km 27 ☏ 65 229 2020, ⓦ hotelawa.cl; map p.301. At this dream in wood and stone, designed by an architect from Santiago, there is tremendous attention to detail – from the suspended wooden sculpture in the airy atrium and the infinity pool overlooking the lake to the Mapuche weavings in the bright, individually decorated rooms with floor-to-ceiling windows. The restaurant (open to non-guests) is the best for miles around, as is the cocktail bar. You'll never want to leave, which is the whole point. **US$400**

Quila Hostal Ruta 225 Km 37 (3km up the dirt road that branches off Ruta 225) ☏ 09 6760 7039, ⓦ quilahostal. com; map p.301. This rambling wooden house with large, spartan twins and doubles (some en suite) is run by a helpful French expat – an outdoors enthusiast who can arrange for you to hike up the surrounding volcanoes (visible from the house) and advise on other outdoor adventures. Breakfast includes eggs and home-made bread and guests socialize over the home-cooked dinners. **US$57**

Parque Nacional Vicente Pérez Rosales and around

Parque Nacional Vicente Pérez Rosales, Chile's first national park, was established in 1926, and covers an area of 2510 square kilometres. It is divided into three sectors: Sector **Osorno**, Sector **Petrohué** and Sector **Peulla**, and comprises some of the most sensational scenery in the Lake District: the emerald **Lago Todos Los Santos**, the thundering turquoise waters of the **Saltos de Petrohué** and the imposing peaks of the area's main **volcanoes**: Osorno, Tronadór and Puntiagudo. Coupled with the fact that this vast chunk of wilderness provides numerous excellent **hiking** opportunities, it's little wonder that it's the most visited park in the whole of Chile. If you are planning to do any extensive hiking, pick up a copy of the water-resistant *Llanquihue* map published by Trekking Chile (ⓦ trekkingchile.com).

Volcán Osorno

Ski season mid-June to early Nov • Ski lift passes CH$20,000/CH$26,000 for a half/full day • ⓦ volcanosorno.com

From the turnoff just short of Ensenada, a paved 14km road snakes up to the picture-perfect conical peak of **Volcán Osorno**. While it has erupted on many occasions in the past, the lava spewed from the craters around its base and this mighty volcano is yet to blow its top. About halfway up the slope you'll come across the signposted **Sendero El**

Solitario (5.6km; 2hr) that leads east through dense forest before emerging on the road to Petrohué, about 1km away from the Saltos de Petrohué.

The **Centro de Ski & Montaña Volcán Osorno** (ⓦvolcanoosorno.com) has two chair lifts and seven runs open to skiers, as well as a "snow park" for snowboarders, a tubing park, a snowshoe route from the top of the first chair lift to a viewpoint overlooking Cráter Rojo and several off-piste possibilities. Conditions can be rather windy, but on the upside, you'll find skiers and snowboarders up here even in early November and equipment is available for rent.

Incidentally, November and December are also the better (and safer) months to **climb the volcano**; while many tour groups in Puerto Varas run half-day hiking trips around Osorno's base (CH$55,000), the ascent of the peak is the region's toughest volcano-bagging challenge (CH$210,000) involving a 5am start, snow- and ice-climbing gear and roping up towards the end. It's about five hours to the summit (two to the snowline, three more to the top), and there are many crevasses; a guide is mandatory

6

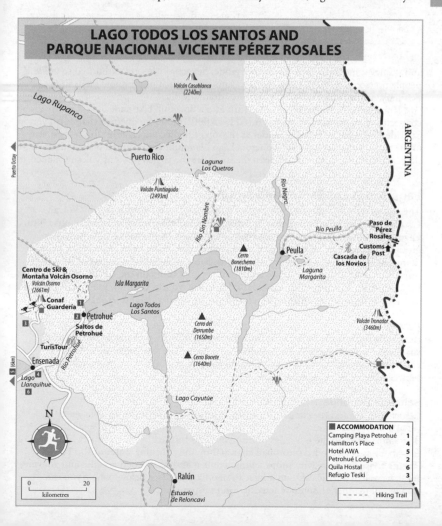

LAGO TODOS LOS SANTOS AND PARQUE NACIONAL VICENTE PÉREZ ROSALES

Lago Rupanco

Puerto Octay

ARGENTINA

Volcán Casablanca (2240m)

Puerto Rico

Laguna Los Quetros

Volcán Puntiagudo (2493m)

Río Sin Nombre

Río Negro

Río Peulla

Paso de Pérez Rosales

Peulla

Customs Post

Cascada de los Novios

Cerro Bonechemo (1810m)

Laguna Margarita

Centro de Ski & Montaña Volcán Osorno
Volcán Osorno (2661m)

Conaf Guardería

Isla Margarita

Lago Todos Los Santos

Petrohué

Saltos de Petrohué

Volcán Tronador (3460m)

Cerro del Derrumbe (1650m)

TurisTour

Cerro Bonete (1640m)

Ensenada

Río Petrohué

Lago Llanquihue

5 (km)

Lago Cayutúe

N

Ralún

Estuario de Reloncaví

0	20
kilometres	

■ ACCOMMODATION
Camping Playa Petrohué	1
Hamilton's Place	4
Hotel AWA	5
Petrohué Lodge	2
Quila Hostal	6
Refugio Teski	3

- - - - - Hiking Trail

6

TREKKING IN PARQUE NACIONAL VICENTE PÉREZ ROSALES

Two good hiking trails set off from the black-sand beach of **Playa Larga** at Petrohué. One 5km trail skirts the lakeshore, while **Sendero Los Alerzales** makes for an enjoyable (7.6km, 4hr 30min return) hike through dense local forest, at one point crossing paths with the **Sendero Paso Desolación**, a tough 13km trek (8hr) that climbs up the northeast side of Volcán Osorno to a height of 1100m and offers a fantastic view of Volcán Tronador and the lake below. The most ambitious hike in the park is the the 25km **Sendero Termas de Callao** (two days) that starts from the northern shores of Lago Todos Los Santos, by the Río Sin Nombre (No-Name River). To reach the trailhead, you'll need to rent a boat from the dock at Petrohué (CH$60,000–70,000 for up to six people). Head up the river – the path is reasonably clear but be sure always to head upwards to the source – and after about three or four hours' climbing you reach the namesake hot springs (free and safe to bathe in) and a basic *refugio*. From here you can either go back down to Lago Todos Los Santos, having asked the boatman to pick you up again, or carry on up to the Laguna Los Quetros (where there's a basic campsite) and then over the pass – another two hours' hike – and then descend to Lago Rupanco, which takes another three hours. From the shores of Lago Rupanco, it's about another hour (west) to Puerto Rico, from where there are buses to Osorno.

---

and it's never more than two hikers per guide. Several outfits are authorised to guide people up (see page 303). Conaf bans ascents once much of the snow melts in February, as the risk of rockslides increases dramatically.

In January and February, the ski runs turn into a downhill **bike park** and the two connected chair lifts stay open all year (CH$12,000/16,000 for one/two chair lifts); you can ride all the way to **Estación Glaciar** at the top of the second chair lift for the best view of the area. To the west you can see across Lago Llanquihue, the central plain and across to the sea, and dominating the skyline to the south are the jagged peaks of Volcán Calbuco.

Lago Todos Los Santos and around

The volcanic rock in the area was part of a tongue of lava sent this way by Volcán Osorno in 1850, an eruption that diverted the Petrohué river from its old course into Lago Llanquihue. At the end of the riverside road lies **Lago Todos Los Santos**, deep green and stunningly clear, one of the most beautiful in the Lake District – it's also known as Lago Esmeralda (Emerald Lake) because of the intense colour of its water. TurisTour (☎65 243 7172, ⊛turistour.cl) offers boat **tours** on the lake (CH$39,000 for a full day), which provide unsurpassed views of Volcán Osorno, the spiked peak of Volcán Puntiagudo and, highest of all, the glacier-covered Monte Tronador.

Petrohué

Accessible by partially paved road from Ensenada, the sleepy hamlet of **PETROHUÉ** sits on the western shore of Lago Todos Los Santos. The settlement dates from the early twentieth century, when one Ricardo Roth began taking tourists across the lakes between Puerto Varas and Bariloche.

Saltos de Petrohué

10km northeast of Ensenada, off the gravel road that leads towards Petrohué • Daily: summer 8.30am–9pm; rest of year 9am–6pm • CH$4000 plus CH$1000 parking fee

The **Saltos de Petrohué** is a series of immense falls formed by an extremely hard layer of lava that has been eroded into small channels by the churning water of Río Petrohue. There's a visitor centre with shops selling woollen and *raulí* wood goodies and gourmet food, as well as a basic café and a First Patagonia office (see below) where you can arrange all manner of outdoor activities on the spot.

The entrance fee gives you access to two short hiking **trails** and another short trail leading to the viewpoints overlooking the falls, where you can watch the incredibly turquoise water roar and swirl below. The waterfalls are particularly impressive on a fine day when Volcán Osorno is visible directly above them.

Peulla

TurisTour (see below) boat excursions depart at 10am (CH$38,000/person including transportation from Puerto Varas or Puerto Montt, or CH$28,000 from Petrohué)

Visitors staying overnight in **PEULLA**, a small scattering of houses spread out along the road at the far end of the lake, have time to do the moderately difficult yet rewarding 8km climb to **Laguna Margarita** (4hr) or take a stroll to the beautiful **Cascada de Los Novios** waterfall nearby.

6

ARRIVAL AND TOURS

By bus Buses run from Puerto Montt via Puerto Varas to Petrohué (peak season Mon–Fri every 30min, Sat & Sun less frequently; rest of the year 2 daily; 1hr 15min).

By boat For details of the Petrohué to Bariloche bus-and-boat journey, see page 296.

Tours From its office at the Saltos de Petrohue visitor centre, TurisTour (see above) arranges rafting on Río

PARQUE NACIONAL VICENTE PÉREZ ROSALES

Petrohue (CH$34,000), full-day catamaran outings on the lake from Petrohue or Puerto Varas/Puerto Montt (CH$28,000/CH$38,000), zip lining (CH$20,000) and guided hikes in Parque Nacional Alerce Andino (from CH$33,000/person for minimum of three).

ACCOMMODATION

Camping Playa Petrohué Petrohué ☎ 09 9499 3226; map p.301. Shaded Conaf-run campsite near the beach, with cold showers and firepits. Sites have space of up to five people. Per site CH$10,000

Petrohué Lodge Ruta 225 Km 60, Petrohué ☎ 65 221 2025, ⓦ petrohue.com; map p.301. Besides the appealing lakeside location, this handsome stone-and-wood lodge features a tower, roaring fireplace in the guest lounge, skylights throughout, fully equipped lakeside *cabañas* (sleeping four to eight) and candle-dotted rooms. Breakfast, packed and regular lunch, *onces* and dinner

available at the decent on-site restaurant (open to non-guests). *Cabañas* US$250, doubles US$264

Refugio Teski Volcán Osorno ☎ 65 256 6622, ⓦ teski. cl; map p.301. This ski-adorned rustic lodge has compact dorms (bring your own sleeping bag), a cosy little café (dish of the day CH$7500) with vibrant photographs of Volcán Osorno's deep-blue ice caves, and one touch of luxury – two outdoor hot tubs (CH$40,000), to be enjoyed with pisco sour in hand while looking down over Lago Llanquihue. Dorms CH$17,000, doubles CH$42,000

Estuario de Reloncaví

On the way back to Ensenada from Parque Nacional Vicente Pérez Rosales, a southern fork, 1km before the town, will take you 33km along a paved road, fringed with large bushes of wild fuchsia and giant rhubarb plants, to the tranquil **Estuario de Reloncaví**. Your first view of the bay comes as you descend to the village of **Ralún**, from which a partially paved road leads you through wild, dramatic scenery deeper into pioneer country and the village of **Cochamó**.

Cochamó

Sitting on the gorgeous Estuario de Reloncaví, against the backdrop of snow-tipped mountains, and presided over by the *alerce*-shingled Iglesia Parroquial Maria Inmaculada, the appealing fishing village of **COCHAMÓ** is an excellent base for exploring the area. Travellers use it as a launching pad for exploring the nearby **Cochamó Valley** and the **Río Puelo Valley**.

6

ARRIVAL AND INFORMATION

COCHAMÓ

By bus Buses Río Puelo pass through en route from Puerto Montt to Puelo and vice versa (up to 4 daily). The most reliable bus towards Puelo passes through around 10am, and in the opposite direction at around 2pm.

By car Route V-69 is paved up to Ralún and beyond; the 12km or so to Cochamó consists of decent gravel road. If you're approaching the village from Puelo, note that the pitted gravel road can be bumpy after heavy rains.

Tourist information A kiosk (Mon–Sat 9am–6pm) on the main street occasionally has surprisingly good maps of the Río Puelo region.

Tours The friendly Southern Trips (Calle Principal s/n; Mon–Fri 8am–7.30pm, Sat & Sun 9am–7pm; ☎ 09 8407 2559, ⓦ southern-trips.com) offers fantastic horseriding in the area, from half-day jaunts to multi-day treks to the Argentinian border. Campo Aventura (see page 296) arranges multi-day horse treks.

ACCOMMODATION

La Bicicleta Hostel Calle Principal 179 ☎ 09 9402 9281, ⓦ labicicletahostel.cl; map p.305. Friendly locals Sixto and his wife welcome backpackers and cyclists (spot the bicycle sculptures out front) into their cosy little bungalow. The four-bed dorms are simple but the mattresses are comfortable and the breakfast and warm welcome get rave reviews. Dorms CH$16,000, doubles CH$38,000

Campo Aventura Riverside Lodge B&B Around 4km south of Cochamó proper, near the turnoff for Río Cochamó Valley ☎ 09 9289 4314 or ☎ 09 9289 4318, ⓦ campo-aventura.com; map p.305. This beautiful, rustic, American-run lodge sits amid a vast riverside property. It accommodates adventurers in its cluster of

rustic but comfortable rooms and lets them camp by the river. They also specialize in horse-riding adventures in the region, particularly multi-day explorations (see page 306). Closed mid-April to Oct. Camping CH$5000, doubles CH$33,000

★ **Eco Hostal Las Bandurrias** Sector El Bosque s/n ☎ 09 9672 2590, ⓦ hostalbandurrias.com; map p.305. High up on a hill above Cochamó (arrange pickup in advance), this gorgeous little hostel consists of a four-bed dorm, a twin and three doubles (shared bathrooms), all with down duvets and run by a friendly and knowledgeable Swiss/Chilean couple. The excellent breakfast includes Sylvie's home-made bread. Dorm CH$14,000, doubles CH$32,000

EATING

The Coffee House Calle Pueblo Hundido s/n ☎ 09 9919 8947. Cochamó's hottest gathering spot is this delightful café, owned by Tatiana from Southern Trips (see above). Here you can find proper coffee, freshly squeezed juice, cakes, sandwiches and reliable wi-fi. Jan–April & Dec daily 11am–9pm.

La Ollita Calle Principal s/n. Right on the main street, and unusually for the region, this local stalwart serves

unexciting yet reliable Chilean standards such as grilled *congrio* or *lomo a lo pobre*. Mains CH$5500–7000. Daily 12.30–10pm.

El Rincón Pirata Calle Principal s/n ☎ 09 9865 8075. Flying the Jolly Roger, this restaurant on the northern approach to the village has earned itself some loyal local and visiting fans with its stone-baked pizzas and grilled meats. Mains CH$7500–11,500. Daily 11am–11pm.

Cochamó Valley and La Junta

The **Cochamó Valley** consists of dense Valdivian rainforest, home to some of the oldest trees in South America, that rises alongside the fast-flowing Río Cochamó. Around 4km east of Cochamó, a dirt road branches off the main Cochamó–Puelo road and runs for 6km to the start of the horse track that cuts through the valley. Follow it for long enough, and you will reach the Argentinian border. Thirteen kilometres along the track is **LA JUNTA**, a cluster of five campsites, plus two rustic lodges, surrounded by a soaring amphitheatre of granite towers. From November to April, this off-the-grid destination attracts thousands of hikers, as well as **rock climbers** who come to take on such world-famous walls as El Monstruo, Trinidad, and Anfiteatro.

ARRIVAL AND INFORMATION

COCHAMÓ VALLEY AND LA JUNTA

On foot It's a 4–6hr hike to La Junta from the beginning of the trailhead, 10km from Cochamó. Several locals offer drop-offs to the trailhead (8am–4pm).

On horseback The only other way to enter the La Junta Valley is on horseback. Southern Trips (see above) and Campo Aventura (see page 296) both arrange horseback trips and/or pack horses.

Tourist information Between mid-Dec and the end of March hikers are allowed access to the La Junta trail only if they have advance reservations with one of the five campsites in La Junta, *Refugio Cochamó* or *Campo Aventura* *Mountain Lodge*. Cars can be parked securely near the trailhead for CH$2000/night. Book accommodation in advance at ⓦreservasvallecochamo.org.

ACCOMMODATION

Campo Aventura Mountain Lodge & Camping La Junta ⓦcampo-aventura.com; map p.305. *Campo Aventura*'s (see page 296) even more rustic outpost in the La Junta Valley, this is a converted farmhouse with bunkrooms, simple doubles and camping spots; *asados* can be organized for guests. The *Mountain Lodge* is used as accommodation for horseback riding trips (four people minimum). The campsite (open to all) has tent sites, some in open pasture and some shaded by trees; there's a *quincho* for cooking. Camping <u>CH$5000</u>, dorms <u>CH$15,000</u>, doubles <u>CH$50,000</u>

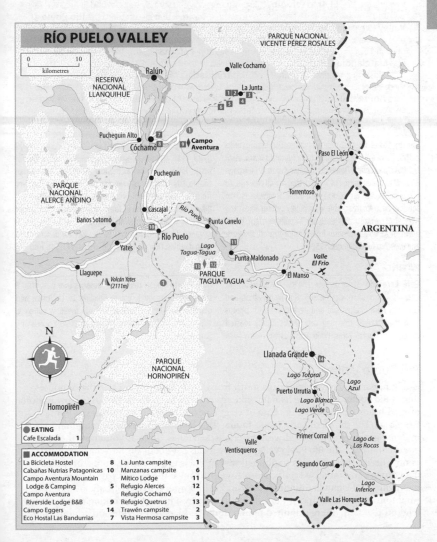

RÍO PUELO VALLEY

● EATING	
Cafe Escalada	1

■ ACCOMMODATION			
La Bicicleta Hostel	8	La Junta campsite	1
Cabañas Nutrias Patagonicas	10	Manzanas campsite	6
Campo Aventura Mountain		Mítico Lodge	11
Lodge & Camping	5	Refugio Alerces	12
Campo Aventura		Refugio Cochamó	4
Riverside Lodge B&B	9	Refugio Quetrus	13
Campo Eggers	14	Trawén campsite	2
Eco Hostal Las Bandurrias	7	Vista Hermosa campsite	3

6

6

TREKKING IN THE COCHAMÓ VALLEY

With the temperate rainforest's gnarly trees "clothed" in lichen, towering *alerces* and granite mountains rising above the forest, it's easy to see how the **Cochamó Valley** acquired its "Yosemite of the South" moniker. The valley is bisected by the remnants of a nineteenth-century logging road (little more than a muddy footpath in places) that now serves as a popular 13km hiking **trail to La Junta** (4–6hr one way), surrounded by mountains that are hugely popular with rock climbers. The initial trail is easy to follow, and very gentle in terms of elevation, but can be extremely muddy, as the horses bringing supplies to the lodge (see page 305) churn up the path in rainy weather. Much of the trail passes through Valdivian rainforest, before emerging amid the granite towers. The rivers all have bridges across them, so there is no need to ford them.

There are five excellent hiking trails around La Junta, as well as the long trail heading east towards the free **El Arco refugio** (15km; 4hr one way); a four-day trek beyond El Arco will take you into Argentina, and it's possible to do a three-day trek that leads you to the **Río Puelo Valley** (see page 306). Three of the day hikes around La Junta are north of the river. The steep hike and scramble to the **Arco Iris viewpoint** (4km; 4–5hr one way) is for seasoned trekkers only and not to be attempted in inclement weather. **Paloma** (3.5km; 3hr 30min one way) and **Matelandia** (2.5km; 2hr one way) trails lead to their namesake rock faces and require a river crossing apiece. South of the river, the **Trinidad** trail (5.5km; 4hr one way) takes you to the base of Cerro Trinidad; the middle section is very steep, but the views are rewarding. The 5km **Anfiteatro** trail (5hr one way), leading to the base of Cerro Anfiteatro, also has very steep sections. A 1km detour from the Anfiteatro trail leads you to some gorgeous waterfalls.

Campsites La Junta ⊕ reservasvallecochamo.org; map p.305. There are five campsites in La Junta: *La Junta, Vista Hermosa, Manzanas, Trawén* and *Campo Aventura* (see page 305). With the exception of *Trawén*, they are all well run. *La Junta* and *Trawén* are next to each other. *Manzanas* is 2km south of *La Junta*, reachable via a pulley system across the river. *Vista Hermosa*, also reachable by pulley system, is just north of *Refugio Cochamó*. Expect solar-heated showers, and *quinchos* for cooking. CH$5000

★ **Refugio Cochamó** La Junta ☎ 09 9289 4314 or ☎ 09 9289 4318, ⊕ cochamo.com; map p.305. This beautiful rustic lodge, run by a friendly American/Argentinian couple, sits amid a vast riverside property across the river from La Junta, reachable via a pulley system. Climbers and hikers exchange stories in the cosy living area, and dinner (pizza or hearty vegetarian mains) has to be booked in advance. Choose between a twelve-person dorm or two snug doubles. Dorm CH$17,000, doubles CH$48,000

EATING

Cafe Escalada 300m before the La Junta trailhead ⊕ cafeescalada.com; map p.305. Run by Jonathan and Elizabeth from Cheltenham and decked out with photos from their travels, this new café serves locally roasted coffee from Puerto Varas, Pudú artisanal ice cream (also from Puerto Varas), cakes and sausages in a bun. They'll store your luggage if you're heading to La Junta, and glamping will be available in a star-lit meadow out back, where there's a beautiful swimming spot in the river. Daily 9am–5pm.

Río Puelo Valley

A 27km, partially paved road runs south from Cochamó to the scattering of houses that is **Río Puelo**, straddling its namesake river. From here, an unpaved, narrow ribbon of road heads east, skirting the base of craggy peaks, before it culminates at **Punta Canelo**, on the shores of **Lago Tagua-Tagua**. This lake, surrounded by mountains clad in dense greenery and flecked with waterfalls, separates Chile as you know it from *huaso* country of the **Río Puelo Valley**, where locals get about on horseback as much as on wheels. That said, this traditional way of life is under threat from a proposed **dam project** and increased traffic from Argentina once the road is paved from the main village of **Llanada Grande** to the Río Puelo border crossing. Many locals offer rural tourism in the shape of horseriding, homestays, fishing and hiking in a bid to fend off the dam. There is limited **phone signal** in Llanada Grande and around **Punta**

Maldonado (better with Entel than Movistar); only some lodgings in Llanada Grande, by Lago Totoral and around Puerto Urrutia offer (slow) **wi-fi**.

Llanada Grande and around

From **Punta Maldonado**, the dock on the side of the lake opposite Punta Canelo, it's a bumpy 32km drive to the one-street main settlement of **LLANADA GRANDE**. Beyond, a 7km road skirts pretty **Lago Totoral** before reaching a fork in the road; the 3km left fork leads west to **Puerto Urrutia**, sitting alongside an aquamarine river (from where fishing excursions can be arranged), while the 13km right fork continues to a lookout over a wide glacial river and a short side road to the tiny settlement of **Primer Corral**. In late 2017, a good gravel road had replaced the horse track for about 7km – halfway towards **Segundo Corral**. If you do make it to Segundo Corral on foot (or horseback), another 4km horse track takes you on to **Lago Inferior**, where it's possible to catch a boat (not daily) all the way across the lake that connects with Argentina's **Lago Puelo**, and then across Lago Puelo to its namesake settlement – where there's public transport to **El Bolsón**.

Adventurous hikers can take on the 47km (2–3 days) trek from **El Manso**, 12km south of Punta Maldonado, all the way to La Junta in the Río Cochamó Valley (see page 304) via the Río Manso Valley, the two-house settlement of Torrentoso and along the west bank of Lago Vidal Gormaz, camping wild en route and buying supplies from isolated farmhouses.

Parque Tagua-Tagua

CH$15,000 • ☎ 65 223 4892, Ⓦ parquetaguatagua.cl • If you want to visit for the day or stay overnight, make arrangements over the phone or online before leaving Punta Canelo in order for the speedboat to meet you at the Punta Maldonado dock for the 10min ride to the park (CH$10,000 return)

Parque Tagua-Tagua, a 3000-hectare slice of Valdivian rainforest, is a private reserve that sits along the south shore of Lago Tagua-Tagua, with a single 18km **trail** that passes by two pretty lakes, kayaking alongside lakeside waterfalls and rock climbing on offer, and the possibility of spotting pudú, pumas and other shy fauna. The first section of the trail is very steep, but it evens out after that.

ARRIVAL AND INFORMATION	**RÍO PUELO VALLEY**

By bus A single bus runs from Puerto Montt (daily 7.45am) to Primer Corral, and there's a daily 9am departure from Primer Corral to Puerto Montt.

By ferry Daily ferries to Punta Maldonado run from Punta Canelo (Jan, Feb & Dec 7.30am, 9am & 1pm, returning at 8.15am, noon & 4.30pm; March–Nov the earliest ferry on each leg does not run; CH$1050/passenger; CH$7000 /car). If driving, get to the dock 1hr before departure to queue.

ACCOMMODATION

Cabañas Nutrias Patagonicas Puelo, around 1km north of the turnoff towards the Lago Tagua-Tagua ferry ☎ 65 280 3662, Ⓦ nutriaspatagonicas.cl; map p.305. These three gorgeous, spotless, spacious *cabañas* are ideal for self-caterers. With a wood-burning stove in the living area and two plush twin rooms with showers apiece, they make an ideal stopover if you're driving to or from the Río Puelo area. Friendly hosts Enrique and Veronica provide a warm welcome. **CH$90,000**

Campo Eggers Signposted just beyond Llanada Grande, near the El Salto waterfall ☎ 2 2196 9212; map p.305. The pioneer home of hospitable Blanca Eggers is a fantastic place to delve into local *huaso* culture. Price includes room with shared facilities, home-cooked meals and wine. Blanca has numerous contacts in the valley and can help organize homestays in Primer Corral and Segundo Corral if you're thinking of trekking into Argentina. Road not recommended for city cars. Solo travellers pay half price. **CH$50,000**

Mítico Lodge North side of Lago Tagua-Tagua ☎ 65 256 6646, Ⓦ miticopuelo.com; map p.305. This handsome lodge is the plushest accommodation inside Parque Tagua-Tagua, with hot tubs and swimming pool, spacious wood-panelled rooms and gourmet cuisine. Fly fishing, trekking, horseriding and kayaking on offer. Full board available. Closed May–Sept. **CH$172,000**

Refugio Quetrus & Refugio Alerces South side of Parque Tagua-Tagua ☎ 65 223 4892, Ⓦ parquetaguatagua.cl; map p.305. The rustic, wood-fire-heated eight-person *Refugio Quetrus* – only

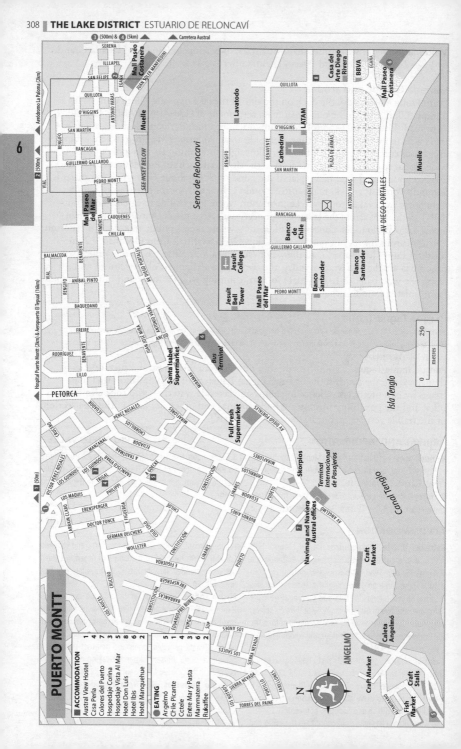

PUERTO MONTT

■ ACCOMMODATION
Austral View Hostel	4
Casa Perla	7
Colores del Puerto	9
Hospedaje Corina	5
Hospedaje Vista Al Mar	3
Hotel Don Luis	8
Hotel Ibis	6
Hotel Manquehue	2

■ EATING
Argelmó	5
Chile Picante	1
Cctele	4
Entre Mar y Pasta	3
Mammaterra	6
Rukaffee	2

Seno de Reloncaví

Isla Tenglo

Canal Tenglo

ANGELMÓ

0   250
metres

N

rentable by a couple or group – and the twenty-person *Refugio Alerces* are reachable via a 5hr 30min and 4hr hike, respectively, from the dock. Bring your own sleeping bag. *Refugio Alerces* dorms ‾CH$15,000‾, *Refugio Quetrus* doubles ‾CH$50,000‾

Puerto Montt

At the southern end of the Lake District and 17km south of Puerto Varas, the Panamericana approaches a large bay – the Seno de Reloncaví – with snowcapped Volcán Calbuco (see page 269) and Volcán Osorno towering beyond. On its edge lies the administrative and commercial capital of the Lake District – **PUERTO MONTT**, founded by the same influx of German colonizers that settled Lago Llanquihue to the north. The city is strung out along the bay, with the central part of town located on a narrow flat area along the main Avenida Diego Portales, and much of the city crowding the hills behind it.

Puerto Montt is an important transportation hub and a busy port, with its formerly $billion-a-year salmon farming industry slowly recovering from the major blow it took in recent years, and the embarkation point for long-distance **ferry trips** (see below). Gritty "Muerto Montt" has few attractions of its own beyond the graffiti-blighted promenade crowned with a couple of redundant steam engines, but it's a worthwhile overnight stop if you want to catch a boat, a plane, or the latest blockbuster at the Mall Paseo Costanera.

Angelmó

The fishing neighbourhood of **Angelmó** sits at the western end of the bay, around 1km west of the bus terminal. Here the *costanera* (coastal road) features an extensive **feria artesanal**, its numerous stalls laden with carved wooden earrings, woven baskets and figures from Chilote mythology, woollen ponchos, sweaters and lapis lazuli jewellery.

FERRIES FROM PUERTO MONTT

One of the main reasons people travel to Puerto Montt is to catch a **ferry** south. From Puerto Montt you can sail to Chaitén and Puerto Chacabuco on the Carretera Austral, the Laguna San Rafael far in the southern fjords, Puerto Natales in Patagonia and Quellón in Chiloé. These ferry trips are almost always fully booked in summer, and you must **reserve ahead**. The quality of your experience will largely depend on the weather. The seas are usually calm as most of the time the ferries are sailing through sheltered fjords, but it can be windy. The exception is the trip to **Puerto Natales**, when the ship heads out to the Pacific across the often-turbulent Golfo de Penas.

PUERTO MONTT TO PUERTO NATALES

The Navimag trip from Puerto Montt to Puerto Natales is an incredible introduction to Patagonia. Lasting four days and three nights, the trip takes you through pristine and deserted waterways, past uninhabited islands and Chile's largest **glacier**, the Piu XI, with frequent sightings of marine life. It passes by **Puerto Edén**, the last remaining settlement of the **Kawéscar** people, before sailing into the cold and little-explored fjords of the south, and finally docking in Puerto Natales on the Seno Última Esperanza. If you're lucky with the weather, you'll not want to leave the deck for the duration of the trip, except to drink at the bar and to enjoy a raucous game of bingo on the last night with a crowd of new friends.

In bad weather, however, at any time of year, it can be a trial: the views shrouded in mist and fog; a sleepless night as the ship navigates the turbulent waters of the open ocean; the equally sickness-inducing waves of the **Golfo de Penas**; your entire trip stuck in the bar or the dining room. In the off-season, you will also be sharing the boat (if not the main deck) with cattle. For ferry operators, see page 310.

6

Just west of the *feria artesanal* lies a thriving **fish market**, a combination of many fish retailers and various restaurants operated by ebullient local women whose steaming vats of *curanto* (see page 320) and delicious aromas of fish cooking attract numerous visitors, particularly at lunchtime. Next to the fish market is another craft market where you can pick up quality woollen clothing, kitchen utensils made from *raulí* wood and other locally produced souvenirs.

ARRIVAL AND DEPARTURE

BY PLANE

Aeropuerto El Tepual (ⓦaeropuertoeltepual.cl) is 16km northwest of the city; there are flights from LATAM (O'Higgins 167 at Urmeneta; ⓦlatam.com) and Sky Airline (ⓦskyairline.cl). Buses Andestur run to and from the airport hourly and meet flights. Cessna flights with Aerocord (ⓣ65 226 2300, ⓦaerocord.cl) and two other small operators serve Chaitén from the Aeródromo La Paloma, off Camino A. Alerce.

Destinations Balmaceda/Coyhaique (2 daily; 1hr); Chaitén (1–2 daily; 40min); Punta Arenas (2–4 daily; 2hr 10min); Santiago (up to 10 daily; 1hr 40min).

BY BUS

The large, well-organized Terminal de Buses (ⓦterminalpm.cl) is at Av Diego Portales 1001 on the waterfront, six blocks west of the town centre. It is served by long-distance buses to many points north and south, and frequent minibuses to regional destinations such as Puerto Varas, Frutillar and Ensenada.

Companies All of the main companies have offices in the terminal (ⓣ65 228 3000), including Tur Bus (ⓣ65 227 3979, ⓦturbus.cl) and Pullman (ⓣ65 225 4399, ⓦpullman.cl), serving all major destinations between Puerto Montt and Santiago, with connections to the north of Chile. Cruz del Sur (ⓣ65 225 2872, ⓦbuscruzdelsur.cl) has the most frequent departures to Chiloé; Queilen Bus (ⓣ65 225 3468, ⓦqueilenbus.cl) also serves Chiloé and has weekly departures for Coyhaique via Argentina, as does Turibus (ⓣ65 225 2872), while Tas Choapa (ⓣ65 225 4828, ⓦwww.taschoapa.cl) and Igi Llaima (ⓣ65 225 9320, ⓦigillaima.cl) head across the border to Argentina. Kemel Bus (ⓣ65 225 6450, ⓦkemelbus.cl) runs to Chaitén via Hornopirén, and Buses Río Puelo (ⓣ09 9123 0838) serves Cochamó and Río Puelo.

Destinations Ancud (every 30min; 2hr); Bariloche, Argentina (4 daily; 6hr); Castro (every 30min; 3hr 30min); Chaitén (2 daily 7am & 11am; 9hr); Coyhaique via Osorno (4 weekly; 24hr); Futaleufú (2 weekly; 12hr); Hornopirén (3–4 daily; 4hr); Osorno (every 30min; 1hr 30min); Puerto Varas (every 15min; 30min); Santiago (every 30min; 14hr); Temuco (hourly; 5hr); Valdivia (every 30min; 3hr).

BY FERRY

The Terminal Internacional de Pasajeros, 700m west of the bus terminal, Av Angelmó 1673, is home to two of the major ferry companies. Shared taxis (*colectivos*) run up and down the *costanera* between the Plaza and Angelmó (CH$500).

FERRY CRUISE OPERATORS

Naviera Austral Terminal Internacional de Pasajeros ⓣ65 227 0430, ⓦnavieraustral.cl. Serves Chaitén (Mon & Thurs 11pm; 9hr; seat CH$17,300, car CH$91,100).

Navimag Terminal Internacional de Pasajeros ⓣ65 243 2360, ⓦnavimag.com. Sails to Puerto Chacabuco (Wed & Sat 11pm, 2 days; CH$51,000 for shared Class C cabin, CH$180,000 for a double in AAA cabin) and Puerto Natales (1–2 weekly 4pm; 3–4 days; US$450 for shared Class CC cabin, US$1050/person in a double in an AAA cabin). Class CC accommodation consists of a bunk with bedding, a locker for storage and a curtain for privacy; bring your own towel. Class AAA gives you your own room with sea view, en-suite bathroom and private dining with the captain; there are several categories in between.

Skorpios Av Angelmó 1660 ⓣ65 225 5050, ⓦskorpios. cl. This luxury cruise company runs two routes: Ruta Chonos, the six-day/five-night voyage to Laguna San Rafael (from US$2200/person if sharing a double) and Ruta Kawéskar, a four-day/three-night fjord cruise from Puerto Natales to remote glaciers and back (from US$1850/person if sharing a double).

BY CAR

All major car companies (Hertz, Avis, Europcar) are represented at the airport. If you wish to drive the Carretera Austral (see page 348) and are thinking of dropping the car off elsewhere, bear in mind that one-way dropoff fees can be crippling (an additional CH$300,000 or more).

INFORMATION

Tourist office Southwestern corner of the Plaza de Armas (Jan–March & Dec daily 9am–9pm; April–Nov Mon–Fri 8.30am–1pm & 3–5.30pm, Sat 9am–2pm; ⓣ65 226 1823; ⓦpuertomonttchile.cl). Well-stocked and helpful.

Hospital Hospital Puerto Montt, Los Aromos 65 (ⓣ65 236 2001).

ACCOMMODATION

Austral View Hostel Bellavista 620 ☎ 09 6284 0751, ⓦ casaperla.com; map p.308. Exuberant hellos from the two resident Bernese mountain dogs greet guests at this friendly guesthouse. Choose between a self-catering two-person *cabaña*, a dorm bed or the snug doubles, and take a drink out onto the terrace high above the city. Dorm CH$16,000, doubles CH$30,000, *cabaña* CH$40,000

Casa Perla Trigal 312 ☎ 65 226 2104, ⓦ casaperla.com; map p.308. Simple rooms and dorms with shared bathrooms in a yellow-shingled Chilean home, packed with antiques and knick-knacks and ruled over by Perla the matriarch. It's an uphill hike to the quiet residential neighbourhood, but pluses include a warm family atmosphere and camping out back; English and German spoken. Camping CH$8000, dorms CH$11,500, doubles CH$27,000

Colores del Puerto Schwerter 207 ☎ 65 248 9360, ⓦ coloresdelpuerto.cl; map p.308. Run by the wonderfully friendly and helpful Tomás, this informal hostel is just a 5min walk from the port and a 10min walk from the bus station, down a quiet street in Puerto Montt's historic neighbourhood. Three twin rooms share facilities. CH$35,000

Hospedaje Corina Los Guindos 329 ☎ 65 227 3948, ⓦ hospedajecorina.cl; map p.308. Guests are full of praise for helpful hostess Corina at this spotless, quiet guesthouse a 10min walk uphill from the waterfront.

Most of the doubles, twins and triples share bathrooms. CH$28,000

Hospedaje Vista Al Mar Vivar 1337 ☎ 65 225 5625, ⓦ hospedajevistaalmar.cl; map p.308. Justly popular guesthouse overlooking the city from a high vantage point and offering excellent value, especially for single travellers, with cosy en-suite rooms. Owner Eliana offers a really good breakfast that includes eggs and home-made bread. CH$30,000

Hotel Don Luis Quillota 146 ☎ 65 220 0302, ⓦ hoteldonluis.cl; map p.308. Central, efficient hotel catering to business and leisure travellers. Rooms are modern and carpeted and come with queen-size beds or twins, plus rain showers in the bathrooms. CH$49,600

Hotel Ibis Huasco 143 ☎ 65 235 1212, ⓦ ibis.com; map p.308. It may be part of a chain, but this efficient, modern hotel has a lot going for it. A central waterfront location, proximity to the bus station (it's right on top of it) and easy access to ferries are just some of them. No parking. CH$21,400

Hotel Manquehue Av Seminario 252 ☎ 65 233 1000, ⓦ hotelmanquehue.cl; map p.308. A few blocks uphill from the *costanera*, this bright, contemporary hotel welcomes you with the grand fireplace in the slate-covered lounge and appealing rooms equipped with all mod cons, livened up with splashes of colour. The service aims to please, and there's a good breakfast buffet. US$120

EATING

Angelmó Next to the fish market, Av Angelmó; map p.308. By far the best spot for an inexpensive seafood meal, this collection of no-frills cafés serves such goodies as *picorocos* (barnacles), *curanto* (see page 320), *almejas* (razor clams), *erizos* (sea urchins) and *chupe de locos* (abalone chowder). Mains from CH$5500. Daily noon–8pm.

★ **Chile Picante** Vicente Pérez Rosales ☎ 09 8454 8923, ⓦ chilepicanterestoran.cl; map p.308. All bright colours and bay views from its lofty location, this compact restaurant (just six tables) fills quickly. The ever-changing three-course daily menu is remarkably good value (CH$10,500), listing such dishes as scallop *ceviche*, gnocchi with crab and calafate berry-flavoured *chapalele* (potato dumplings) with apple granita. Reservations a must. Mon–Sat 12.30–3.30pm & 7.30–11pm.

★ **Cotele** Manfredini 1661, Pelluco ☎ 65 227 8000, ⓦ cotele.cl; map p.308. You have to travel 3km east of the centre to Pelluco for these exceptional steaks. Choose between the fillet, sirloin and the ultra-popular rib-eye, complemented by the extensive menu of Chilean reds,

and watch the chef in action as he cooks your cut to the desired degree. Mains from CH$12,000. Mon–Sat 1–4pm & 8pm–midnight.

Entre Mar y Pasta Egaña 311 ☎ 09 7893 0080; map p.308. Refined, aptly named restaurant that plays to its two strengths: seafood and pasta. Choose from the likes of superlative mixed fish *ceviche*, sea urchins with pepper and squid-ink pappardelle with seafood, and wash it down with a signature mint lemonade. Mains from CH$10,000. Mon–Sat 1–3.30pm & 7–11.15pm, Sun 1-4.30pm.

Mammaterra Illapel 10, Mall Paseo Costanera, local 315B ☎ 65 271 3918, ⓦ mammaterra.cl; map p.308. This place distinguishes itself by specializing in vegetarian "fast good". Expect quinoa burgers and felafel, beetroot-and carrot-infused burger baps and ample salads. Daily 10am–9.30pm.

Rukaffee Egaña 31 ☎ 65 227 4696; map p.308. Arguably Puerto Montt's best espressos, along with a wide assortment of cakes and a few sandwiches. Skip the sushi, though. Mon–Fri 7.30am–9pm, Sat 9.30am–9.30pm.

6

Chiloé

PARQUE NACIONAL CHILOÉ

Chiloé

Located immediately south of the Lake District, the fascinating Chiloé archipelago – part of a mountain range that sank below the waves following the last Ice Age – is a haven of rural tranquillity. The focus for travellers is Isla Grande, the second largest island in South America. Sliced in half lengthways by the Panamericana, it connects the two main towns, Ancud and Castro, with the port of Quellón. The densely forested Parque Nacional Chiloé and Parque Tantauco offer great opportunities to explore unique Chilote wilderness, while coastal villages and islands off Isla Grande's east coast – the most accessible being Isla Quinchao and Isla Lemuy – provide glimpses into traditional life.

Chiloé was originally populated by the native Chonos and Huilliche (southern Mapuche), who eked out a living from fishing and farming before the Spanish took over the island in 1567. For more than three hundred years, Chiloé was isolated from mainland Chile owing to the fierce resistance of the mainland Mapuche to European colonists. As a result, the slow pace of island life saw little change. **Ancud**, in fact, was the last stronghold of the Spanish empire during the wars of Independence, before the final defeat by pro-independence forces in 1826. Despite being used as a stopover during the California Gold Rush, Chiloé remained relatively isolated until the end of the twentieth century, though now it draws increasing numbers of visitors with its unique blend of architecture, myths and legends, and its distinctive cuisine.

More than 150 eighteenth- and nineteenth-century **wooden churches** and **chapels** dot the land. Chiloé is also one of the few places in the country where you can still see **palafitos**, precarious but picturesque timber houses on stilts, once the traditional dwellings of most fishermen in southern Chile. Much of the old culture has been preserved, assimilated into Hispanic tradition by a profound mixing of the Spanish and indigenous cultures, making today's Chiloé more "pagan Catholic" than Roman Catholic.

Today the archipelago faces a number of **challenges**. Some far-flung islands are still without running water or electricity, and a proposed wind farm threatens a nature reserve. Most controversially of all, the government plans to build a bridge between **Isla Grande** and the mainland. Although this is a popular plan with the salmon and lumber industries, locals fear the bridge would damage the local ecosystems and the traditional way of life, arguing the money would be far better spent on a modern hospital or public university.

ARRIVAL AND DEPARTURE CHILOÉ

By ferry There are regular ferry services from Pargua, 59km southwest of Puerto Montt on the mainland (daily 6am–1.20am every 30min; 35min; cost included in bus tickets to either Ancud or Castro) to the village of Chacao on Isla Grande's northern shore. Scheduled ferry services also crisscross the gulf, linking Puerto Montt, Chaitén, Castro and Quellón.

MARINE OTTERS, PARQUE NACIONAL CHILOÉ

Highlights

❶ **Curanto** Tuck into Chiloé's traditional dish, a savoury hotchpotch of meat, seafood and potato dumplings, cooked either in a pit in the ground or a cast-iron pot. See page 320

❷ **Magellanic penguins** Go penguin- and sea-otter-spotting on a boat trip from Puñihuil, easily reachable from Ancud. See page 323

❸ **Chepu Valley** Explore this tranquil valley's sunken forest, created by the 1960 tsunami, in a kayak at dawn. See page 322

❹ **Isla Quinchao** A soothing spot to experience the slow pace of Chiloé's lesser isles and see one of the archipelago's most celebrated wooden

churches. See page 327

❺ **Castro's palafitos** Undeniably picturesque, Castro's traditional fishermen's houses on stilts are the sole remaining examples in the country. See page 330

❻ **Parque Nacional Chiloé** Hike through this region's once vast forests, home to foxes, pygmy deer and *chungungo* (marine otters). See page 332

❼ **Parque Tantauco** A vast private nature reserve with a well-designed infrastructure offering access to pristine and remote corners of southern Chiloé. See page 339

HIGHLIGHTS ARE MARKED ON THE MAP ON PAGE 316

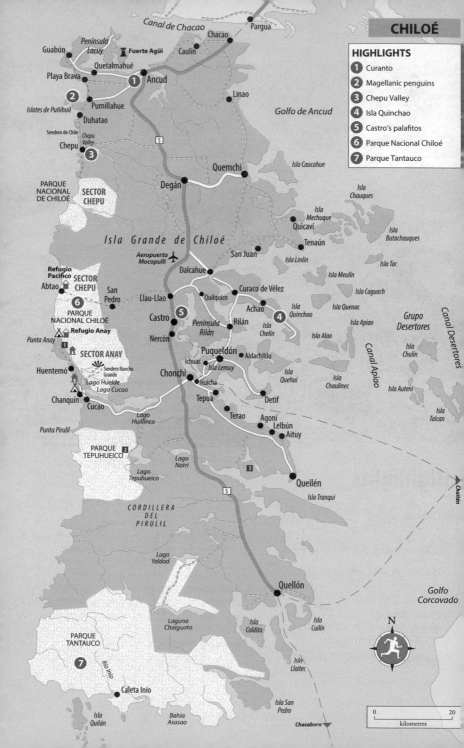

MAQUÍ – THE WONDER BERRY

Stronger than a blueberry, more powerful than açai, able to battle ageing and neurodegenerative diseases: the **maquí berry** (*Aristotelia chilensis*), or Chilean wineberry, is native to Chile's Valdivian rainforests. It has been used by the Mapuche for centuries, both as a foodstuff and to prepare *chicha* (an alcoholic drink made from fermented berries). In recent years, scientific studies have discovered that maquí has far higher antioxidizing properties than its nearest competing "superfoods" – blackberries, açai and blueberries. While studies are still limited, it is believed the consumption of antioxidants helps to prevent diseases like cancer and Alzheimer's. Maquí products are found throughout Chiloé and at ⓦislanatura.com.

Ancud

The low-key fishing port of **ANCUD** is built on a small, square promontory jutting into the Canal de Chacao and the Golfo de Quetalmahue. The town centres on the **Plaza de Armas**, decorated with figures from Chilote mythology and abuzz with craft stalls and street musicians in summer. The colourful **Mercado Municipal**, one block north, offers inexpensive meals and local crafts, as does the **Feria Municipal**, a few blocks east of the centre along Arturo Prat.

Ancud was founded in 1769 as a Spanish stronghold and, after Peruvian independence in 1824, became the crown's last desperate foothold in South America. Its forts resisted one attempt at capture, but finally fell in January 1826 when the lonely and demoralized Spanish garrison fled into the forest in the face of a small *criollo* attack. The remains of these Spanish forts – **Fuerte San Antonio** in town and lonesome, cannon-studded **Fuerte Agüi** on Península Lacuy to the northwest – can still be visited.

Fuerte San Antonio

Lord Cochrane s/n, 750m north of the main plaza • Mon–Fri 8.30am–9pm, Sat & Sun 9am–8pm; reduced hours in the winter • Free

From the harbour, a promenade heads south past half a dozen intriguing pieces of **sculpture**, while Calle Lord Cochrane follows the coast to the north to the reconstructed walls of the Spanish **Fuerte San Antonio**. The fort affords a sweeping view over the Golfo de Quetalmahue and out to the Pacific Ocean, while its sixteen cannon, combined with the fifteen in Fuerte Agüi (on the Península Lacuy across the water), could sink any ship entering the Bahía de Ancud.

Calle Bellavista, parallel to Cochrane, leads further north to the **Playa Arena Gruesa**, a popular swimming beach.

Museo Regional de Ancud

Libertad 370 • Jan & Feb Tues–Fri 10am–5pm, Sat & Sun 10.30am–3.30pm; March–Dec Tues–Fri 10am–5pm, Sat & Sun 10.30am–1.30pm • Free • ☏ 065 262 2413, ⓦ museoancud.cl

The patio of the **Museo Regional de Ancud** houses a replica of the *Goleta Ancud*, a **schooner** with which the first Chilean settlers took possession of the Magellan Strait in September 1843. It was the culmination of a great tradition of Chilote boat-building, which included boats made from rough planks lashed together with vines and caulked with *alerce* bark. Nearby is the skeleton of a blue whale.

Inside, Spanish-language exhibits cover various aspects of life in the archipelago, including fishing, textiles and pottery, the natural environment and wildlife, European conquest, archeology and religious art. Striking photographs illustrate the impact of the 1960 earthquake, and you can see a vaguely menacing stone **Trauco** (see page 325).

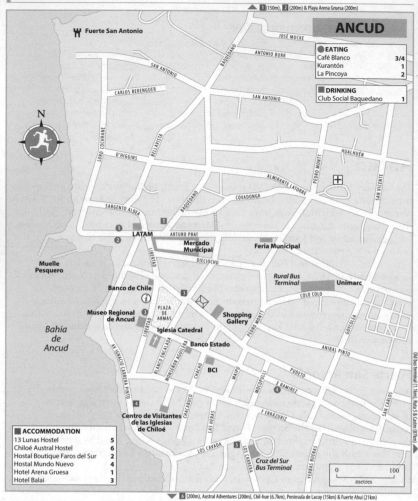

Map legend:

ANCUD

● EATING
Café Blanco	3/4
Kurantón	1
La Pincoya	2

■ DRINKING
Club Social Baquedano	1

■ ACCOMMODATION
13 Lunas Hostel	5
Chiloé Austral Hostel	6
Hostal Boutique Faros del Sur	2
Hostal Mundo Nuevo	4
Hotel Arena Gruesa	1
Hotel Balai	3

Centro de Visitantes de las Iglesias de Chiloé

Federico Errázuriz 227 • Jan & Feb Mon–Fri 9am–7pm, Sat & Sun 10am–6pm; March–Dec Mon–Fri 9.30am–6pm • Suggested donation CH$500 • ⓦ iglesiasdechiloe.cl

If you are planning to visit Chiloé's spectacular **churches** (see page 327), the **Centro de Visitantes de las Iglesias de Chiloé**, an excellent museum/visitor centre/gift shop, is a perfect starting point. Exhibits inside this church building include antique doors and other fragments, hung in the centre of the room, and illuminated to great effect by the light from the stained-glass windows. Diagrams show each stage of construction of a typical Chilote church, but the biggest draw are the incredibly detailed scale models. Staff are a good source of information.

ARRIVAL AND DEPARTURE

ANCUD

By bus Most long-distance buses – including Cruz del Sur – arrive at the Terminal de Buses on Los Carrera 850, a 5min walk from the Plaza de Armas. Queilén Bus still uses the largely abandoned and inconveniently located old bus terminal 1.5km along Arturo Prat. The rural bus terminal, serving numerous villages, is on Colo Colo, above the Unimarc supermarket; there are no Sun departures. Schedules are notoriously prone to change, so check before setting out.

Destinations from the Cruz del Sur terminal Castro (every 30min–1hr; 1hr 15min–1hr 45min); Puerto Montt (every 30min; 1hr 30min–2hr); Quellón (16 daily; 4hr).

Destinations from the rural bus terminal Caulín (Mon–Sat 1–4 daily; 30min); Chacao (Mon–Sat every 15min; 30min); Chepu (Mon, Wed & Fri 4pm; 1hr); Península Lacuy and Fuerte Agüi (Mon–Sat 1–2 daily; 45min); Puñihuil (Mon–Sat 2–3 daily; 1hr); Quemchi (Mon–Sat up to 12 daily; 1hr); Quicaví (Mon–Sat 1–2 daily; 1hr 45min).

GETTING AROUND AND INFORMATION

Car rental Salfa Sur, Arturo Prat 270, at Pedro Montt (w salfasur.cl).
Tourist office Plaza de Armas at Libertad 665 (Mon–Thurs 8.30am–5.30pm, Fri 8.30am–4.30pm; ☎ 65 262

2800, w ancud.cl/turismo). Offers information on the entire archipelago.
Websites w chiloe.cl and w www.interpatagonia.com.
Hospital Almirante Latorre 301 (☎ 65 232 6478, w hospitalancud.gov.cl).

ACTIVITIES AND TOURS

Austral Adventures Av Costanera 904 ☎ 65 262 5977, w austral-adventures.com. Established American-run outfit offering kayaking, trekking, birdwatching and

cultural experiences. Tailor-made and self-drive trips available.

7

ACCOMMODATION

Ancud has several good **budget** options, but a severe lack of decent mid-range (and no top-end) hotels.

★ **13 Lunas Hostel** Los Carrera 855 ☎ 65 262 2106, w 13lunas.cl; map p.318. It's hard to miss this bright lime and yellow hostel, a beautifully renovated, shingled wooden house opposite the Cruz del Sur bus station. It has spacious rooms, ample common spaces with guitars, TV and table football, a BBQ area, spacious guest kitchen and outdoor terraces. A basement double lacks windows but there are bonus points for extras such as bike rentals, tour info and spirit of camaraderie. Dorms CH$10,500, doubles CH$30,000

Chiloé Austral Hostel Anibal Pinto 1318 ☎ 65 262 4847, w ancudchiloechile.com; map p.318. Its snug, wood-panelled rooms overlooking the Bay of Ancud, this blue-shingled house has good-value singles, doubles and triples. While little English is spoken, Roberto and his family go out of their way to make guests feel welcome. CH$23,000

Hostal Boutique Faros del Sur Costanera Norte 320 ☎ 65 262 5799, w farosdelsur.cl; map p.318. This clifftop guesthouses boasts homely en suites, all with sea views; for the best vistas, go for the corner suite (CH$63,000). The most striking feature, however, is the splendid wood-panelled guest lounge with tall ceilings, chunky stone fireplace and light streaming in from the vast windows. Guest kitchen available. CH$49,000

★ **Hostal Mundo Nuevo** Costanera 748 ☎ 65 262 8383, w newworld.cl; map p.318. A long-standing

favourite, this guesthouse on the *costanera* offers bright, top-notch dorms and rooms (shared or private bathrooms) with polished wooden floors, a great ratio of guests/shared bathroom, communal kitchen and handy folders full of info. Sit down to a good breakfast (which includes home-made bread), ask helpful owner Martin for help with arranging excursions, or simmer in the hot tub (CH$12,000/hour for guests; CH$18,000 for non-guests). Dorms CH$14,000, doubles CH$41,000

Hotel Arena Gruesa Constanera Norte 292 ☎ 65 262 3428, w hotelarenagruesa.cl; map p.318. At this great clifftop location, a few minutes' walk from Arena Gruesa beach, there are three choices of accommodation: a large campsite with excellent sea views, hot water and individual shelters with lights; several fully equipped *cabañas* sleeping up to ten; and well-kept, wood-panelled en suites in the white-shingled hotel. Camping CH$7000, *cabañas* CH$35,000, doubles CH$46,000

Hotel Balai Pudeto 169 ☎ 65 262 2966, w hotelbalai. cl; map p.318. "Quirky" and "whimsical" are two words that come to mind when you're confronted with Victorian diving suits, mermaid figureheads and other nautical knick-knacks that clutter the common spaces. The wood-panelled rooms are a little gloomy and the attached bathrooms are tiny, but the location couldn't be more central. CH$36,000

EATING

★ **Café Blanco** Ramirez 359 and Libertad 669 ☎ 65 262 0197, w facebook.com/CafeBlancoChiloe; map p.318. The Ramirez branch of this mini chain (there's a

smaller branch on the main square, plus a couple in Castro; see page 331) is a haven, particularly on a cold, wet day. As well as the town's best coffee (from CH$1200), there's a

HOT ROCKS: THE CULINARY SECRETS OF CURANTO

Chiloé's signature dish, **curanto**, has been prepared for centuries using cooking methods very similar to those used in Polynesia, testimony to the legendary sailing prowess of the Polynesians. First, extremely hot rocks are placed at the bottom of an earthen pit; then, a layer of shellfish is added, followed by chunks of smoked meat, chicken, *longanisa* (sausage), potatoes, *chapaleles* and *milcaos* (potato dumplings). The pit is then covered with *nalca* (Chilean wild rhubarb) leaves; as the shellfish cooks, the shells spring open, releasing their juices onto the hot rocks, steaming the rest of the ingredients.

Traditional *curanto* (*curanto en hoyo*) is **slow-cooked in the ground** for a day or two, but since traditional cooking methods are only used in the countryside, most people end up sampling *curanto en olla*, also known as *pulmay*, oven-baked in cast-iron pots. The dish comes with hot shellfish broth to be drunk (and used for dipping your shellfish) during the meal.

Good bets for *curanto en hoyo* are *Al Norte del Sur* (see page 321) and *Agroturismo San Antonio* (page 322), while *Kurantón and La Pincoya* in Ancud (see page 320), and some of the restaurants in the Yumbel market in Castro (see page 330), whip up excellent *curanto en olla*.

7

range of teas, cakes, and snacks. Mon–Fri 9am–9.30pm, Sat 10am–9.30pm.

Kurantón Prat 94 ☎65 262 3090; map p.318. The legend reads: "Curanto: helping people to have good sex since 1826". Tuck into this veritable mountain of shellfish and potato dumplings amid photos of old Ancud, carvings of Chilote mythical creatures and nautical paraphernalia.

Mains CH$6,000–10,000. Daily 12.30–3pm & 7–11.30pm.

La Pincoya Prat 61 ☎65 262 2613; map p.318. Overlooking the harbour, this faded, family-run restaurant with an old-school, bow-tie-clad waiter, is a good bet for fish and seafood (CH$5000–10,000), such as *curanto en olla* and salmon *cancato*. Daily 11am–3pm & 7–10pm; erratic hours in the off-season.

DRINKING

Club Social Baquedano Baquedano 469 ☎065 262 3633; map p.318. Billing itself a "restaurant and *cantina*", this is one of the smarter eating/drinking spots, with an attractive wood-panelled dining room and terrace seating.

Draft beer and good food (from CH$5000) are on offer. Mon–Fri 12.30pm–3am, Sat 1pm–5am, Sun 6pm–3am (reduced hours out of high season).

Around Ancud

West of Ancud lies **Península Lacuy**, its clifftop **Fuerte Agüi** famous as Spain's last stronghold in Chile, while south of the town is **Islotes de Puñihuil**, a thriving penguin colony. Further south still, **Chepu Valley**, formed by the powerful tsunami after the earthquake of 1960, is a top destination for birders, its wetlands home to an abundant wealth of bird life. East of Ancud, a turn-off leads to **Caulín**, one of the best spots in Chile for oysters.

Caulín

Nine kilometres along the Panamericana on the way to Ancud from Chacao, a turn-off to the right leads to the hamlet of **CAULÍN** on the edge of a windswept, 1km-wide sandy beach, where you can often see locals collecting and laying out a stinking grey seaweed to dry. Called *pelillo* ("fine hair"), it has a dual purpose: agar-agar, a gelatinous substance used in the food and cosmetics industries can be extracted from it, or the seaweed can be woven into a fibre. Caulín is famous for its small, sweet **oysters**, the likes of which are only otherwise found in New Zealand.

ARRIVAL AND DEPARTURE

By bus Buses Caulín (☎ 09 9222 8223) run to Caulín (Mon–Sat 1–4 daily; 30min) from Ancud's rural bus terminal.

EATING

Ostras Caulín Seafront ☎09 9643 7005, ⓦ ostrascaulin.cl. Oysters come in a variety of guises at this fine restaurant, including fried, in a cocktail, as a cream of oyster soup and, the most popular choice, as an oyster platter featuring one of three types of oysters on the half shell (CH$4000–10,000). Daily dawn–dusk.

Península Lacuy

A paved road leads west out of Ancud, passing the turn-off towards Pumillahue and the Islotes de Puñihuil at 14km, and bisecting the tiny fishing community of **Quetalmahue** before reaching the **Península Lacuy**. The road forks: the left (unpaved) branch leads to the wind-whipped sand dunes and cliffs of **Playa Guabún**; if you have your own vehicle, you can follow the picturesque loop of a dirt road past the beach, through Chilote countryside, to where you started from. Chiloé's northernmost section of the **Sendero de Chile** (see page 335) also starts at Guabún, though much of the trail consists of dirt roads. The right branch continues to **Faro Corona**, an isolated lighthouse, with yet another (unpaved) fork splitting off to the right after 13km, depositing you below **Fuerte Agüi** (no set hours; entry CH$500), the last toehold of the Spanish Empire in South America. The forlorn cannons are still in place, and from the ruins you get great views of the bay of Ancud and beyond.

7

ARRIVAL AND DEPARTURE

By bus Minibuses Ahuí depart from Ancud's rural bus terminal for Fuerte Agüi (Mon–Sat 1–2 daily; 1hr).

By car Take Av Costanera south out of Ancud and follow the signposted road.

ACCOMMODATION AND EATING

★ **Chil-hue** Camino Lechagua Km 6.4 ☎ 09 9644 2578, ⓦ chil-hue.com. Describing itself as a "Sanctuary by the Sea", *Chil-hue* has three unique living spaces – the open-plan, wooden-beamed *Beach House* (sleeping up to six; US$200) and the wood-shingled *Tower* and *Studio* (both sleeping up to three) beckon travellers who come to this deserted beach in search of silence, communion with nature and dolphin sightings from their window. Gourmet meals and cookery lessons (US$80) are offered; yoga sessions also available. US$120

Al Norte del Sur 300m up the road to Guabún from the road fork ☎ 09 9919 5445, ⓦ agroturismo. alnortedelsur.cl. This homely little restaurant is a rising star of the *agroturismo* movement, and there's no menu; you'll get whatever's been cooked up on the day. *Curanto en hoyo* (see page 320) and lamb *asado* are the house specialities, accompanied by organic veg from their own garden. Dinner costs CH$7500. Rustic accommodation is also available. Daily 10am–10pm. CH$35,000

Restaurant Quetalmahue Quetalmahue, 12km west of Ancud en route to Península Lacuy ☎ 09 8791 9410, ⓦ restaurantequetalmahue.es.tl. In the tiny village of Quetalmahue, with wooden carvings of mythological Chilote figures on the patio and its grounds covered in discarded mussel shells, this rural restaurant (mains CH$7000–12,000) is an excellent bet for *curanto en hoyo*. Generally daily 2–9pm, but phone ahead.

Islotes de Puñihuil

Puñihuil · Jan–March & Sept–Dec daily 10.30am–5.45pm · CH$8000 · ☎ 09 8317 4302, ⓦ pinguineraschiloe.cl · Driving to Pumillahue from Ancud is straightforward if you take Av Costanera south and follow the signs; you can also catch a bus – Buses Mar Brava (☎ 65 262 2312) runs a regular service from Ancud's rural bus terminal (Mon–Sat 1 daily; 30min) – or share a taxi (around CH$20,000 one-way); for the islands, you can come on an organized tour from Ancud or Castro (around CH$20,000; approx 3hr) or hop on a boat excursion; they depart directly from the beach (at least hourly; 40min); reserve in advance in Jan & Feb

Reachable from Ancud along a mostly paved 28km road is the seaside village of **Pumillahue**. Just off the coast lies the rocky outcrop of the **Islotes de Puñihuil**, a **penguin colony** monitored by Ecoturismo Puñihuil, a local organization dedicated to the protection of the penguins. This thriving colony is unique to Chile in that it is visited by both Magellanic and Humboldt **penguins** in the breeding and rearing season. The adults fish most of the day, so try to visit in the morning or mid-to-late afternoon.

Three companies based in the guesthouse and restaurants on the beach pool their customers and run informative **boat trips** to see the penguins and other marine fauna, including the sleek *chungungos* (marine otters). At the time of writing there were controversial plans to build a wind farm nearby.

Chepu Valley

Heading south towards Castro, Ruta 5 (which traverses the island) passes two rough, gravelled tracks to Chepu – one at 12.5km south and the other at 25km south, both leading through farmland to the **Chepu Valley**. You'll see undulating pastureland and, making up the scattered settlement of Chepu, a few farmhouses spread out along the gravel roads. The main attraction is a large stretch of **wetlands**, created in 1960 when the tsunami caused by the most powerful earthquake ever recorded flooded a section of coastal forest. Today, the sunken forest provides a thriving habitat for over a hundred different bird species, as well as ground for **kayaking** and fishing.

ARRIVAL AND DEPARTURE CHEPU VALLEY

By bus Buses Peter runs from Ancud's rural bus terminal to Chepu (Mon, Wed & Fri 4pm; 1hr).

By car Take the Panamericana from Ancud and then either the gravel road to Chepu from Km 25; or take another

gravel road from the Km 12 turn-off, though this route is longer and rougher. Immediately beyond Chepu, the track descends sharply; don't try to drive it – cars have been stranded in the past.

ACCOMMODATION AND EATING

Agroturismo San Antonio Camino a Chepu Km 2 ☎09 9643 7046, ✉agroturismosanantonio@gmail.com. Set amid beautiful flowering gardens, the rural home of the Dimter Maldonado family welcomes you into its fold, largely thanks to the efforts of super-friendly hostess María Louisa. The rooms are simple yet comfortable, and if there are enough takers, the family cooks up a fantastic *curanto*

en hoyo (CH$12,000). To get here, take the first turn-off to Chepu from Ancud for 2km. **CH$30,000**

Chepu Adventures Camino a Chepu Km 13.2 ☎09 9227 4517 or ☎65 284 0543, ⊛chepu.cl. This wonderful, award-winning ecolodge is currently closed as the owners are looking to sell; check the website for updates.

Quemchi

East from the Panamericana, 41km south of Ancud, a coastal road leads to **QUEMCHI**, an attractive little fishing town with narrow streets sloping down to the water's edge. On a sunny day, the sight of snow-tipped volcanoes beyond makes for an impressive sight. A couple of kilometres south, there's a tiny wooded island, **Isla Aucar**, only accessible by a 500m-long footbridge. Nestled on the island is a small **church** with a duck-egg-blue roof.

ARRIVAL AND DEPARTURE QUEMCHI

By bus Quemchi is served by up to ten daily buses (1hr) from Ancud's rural bus terminal. There are also buses from Castro (Mon–Sat 18 daily, Sun 3; 1hr 15min).

EATING

El Chejo Diego Bahamonde 251 ☎65 269 1490. Wander into the kitchen at this family-run restaurant and peer into the pots to see what Elsa is cooking; the menu ranges from grilled fish to *casuela Chilote* (Chilote stew with *cochayuyo*

seaweed) and *curanto*. Many consider the seafood *empanadas* the best on the island. Dishes from CH$2000. Daily 1–3.30pm & 7.30–10.30pm.

Dalcahue

The bustling, historical town of **DALCAHUE** lies 20km northeast of Castro via the turn-off at Llau-Llao. It is famous for its boat-building industry and the Sunday **Feria Artesanal**, a much better bet for Chilote goods than Castro. Dalcahue also provides the only link with nearby **Isla Quinchao** (see page 327), the second largest island in the archipelago.

Most of the action is centred around the attractive **Plaza de Armas** and the open-sided market building on the waterfront. On the plaza rises the imposing, UNESCO-listed **Iglesia de Nuestra Señora de Los Dolores**, which dates back to 1893 and boasts a unique nine-arched portico.

ARRIVAL AND DEPARTURE
DALCAHUE

By bus Buses Dalcahue Expreso run daily from Castro (Mon–Sat every 15min, Sun every 30min; 30min).

ACTIVITIES AND TOURS

Altué Expeditions ☎ 09 9419 6809, ⓦ seakayakchile. com. Excellent outfit offering multi-day trips around the archipelago complete with lodging at their kayak centre near Dalcahue. Combination trips in the Lake District and Patagonia are also on offer.

ACCOMMODATION

Hostal Encanto Patagón Montt 146 ☎ 65 264 1651 ⓦ hostalencantopatagon.blogspot.com. On the *costanera* (waterfront), this venerable 120–year-old house with sloping wooden floors has a clutch of singles, doubles and triples named after locations on the Carretera Austral. The owners whip up delicious meals and can help plan trips to some of the far-flung islands. CH$32,000

Hostal Lanita O'Higgins 50 ☎ 65 264 2020, ⓦ lanitahostal.blogspot.com. You'll feel part of the family at this homely little hostel. Besides the snug five-bed dorm there's a double and a triple. The only downside is the occasional queue for the two bathrooms. Dorms CH$13,000, doubles CH$32,000

Refugio de Navegantes San Martín 165 ☎ 65 264 1128, ⓦ refugiodenavegantes.cl. Attached to the cafe-restaurant-souvenir shop of the same name (see below), this boutique hotel is a delightful place to stay, with elegant, well-equipped (coffee machines, TVs, etc) en suites, some with church views. CH$115,000

EATING

★ **Café Artesanías Casita de Piedra** Montt 144 ☎ 09 9489 9050. Bringing a touch of urban sophistication to Dalcahue's *costanera*, at this split-level boutique/café you can buy woollen goods downstairs and then head up to the cheerful yellow café for a hit of espresso or a *ristretto* (coffee from CH$1400). Tues–Sat 10.30am–2pm & 3.30–8pm, Sun 10.30am–2pm.

Las Cocinera Dalcahue Next to the Feria Artesanal. This establishment, resembling an upturned boat, is an excellent place to try inexpensive Chilote specialities. Shop around the various food stalls as local women dish up *curanto*, *empanadas*, *milcaos* (flat potato dumplings studded with smoked pork) and sweet baked twists known as *calzones rotos* (literally "torn underpants"). Doña Lula, Puesto 8, does fabulous empanadas; Tenchita, Puesto 2, is a favourite for *canacato*, while La Nenita, Puesto 4, offers very fresh salmon ceviche. A good feed will set you back less than CH$5000. Daily 9am–7/8pm.

Refugio de Navegantes San Martín 165 ☎ 65 264 1128, ⓦ refugiodenavegantes.cl. With its vast slate fireplace and stellar plaza location, this shingled house surrounded by monkey puzzle trees is a port in a storm for travellers in search of comfy seats to sink into and a menu of delicious light bites (mains from CH$5500). There are souvenirs for sale, and you can also stay the night (see above). Jan & Feb Mon–Wed 9am–11pm; Thurs 1–10pm, Fri & Sat 9am–11pm, Sun 11am–8pm; March–Dec reduced hours.

Around Dalcahue

For visitors wishing to witness **traditional Chilote life** in settlements where time seems to stand still, there are few better places to do so than the **east coast**. If you have your own vehicle, take the gravel roads to tiny, sleepy coastal villages, where on a grey and

CHILOTE MYTHOLOGY

The islands of Chiloé have long been rife with **myths** and legends, especially in the remote rural regions, where tradition and superstition hold sway, with colourful supernatural creatures cropping up in stories throughout the archipelago.

Basilisco A snake with the head of a cockerel, the Basilisco turns people to stone with its gaze. At night, the Basilisco enters houses and sucks the breath from sleeping inhabitants, so that they waste away into shrivelled skeletons. The only way to be rid of it is to burn the house down.

Brujo This is the general term for a witch; in Chiloé, there are only male witches and their legendary cave is rumoured to be near the village of Quicaví. To become a witch, an individual must wash away baptism in a waterfall for forty days, assassinate a loved one, make a purse out of their skin in which to carry their book of spells and sign a pact with the devil in their own blood, stating when the evil one can claim their soul. Witches are capable of great mischief and can cause illness and death, even from afar.

Caleuche This ghostly ship glows in the fog, travels at great speeds both above and below the water, emitting beautiful music, carrying the witches to their next stop. Journeying through the archipelago, it's crewed by shipwrecked sailors and fishermen who have perished at sea.

Fiura An ugly, squat woman with halitosis, she lives in the woods, clothed in moss. The coquettish Fiura bathes in waterfalls, where she seduces young men before driving them insane.

Invunche Stolen at birth by witches, and raised on the flesh of the dead and cats' milk, the Invunche was transformed into a deformed monster with one leg crooked behind his back. He feeds on goats' flesh and stands guard at the entrance to the legendary witches' cave, the Cueva de Quicaví, grunting or emitting bloodcurdling screams. If you're unlucky enough to see him, you'll be frozen to that spot forever.

Pincoya A fertility goddess of extraordinary beauty, Pincoya personifies the spirit of the ocean and is responsible for the abundance or scarcity of fish in the sea. She dances half-naked, draped in kelp, on the beaches or tops of waves. If she's spotted facing the sea, the village will enjoy an ample supply of seafood. If she's looking towards the land, there will be a shortage.

Trauco A deformed and ugly troll who dwells in the forest, Trauco dresses in ragged clothes and a conical cap and carries a stone axe or wooden club, a *pahueldœn*. His breath makes him irresistible to women, and he is blamed for all unexplained pregnancies on the island.

Voladora The witches' messenger, the Voladora is a woman who transforms into a black bird by vomiting up her internal organs. The Voladora travels under the cover of night and can only be detected by her terrible cries, which bring bad luck. If the Voladora is unable to recover her innards at the end of the night, she is stuck in bird shape forever.

7

misty day you can almost imagine the characters from Chiloé's **mythology** (see above) coming to life. On public transport you can cross over to **Isla Quinchao**, characterized by its rolling farmland, small towns with striking traditional churches and the daily market in Achao.

Península Rilán

Between Dalcahue and Castro, the tranquil, rural **Península Rilán** is increasingly popular. In addition to the UNESCO-listed **Iglesia de Santa María de Rilán**, the peninsula boasts rich **bird life** thanks to its extensive wetlands, as well as several smart hotels.

ARRIVAL AND DEPARTURE   PENÍNSULA RILÁN

By bus Several daily buses run from Castro's rural bus terminal to the village of Rilán (1hr 15min), but it's best to have your own transport.

7

ACCOMMODATION AND EATING

Hotel Parque Quilquico Quilquico ☎65 297 1100, ⓦhpq.cl. Overlooking a peaceful valley, this horseshoe-shaped, *alerce*-shingled hotel has won awards for its efforts towards sustainability. It's visually stunning, with grass growing on the roofs of its corridors, *palafito*-style rooms on stilts and an indoor pool and hot tub. Even if you're not staying, the restaurant is worth the trip, and guests have access to walking trails. Rates include half board. U̲S̲$̲3̲0̲2̲

★ **Rucalaf Putemún** Camino de Rilán Km 3.6 ☎09 9579 7571, ⓦrucalafputemun.cl. A short drive out of Castro, en route to the Rilán peninsula, this roadside treasure has won accolades for its imaginative fusion cuisine. Surrounded by colourful modern prints, you can treat yourself to the likes of salmon carpaccio, suckling pig and lime cheesecake with rhubarb compote (mains CH$7000–12,000). There's also a well-chosen drinks list. Tues–Sat 1–4pm & 7.30–10pm.

★ **Tierra Chiloé** San José Playa ☎65 277 2080, ⓦwww.tierrahotels.com. Overlooking a gorgeous bay, this eye-catching, award-winning hotel is constructed from a mix of native woods and concrete, and blends in perfectly with its surroundings. As well as exquisite en suites with huge windows and great views, *Tierra Chiloé* has an excellent restaurant (open to non-guests; book on erecepcion@tierrachiloe.com), a good spa and a high level of service: it's the best place to stay on the archipelago. Two-night minimum stay; full board, drinks, transfers and daily excursions, which range from boat cruises to cultural trips, included. U̲S̲$̲1̲5̲5̲0̲

Tenaún

From Dalcahue, an attractive gravel road heads northeast towards Quemchi, following the coast. Some 37km kilometres along, a small bumpy road with two forks (first take the left, then the right) heads down to the somnolent coastal village of **TENAÚN**. Smiling down at the attractive waterfront and quaint little fishermen's cottages is arguably Chiloé's most extraordinary **church**. Founded in 1734 but rebuilt in 1861, and since spruced up, it's dazzling: painted white with two huge pale blue stars daubed onto the wall above the entrance, and topped by three vibrant blue and red towers.

ARRIVAL AND DEPARTURE   TENAÚN

By bus There are regular buses to Tenaún (at least 4 daily; 1hr 15min) from Castro with Expresos Catalina and Expresos Tenaún.

ACCOMMODATION

Hospedaje Mirella Tenaún ☎09 9647 6750, ⓔmirellamontana@gmail.com. Part of the *Agroturismo* network, this friendly family-run guesthouse has room for seven guests in a few basic but comfy rooms and is run by the hospitable Mirella and the Soto family. *Curanto en hoyo* is sometimes on offer. C̲H̲$̲2̲8̲,̲0̲0̲0̲

Quicaví

Six kilometres beyond Tenaún on the main road, a turn to the east leads, after 7km, to the tiny seafront village of **QUICAVÍ**, whose sleepiness belies its importance in Chilote mythology. It's said that somewhere along the nearby coast lies the legendary **Cueva de Quicaví**, where a Spanish warlock left a powerful book of spells for the resident *brujos* after being defeated in a magic duel. The Spanish Inquisition, and many others besides, have searched for the cave in vain. Perhaps because of this wealth of superstition, the missionaries built a larger than usual **church** here.

ARRIVAL AND DEPARTURE   QUICAVÍ

By bus Buses Expreso Quicaví (☎09 9248 4362) has services from Ancud (Mon–Sat 1–2 daily; 1hr), as does Buses Rony Velásquez (Mon–Fri 1 daily).

Isla Mechuque

Small launches depart from Tenaún and Quicaví for the beautiful **Isla Mechuque**, the largest and most easily accessible island of the Chauques subgroup. Since a quorum of

CHILOTE CHURCHES

It is impossible to visit Chiloé and not be struck by the sight of the archipelago's incredible **wooden churches**. In the early nineteenth century these impressively large buildings would have been the heart of a Chilote village. Several of the churches have been declared national monuments, an honour crowned in 2001 when UNESCO accepted sixteen of them on its prestigious World Heritage list. Of these (Colo, Tenaún, San Juan, Dalcahue, Achao, Quinchao, Caguach, Rilán, Chelín, Nercón, Chonchi, Ichuac, Aldachildo, Detif, Vilupulli and Castro) only fourteen are on Chiloé Island proper; Chelín and Caguach are found on tiny islands off the east coast, with the last particularly far-flung and difficult to reach.

The churches generally face the sea and are built near a beach with an open area, plaza or *explanada* in front of them. The outside of the churches is almost always bare, and the only thing that expresses anything but functionality is the three-tiered, **hexagonal bell tower** that rises up directly above an open-fronted portico. The facades, doors and windows are often brightly painted, and the walls clad with *tejuelas* (wooden tiles or shingles). All the churches have three naves separated by columns, which in the larger buildings are highly decorated, supporting barrel-vaulted ceilings. The ceilings are often painted, too, with allegorical panels or sometimes with golden constellations of stars painted on an electric blue background.

HISTORY

Only the *pueblos* with a priest had a main church, or **iglesia parroquial**. If there was no church, the missionaries used to visit once a year, as part of their so-called *misión circular*. Using only native canoes, they carried everything required to hold a mass with them. When the priest arrived, one of the eldest Chilotes would lead a procession carrying an image of Jesus, and behind him two youths would follow with depictions of San Juan and the Virgin. They would be followed by married men carrying a statue of San Isidro and married women carrying one of Santa Neoburga.

If the *pueblo* was important enough there would be a small *capilla* (bell tower) with altars to receive the statues. The building where the missionaries stayed was known as a *residencia*, *villa*, *casa ermita* or *catecera*, and was looked after by a local trustee called a *fiscal*, whose function was somewhere between that of a verger and lay preacher. This honorary position still exists and, in Chiloé's remoter areas, the *fiscal* commands great respect in his community. For more **information** on Chiloé's churches, check out the informative Ⓦinterpatagonia.com/iglesiaschiloe.

passengers is required, the surest way of making this magical trip past unspoiled island scenery is to go on an organized excursion from Castro in the summer (see page 331). The highlight of trips to the tiny village of **Mechuque**, with its shingled *palafitos*, is a genuine *curanto en hoyo* (organize in advance).

Isla Quinchao

For some, **Isla Quinchao** is the cultural heart of Chiloé. Rich in traditional wooden architecture, the island is a mere ten-minute ferry ride from Dalcahue. A paved road runs across Quinchao through the only two towns of any size, **Curaco de Vélez** and **Achao**, both of which offer a taste of traditional Chilote life. They can be seen on a day-trip from Castro or Dalcahue.

Curaco de Vélez

Twelve kilometres from the ferry terminal, **CURACO DE VÉLEZ** comprises a couple of streets of weather-beaten shingled houses set around a beautiful bay and bordered by rolling hills. The Plaza de Armas features a bust of locally born hero Almirante Riveros, who commanded the fleet that captured the Peruvian, ironclad *Huáscar* during the War of the Pacific (see page 474). From November to March, the kiosks just off the plaza host a **Feria Artesanal** (Jan & Feb daily; March, Nov & Dec Sat & Sun).

Achao

Fifteen kilometres southeast of Curaco lies the fishing village of **ACHAO** with its scattering of houses clad in colourful *tejuelas* (shingles), set against a backdrop of snowcapped volcano peaks. It is famous both for its **church** and two simultaneous **festivals** in early February: Encuentro Folklórico de las Islas del Archipiélago, a folk festival that draws musical groups from all over Chiloé, and Muestra Gastronómica y Artesanal, which gives you a chance to sample traditional Chilote cuisine and pick up handicrafts.

Iglesia Santa María de Loreto

Plaza de Armas • Tues–Sun 11am–12.45pm & 2–4pm • Free

Dominating the Plaza de Armas and dating back to 1764, **Iglesia Santa María de Loreto** is a prime example of a typical Chilote church and is thought to be the oldest in the archipelago. The main framework is made from *ciprés de las Guaitecas* and *mañío*, a tree still common in southern Chile. The original *alerce* shingles which covered the exterior have mostly been replaced with *ciprés* boarding. Restoration work is a constant and expensive necessity – if you look around the *luma* wood floorboards, you can see the church's foundations. All the joints have been laboriously fixed into place with wooden plugs and dowels made from *canelo*, another type of Chilean wood.

ARRIVAL AND DEPARTURE ISLA QUINCHAO

By boat Ferry services run from the Dalcahue dock (every 30min, 7am–11pm; foot passengers free, cars CH$4000 return).

By bus Achao's Terminal de Buses (Miraflores at Zañartu), a couple of blocks east of the Plaza, has daily departures for Dalcahue (every 20min, 7.15am–8.30pm; 40min) via Curaco de Vélez. Bus tickets include the ferry journey.

ACCOMMODATION AND EATING

Hospedaje Sol y Lluvia Ricardo Jara 9, Achao ☎65 266 1383. The nicest guesthouse in town, with a burned-orange exterior that hides spacious, comfortable rooms, some with shared bathrooms. The owners offer breakfast that is above and beyond the usual bread-and-instant-coffee combo and solo travellers pay exactly half. **CH$26,000**

Ostras Los Troncos Francisco Bohle s/n, Curaco de Vélez. Follow the road downhill from the Plaza de Armas to the coastal road and look out for the sign that'll direct you to the garden, festooned with fishing nets and lined with rough-hewn wooden tables and seats – a superb spot for slurping a dozen or two local oysters (around CH$500/oyster). Jan–March & Dec daily 11am–7pm.

Castro

Built on a small promontory at the head of a 20km fjord, lively **CASTRO** occupies an unusual position physically and historically. Founded in 1567, it's the third-oldest city in Chile, but it never became strategically important because it's a terrible harbour for sailing ships, only flourishing because the Jesuits chose to base their mission here. Today, little remains of old Castro, though some buildings have miraculously survived, such as the clusters of colourful **palafitos** – shingled fishermen's houses on stilts – on the waterfront to the north and south of town, many of which have now been turned into some of Chiloé's best lodgings and cafés. Castro is as cosmopolitan as the archipelago gets, with a clutch of good restaurants, plus excellent transport.

Iglesia de San Francisco de Castro

Northeast corner of the central Plaza de Armas • Summer daily 9.30am–10pm; rest of the year Mon–Sat 9.30am–12.30pm & 3.30–8.30pm, Sun 9am–12.30pm & 3–8.30pm • Free

The national monument of **Iglesia San Francisco de Castro** is one of Chiloé's sixteen UNESCO-recognized churches (see page 327), its iron-clad wooden structure a mix of Classical and neo-Gothic styles, designed in 1906 by the Italian Eduardo Provasoli. The impressive interior comprises a harmonious blend of the island's native hardwoods and rows of stained-glass windows, while the exterior is a violent clash of yellow and purple.

Museo Regional

Calle Esmeralda • Jan & Feb Mon–Fri 9.30am–7pm, Sat 9.30am–6.30pm, Sun 10.30am–1pm; March–Dec Mon–Fri 9.30am–1pm & 3–6.30pm, Sat 9.30am–1pm • Free, but donations welcome

Located just off the Plaza de Armas, the small but well-laid-out **Museo Regional** displays Huilliche artefacts and traditional farming implements, as well as black-and-white photographs of the town, before and after it was devastated by the 1960 earthquake.

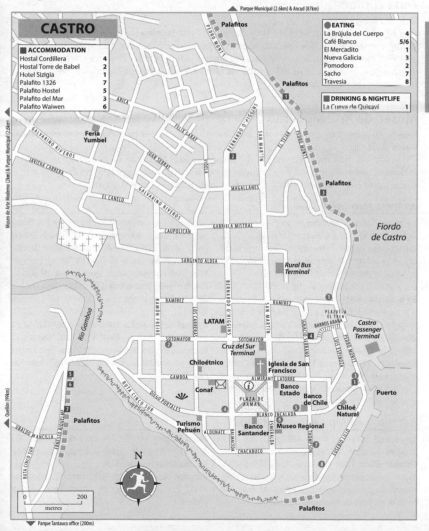

CASTRO

ACCOMMODATION
Hostal Cordillera	4
Hostal Torre de Babel	2
Hotel Sizigia	1
Palafito 1326	7
Palafito Hostel	5
Palafito del Mar	3
Palafito Waiwen	6

EATING
La Brújula del Cuerpo	4
Café Blanco	5/6
El Mercadito	1
Nueva Galicia	3
Pomodoro	2
Sacho	7
Travesia	8

DRINKING & NIGHTLIFE
La Cueva de Quisaví	1

7

7

CASTRO'S PALAFITOS

Though deemed unsanitary by some locals, Chiloé's famous **palafitos** are still found at several locations around Castro. Perched precariously on stilts above the water, these brightly painted, *alerce*-shingled, traditional wooden fishermen's dwellings are an unforgettable sight. The idea was that you could moor your boat at your back door and walk out onto the street through the front one. The most impressive examples are at the north end of town, off **Pedro Montt**, where they are perfectly reflected in the grubby mini-lake by the roadside. More are found slightly south along the same street, while others are used as restaurants at the southern end of town, by the **Feria Artesanal**. A final batch can be seen from the western end of Lillo, across the **Río Gamboa** – and a number have now been converted into atmospheric lodgings and restaurants (see page 331).

Feria Yumbel

Yumbel 863 • Mon–Sat 8am–7pm

In a new location, northwest of the centre, the **Feria Yumbel** is a large covered market selling the woollen goods that the region is famous for. There are also some Peruvian and Bolivian offerings, so pay attention to what you purchase. Produce stalls sell anything from necklaces of dried mussels to fresh fruit, and you'll find several inexpensive places to eat.

Museo de Arte Moderno

Pasaje Diaz 181, 4km northwest of downtown • Mid-Jan to mid-March daily 10am–6pm • Free, but donation welcomed • ☎ 65 263 5454, ⓦ mamchiloe.cl

Only open during the high season, the **Museo de Arte Moderno** (also known as MAM) is housed inside a group of five restored wooden barns inside a park. The displays are made up of edgy contemporary works by Chilean (and Chilote) artists.

ARRIVAL AND DEPARTURE   CASTRO

By plane Castro is connected to Santiago by LATAM flights; there's an office at O'Higgins 412 (☎ 600 526 2000, ⓦ latam.com). Transfers to the airport, 19km north of the city centre and currently undergoing an expansion, can be organized by your hotel (around CH$4500).
Destinations Santiago (5 weekly; 1hr 55min).
By bus Castro's long-distance (Cruz del Sur) bus terminal is at San Martín 486, a block north of the Plaza de Armas, while the rural bus terminal is at San Martín 667, down an alley two and a half blocks north of the Plaza.
Destinations from the long-distance bus terminal Ancud (every 30min–1hr; 1hr 15min–1hr 45min); Chonchi (every 30min–1hr; 30min); Puerto Montt (hourly–every 2hr; 3hr); Punta Arenas, via Argentina (3 weekly; 28hr); Quellón (hourly; 2hr 15min).

Destinations from the rural bus terminal Achao (Mon–Sat every 30min; fewer on Sun; 1hr 50min); Chonchi (every 30min; 30min); Cucao and the Parque Nacional Chiloé, sector Anay (up to 15 daily; 1hr 15min); Curaco de Vélez (Mon–Sat every 30min, fewer on Sun; 1hr 30min); Dalcahue (every 30min; 30min); Puqueldón (Mon–Sat 2–3 daily, Sun 1; 1hr 15min); Queilén (hourly–every 2hr; 1hr 15min).
By boat Naviera Austral (ⓦ www.navieraustral.cl) runs a weekly boat to Chaitén in summer (days and times subject to change, so check in advance; 5hr 30min) from Castro's passenger terminal. Book tickets via Turismo Pehuén (see page 331).

GETTING AROUND AND INFORMATION

Car rental Salfa Sur, Mistral 499 (☎ 65 263 0422, ⓦ salfasur.cl); ask also at *Hostal Cordillera* (see page 331).
Tourist office Plaza de Armas (daily 10am–8pm; ✉ turismo@municastro.cl). A large and well-stocked office (though the brochures are hidden behind the desk) that keeps erratic hours in spite of the set timetable.

Conaf Gamboa 424 (Mon–Fri 10am–12.30pm & 2.30–4pm; ☎ 65 253 2503). Limited information about Parque Nacional Chiloé (see page 334).
Hospital Hospital Augusta Rifat, Freire 852 (☎ 65 263 2445, ⓦ hospitalcastro.gov.cl), offers basic medical services.

ACTIVITIES AND TOURS

Chiloé Natural Blanco 100 ☎ 65 253 4973, ⓦ chiloenatural.com. An experienced, English-speaking outfit offering day-trips and multi-day treks in Parque Tantauco, as well as horseriding, trips to Parque Nacional Chiloé, *curanto*-eating outings to Chelín by catamaran, excellent kayaking adventures and day-visits to seven churches. Tailor-made trips are arranged and kayaks, mountain bikes and camping equipment are available for rent; there's also a detailed map of Chiloé for sale in the small attached shop. They run a free walking tour of Castro, departing from the main plaza (Jan & Feb daily 10am).

Chiloétnico Los Carrera 435 ☎ 65 263 0951, ⓦ chiloetnico.cl. Juan Pablo is an enthusiastic, English-speaking, experienced guide who arranges anything from trips to Parque Tantauco, Tepuhueico and Parque Nacional Chiloé to multi-day cultural immersions in traditional Chilote culture or a half-day horseriding jaunt to Nercón. Mountain bike, tent and sleeping bag rental also on offer.

Turismo Pehuén Chacabuco 498 ☎ 65 263 5254, ⓦ turismopehuen.cl. Established company specializing in day-trips, from boat outings to Isla Mechuque to gastronomic tours and church tours. Also car rental.

ACCOMMODATION

Castro has seen a proliferation of boutique-type **accommodation** inside converted, renovated *palafitos*. A short drive away, tranquil **Península Rilán** (see page 325) has some luxury hotels.

7

Hostal Cordillera Barros Arana 175 ☎ 09 9512 2667, ⓦ hostalcordillera.cl; map p.329. Less atmospheric than its budget competitors, but still a solid choice, with reasonable rooms with shared or private bathrooms; solo travellers pay half the price of a double. There's also a cabin sleeping up to seven people, and a useful rent-a-car service. Doubles CH$36,000, cabin CH$100,000

Hostal Torre de Babel O'Higgins 965 ☎ 65 253 4569, ⓦ hostaltorredebabel.com; map p.329. Travellers from around the world find a common language in the vast, wood-stove-heated, beanbag-strewn lounge of this welcoming hostel. Young, helpful owner Louis is happy to give advice, and the simple wood-panelled rooms are comfortable, if a bit gloomy. Dorms CH$18,000, doubles CH$36,000

Hotel Sizigia Pedro Montt 817 ☎ 9 92225453, ⓦ sizigia.cl; map p.329. Owned by a local writer-photographer, this boutique *palafito* hotel has stylish, minimalist en suites, many of which have huge windows offering views directly of the water (#8 is the best). Downstairs is a charming café-bar, and a small shop filled with tasteful souvenirs. CH$110,000

★ **Palafito 1326** Riquelme 1326 ☎ 65 253 0053, ⓦ palafito1326.cl; map p.329. This boutique *palafito* hotel combines traditional Chilote design (walls made of native cypress and *tepú* wood, thick woollen throws and pillows) with floor-to-ceiling windows, subtle lighting, immaculate, modern bathrooms and a first-rate café-bar

(featuring local craft beers) upstairs with estuary views. Tours can be arranged. CH$89,000

★ **Palafito Hostel** Riquelme 1210 ☎ 65 253 1008, ⓦ palafitohostel.com; map p.329. Its curved wooden walls reminiscent of a ship, this revamped *palafito* has a selection of beautiful rooms (all en suite; two with sea-view balconies), a four-bed dorm, an appealing common space upstairs, adorned with contemporary art and woollen hangings, and an outdoor deck overlooking the water. Staff can organize tours, including horseriding in Parque Nacional Chiloé. Dorms CH$17,000, doubles CH$58,000

★ **Palafito del Mar** Av Pedro Montt 567 ☎ 65 263 1622, ⓦ palafitodelmar.cl; map p.329. With just five suites, a double and a triple, this elegant boutique *palafito* hotel is run by an engaging young couple. All rooms have terraces with sea views and the gorgeous common area, flooded with natural light and sporting quirky furniture, was instrumental in securing architectural awards. You can kayak right off the sea terrace out back, too. The same couple also offer four-person apartments at *Apart Hotel El Palacito* next door. Doubles CH$70,000, apartments CH$140,000

★ **Palafito Waiwen** Riquelme 1236 ☎ 65 253 3888, ⓦ palafitowaiwen.com; map p.329. Another *palafito*-based hostel, in the pretty Gamboa neighbourhood, *Waiwen* has attractive wood-panelled en-suite rooms and slightly cramped four-bed dorms, some with wonderful views. Dorms CH$15,000, doubles CH$50,000

EATING

CAFÉS AND CHEAP EATS

La Brújula del Cuerpo O'Higgins 308 ☎ 65 263 3229, ⓦ facebook.com/LaBrujulaDelCuerpo; map p.329. Travellers and locals alike gravitate to "The Body's Compass" – a busy café on the main square specializing in inexpensive burgers, salads, sandwiches, and ice cream sundaes (CH$2900–4100 for the last), plus a good-value set lunch for around CH$5000. Mon–Thurs 9.30am–

11pm, Fri 10am–midnight, Sat 11am–midnight, Sun 12.30–9pm.

Café Blanco Blanco 215 and Blanco 268 ☎ 65 253 4636, ⓦ facebook.com/CafeBlancoChiloe; map p.329. Part of a mini-chain, with two branches on the same road and another pair in Ancud (see page 319), *Café Blanco* is a treat, with more than a dozen coffees (CH$1200–3300), Twinings and Clipper tea, great cakes and light meals

FESTIVAL COSTUMBRISTA

At the northwest end of Castro lies the **Parque Municipal**. In mid-February the park hosts an enormous feast, the culmination of the **Festival Costumbrista**, a celebration of traditional Chilote life, when *curanto* is cooked in great cauldrons, *chicha* (cider) flows freely and balls of grated potato – *tropón* – are baked on hot embers. The inevitable burned fingers and resultant hot-potato juggling that results from picking them up is known as *bailar el tropón* (dancing the *tropón*). From early January until the end of February, the Festival Costumbrista is held every weekend in a different part of Chiloé, with events held by both the Castro and Ancud municipalities.

including burgers, sandwiches and salads. Mon–Fri 9am–9.30pm, Sat 10am–9.30pm.

RESTAURANTS

In addition to the places reviewed below, the **Feria Yumbel** (see page 330) has a range of inexpensive places to eat.

★ **El Mercadito** Montt 210 ☎65 253 3866, ⓦelmercaditodechiloe.cl; map p.329. Excellent, inventive restaurant close to the dock. The menu features imaginative, often fusion, creations conjured up from local, seasonal ingredients: try fresh local oysters (CH$8000 for a dozen and a glass of wine) and a hearty chori buger (with chorizo; CH$7200). Daily 1–3.30pm & 7.30–10.30pm.

Nueva Galicia Montt 38 ☎65 253 2828; map p.329. Inside this nautically themed, white-linen restaurant, waiters serve up Chilote standards such as *curanto* and *cancato* (salmon steamed with sausage and cheese), as well as more imaginative fusion dishes including king crab lasagne. Accompaniments may include quinoa as well as Chilote potatoes. Mains from CH$8000. Tues–Sun 1.30–3.30pm & 7.30–10.30pm.

Pomodoro Sotomayor 520 ☎65 263 4141, ⓦfacebook.com/pomodorotrattoria; map p.329. A standout Italian restaurant, offering everything from *vitello tonnato* to stone-baked pizzas, house-made pastas to tiramisu (mains CH$7000–10,000); ask about off-the-menu specials, which sometimes include king crab cannelloni. Tues–Sat 1–10pm, Sun 1–4pm.

Sacho Thompson 213 ☎65 263 2079; map p.329. The upstairs dining area of this local institution offers excellent views across the fjord. It's difficult to go wrong with anything clam or fish based, though there is also a good selection of Spanish-style omelettes, *milanesas* and steaks (mains CH$4500–10,000): the *cancato* stands out. Mains from CH$7000. Mon–Sat noon–3.30pm & 8–11.30pm.

Travesia Lillo 188 ☎65 263 0137, ⓦfacebook.com/restaurantravesia; map p.329. An excellent place to sample traditional Chilote, fusion and global dishes (mains CH$8000–10,000), cooked and served with a contemporary flourish. The chef has also written a (Spanish-language) cookbook – *Chiloé contado desde la cocina* – about Chilote cuisine and culture; it's well worth picking up if you can find a copy. Mon–Sat 1–11pm, Sun 1–4pm.

DRINKING AND NIGHTLIFE

In addition to the establishment below, *Palafito 1326* and *Hotel Sizigia* (see page 331) also have appealing **bars** with views across the water.

La Cueva de Quicaví Encalada 55; map p.329. Despite a garish entrance guarded by a demon, and a rough-and-ready interior, this is actually a pretty welcoming place for a drink (and sometimes a dance). Live music is luck of the draw – local death metallers one night, reggae the next – but there's usually a lively crowd after midnight and a good beer selection. Tues–Sat 7pm–2/3am.

Parque Nacional Chiloé and around

59km southwest of Castro · Daily 9am–7pm · CH$4000 · ☎065 248 6102, ⓦwww.conaf.cl

On the island's western coast, the **Parque Nacional Chiloé** comprises more than 420 square kilometres of native evergreen forest, covering the slopes and valleys of the **Cordillera de Piuchén**, largely unexplored and harbouring flora and fauna unique to the archipelago, as well as deserted beaches and long stretches of **rugged coastline**, home to dozens of seabird species, penguins and sea lions.

HIKING IN PARQUE NACIONAL CHILOÉ

A couple of short **hikes** start from the visitor centre at the Conaf ranger post. Besides two ultra-short interpretative trails, one is the circular, 770m **El Tepual**, running through an area of *tepu* forest, a tree which thrives in this humid bogland; there are log walkways across the wetter sections of these enchanted-looking woods, with twisted moss-covered trunks intertwined with other native species. The second hike is the **Sendero La Playa**, which leads you through patches of *nalca* (native rhubarb) and tunnels of dense vegetation before emerging on the regenerating scrubland that takes you via sand dunes to the exposed Pacific coast. A little more taxing is the 3km (one-way) walk along the beach to Lago Huelde, where you pick up a 9km trail known as **Sendero Rancho Grande**, along the Río Deñal up to the edge of the tree line, revealing beautiful views below.

The park's longest hike is the beautiful 25km (6hr) **Sendero Chanquín**, which alternates between stretches of coastline, pounded by the fierce Pacific surf, and dense, native evergreen forest, before finishing up by the rustic Conaf *refugio* and campsite at Cole Cole (overseen by the Huentemó community). There's also a summer-only Conaf ranger post. The trail then technically continues another 8km north to the *Refugio Anay*, though there's a river that has to be crossed and hiking further than the Huentemó community can be difficult; due to tensions between the villagers and Conaf (and the villagers and some unscrupulous home-grown backpackers stealing chickens after they'd run out of camping supplies), whether or not you're allowed to pass through depends on the whim of the villagers. Some days you're waved on; on others they may demand an exorbitant CH$20,000 entry fee.

The park is divided into three sectors. The most accessible, **Sector Anay**, is reached by a 25km paved road that shoots west from a junction on the Panamericana, 20km south of Castro. At the end of the road is the gateway to the park, **Chanquín** – a scattering of guesthouses across the bridge from the ramshackle village of **Cucao**, where you can buy last-minute provisions. Due to the somewhat limited trail system, you can see the park's highlights in a couple of days, staying overnight in Chanquín (see page 335).

Sector Anay

Every summer, backpackers descend on the park's **Sector Anay**, keen to camp on its 20km of white-sand beach and to explore the dense forest. This section of the national park covers 350 square kilometres of the Cordillera de Piuchén, rising up to 800m above sea level, and comprises vast chunks of native flora, including *coigüe* and *mañío* woodlands, and the magnificent *alerce*. Besides potentially catching glimpses of the shy Chilote fox, the elusive *pudú* (pygmy deer), marine otters and a wealth of native birds, the depths of primeval Chiloé forest allow you to experience a sense of true wilderness.

Sector Chepu

Thirty kilometres **south** of Ancud and to the north of Sector Anay is the northernmost section of Parque Nacional Chiloé, **Sector Chepu**, known for its birdlife-rich **wetlands** (drivers should watch out here; see page 322). Though the Chiloé section of the **Sendero de Chile** (see page 335) technically starts from the village of Guabún on Península Lacuy (see page 321), it's not well marked, so it's best to start from the bridge at the village of Duhatao, south of Pumillahue. From here, a trail combining coastal footpaths, stretches of beach and wooden walkways runs all the way to Chepu Valley (see page 322). Take the trail to the beach which can be crossed at low tide; at high tide, take the first trail up the hill, and follow the power lines. There are some nice little detours with great sea views. It's a six- or seven-hour walk that's as rugged as it is beautiful; be prepared for mud during the two-hour stretch that runs through the forest, and bear in mind that when crossing Chepu Beach, you'll have to ford a stream. The trail finishes at Río Chepu, and a road runs uphill from the coast through Chepu

> **SENDERO DE CHILE**
>
> The **Sendero de Chile** (⊕fundacionsenderodechile.org) is a hugely ambitious project, aimed at creating the **world's longest continuous hiking trail** to span the entire length of Chile, allowing hikers to traverse the country's varied landscapes and interact with local communities en route. The 8500km-long trail was officially completed in 2010; much of the work revolved around linking existing trails within national parks with each other, as a result of which the route comprises some secondary roads as well as bona fide hiking trails. **Maintenance** is a problem; while sections that pass through national parks are properly maintained and signposted, other sections of the Sendero are not.

Valley; it's another 45-minute walk to the hamlet of Chepu and the bridge that the bus leaves from three times weekly (Mon, Wed and Fri). Given that departures are early morning only, however, you have no choice but to stay in Chepu overnight.

ARRIVAL AND INFORMATION

By bus Buses Ojeda and Buses Interlagos both run services from Castro to Cucao (up to 15 daily between them in peak season; 1hr 15min).

Conaf At the park entrance (daily 9am–7pm; visitor centre daily: Jan & Feb 9.30am–8pm; March–Dec 9am–1pm & 2–6pm; ☎065 248 6102, ⊕conaf.cl). Pay the park fee at the Conaf ranger post, where there's also an interpretative centre.

PARQUE NACIONAL CHILOÉ

Palafito Trip ☎09 8849 5522, ⊕palafitotrip.cl. Based at *Palafito Cucao* (see page 335), this reliable operator offers outings in Parque Nacional Chiloé on foot or horseback, kayaking and trekking excursions, and numerous other tours. The owner, Pato, only speaks Spanish, but if contacted in advance can round up an English-speaking guide.

ACCOMMODATION AND EATING

All Parque Nacional Chiloé **accommodation** options are situated in and around Chanquín. The **refugios** in the park are not in a great state of repair and are only open in peak season. They are not always staffed and you must bring own sleeping bags.

El Arrayán Near the park entrance. This is the only reliable restaurant around, with rough-hewn wooden furniture, friendly service and a menu of simple but well-executed meat and seafood dishes. Mains from CH$6500. Jan–March & Dec daily noon/1pm–10pm; outside high season reduced hours.

Camping del Parque 200m past the Conaf visitor centre ☎09 9507 2559, ⊕parquechiloe.cl. This campsite offers 25 camping spots with fire pits, showers and picnic tables. There are also four fully equipped cabins sleeping up to six people. Camping CH$5000, cabins CH$50,000

★ **Hostel Palafito Cucao** 200m from the park entrance ☎65 297 1164 or ☎09 8403 4728, ⊕hostelpalafitocucao.cl. This shingled guesthouse is ideally situated for the park, boasting views of Lago Cucao from its rooms and dorm. Guests congregate in the cosy lounge, heated by a wood-burning stove, watch the sunset from the deck or simmer in the hot tub. Nab the corner room for the best views. Dorms CH$18,000, doubles CH$65,000

Parque Tepuhueico

Next to the Parque Nacional Chiloé and reachable via a well-signposted, bumpy gravel road that branches off the road to Cucao at around Km 9, **Parque Tepuhueico**, a 200km-square private reserve between the Pacific coast and Lago Tepuhueico, consists largely of dense cypress, *tepué*, *canelo* and *coigue* forest. It is home to more than a hundred bird species and native fauna such as Darwin's fox, the *pudú* and *monito del monte* – a tiny marsupial whose species is more than forty million years old. At the heart of the reserve sits *Tepuhueico Ecolodge* (see page 336), and two beautiful walking trails run near the property, making a loop of sorts. The most spectacular is the **Catedral de Arrayanes**, a slippery twenty-minute ramble through an enchanted-looking, lichen-covered tangle of gnarly trees. The prize at the end is a gorgeous thicket of red-

7

THE BRIDGE TO NOWHERE

Reachable via a rough, unpaved 45-minute drive south from Cucao, the privately owned **Punta Pirulil** headland is the stage for a beautiful, wind-whipped walk over the hills and along wave-battered cliffs. Indigenous Huilliche legends have it that this part of the island acts as a bridge between this world and the next, with the souls of the dead calling out to the boatman to ferry them across. The story goes that one day, a foreigner who was very much alive summoned the boatman; the boatman turned him away. The following year, the foreigner died and his soul tried to summon the boatman, but the boatman assumed that it was another trick, so the restless soul of this foreigner is said to still wander these hills, emitting eerie cries (which you'll get to hear). A symbolic **Muelle de las Almas**, a bridge to nowhere that ends halfway, has been built here to illustrate the legend, facing the bay, and the walk to and from the bridge takes a couple of hours.

The trailhead is accessible only by 4WD and to unlock the gate you have to call at the farmhouse directly before the only bridge you cross en route to the trailhead. This is where you pay the entry fee (CH$1500); Don Carmelo will then hand you a key and can show you his extensive collection of fossils and his personal contribution to the demise of endangered endemic fauna in the shape of pelts lining the wall. It's easiest to get to Punta Pirulil via a half-day tour with Palafito Trip (see page 335) or another operator.

The artist behind the Muelle de las Almas has since built a successor, the **Muelle de la Luz** (ⓦfacebook.com/muelledelaluz), near Chepu. Although scenic, it is pricey to visit (CH$5000) and doesn't have the mythical heft of its predecessor.

---

gold myrtle trees that reach for the sky. This trail joins up with the riverside trail that skirts the rushing river, where guests can go kayaking. Parque Tepuhueico is accessible either for hotel guests or those taking a tour (see below).

ACCOMMODATION AND EATING

PARQUE TEPUHUEICO

Tepuhueico Ecolodge About 25km inside Parque Tepuhueico ⓦparquetepuhueico.cl. This wood-shingled keep sports a circular, split-level dining and lounge area with vast ceilings. The two secluded, triple-level *cabañas* for up to six people continue the innovative architecture theme, with open-plan bedrooms, terraces overlooking the lake, and wood-burning stoves. The rooms inside the main building are plush but darker, with powerful showers and cute touches in the form of Chilote woollen dolls and wall hangings. Rates include full board and tours. <u>US$458</u>

Chonchi

Some 23km south of Castro lies the attractive working town of **CHONCHI**. Founded in 1767, the town was home to the wood baron Ciriaco Alvarez, who earned the name *El Rey de Ciprés* (The Cypress King) by stripping the archipelago of almost all of its native forest. The most sheltered harbour on the island is lined with beautiful old wooden buildings, and during low tide you can see local women digging for razor clams on the beach.

In February, the town comes alive during the **Semana Verano Chonchi** – a festival featuring dancing, music, art and rodeo skills. Chonchi is also the home of the golden *licor de oro*, a potent combination of saffron, vanilla, milk, lemons, cloves, cinnamon and other ingredients to storm your palate.

Otherwise, the attractions of this sleepy town are limited to the **Iglesia San Carlos de Borromeo** (1900) on the main Calle Centenario (daily 9am–7pm; free), whose Neoclassical facade is among the island's finest.

ARRIVAL AND DEPARTURE

CHONCHI

By bus There are frequent departures with operators such as Cruz del Sur, Transchiloé, Expresos Interlagos and Queilén Bus. Larger buses stop alongside the Plaza, while minibuses stop along the little triangular *plazuela* along Centenario.

Destinations Castro (14 daily; 30min); Quellón (14 daily; 1hr 45min).

ACCOMMODATION AND EATING

Hostal La Turtuga Pedro Montt 241 ☏ 09 9098 2925, ⓦ hostallatortuga.com. In a historic wood-shingled house right next to the Cruz del Sur bus station, this rambling guesthouse is run by a friendly owner. Rooms (some with private bathrooms) are spartan, their crooked floors testimony to the building's 120-year-plus history. Breakfast costs extra. **CH$26,000**

El Trebol Irarrázaval 187 ☏ 65 267 1203. At the southern end of the waterfront above the local market, this is a beloved local institution, serving primarily fish and seafood dishes (from CH$5500) to a satisfied clientele. Mon–Sat 10am–10.30pm.

Isla Lemuy

On the coast, a 4km walk south of Chonchi at **Huicha**, a ferry heads to **Isla Lemuy**. Boasting three of Chiloé's sixteen UNESCO churches (see page 327), the island is dotted with traditional rural settlements, each comprising just a few houses; the celebrated churches are in the villages of **Ichuac**, **Aldachildo** and **Detif**. The last is the remotest of them all, on an isolated, bleak headland at the far eastern end of the island, about 20km from Puqueldón, Lemuy's main settlement. The drive to Detif is particularly picturesque.

7

ARRIVAL AND DEPARTURE   ISLA LEMUY

By bus Buses Gallardo (☏ 65 264 3541) runs to Puqueldón from Castro (1–4 daily; 1hr); the bus crosses to the island on the ferry.

By boat Ferries departs from a terminal 3km south of Chonchi (8am–8pm: Mon–Sat every 30min; Sun hourly; 20min; free for passengers, CH$4500/car).

ACCOMMODATION AND EATING

El Castaño Aldachildo ☏ 09 7445 0886, ⓦ autenticochiloe.com. Rural life needs no better introduction than a stay at this rustic *Agroturismo* guesthouse run by a friendly Italian/Chilean couple. There are just three doubles with neither TVs nor internet to distract you from your spectacular natural surroundings. Witness sheep-shearing or cider making, or go horseriding. **CH$35,000**

Parque Yayanes 1.5km from Puqueldón en route to Lincay ☏ 09 8861 6462, ⓦ parqueyayanes.cl. The best place to stay on the island consists of three adorable *cabañas* (think polished wooden floors and wood-burning stoves). The two six-person *cabañas* and a two-person *cabaña* have kitchenettes and TVs. The owners are hospitable and there's a good restaurant. **CH$30,000**

Queilén and around

The paved road to Queilén runs above a string of pretty little villages down by the sea. **TEPUA** in particular is worth a visit to see its graveyard filled with *mausoleos*, traditional shelters that protect mourners from the elements when they visit the graves of the dead, some of which are splendidly ornate. You'll either need a sturdy vehicle to tackle the steep dirt paths leading to the villages, or be prepared for a lot of walking.

Forty-six kilometres from Chonchi, the road pulls into **QUEILÉN**, a sleepy little fishing town whose two main streets, Pedro Aguirre Cerda and Alessandri, bisect the neck of a long, sandy peninsula. The western end of town is very picturesque, lined with fishermen's houses built on a long beach sheltered by the nearby **Isla Tranqui**. In February, the town hosts a **craft fair**.

ARRIVAL AND DEPARTURE   QUEILÉN AND AROUND

By bus Queilén Bus (☏ 65 263 2173) runs services to Queilén from Castro (hourly–every 2hr; 1hr 15min).

ACCOMMODATION AND EATING

Espejo de Luna Ruta Chonchi a Queilén Km 35 ☎09 7431 3090 or ☎09 7431 3091, ⓦespejodeluna. cl. Difficult to miss due to the distinctive shape of its restaurant, which resembles a boat on its side, this nature retreat combines thoughtful design (including a lift down to the private beach for disabled guests) with somewhat overpriced flair – spacious, light rooms in the lodge and private *cabañas* (sleeping up to five) hidden in the greenery. Non-guests can stop by for lunch or dinner. Doubles US$165, *cabañas* US$216

★ **Isla Bruja Lodge** Overlooking an isolated bay near Pailldad (get directions if driving) ⓦislabrujalodge. com. This beautiful lodge is the picture of rural tranquillity, with delightful antique touches throughout, such as a genuine Singer sewing machine. The four luxurious en suites and one cabin (sleeping up to five) are presided over by the wonderfully welcoming American/Chilean owners, as well as Lana the dog and Torpe the pet sheep. Perks include a hot tub, gourmet food and free use of kayaks and mountain bikes. Doubles CH$93,000, cabin CH$85,000

Refugio de Navegantes Av Balneario 253 ☎65 2611310, ⓦrefugiodenavegantes.cl. An offshoot of the popular *Dalcahue* hotel/restaurant (see page 324), *Refugio de Navegantes* has four colourful cabins and a fully fitted apartment with sea views (all sleep up to four people), as well as a delightful café. Cabins CH$50,000, apartment CH$70,000

Quellón

If you follow Ruta 5 south from the turn-off for Chonchi, after 70km you reach **QUELLÓN** – the official end of the Panamericana, which starts in Alaska, and the end of Chiloé. Formerly a logging port, more recently the centre of a major salmon-farming industry, Quellón is still recovering from Infectious Salmon Anaemia, the blight that affected Chile's salmon between 2005 and 2010, with production falling dramatically. Unemployment remains high and the port area is dodgy at night. The main reason to come is to catch a **ferry** across to Chaitén (see page 353) or down to Chacabuco (see page 366). You can also organize transport to Parque Tantauco (see page 339), though that can equally be done in Castro (see page 328).

ARRIVAL AND TOURS

QUELLÓN

By bus Cruz del Sur and Transchiloé buses run to Castro (hourly; 2hr) and Puerto Montt (hourly–every 2hr; 6hr) via Chonchi (1hr 20min) from the terminal a block west of the main plaza on Pedro Aguirre Cerda.

By boat The Don Baldo ferry – operated by Naviera Austral at Montt 457 (☎65 268 2207, ⓦnavieraustral.cl) – calls at the harbour a block south of the main plaza. Ferries may be subject to delays and cancellations, so check the exact departure time in advance. Fewer services outside peak season.

Destinations Chaitén (2–3 weekly; 5hr); Puerto Chacabuco (2–3 weekly; 28hr).

Excursiones Quellón Av Jorge Vivar 382B ☎09 7402 2456, ⓦexcursionesquellon.cl. This operator runs buses to Parque Tantauco (see page 339) in Jan and Feb, and offers kayaking and boat trips.

ACCOMMODATION

Hotel Chico Leo Montt 325 ☎65 268 1567. The pick of a mediocre waterfront bunch of budget hotels, offering (mostly) spick-and-span rooms, some with shared facilities. The water in the showers is reliably hot, but the restaurant gets mixed reviews. CH$26,000

Hotel Patagonia Insular Ladrilleros 1737 ☎65 268 1610, ⓦhotelpatagoniainsular.cl. This modern, glass-fronted hotel enjoys an enviable hilltop location just west of the centre. The large, comfortable rooms have porthole windows in the bathrooms and all the mod cons you'd expect from a four-star; the suite (CH$103,000) even has a jacuzzi. There's a good restaurant. CH$68,000

EATING

Cafe Isla Sandwich Ladrilleros 190 ☎65 268 0683. As the name suggests, this trendy, popular café offers an array of imaginative sandwiches (CH$4000–6000), as well as cakes, coffee and fresh juices. Mon–Fri 10am–9pm, Sat 4–9pm.

Romeo Alfa Montt 554 ☎09 8858 0232. Right on the water, this restaurant is a solid but unspectacular choice for fish and seafood (CH$5000–8000); try the *ceviche* or the grilled catch of the day. Daily 12.30–3.30pm & 7.30–11.30pm.

Parque Tantauco

To the south of Isla Grande and 30km to the northwest of Quellón • Jan–March & Dec daily 9am–8pm • CH$3500 • Access by bus, boat or plane can be arranged via the Castro-based Parque Tantauco office (see page 341), or via Chiloé Natural or Chiloétnico (see page 331)

Parque Tantauco (ⓦ parquetantauco.cl) is Chiloé's largest natural attraction with nearly 1200 square kilometres of unspoiled wilderness, more than double the size of Parque Nacional Chiloé. The park, funded by the Fundación Futuro, is the brainchild of **Sebastián Piñera**, billionaire owner of LATAM and Chile's current president.

After Parque Pumalín (see page 350), Piñera was inspired to start his own conservation project to "protect and conserve vulnerable ecosystems and species, and those at risk of extinction", as well as to restore a large chunk of the park's territory that was devastated by a forest fire in the 1940s, by replanting native species in the affected area. The park is located in one of the world's 25 "biodiversity hotspots", with unique ecosystems and wildlife habitats, and home to such species as the Chilote fox, the *pudú*, the *huillín* (otter) and the blue whale.

Consisting of **Zona Sur** and **Zona Norte**, Tantauco boasts more than 130km of well-signposted, meticulously maintained hiking trails of varying length and difficulty, encompassing both the coastal areas and Chilote rainforest. These trails are part of an **excellent infrastructure** that also includes fully equipped campsites and unmanned, basic *refugios*. Owing to the park's remoteness, moreover, it's not overrun by visitors in the summer, and away from **Lago Chaiguata** and **Caleta Inío**, the gateways to Zona Norte and Zona Sur, respectively, you can hike practically in solitude for a week or more.

There are **two long trails** in the park which form a T-shape: the east-west Ruta Caleta Zorra from Lago Chaiguata (41km one-way; seven days return), and the north-south Ruta Transversal (52km; five days one-way) from Lago Chaiguata to Caleta Inío, which turns south halfway along to Caleta Zorra. The two combined create Ruta Tantauco (94km; eight/nine days one-way): Lago Chaiguata to Caleta Zorra and Caleta Zorra to Caleta Inío, though inevitably the T-shape of this route entails some retracing of steps.

Zona Sur is accessible on foot from Zona Norte, as well as by boat and Cessna flights. Bring all the necessary gear, including waterproof clothing.

Zona Norte

It's possible to visit **Zona Norte** in a day; Chiloé Natural and Chiloétnico (see page 331) run day-trips. There are a couple of nice short hikes, such as the **Sendero Siempreverde**, an interpretive walk leading through evergreen forest, and the **Circuito Muelle**, which goes from *Camping Chaiguata* along the banks of Lago Yaldad. Alternatively, the **Sendero Lagos Occidentales**, a 6km walk of moderate difficulty, leads you through evergreen forest from Lago Chaiguata to Lago Chaiguaco, where you can overnight at the *Refugio Chaiguaco*.

From *Refugio Chaiguaco*, the trail continues through the forest to *Refugio Pirámide* (15km; 5hr), next to a tiny lagoon. From there you can either head south towards Caleta Inío, or continue west to Caleta Zorra on the coast along the river, stopping at the *Refugio Emerenciana* on the banks of the picturesque Laguna Emerenciana along the way (15km; 7–9hr), from where it's an additional tough 6km (5–6hr) to *Camping Agreste* by a beautiful cove.

A densely wooded trail heads south from *Refugio Pirámide*, reaching *Refugio Huillín* after six hours (14km). From there it's a further four to six hours (7.5km) to *Refugio Miradór Inío*, the highest point of the trek; you get a great overview of the landscape from the watchtower. To get to the fishing village of Caleta Inío in Zona Sur it's another five to seven hours (9.6km).

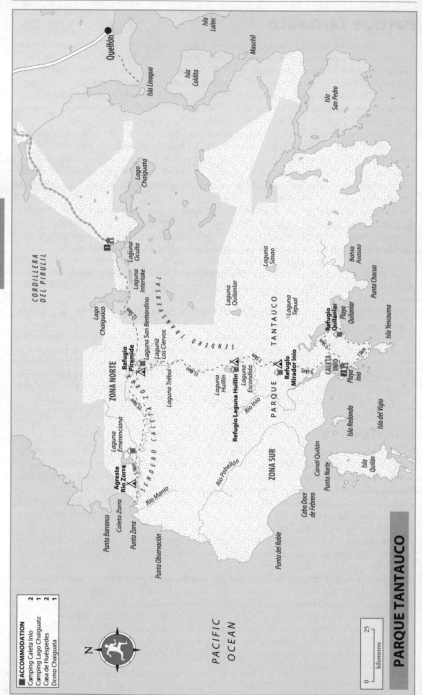

7

PARQUE TANTAUCO

Quellón

Isla Laitec

Isla Linagua

Isla Coldita

Mauchil

Isla San Pedro

Lago Chaiguata

Laguna Oculta

CORDILLERA DEL PIRULIL

Lago Chaiguaco

Laguna Interlake

Laguna Sasao

Bahía Asasao

Laguna San Bernardino

Laguna Quilanlar

Laguna Tepual

Punta Chacua

Refugio Quilanlar

Playa Quilanlar

Refugio Pirámide

Laguna Los Ciervos

SENDERO TRANSVERSAL

PARQUE TANTAUCO

Isla Yencouma

Laguna Trébol

ZONA NORTE

SENDERO CALETA ZORRA

Refugio Laguna Huillín

Laguna Huillín

Laguna Escondida

Refugio Mirador Inio

CALETA INIO

Playa Inio

Río Inio

Laguna Emerenciana

Agreste Río Zorra

Río Manio

Río Pabellón

ZONA SUR

Punta Barrana

Caleta Zorra

Punta Zorra

Punta Observación

Punta del Roble

Cabo Doce de Febrero

Punta Norte

Canal Quilán

Isla Redonda

Isla del Vigía

Isla Quilán

PACIFIC OCEAN

N

ACCOMMODATION
Camping Caleta Inio   2
Camping Lago Chaiguata   1
Casa de Huéspedes   2
Domo Chaiguata   1

0   25
kilometres

Zona Sur

Around Caleta Inío in **Zona Sur**, you can explore the coastal caves where the indigenous Chonos once resided, as well as the pristine beaches and islets off the coast. A beautiful two-day circuit takes in stunning viewpoints and stretches of beach and forest; you can overnight at the *Refugio Quilanlar* (13km or 9.5km from Caleta Inío, depending on which half of the loop you take). The extensive beaches near Inío are sheltered from the Gulf of Corcovado by small offshore islands and the numerous coastal inlets are ideal for **kayaking** – rental is available in Caleta Inío (CH$5000/half-day).

ARRIVAL AND DEPARTURE

PARQUE TANTAUCO

By car Zona Norte can be accessed by vehicles with high clearance (pickup trucks or 4WDs) along a dirt road branching off from the Panamericana, 14km north of Quellón, and labelled "Colonia Yungay". The 18km drive brings you to the park administration office by Lago Yaldad (see below), from where it's an additional 20km to Lago Chaiguata.

By bus In Jan and Feb, there are buses from Quellón to Zona Norte (Mon, Wed & Sat 9am, returning 4pm; book via Excursiones Quellón – see page 338).

By boat A private boat can be chartered from Quellón via Castro's Parque Tantauco office or Chiloé Natural or

Chiloétnico (see page 331) – these either drop people off at Caleta Inío or pick people up (around CH$60,000/person). It's sometimes possible to catch a ride from Caleta Inío to Quellón with a local fishing boat, but allow plenty of time.

By plane A four-person Cessna from Castro airport can be chartered through Castro's Parque Tantauco office, Chiloé Natural or Chiloétnico (see page 331) to fly to Caleta Inío, taking either three passengers and no luggage or two passengers with luggage (around CH$360,000 for the whole plane or CH$120,000/person for a day-trip).

INFORMATION AND TOURS

Park office The main park office is just south of Castro, across the street from the casino, on ruta 5 Sur 1826, Castro (Jan–March & Dec daily 9am–6pm; April–Nov Mon–Fri 9am–6pm; ☎ 65 263 3805, ⓦ parquetantauco.cl).

Park administration office Lago Yaldad (Jan–March & Dec daily 9am–8pm). The office is permanently staffed

only during the months indicated. The park entry fee (CH$3500) includes a detailed trail map. There's also a small visitor centre in Caleta Inío (open on request).

Tours and activities Chiloé Natural and Chiloétnico (see page 331) both run excursions, ranging from day-trips to Lago Chaiguata to multi-day treks.

ACCOMMODATION

All **accommodation** apart from the basic campsites and *refugios* has to be reserved via the park offices (see above) and paid for on arrival. The only place to buy limited food supplies is Caleta Inío; otherwise bring all supplies with you.

Camping and refugios Basic campsites and *refugios* are deliberately arranged with a day's hike between each site, and drinking water is found at every site apart from *Refugio Mirador Inío*, the highest of the sites; bring two days' worth of water from either *Camping Caleta Inío* or *Refugio Laguna Huillín*. Camping wild is not allowed. There's a standard camping price/night throughout, with the exception of the fully equipped campsites at Lago Chaiguata and Caleta Inío (see below). Smaller campsites along the trails consist of four to six camping spots each. Basic *refugios* are each equipped with eight bunk beds (bring own bedding) and are also priced at a standard rate. Camping CH$12,000, dorms CH$15,000

Camping Caleta Inío Caleta Inío; map p.340. Large campsite consisting of 24 spaces, complete with showers, fully equipped indoor cooking area, a large *fogón* for barbecue and even a *curanto* pit. CH$15,000

Camping Lago Chaiguata Lago Chaiguata; map p.340. Camping site with fifteen spaces, some with sheltered picnic tables. Access to showers and *quincho*. Ranger station nearby. There's also a restaurant and visitors can book a hot tub (CH$35,000) in advance. Sites with sheltered picnic table cost slightly more. CH$15,000

Casa de Huéspedes Caleta Inío; map p.340. Attractive guesthouse offering six homely, wood-panelled rooms with down duvets: three en-suite twins, a standard double and two doubles with shared facilities. There's a guest kitchen and a large lounge. CH$60,000

Domo Chaiguata Lago Chaiguata; map p.340. Six geothermal domes with central heating and four or eight beds each for those who prefer glamping to camping. Facilities include a restaurant and hot tub. Bring your sleeping bag. CH$84,000

7

Northern Patagonia

FLOWERING LUPINS, CARRETERA AUSTRAL

Northern Patagonia

From Puerto Montt, the Carretera Austral, or "Southern Highway", stretches more than 1000km south through the wettest, greenest, wildest and narrowest part of Chile, ending its mammoth journey at the tiny settlement of Villa O'Higgins. Carving its path through tracts of untouched wilderness, the route takes in soaring, snowcapped mountains, Ice Age glaciers, blue-green fjords, turquoise lakes and rivers, and one of the world's largest swathes of temperate rainforest. Most of it falls into Aysén, Chile's "last frontier", the final region to be opened up in the early twentieth century. A hundred years on, the region remains very sparsely populated, and still has the cut-off, marginal feel of a pioneer zone.

Leaving Puerto Montt, you can travel through both **Parque Nacional Alerce Andino** and **Parque Nacional Hornopirén**, before taking the boat over to Caleta Gonzalo, where the Carretera cuts a passage through virgin temperate rainforest of **Parque Nacional Pumalín Douglas R. Tompkins**, and finally emerging in the volcano-ravaged town of **Chaitén**.

South along the Carretera from Chaitén is the nondescript settlement of Villa Santa Lucía. From here, one branch of the road heads east, to the border village of **Futaleufú**, one of the world's top destinations for **whitewater rafting**. Continuing south, the Carretera emerges at the **Parque Nacional Queulat**, whose extraordinary hanging glacier and excellent trails make it one of the most rewarding places to get off the road. Don't miss the chance to luxuriate in the secluded hot pools of the luxurious **Termas de Puyuhuapi**.

The main town of **Coyhaique** marks the centre of the Carretera; to the west, **Puerto Chacabuco** is a starting point for boat excursions to the sensational **Laguna San Rafael glacier**, the other being **Puerto Río Tranquilo** further south, a jumping-off point for kayaking, boating and hiking on a nearby glacier. Here, the road skirts South America's second largest lake, **Lago General Carrera**, with a branch shooting off towards **Chile Chico** and the Argentinian border. The final stretch of the Carretera passes by the turnoff to **Parque Nacional Patagonia**, the region's newest and most exciting protected area, with ample hiking opportunities, before connecting the ranching town of **Cochrane** to the isolated hamlet of **Villa O'Higgins**, with another road branching off en route to the highly unusual logging settlement of **Caleta Tortel**.

Brief history

The original inhabitants of this rain-swept land were the nomadic, hunter-gatherer **Tehuelche** of the interior, and the canoe-faring **Kawéshkar**, who fished the fjords and channels of the coast, though now only a handful of the latter remain. In 1903, the government initiated a colonization programme that ultimately handed over thousands of hectares of land to three large livestock companies. At the same time, a wave of individual pioneers – known as **colonos** – came down from the north to try their

WHITEWATER RAFTING ON THE FUTALEUFÚ RIVER

Highlights

❶ The Carretera Austral Drive Chile's most spectacular – and most challenging – road. See page 348

❷ Parque Nacional Pumalín Douglas R. Tompkins Hike the trails and sail the fjords in one of Chile's new national parks. See page 350

❸ Whitewater rafting at Futaleufú "Purgatory", "Hell" and "Terminator" are just three of the world-class rapids on the "Futa". See page 356

❹ Ventisquero Colgante Gawk at the suspended glacier that seems to defy gravity in Parque Nacional Queulat. See page 359

❺ Termas de Puyuhuapi Soak your bones while gazing at the southern night skies in

Chile's premier spa resort. See page 360

❻ Parque Nacional Patagonia This newly created national park, 1.5 times the size of Torres del Paine, acts as an important wildlife corridor. Hike past dazzling highland lagoons and drive what may be Chile's most gorgeous road. See pages 370, 373 and 375

❼ Puerto Río Tranquilo Kayak to otherworldly marble formations, go ice hiking on Glaciar Exploradores and take a boat ride to Laguna San Rafael to see its namesake glacier. See page 371

❽ Villa O'Higgins border crossing Crossing into Argentina on foot and by boat, through spectacular scenery. See page 377

HIGHLIGHTS ARE MARKED ON THE MAP ON PAGE 346

NORTHERN PATAGONIA

HIGHLIGHTS

1. The Carretera Austral
2. Parque Nacional Pumalín Douglas R. Tompkins
3. Whitewater rafting at Futaleufú
4. Ventisquero Colgante
5. Termas de Puyuhuapi
6. Parque Nacional Patagonia
7. Puerto Río Tranquilo
8. Villa O'Higgins border crossing

PACIFIC OCEAN

MAR CHILENO

Isla de Chiloé

ARGENTINA

N

0   40
kilometres

luck at logging and farming, resulting in massive deforestation and destruction of the natural environment.

Faced with Argentina's encroaching influence, the government set out to actively "Chileanize" this new zone. Over the years, the perceived need for state control of the region did not diminish, explaining the rationale behind the construction of the Carretera Austral, initiated by earlier governments but with the greatest progress achieved under **General Pinochet**. Building the road was a colossal and incredibly expensive undertaking: the first section was finished in 1983 and engineers completed the final 100km in 2000, from tiny Puerto Yungay to the frontier outpost of Villa O'Higgins, by the Argentine border.

Parque Nacional Alerce Andino

47km south of Puerto Montt • CH$4000 • ⓦ conaf.cl/parques/parque-nacional-alerce-andino • Take southbound Ruta 7 to Cohuín or Lenca; the park entrance is to the left

Parque Nacional Alerce Andino was created in 1982 to protect the region's ancient and rapidly depleting *alerce* forests (see below), threatened with extinction by intense logging activity. Almost 200 square kilometres – half the park's land area – are covered by the massive, millenia-old *alerces*, mixed in with other native species including *coigüe* and *lenga*. This dense covering is spread over a landscape of steep hills and narrow glacial valleys dotted with dozens of lakes. The park is home to the tiny endemic marsupial *monito de monte*, pudú deer, the güiña (the smallest cat in the Americas) and the puma.

There are **two entrances** to the park: **Correntoso** and **Chaicas**. A paved road runs from Coihuín, 7km south of Puerto Montt, to Correntoso, from where a gravel road runs to the Correntoso ranger station, which is connected to the Sargazo ranger station, near Laguna Sargazo, by a poor gravel road. Some 40km down the road – just beyond the Puente de Lenca – a signed track, suitable only for high clearance cars, branches left and leads 7km to the Chaicas (southern) entrance of the park, where you'll find a small **Conaf** hut (daily 8am–5pm), a ranger station and a basic **camping** area.

Hikes in Parque Nacional Alerce Andino

For a short walk, you can take the 1km-long interpretative "Huillifotem" trail from the **Correntoso** ranger station. From the **Sargazo** station a 9.5km (9hr return) hike passes

8

ALERCE TREES

Endemic to southern Chile and Argentina, the famed **alerce** trees – accorded national monument status by the government in 1976 – grow in high, soggy soil, usually on mountainsides between 600m and 800m above sea level. Among the **largest and oldest trees in the world**, they can rise to a height of 45m, with a trunk diameter of up to 4m, and live for more than three thousand years. After shooting up rapidly during their first hundred years, they slow down dramatically, their diameter increasing just 1mm every three years. As they grow, they lose their lower branches, keeping only their top crown of dark-green, broccoli-like leaves. The lighter, lower leaves belong to parasite trees, which often prove useful to the ancient *alerces*, supporting them when they topple and keeping them alive. The trees' grey, papery bark conceals a beautiful, reddish-brown and extremely **valuable wood**; a large tree is worth tens of thousands of dollars. In the late nineteenth and early twentieth centuries, the trees were chopped down at random by early colonizers – sometimes to be used for telegraph poles or shingles, but often just to clear land which was later found to be useless for agriculture. Today, it's illegal to chop down an *alerce* owing to their protected status, but it's not forbidden to sell the wood of dead trees, hence the untimely death of many *alerces*.

"DOING" THE CARRETERA AUSTRAL

The words "Carretera Austral" – or Southern Highway – conjure up images of a smooth, paved, multi-lane road, right? Wrong. The Carretera is still very much a "triumph" of humans over nature; though parts of the road are being tamed through paving as we type, it is still Chile's most challenging and spectacularly scenic road trip. "Doing" the Carretera Austral thus requires a certain amount of forward **planning**, and time should be allowed for unexpected delays such as landslides, which tend to affect the northern half of the road from the Puerto Cisnes turnoff onwards during rainy weather. Just before Christmas 2017, a glacier calved and the resulting mudslide swept away part of Villa Santa Lucia, killing at least sixteen people and taking a section of the road with it. At the time of writing, Chaitén was cut off from the rest of the Carretera Austral as a consequence, and a car ferry service had temporarily replaced a section along the Puyuhuapi fjord due to a landslide.

It's worth noting that **Coyhaique** is the only place on the Carretera Austral where you can reliably withdraw **cash**. Elsewhere there is usually a single cash machine that's not to be relied on.

BY CAR

What type of car do I need? Most car rental agencies will insist that you rent a 4WD or a pickup truck for the journey, but while certain sections may be easier to drive in a high-clearance vehicle, the whole of the Carretera Austral is perfectly doable in a regular car. A high-clearance vehicle is highly recommended for some side trips, such as the road that passes through Parque Nacional Patagonia (see page 373) en route to the Argentinian border, or the road from Chile Chico to Parque Nacional Patagonia's Sector Jeinimeni.

What are the road conditions like? Some sections are more challenging than others; see below for a brief guide to the different stretches of road.

Will there be anywhere to buy petrol? The vast majority of settlements along the Carretera Austral have petrol stations. Fill up regularly, and you needn't worry about running dry.

What essentials should I bring? Bring a spare tyre (*neumático*), and all equipment necessary to change it (all typically provided by rental car companies), as you'll only be able to rely on yourself and passing motorists for roadside assistance. Carry food, water and a sleeping bag, just in case.

What about crossing the border into Argentina? You'll need to have the required paperwork from your car rental company.

Any other precautions? Try to avoid driving when it's dark, as not all curves in the road are marked with reflectors. Driving too close to other cars is a bad idea as the loose gravel flying out from under the wheels of the vehicle in front of you can crack your windscreen. Do not take

by Laguna Sargazo and leads to tiny Laguna Fria, while a shorter, easier trail (2.5km) leads to the west shore of Laguna Sargazo. There's also a good, long **day-hike** from the **Chaicas** Conaf hut; the path follows the Río Chaica for 5km as far as the pretty **Laguna Chaiquenes**, surrounded by steep, forested hills. On the way, about an hour from the hut, you pass some impressive waterfalls and, twenty minutes later, a huge, 3000–year-old *alerce* tree. From Laguna Chaiquenes, the now deteriorating path heads north for a further 4km, as far as the long, thin **Laguna Triángulo**, where it peters out. Count on taking around three hours to get to Laguna Chaiquenes, and another two hours to get to Laguna Triángulo.

Hornopirén and around

The sheltered, sandy cove of **La Arena** lies 13km south of the turnoff to Parque Nacional Alerce Andino; it's the departure point of a thirty-minute **ferry** crossing (see page 349) to tiny **Caleta Puelche**, from where the road winds through 58km of thickly forested hills before arriving at the village of **HORNOPIRÉN**. Here you catch another (Naviera Austral) ferry to Caleta Gonzalo, where the Carretera continues.

corners at high speeds on the *ripio* (dirt and gravel) sections of the road. If you're travelling via Hornopirén and Caleta Gonzalo, and wish to take the ferry between Puerto Ibañez and Chile Chico, book ferry tickets a week in advance. If you have a mobile phone, bear in mind that only Entel works in all villages on the Carretera Austral (see page 378).

BY PUBLIC TRANSPORT

It is possible to travel the Carretera Austral by **bus**, but plan ahead since stretches such as Villa O'Higgins–Cochrane and La Junta-Chaitén are served only twice weekly. In peak season, the villages are covered by a combination of minibuses, ferries and local flights, but outside the December–March period there may be fewer services between some destinations; call and enquire in advance.

BY BICYCLE

Cycling the Carretera Austral is a challenge. While large stretches of the northern half of the Southern Highway are now paved, equally there are steep, narrow and unpaved sections and long sections of washboard-type gravel road, particularly south of Villa Cerro Castillo. Always cycle defensively to avoid the reckless drivers and be particularly careful south of Cochrane, as the road is frequently narrow and features blind turns. Carry all necessary spare parts and supplies, because of the absence of bike shops (barring in Coyhaique) and be prepared for rain.

ROAD CONDITIONS BY SECTION

Chaitén to Villa Santa Lucia Was completely paved before the December 2017 mudslide; a section of the road was being rebuilt at research time.

Villa Santa Lucía to Futaleufú Valley Somewhat potholed, mostly good gravel road; some landslide-prone sections.

Villa Santa Lucía to Puyuhuapi Mostly paved, but the section between La Junta and Puyuhuapi is prone to landslides.

Puyuhuapi to Puerto Cisnes crossroads The most challenging section is the Paso Queulat – narrow, steep, deeply rutted and with tight curves. Sections were being paved at research time.

Parque Nacional Queulat to the turnoff for Puerto Aysén Completely paved.

Coyhaique to Puerto Aisén Completely paved but with some blind turns.

Coyhaique to Cochrane Paved between Coyhaique and Cerro Castillo; otherwise mostly good gravel road with few potholes and some narrow and "washboard" sections.

Cruce El Maitén to Chile Chico Mostly good gravel road, but narrow in places, with "washboard" sections, and with a precipitous drop on one side.

Cochrane to Caleta Tortel/ Villa O'Higgins Mostly good gravel road, steep and narrow in parts; ferry crossing required at Puerto Yungay; some blind turns and sheer drops to one side.

8

Perched on the northern shore of a wide fjord, at the foot of **Volcán Hornopirén**, the village enjoys a spectacular location. Originally founded in 1890 by settlers from Chiloe, Hornopirén grew until the 1970s thanks to the *alerce* logging trade; salmon farming and tourism have since taken over as main industries. If you're lucky, you'll spot Austral dolphins frolicking in the estuary on which the town sits. It's worth hiking the short **trails** on the headland next to *Ecocamping Patagonia El Cobre* (see page 350); one leads to a dolphin outlook (1hr return), while another crests the steep hill (3hr return), leading to a viewpoint.

ARRIVAL AND DEPARTURE   HORNOPIRÉN

By bus Kemel Bus (☎ 65 225 3530) runs from the corner of the town's main square to Puerto Montt (3–4 daily; 3hr) and passes through en route to Chaitén at around 10am (1 daily; 5hr).

By car The road from Puerto Montt to Caleta Arena is paved, and Caleta Puelche to Hornopirén is largely paved, but if you're looking to drive from Hornopirén towards Cochamó (see page 303) via the V-69 that leads east from

Caleta Puelche, allow yourself an hour to cover the poorly maintained 36km road to Puelo.

By ferry The La Arena–Caleta Puelche ferry is operated by Transportes del Estuario (6.30am–10.30pm; every 30min; CH\$9800/car, passengers free; ✆ transportesdelestuario.cl). Transportes Austral (☎ 600 401 9000, ✆ taustral.cl) covers the two-stage ferry crossing between Hornopirén and Caleta Gonzalo, with daily ferries from Hornopirén departing for

Leptepú at 10.30am, and ferries sailing from Caleta Gonzalo, at the north end of Parque Nacional Pumalín Douglas R. Tompkins, at 1pm. There's an extra daily departure from both ends in Jan and Feb. Rates are CH$5600 for passengers and CH$33,600 for cars; in peak months, book the Hornopirén–Caleta Gonzalo leg online, well in advance.

ACCOMMODATION

★ **Ecocamping Patagonia El Cobre** Playa El Cobre ☎ 09 8227 5152 or ☎ 09 7809 0799, ✉ patagoniaelcobre@gmail.com. Follow the beach round from the ferry ramp for 500m to reach this eco-campsite and dorm, partially hidden in a woodland. Owner Roberto is serious about permaculture and recycling, and there's a café/hangout space for campers and visitors alike. Bikes and kayaks for rent, too. Camping CH$5000, dorm CH$14,000

Hostería Catalina Av Ingenieros Militares s/n ☎ 65 221 7359. Attractive, shingled B&B with snug, wood-panelled en-suite rooms, two fully equipped *cabañas* sleeping six, attentive host Wladimir and a guests-only restaurant. On the downside, the thin walls can make you feel as if you're in bed with your neighbours. Doubles CH$42,900, *cabañas* CH$72,900

Hotel Hornopirén Ignacio Carrera s/n ☎ 65 221 7256. Right on the waterfront, this is the town's oldest hotel, built more than fifty years ago from *alerce* wood. It's a characterful place, with low ceilings and creaky floors; the largest doubles are en suite. The extensive breakfast includes home-made jams, and other meals can be arranged on request. CH$35,000

Hotel Oelckers Lago Pinto Concha at Los Colonos ☎ 65 221 7450 ⊚ hoteloelckers.cl. The plushest option in town, this handsome stone and wood-shingled lodge has snug, centrally heated, wood-panelled en suites in various configurations – single, twin, triple, double, plus a restaurant (guests only). CH$37,000

EATING

Entre Montañas Carretera Austral s/n ☎ 09 5642 2463. The town's fanciest restaurant is on the northern approach to Hornopirén, just off the Carretera Austral. Expect steaks, seafood stews and grilled fish, coupled with a rustic ambience and several mounted deer heads on walls. Mains CH$7500–12,000. Daily noon–9pm.

Faros Cafe Av Ingenieros Militares s/n. Right by the ferry ramp, this thimble-sized café serves real coffee (from CH$1000) and *empanadas* (CH$2000). Jan & Feb daily 7.30am–9pm; March–Dec shorter hours.

El Pescador Río Barceló s/n ☎ 09 9508 9534. A short walk up from the ferry ramp, this one of the town's two main restaurants is a reliable bet for *merluza a la plancha* (grilled hake) and other Chilean standards. Mains CH$5000–7500. Daily 10am–10pm.

Parque Nacional Volcán Hornopirén

16km east of Hornopirén • ⊚ conaf.cl/parques/parque-nacional-hornopiren

To the east of Hornopirén unfold the 482 square kilometres of protected wilderness that make up **Parque Nacional Volcán Hornopirén**. The park's namesake and centrepiece, 18km the village, is the perfectly conical **Volcán Hornopirén** (1572m). It's possible to climb the volcano without a guide if you're an experienced hiker. A decent gravel road runs from Hornopirén for 11km, followed by a signposted road into the park, consisting of 7km or potholed gravel, until it reaches a car park. From there's it's a 10km, six-hour hike to **Lago General Pinto Concha** along a well-marked trail that climbs through native forest to the lakeshore, where there's a basic camping area and Conaf shelter. From the campsite, a 3.5km (5hr return) trail leads to the base of the 2111m **Volcán Yates** and ascends to the southern edge of the crater, with panoramic views of the park and the Hornopirén fjord from the top.

Parque Nacional Pumalín Douglas R. Tompkins

30km north of Chaitén • ⊚ www.parquepumalin.cl

South of Hornopirén, connected to it by two ferries, lies **Parque Nacional Pumalín Douglas R. Tompkins**, formerly the world's largest privately owned conservation

DOUG TOMPKINS AND THE PUMALÍN PROJECT

In 1995 it was publicly announced that a North American billionaire, **Doug Tompkins**, had used intermediaries to buy a 3000-square-kilometre chunk of southern Chile – marking the beginning of a five-year national soap opera that transformed Tompkins into one of the most controversial public figures in the country. In 1991, the 49-year-old Californian, increasingly committed to environmental issues, sold his share in the North Face and Esprit clothing empire, bought an abandoned ranch on the edge of the **Reñihué fjord**, 130km south of Puerto Montt, and moved there with his wife Kris. Inspired by the "deep ecology" movement pioneered by the Norwegian environmentalist **Arne Naess**, Tompkins set out to acquire more of the surrounding wilderness, with the aim of protecting it from the threat of commercial exploitation. As he did so, he was seized with the idea of creating a massive, privately funded national park, which would ensure permanent protection of the **ancient forest** while providing low-impact facilities for visitors.

THE MEDIA BACKLASH

Over the next four years Tompkins spent more than US$14 million buying up adjoining tracts of land, in most cases hiding his identity to prevent prices from shooting up. His initial secrecy was to have damaging repercussions, however, for once his land acquisitions became public knowledge, he was engulfed by a wave of suspicion and hostility, fuelled by several right-wing politicians and the press, with his motives questioned by everyone. The biggest cause for alarm, it seemed, was the fact that Tompkins' land stretched from the Argentine border to the Pacific Ocean, effectively "cutting Chile in two". Tompkins appeared on national television, explaining his intentions to create **Parque Nacional Pumalín**, a nature sanctuary with free access, slowly winning over some of the public.

SUCCESS WITH STRINGS

Eventually, the government agreed to support Tompkins' aims to establish the park – on the condition that for one year he would not buy more than 7000 contiguous hectares (17,250 acres) of land in the south of Chile. Tompkins was also prevented from purchasing Huinay, a 740,000-acre property owned by the Catholic University of Valparaíso, separating the two chunks of his land, which was instead sold to ENDESA, Chile's largest energy corporation.

Tompkins, determined to save a little more unspoiled terrain from development, purchased another chunk of land in 2001 near the Termas del Amarillo, south of Chaitén, while in 2005, the park, by this point managed by the Chilean Fundación Pumalín (whose board includes Tompkins' wife, Kristine), was finally declared a **santuario de la naturaleza** (nature sanctuary), which gave it additional protection.

THE TOMPKINS' LEGACY

Pumalín was only the start of the Tompkins' environmentalist legacy in Chile and Argentina. While Doug died in a kayaking accident in 2015, **Kris** continues to be involved in numerous conservation projects in both Chile and Argentina, purchasing tracts of land, restoring the original ecosystems and donating them to the respective countries as national parks. On January 29, 2018, the Tompkins Foundation made the largest gift of private land in history to the state of Chile, resulting in the creation of five new national parks (see page 42), including Pumalín and **Parque Nacional Patagonia** (see pages 370, 373 and 375).

8

area, covering 2900 square kilometres of land, and as of January 2018 one of Chile's newest national parks. The Pumalín Project, founded by North American billionaire philanthropist Doug Tompkins to protect one of the world's last strongholds of temperate rainforest, originally generated a considerable amount of controversy, yet few would deny today that the park represents a magnificent environmental achievement. It's a place of overwhelming natural beauty, with calm lakes reflecting stands of endangered *alerce* trees, ferocious waterfalls gushing through chasms of dark rock and high, snowy-peaked mountains. The park consists of **three sectors**; the **southern sector** is the most visited.

Northern sector

The largely inaccessible **northern sector** features the gloriously isolated **Termas de Cahuelmó**: a series of natural hot pools, carved out of the rock at the end of a steep, narrow fjord, reachable only by private boat from Hornopirén. There's a manned campsite there also. Though there are two remote hiking trails in the northern section, they are difficult and expensive to reach, so visitors to this less-explored part of the park do so by kayak (see page 354) or by renting a boat.

Southern sector

The **southern sector** has the most infrastructure geared towards visitors, with trails and campsites branching off the 58km of the Carretera Austral. Near the ferry ramp at Caleta Gonzalo, the **Sendero Cascadas** climbs steeply through a canopy of overhanging foliage up to a 15m waterfall (3hr return). Other trails have been carved out of the forest, branching off from the Carretera Austral as it heads south through the park, passing the splendid Lago Blanco and other numerous natural highlights. Twelve kilometres south of Caleta Gonzalo, **Sendero Laguna Tronador** (4.8km; 4hr return) is relatively challenging, crossing a narrow gorge filled with a rushing, whitewater stream, and climbing steeply up a series of wooden stepladders to a look-out point with fabulous views onto Volcán Michinmahuida, and ending at the pristine lake with a camping area alongside.

One kilometre south of the Sendero Laguna Tronador trailhead, across the Río Blanco, the 700m **Sendero Los Alerces** is an enjoyable twenty-minute circular route, dotted with information panels, through a grove of millennia-old, colossal *alerces*. Another kilometre down the road, the **Sendero Cascadas Escondidas** is an easy two-hour return through the forest to three high, slender waterfalls; you reach the first one after 25 minutes or so, and the other two half an hour after that.

Closer to Chaitén are two other trails: the **Sendero Volcán Michinmahuida**, a gentle 12km climb to the base of the eponymous volcano (8–10hr return), and the **Sendero Volcán Chaitén**, a popular 2.2km trail that climbs steeply up to the rim of the cantankerous volcano that has wreaked so much havoc in the area (3hr return).

El Amarillo sector

Next to the village of the same name, 24km south of Chaitén, the **El Amarillo sector** is the newest part of the park. Just over 4km from the entrance is the start of the **Sendero Darwin**, a 2.5km (1hr) interpretative loop that runs through dense forest. From the Ventisquero campsite, the flat 10km (6hr return) **Sendero El Amarillo Ventisquero** runs to the base of the Michimahuida glacier, with superb views en route, making it a really good, easy day hike. Starting from the road to the Ventisquero campsite, the 2.2km (1hr) **Sendero El Mirador** climbs steeply along the slope of three volcanic cones before descending to the campsite itself.

Not strictly in the El Amarillo sector, 2km uphill from the park entrance are the **Termas El Amarillo**, a set of relaxing hot-spring-fed outdoor pools (CH$5000).

ARRIVAL AND DEPARTURE   **PARQUE NACIONAL PUMALÍN DOUGLAS R. TOMPKINS**

NORTHERN SECTOR

By organized tour One option is to join a multi-day kayaking adventure trip with Alsur Expediciones (☏65 223 2300, ⊛alsurexpeditions.com) or Yak Expediciones (☏09 9299 6487, ⊛yakexpediciones.cl). It's also possible to charter a boat in Hornopirén.

SOUTHERN SECTOR

By bus Kemel Bus services (☏65 225 3530, ⊛kemelbus. cl) pass through the southern section en route from Puerto Montt to Chaitén (2 daily) and can drop you off on the way.

By car There are daily car ferries (Jan–March & Dec 10.30am & 3pm; 8.30am & 1pm return; April–Nov 10.30am; 1pm return) from Hornopirén to Caleta Gonzalo (see page 349), the entry point to the park. Book well in advance with Transportes Austral (W taustral.cl).

By organized tour From November to March Chaitur, Chaitén Nativo and Natour (see page 354) all offer guided treks in the park from Chaitén.

EL AMARILLO SECTOR

By bus Any bus between Chaitén and destinations south can drop you off at El Amarillo village.

By car The *Ventisquero El Amarillo* campsite (see page 353) can only be reached by pickup truck or 4WD, but the other dirt roads are fine.

By organized tour Chaitur, Chaitén Nativo and Natour (see page 354) all run tours to the Termas El Amarillo (CH$30,000) and can drop you at the entrance to the Amarillo sector. You'd have to hitchhike back. It's also possible to arrange a transfer with all three if they are not too busy with actual tours.

INFORMATION

Park information The park has two Centros de Visitantes: at Caleta Gonzalo and El Amarillo, across the road and uphill from the park entrance (Jan, Feb & Dec Mon–Sat 9am–7pm, Sun 10am–4pm; March–Nov Mon–Sat 9am–

2pm & 4–8pm, but check in advance; W parquepumalin. cl). You can get advance info on the park at Casa Puma in Puerto Varas at Klenner 299 (Mon–Fri 9am–5pm; T 65 225 0079).

ACCOMMODATION AND EATING

There are five well-equipped, beautifully located campsites in the **southern sector** and two in the **El Amarillo sector** – including *Camping Ventisquero Amarillo*, the park's largest site and the one with the loveliest setting. At all the campsites, it's possible for groups and families to rent *quinchos* (CH$16,000 for up to four people), while motorhomes are charged CH$10,000.

SOUTHERN SECTOR

Cabañas Río Gonzalo Caleta Gonzalo T 65 225 0079. At Caleta Gonzalo, these seven *cabañas* (sleeping 2–5) are the epitome of rustic luxury, each individually designed, with comfy loft beds and ocean views. There's also a good camping spot nearby with cold showers and sheltered cooking spaces. Camping **CH$6000**, *cabañas* **CH$90,000**

Café Caleta Gonzalo Caleta Gonzalo T 65 225 0079. This appealing restaurant with massive copper-plated fireplace serves Chilean dishes cooked with organic vegetables (dish of the day CH$8000), and there are sandwiches to take away. Summer daily noon–10pm.

Camping Lago Blanco 36km north of Chaitén. This campsite has fantastic views of Lago Blanco from the covered sites, as well as hot showers and fire pits. **CH$6000**

Camping El Volcán Halfway between Chaitén and Caleta Gonzalo. Large, tree-fringed campsite; each site comes with its own cooking area, barbecue and drinking water access. **CH$6000**

EL AMARILLO SECTOR

Camping Grande 3.3km from park entrance. Attractive campsite with sites scattered around giant *nalca* patches and surrounded by trees. Comes with bathrooms and *quinchos* for cooking. **CH$6000**

Camping Ventisquero Amarillo 8km from park entrance. Dubbed "The most beautiful campsite in Chile", albeit the furthest from the park entrance, this tree-fringed spot comes with spectacular views of the hanging glacier, as well as cooking shelters and bathrooms. **CH$6000**

Yelcho En La Patagonia Puerto Cárdenas, 19km south of El Amarillo T 65 257 6005, W yelcho.cl. This luxurious retreat consists of a boutique hotel with eight intimate rooms, and fishing and horseriding trips on offer. Nearby is a large lakeside campsite; each pitch comes with a cooking shelter, firepit and firewood, and hot shower access. Camping **CH$4000**, doubles **US$175**

SHOPPING

Puma Verde Carretera Austral s/n. By the El Amarillo petrol station, this is an excellent store selling varied foods

as well as camping supplies and even outdoor gear. Mon–Sat 9am–6pm.

Chaitén

On May 2, 2008, **Volcán Chaitén**, at the foot of which nestles its namesake town, erupted for the first time in more than nine thousand years, taking the local residents completely by surprise. **CHAITÉN**, and much of the surrounding area, had to be evacuated as the 30km plume of ash and steam from the volcano affected the local water sources and a mudslide caused floods that devastated the town. Chaitén has been rebuilt since (though several eerie, wrecked houses half-buried in volcanic detritus have been left standing off Calle Río Blanco as a macabre outdoor museum) and is a useful transport hub and a good base for visiting Parque Nacional Pumalín Douglas R. Tompkins.

ARRIVAL AND DEPARTURE

CHAITÉN

By bus Buses Becker (☎67 223 2167, ⓦbusesbecker. com) run to Coyhaique via La Junta and Puyuhuapi; Buses Cardenas (☎67 272 1214) serve Futaleufú; Buses Cumbres Nevadas (☎09 8597 6405) run both to Futaleufú and Palena; and Kemel Bus (☎65 225 3530 ⓦkemelbus.cl) runs to Puerto Montt via Hornopirén.

Destinations Coyhaique (Fri 11.30am; 8hr); Futaleufú (Mon–Sat 8am & 4pm; 2hr 30min–4hr); Hornopirén (daily 8.30am & 2pm; 4hr 30min); Palena (daily 8am & 4pm; 2hr 30min); Puerto Montt (daily 8.30am & 2pm; 7hr).

By boat The Naviera Austral/Transportes Austral office at Almirante Riveros at Todesco (☎65 273 1011, ⓦnavieraustral.cl or ⓦtaustral.cl) sells tickets for ferries to Quellón, Puerto Montt and the Caleta Gonzalo–Hornopirén

car ferry north of Parque Nacional Pumalín Douglas R. Tompkins.

Destinations Puerto Montt (Thurs noon, Sun midnight; 9hr); Quellón (Tues 10am, Thurs 1am; 5hr).

By car From the north, you can drive via Hornopirén, booking the Caleta Gonzalo ferry in advance (see page 349). It's possible to take the car ferry from Quellón, but prices are steep.

By plane Pewen Air Services (☎65 222 4000, ⓦpewenchile.com), CieloMarAustral (☎65 226 4010 ⓦcielomaraustral.cl) and Aerocord (☎65 226 2300, ⓦaerocord.cl) all have scheduled flights to Puerto Montt from the Santa Barbara airstrip (CH$50,000 one way).

Destinations Puerto Montt (at least one daily; 45min).

INFORMATION

Tourist information There's a kiosk on the *costanera* (promenade), but it's rarely staffed or open.

Banks and exchange A Banco Estado on the plaza has an ATM which accepts some foreign cards, but not others. Change your euros, dollars and Argentinian pesos here.

ACTIVITIES AND TOURS

Chaitén Nativo Libertad 253 ☎65 273 1333 or ☎09 7764 5891, ⓦchaitennativo.cl. Besides outings to Termas de Amarillo, kayaking and mountain biking excursions, this knowledgeable, local one-man show also leads bilingual guided treks to different parts of Parque Nacional Pumalín Douglas R. Tompkins. Bikes available for rent.

Chaitur O'Higgins 67 ☎65 273 1429 or ☎09 7468 5608, ⓦchaitur.com. The HQ of American expat Nicolas La Penna – a treasure trove of local information – doubles as the local bus terminal and organizes day tours to Parque

Nacional Pumalín Douglas R. Tompkins and Termas de Amarillo. If Nicolas is not at the office (which is often), ask a local to point out his house.

Natour O'Higgins 176 ☎09 4234 2803, ⓦnatour.cl. This energetic German/Chilean couple runs guided tours of Parque Nacional Pumalín Douglas R. Tompkins, sea kayak safaris from nearby Santa Barbara, boat trips in the bay in search of wildlife and transfers to the airstrip. They also rent bicycles.

ACCOMMODATION

Brisas del Mar Av Corcovado 287 ☎09 9515 8808, ⓦbrisasdelmarchaiten.cl. Particularly good value for groups or families, these well-equipped, centrally heated cabins are slightly set back from the coastal road. CH$45,000

Hostal Don Carlos Riveros 53 ☎65 273 1287. Popular family-run guesthouse a block from the waterfront, with compact, functional rooms, some lacking in natural light. En suites with cable TV are pricier. Hosts won't win congeniality prizes and the breakfast is just OK. CH$26,000

Hostel & Camping Las Nalcas Ercilla 342 ☎09 9619 9042, ⓦhostel-las-nalcas.webnode.cl. Run by a friendly couple, this is the closest Chaitén gets to a hostel. There are camping spots in the garden out back, with a kitchen and reliable hot showers, plus a handful of cosy rooms. Camping CH$4000, doubles CH$25,000

Hostería Llanos Corcovado 387 ☎65 273 1332. Spotless, family-run seafront residence with a clutch of wood-panelled rooms, some en suite, and a couple of swing-a-cat singles. CH$24,000

EATING

Natour Cafe O'Higgins s/n ☎09 4234 2803. A block from the bus station, this green bus doubles as a popular café. Come for your morning coffee and the breakfast of

champions – involving omelettes – and take heart from their motto: "Eat Well. Travel Often." Mon–Sat 9am–2pm.

Pizzeria Reconquista Portales at O'Higgins. The walls at this locally beloved pizzeria are hung with photos of ye olde Chaitén and the spectacular eruption, and the bar serves Austral, Kunstmann and Kross beers. Pizzas are thin and crispy and sport some exotic ingredients. Pizzas CH$6500–8800. Daily 12.30–3.30pm & 7–10pm.

★ **El Rincón del Mate** Libertad at Padre Juan Todesco ☎09 9195 8229. This ecodome, decked out with striking photos of the region, is both base camp and gourmet restaurant. The *ceviche* and the *ostiones parmesana* (scallop fondue) are among the best in Chile, and apart from the good selection of regional craft beers, there are also spectacular calafate sours and a supporting cast of burgers and *quesadillas*. Mains CH$7000–10,000. Daily 12.30–11pm.

Futaleufú Valley

The 80km trip up the **Futaleufú Valley** is one of the most enjoyable diversions off the Carretera Austral. Heading east from the drab crossroads settlement of Villa Santa Lucía, south of Chaitén, you first skirt the southern shore of Lago Yelcho for 30km, before arriving at a fork in the road. The right turn goes to the quiet border village of **Palena**, while the left branch follows the turquoise **Río Futaleufú** for 17km through towering gorges, lush forests and snow-streaked mountain peaks to its namesake town.

Futaleufú

Sitting on the **Río Futaleufú**, near its confluence with the **Río Espolón**, and surrounded by forested, snowy peaks, **FUTALEUFÚ** more than earns the grandiose description – "A landscape painted by God" – applied to it by early inhabitants. With its big "explosion waves" and massive "rodeo holes", the Futaleufú is regarded by many professional rafters and kayakers as one of the most challenging **whitewater** rivers in the world, with sections of the river known as "Hell" and "The Terminator"; the toughest Class V rapids are "Trono" and "Zeta".

An attractive little town, Futaleufú serves as a popular summer base for rafting, kayaking, hiking and horseriding. Since it's very close to the Argentinian border, it also makes for an easy transfer to Esquel and Trevelín.

8

ARRIVAL AND DEPARTURE
FUTALEUFÚ

By bus Kemel Bus (☎09 7714 6122 ⓦ kemelbus.cl), Buses Absa (☎09 9256 6673, ⓦ busesabsa.cl) and Buses Palena (☎65 274 1319) run to Puerto Montt via Argentina, while Buses Futaleufú runs across the border to Esquel. Buses Becker (☎67 223 2167) runs to Coyhaique (via La Junta and Puyuhuapi) and Chaitén (though the latter was suspended at research time due to a mudslide at Villa Santa Lucia). All buses except those to Esquel depart from the corner of Prat and Balmaceda. Note that at the time of research, bureaucracy decreed that Esquel-bound buses stop at the Chilean border. Passengers then have to walk 400m with their luggage and transfer to a connecting bus on the Argentinian side.

Destinations Coyhaique (Wed & Sun 10am; 8hr); Esquel (Argentina; Mon, Wed & Fri 9am & 7pm; 30min); Puerto Montt (daily except Wed & Sat 7.30am; 12hr).

INFORMATION

Tourist office O'Higgins 536, south side of the Plaza de Armas (summer daily 9am–9pm). Very helpful, with bus timetables and information on tour operators and all accommodation options.

Banks and exchange There's a single ATM at Banco Estado, on the plaza, but it doesn't accept some foreign cards, so bring plenty of cash.

ACTIVITIES AND TOURS

Most people come to Futaleufú for the **whitewater rafting** and kayaking (see page 356), though you needn't stop there: the area around Futa lends itself to a range of outdoor activities including hiking, horse-trekking, mountain biking, drifting down the tamer Río Espolón on an inner-tyre tube, canyoning (abseiling down waterfalls) and stand-up paddleboarding.

WHITEWATER RAFTING ON THE FUTA AND ESPOLÓN

A number of Chilean and US operators offer **rafting** trips down the **Río Futaleufú**, a body of water that runs through a basalt gorge known as the Gates of Hell, and boasts more than forty class IV–V rapids. You don't have to have prior rafting experience, because you'll be taught all the safety instructions and commands, but you do have to be reasonably fit and a decent swimmer. Futa is a serious river and even a half-day excursion (1hr 30min–2hr on the water) will expose you to some drenching, **heart-stopping fun** amid raft-battering turquoise waves. The standard half-day outing is the "Bridge to Bridge" section, which comprises around twelve rapids, mostly Class III+ and IV, and one V ("Mundaca"). Tour operators take safety seriously and a raft or two is accompanied by rescue catarafts and kayaks. Occasionally people fall out of rafts, and sometimes a raft will flip; you will be taught what to do in each situation and rescuers will be nearby. Expect to pay around CH$50,000 for a half-day excursion, or CH$90,000 for a full day, which includes tackling numerous Class V rapids. For something gentler you could pay CH$25,000 for a relatively simple run down the **Río Espolón**.

RAFTING OPERATORS

Bochinche Expediciones Cerda 697 ☎09 8847 6174, ⊛bochinchex.com. This excellent operator is the only one to offer full days on the Futa even when the water level is too high for others; they have catarafts, which are more stable than rafts, and twice the safety personnel. They are also the only operator to offer riverbug and tandem kayaking. Week-long activity packages (US$2500) also available.

Condorfu O'Higgins at Rodríguez ☎09 4213 9636, ⊛condorfu.cl. Highly professional outfit, offering standard rafting excursions, as well as 2hr canyoning trips for beginners and those with experience

(CH$25,000). Whitewater kayaking tuition, too (CH$25,000).

Expediciones Chile Mistral 296 ☎1 208 629 5032, ⊛exchile.com. With its own riverfront camp, this American/Chilean outfit specializes in multi-day rafting on the Futa. Half-day and full-day outings, whitewater kayaking lessons and small-group, multi-day trekking and ranch stays.

Patagonia Elements Cerda 549 ☎09 7499 0296, ⊛patagoniaelements.com. Right on the plaza, this reputable, safety-conscious Chilean operator is an excellent bet for half- and full-day rafting on the Futa.

Carpintero Negro Aventuras Cerda between Prat and Aldea ☎09 5825 4073, ⊛carpinteronegro.com. Offering cultural immersion and landbound activities, this enthusiastic operator specializes in guided treks around

Futa, from half-day outings to three-day hikes around Lago Espolon, complete with camping and traditional *asados* (barbecues).

ACCOMMODATION

Antigua Casona Rodriguez 215 ☎65 272 1311, ✉antiguacasono.futa@gmail.com. When you step inside the living/dining area of this adorable boutique hotel, you're immediately surrounded by nautical memorabilia and other intriguing little touches from all over Europe. A friendly Chilean/Italian family oversees the appealing, wood-panelled rooms upstairs and the restaurant, which serves excellent Italian dishes. CH$70,000

Camping Los Coihues Next to the bridge, just south of town ☎09 9326 8777, ⊛campingfutaleufu.cl. With its own riverside beach and a sheltered part of Río Espolón for swimming, this well-located, large, tree-shaded campsite is the best in town. There are reliable hot showers, a *quincho* for cooking and even a laundry service. Each car is charged CH$2000. Camping CH$7000, motorhomes CH$10,000

★ **La Gringa Carioca** Aldea 498 ☎65 272 1260, ⊛hostallagringacarioca.cl. South African Adriana is the

effusive hostess at this intimate cottage in the middle of a large garden on the edge of Futa. The four light, bright, spacious doubles may all be individually decorated but have in common the high-quality beds and linens. An extensive breakfast seals the deal. Closed May–Aug. CH$65,000

★ **Hostal Las Natalias** O'Higgins 302 ☎09 9631 1330, ⊛hostallasnatalias.info. A 10min walk west of town along Calle Cerda, Futa's only bona fide hostel is run by hospitable American-Argentinian Nate, a fount of local knowledge who offers whitewater kayaking lessons. The huge open-plan communal area/kitchen is a very sociable place, and the dorms and private rooms are airy and spacious. Guests find themselves extending their stay, seduced by the easy-going vibe. Dorms CH$15,000, doubles CH$32,000

Lodge El Barranco Bernardo O'Higgins 172 ☎65 272 1314, ⊛elbarrancochile.cl. The hospitable owners of this upscale option on the outskirts of town can help organize fishing, rafting and horseriding excursions. The spacious, wood-panelled rooms have comfortable beds with crisp linens and there's a small swimming pool for guests. The restaurant (dinner only; open to non-guests) is the best in town, with a good mix of seafood and Thai dishes (mains from CH$11,000). **CH$130,000**

Uman Lodge Fundo La Confluencia s/n, 4km south of Futaleufú ☎ 65 272 1700, ⓦ umanlodge.cl. Reachable via a steep road, this shingled wonder of a hotel sits on a bluff overlooking the river far below. The hotel's enticing features include a library/lounge with high ceilings, a first-class restaurant (open to non-guests) and an infinity pool. The open-plan rooms with free-standing tubs are luxurious and stylish, and numerous outdoor activities are on offer. **US$460**

EATING

Cafe Mandala Cerda 545 ☎ 09 6168 4925. Decorated with colourful mandalas, this thimble-sized café right on the square is your best bet for proper coffee (Patagonian Blend). Excellent *kuchen* of the calafate, blueberry and raspberry variety, also. Mon–Fri 9am–8pm, Sat & Sun noon–9pm.

Martín Pescadór Balmaceda 603 ☎ 65 272 1279. Inside this wooden *quincho*-like structure with a soaring roof and stone fireplace, the chef makes great use of her own organic vegetables and ingredients from local suppliers to create memorable dishes, such as gnocchi in morel sauce, slow-cooked lamb and prawns on a quinoa biscuit. The wine list is extensive. Mains from CH$10,000. Daily 7.45–11.30pm.

★ **Pizzas de Fabio** Carnicer 280 ☎ 09 8577 8334. Come to this diminutive takeaway for the best pizza in the south of Chile (and we do not make this claim lightly). Whether is Quatro Quesos or Hawaii en Futa, the thin and crispy pizzas are cooked to perfection and the ingredients are top-notch. The owner plans to add seating. Daily noon–10pm.

Rocoto Patagón Pratt 262 ☎ 09 7499 0296. Tucked away in the Pueblito Artesanal, off the plaza, this Peruvian fusion hole-in-the-wall is a good spot for *ceviche* (though without the Peruvian heat), *arroz con mariscos* (seafood rice), *aji de gallina* (chicken in spicy yellow sauce) and a flavourful seafood soup. Mains from CH$7000. Mon–Sat noon–3pm & 7–10pm.

Puerto Raul Marín Balmaceda

A couple of kilometres north of La Junta and around 75km south of the crossroads settlement of Villa Santa Lucía – where the road to the Futaleufú Valley branches off from the Carretera Austral – a westbound, 73km-long gravel road splits off from the Carretera, running along the banks of Río Palena to **Puerto Raúl Marín Balmaceda**. Founded in 1889, this fishing village is the oldest in the region (though it only acquired road access in 2009), with the most attractive setting along the whole of the Carretera Austral. The cluster of houses, hiding behind greenery along several sandy streets, sits on an island in the river delta, reachable by car ferry (see page 358) and boasting attractive white sand beaches; note that you have to drive an additional 9km post-ferry to get to the village after the initial 64km drive to the river. The bay is full of marine life, such as seals and cormorants, and it's possible to see dolphins and even blue whales if you do a boat excursion (see page 358).

Termas El Sauce

21km northwest of La Junta and 54km east of Raúl Marín Balmaceda • Daily 10am–8.30pm • CH$6000; plus CH$1000 for private pools • ☎ 09 9452 2711

The well-kept hot springs of **Termas El Sauce**, 3km from the main road, are a worthy detour en route to or from the village. Surrounded by lush vegetation, there is one hot pool fed by two thermal springs (40ºC) and two smaller private pools, as well as two refreshing river water pools to dunk yourself in. You can dip in the thermal pool for free outside regular opening hours if you **camp** here (CH$12,000).

ARRIVAL AND INFORMATION   PUERTO RAUL MARÍN BALMACEDA

By bus Buses Transportes Willy (☎ 09 3207 9076 or ☎ 09 9427 6625) run to Raúl Marín Balmaceda from La Junta (daily 5.30am & noon, returning 8am & 2pm; 2hr).

By car Allow 2hr for the drive from La Junta; it's a scenic but at times treacherously narrow road, with tight bends and steep sections. Be mindful of ferry crossing times.

8

By ferry The free car ferry that connects the village to the Carretera Austral runs back and forth (5min) from 8.30am to 1pm and 1.30pm to 5.30pm. In peak season, hours may be extended. Naviera Austral ferries (@navieraustral.cl) stop here en route between Puerto Chacabuco and Quellón. Turismo Valle de Palena (see below) sells ferry tickets.

Services There is no ATM or petrol station in the village, and Entel signal only for mobile phones.

ACTIVITIES AND TOURS

Kawelyek Expediciones Las Hermanas s/n ☏09 5742 9056, @kawelyek.cl. Local guide Patricio runs three different tours: a 2hr boat tour that takes you dolphin- and sea-bird-spotting, a 4hr wildlife-watching boat tour that runs up the Estuario Pitipalena and a 6hr tour up Canal Garrao, which can be done in a boat or sea kayak.

Turismo Valle de Palena Las Hermanas s/n ☏09 6608 9537. Jonathan Hechenleitner, owner of the *Hostería Valle del Palena*, can organize all manner of outdoor tours; his office also acts as the village tourist office and Naviera Austral ticket office. Maps available and English spoken. Daily 3–7.30pm.

ACCOMMODATION AND EATING

★**Fundo Los Leones** ☏09 7898 2956, @fundolosleones.cl. You'll find this delightful ecotourism lodge that formerly belonged to Doug Tompkins (see page 351) on the outskirts of Raúl Marín Balmaceda, 3km away. The wood-panelled *cabañas* (sleeping two) are bright and individually decorated, the extensive private beach is a good place to spot dolphins and sea lions, and the lodge offers wildlife-viewing boat trips, horseback riding and fishing excursions. Internet in the main building only; there's an outdoor hot tub for relaxation. **US$180**

Hostal El Viajero Av Costanera s/n ☏09 6608 4858. Popular guesthouse a short walk from the ferry port. Upstairs is a clutch of snug, simple, wood-panelled rooms that share facilities, while downstairs is a kitchen for guest use. Singles are half the price of doubles. **CH$24,000**

Hostería Isla del Palena Las Hermanas s/n ☏09 6608 9537, ✉isladelpalena@gmail.com. Of the two places to eat in the village, this is by far the best, with excellent seafood dishes such as *puye al pilpil* and *chupe de jaiba*. Mains from CH$8000. There are decent en-suite rooms here, too. Daily 8am–9pm. **CH$30,000**

La Junta and Reserva Nacional Lago Rosselot

South of the turnoffs for Raúl Marín Balmaceda and Lago Verde, and just before the northern boundary of Parque Nacional Queulat, the Carretera Austral passes through **LA JUNTA**, a collection of tin houses established in 1983 as one of General Pinochet's "new towns", and home to a controversial unauthorized monument to the dictator. La Junta is the access point to the **Reserva Nacional Lago Rosselot**, popular with the fly-fishing set, but is otherwise an unremarkable transport hub with little to detain you.

ARRIVAL AND INFORMATION

LA JUNTA

By bus Transportes Terraustral (☏67 225 4335) runs to Coyhaique (via Puyuhuapi) and Chaitén. Buses Becker (☏67 223 2167, @busesbecker.com) also serves Chaitén, as well as Futaleufú. Transportes Willy (☏09 3207 9076 or ☏09 9427 6626) runs to Raúl Marín Balmaceda. Most buses depart from the plaza.

Destinations Chaitén (2 weekly; 3hr 30min); Coyhaique (several weekly; 6hr); Futaleufú (1 weekly Tues around noon, returning around 2pm on Wed; 3hr); Raúl Marín Balmaceda (daily 5.30am & noon; 2hr 30min).

Tourist office Plaza de Armas (Jan–March & Dec daily 9am–9pm; shorter hours rest of year ☏65 272 1239).

ACCOMMODATION AND EATING

★**Alto Melimoyu Hotel & Patagonia** Carretera Austral 375 ☏67 231 4320, @altomelimoyu.cl. The young owners of this beautiful guesthouse offer numerous excursions for active travellers, from hiking in Reserva Nacional Lago Rosselot to kayaking and mountain biking. Bright rooms come with all manner of creature comforts (including satellite TV). **CH$93,000**

Espacio y Tiempo Hotel de Montaña Carretera Austral 399 ☏67 231 4141, @espacioytiempo.cl. With appealing rustic interior and nine spiffy, centrally heated rooms, this wood-and-stone mountain lodge just off the Carretera Austral allows easy exploration of the Río Palena watershed on horseback, or just lets you curl up by the fireplace in the cosy guest lounge. The restaurant, open to non-guests, serves good Chilean staples. **CH$95,000**

Hostería Valderas Varas s/n ☏67 231 4195. One of several guesthouses of comparable quality, the Lagos family home sits a couple of blocks from the plaza. Rooms, some en suite, are clean and basic. The proprietress can cook up simple meals on request. **CH$26,000**

Mi Casita de Té Carretera Austral at Patricio Lynch ☎ 67 231 4206. Welcoming café where Eliana and her daughters serve slabs of grilled fish, *lomo a lo pobre* (meat with fried egg), *cazuela* (stew) and regional beers. Mains CH$6000. Mon–Sat 12.30–10pm, Sun 12.30–3.30pm.

Parque Nacional Queulat and around

22km south of Puyuhuapi • CH$5000, payable only if you enter Sector Ventisquero Colgante

Consisting of rugged, mountains, dense forest, raging glacial rivers and its namesake hanging glacier, the 1540-square-kilometre **Parque Nacional Queulat** is one of the region's most impressive natural attractions, as beautiful as it is remote and as rainy as it is beautiful. It is divided into three sectors. The Carretera Austral enters the park's northern boundary 15km north of the village of Puyuhuapi and crosses its southern limit 55km further south, just beyond the Portezuelo de Queulat pass. The **main entrance** – where you find most accommodation and trails – lies 2.5km along a signposted turnoff from the Carretera Austral.

Sector Angostura

Beyond Puyuhuapi, in the northern sector of the park, a track pulls off the road to the Conaf *guardería*, on the shores of the long, thin **Lago Risopatrón**. The lake, flanked by steep mountains jutting abruptly out of its deep-blue waters, is a lovely spot, and the **camping** area (see page 360) near the Conaf hut is one of the prettiest along the entire road. By the *guardería*, the **Sendero Laguna Los Pumas** (13km; 5hr return) starts with a steep ascent, climbing to 1100m. From the plateau at the top, you get sweeping views onto surrounding mountains and out to the fjord. The trail then descends through a pass, leading to the shimmering Laguna Los Pumas.

Sector Ventisquero Colgante

The central and most popular section of the park, **Sector Ventisquero Colgante**, is named after the incredible "hanging glacier". Wedged between two peaks, forming a V-shaped mass of blue-white ice, the glacier indeed seems to hang suspended over a sheer rock face above a glacial lake. From the parking area 2km beyond the ranger post, follow the signposted 250m **Sendero Mirador Panorámico**, a muddy fifteen-minute return trip up to a viewpoint overlooking the raging glacial river. For a closer look at the glacier, cross the suspension bridge over the river, and turn right, taking the 600m **Sendero Laguna Témpanos**, a non-strenuous trail (30min return) through overgrown woods that skirts the river and leads to the glacial emerald lagoon, fed by two thundering waterfalls plummeting down from the glacier.

At the lake or in Puyuhuapi (see page 360) it's possible to organize a boat outing on the lagoon (CH$5000/person) for a closer peek at the Ventisquero Colgante. Left of the bridge, the steep **Sendero Ventisquero Colgante** climbs 3.2km (2hr return) to a higher viewpoint overlooking the glacier.

Sector Portezuelo Queulat

Just beyond the southern entrance to the park, in the **Sector Portezuelo Queulat**, a short trail leads west to a mighty waterfall, the 40m-high **Saltos del Cóndor**. Five kilometres beyond, the Carretera Austral narrows and zigzags its way down the steep **Cuesta de Queulat**, through sheer-sided mountains crowned with glaciers. A signposted 2km trail, **Sendero Bosque Encantado**, makes for an easy but exhilarating hike (3hr 30min return), branching off to the left from the road just before the Portezuelo de

Queulat, and leading 1.7km through moss-covered ancient trees before ending at the Río Cascadas.

From here, follow the river up the hill for another 800m, and you'll arrive at its source – a jade-green lake at the foot of a granite cliff, topped by a glacier and streaked by waterfalls. Just beyond the Portezuelo de Queulat pass is Sendero Padre García, with a 100m-staircase leading down to the **Salto Padre García**, a powerful waterfall dropping 30m into the Río Queulat.

ARRIVAL AND DEPARTURE
PARQUE NACIONAL QUEULAT

By bus From Coyhaique, you can get any northbound bus that goes to Puyuhuapi or beyond, or any Coyhaique-bound bus from any destination north of Parque Nacional Queulat, to drop you off by the main entrance to the park. Book a bus seat in advance for the day you plan to leave the park.

By organized tour Several tour companies run day-trips to the Ventisquero Colgante from Coyhaique during the summer (see below), and one from Puyuhuapi (see page 360).

ACCOMMODATION

Camping Angostura Sector Angostura. Beautiful campsite on the shores of Lago Risopatrón near the Conaf ranger hut; each site comes with its own picnic table and *fogón* (barbecue area). Cold showers only. **CH$4000**

Camping Ventisquero Sector Ventisquero Colgante. Though the ground is rocky and hard, the ten emplacements come equipped with picnic tables and *fogones*. Make use of the firewood to get over the freezing cold showers. **CH$6000**

★ **Eco Camping Los Arrayanes** Carretera Austral Norte Km 227 ☎ 09 9078 5896. Located 5km north of Puyuhuapi, this is a gorgeous waterfront campsite surrounded by a myrtle grove. It's clean and orderly, with its own beach and access to hot showers, *fogones* for cooking and kayaks and canoes for rent. **CH$6000**

Puyuhuapi and around

Sitting at the head of the narrow Ventisquero fjord, surrounded by steep, wooded hills and frequently shrouded in low-hanging mist, **PUYUHUAPI** was founded in 1935 by four young German immigrants from Sudetenland who married Chilean women. It's a great place to break your journey along the Carretera Austral in either direction, not only for the wild beauty of its setting, but also for its proximity to the **Termas de Puyuhuapi** – an upmarket hot springs resort that can be visited on a day-trip – and its convenience as a base for exploring **Parque Nacional Queulat** (see page 359). The town's historic **textiles factory** has mostly switched production to craft beer these days, producing the very good Hopperdietzel tipples. Pick up a brochure at the tourist office (see page 361) for a self-guided walk around the village and check out the cemetery of the first colonists, the surviving original houses and walking trails.

Termas Ventisquero

6km south of town along the Carretera • Jan, Feb & Dec 7am–9pm; March–Nov shorter hours • CH$20,000 • ☎ 09 7966 6805, ⓦ termasventisqueropuyuhuapi.cl

A cheaper alternative to the plush Termas de Puyuhuapi is the more easily accessible **Termas Ventisquero**, with two simple outdoor pools fed by thermal springs (temperatures vary), a beautiful view over the fjord and an on-site café.

Termas de Puyuhuapi

17km south of Puyuhuapi and across the bay • Day visit CH$55,000 for outdoor pools, indoor pool and jacuzzis; price includes return boat ride • ☎ 67 245 0305, ⓦ puyuhuapilodge.com • Boat departs from a signposted wooden jetty 15km south of Puyuhuapi (Jan–March & Dec 4 daily, typically 10am, 1pm, 3.30pm & 7pm; less frequently off-season; call for updated schedule; 10min)

The luxurious thermal baths, lodge and spa at **Termas De Puyuhuapi** enjoy a fantastic location, marooned on the edge of a peninsula on the opposite side of the fjord from the Carretera Austral. You don't need to be an overnight guest (see below) to visit, but you should phone ahead to book.

The thermal baths used to be a handful of ramshackle cabins that were transformed into a series of low-lying, beautifully designed buildings made of reddish-brown *alerce* timber and lots of glass by the East German shipbuilding magnate Eberhard Kossman in the late 1980s. Apart from its spectacular location, the main reason to come here is to soak in the steaming **hot springs**, channelled into three outdoor pools reached by a short walk through the forest. Two of the pools are large enough to swim in, and sit right on the edge of the fjord, while the third one, containing the hottest water, is a small pond enclosed by overhanging ferns and native trees. There's a state-of-the-art **spa**, specializing in a range of treatments and massages, an indoor pool with "waterfall", a cold water pool and two jacuzzis.

ARRIVAL AND DEPARTURE
PUYUHUAPI

By bus Buses Terra Austral (☎67 225 4335), Buses Becker (☎67 272 1248) and Interlagos (☎67 224 0840) serve Coyhaique and Futaleufú; Buses Becker is due to resume services to Chaitén when the road from Villa Santa Lucia is cleared and rebuilt (see page 348).

Destinations Coyhaique (Terra Austral: daily 6am; Buses Becker: Wed–Sun 3.30pm; Interlagos: Mon, Wed & Fri 3pm; 6hr); Futaleufú (Terra Austral: Mon, Tues, Thurs & Fri 7am; Buses Becker: Tues–Sat noon; Interlagos: Tues, Thurs & Sun 4.30pm; 4hr).

INFORMATION AND TOURS

Tourist office Av Übel (daily 9am–1pm & 3–8pm; ⓦpuertopuyuhuapi.cl). This well-stocked and helpful tourist office is in the centre of town; they have maps, bus timetables and lots of information on accommodation.
Experiencia Austral Av Übel (☎09 8744 8755, ⓦpuertopuyuhuapi.cl). New operator offering kayaking

both on the fjord and beneath the hanging glacier in Parque Nacional Queulat. Also, bicycles and outdoor equipment for rent, plus boat outings beneath the glacier.
Services There is no ATM in Puyuhuapi and most businesses only accept cash.

ACCOMMODATION

★ **Casa Ludwig** Otto Uebel 202 ☎67 232 5220, ⓦcasaludwig.cl. This rambling yellow chalet – a historical monument in its own right – has comfortable singles and doubles (some en suite), polished wooden floors, excellent breakfast, a library and great views. It's run by English- and German-speaking Louisa – the daughter of one of the original colonists – who is a wealth of information on the area. Management may change in 2019. CH$42,000
Hostal Augusto Grosse Camilo Henriquez 4 ☎67 232 5150, ⓦhostalaugustogrosse.cl. This tiny hostel consists of a couple of dorms and doubles, all decked out with beautiful wooden furniture hand-carved by the owner. Guests gather in the tiny wood-stove-heated living area and are welcome to use the kitchen. Breakfast CH$1500. Dorms CH$12,000, doubles CH$26,000

Hostería Aonikenk Hamburgo 16 ☎67 232 5208, ⓦaonikenkpuyuhuapi.cl. A helpful hostess presides over this collection of compact doubles and fully equipped *cabañas* (three to five people) with balconies. Meals are served in the cheery dining area of the main house, and there's a lounge area upstairs for chilling out. Doubles CH$54,000, cabañas CH$70,000
★ **Puyuhuapi Lodge & Spa** Bahía Dorita ☎2 2225 6489, ⓦpuyuhuapilodge.com. This elegant, wood-shingled lodge sits right on the tranquil fjord. The spacious, carpeted rooms come with king-size beds and terraces overlooking the water and guests can choose whether to have access just to the outdoor hot springs or also to the indoor spa/pool complex. The restaurant serves delicious three-course meals made with fresh local produce, and the inclusive breakfast buffet is the best in the region. Half board and full board available. US$320

EATING

El Muelle Otto Uebel s/n ☎09 7654 3598. This fjordside restaurant is the only place in the village that's reliably open for meals and its wonderfully fresh catch-of-the-day dishes do not disappoint. Their grilled hake is a winner and the home-made *kuchen* with wild berries hits the spot. Mains CH$6000–9000. Daily 12.30–3.30pm & 7–10pm.

Mi Sur Otto Uebel 36 ☎09 7550 7656. With Bob Marley singing in the background and a generally mellow vibe, this new spot aspires to haute cuisine. The gravlax, risotto and "*creacion de chef*" are well worth a try, washed down with a local Hopperdietzel craft beer or pisco cocktail. Mains CH$7500. Daily 1–3pm & 6–10pm.

8

Coyhaique

After the smattering of small villages scattered along the Carretera Austral, Aysén's lively regional capital, **COYHAIQUE**, can be a welcome change. The city's fifty thousand or so inhabitants make up half the region's population, and it's the only place along the Carretera that offers a wide range of services – including ATMs. It's also a good launch pad for some great **day-trips** (see page 363). Coyhaique's most unusual feature is its large, five-sided **Plaza de Armas**, from which the main streets radiate like a spider's web; even with map in hand, travellers often find themselves wandering around in circles (or pentagons).

ARRIVAL AND DEPARTURE

BY PLANE

LATAM and Sky Airline tickets can be purchased online or at Turismo Prado, 21 de Mayo 417 (☎67 221 3815, ⓦturismoprado.cl); the latter also sells tickets to Laguna San Rafael (see page 367).

Aeropuerto de Balmaceda Sky and LATAM flights to and from Santiago, Puerto Montt and Punta Arenas, plus DAP flights to Punta Arenas, land at the Aeropuerto de Balmaceda, 55km south of Coyhaique, and are met by three minibus transfer companies that take passengers to their hotels (CH$5000).

Destinations Puerto Montt (2 daily; 1hr 15min); Punta Arenas (Tues & Thurs; 1hr 45min); Santiago (2 daily; 3hr).

Aeródromo Teniente Vidal Charter flights over the San Rafael glacier with Aerocord (General Parra 21; ☎67 224 6300, ⓦaerocord.cl), plus weekly flights to Villa O'Higgins and charter flights to Chile Chico and other destinations along the Carretera Austral, take off from the Aeródromo Teniente Vidal, 5km west of town.

Destinations San Rafael glacier (on demand in season; 2hr); Villa O'Higgins (Mon & Thurs 10am; 1hr 15min).

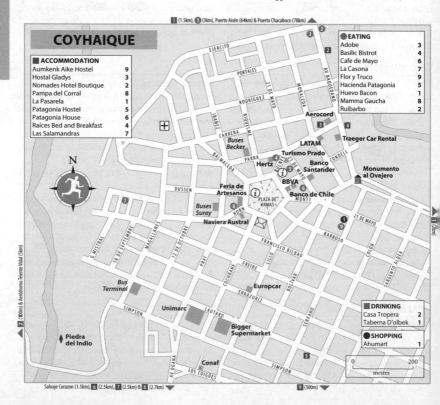

COYHAIQUE

ACCOMMODATION
Aumkenk Aike Hostel	9
Hostal Gladys	3
Nomades Hotel Boutique	2
Pampa del Corral	8
La Pasarela	1
Patagonia Hostel	5
Patagonia House	6
Raíces Bed and Breakfast	4
Las Salamandras	7

EATING
Adobe	3
Basilic Bistrot	4
Cafe de Mayo	6
La Casona	7
Flor y Truco	9
Hacienda Patagonia	5
Huevo Bacon	1
Mamma Gaucha	8
Ruibarbo	2

DRINKING
Casa Tropera	2
Taberna D'olbek	1

SHOPPING
Ahumart	1

BY BUS

Most buses pull in at the central terminal on the corner of Lautaro and Magallanes, though a few arrive at, and depart from, their respective company offices.

Destinations Castro via Ancud, Puerto Montt & Osorno (Queilen Bus ☎67 224 0760; Mon, Wed & Fri 2pm; 28hr); Chaitén via La Junta & Puyuhuapi (Buses Becker, General Parra 335 ☎09 8465 2959, ⓦbusesbecker.com; Tues & Sat 8am); Cochrane via Villa Cerro Castillo, Puerto Río Tranquilo, Cruce El Maitén and Puerto Bertrand (Buses Acuario 13 ☎67 252 2143; Buses Don Carlos ☎67 252 2150; Buses Sao Paulo ☎67 225 5726; 1–2 daily 9am & 9.30am); Comodoro Rivadavia, Argentina (Transaustral ☎67 223 2067; Mon & Fri 9am; 9hr); Futaleufú (Buses Becker; Sat 8am; 12hr); Puerto Aysén & Puerto Chacabuco (Buses Suray, Prat 265 ☎67 223 8387; Buses Ali, Dussen 283 ☎67 223 2788; every 30min); Puyuhuapi (Buses Becker and Buses Terra Austral ☎67 225 4335; 1–2 daily; 4hr 30min); Puerto Ibáñez (Miguel Acuña ☎67 225 1579; Buses Carolina ☎09 8952 1592; Transporte Alonso ☎09 4247 1135 – schedules linked to ferry departure; 1–2 daily; 2hr 30min).

BY FERRY

Navimag, Lillo 91 47 (☎67 223 3306, ⓦnavimag.com) runs to Puerto Montt from nearby Puerto Chacabuco (see page 366) frequently during summer, less often in winter. Naviera Austral, Horn 40 (☎67 221 0727, ⓦnavieraustral.cl) connects Puerto Chacabuco with Quellón via Puerto Cisnes and Raul Marín Balmaceda (see page 357).

GETTING AROUND AND INFORMATION

Car rental Reserve in advance, particularly in peak season. Driving the Carretera Austral requires a certain amount of forward planning (see page 348). Reputable car rental companies include Traeger, Baquedano 457 (☎67 223 1640, ⓦtraeger.cl); Hertz, General Parra 280 (☎67 224 5780, ⓦhertz.cl); and Europcar, Errázuriz 454 (☎67 225 5171, ⓦeuropcar.cl). All have airport branches at Balmaceda.

Tourist office Bulnes 35 (Jan & Feb daily 8.30am–8.30pm; March–Dec Mon–Fri 8.30am–5.30pm; ☎67 227 0290, ⓦsernatur.cl). Pick up a wealth of brochures on the region at this ultra-helpful office.

ACTIVITIES AND TOURS

Salvaje Corazón Casilla 311 ☎67 221 1488, ⓦsalvajecorazon.com. Recommended operator offering expeditions to the Southern Icefields, trekking in the San Lorenzo Massif, photo safaris across Patagonia, and multi-day trips along the northern half of the Carretera Austral that take in Parque Nacional Pumalín Douglas R. Tompkins, Futa and Parque Nacional Queulat. Reckon on around US$1500 for a nine-day trip.

ACCOMMODATION

HOTELS AND B&BS

Hostal Gladys Parra 65 ☎67 224 5488, ⓦhostalgladys.cl; map p.362. As central as you can get, this long-established guesthouse offers rooms with skylights (instead of windows), most en suite. Breakfast includes freshly brewed coffee, eggs and home-made jams. CH$40,000

★ **Nomades Hotel Boutique** Av Baquedano 84 ☎67 223 7777, ⓦnomadeshotel.com; map p.362. This handsome edifice of rough-hewn stone chunks slotted together hides seven luxurious rooms with rain showers, some with splendid terrace views of Río Coyhaique down below. The decor pays homage to Coyhaique's pioneer heritage, with wool throws, cowboy lassos and deer antler chandeliers, and the massive slate fireplace warms the lounge. US$200

Pampa del Corral Camino Campo Alegre, Lote AB1 ☎09 8528 5680, ⓦpampadelcorral.com; map p.362. This four-room, hilltop boutique lodge is run by an enthusiastic local couple, with several friendly dogs underfoot. There are power showers, each of the excellent beds has an individual headboard painting by local children, the gourmet breakfast makes extensive use of local produce and there's a hot tub to simmer in on the leafy property. US$151

La Pasarela 1.5km north of Coyhaique ☎67 239 1716, ⓦlapasarela.cl; map p.362. Just before the main road continues to Puerto Aysen, a minor road dips down towards a suspension bridge across Río Simpson. Across the river, guests are lulled into relaxation at this enticing lodge by the sounds of the fast-flowing river. There's a hot tub on the river bank and the on-site restaurant (not open to non-guests) offers half-board options. Wi-fi in common area only. CH$60,000

★ **Patagonia House** Camino Campo Alegre, Quinta 18 de Julio ☎67 221 1488, ⓦpatagonia-house.com; map p.362. Set on a hillside above Coyhaique, the eight rooms of this boutique lodge have panoramic windows, rain showers and wood-shingled headboards. The chef cooks gourmet dishes for the changing daily menu, the breakfast spread is the best in the south of Chile and the attention that friendly owner Ruth gives her guests is difficult to fault. US$160

Raíces Bed and Breakfast Av Baquedano 444 ☎67 221 0490, ⓦraicesbedandbreakfast.com; map p.362. This B&B has some of the most attractive rooms

8

in town – wood-panelled, full of light, decorated in whites and creams with woollen accents (the owner sells high-quality knitwear). The breakfast is above par, too. CH$80,000

HOSTELS

Aumkenk Aike Hostel Simpson 1443 ☎ 09 9670 3853; map p.362. Run by enthusiastic English teacher Fareed, this guesthouse is a 15min walk from the plaza. Guests are housed in a clutch of spotless singles and doubles, with resident feline Pumi wandering around the common areas. Kitchen access, barbecue, and plenty of local info seal the deal. US$34

★**Patagonia Hostel** Lautaro 667 ☎ 09 6240 6974, ⌨ patagonia-hostel.com; map p.362. The only proper backpacker/cyclist hostel in town has just ten beds (two doubles and a six-bed dorm) and they book up fast. The beds and bunks are large and comfortable, with a personal reading light above each one; the lounge encourages socializing and the young, energetic German owners, Thomas and Sandra, run their own tour agency and can assist with kayaking trips and more. Dorms CH$18,000, doubles CH$42,000

Las Salamandras Carretera Teniente Vidal Km 2.5 ☎ 67 221 1865, ⌨ hostalsalamandras.com; map p.362. Set in a woodland property by a river 2.5km from Coyhaique, this hostel, popular with backpackers and cyclists, offers the use of a kitchen, mountain-bike rental and a range of excursions, including to Parque Nacional Queulat and cross-country skiing trips. Hot tub available (CH$20,000). Camping CH$10,000, dorms CH$18,000, doubles CH$42,000,

EATING

CAFÉS AND CHEAP EATS

Basilic Bistrot Parra 220 ☎ 09 7766 2794; map p.362. Lined with photos depicting life in coastal fishing communities, this bright little bistro is a good spot for freshly squeezed juices, teas and a gourmet three-course *menú del día* (CH$7000) that is both delicious and excellent value. Typically vegetarian, it may include the likes of mushroom carpaccio, gnocchi and apple pie. Tues–Fri 10.30am–7.30pm, Sat & Sun noon–9pm.

Cafe de Mayo 21 de Mayo 543 ☎ 09 9709 8632; map p.362. This is the best of the centrally located coffee shops in which to catch up on your emails over an extensive menu of excellent coffees. Teapots and enamel mugs dangling from the ceiling and a wall of potted flowers flanking the covered outdoor terrace add to the homely ambience. Mon–Sat 9am–9pm.

Flor y Truco Serrano 139 ☎ 09 9883 7885; map p.362. This is primarily a Colombian-run shop selling gourmet coffee, chocolate and hard-to-get vegan items. But you can also find excellent gelato-like artisanal ice cream, plus sandwiches and arguably Coyhaique's best coffee to take away. Mon–Sat 9am–6pm.

Huevo Bacon Carretera Austral Km 3 ☎ 09 9933 3606; map p.362. A little way out of town, towards Puerto Aysén, this is Coyhaique's only breakfast/brunch diner. Apart from eggs and bacon prepared several ways (including egg-and-bacon-stuffed avocados), there are breakfast sandwiches, good coffee and excellent *Kuchen*, courtesy of the part-German pastry chef. Mains from CH$5500. Mon–Fri 7.30am–10pm, Sat & Sun 9am–10pm.

RESTAURANTS

★**Adobe** Baquedano 9 ☎ 67 224 0846, ⌨ adobecoyhaique.cl; map p.362. Choose one of the regional craft beers (Puyuhuapi's Hopperdietzel, Puerto Cisnes' Finisterra, or a local D'olbek) and join the locals on the outside terrace with a *tabla* (cold cut sharing plate) or burger. This is one of those rare places where the food is as good as the drinks – including an extensive list of signature cocktails. The *ceviche* stands out. Mains from CH$8000. Mon–Sat 12.45pm–2am.

★**La Casona** Vielmo 77 ☎ 67 223 8894; map p.362. Set on a quiet street, this homely, family-run restaurant is a decent option for well-prepared Chilean food, with a menu full of steaks and seafood dishes. The *filete casona* is a top choice for the carnivorously inclined, and the service is attentive. Mains from CH$8000. Daily 12.30–3pm & 7.30–11pm.

Hacienda Patagonia 21 de Mayo 461 ☎ 67 223 3933, ⌨ haciendapatagonia.cl; map p.362. Professional service and a refined setting at this upscale spot where the Patagonian dishes range from grilled meats (including sweetbreads and other offal) to *chupe de jaibas* (crab pie) and *papillote de merluza*. Mains CH$6000–14,000. Tues–Sun 12.30–3.30pm & 7.30–11.30pm.

★**Mamma Gaucha** Horn 47 ☎ 67 221 0712, ⌨ mammagaucha.cl; map p.362. At this Italian trattoria-meets-Patagonia, efficient staff serve wood-fired pizzas, lamb-filled ravioli, *crudos* (steak tartare) on toast, vast salads and imaginative desserts (try the blueberry *crème brulée*), amid black-and-white photos of the region. Mains from CH$7000. Mon–Sat 10am–2am.

★**Ruibarbo** Av Baquedano 208 ☎ 67 221 1826; map p.362. This intimate restaurant looks unassuming, but the dishes here are some of Coyhaique's more creative offerings. Come for the risotto *de la costa* (with *cochayuyo* seaweed), cherry-glazed lamb chops and conger eel with quinoa. Mains CH$9000–15,000. Mon–Sat 1–3.30pm & 7.30–10.30pm.

DRINKING

★ **Casa Tropera** Camino Aeródromo Teniente Vidal Km 1.5 ☎09 6597 0585, ⌨tropera.cl; map p.362. One of Coyhaique's two main craft beer breweries, Tropera brews eight beers, from the blond Bota Sucia and amber Horn 47 to the Crazy Juan brown ale and the Ranita de Darwin bitter double IPA. The beer terrace is often packed, and accompanying nibbles include truly excellent burgers (try the Annapurna). Mon–Sat noon–2am.

Taberna D'olbek Baquedano 1895, 2km east of centre ☎67 223 9385; map p.362. Owned by the former owner of Estancia Chacabuco, which the Tomkinses turned into Parque Nacional Patagonia (see page 373), this appealing brewpub decked out with creeping greenery is a popular gathering place for locals. There are three brews to choose from, including a maqui-berry-flavoured ale, as well as sandwiches, burgers, *crudos* (steak tartare) and *tablas* (sharing platters of cold cuts). Daily noon–1am.

SHOPPING

Ahumart Serrano 133 ⌨ahumart.cl; map p.362. This excellent speciality shop is the place to stock up on gourmet crisps, a wide variety of cheese and locally smoked meats plus terrific locally produced jerky and jams before hitting the road. Mon–Sat 9.30am–1pm & 3–8pm.

DIRECTORY

Banks and exchange The following banks have ATMs: Banco Santander, Condell 184, Banco de Chile, Condell 298, and BBVA, Condell 254. *Cambios* include Emperador at Freire 171.

Hospital The regional hospital is at Jorge Ibar 168 (☎67 221 9100).

8

West of Coyhaique

West of Coyhaique, a paved section of the Carretera Austral runs towards the coast, past a modest nature reserve, to the port of **Puerto Aysén**, 65km away – a small town you have to pass through on the way to the even more nondescript **Puerto Chacabuco**, one of the gateways to **Parque Nacional Laguna San Rafael**.

Puerto Aysén and Puerto Chacabuco

The former cattle-shipping port of **PUERTO AYSÉN** literally became a backwater when its harbour silted up, forcing commercial vessels to use nearby **PUERTO CHACABUCO** from 1960. Your only reason for coming to the latter would be to take a boat to the **Laguna San Rafael** glacier or to catch a Navimag or Naviera Austral **ferry**.

ARRIVAL AND DEPARTURE   PUERTO AYSÉN AND PUERTO CHACABUCO

By bus Buses Suray, in Puerto Aysén at Eusebio Ibar 630 (☎67 233 6231), serves Puerto Chacabuco and Coyhaique. Destinations Coyhaique (every 30min; 45min); Puerto Chacabuco (at least 20 daily; 20min).

By ferry Chacabuco is the departure point for Naviera Austral ferries (⌨navieraustral.cl) to Quellón (CH$16,650), Navimag (⌨navimag.com) ferries to Puerto Montt

(from CH$51,000) and Catamaranes del Sur catamarans (⌨catamaranesdelsur.cl) to Laguna San Rafael. Destinations Laguna San Rafael (2 ferries weekly; 16hr; catamaran several weekly in season; 5hr one way); Puerto Montt (Tues & Fri; 24hr); Quellón via Puerto Cisnes, Puerto Gaviota and Raúl Marín Balmaceda (Mon & Fri; 28hr).

ACCOMMODATION

Patagonia Green Camino Lago Riesco, Puerto Aysén ☎67 233 6796, ⌨patagoniagreen.cl. A delightful hotel on the edge of town, with a good restaurant and good-value cabins for up to five people. Doubles CH$70,000, cabins CH$78,000

Parque Nacional Laguna San Rafael

125 nautical miles south of Puerto Chacabuco • CH$7000, payable only if you land • Ⓦ conaf.cl/parques/parquet-nacional-laguna-san-rafael

Almost half of the remote 12,000-square-km **Parque Nacional Laguna San Rafael** is covered by the immense ice field known as the **Campo de Hielo Norte**; it feeds eighteen other glaciers on top of the San Rafael Glacier and contains more than 250 lakes and lagoons. The 4058m **Monte San Valentín**, the highest peak in the southern Andes, towers over the frozen plateau.

Laguna San Rafael

A boat ride either from Bahía Exploradores or Puerto Chacabuco through the labyrinthine fjords of Aysén brings you to the dazzling **San Rafael glacier**, spilling into the broad **Laguna San Rafael**. The journey is a spectacle in itself, as boats edge their way through channels hemmed in by precipitous cliffs dripping with vegetation, passing the odd sea lion colony along the way. After sailing down the long, thin Golfo de Elefantes, the boat enters the seemingly unnavigable Río Témpanos, or "Iceberg River", before emerging into the lagoon. Floating here are dozens of **icebergs**, fashioned by wind and rain into monumental sculptures, with such a vibrant electric-blue colour that they appear to be lit from within.

San Rafael glacier

You approach the giant **San Rafael glacier** at the far end of the lagoon. More than 4km wide, and rearing out of the water to a height of 70m, it really is a dizzying sight. While the cruise boat keeps at a safe distance, you'll be given the chance to get a closer look from an inflatable motor dinghy – but not too close, as the huge blocks of ice that calve off into the water with a deafening roar create dangerous waves. What you can see from the boat is in fact just the tip of the glacier's "tongue", which extends some 15km from its source.

The glacier is retreating fast, however, frequently by as much as 100m a year. Early explorers reported that in 1800 the glacier filled three-quarters of the lagoon, and archive photographs from the beginning of the twentieth century show it as being far longer than it is today. It is estimated that by the year 2030, the glacier will be gone.

ARRIVAL AND DEPARTURE

PARQUE NACIONAL LAGUNA SAN RAFAEL

The glacier is currently accessible *only* by **boat** or **plane**, though you can drive up Valle Exploradores from Puerto Río Tranquilo (see page 371) and take a three-hour boat ride to reach the lagoon from Bahía Exploradores – or a much longer boat trip from Puerto Chacabuco – with three hours at the glacier itself.

By plane Cessna flights from Coyhaique are operated by Aerocord, Gral Parra 21 (Ⓣ 67 224 6300, Ⓦ aerocord.cl), and usually require the full quota of five passengers (1hr 30min each way; around CH$200,000/person). Passengers touch down at Monte San Valentín with barely enough time to take the 7km trail from the Conaf *guardería* to a breathtaking viewpoint platform over the sprawling, icy tongue (allow around 2hr up and slightly less coming down).

ACTIVITIES AND TOURS

Day-trips Year-round, Catamaranes del Sur (Ⓣ 22 231 1902, Ⓦ catamaranesdelsur.cl; CH$200,000) offers day-trips to the glacier (check website for dates; 5hr each way). Trips include three meals and an open bar – it is a tradition to drink a whisky or cocktail containing "thousand-year-old ice cubes" chipped from an iceberg. You can buy tickets at Turismo Prado in Coyhaique (see page 362).

Kayaking If you're looking for a physically tough multi-day adventure, contact Puerto Aysén-based Agua Hielo (Ⓣ 09 7605 3580, Ⓦ aguahielo.cl), which runs seven- to eight-day sea kayaking ventures to Laguna San Rafael and also the Jorge Montt glacier.

Trekking Another way to explore the park is on foot: Patagonia Adventure Expeditions (Ⓣ 09 8182 0608, Ⓦ patagoniaadventureexpeditions.com) is a pioneering operator that offers three superb multi-day treks, the longest being the challenging ten-day Aisén Glacier Trail. If you have less time, the six-day Fault Line trek and the four-day Nunatak trek are very worthwhile.

8

Parque Nacional Cerro Castillo

75km south of Coyhaique along the Carretera Austral · CH$2000 · Take any southbound bus from Coyhaique

About an hour's drive south of Coyhaique, the Carretera Austral crosses the northern boundary of the **Parque Nacional Cerro Castillo**, a 445,000-acre protected area that is home to the elusive *huemúl* deer. Spread out below you is a broad river valley flanked by densely forested lower slopes that rise to a breathtaking panorama of barren, rocky peaks. Dominating the skyline is the reserve's eponymous centrepiece, **Cerro Castillo** (2675m) whose needlepoint spires loom over the valley like the turrets of a Transylvanian castle. Further north, 67km from Coyhaique, by Laguna Chaguay, you pass the *guardería* on your left, which has a basic **camping** area (see below). Just south of Parque Nacional Cerro Castillo, Villa Cerro Castillo is the ending/starting point for the **Sendero Cerro Castillo**.

Sendero Cerro Castillo

75km south of Coyhaique along the Carretera Austral · Take any southbound bus from Coyhaique

The rewarding 40km **Sendero Cerro Castillo**, which takes four days to complete, starts at Km 75, branches right (west) from the road 6km south of the *guardería*, and follows the Río La Lima upstream to a 1450m pass on the east side of Cerro Castillo through *coigüe* and *ñire* forest. On the way, you pass the stunning **Laguna Cerro Castillo**, at the foot of a glacier suspended from the mountainside, before descending to the village of **Villa Cerro Castillo** (see page 370). Note that the trail is poorly marked; you should buy an IGM map in advance in Coyhaique and get more detailed route advice from Conaf at the *guardería*, where you should register with the park rangers before you set off. It may be easier to start at the Villa Cerro Castillo trailhead and hike the trail in reverse, especially since it means fewer uphill stints. The mountain scenery here is spectacular and you're likely to have it to yourself.

ACCOMMODATION   PARQUE NACIONAL CERRO CASTILLO

There are five basic **campsites** along the Sendero Cerro Castillo with toilets and fireplaces.

Camping Laguna Chiguay Carretera Austral Km 75.
This Conaf-maintained campsite at the start of the Sendero

Cerro Castillo has basic sites and access to hot showers. <u>CH$5000</u>

Around Lago General Carrera

Just beyond the southern boundary of Parque Nacional Cerro Castillo, a 31km side road shoots southeast from the Carretera Austral to the tiny village of **Puerto Ibáñez**, on the northern shore of **Lago General Carrera**. This lake, encircled by rocky, sharp-peaked mountains, is the second largest in South America, and stretches east into Argentina. Regular ferries connect Puerto Ibáñez with the sunny, cherry-growing town of **Chile Chico**, on the opposite shore; an attractive alternative to following the Carretera Austral around the lake. From Chile Chico, a 128km road skirts the lake's southern shore, joining the Carretera just beyond the village of **Puerto Guadal**.

Puerto Ibáñez

Sitting in a green, fertile plain, divided up by rows of soldier-like poplars, **PUERTO IBÁÑEZ** is a shrinking village. Once an important port, connecting Coyhaique with Chile Chico and the remote *estancias* on the Lago General Carrera's southern shore, it fell into decline with the construction of the Carretera Austral bypass, and most travellers pass through only to catch the ferry to Chile Chico (see page 369).

ARRIVAL AND DEPARTURE

By bus Miguel Acuña (☎ 67 225 1579) and Buses Carolina (☎ 09 8952 1592) are two of five bus companies that run minibuses to Puerto Ibañez from Coyhaique, the latter timed to coincide with the arrival and departure of the ferry to Chile Chico. Book in advance to be picked up from your place of residence.

By ferry The Sotramin office in Puerto Ibañez is at Carrera 202 (☎ 67 252 6992, ⍰ sotramin.cl; see page 369).

Chile Chico

Sitting on the southern shore of Lago General Carrera, the small agricultural town of **CHILE CHICO** is a sunny place with its own microclimate and an attractive Plaza de Armas, lined with apricot trees and pines. It is famous for its fruit festival at the end of January, and lays claim to growing Chile's best cherries. The town was settled by farmers who crossed over from Argentina in 1909, causing a conflict known as the "Chile Chico war" when they refused to hand over land to the concessionaires given grants by the government. The new settlement depended entirely on Argentina until a road was built between Coyhaique and Puerto Ibáñez in 1952, after which Chile Chico's orchards became Coyhaique's main source of fresh fruit. You get a great view of the town and the lake from the hill opposite the dock. Chile Chico makes a good base for the exploration of the gorgeous Jeinimeni sector of Parque Nacional Patagonia (see page 370).

ARRIVAL AND INFORMATION

By bus From the bus terminal on the plaza, Buses Costa Carrera (☎ 09 8739 2544) and Buses Marfer (☎ 09 7756 8234) run to Cochrane via Puerto Guadál, Cruce El Maitén and Puerto Bertrand. Transportes Eca (☎ 67 243 1224) and Transportes Seguel (☎ 67 243 1214) run to Puerto Guadál. Transportes Pia (☎ 09 9133 6363) and Transporte Martín Pescador (☎ 09 9786 5285) serve Puerto Río Tranquilo. At research time there were no cross-border transfers to Los Antiguos in Argentina; you can take a taxi to the border (CH$6000) and then walk for 2km into Argentina to connect with buses going up and down Ruta 40.

Destinations Cochrane (Mon 8am & 6pm, Wed 4pm, Fri 4pm, Sun 2pm; 5hr); Puerto Guadál (Mon–Fri 4pm; 3hr); Puerto Río Tranquilo (daily 10am & 10.30am; 5hr).

By ferry Transbordador *La Tehuelche* run by Sotramin (☎ 67 241 1003, ⍰ sotramin.cl, ⍰ barcazas.cl) crosses Lago General Carrera from Chile Chico to Puerto Ibañez (passengers CH$2500, vehicles CH$19,800); book tickets a week in advance in peak season if you want to transport your car, otherwise a couple of days in advance. Check times well ahead, because they are subject to change; reservations are a must. When buying your ticket at the bus terminal it's possible (and a good idea) to buy an onward minibus ticket to Coyhaique from Puerto Ibañez. Be at the dock an hour before departure.

Destinations Puerto Ibañez (Mon, Tues & Thurs 8am, Wed 4pm, Fri 5pm, Sat 9am, Sun 3pm; 2hr 15min).

Tourist office O'Higgins 333 (Mon–Fri 9am–2.30pm & 4–6.30pm, Sat 10am–2pm; ☎ 67 241 1303, ⍰ chilechico. cl). Very helpful, with maps of town, plenty of brochures and info on Jeinimeni.

ACTIVITIES AND TOURS

Patagoniaxpress O'Higgins 333, local 4 ☎ 09 4484 0511. Andrés runs half- and full-day hiking trips into the Jeinimeni sector of Parque Nacional Patagonia, as well as mountain biking and fishing trips.

Turismo Tramal Rodríguez 487 ☎ 09 7538 0178. Full-day trips to the Capillas de Mármol in Puerto Río Tranquilo (CH$45,000/person). If you're looking to travel up or down the Carretera Austral, you can just take a one-way trip.

ACCOMMODATION AND EATING

Hospedaje Brisas del Lago Rodríguez 443 ☎ 67 241 1204. A block and a half from the waterfront, this simple guesthouse is a good place to gather info on onward travel. Rooms are simple, and some share facilities, but wi-fi is decent. CH$26,000

Hospedaje & Camping Kon Aiken Rodríguez at Burgos ☎ 67 241 1598. Friendly Fidelina's back garden seems to attract most of the campers in town, who make use of the *quincho*, hot shower and outdoor barbecue. There are some tiny, cramped rooms upstairs that share the campsite bathroom, plus a couple of well-equipped two-person *cabañas*. Camping CH$5000, *cabañas* CH$30,000

Hostería de la Patagonia Camino Internacional Chacra 3-A ☎ 09 8159 2146, ⍰ hosteriadelapatagonia. cl. A charming Belgian-/Chilean-owned house with comfortable en-suite rooms, sheltered camping spots

8

with access to hot showers, good home-cooked food and outdoor excursions on offer, tucked away in a large garden on the eastern edge of town. You can also choose to sleep inside a boat. Camping <u>CH$5000</u>, doubles <u>CH$62,000</u>
Jeinimeni Restaurante Blest Gana 120 ☎ 09 8139 7738. The dishes at this good-value place are simple but filling, and the dining room is perpetually full. Expect the likes of grilled salmon, *empanadas*, mountains of potato topped with meat, and Hudson craft beer from

Puerto Ibañez. Mains CH$7000. Daily 1–3.30pm & 7.30–10.30pm.
★ **El Petiso Patagón** Carrera 321-B ☎ 09 6240 2947. Its stone walls decorated with woodcut scenes of gaucho life, this excellent restaurant specializes in monster portions of *cordero al palo* (Patagonian-style lamb), along with a supporting cast of *milanesa* steaks and *bife a lo pobre* (meat topped with fried egg). Mains CH$7500–12,000. Daily 1–3.30pm & 7.30–11.15pm.

Parque Nacional Patagonia: Sector Jeinimeni

52km southwest of Chile Chico • CH$3000 • ⓦ conaf.cl/parques/reserve-nacional-lago-jeinimeni • A regular car can make it to the main entrance to the park, though there are a couple of minor streams to cross and the last section is bumpy; a high-clearance vehicle is a better bet, and essential for driving up to the car park in the first section of the park – alternatively, day excursions to this and the sector accessed via the main entrance are run by Patagoniaxpress in Chile Chico (see page 369)

Now the northern gateway to **Parque Nacional Patagonia**, created in January 2018, the beautiful, lightly visited **Sector Jeinimeni** comprises Patagonian steppe, russet-coloured mountains and azure lakes, and is home to guanacos, vizcachas (a cross between a rabbit and a squirrel), puma and a smaller forest cat, among others. Most trails start from the main entrance, 52km from Chile Chico.

Twenty-five kilometres along the road is the first entrance to a separate part of the park. Here you can hike the excellent 6km loop trail, **Sendero Piedra Clavada** (3hr), with some steep sections; it passes by the Cueva de los Manos – a cave with millennia-old Tehuelche cave paintings, as well as a lookout overlooking the Valle Lunar – an arid moonscape of jagged red rock formations. From the campsite beyond the main entrance to the park you can take the **Sendero El Mirador**, an 800m ascent to a viewpoint overlooking the lake via *lenga* forest. Also from the campsite, **Sendero Escorial del Silencio**, an ascent of 837m, passes five viewpoints along the way with sweeping views of the park. Meanwhile, the largely flat **Sendero Lago Verde**, a 5.2km, two-hour round trip to the eponymous lake, skirts the cerulean Lago Jeinimeni.

The most ambitious hiking trail, however, is the three-day, 47km **Sendero La Leona**, which starts at the Conaf ranger station, several hundred metres before the campsite, skirts the southern shore of Lago Jeinimeni, climbs up to the Cordón La Gloria before touching the northern tip of Lago Verde, and then follows Valle Hermoso and Valle Áviles to Casa Piedra in the central section of Parque Nacional Patagonia (see page 373), with the latter part of the trail following Río Áviles. The trail isn't always easy to follow and there are minor rivers to ford, so good wilderness skills are necessary.

Parque Nacional Patagonia has two further sectors: **Sector Central** (see page 373) and **Sector Tamango** (see page 375).

Villa Cerro Castillo

Looping around Lago General Carrera along the Carretera Austral offers spectacular panoramas of the grey and pink mountains west of the road, plus a few glimpses of the Campo de Hielo Norte (see page 367). Nine kilometres on from the turnoff to Puerto Ibáñez, you pass **Villa Cerro Castillo**, a rather bleak pioneer settlement whose sole draw is the rugged hiking around Cerro Castillo (see page 368).

Monumento Nacional Manos de Cerro Castillo

Just across the bridge outside Villa Cerro Castillo, up a signed 2km track • Dec–April • CH$2000

A track leads steeply uphill to **Monumento Nacional Manos de Cerro Castillo**, a dense collection of more than one hundred handprints (some belonging to children), in three separate panels at the foot of a sheer basalt rock face. The images, mostly negative prints against a red background, are thought to have been left by the Tehuelche people between three and five thousand years ago.

ARRIVAL AND DEPARTURE

VILLA CERRO CASTILLO

By bus Buses Acuario 13 (☎67 252 2143), Aguilas Patagonicas (☎67 221 1288) and Buses Sao Paulo (☎67 252 2143) all stop along the main street of Villa Cerro Castillo en route between Coyhaique and Cochrane.

Destinations Cochrane (at least 2 daily; 4hr 30min); Coyhaique (at least 2 daily; 1hr 30min).

ACCOMMODATION AND EATING

Cabañas El Tropero Carretera Austral 305 ☎09 7759 5766, ⓦeltropero.cl. This friendly, family-run place offers two two-storey cabins for up to six people each. With simple, wood-panelled rooms, both come fully equipped with wood-burning stove for heating, cable TV and small kitchen. Rates are charged according to number of people. CH$45,000

Camping & Hostel Senderos Patagonia Carretera Austral s/n ☎09 6224 4725, ⓦaysensenderospatagonia.com. At the southern approach to Cerro Castillo, mountain guides Mary and

Christian run this appealing, sheltered campsite and hostel (one dorm). Guided treks and horseback riding are on offer, and there's an occasional *asado* (barbecue). Camping CH$5000, dorm CH$10,000

El Puesto Huemul Camino Estero del Bosque ☎09 9218 3250. An unexpected treat in this small pioneer town, this Argentinian-run restaurant really delivers when it comes to imaginative dishes such as lamb ravioli, barbecued lamb, freshly baked *empanadas* and gnocchi with wild mushrooms. Mains from CH$7500. Daily noon–11pm.

Puerto Río Tranquilo

8

Some 25km south of the turnoff for Puerto Murta, a tiny cattle-farming community, you'll reach **PUERTO RÍO TRANQUILO**, a picturesque village on the shore of Lago General Carrera. Puerto Río Tranquilo has been a popular traveller stop for many years due to its proximity to the **Capilla de Mármol** ("Marble Chapel"), an impressive limestone cliff looming out of the water, streaked with blue-and-white patterns and gashed with caves which can be entered by boat. Also reachable by boat from Puerto Tranquilo are the **Cavernas de Mármol** ("Marble Caves"), near the tiny village of Puerto Sánchez. All the dozen or so kiosks on the *costanera* (promenade) offer a boat trip to Capilla de Mármol, leaving throughout the day (CH$10,000/person or CH$60,000–70,000 for a whole boat). The light is best early in the morning and late in the afternoon. For something more adventurous, you can opt for a kayaking or stand-up paddleboarding trip instead (see below).

In the last few years, the village's appeal has skyrocketed due to the opening of **Valle Exploradores**, a stupendously scenic, narrow road that snakes its way past glacial lakes and mountains for 82km to Bahía Exploradores, the launchpad for boat trips to Laguna San Rafael (see page 367). Since Puerto Río Tranquilo is considerably closer to **Glaciar San Rafael** (see page 367) than Puerto Chacabuco, the three-hour boat trip to the icy lagoon is an enticing alternative for those who don't wish to spend all day on a boat. That's not all: 55km west along the Valle Exploradores road is the starting point for the guided trek and ice hike (see below) on the vast **Glaciar Exploradores**, the northern tongue of ice that extends from the Campo de Hielo San Valentín.

ACTIVITIES AND TOURS

PUERTO RÍO TRANQUILO

El Puesto Expediciones Lagos at Exploradores ☎09 6207 3794, ⓦelpuesto.cl. Established agency offering glacier treks (CH$70,000 including transport), ice climbing (CH$85,000), 3hr kayak trips to the Capilla de Mármol (CH$55,000) and full-day kayak outings to the Cavernas de Mármol (CH$105,000).

Latitud 47 Expediciones Carretera Austral s/n ☎09 8186 1715, ⓦlatitud47.cl. One of the waterfront kiosks, this operator is the only one to offer stand-up paddleboarding trips around the marble caves (2hr 30min; CH$40,000), as well as standard glacier treks and kayaking jaunts.

Río Exploradores ☎ 09 8259 4017, ⓦ exploradores-sanrafael.cl. This operator offers full-day excursions (CH$145,000) and multi-day excursions to Laguna San Rafael from Km 75 (you need own wheels to get there), as well as helicopter flights over the glacier.

Valle Exploradores ☎ 61 261 4681, ⓦ valleexploradores.cl. Attached to the hotel of the same name, this operator offers full-day trips to Laguna San Rafael with its own comfortable 22-person boat. It's CH$140,000/person, and an extra CH$15,000 for transfers to the boat landing if you don't want to drive yourself.

ACCOMMODATION AND EATING

Camping Pudú 1km south of Puerto Río Tranquilo ☎ 67 257 3003, ⓦ puduexcursiones.cl. Attractive, sheltered lakeside campsite with hot showers and access to laundry service and sauna. The fully equipped six-person *cabaña* features terrific lake views. The owners are happy to organize excursions to the Capilla de Mármol. Camping CH$5000, *cabaña* CH$50,000

Cervecería Río Tranquilo (Arisca) Carretera Austral s/n ☎ 09 9895 5577. Facing the waterfront, right in the centre of town, this microbrewery does a decent golden ale, amber ale and stout and complements it with massive *chorillana* plates to share (CH$10,000), chunky *churrasco* and chicken sandwiches and salmon tartar. Daily noon–midnight.

Hostería-Suite Los Pinos Godoy 51 ☎ 67 241 1572, ⓔ lospinos-hosteriasuite@hotmail.com. Opposite the Copec petrol station, this basic guesthouse with friendly management is popular with dusty motorcyclists and cyclists in search of a treat, with its clutch of compact, carpeted en-suite singles and doubles. No breakfast or wi-fi. CH$35,000

La Provençale Lagos at Exploradores. A block from the waterfront, this French-run food truck gets high marks for its waffles with multiple toppings and grilled panini sandwiches that are fancier than other in-town offerings: think ham, cheese, caramelized onions and sun-dried tomatoes, among others. Sandwiches CH$4500. Daily 10am–9pm.

El Puesto Lagos 258 ☎ 09 6207 3794, ⓦ elpuesto.cl. This beautiful but overpriced boutique guesthouse is the nicest in town and consists of ten bright, stylish en-suite singles, doubles, triples and quads with crisp linens and down duvets. Packed lunch and other meals available on request and there are bikes and kayaks for rent. CH$120,000

Puerto Guadal and around

Thirty-five kilometres south of Puerto Tranquilo lies the outlet of **Lago General Carrera**, which drains into the adjacent Lago Bertrand. Shortly afterwards, you'll reach **Cruce El Maitén**, a fork in the road with a couple of lodges. The eastern fork skirts the southern edge of Lago General Carrera to **PUERTO GUADAL**, a picturesque little village with an excellent stretch of beach, before the precipitous and sometimes narrow road continues to Chile Chico (see page 369).

ACCOMMODATION   PUERTO GUADAL

Hospedaje Janito Las Camelias 169 ☎ 09 9775 8659. If you happen to get stuck in Puerto Guadal for a night, this homey guesthouse, run by a friendly, middle-aged couple, is a decent bet. It has tiny rooms, creaky floors, temperamental wi-fi and spotless bathrooms. Singles are half the price of doubles. CH$24,000

★ **El Miradór de Guadál** Camino a Chile Chico Km 2 ☎ 02 2813 7920, ⓦ elmiradordeguadal. With floor-to-ceiling windows letting in plenty of light and stunning lake views, these attractive cabins (for two or four people) are all individually decorated, well heated, tree shaded and spaced far enough apart to give you privacy. The Dutch/Chilean owners serve meals in the reception area overlooking the lake and organize guided hikes and horse rides. US$120

Puerto Bertrand

Twenty-five kilometres south of Cruce El Maitén you arrive at the charming little village of **PUERTO BERTRAND**, sitting pretty much on top of the turquoise waters of Lago Bertrand. With fishing lodges nearby, Puerto Bertrand is also a base for rafting adventures on the Río Baker and multi-day trekking expeditions on the Campo de Hielo Norte.

ACTIVITIES AND TOURS	PUERTO BERTRAND

Baker Patagonia Aventura Costanera s/n ☎ 09 8817 7525, ⓦ bakerpatagonia.com. Río Baker rafting trips, ranging from Class III half-day floats (from CH$35,000/person) to multi-day expeditions.

ACCOMMODATION

Green Baker Lodge Camino a Cochrane Km 3 ☎ 09 9159 7757, ⓦ greenlodgebaker.com. This attractive wooden lodge on the bank of Río Baker, 3km south of Puerto Bertrand, caters to anglers and other outdoor enthusiasts with seven comfortable *cabañas* (two to four people) and a mini-hotel. Non-fishing guests can enjoy horseback riding, rafting on the Río Baker and ice trekking, among other adventures. Doubles CH$70,000, *cabañas* CH$90,000

South of Lago General Carrera

South of the great lake, a gravel road winds its way along the river towards **Cochrane**, the last settlement of any size. Seventeen kilometres north of Cochrane, one of the most gorgeous roads branches off east to the central sector of **Parque Nacional Patagonia** before crossing the Argentinian border beyond. South of Cochrane, the road snakes its way through a dense carpet of evergreens and giant *nalca*. After just over 100km south, you come to the embarcadero de Río Vagabundo, the launching spot for boats to the tiny, remote logging village of **Caleta Tortel**, also reachable by the gravel road that forks west from the Carretera. Further south, at Puerto Yungay, a car ferry crosses Fiordo Mitchell and a precarious road leads to the Carretera's final stop – the pioneer settlement of **Villa O'Higgins**.

Parque Nacional Patagonia: Sector Central

17km north of Cochrane • ⓦ patagoniapark.org • High-clearance vehicle recommended

The central section – **Sector Central** – of the newly created **Parque Nacional Patagonia**, which stretches along the little-travelled X-83 all the way to the Argentinian border, is a triumph for ecologists in general and for the non-profit foundation Conservación Patagónica (ⓦ conservacionpatagonica.org) in particular. The Kris-Tompkins-led initiative (see page 351) has seen incredibly hard work from scores of volunteers as they laboured to restore the heavily damaged steppe from damage caused by sheep from the historic Estancia Valle Chacabuco. Invasive non-indigenous plants were ripped out by hand and replaced by endemic species, and today the park is home to diverse fauna such as the endangered *huemúl*, as well as guanacos, puma and the four-eyed Patagonian frog.

The gravel road that bisects the central section of the park is one of the most gorgeous drives in the country, passing through a varied landscape of snow-tipped mountains, icy highland lakes, shallow lagoons teeming with flamingos, and wind-battered steppe and scrubland.

ARRIVAL AND INFORMATION	PARQUE NACIONAL PATAGONIA: SECTOR CENTRAL

By car There's currently no public transport to Parque Nacional Patagonia. To get to the main lodge/administration area any car suffices, but to proceed any further towards the Argentinian border, a vehicle with high clearance is highly recommended.

Administration office 17 km east of the park entrance, at Park Headquarters (Mon–Fri 8.30am–12.30pm & 2–6pm, Sat 8.30am–1pm; ☎ 65 297 0829, ⓦ patagoniapark.org). Register and pay for camping and pick up a basic map, or buy a detailed map of the park at the gift shop of nearby *El Rincón Gaucho*.

Wi-fi and phone There is no phone reception inside the park and wi-fi only at *El Lodge* (see page 374).

8

PARQUE NACIONAL PATAGONIA: CENTRAL SECTOR HIKES

Of the five existing trails in this section of the park, the 21km **Sendero Lagunas Altas** starts by *Camping Westwinds* (see below), climbing gently uphill through scrubland and snow-brushed forest to a lagoon-dotted plateau with snowy mountains in the distance. The trail meanders between the lagoons, with splendid views of the valley below along the way, before descending along scrubland-covered hill slopes to a spot near the park headquarters. The 47km **Sendero Avilés** starts at the *Casa Piedra* campsite (see below). Taking around three days to hike, much of the trail meanders through the Avilés Valley before turning east into Valle Hermoso, skirting the northern shore of Lago Verde, traversing the Cordón la Gloria and coming to an end by the ranger headquarters of Lago Jeinimeni.

It is also possible to hike from **Sector Jeinimeni** (see page 370) through to the entrance of **Sector Tamango** (see page 375) – a continuous week-long hike – with the trail into Tamango branching off from the Sendero Lagunas Altas.

From the *Alto Valle* campsite (see below), 9km or so east of *Casa Piedra* along the road to Argentina, a 6km 4WD track ascends to the **Mirador Douglas Tomkins** that overlooks two gorgeous glacial lakes nestling between snow-peaked mountains. Two new trails in this sector of the park – **Sendero Los Gatos** and **Sendero Lago Chico** – branch off the 4WD track at 4.6km and 5.5km, respectively.

ACCOMMODATION AND EATING

The **campsites** (first come, first served) and **lodge** are open October through to April.

Camping Alto Valle 35km east of the Park Headquarters. Sheltered campsite nestling among trees at the base of a hill. There are two large *quinchos* for large groups, six smaller ones for individual campers, plus solar-heated showers. CH$8000

Camping Casa Piedra Around 25km east of the Park Headquarters along the X-83. Sheltered campsite in a splendid steppe location. CH$8000

Camping Westwinds 2km from the Park Headquarters. This tree-shaded campsite has sheltered areas for cooking and bathrooms with solar-power-heated showers. Closed late April to Sept. CH$8000

★ **El Lodge** Park Headquarters, 17km east of the park entrance ☎ 65 297 0829. The six individually styled rooms at this handsome, *estancia*-style stone lodge combine original wildlife photography and antique furniture with thoroughly modern rain showers heated by solar power. In the lounge you can sink on to the leather sofas and peruse the collection of coffee-table books on Patagonia's wild spaces, or watch guanacos grazing outside your window. If you're travelling with family or friends, the quad is a very good deal. Wi-fi access. US$500

★ **El Rincón Gaucho** Park headquarters, 17km east of the park entrance. All high beams and stone, the park restaurant serves fantastic food, making full use of greens from the on-site greenhouses, local lamb, and more. The menu changes seasonally and you can expect anything from a Patagonian-style *asado* buffet in the evenings to goat's cheese and caramelized onion sandwiches for lunch. Choose from set menu or à la carte. Lunch CH$16,000, dinner buffet CH$26,000. Daily 12.30–3pm & 7.30–10pm.

Cochrane

The ranching settlement of **COCHRANE** lies 50km south of Puerto Bertrand. The town's paved, orderly grid of streets spreading out from the neat Plaza de Armas, and its array of limited services, make it a prime spot to rest up after the wildness of the Carretera Austral, to fill up on fuel if heading south, or to pick up provisions if you're looking to hike into Parque Nacional Patagonia (see pages 373 and 375).

ARRIVAL AND DEPARTURE COCHRANE

By bus Buses depart from the new bus terminal off Caucahues, two blocks north of the plaza. Buses Acuario 13 (☎ 67 252 2143), Buses Don Carlos (☎ 67 221 4507) and Buses Sao Paulo (☎ 67 252 2470) run to Coyhaique, while Buses Aguilas Patagonicas (☎ 09 6725 3730) serve Villa O'Higgins as well as Coyhaique. Caleta Tortel is served by Buses Aldea (☎ 67 263 8291), Buses Patagonia (☎ 67 252 2470), Buses Katalina (☎ 09 9932 4320), Buses Cordillera (☎ 09 8134 4990) and Buses Pachamama (☎ 09 9411 4811). Chile Chico, via Puerto Bertrand and Puerto Guadal, is served by Buses Marfer (☎ 09 9645 3621). Buses Marfer and Buses Katalina also run to Puerto Río Tranquilo.

Destinations Caleta Tortel (2–4 daily; 3hr); Chile Chico, via Puerto Bertrand and Puerto Guadal (Wed & Fri 8am, Sun 5pm; 5hr); Coyhaique (3–4 daily; 6–7hr); Puerto Río Tranquilo (daily 8am plus Mon–Fri 3pm); Villa O'Higgins (Mon, Wed & Sat 8.30am; 7hr).

INFORMATION AND TOURS

Tourist office Plaza de Armas (Jan–March & Dec Mon–Sat 10am–1pm & 3–7pm; ⓦ cochranepatagonia.cl). There's also an information booth at the bus terminal (daily 9am–1pm & 2.30–6.30pm).
Conaf Río Nef 417 (Mon–Fri 10am–5pm; ☎ 67 252 2164). This is a good place for information on the Tamango sector of Parque Nacional Patagonia; trail maps are sometimes available.

COCHRANE

Jimmy Valdes Lago Brown 388 (☎ 09 82678155, ⓦ lordpatagonia.cl). Experienced local guide Jimmy specializes in treks around the San Lorenzo and Calluqueo glaciers. Horseback riding along the Ruta de los Pioneros is also arranged.
Banks and exchange Bring plenty of cash. The Banco Estado ATM off the plaza accepts some foreign cards but not others and is not to be relied on.

ACCOMMODATION

Cabañas Sol y Luna Camino a Tamango Km 1 ☎ 09 8157 9602, ⓦ turismosolyluna.cl. Located a 15min walk from Cochrane, towards the Tamango entrance to Parque Nacional Patagonia, these rustic, well-heated *cabañas* are run by friendly Ximena and the setting is wonderfully tranquil. There's a sauna and hot tub and Ximena also brews craft Baker Beer. CH$40,000
Hostal Lago Esmeralda San Valentín 141 ☎ 09 9718 6805. Particularly good for solo travellers (six of the seven rooms are singles, and cost half the price of the double), this basic guesthouse has a decent restaurant. CH$30,000
Hotel Ultimo Paraíso Lago Brown 455 ☎ 67 252 2361, ⓦ hotelultimoparaiso.cl. As close as you get to paradise in Cochrane, the only upscale hotel in town is split into seven beautiful wood-panelled rooms with wood-burning stoves and cable TV. Breakfast includes Spanish specialities, and owner Carlos arranges fishing – and other – excursions. CH$90,000
Residencial Cero a Cero Lago Brown 464 ☎ 67 252 2158. This rambling maze of a family home caters to backpackers and cyclists with their clutch of small twins and doubles. They're unheated, but plenty of woolly blankets are provided. It's run by a friendly family, breakfast is basic and wi-fi works in the tiny lounge area by the stove. CH$26,000

EATING AND DRINKING

Ada's Restaurant Teniente Merino 374 ☎ 09 8399 5899. This large, family-run restaurant has an extensive menu of nicely cooked steaks, standard fish dishes, strong signature cocktails and pints of beer. Good wine list also. Mains from CH$8000. Daily 1.30–3.15pm & 8.30–10.30pm.
Café Tamango Esmeralda 464 ☎ 09 9158 4521. Just off the main square, this bright and wholesome café is a favourite gathering spot for cyclists checking their emails. Lots of veggie options, including quiches, soup and lentil burgers, plus good coffee and fresh juices. Mon–Sat 9am–8pm.

★ **Cervecería Tehuelche** Teniente Merino 372 ☎ 09 6628 3961. Its walls decked out with prehistoric hunting scenes, Cochrane's best microbrewery has two own brews on tap, a porter and an amber ale, as well as a D'olbek beer from Coyhaique, and the food doesn't let the side down. The grilled fish (CH$8500) is super-fresh, and if beer is not your thing, you can sip a fresh fruit juice or a calafate sour on the outdoor terrace. Daily 12.30pm–late.
Naciónpatagonia Steffens at Las Golondrinas. Adorable little café, with hospitable owners, serving real coffee (from CH$1200) and delicious home-made cakes. Good place for gathering local ecological info. Daily 9am–1pm & 3.15pm–9pm.

Parque Nacional Patagonia: Sector Tamango

6km east of Cochrane • ⓦ conaf.cl/aniversario-50-reserva-nacional-tamango • No public transport, but it's possible to walk 6km to the entrance from Cochrane by taking Pasaje 1 north and then east from San Valentín and Colonia

Parque Nacional Patagonia sits on the banks of **Lago Cochrane**, a skinny, twisting lake that straddles the Argentine border. The eight rewarding trails from the **Sector Tamango** entrance vary in difficulty and range (40min to 6–8hr); the longest leads to Laguna Tamanguito, seamlessly connecting Sector Tamango with the Lagunas Altas trail in the central sector (see page 374); bring windproof clothing. This sector is notable for its population of around eighty *huemúl* (native deer); if you're lucky, you may spot one, particularly along the Sendero Los Huemules from the ranger station at the entrance to Refugio El Húngaro (5km; 2hr).

Caleta Tortel

Perhaps the most unusual village in Chile, **CALETA TORTEL** consists of a scattering of houses on forested slopes surrounding a pale emerald bay. Located at the mouth of the Río Baker between the northern and southern ice fields, Tortel, founded in 1955 as a logging spot for a lumber company, soon grew into a scattered settlement, each house with its own jetty, linked by a network of walkways and bridges made of fragrant cypress. There are no streets, and even the police "car" and the fire engine are boats.

Hitting the spotlight when the UK's Prince William worked on an Operation Raleigh project here during his gap year, Tortel is also renowned for a mysterious incident that gave its name to a nearby island, the **Isla de los Muertos**. 2018 saw a flurry of activity, with numerous new houses being built, and with the fairly recent addition of the Entel mobile network and temperamental, slow wi-fi, Tortel has joined the digital world.

The village itself is divided into **five sections**: Rincón Alto (the upper section of the village, closest to the car park), Rincón Bajo (below Rincón Alto), Rincón Base (the centre of the village), Playa Ancha (further up along the coast from Rincón Base) and Junquillo, uphill from Playa Ancha.

Isla de los Muertos

3km off shore · Expediciones Patagonia Landeros (☎ 09 8238 6781) and Borde Río Tortel Expeditions (☎ 09 9940 8265) run boat trips from Tortel (CH\$50,000 for up to six passengers)

You can visit the morbid but beautifully unspoiled **Isla de los Muertos** on a forty-minute boat trip; you can disembark and have a look at the graveyard. The island assumed its grisly moniker in 1906 after almost seventy employees involved in a timber-felling scheme suddenly died in unexplained circumstances. Officially the cause was an epidemic of some kind, possibly scurvy, but rumours suggested they were poisoned, maybe deliberately so that the company didn't have to pay their wages.

ARRIVAL AND DEPARTURE — CALETA TORTEL

By boat Transbordadora Austral Broom (☎ 09 6232 2798, ⓦ tabsa.cl) sails weekly to Puerto Natales in southern Patagonia between Dec and Feb, and weekly for three weeks out of four during the rest of the year (passenger CH\$132,000, bicycle CH\$28,300). The car ferry picks up cargo first at Puerto Yungay, then foot passengers in Tortel. There's a ticket office in Rincón Base, near *Residencial Estilo*. **Destinations** Puerto Natales (Sat 11pm; 8pm from Puerto Yungay; 40hr).

By bus Buses stop in the car park in Rincón Alto, next to the tourist office. Between Nov and April, there are direct services to Villa O'Higgins. Buses Aldea (☎ 67 263 8291), Buses Patagonia (☎ 67 252 2470), Buses Katalina (☎ 09 9932 4320), Buses Cordillera ☎ T09 8134 4990) and Buses Pachamama (☎ 09 9411 4811) run to Cochrane. **Destinations** Cochrane (daily 9.30am, some days also 8am, 10am, 2pm & 8.15pm; 3hr); Villa O'Higgins (Mon, Thurs & Sat 4.30pm; 4hr).

INFORMATION

Tourist information The very helpful kiosk, with plenty of info on Tortel, is in the car park at the upper entrance to the village (daily 10am–8pm in peak season).

Money and exchange There are no banks or ATMs, so bring plenty of cash.

ACCOMMODATION AND EATING

There's a free **campsite** with no facilities at Playa Ancha, a 45min walk from the car park. Most guesthouses charge/person, so singles are half the price of doubles.

Hospedaje Brisas Del Sur Playa Ancha ☎ 09 9698 8244. Presided over by friendly Valeria, this budget option consists of basic but comfortable rooms, many with sea views. Avoid the downstairs room. Valeria's brothers run boat tours to Isla de Los Muertos and glaciers. CH\$30,000

8

Hospedaje Costanera Rincón Base ☎ 09 6670 0236. Friendly Louisa Escobar houses her guests in a clutch of simple, carpeted rooms with wood-burning stoves. Some rooms lack natural light, so have a look at several if possible. CH$30,000

★ **Lodge Entre Hielos** Rincón Bajo ☎ 09 9579 3779, ⓦ entrehielostortel.cl. Beautiful upscale lodge uphill from the boardwalk, with attractive woollen details and bright throws in the six plush rooms with rain showers. The restaurant serves fine Patagonian cuisine with emphasis on local ingredients (three-course dinner CH$23,000);

non-guests may dine with prior reservations. Staff organize boat trips and glacier hikes. CH$116,000

Residencial Porvenir Junquillo ☎ 09 7652 1937. The welcoming Iñiguez family offers several wood-stove-heated twins and doubles with colourful beadspreads and home-cooked meals on request. CH$26,000

★ **Sabores Locales** Rincón Bajo. The indomitable Maritza serves up large portions of ultra-fresh fish dishes, hearty shellfish soup and vegetables from her own garden, as well as locally brewed craft beer. She's a great source of local info and has a guidebook of particular interest to cyclists. Mains around CH$9000. Daily 12.30–11pm.

Puerto Yungay to Río Bravo

Dec–Feb 4 free ferries south daily at 10am, noon, 3pm & 6pm; rest of year 2 ferries daily (noon & 3pm) each way; return trips 1hr later; double-check timetable locally; 45min

Villa O'Higgins is reached via the very final – and particularly spectacular – 100km stretch of the Carretera beyond the small military camp of **PUERTO YUNGAY**, 20km beyond the turnoff to Caleta Tortel, where you must cross the Fiordo Mitchell via ferry. If driving, confirm departure times in Cochrane and arrive at least half an hour early to guarantee a space. Puerto Yungay is the last port of call for weekly ferries from Puerto Natales (see page 393).

8

Villa O'Higgins and around

Tiny **VILLA O'HIGGINS** was built on a simple grid, with the Carretera Austral running along the western side all the way down to the Bahía Bahamondez on the enormous glacial **Lago O'Higgins**, 7km away. Most of the earliest settlers – who came at the beginning of the twentieth century, when it was most easily accessible from Argentina – were British. The first Chilean settlers did not arrive until the 1920s, and the town wasn't officially founded and given its present name until 1966. Until 1999, this orderly collection of wooden houses huddled against a sheer mountain face was reachable only by a small prop plane from Coyhaique or by boat from Argentina. A ten-minute hike up to the **Miradór Cerro Santiago** gives you a bird's-eye view; a longer, two-hour hike carries on up to the even higher **Miradór La Bandera**.

Villa O'Higgins is the starting and finishing point for cyclists "doing" the Carretera Austral, as well as a springboard for hiking to some of the area's remote glaciers.

ARRIVAL AND DEPARTURE   VILLA O'HIGGINS

By bus Buses Águilas Patagónicas (☎ 67 252 3730) serves Cochrane (arriving in O'Higgins the day before), departing from Calle Lago Christie at Río Bravo. Buses VulTur Patagonia (☎ 09 9350 8156) runs to Tortel between Nov and April from Calle Lago Cisnes at Río Bravo. Buy tickets in advance.

Destinations Cochrane (Tues, Thurs & Sun 8.30am; 7hr), Tortel (Mon, Thurs & Sat 8.30am, 4hr).

By plane Aeercord (Calle Lago O'Higgins between Río Pascua and Río Mayer; ⓦ aerocord.cl) serves Coyhaique (CH$45,000 one way).

Destinations Coyhaique (Mon & Thurs; 1hr 15 min).

INFORMATION AND TOURS

Tourist office On the plaza (summer Mon–Fri 10am–2pm & 3–7pm; ⓦ villaohiggins.com, ⓦ ohigginspatagonia.cl). The staff at the tourist office provide information on the surrounding area.

Tour operators Hielo Sur, next to *Robinson Crusoe* (see page 379; ⓦ hielosur.com), runs boat trips to the

Ventisquero O'Higgins (see page 379) and Ventisquero Chico, as well as single and multi-day hikes, and provides info for self-guided ventures. Wings (ⓦ wingspatagonia. cl) offers scenic, hour-long flights over the Southern Ice Field and its tremendous glaciers in a Cessna P206, as well as longer flights over the Northern Ice Field. At around

ARGENTINA THE HARD WAY: THE EL CHALTÉN CROSSING

The crossing between **Villa O'Higgins** and Argentina's **El Chaltén** remains remote and challenging, yet more and more travellers are prepared to take the boat, followed by a 20km hike over the border and then another lake crossing. The sixty-passenger *Quetru*, connected to Villa O'Higgins by the 7.50am transfers run by *Robinson Crusoe Deep Patagonia* lodge (CH$2500), leaves Bahía Bahamondez at 8.30am (Jan, Feb & Dec Mon, Wed, Thurs & Sat; March & Nov Mon, Wed & Sat; Sept, Oct & April weekly; CH$36,000) and arrives at the hamlet of **Candelario Mancilla**, the border post across the lake, at 11.15am. Just beyond the dock a signposted dirt track leads to *Hospedaje Candelario Mancilla* (☎67 256 7189) – a **campsite** with access to showers (CH$2500) and two or three basic **rooms** available at owner Rodrigo's house (CH$8000/person); the latter can provide meals on request. Get your passport stamped by **Chilean border control** further up the main road before you set off for Argentina.

TO THE BORDER

Beyond Candelario Mancilla, a gravel road winds uphill through patches of woodland to the international border. Beyond the border, marked by signs welcoming you into Chile and Argentina, the 7.5km stretch of trail to the **Argentine Gendarmería** (no set hours) on the banks of the **Lago del Desierto** becomes a narrow, muddy footpath snaking its way through hilly forest and scrubland; cyclists have to push and sometimes carry their bikes. After getting stamped into Argentina, you can either pitch a tent at *Camping Lago del Desierto* (US$8), or stay in the basic *cabaña* run by the gendarmes (US$20). The next day, you can catch the motor launch *Huemul* across the lake (Jan–March, Nov & Dec daily 11am & 5pm; 30–45min; CH$28,000/AR$950; ⓦexploradoreslagodeldesierto.com) or hike the remaining 16km (5hr) along a steep, thickly forested path on the east side of the lake, emerging by the pier on the south side.

Minibuses to **El Chaltén** meet the arriving motor launches (1.30pm, 4pm & 8pm; CH$21,000/AR$500). If crossing from El Chaltén to Villa O'Higgins, bring enough food for at least three days, as boat schedules are weather-dependent and you can get stuck for a day or two at Candelario Mancilla. To book a guide and packhorses (CH$40,000/packhorse, two-horse minimum), or a 4WD to drop you at the border (CH$15,000/person) visit ⓦvillaohiggins.com.

US$250/person (based on five people maximim), it's not cheap, but it is a once-in-a-lifetime experience. Contact Vicente the pilot (☎09 9162 5137) or Daniel the manager (☎09 9357 8196).

Banks and exchange Since there are no banks or ATMs, bring plenty of cash. If you've just crossed the border from Argentina and have a surplus of Argentine pesos but no

Chilean currency, you can change a limited amount of cash on the *Quetru* boat (see above); some lodgings can unofficially change Argentinian pesos at a poor rate.

Phone and wi-fi Entel is the only mobile network that works in O'Higgins (including data). Most lodgings have wi-fi, but it's painfully slow.

ACCOMMODATION AND EATING

Eco Camping Tsonek Carretera Austral s/n, 1km north of Villa O'Higgins ☎09 7892 9695, ⓔinfo@tsonek.cl. Run by ornithologist Mauricio (who can arrange birdwatching and trekking tours), this ecologically sustainable campsite has wooden platforms for tents, a composting toilet, hot showers and a communal building for cooking and reading. Electricity is provided by a solar panel and a bicycle-powered generator. CH$6000

Entre Patagones Carretera Austral 1 ☎67 243 1810, ⓦentrepatagones.cl. Pretty much the only restaurant in town, this large wooden lodge dining hall fills up nightly; dishes are simple and portions are large. Expect the likes of cheese *empanadas* and grilled hake; if you're lucky, you'll be there on *asador patagónico* (spit-roasted lamb)

night. Mains around CH$10,000. Daily 12.30–3pm & 7.30–11pm.

Hostería Fitz Roy Río Teniente Merino at Río Mayer ☎61 239 0288. Run by helpful teacher Yaline, this cosy guesthouse in the southwest corner of town has four warm, comfortable rooms with decent beds: an en-suite family room, plus a twin, double and single with shared facilities. CH$25,000

★ **El Mosco** Carretera Austral Km 1240 ☎67 243 1819. With its hammock-festooned porch, the town's only hostel acts as a hiker and biker magnet. Friendly Orfelina offers plenty of info on travel around the Carretera Austral. Campers can use the hot showers, kitchen and lounge; the dorms are spacious, there are snug rooms upstairs (some en suite) and a tower and cabin for groups. Splurge on a

Finnish sauna (CH$15,000) or hot tub (CH$30,000). Closed June–Aug. Camping CH$6000, dorms CH$10,000, doubles CH$30,000,

Robinson Crusoe Deep Patagonia Carretera Austral Km 1240 ☎ 67 243 1821, ⓦ robinsoncrusoe.com. O'Higgins' only high-end option, this beautiful lodge near the north end of town has twelve spacious, light-filled, centrally heated rooms with excellent beds, rain showers and a high-ceilinged, wood-stove-heated guest lounge. The outdoor hot tubs are great for a post-hike soak. Non-guests may dine here. US$230

Hikes and glaciers around Villa O'Higgins

Note that before embarking on any of the treks, you have to register with the *carabineros* in town. Directly from the town, a footpath from Calle Lago Cisnes runs through **Parque Cerro Santiago** up to two viewpoints (30min return); from the second viewpoint, the path continues on towards the ice "tongue" of the **Ventisquero Mosco**, the nearest hanging glacier. It's a tough 11km one way, around 10hr return, with a basic *refugio* about 8km along; a guide is recommended unless you're an experienced wilderness trekker. Two kilometres along this trail is the gorgeous **Mirador del Valle** (3hr return).

Further afield, around 6km south of Villa O'Higgins, is the trailhead for **Cerro Submarino**, a steep but rewarding 7km ascent (6hr return).

Several **glaciers**, including Ventisquero O'Higgins, spill into Lago O'Higgins from the massive Campo de Hielo Sur – a titanic ice cap that blocks any further progress southwards for the Carretera. These can be visited by boat (see page 395).

From the boat dock at Bahía Bahamondez, in the spring and summer months (Jan–March, Nov & Dec), a cross-lake ferry travels to the Argentine side, from where it's possible to walk to Argentina's **El Chaltén** along a route that's become very popular with intrepid hikers and particularly with bikers. The boat crosses over to the hamlet of **Candelario Mancilla** (see page 378) – the starting point for the rewarding 7km Sendero de Chile hike that climbs steeply through *lenga* forest to the Dos Lagunas pass, where you get sweeping views of the O'Higgins, Chico and Pirámide glaciers, before descending to the *refugio* by Lago O'Higgins' Brazo Sur. You can arrange to be picked up at Candelario Mancilla by the boat that runs tours to the glaciers.

8

Southern Patagonia

GAUCHO, PARQUE NACIONAL TORRES DEL PAINE

9 Southern Patagonia

Patagonia lies tucked away right at the southernmost tip of the Americas – indeed of the world's landmass, not counting Antarctica. While the very name holds a fascination for many travellers, the reality can be harsh: the place is cursed by a persistent wind, the *Escoba de Dios* (God's Broom); trees grow horizontally here, sculpted by the gales; winters are long and summers short. Geographically ill-defined, "Patagonia" usually refers to the narrow triangle of land south of a line between Puerto Montt, in Chile, and Argentina's Península Valdés. In Chile the term is actually usually reserved for Southern Patagonia, where the Andes take a last, dramatic breath before plunging into the ocean.

While much of Argentine Patagonia is flat rolling **pampa**, the land rises in the western sliver of land shared by both countries; people on both sides of the border think of themselves as Patagonians first, and Chileans or Argentinians second, united by a common ranching culture that has long been in decline. These days, large numbers of Chileans and non-Chilean visitors alike come to Patagonia to hike – in Chile's most famous and stunning national park, **Parque Nacional Torres del Paine**, a massif crowned with otherworldly granite towers and accessed from the superbly located gateway town of **Puerto Natales**. Others come to follow in the footsteps of the region's famous travellers – navigator Ferdinand Magellan, naturalist Charles Darwin and author Bruce Chatwin; to gaze at the region's many spectacular **glaciers**; or to visit the **penguin colonies** from the lively provincial capital of **Punta Arenas** – a port city sitting on the shore of the stormy Magellan Strait. The broad expanse of frigid grassland between Puerto Natales and Punta Arenas stretches to the Atlantic coast, taking in the desolately beautiful **Parque Nacional Pali Aike**. Fewer visitors make it to the remote **islands** of the Pacific coast.

Since the whole of this region is physically cut off from the rest of Chile by two vast ice caps, the only links with territory to the north are by air or water or through **Argentina**. The last option allows you to visit traditional **estancias** and some of Argentina's finest landscapes, including the **Parque Nacional Los Glaciares**, where the **Fitz Roy Massif**, near the tiny town of **El Chaltén**, offers incredible hiking and climbing opportunities, while **Glaciar Perito Moreno**, accessible from the tourist hub of **El Calafate**, is visually arresting, not to mention the most accessible of all South American glaciers.

Brief history

Chilean Patagonia, the site of the some of the continent's oldest human habitation, was originally populated by Tehuelche hunter-gatherers, who stalked roaming guanacos in the interior, and the sea-faring Kawéscar who dived naked for shellfish in the frigid waters around the southern fjords. The first European to discover the area was **Ferdinand Magellan**, a Portuguese navigator who sailed through the strait now bearing

MAGELLANIC PENGUINS, ISLA MAGDALENA

Highlights

❶ Cemetery at Punta Arenas Visit this moving – and beautiful – memorial to the pioneers from Britain and Spain, Croatia and Italy. See page 388

❷ Cabo Froward Hike to the southernmost tip of the South American continent, fording rivers as you go. See page 392

❸ Penguins at Isla Magdalena Watch the birds' comic antics on this island sanctuary – the second largest colony of Magellanic penguins in South America. See page 392

❹ Hiking Parque Nacional Torres del Paine Set aside at least a few days to trek through Chile's most popular, spectacular park. See page 398

❺ Parque Nacional Los Glaciares Hike and boat your way to the remotest corner of the park and watch glaciers crumble into a pristine, ice-filled lagoon. See page 407

❻ Glaciar Perito Moreno Admire Argentine Patagonia's most spectacular glacier from afar, take a boat right up to its face or go ice-hiking on its surface. See page 409

HIGHLIGHTS ARE MARKED ON THE MAP ON PAGE 384

9

his name. Spanish colonization attempts failed catastrophically and no European tried to settle the place again for another 250 years.

The voyages of the *Beagle*, from 1826 to 1834, the second one bearing young Charles Darwin, renewed interest in the area, prompting continued Chilean and Argentine attempts to colonize the area. In the 1870s the two narrowly avoided war over the territory, not for the last time. From 1849, Punta Arenas was boosted by sea traffic en route to the California Gold Rush; while it didn't last long, the introduction of sheep

SOUTHERN PATAGONIA

HIGHLIGHTS

1. Cemetery at Punta Arenas
2. Cabo Froward
3. Penguins at Isla Magdalena
4. Hiking Parque Nacional Torres del Paine
5. Parque Nacional Los Glaciares
6. Glaciar Perito Moreno

farming created sprawling **estancias** (ranches) and brought great wealth to their owners – and misery to the indigenous populations – in the late nineteenth century. The city was also a stopover for Antarctica-bound explorers, which it remains to this day, as well as a base for Tierra del Fuego-bound travellers.

Wool has now been replaced by **oil**, commercial salmon farming and tourism as the region's main resources. The Chileans call the area the province of **Magallanes**, in the explorer's honour, and it has its own flag.

Punta Arenas and around

Seen from above, **PUNTA ARENAS**, 2190km south of Santiago, is a patchwork of galvanized tin roofs and brightly coloured houses climbing up from the shores of the Magellan Strait. In the centre, glass and concrete office buildings sit alongside grand nineteenth-century stone mansions built by local wool barons. Across Avenida España to the west, steps lead up to the **Mirador Cerro la Cruz**, where you can enjoy a sweeping view of the city's multicoloured roofs and the wind-whipped sea.

A short drive south is **Puerto Hambre**, where the first colonists of the area perished, as well as the rebuilt **Fuerte Bulnes**. Even further south starts the trailhead to **Cabo Froward**, the southernmost tip of the South American mainland. It's possible to sail from Punta Arenas to **Monumento Natural Isla Magdalena**, Chile's largest Magellanic penguin colony, while a short drive north of town is **Parque Nacional Pali Aike**, a surreal landscape of old lava flows.

Plaza Muñoz Gamero

The tranquil **Plaza Muñoz Gamero**, featuring shady pathways under magnificent century-year-old Monterey cypresses, teems with strolling families and souvenir vendors. In the middle rises an imposing **monument to Ferdinand Magellan**. Below Magellan sits a Selk'nam man – one of only two references to the now extinct people that you'll find in the city (see page 388). If you touch (some say kiss) the Selk'nam man's polished toe, local legend has it that you'll return to Punta Arenas. The two blocks of Magallanes running from the square's northeast corner are all that remains of the city's oldest original street, originally named Calle María Isabel.

Palacio Sara Braun

Plaza Muñoz Gamero • Daily except Tues 10.30am–5pm • CH$1500

Around the plaza rise several grand houses dating from the wool boom, but the only one you can visit is the **Palacio Sara Braun**, on the northwestern corner, designed by a French architect, Numa Mayer, for Sara Braun, widow of the great sheep baron José Nogueira. While it is now divided between the *Club de la Unión* and the *Hotel José Nogueira* (see page 390), visitors can stroll through the elegant, period furniture-lined rooms of the *Club de la Unión* section, and marvel at the opulence of the frescoes.

Museo Regional Braun Menéndez

Magallanes 949 • Daily except Tues: May–Sept 10.30am–5pm; Oct–April 10.30am–2pm • CH$1500 • ⓦ museodemagallanes.cl

Half a block north of the square sits the **Palacio Braun Menéndez** – the former family residence of the marriage that united the two wealthiest and most powerful families in Punta Arenas, and now housing the **Museo Regional Braun Menéndez**. The beautifully preserved private quarters of this early twentieth-century family home offer a window onto a wealthy middle-class lifestyle achieved by few who came to Patagonia in search of it: a dining room and bedrooms filled with French Art Nouveau furnishings and the billiard room where men discussed affairs of state.

9

Hospital Regional (2km), Zona Franca (3km), Ferry Terminal (5km), ▲
Nao Victoria Museum (7km) ▲
1 (350m) ▲
Transbordadora Austral Broom Ferry (5km) & Airport (20km) ▲

● **EATING**

Amaranta Tea House	3
Café Inmigrantes	1
Café Tapiz	7
La Cuisine	5
History Coffee	6
Kiosko Roca	8
La Marmita	2
La Mesita Grande	4
Parrilla Los Ganaderos	9
Wake Up	10

■ **DRINKING**

Sky Bar	2
La Taberna del Club de la Unión	1

■ **ACCOMMODATION**

Apart Hotel Quillango	3
Cabañas Shenu	4
Dreams del Estrecho	11
Hospedaje Costanera	1
Hospedaje Magallanes	2
Hostal Independencia	12
Hostal Labarca	13
Hostal Ventisqueros	6
Hotel José Nogueira	9
Hotel Rey Don Felipe	8
Ilaia	7
Innata Patagonia	5
Patagonia B&B	10

Cementerio Municipal

ANGAMOS

MAIPÚ

AVENIDA MANUEL BULNES

Museo Salesiano

SARMIENTO DE GAMBOA

Santuario María Auxiliadora

CROACIA

CROACIA

JORGE MONTT

AV ESPAÑA

MEJICANA

MEJICANA

A SANHUEZA

CHILOÉ

BORIES

Cine Estrella

MAGALLANES

SAMPAIO

NAVARRO

O'HIGGINS

CARRERA PINTO

CARRERA PINTO

Buses Fernández/ Turibus/ Cruz del Sur/ Bus El Pinguino

Pullman Bus

Río de las Minas

Bus Sur

Buses Pacheco

AVENIDA COLÓN

JORGE MONTT

Bus Sur

LATAM

JOSÉ MENÉNDEZ

Aerovías DAP

Castillo Milward

Hertz

† St James

Museo Regional Braun Menéndez

Techni Austral Buses

WALDO SEGUEL

Palacio Sara Braún

PEDRO MONTT

Iglesia Matriz

PLAZA MUÑOZ GAMERO

Banco Santander

Museo Naval y Marítimo

FAGNANO

Turismo Comapa

ROCA

ⓘ

Whalesound

A SANHUEZA

ERRÁZURIZ

CHILOÉ

NOGUEIRA

21 DE MAYO

NAVARRO

COST

Port

Solo Expediciones

BALMACEDA

Magellan Strait

AV INDEPENDENCIA

PUNTA ARENAS

0	200
	metres

Mirador Cerro de la Cruz (100m)

▼ **13** (250m)
▼ Fuerte Bulnes (51km) & Puerto Hambre (51km)

MAGELLAN, PIONEER OF GLOBAL EXPLORATION

Fernão de Magalhães, known to English-speakers as **Ferdinand Magellan**, was born in about 1480 in northern Portugal, and had an adventurous early life: in his 20s he saw service with the Portuguese fleets in their wars against the Muslims of the Indian Ocean, and by 1515 he was a veteran of the campaigns in Morocco. In 1516, after being refused a rise in his pension by the king of Portugal, Magellan took his services to the Spanish crown.

Those days were the beginning of European exploration, prompted mainly by the desire to seek out **new routes** to the East and its valuable **Spice Islands** (the Moluccas of Indonesia). Magellan believed that the answer lay to the west, under or through the newly discovered American continents, and he asked the king of Spain, Carlos I, to fund his search. Charles agreed, eager to prove that the Spice Islands lay in the half of the New World that the pope had just assigned to Spain.

THROUGH THE STRAITS TO THE PACIFIC

On September 20, 1519, Magellan sailed west as admiral of a fleet of five ships, including the *Nao Victoria*, a life-sized replica of which can be seen at the Nao Victoria Museum (see page 388). They crossed the Atlantic Ocean, and started to search the coast of South America for the elusive passage. It was a long and hard hunt, and not all Magellan's fleet believed there was a strait: on Easter Day 1520, Magellan had to quash a mutiny by his Spanish captains. But on October 21, 1520, his flagship, the *Trinidad*, finally rounded Cabo Virgenes and entered the **strait** that now bears his name. Thirty-six days later the open seas of an ocean were sighted; they named the new ocean **"the Pacific"** for its calmness after the storms of the strait, and set out across it, not expecting it to be so wide. Seeing the smoke from countless fires of the Selk'nam and the Yamaná people on the coast of the immense island on the southern side of the Strait, Magellan gave it its present name: Tierra del Fuego (Land of Fire).

BACK TO SPAIN

They sailed for four months without seeing land. When Magellan himself was **killed** in a fight with the natives of Mactán Island, the fleet didn't turn back; petrified of attempting to go through the straits at the bottom of South America for a second time, they took the longer route round the Cape of Good Hope. Three years after they'd set out, just one of Magellan's original five ships finally limped back to Spain. It was loaded with spices (cloves and nutmeg) and manned by just eighteen of the original crew, men wasted and half-dead. The voyage's chronicler said he could not imagine the journey ever being repeated.

Several rooms are devoted to a permanent exhibition detailing the colonization of Patagonia and Tierra del Fuego, with pioneer articles, historical photos and bilingual displays on the maritime and farming history of the region, as well as the region's **indigenous peoples** – the Kawéscar and the Selk'nam. Dusty old account books and documents reveal that the founding families controlled not only the sheep trade, but also an immense range of other commercial activities. In effect, they *were* the city.

Museo Naval y Marítimo

Pedro Montt 981 • Tues–Sat 9.30am–12.30pm & 2–5pm • CH$1200

Housed in the former naval headquarters, the engaging **Museo Naval y Marítimo** focuses on Chile's naval history and the exploration of the southern waters. The ground floor features a collection of minutely detailed scale models of ships that have sailed these southern waters, including Sir Ernest Shackleton's *Endurance* and the *Yelcho* that ended up rescuing Shackleton's crew, as well as a block of Antarctic ice. Upstairs you can play around in the area decked out as a ship, complete with nautical equipment, maps, charts and interactive displays of sailing routes and Chile's southernmost lighthouses.

9

Museo Salesiano Maggiorino Borgatello

Av Manuel Bulnes • Tues–Sun 10am–12.30pm & 3–5.30pm • CH$3000

Besides a plethora of taxidermied local wildlife, the exhibits at the absorbing **Museo Salesianno Maggiorino Borgatello** focus largely on the indigenous peoples of Southern Patagonia and Tierra del Fuego and their evangelization by the Salesian religious order. The exhibits suggest that the missionaries acted as mediators between the locals and the settlers, failing to point out the evangelizers' roles in the demise of native culture.

Standout displays vividly depict the daily life of the Kawéscar and the weapons they used for hunting and fishing. Another choice exhibit is the unparalleled collection of photographs of the region and its inhabitants, taken by the Italian mountaineering priest, Alberto de Agostini, who spent many years among the indigenous people of Patagonia and Tierra del Fuego.

Cementerio Municipal

Av Bulnes • Daily 8am–8pm • Free

The city's magnificent **Cementerio Municipal** extends over four city blocks. Crisscrossed by a network of footpaths lined with immaculately clipped cypresses, this eclectic necropolis reflects the turbulent history of Patagonia. The monumental tombs of the city's ruling families, such as Menéndez and Nogueira – some made of the same Italian marble as Michelangelo's *David* and elaborately engraved with the English and Spanish names – mingle with the Croatian and Scandinavian names of immigrant labourers, etched on modest gravestones and funerary urn receptacles.

A monument depicting a **Selk'nam** man is surrounded with plaques conveying the gratitude of those whose wishes it allegedly granted. Try to spot the onion-domed crypt of the Braun family – one of the city's founding dynasties – and the simple gravestone of Charles Milward (a map inside the main entrance highlights the more famous graves).

Nao Victoria Museum

Río Seco, Km 7.5 north • Daily 9am–7pm • CH$4000 • ⓦ naovictoria.cl • Buses run to Río Seco from the corner of Carrera Pinto and Chiloé

Well worth the 7.5km drive north of town, the interactive **Nao Victoria Museum**, by the sea, consists of four full-size replicas of famous nautical vessels associated with the history of the Magellan Strait. Climb down into the hold of Magellan's *Nao Victoria* carrack that took him around Cape Horn, view the surprisingly compact *Goleta Ancud* that brought the colonists to Punta Arenas, check out the HMS *Beagle* that carried Charles Darwin to Patagonia and see Shackleton's lifeboat, *James Caird*. The last carried the explorer and five crew members to South Georgia through the most violent stretch of ocean on earth after the *Endurance* was crushed by ice.

ARRIVAL AND DEPARTURE   **PUNTA ARENAS**

By plane Most travellers arrive at the user-friendly Aeropuerto Presidente Ibañez, 20km north of town. Scheduled LATAM (office Menéndez at Bories; ☎ 61 224 1100, ⓦ latam.com) and Sky Airline (ⓦ skyairline.cl) flights leave Punta Arenas for Coyhaique (Balmaceda), Puerto Montt and Santiago. There's also a weekly LATAM flight to the Falkland Islands (CH$250,000). In summer, Aerovías DAP (O'Higgins at Menéndez; ☎ 61 261 6100, ⓦ dapairline.com) runs flights to Puerto Williams (CH$75,500) and Antarctica (US$5500/US$6500 for full day/overnight stay), plus year-round flights to Porvenir (CH$29,000) Taxis to the centre charge CH$10,000, while door-to-door minibuses charge CH$5000. Buses heading to Puerto Natales also stop at the airport.

Destinations Antarctica (Nov–March several monthly; 6hr round-trip); Balmaceda (Tues & Thurs; 1hr 30min); Falkland Islands (1 weekly on Sat; 1hr 30min); Porvenir (Mon–Sat 2–3 daily; 12min); Puerto Montt (2 daily; 2hr); Puerto Williams (summer Mon–Sat 1 daily 10am; winter 3 weekly; 40min–1hr 20min); Santiago (4–5 daily; 3hr 20min).

By bus Each bus company has its own terminal in the centre of Punta Arenas. Buses Tecni Austral, Navarro 975 (☎ 61 261 3420), Buses Pacheco, Av Colón 900 (☎ 61 224 2174, ⓦ busespacheco.co.cl), Buses Barria, Av España 264 (☎ 61 224 0646) and Bus Sur, Av Colón 842 (☎ 61 261 4224, ⓦ bussur.com) serve Ushuaia via Río Grande; book ahead in peak season. Bus Sur, Buses Pacheco and Buses Fernández

(Sanhueza 745; ☎ 61 224 2313, ⊛ busesfernandez.com) go to Puerto Natales. Bus El Pingüino, Sanhueza 745 (☎ 61 222 1812) and Buses Pacheco serve Río Gallegos. Buses Queilén, Navarro 975 (☎ 61 222 2714, ⊛ queilenbus. cl), Turibus/Cruz del Sur, Sanhueza 745 (☎ 61 222 7970, ⊛ busescruzdelsur.cl) and Pullman, Av Colón 568 (☎ 61 222 3359, ⊛ pullman.cl) run to Osorno, Puerto Montt, Ancud and Castro. Bus journeys to Ushuaia involve a 40min ferry crossing and don't always include a meal stop, so bring food with you.

Destinations Ancud and Castro via Puerto Montt and Osorno (Mon, Wed & Sat 9am; 27hr); Puerto Natales (16 daily; 3hr); Río Gallegos, Argentina (1–2 daily; 4hr); Ushuaia, Argentina, via Río Grande (daily 8.30am/9am; 12hr).

By ferry The ferry terminal at Tres Puentes, 5km north of town, is a short *colectivo* (CH$1000) or taxi ride

(around CH$5000) from downtown, along the Natales road to the north. Transbordadora Austral Broom ferries, Juan Williams 6450 (☎ 61 272 8100, ⊛ tabsa.cl), serves Porvenir in Tierra del Fuego and Puerto Williams on Isla Navarino, as well as the Primera Angostura crossing between Punta Delgada on the Patagonian mainland and Bahía Azul (Puerto Espora) in Tierra del Fuego. Timetables are weather-dependent; if taking a car to Porvenir, book a space in advance.

Destinations Porvenir (daily 9am; 2hr 30min; passenger CH$6200, car CH$39,800); Primera Angostura (summer daily 8.30am–11pm every 45min; rest of the year less frequently; 20min; passenger CH$1700, car CH$15,000); Puerto Williams (Jan–March, Nov & Dec Thurs 6pm, also some Mons 1am; 32hr; Pullman seat CH$108,000, sofa-berth CH$151,000).

GETTING AROUND AND INFORMATION

Car rental All main car rental companies have a booth at the airport. Reserve in advance in peak season. Europcar, O'Higgins 964 (☎ 61 220 2720, ⊛ europcar.cl); Hertz, O'Higgins 931 (☎ 61 261 3087, ⊛ hertz.cl)

Conaf Bulnes 309, fourth floor (Mon–Thurs 8.30am–5pm, Fri 8.30am–4pm; ☎ 61 223 8554). Information on the area's national parks and reserves.

Tourist office Fagnano 643 (Mon–Fri 8.30am–8pm, Sat 10am–6pm; ☎ 61 224 3790) ⊛ patagonia-chile.com). Lots of information on the city and the region.

ACTIVITIES AND TOURS

Most tour companies offer trips to Fuerte Bulnes (CH$30,000) and Parque Nacional Pali Aike (CH$65,000). The following are reputable operators offering standard and specialized excursions.

Kayak Agua Fresca ☎ 09 9655 5073, ⊛ kayakaguafresca.com. Highly recommended outfit specializing in sea kayaking trips, including a half-day paddle along the Magellan Strait (CH$70,000) and a day-long outing around Cabo San Isidro (CH$230,000).

Solo Expediciones Nogueira 1255 ☎ 61 271 0219, ⊛ soloexpediciones.com. With their fast, covered speedboat, these guys whisk passengers off on half-day trips to Isla Magdalena (CH$70,000), stopping at the sea lion colony of Isla Marta. They sail from Laredo pier, rather than Punta Arenas itself, which means far less time on the water than with Comapa (see below), though their boat is more weather-dependent.

Turismo Comapa Navarro 1112 ☎ 61 220 0200, ⊛ comapa.com. This longstanding operator offers ferry excursions to Isla Magdalena (see page 392; CH$50,000) that involve 4hr on the boat in total. Land excursions to Fuerte Bulnes and Reserva Magallanes also on offer.

Whalesound Navarro 1191 ☎ 61 222 1935, ⊛ whalesound.com. Responsible operator offering humpback whale-watching trips in Coloane Marine Park (Jan–May & Dec), ranging from two to four days and overnighting on Carlos III island or Faro San Isidro (two-day, two-night, all-inclusive trip US$1500).

ACCOMMODATION

HOTELS AND B&BS

Dreams del Estrecho O'Higgins 1235 ☎ 61 220 4648, ⊛ mundodreams.com; map p.386. All chrome and glass, this tower would look more at home in Dubai than Punta Arenas, but *Dreams* is the city's most modern, luxurious business hotel, with a killer location overlooking the sea. Its rooms and suites come with king-size beds and every convenience you'd expect. Perks include swimming pool, spa, gym, swanky bar (see page 391) and casino. US$208

Hostal Labarca Chiloé 1581 ☎ 61 224 2979, ⊛ hostallabarca.cl; map p.386. A few blocks north of the plaza, a friendly, helpful hostess presides over a clutch of homely, frilly, comfortable doubles and twins (some with bathroom). Some rooms are rather compact, but you will be made to feel welcome. A little English spoken. CH$40,000

Hostal Ventisqueros O'Higgins 745 ☎ 61 232 4320, ⊛ contacto@hostalventisqueros.cl; map p.386. Run by a friendly local family, this guesthouse offers a clutch

9

of cosy, carpeted, centrally heated rooms, some with bathrooms. There's a good mix of international and Chilean guests, but sadly no common area for mingling. US$80

Hotel José Nogueira Bories 959 ⊙61 271 1000, ⓦhotelnogueira.com; map p.386. This historic hotel boasts a prime location on the plaza, inside the Palacio Sara Braun, former home to the city's most powerful family (see page 385). Here's your chance to reside in the style of nineteenth-century wool barons (with the added benefit of central heating and cable TV). Not all rooms are the same size. US$182

Hotel Rey Don Felipe Sanhueza 965 ⊙61 229 5000, ⓦhotelreydonfelipe.com; map p.386. The handsome mock-Tudor facade is a fitting introduction to a luxury hotel that gets all the important details right: all rooms are spacious, with classic decor and king-size or twin beds, rain showers in the modern bathrooms and a very good restaurant. A gym, sauna and jacuzzi are nice extras and service is very attentive. US$180

★ **Ilaia** Carrera Pinto 351 ⊙61 222 3592, ⓦilaia.cl; map p.386. This small boutique hotel places emphasis on the rejuvenation of body and spirit, with minimalist, individually decorated rooms with plenty of space, wood-panelled walls, light, bright touches and an absence of TVs. You can take part in hatha yoga, reiki and meditation; breakfast nourishment consists of home-made muesli, chapatis, fruit and yogurt. US$110

★ **Innata Patagonia** Magallanes 631 ⊙9 6279 4254, ⓦinnatapatagonia.com; map p.386. This brand new B&B is an absolute delight. It's within easy walking distance of most attractions, restaurants and bus stations, the helpful, bilingual staff can help you with onward travel and the whitewashed, spotless rooms are en suite and come with mini-kitchenettes, central heating and powerful showers. US$80

Patagonia B&B España 1048 ⊙61 222 7243, ⓦpatagoniabb.cl; map p.386. Set back from the main street and thus shielded from the noise, this is a beautiful, modern, hotel-like B&B; all twins and doubles are bright, spacious and en suite, with cable TV and bright splashes of colour. The CH$20,000 discount for solo travellers makes this a great bargain, but breakfast is lacklustre. CH$55,000

CABAÑAS AND APARTMENTS

★ **Apart Hotel Quillango** Av República 363 ⊙61 224 8316, ⓦahpuq.com; map p.386. Just a few blocks from the city centre, these spacious, stylish, modern one- and two-bedroom apartments are ideal for self-caterers. Expect plenty of light, fully equipped kitchens, colourful throws in otherwise austere surroundings, and helpful service from the owners. CH$60,600

Cabañas Shenu Quillota 658 ⊙61 237 1573, ⓦshenupatagonia.cl; map p.386. These four gorgeous, compact, luxurious stone-and-wood *cabañas* sit in a quiet residential neighbourhood several blocks from the plaza. All come with high-quality fittings, bathtubs and rain showers, a cosy double, a sofa-cum-double-bed and a folder full of info on the city. Cribs are provided for young children and there's even a little playground on the property. CH$72,000

HOSTELS

★ **Hospedaje Costanera** Correa 1221 ⊙61 224 0175, ⓦhospedaje-costanera.hostel.com; map p.386. In a quiet neighbourhood around a 20min walk from main attractions, this hostel gets rave reviews for its helpful owners and "home from home" vibe. Guest kitchen, luggage storage and a wealth of local info are some of the perks. Dorms CH$14,000, doubles CH$30,000

Hospedaje Magallanes Magallanes 570 ⊙61 222 8616, ⓦhospedaje-magallanes.com; map p.386. There are five simple doubles (one windowless, one en suite) and a six-bed dorm on offer at this family home, which you'll share with gregarious owner Marisol. Outdoor activities and tours of the surrounding area organized on request. Dorms CH$18,000, doubles CH$45,000

Hostal Independencia Independencia 374 ⊙61 222 7572, ⓦhostalindependencia.es.tl; map p.386. Friendly young owners allow camping cheek by jowl in the yard and can rent out equipment and organize tours of the area. Dorms and rooms are too small to swing a cat, but the warmth of the owners and generous breakfast (CH$1500) make up for it. Camping CH$4000, dorms CH$8000, doubles CH$15,000

EATING

CAFÉS AND CHEAP EATS

Amaranta Tea House Av Colón 822B ⊙61 237 1132, ⓦfacebook.com/amarantatearoom; map p.386. Amid flowery seats, colourful mandalas and pastel-coloured walls, this cute café serves eleven types of loose-leaf tea, tempting cakes and a great-value daily menu (CH$5900) that typically involves veggie lasagne or the like. Mon–Sat 10am–9pm.

Café Inmigrantes Quillota 559 ⊙61 222 2205, ⓦinmigrante.cl; map p.386. Located on a corner in the

quiet Croatian neighbourhood, this homely café is filled with knick-knacks and sports sepia prints of historic Punta Arenas. Come here for chunky sandwiches overstuffed with locally smoked salmon, meats and more, and don't leave without sampling the home-made cakes. Sandwiches from CH$6000. Mon–Sat 2.30–9pm.

Café Tapiz Roca 912 ⊙09 8730 3481, ⓦcafetapiz.cl; map p.386. This wood-shingled café has been drawing locals and travellers alike with its salads, sandwiches (try the smoked salmon with capers and cream cheese;

CH$5000), grilled cheese toasties, real coffee and excellent home-made cake selection. The fruit juices are not watered down and will give you a big vitamin boost. Mon–Sat 9am–9pm.

History Coffee Navarro 1065 ☎ 61 222 0000; map p.386. At this aptly named café you're surrounded by history (ye olde photos of Punta Arenas, antique coffee grinders) and coffee (beans embedded in your table). The brew is decent, there's a good selection of sweet and savoury crêpes, *churrascos* and burgers (CH$4000–5200), and the service is sweet and prompt. Mon–Sat 9am–9pm.

Kiosko Roca Roca at Navarro; map p.386. To get at this hole-in-the-wall's specialities – banana milk, *choripan* (mini grilled chorizo sandwich, CH$1500), *choripan con queso* (the same with cheese) – push through the locals propping up the bar. It's worth it. Mon–Sat 7am–7pm.

★ **Wake Up** Errázuriz 944 ☎ 61 237 1641; map p.386. A welcome addition to the Punta Arenas dining scene, *Wake Up* is the place to come for great coffee or an all-day breakfast. Choose from a stack of American pancakes, French toast, eggs Benedict and more. There's usually a lunchtime dish of the day, as well. Mains CH$4500–6000. Mon–Fri 7am–8pm, Sat 9am–4pm, Sun 10am–4pm.

RESTAURANTS

★ **La Cuisine** O'Higgins 1037 ☎ 61 222 8641; map p.386. With his good-value lunch menu (CH$6500), French chef Eric has earned himself a loyal local clientele. While the set menu is not bad, his cooking shines on dinnertime a la carte choices such as *boeuf bourguignon*, king crab lasagne and salmon in a red wine reduction,

served amid clichéd "French" decor – murals of the Eiffel Tower and ladies doing the cancan. Service is leisurely. Mains CH$7000–12,000. Mon–Sat 12.30–3pm & 7.30–11pm, Sun 1–3.30pm.

★ **La Marmita** Plaza Sampaio 678 ☎ 61 222 2056, ⓦ marmitamaga.cl; map p.386. Among the colourful rugs, weavings, collections of teapots and other eclectica you'll find some of the best flavours for miles around and attentive service from the young staff. The pisco (and berry) sours are the best in town, and you can feast on the likes of *ceviche*, vegetable risotto and hare casserole with black beer. The chef's signature dessert is the sublime chocolate pyramid with calafate berry mousse. Mains CH$8000–14,000. Mon–Sat 12.30–3pm & 7–11pm, Sun noon–midnight.

La Mesita Grande O'Higgins at Montt ☎ 61 224 4312, ⓦ mesitagrande.cl; map p.386. This Puerto Natales transplant has taken the city by storm, with its thin and crispy pizzas and lively, communal ambience, encouraged by the long wooden tables and benches. The *matavampiros* (mozzarella with roasted garlic) is excellent. Pizzas from CH$5300. Daily 12.30–11pm.

Parrilla Los Ganaderos O'Higgins 1166 ⓦ losganaderos.cl; map p.386. A resplendent grill with stake-roasted lamb is the focus of the room, with large platters of meat served by waiters dressed like Patagonian cowboys. The mixed grill for two (CH$23,000) and the Patagonian lamb are excellent; the steaks are merely good. Mains from CH$11,000. Daily noon–3pm & 8pm–midnight.

DRINKING

Sky Bar O'Higgins 1235 ☎ 61 292 2900; map p.386. Occupying a lofty spot inside the *Dreams del Estrecho* hotel (see page 389) this glass-and-chrome bar has a wide selection of spirits and cocktails, complemented by views of the Magellan Strait. Daily 7pm–3am.

La Taberna del Club de la Unión Plaza Muñoz Gamero 716 ☎ 61 224 1317; map p.386. In the basement of the Palacio Sara Braun (see page 385), you can nurse a whisky or cocktail at this atmospheric former gathering spot for the city's most powerful men, decorated with black-and-white maritime photographs. Daily 7pm–2am.

DIRECTORY

Hospital Hospital Regional, Angamos 180, between Señoret and Zenteno (☎ 61 224 4040).

Pharmacy There are several well-stocked pharmacies along Bories.

Puerto Hambre

Some 58km south of Arenas along the beautiful, shore-hugging road, you'll see a large **white obelisk** – a monument to the "navel of Chile": the country's geographical centre, which takes into account Chilean Antarctic territory right down to the South Pole. The road to the left of the obelisk leads 2km south to **Puerto Hambre** ("Port Famine"). One of the first two Spanish colonies on the Magellan Strait, Puerto Hambre is the site of the ambitious 1584 colony founded by Pedro Sarmiento de Gamboa – "Ciudad del Rey Don Felipe" – which ended in the starvation of most of its 337 colonists. Two remaining men were rescued by English privateer Thomas Cavendish, one of whom

9

HIKING TO CABO FROWARD

Ninety kilometres south of Punta Arenas lies **Cabo Froward**, the southernmost mainland point on the continent, marked with an enormous cross, erected in honour of the 1987 visit by Pope John Paul II. The cape can be reached via a starkly picturesque two-day wild hike on pristine beaches, through forest, scrambling among rocks and following weather-beaten cliffs by any reasonably fit individual. The **50km trail** is much better signposted than it used to be, but the trail is still not always obvious and this is a challenging hike that requires you to ford or even swim across several narrow but deep rivers along the way (having your gear in a waterproof canoe bag is best), depending on the tides. You can either join a guided expedition with Erratic Rock (see page 395) or with a hiking partner (it is not advisable to go alone), taking all necessary supplies with you, as well as a good map: *SIG Patagon* maps of the Cabo Froward trail are the most up-to-date. To get to the trailhead, arrange a lift or check the schedule for the thrice-weekly municipal bus from Punta Arenas that goes almost to the start of the trail along the road to the extreme right of the obelisk near Fuerte Bulnes (see below). There are very basic camping facilities en route, as well as a rustic *refugio* (bring your own bedding).

then died on board the ship. All that's left on a little promontory is a plaque, together with a palpable sense of desolation.

Fuerte Bulnes

62km south of Punta Arenas along the Y-621 and 4km from Puerto Hambre • Jan to mid-April, Nov & Dec daily 8.30am–8pm • CH$14,000
• Many tour companies run half-day tours from Punta Arenas to Fuerte Bulnes and Puerto Hambre

The road to the right of the obelisk near Puerto Hambre leads to the overpriced **Fuerte Bulnes**, a 1940s reconstruction of the first Chilean settlement in the area. Fuerte Bulnes was founded in September 1843 (and named after President Manuel Bulnes) by a boatload of sailors from Chiloé who arrived in the *Goleta Ancud*, captained by one John Williams. They came to pre-empt colonization from Europe, and only just made it: a few hours after they arrived, a French warship, the *Phaeton*, planted the tricolour on the shore. After Williams protested, the French moved off and annexed Tahiti in the Pacific instead. The location was less than ideal for a settlement owing to a lack of drinking water and pasture land, which prompted Williams to move the colony to the site of present-day Punta Arenas. A restored stockade surrounds a number of old cannons, sturdy log cabins, a gaol building, a lookout tower, the governor's house and a small wooden chapel.

Monumento Natural Isla Magdalena

35km northeast of Punta Arenas • Tours with Solo Expediciones (see page 389) or Turismo Comapa (see page 389)

One of the largest penguin colonies in southern Chile, **Monumento Natural Isla Magdalena** is home to around 100,000 Magellanic **penguins**. The small island, just one square kilometre in size and topped by a pretty red lighthouse, is two hours away from Punta Arenas by boat. The penguins dig their burrows under the tufts of grass covering the 15m-high cliffs.

In October each year, the birds migrate back here and find their mate – they're monogamous and remain faithful to one partner all their lives. The female lays two eggs in the nest and when the chicks hatch, in November, both parents nurture the young, one adult remaining with the chick, the other going fishing. In late January, the chicks shed their baby feathers and get ready for their first trips into the ocean. By the end of March the penguins have returned to sea again. You can get very **close to the birds** as they half hide in the waving grass and lounge by the sea. Both Solo Expediciones and Turismo Comapa (CH$50,000/person) give you an hour on the island; Solo Expediciones offers an additional stop at the Isla Marta **sea lion colony**.

Parque Nacional Pali Aike

146km north of Punta Arenas • Jan–April & Oct–Dec daily 9am–6pm • CH$3000 • No public transport; several companies run full-day
tours from Punta Arenas (CH$35,000/person)

Eleven kilometres beyond the turning for the Punta Arenas ferry (see page 389) is
the small town of **Punta Delgada**, from where a good gravel road heads 28km north
to Chilean Patagonia's seldom-visited **Parque Nacional Pali Aike**. The park's entrance
looms up out of the barren rolling plains, green roof first; the sight explains its
Tehuelche name, meaning "desolate place of bad spirits". There's a strange magic to the
otherworldly volcanic formations that dot the heath and the small lagoons ringed by
white tidemarks; this seemingly barren place is home to a surprising amount of smaller
wildlife – from well-camouflaged lizards to owls.

Cueva Pali Aike and around

From the *guardería*, the main gravel road runs north to the remote, picturesque **Laguna
Ana**, where you can occasionally spot flamingos, and the start of the park's longest
hike: a 9km (2hr 45min) **walk** across flat, windy, exposed terrain to **Cueva Pali Aike**,
a 17m-deep cave in a tall ridge of congealed lava. It was excavated by the famous
archeologist Junius Bird in 1937, and was found to contain evidence of prehistoric
habitation, including bones of a *milodón* and the *Onohippidium*, an extinct American
horse, dating from nine thousand years ago.

An 8km gravel road branches off from the main one, heading east to the cave via the
starting point for the park's other two hikes: a 1700m (30min) wander through the
largely flat old lava beds to the volcano rim of the **Crater Morada del Diablo** ("Dwelling
of the devil"), followed by a 2000m (45min) ascent through the fields of jagged
volcanic rock to the **Pozos del Diablo** ("devil's wells") – dozens and dozens of somewhat
sinister craters.

Puerto Natales and around

Chilean Patagonia's second-largest settlement, **PUERTO NATALES**, 250km north of
Punta Arenas, is the gateway to the **Parque Nacional Torres del Paine**. In spite of its
popularity, Natales retains a pioneer feel, its history reflected in its simple wood-and-
tin buildings. It makes a useful base for visiting the **Cueva del Milodón**, the glaciers of
the **Parque Nacional Bernardo O'Higgins** and, across the border in Argentina, **Parque
Nacional Los Glaciares**. Natales is also a good transport hub, home to the terminal of
the **Navimag** ferry from Puerto Montt in the Lake District, and linked to Punta Arenas,
Torres del Paine and Argentina by bus.

Puerto Natales sits on the wind-whipped **Seno Ultima Esperanza** ("Last Hope
Sound"), fringed by tall peaks, with the powerful wind stirring up waves on the
turquoise channel where the remnants of a wooden pier bedecked with cormorants
stretch into the distance. The channel's name comes from the 1557 explorer, Juan
Ladrilleros, who came upon it when he was at the end of his tether while searching for
the western entrance to the Magellan Strait. He found the strait, but almost all his crew
died in the attempt.

Museo Histórico Municipal

Bulnes 285 • Mon–Fri 8am–7pm, Sat 10am–1pm & 3–7pm • CH$1000

A couple of blocks west of the Plaza de Armas is the small **Museo Histórico Municipal**,
with attractively laid-out bilingual exhibits on the region's European settlement, natural
history, the Milodón's cave and the indigenous Aonikenk and Kawéskar tribes who
dwelled in this inhospitable land, illustrated with black-and-white photos. Besides
displays on Aonikenk funeral customs and photos of present-day indigenous people

PUERTO NATALES

▲ 🛫 ▮1(1.5km), ❶(6km), ▮2(6km), Estancia Travel (10km), Cueva de Milodon (21km), Torres del Paine (112km) & Punta Arenas (250km)

■ **DRINKING**

Base Camp	3
Cervecería Baguales	1
Last Hope Distillery	2

■ **ACCOMMODATION**

Erratic Rock	13
Hostal America	10
Hostal Morocha	12
Hostel Camino de Santiago	14
Hotel If Patagonia	4
Hotel Vendaval	6
Kau Patagonia	3
El Muelle Hotel Boutique	8
NOI Indigo	5
Remota	1
The Singular Patagonia	2
Treehouse Patagonia	11
Wild	7
Yagan House	9

● **EATING**

Afrigonia	7
Angelica's Boutique Gourmet	9
El Asadór Patagónico	5
Cangrejo Rojo	10
Forestera	4
Lenga	3
El Living	2
La Mesita Grande	6
The Singular	1
Vinnhaus	8

living in remote Puerto Edén, a highlight is the room dedicated to the region's first settler, a rather fierce-looking nineteenth-century German, Herman Eberhard; look out for his ingenious collapsible boat that turns into a suitcase.

ARRIVAL AND DEPARTURE PUERTO NATALES

By plane There's a tiny airport just north of Puerto Natales. In high season, LATAM (ⓦlatam.com) serves Santiago, while DAP (ⓦdapairline.com) flies to El Calafate (CH$168,00).

Destinations El Calafate (Jan–April, Nov & Dec Thurs & Sun; 35min); Santiago (4 weekly, 3hr 30min).

By bus The bus terminal, Rodoviario Puerto Natales (Av España 1455) is a 10–15min walk east from the centre; taxis cost CH$1500 within town. Some bus companies have offices in town; while you can buy tickets at the offices, buses depart from the main terminal. Services to El Calafate and Torres del Paine only operate Jan–

April & Oct–Dec. Buses Becker (ⓣ09 8554 7774) runs to Coyhaique; Buses Cootra (ⓣ61 241 2785) runs to El Calafate; Buses Fernández, Ramírez 399 (ⓣ61 241 1111, ⓦbusesfernandez.com) and Buses Magallanes (ⓣ61 241 0101) serve Punta Arenas; Buses Pacheco, Ramírez 224 (ⓣ61 241 4800, ⓦbusespacheco.com) runs to Punta Arenas, El Calafate, Ushuaia and Río Gallegos; Bus Sur, Baquedano 668 (ⓣ61 241 0784, ⓦbussur.com) runs to Punta Arenas, Río Gallegos and Ushuaia; Turismo Zaahj, Prat 236 (ⓣ61 241 1355, ⓦwww.turismozaahj.co.cl), Buses JB, Prat 258 (ⓣ61 241 0242, ⓦbusesjb.cl) and Buses Gómez, Prat 234 (ⓣ61 241 1971, ⓦbusesgomez.

com) run to Torres del Paine, while Turismo Zaahj also serves El Calafate.

Destinations El Calafate, Argentina (2–3 daily; 5hr); Coyhaique (Wed noon; 17hr); Parque Nacional Torres del Paine (numerous daily; 2hr 30min); Punta Arenas (hourly; 3hr); Río Gallegos, Argentina (3 weekly; 5hr); Ushuaia, Argentina (2 daily; 12hr).

By ferry The Navimag ferry terminal is on Pedro Montt 308, four blocks west and one block south of the Plaza de Armas (●61 241 1421, ⓦnavimag.c1). Transbordadora Austral Broom (●61 272 8100, ⓦtabsa.c1) at Montt 605 connects Caleta Tortel and Puerto Yungay on the Carretera Austral to Natales via Puerto Edén.

Destinations Caleta Tortel (Thurs 5am; 41hr); Puerto Montt (summer every Tues, less often at other times of year; around 70hr).

GETTING AROUND AND INFORMATION

Car rental Europcar, Manuel Bulnes 100 (●61 241 4475, ⓦwww.europcar.cl) and Hertz, Blanco Encalada 353 (●61 241 4519, ⓦhertz.cl).

Tourist office Pedro Montt s/n (Mon–Fri 8.30am–8pm, Sat & Sun 10am–6pm; ●61 241 2125). The small office by the water has basic maps of town and brochures on attractions.

Torres del Paine National Park information Visitors heading to the National Park (see page 398) shouldn't miss the daily 11am and 3pm talks at the Erratic Rock Equipment Rental Center, Baquedano 955, where experienced local trekkers will give you the lowdown on what to expect and how best to tackle the park.

Camping equipment rental Try Erratic Rock Equipment Rental Center.

ACTIVITIES AND TOURS

Baqueano Zamora Baquedano 534 ●61 261 3531, ⓦbaqueanozamora.cl. Horse-trekking in Torres del Paine (CH$35,000/55,000 for half-/full-day) arranged by this longstanding operator. It operates out of the Estancia Tercera Barranca near Torres del Paine.

BigFoot Montt 161 ●61 241 4611, ⓦbigfootpatagonia.com. Operating out of *Refugio/ Campamento Grey* in Torres del Paine (see page 406), and with an office in *Kau Patagonia* (see page 396), this longstanding operator offers twice-daily (11am & 4pm) 5hr ice hikes on Glaciar Grey (CH$105,000) as well as kayaking (CH$66,000) amid the house-sized chunks of ice. Book in advance to get a discounted boat trip across Lago Grey/ice trekking combo (CH$130,000).

Erratic Rock Baquedano 719 ⓦerraticrock.com. Experienced operator with an excellent reputation, running multi-day trekking trips to Cabo Froward (see page 392) and in Torres del Paine, as well as rock climbing ascents of Torre Norte and dog sledding jaunts in Ushuaia.

Estancia Travel Puerto Bories 13B ●61 241 2221, ⓦestanciatravel.com. Highly recommended horseriding trips, from half-day rides to the Cueva de Milodón to twelve-day *estancia* expeditions by an English/Chilean outfit.

Fantástico Sur Esmeralda 661 ●61 261 4184, ⓦfantasticosur.com. Makes bookings for the Torre Norte, Torre Central, Chileno and Los Cuernos *refugios* and campsites, as well as *Campamento Serón* and *Camping Francés*.

Turismo 21 de Mayo Eberhard 560 ●61 261 4420, ⓦturismo21demayo.cl. Sailing excursions to see the Balmaceda and Serrano glaciers in Parque Nacional Bernardo O'Higgins on their private cutter, *21 de Mayo* (CH$90,000), and combo sailing day trips that include a tour of Torres del Paine. Multi-day adventures include yachting, horseriding and a stay at the *Estancia Perrales*.

Tutravesia Barros Arana 176 ●61 269 1196, ⓦtutravesia.com. Established kayaking outfit offering multi-day trips for beginner and advanced kayakers alike – from a day-long paddle Río Grey and three-day trips to Glaciar Tundall to the spectacular four-day Ruta de Hielo, which ends in a lake filled with icebergs.

Vertice Patagonia Bulnes 100 ●61 241 2742, ⓦverticepatagonia.com. Bookings for Paine Grande, Lago Grey, Los Perros and Dickson *refugios*, as well as campsites in Torres del Paine.

ACCOMMODATION

HOTELS

Hotel If Patagonia Magallanes 73 ●61 241 0312, ⓦhotelifpatagonia.com; map p.394. The light-filled atrium of this excellent mid-range hotel puts you in mind of an M.C. Escher work, leading up as it does to a rooftop terrace with superb views of Last Hope Sound. The rooms are bright (though with little luggage space), characterized by warm touches of woven art, and the superior doubles have jacuzzis. <u>US$150</u>

★ **Hotel Vendaval** Eberhard 333 ●61 269 1760, ⓦhotelvendaval.com; map p.394. Inside this eye-catching red metal structure, there are 23 bright rooms with ultra-comfortable king-size beds and contemporary bathrooms. There are great views of Natales' tin roofs from the roof terrace, and the small bar

9

serves beer, wine and cocktails. Super-central and great value. US$255

El Muelle Hotel Boutique Bulnes 37 ☎ 61 241 4995, ⊛ elmuellehotel.com; map p.394. This intimate boutique hotel consists of just seven bright, centrally heated rooms with a nautical theme, just a block away from the water. The interior is decorated with scenic photos of the region. Closed June & July. US$150

NOI Indigo Ladrilleros 105 ☎ 61 274 0670, ⊛ noihotels.com; map p.394. With 29 rooms spread across five floors, and a full spa for guests and non-guests alike, the *Indigo* is the plushest option in central Natales. Its sloping floors, whitewashed walls and sliding wooden shutters are Navimag-inspired, and the compact rooms resemble cabins. Good breakfast buffet. US$239

★ **Remota** Ruta 9 Norte, Km 1.5 ☎ 2 2387 1500, ⊛ remotahotel.com; map p.394. Drawing on the area's *estancia* heritage, this award-winning piece of architecture combines the comfort of the king-size beds and rain showers with deliberate sparseness of decor – a gaucho's woollen poncho gracing a wall instead of a TV. The two grass-roofed corridors are an aesthetic representation of a sheep yard and huge windows let in the wilderness beyond. The rooms and the glass-walled "beach" appeal to visitors seeking silent contemplation. The excellent restaurant specializes in international-Patagonian fusion, and there is an ample breakfast buffet. Full board available. US$370

★ **The Singular Patagonia** Puerto Bories ☎ 61 272 2030, ⊛ thesingular.com; map p.394. This former meatpacking factory turned five-star-hotel is unique in concept and design. Lovingly restored by the descendents of two pioneer families, it has kept its original machinery in vast, stripped-down brick halls. A funicular whisks you to the rooms, with immense floor-to-ceiling windows gazing out over Last Hope Sound. Besides the tranquil spa and indoor/outdoor pool, the restaurant is one of the best in Patagonia. All-inclusive packages are available, with a choice of 25 excursions. US$390

B&B AND GUESTHOUSES

Hostal America Miraflores 1045 ☎ 09 7897 5567; map p.394. This new guesthouse may be a bit impersonal, but if you're looking for a spotless, centrally heated, en-suite room with good beds, then your search is over. The breakfast is a Chilean affair. CH$50,000

Hostal Morocha Barros Luco 688 ☎ 09 9708 1250, ⊛ hostalmorocha.com; map p.394. With just five individually decorated rooms (expect James Dean quotes!), a most satisfying breakfast spread and welcoming, knowledgeable owners (Pablo is a porter in Torres del Paine), this is an excellent choice for visitors who want some privacy without breaking the budget. Doubles have their own bathrooms; the twin and the singles share facilities. CH$40,000

Kau Patagonia Montt 161 ☎ 61 241 4611, ⊛ kaulodge. com; map p.394. The sparse decor and design of these luxurious rooms feels appropriate in Patagonia, with plenty of space, light and views of the Sound from all windows, plus a colour scheme of creams and blues and a single wooden wall reminiscent of forests. Four of the nine rooms have generous bunk beds (US$100). The *Coffee Maker* café downstairs serves good espressos and home-made cakes. US$115

HOSTELS

★ **Erratic Rock** Baquedano 719 ⊛ erraticrock.com; map p.394. Owner Bill, self-styled "burnt-out hippie from Oregon" got it exactly right: the atmosphere is laidback, hostel cat Clyde wanders about, dorms and rooms are snug and there's a real sense of camaraderie between the trekkers who bunk here. The early morning breakfast – among the best in town – sustains hikers heading to Torres del Paine. Onward transport and tours can also be booked (see page 395). Walk-ins only. Dorms CH$12,000, doubles CH$30,000

Hostel Camino de Santiago Ramírez 952 ☎ 09 9304 1094, ⊛ hostalcaminodesantiago.cl; map p.394. One of the better additions to Natales' hostel scene, run by a Spanish/Chilean couple. There's a guest café and bar downstairs and mountain bikes for rent. The quality bunks and beds in the four-bed dorms and bright twins and doubles make for a good night's rest. Dorms CH$21,000, doubles CH$60,000

★ **Treehouse Patagonia** Chorillos 653 ☎ 09 8417 4514; map p.394. Beautifully designed by its welcoming architect owner, Pancho, this intimate hostel has room for just ten guests. Choose between the snug four-bed dorm with large lockers or one of the three gorgeous en suites – a double and two twins – with high ceilings and woollen hangings. Guests gather in the combined kitchen/living area and the garden is ready for barbecues. Closed June–Aug. Dorm CH$14,000, doubles CH$40,000

Wild Bulnes 555 ☎ 09 7715 2423, ⊛ wildhostel.com; map p.394. There's a lot to like about *Wild*, from its name spelled across a wall in tree branches and the eye-catching white, crimson and lime green decor to a plethora of amenities including an on-site bar and café. Bed down in one of the upstairs dorms or choose a garden double (or deluxe suite with kitchen). Equipment rental shop attached. Dorms CH$14,000, doubles CH$45,000

Yagan House O'Higgins 584 ☎ 61 241 4137, ⊛ yaganhouse.cl; map p.394. Excellent beds with down duvets, warm red-and-cream decor, ecofriendly practices and a guest lounge with a roaring fire distinguish this intimate hostel. The owners throw an occasional Patagonian barbecue and extras include gear rental, a small bar and laundry service. Dorms CH$15,000, doubles CH$45,000

EATING

CAFÉS AND CHEAP EATS

Angelica's Boutique Gourmet Bulnes 501; map p.394. This bakery-cum-coffee shop serves good coffee, gooey brownies, home-made cheesecake and inexpensive daily specials, such as calzones, Greek salad and pizza with goat's cheese (from CH$6500). Also sells tiny wine bottles – ideal for taking to Torres del Paine. Daily 9am–4pm & 5–10pm.

Forestera Baquedano 699 ☎09 8295 2036; map p.394. This gourmet burger joint grills a devil's dozen of beef, lamb, chicken and vegetarian burgers (CH$7000) to your specifications. The Forestera – with caramelized onions and bacon – is a classic, while "del Puerto" comes topped with sheep's cheese and spinach. Regional Coirón and Fernando de Magallanes microbrews are a good acoompaniment. Mon–Sat 1–3pm & 7.30–11pm.

★ **El Living** Arturo Prat 156 ☎61 241 1140, ⓦel-living.com; map p.394. An excellent vegetarian restaurant and lounge café, with chillout music in the background and comfortable sofas to sink into. Treats include three cheese and walnut ravioli, borscht, hummus and chunky sandwiches, such as avocado, camembert and olive. Their cakes and home-made honeycomb ice cream are equally good. Mains CH$5600–8200. Jan–March & Dec Mon–Sat 11am–10pm.

La Mesita Grande Eberhard 508 ☎61 241 1571, ⓦmesitagrande.cl; map p.394. Hordes of hungry hikers stage a daily invasion of the best pizzeria in Patagonia, drawn by the generous portions of superb thin-crust pizzas (from CH$6800), home-made pasta and interesting desserts (including sweet pizza with *dulce de leche*). The two long wooden tables make for a communal dining experience and encourage mingling. Daily 12.30–3.30pm & 7–11.30pm.

Vinnhaus Bulnes 499 ☎09 8269 2510, ⓦvinnhaus. com; map p.394. Attached to the eponymous hostel, this cosy café and bar has become a traveller's haunt, whether you're after coffee, cake and quiche, craft beer from a regional brewery, or glass of wine. Daily 11am–10.30pm.

RESTAURANTS

★ **Afrigonia** Magallanes 247 ☎61 241 2877; map p.394. One of Natales's most imaginative restaurants serves delectable African/Patagonian fusion dishes. Standouts include *ceviche* with mango, melt-off-the-bone Patagonian lamb and spicy seafood curry with *wali* (rice with almonds and raisins). Be prepared for a leisurely dinner. Mains CH$10,000–14,000. Daily 1–10.30pm.

El Asador Patagónico Arturo Prat 158 ☎61 241 3553; map p.394. The signature *asado Patagónico* – lamb roasting on a spit in the barbecue pit by the window – acts as a magnet for keen carnivores. The expertly grilled steaks at this established *parrilla* are not quite as good, but portions are ample. Mains from CH$14,000. Daily 12.30–3pm & 7.30–11pm.

Cangrejo Rojo Santiago Bueras 782 ☎61 241 2436; map p.394. Strategically strewn with fishing nets, buoys, snorkelling masks and other nautical paraphernalia, this cute restaurant specializes in fish and seafood. Among the likes of *ceviche* and grilled conger eel with squid-ink rice you'll find more unusual items, such as grilled sheep's testicles. Mains from CH$8000. Mon–Sat 1–11pm.

★ **Lenga** Bories 221 ☎61 269 1187; map p.394. "Cook free or die" is the motto at this creative, intimate restaurant with a seasonally changing menu that makes the most of Patagonian ingredients. Presentation is striking, flavours are faultless, and you can expect the likes of scallop *ceviche* with edible flowers, slow-cooked lamb shanks and chocolate brownie with calafate berry sorbet. Reservations recommended. Mains CH$10,000–14,000. Tues–Sun 6–11pm.

★ **The Singular Patagonia** Km 5.5 Norte ☎61 272 2030, ⓦthesingular.com; map p.394. The best restaurant in the region is reached via a funicular and a short walk through stark former abattoir warehouses. Inside, it's all leather and chrome – gentlemen's club meets bistro. Chef Pasqualetto combines French techniques with local ingredients to create such dishes as king crab pie, sweetbreads with apple, *ceviche* and terrific salads, plus varied vegetarian dishes. Mains CH$10,000–14,000. Reserve. Daily 1–2.30pm & 7.30–10.30pm.

DRINKING

Base Camp Baquedano 731 ⓦerraticrock.com; map p.394. Next door to the most popular hostel in town, this former brothel turned lively pub is usually full to the brim with pre- and post-Torres hikers, contentedly drinking local brews and eating thin and crispy pizzas. Expect occasional performances by local bands, themed nights and spontaneous barbecues. Daily 6pm–1am.

Cervecería Baguales Bories 430 ☎61 241 1920, ⓦcervezabaguales.cl; map p.394. If the one thing that would make your Patagonian hiking experience complete

is returning to a cosy microbrewery serving ample platters of fiery buffalo wings, quesadillas, tacos and other Tex-Mexicana, accompanied by a home-made light, dark and amber brew, then you're in luck: look no further than this Californian/Chilean pub. Beers CH$2200; mains CH$6000–12,500. Mon–Sat 1pm–2.30am.

★ **Last Hope Distillery** Esmeralda 882 ☎09 7201 8585; map p.394. When Aussies Matt and Kiera couldn't find an après-trek beverage they wanted, they opened a gin and whisky distillery of their own. Choose from

9

THE STRANGE CASE OF THE GIANT SLOTH SKIN

In 1900 an **expedition** sponsored by London's *Daily Express* arrived to investigate the rumours of a **giant sloth** in a cave near Puerto Natales, but no live creatures were found. The skin, it turned out, was so well preserved because it had been deep-frozen by the frigid Patagonian climate. Shortly after the 1900 expedition an unscrupulous gold prospector dynamited the cave's floor, uncovering and then selling the remaining skin and bones. Two pieces made their way to Britain: one to the Natural History Museum in London, and the other to Charley Milward's family, the very same which was to fire the imagination of a young **Bruce Chatwin**.

country-specific whisky flights – their whisky selection is unparalleled in Natales – or original cocktails including the signature G&T made with their own calafate berry gin.

Snacks span the globe: *Last Hope* is the sort of place you find yourself lingering in until the wee hours. The distillery itself offers afternoon tours. Wed–Sun 5pm–2am.

Cueva del Milodón

21km north of Puerto Natales • Daily 8am–8pm • CH$5000

The vast **Cueva del Milodón** is an impressive 30m high, 80m wide and 200m deep. In 1895, the German settler Herman Eberhard, who owned the land bordering the cave, discovered a large piece of skin from an unidentifiable animal, which was eventually traced to a giant sloth called a milodón. This creature was thought to be long extinct, but the excavated skin looked so fresh that rumours began to circulate that it might still be alive. An expedition was mounted (see above), though no live sloth was ever found. Along the short boardwalk leading to the cave there are displays on Patagonia's (mostly) extinct prehistoric animals, such as the sabre-tooth tiger, the panther and the ancestor of a horse. Inside the cave, a small display features part of a young milodón femur and some skin and hair, as well as a life-size replica.

The Balmaceda and Serrano glaciers

136km northwest of Puerto Natales

Northwest of the Cueva del Milodón, the Seno Ultima Esperanza continues on for about 100km until it meets the Río Serrano, which, after 36km, arrives at the **Balmaceda** and **Serrano glaciers**. A boat trip here (see page 395) is one of the most beautiful in the entire area. It takes seven hours and you pass a colony of cormorants and a slippery mass of sea lions. The glaciers themselves make an impressive sight, especially when a chunk of ice the size of a small building breaks off and crashes into the water. They form the southern tip of **Parque Nacional Bernardo O'Higgins**, the largest and least-visited national park in all Chile. The east of the park is almost entirely made up of the Campo de Hielo Sur (the Southern Ice-Field); the west comprises fjords, islands and untouched forest.

Parque Nacional Torres del Paine

102km north of Puerto Natales via Ruta 9 • CH$21,000 • ⓦ torresdelpaine.com

Nothing really prepares you for your first sight of **Parque Nacional Torres Del Paine**. The **Paine Massif**, the unforgettable centrepiece of the park, appears beyond the turquoise lakes long before you get close to it. The finest views of the massif are from the south bank of Lago Nordenskjöld, whose waters act as a great reflecting mirror. If driving through the park, take the southern entrance to constantly have the best views in front of you.

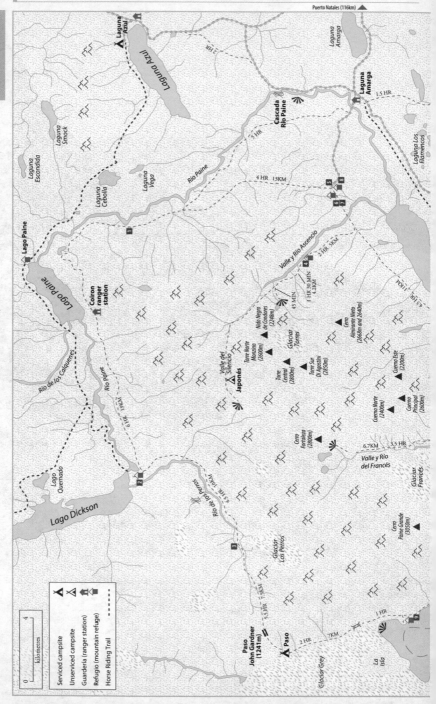

Puerto Natales (116km)

Laguna Azul

Lago Azul

Laguna Amarga

Laguna Amarga

1.5 HR

Cascada Río Paine

2 HR

Laguna Smock

Laguna Escondida

Laguna Cebolla

Laguna Vega

Río Paine

Laguna Los Flamencos

4 HR 13KM

Lago Paine

Valle y Río Ascencio

Colrón ranger station

2 HR 5KM

1 HR 30 MIN 4.2KM

45 MIN

4.5 HR 11KM

Nido Negro de Cóndores (1248m)

Cerro Almirante Nieto (2660m and 2640m)

Lago Paine

Río de los Calafquenes

Río Paine

Valle del Silencio

Japonés

Torre Norte Monzino (2600m)

Glaciar Torres

Torre Central (2800m)

Torre Sur DI'Agostini (2850m)

Cuerno Este (2200m)

Cuerno Norte (2400m)

Cuerno Principal (2600m)

Cerro Fortaleza (2800m)

6.7KM 3.5 HR

Valle y Río del Francés

Lago Quemado

Río de los Perros

4.5 HR 10KM

Glaciar Francés

Lago Dickson

Glaciar Los Perros

Cerro Paine Grande (3050m)

Paso John Gardner (1241m)

Paso

5.5 HR 7.5 KM

2 HR 7KM

1 HR

Glaciar Grey

La Isla

kilometres
0   4

Serviced campsite
Unserviced campsite
Guardería (ranger station)
Refugio (mountain refuge)
Horse Riding Trail

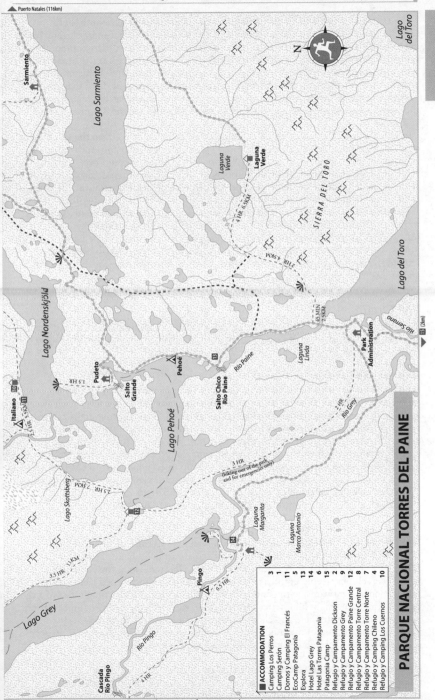

▲ Puerto Natales (116km)

Lago del Toro

Lago Sarmiento

Sarmiento

Laguna Verde
Laguna Verde

SIERRA DEL TORO

Lago del Toro

4 HR 6.5KM

2 HR 4.5KM

45 MIN 2.5KM

Park Administration

Río Serrano

13 (2km) ▶

Lago Nordenskjöld

Pudeto
Salto Grande

Pehoé
Salto Chico Río Paine

Río Paine

Laguna Linda

2 HR
Río Grey

1.5 HR

Italiano
2.5 HR 5.5KM

Lago Pehoé

Lago Skottsberg
2.5 HR 7.8KM

3 HR
(hiking out of the park
and for emergencies only)

Laguna Margarita

Laguna Marco Antonio

12

3.5 HR 11KM

Pingo
0.5 HR

14

Lago Grey

Río Pingo

4 HR

Cascada
Río Pingo

▲ Campamento Zapata (1km), Glacier Pingo (3km) & Mirador Zapata (2km)

PARQUE NACIONAL TORRES DEL PAINE

■ ACCOMMODATION

Camping Los Perros	3
Camping Serón	1
Domos y Camping El Francés	11
EcoCamp Patagonia	5
Explora	13
Hotel Lago Grey	14
Hotel Las Torres Patagonia	6
Patagonia Camp	15
Refugio y Campamento Dickson	2
Refugio y Campamento Grey	9
Refugio y Campamento Paine Grande	12
Refugio y Campamento Torre Central	8
Refugio y Campamento Torre Norte	7
Refugio y Camping Chileno	4
Refugio y Camping Los Cuernos	10

9

The centrepiece is made up of the twin peaks of **Cerro Monte Almirante Nieto** (2668m and 2640m). On the northern side are the soaring, unnaturally elegant **Torres del Paine** ("Paine Towers"), the icon of the park, and further west the sculpted, dark-capped **Cuernos del Paine** ("Paine Horns"). To the west of the park is the broad ice river of **Glaciar Grey**, and on the plains at the mountains' feet, large herds of **guanacos** and the odd *ñandú* (rhea) still run wild; you're more likely to spot these than the park's more elusive fauna: pumas and the rare *huemul* deer, the latter present largely in the western part of the park and the former more plentiful around Lagunas Sarmiento and Amarga.

In January and February the park is crammed with holidaymakers, so the **less busy months** to visit are October, November and December or March and April. Although in **winter** (June–Sept) temperatures can fall to -10°C (14°F) or even lower, freezing lakes and icing over trails, the small numbers of visitors, lack of wind and often clear visibility can also make this another good time to come – just wrap up warmly and note that in winter visitors are only allowed in the park with a certified guide.

This may not be the place to taste true wilderness, but there are still plenty of places to lose the crowds. The most popular hike is the **"W"**, so-called because the route you follow looks like a "W", up three valleys, taking you to the "stars" of the park – Las Torres, Valle del Francés and Glaciar Grey – while the "**Circuit**", which leads you around the back of the park, is less peopled. Allow at least five days for the "Circuit" and at least four for the "W".

The Circuit

The only way visitors are allowed to hike the "**Circuit**" is anticlockwise; it means that you'll have excellent views of Glaciar Grey in front of you when you come to tackle the most challenging part of the hike – the Paso John Gardner.

Hostería Las Torres to Las Torres

From **Hostería Las Torres**, go southwest along the foot of the massif. Just after a bridge, the track veers to the north up Valle Ascencio along a scree-strewn trail; after a relatively steep 5.5km, two-hour climb it's possible to spend the first night at the *Refugio y Camping Chileno*. From *Chileno*, the 3.7 km trail continues up and down exposed inclines (beware of sudden gusts of wind), and then through *lenga* brush, crossing a stream, to the now-closed *Campamento Torres*; allow ninety minutes. From here it's a knee-popping 600m, 45-minute climb up uneven boulders to **Las Torres**. If the weather is clear you are treated to a stunning postcard view across Laguna Torres up to the three strange statuesque towers that give the park its name – **Torre Norte Monzino** (2600m), **Torre Central** (2800m) and **Torre Sur Di Agostini** (2850m).

Hostería Las Torres to Refugio Lago Dickson

From **Hostería Las Torres**, *Campamento Serón* is an easy 13km, four-hour walk northwards up and down gentle inclines and across vast daisy fields. From *Campamento Serón*, it's a six-hour hike to *Refugio Dickson*, with a flat trail along the Río Paine, which then climbs steeply uphill as you pass a small horseshoe-shaped lagoon. The trail meanders westwards, with gentle descents and ascents and sweeping views of Lago Paine to the right. Eight kilometres into the hike, you reach the Coirón ranger station; all hikers must register here and show their reservations for Dickson, Los Perros and Paso. The final section of the trail descends steeply to *Refugio Lago Dickson* in its scenic setting at the southern end of iceberg-flecked Lago Dickson.

Refugio Lago Dickson to Campamento Los Perros

Campamento Los Perros lies an 11km, four or five-hour hike from **Refugio Lago Dickson** southwest along a largely uphill trail that snakes through dense forest for most of the way. You cross two bridges over large glacial streams and pass a waterfall, before emerging at an exposed, rocky section, which treats you to a fabulous view of Glaciar Los Perros, before continuing to a patch of forest which partially shields the campsite.

Across Paso John Gardner

The weather has to be in your favour before you start on a three to five-hour climb to the top of **Paso John Gardner** (1241m). It is too dangerous to cross the pass in gale-force wind. From *Los Perros* you cross a stream using a wooden bridge, followed by an hour's muddy trudge. Above the tree line, it's a straightforward uphill slog along the rock-strewn slope before reaching the exposed pass. The reward for all this is the sudden, staggering view over the icy pinnacles of **Glaciar Grey**, more than 7km wide at its largest point, and the vast immaculate expanse of the **Campo del Hielo Sur** – over ten thousand square kilometres of ice cap and one of the largest icefields outside the polar regions.

On the other side of the pass steps descend steeply into *lenga* forest. It takes a couple of hours to reach the small, basic *Campamento Paso*, 7.5km from Los Perros.

Campamento Paso to Refugio y Camping Lago Grey

It takes three hours or so to descend through lenga forest the 7km from **Campamento Paso** to **Refugio y Camping Lago Grey**. In two places, there are bridges to cross. The campsite is beautifully sited on the beach at the foot of Glaciar Grey, while the *refugio* building is just uphill from it. It's possible to catch a boat to *Hotel Lago Grey* in summer; the boat sails alongside the glacier before making its way along the length of the lake (CH$65,000 one way) four times daily in high season. If you're staying overnight at *Refugio y Camping Lago Grey*, it's also possible to go ice hiking on the glacier or kayaking around it with Bigfoot (see page 395).

Refugio y Camping Lago Grey to Paine Grande Lodge

From **Refugio y Camping Lago Grey**, the 11km trail runs alongside the lake, before the largely exposed trail almost doubles back on itself, climbing steeply, after which it runs mostly uphill through the **Quebrada de los Vientos** ("Windy Gorge"), with several viewpoints from which to admire the lake. It then ducks into the burnt remains of *ñire* glen, passing the small Laguna Los Patos on the right-hand side, and descends to the **Paine Grande Lodge** and campsite, situated on the bank of the stunning glacial Lago Pehoé, around four hours later. From here you can continue along the "Circuit"; this is also the ideal place to start the "W".

The "W"

Like the "Circuit", it's best to follow the "**W**" anti-clockwise, leaving the steepest hike to Las Torres until last, by which time you will have consumed most of your supplies. The first leg of the "W" is the hike there and back from *Paine Grande Lodge* to Glaciar Grey (see above).

Paine Grande Lodge to Valle del Francés

From **Paine Grande Lodge**, take the signposted 7.5km trail that runs along the southern side of the Paine Grande massif along Lago Skottsberg, and a couple of smaller lagoons on the right-hand side, before crossing a suspension bridge across Río Francés to *Campamento Italiano*; it's a trip of around two and a half hours. Leave your gear here before heading north up the **Valle del Francés**.

It's a rather steep 5km, three or four-hour hike with great views of the **Glaciar Francés** up to the viewpoint from which you can admire **Paine Grande**, the massif's highest peak at 3050m, to your west, and the **Cuernos del Paine**, a set of incredibly carved towers capped with dark rock peaks, guarding the entrance to the valley to the southeast.

9

BEYOND THE W: TORRES DEL PAINE ALTERNATIVES

There is more to Torres del Paine than just the "Circuit" and the "W"; the following **shorter hikes** can be very worthwhile.

MIRADOR LAGO GREY AND MIRADOR FERRIER

From the **Lago Grey** ranger station near *Hotel Lago Grey*, a short trail leads through the forest to the lake's vast windswept beach, where you can watch huge chunks of bluish ice bobbing on the pale waters. To the left of the beach, by the jetty, a fairly steep unmarked trail skirts around the cliff before giving you an unobstructed view of Glaciar Gray. The most spectacular viewpoint of them all, **Mirador Ferrier**, lies a steep 2km, two-hour hike up from behind the ranger station. From up there, you get a jaw-dropping vista over the park's many lakes, their colours ranging from aquamarine to greyish white. At the top, you make your way through forest before emerging among exposed rocks.

LAGUNA AZUL

From Laguna Amarga it's 18km by road to the *guardería* at **Laguna Azul**, a secluded and little-visited lake in the northeast. From there, a mostly gentle 9km, five-hour trail leads to **Lago Cebolla**. It's possible to continue on horseback to Lago Paine and beyond to *Refugio Dickson*, wading across Río Paine or else continue along this trail to a viewpoint overlooking Glaciar Dickson near the border guard post.

LAGUNA VERDE

A scenic 14.5km, seven-hour trek runs from the bridge, 2.6km north of the Administration building, to the *guardería* at **Laguna Verde**, passing the **Miradór del Toro** an hour into the trek, with views over the pretty Laguna Los Ciervos.

MIRADOR ZAPATA

Another seldom-trod path takes you up to **Mirador Zapata**, a steep 16km, seven- to nine-hour climb from *Guardería Lago Grey* at the southern tip of Lago Grey, near *Hotel Lago Grey*, rewarding you with views of the ice cap and the magnificent Glaciar Pingo. *Campamento Pingo* is an hour or so into the trek, and *Campamento Zapata* ninety minutes from the *mirador*, making it an ideal overnight stop. If you're planning on overnighting, you may only do this hike with a licensed Torres del Paine guide; enquire at the Administration building.

Valle del Francés to Refugio y Camping Los Cuernos

From *Campamento Italiano* in the **Valle del Francés** it's a steep 5km ascent (allow 2hr 30min) along the pale blue waters of the icy Lago Nordenskjold to the bustling **Refugio y Camping Los Cuernos**, which nestles in a clearing in the shadow of Los Cuernos. Around 1.5km (45min) into the hike you reach Domos y Camping Francés.

Refugio y Camping Los Cuernos to Hostería Las Torres

From **Refugio y Camping Los Cuernos**, it takes around four or five hours to reach the *Hostería Las Torres*; the 12km trail runs along gentle inclines through low shrubbery and then along green hills. You will pass two shortcuts to Las Torres, and shortly before reaching the *Hostería Las Torres*, you will see the signposted trail leading up Valle Ascencio (see page 402).

ARRIVAL AND DEPARTURE	PARQUE NACIONAL TORRES DEL PAINE

By bus The only entrance to the park for visitors coming by bus from Puerto Natales (daily 7.30am & 2.30pm; 2hr 30min) is 117km from the town at Laguna Amarga, where you pay the park fee at the Conaf station. From here, minibuses meet bus arrivals from Natales for the transfer to *Hostería Las Torres* (see page 402; CH$3000). The buses from Natales continue along Lago Nordenskjöld for another 19km to the *guardería* at Pudeto, the departure point for the catamaran to *Paine Grande Lodge*; the morning buses arrive in time for the noon boat. The bus continues beyond here, past *Hostería Pehoé*, *Camping Pehoé* and *Explora* (see page 405), opposite Salto Chico, to reach the Park Administration 18km further on, where there's a visitor centre, a *refugio*, a grocery store and a *hostería*. In peak months, book your bus tickets into the park at least a day in advance. From Argentina's El Calafate, Always Glaciers and

South Road (see page 407) run day-trips and transfers to Torres del Paine.

By car Driving up from Puerto Natales, you have a choice: to reach the southern entrance of the park, take the gravel Y-290 turn-off towards the Milodón Cave from the main, paved Ruta 9 towards Cerro Castillo. Ruta 9 from Natales continues to the park's north entrance at Laguna Amarga. A few kilometres before Laguna Amarga, you can turn off towards Lago Nordenskjöld.

GETTING AROUND

By catamaran From the *guardería* Pudeto, a Hielos Patagónicos catamaran (🚣 hipsur.com; Jan–March & Dec daily 9am, 11am, 4.15pm & 6pm; April daily 11am & 6pm; May–Aug 1st & 15th of every month 11am; Oct daily noon; Nov daily 11am & 6pm; 35min; CH$18,000 one-way, CH$28,000 return; tickets sold on board) runs across Lago Pehoé. Return trips from *Paine Grande Lodge* leave 30min after the arrival times and are met by buses heading back to Puerto Natales. From Pudeto and Laguna Amarga there are two buses to Puerto Natales, leaving at 2pm and 7pm, and 2.30pm and 7.45pm, respectively. From the Las Torres visitor centre, transfers connect with the Puerto Natales buses at Laguna Amarga, leaving 45min before the bus departs.

By car The gravel road that runs through the park is reasonably well maintained. Take the bends slowly as loose gravel is a hazard.

INFORMATION AND TOURS

Park Administration Centre The Park Administration Centre at the park's southern entrance (Jan, Feb & Dec daily 8.30am–8pm; ☎ 61 269 1931) has detailed displays on the park's fauna and flora. However, all the *guarderías* provide information about trail conditions and you'll be given a basic trail map when you pay your entrance fee and watch the park safety video.

Climbing To climb in the park, you'll need to get a permit from the Park Administration Centre; it costs CH$90,000 and covers any ascent.

Park rules Follow park guidelines regarding never lighting fires (human negligence in 2005 and in 2011 led to the destruction of a large chunk of the park) and carry *all* your rubbish back to Puerto Natales.

Tours It's possible to go ice trekking on Glaciar Grey and kayaking on Lago Grey (see page 395). Horseback rides in the park are arranged by several hotels, as well as operators in Puerto Natales (see page 395).

ACCOMMODATION

Overnight visitors to Torres del Paine must have **reservations** for all the nights they intend to spend in the park; these are rigorously checked at every lodging and Conaf ranger station. You'll need to book your accommodation for peak season around four months in advance. The park's **accommodation** is divided into serviced campsites and *refugios* run by Vertice Patagonia (see page 395) or Fantástico Sur (see page 395) and basic campsites run by Conaf (see page 406), as well as top-end *hosterías* and hotels and privately owned campsites. All the restaurants are attached to hotels; *refugios* offer pricey, high-quality meals.

HOSTERÍAS AND HOTELS

★ **EcoCamp Patagonia** Overlooking Las Torres ☎ 2 2334 9255, 🌐 ecocamp.travel; map p.400. Using solar power and hydropower, this carbon-neutral luxury camp boasts terrific views of Las Torres from its bluffside location. Lodging ranges from basic geodomes with shared facilities to luxurious loft suite domes, and the dining is first rate. Tours of Torres del Paine – from exciting day jaunts up Valle Francés and to Las Torres to multi-day cycling and kayaking adventures – are conducted by enthusiastic bilingual guides. This is also the only hotel inside the park to offer fully supported "W" and "Circuit" treks. Minimum two-night stay. Geodome all inclusive US$295

Explora Overlooking Lago Pehoé ☎ 2 2395 2800, 🌐 explora.com; map p.400. The most exclusive five-star hotel in the park, this sleek white building overlooks Lago Pehoé, with incredible views from every room. A boardwalk leads down past nearby Salto Chico to the lakeside swimming pool and open-air hot tubs. The restaurant serves excellent fusion cuisine and you can choose from 25 tours with knowledgeable bilingual guides, from day treks to horseriding. Obligatory four- to eight-night all-inclusive packages. US$2090

Hotel Lago Grey Lago Grey ☎ 61 271 2190, 🌐 lagogrey.com; map p.400. Sitting amid beech trees, this hotel has splendid views of the eponymous lake and glacier, with several good hiking trails nearby. The location is rather isolated from the rest of the park, but it has a good restaurant and there are four daily boat trips during high season to Glaciar Grey. US$360

Hotel Las Torres Patagonia Foot of Cerro Paine ☎ 61 261 7450, 🌐 lastorres.com; map p.400. Conveniently located, with beautiful, comfortable (compact) rooms and a good restaurant (open to non-guests) make this a good

9

choice, if rather pricey. All-inclusive packages are available, offering activities from horseriding to guided treks. There's also a spa. US$290

★ **Patagonia Camp** Overlooking Lago Toro ☎ 2 2334 9255, ⓦpatagoniacamp.com; map p.400. A short drive from the Administración entrance to the park, this eco-conscious hotel consists of twenty luxury yurts peeking through the trees, with boardwalks built around them. Each yurt is centrally heated, with a skylight for stargazing, a bathtub and supremely comfortable beds. Dishes at the light-filled restaurant are beautifully executed, traditional Patagonian barbecues are held in the *quincho* and guests may choose from all-inclusive rates (complete with numerous excursions – from treks in the park to custom-made activities) or B&B. Minimum two-night stay. US$440

CAMPSITES AND REFUGIOS

Wild camping isn't permitted. Most **campsites** tend to be open Oct–April, though the ones on the Circuit open later in the season. Bring a sturdy waterproof tent and all necessary camping equipment. All Fantástico Sur and Vertice Patagonia *refugios* and campsites either rent sleeping bags and tents or else you can book a premium camping spot – a ready mounted tent on wooden platform with bedding provided. **Reservations** for a spot must be made on the relevant website, whereas arrangements to rent gear at each respective site must be made in advance with the relevant offices in Puerto Natales. All the **serviced campsites** are listed below; **basic campsites** – *Japonés* (climbers with permits only), *Italiano* and *Paso* on the Torres del Paine Circuit – are free and are basically offer just a flat patch of land, a place to cook and pit toilets. Early booking for *Paso* is crucial since hikers are not allowed to continue beyond *Los Perros* or *Dickson* (see below) if they don't have advance reservations either for *Paso* or *Grey* (see below) and *Paso* is small and fills up very quickly. If camping you'll need to bring your own **food** (the small shops attached to *refugios* and campsites have a limited selection); drinking water, however, can be collected from streams. Note, however, that *Chileno* – along with *Francés* and *Cuernos* – offer no cooking facilities; full board is the only option. *Refugios* provide **hot meals** for around CH$13,000/CH$19,000/CH$25,000 for breakfast/lunch/dinner.

Camping Los Perros (Vértice Patagonia) Last campsite before the John Gardner pass; map p.400. Located in a wooded area, with a small food shop, cold showers and a cooking hut. CH$5000

Camping Serón (Fantástico Sur) Beside Río Paine; map p.400. Partially shaded campsite with picnic tables, cooking hut, cold showers and a small shop in a pleasant meadow setting at the bottom of the massif's northeast

corner. Camping US$13, camping *platforma* US$80, camping *platforma* full board US$240

Domos y Camping El Francés (Fantástico Sur) Overlooking Lago Nordenskjöld; map p.400. A short, steep hike down from the trail between *Campamento Italiano* and *Refugio Los Cuernos*, with two multi-person geodomes (bring own bedding or rent it here). Camping US$13, camping *platforma* US$80, camping *platforma* full board US$240, geodome US$130, geodome full board US$210

Refugio y Campamento Dickson (Vertice Patagonia) Lago Dickson; map p.400. On the northern part of the Circuit, this is the most remote refuge in the park. There's a well-stocked shop and cooking facilities, plus a campsite with cold showers and toilets. Camping US$8, dorms US$32, dorms full board US$82

Refugio y Campamento Grey (Vertice Patagonia) Overlooking Lago and Glaciar Grey; map p.400. A popular *refugio* with a beachside campsite, hot showers and a small on-site grocery store. Add US$50 for full board. Camping US$8, dorms without bedding US$32, dorms with bedding US$80

Refugio y Campamento Paine Grande (Vertice Patagonia) Lago Pehoé; map p.400. This modern structure has a scenic location and a café, restaurant and small store within the lodge. You can camp in the adjoining grassy fields and there are separate toilets and hot showers, as well as a cooking hut for campers. Add US$50 for full board. Camping US$10, dorms without bedding US$50, dorms with bedding US$80

Refugio y Camping Chileno (Fantástico Sur) Halfway along the Valle Ascencio; map p.400. A popular stop, this small *refugio* offers just 32 beds and has a small provisions shop as well as offering hot meals. Full board only. Dorms US$170, camping platform US$240

Refugio y Camping Los Cuernos (Fantástico Sur) Northern shore of Lago Nordenskjöld; map p.400. This *refugio* sits in a clearing beneath the Cuernos del Paine, with private *cabañas* as well as a cafeteria, cooking room for campers, tree-shaded campsite with platforms and hot showers. Full board only. Camping US$70, dorms US$170, camping *platforma* US$240, *cabañas* US$470

Refugio y Campamento Torre Centro & Refugio y Campamento Torre Norte (Fantástico Sur) Near the entrance to the park and the Hostería Las Torres; map p.400. This *refugio* is split between two buildings (*Torre Norte* is dorms only) and has comfortable bunks, a small shop and gear rental. Hearty meals are served in the large dining room. The campsite has hot showers, picnic tables and fire pits. Camping US$130, camping *platforma* US$80, *Refugio Torre Norte* dorms full board US$170, *Refugio Torre Central* dorms US$120, *Refugio Torre Central* dorms full board US$200

Parque Nacional Los Glaciares

The vast majority of travellers to Patagonia don't limit themselves to the Chilean side alone. Just over the easily crossed border lies Argentina's most spectacular national park – **Parque Nacional Los Glaciares** – home to two of the region's star attractions. The first is the craggy blue face of the **Glaciar Perito Moreno** – regularly cited as one of the world's natural wonders, and situated near the tourist hub of **El Calafate**. The second is the trekkers' and climbers' paradise of the **Fitz Roy mountain range** in the north of the park, accessed from the relaxed little town of **El Chaltén**.

El Calafate

Settled by wool traders in the 1920s and named after the edible purple berry that pops up on thorny bushes in summertime, **EL CALAFATE** expanded rapidly following the creation of Parque Nacional Los Glaciares in 1937. The **Perito Moreno glacier** is the main draw for the many visitors who flood the town, which is busiest between December and March. The glacier aside, El Calafate makes an excellent base for other park-related activities: boat trips, ice trekking, visits to nearby *estancias* and hikes into the remotest corners of this slice of wilderness. The main drag, **Avenida Libertador**, is lined with tourism outfits and restaurants.

Glaciarium

6km west of El Calafate along Ruta 11 • Daily: May–Aug 11am–7pm; Sept–April 9am–8pm • AR$360 • ⓦ glaciarium.com • Hourly free transfers (daily 11am–6pm) from the car park in front of the Santa Cruz Province Touristic Bureau, 1 de Mayo between Libertador and Roca

The **Glaciarium** is a superb interactive museum dedicated to glaciers. Illuminated displays in the strategic semi-gloom cover the discovery and research of the two Patagonian ice fields and reveal the tiny creature that's adapted to live on the ice: the Patagonian dragon, also known as the stonefly. The movies – a striking 3D documentary on the Parque Nacional Los Glaciares and another on environmental issues – are particularly worthwhile. End the visit with a drink at the on-site *Glacio Bar Branca* – the first (and still best) ice bar in Argentina.

ARRIVAL AND DEPARTURE · EL CALAFATE

By plane El Calafate's airport (ⓦ aeropuertoelcalafate.com) is 22km east of town; taxis (AR$300) and minibuses run by Ves Patagonia (ⓣ 02902 494355, ⓦ vespatagonia.com.ar; AR$150) connect with El Calafate. El Calafate is linked by frequent Aerolíneas Argentinas and LADE flights to a number of Argentinian destinations. DAP (ⓦ dapairline.com) flies to Puerto Natales and Punta Arenas.

Destinations Bariloche (daily; 1hr 45min); Buenos Aires (5 daily; 3hr); Punta Arenas (3 weekly; 1hr 15min); Puerto Natales (Jan–March & Dec Thurs & Sun; 35min); Rosario (3 weekly; 3hr 30min), Trelew (3 weekly; 1hr 30min); Ushuaia (3 daily; 1hr 20min).

By bus Buses to and from Puerto Natales and various Argentine destinations arrive at the new Terminal de Omnibus (ⓣ 02902 491476) on the outskirts of town, off Av Pluschow. It's a 10min walk to central El Calafate. Chaltén Travel (ⓣ 02962 493022, ⓦ chaltentravel.com), Taqsa/Marga (ⓣ 02966 4442 033, ⓦ taqsa.com.ar) and Cal-tur (ⓣ 02962 493150, ⓦ caltur.com.ar) all serve El Chaltén during high season, typically at 8am, 1pm and 6.30pm; Chaltén Travel and Taqsa/Marga also run buses up Ruta 40 (Jan–April, Nov & Dec daily). Taqsa/Marga also run to Río Gallegos; change there for daily departures to Ushuaia. Cootra (ⓣ 02902 491444, ⓦ cootra.com.ar) and Turismo Zaahj (ⓣ 02902 491631, ⓦ turismozaahj.com) run daily services to Puerto Natales in peak season.

Destinations Bariloche (summer only; 1–2 daily; 27hr); El Chaltén (up to 9 daily; 3hr); Puerto Natales (Chile; 1–2 daily; 6hr); Río Gallegos (3 daily; 4hr–4hr 30min).

By private bus In addition to regular bus companies, Always Glaciers, Av Libertador 924 (ⓣ 02902 493961, ⓦ alwaysglaciers.com) runs private bus transfers to Torres del Paine in Chile, as does South Road, Av Libertador 1215 (ⓣ 02902 492393, ⓦ southroad.com.ar); the latter has rugged vehicles that take a shortcut on the Argentinian side.

9

GETTING AROUND AND INFORMATION

Car rental Companies include Europcar, Av Libertador 1741 (☎02902 493606) and Hertz at the airport (☎02902 492525).

Tourist office The semi-helpful and poorly stocked tourist office is on the corner of the Anfiteatro del Bosque, a centrally located park off Av Libertador (daily: summer 8am–9pm; rest of year 9am–7pm; ☎0800 222 2252 3283, ⓦelcalafate.tur.ar). There's also a kiosk inside the bus terminal.

National park information The national park office, Av Libertador 1302 (Mon–Fri 8am–6pm, Sat & Sun 9am–6pm; ☎02902 491005, ⓦparquesnacionales.gov.ar), has maps, sells fishing licences and can provide up-to-date information.

BAFT (Backpacking Free Travel) Gregores at 9 de Julio (daily 9am–7pm; ⓦbaftravel.com). Excellent information centre aimed at backpackers and staffed by an energetic young team who can help book accommodation and onward travel. Also rents trekking equipment.

ACTIVITIES AND TOURS

Virtually every tour agency in El Calafate runs day-trips to the **Perito Moreno** glacier, allowing around 4hr at the ice face. For more **specialized excursions**, try the established operators listed below.

Cruceros MarPatag Av Libertador 1319 ☎02902 492118, ⓦcrucerosmarpatag.com. Full-day boat trips aboard the luxurious *Crucero Maria Turquesa*, taking in all three main glaciers – Upsala, Spegazzini and Perito Moreno. AR$3950/person.

Glaciar Sur 9 de Julio 57, Local 2 ☎02902 495050, ⓦglaciarsur.com. The only operator allowed to take small groups of visitors into the pristine, remote southwestern corner of Parque Nacional Los Glaciares (see page 407).

Hielo y Aventura Av Libertador 935 ☎02902 492205, ⓦhieloyaventura.com. "Mini Trekking" (AR$2700) and "Big Ice" (AR$5200) ice-trekking trips on Glaciar Perito Moreno, as well as boat excursions to the glacier (AR$500).

Southern Spirit Av Libertador 1319 ☎02902 491582, ⓦsouthernspiritfte.com.ar. The only company to run a boat cruise to the so-called hidden glacier, Glaciar Mayo; the full-day trip includes a short hike. AR$2000/person.

Viva Patagonia Av Libertador 1037 ☎02902 491133, ⓦvivapatagonia.com. Half-day kayaking excursions (US$50) along the Perito Moreno glacier. Beginners welcome.

ACCOMMODATION

HOTELS AND B&BS

★ **Madretierra** 9 de Julio 239 ☎02902 498880, ⓦmadretierrapatagonia.com. The main draws of this family-run boutique hotel are the personal touches (your name on the door), the wonderfully attentive hosts, the snug, stylish rooms with excellent showers and beds, and a funky lounge with plenty of glossy books on Patagonia to leaf through. Effusive owner Mariano is an experienced guide happy to organize outdoor adventures to suit your taste. US$200

Miyazato Inn Feruglio 150 ☎02902 491953, ⓦmiyazatoinn.hol.es. A handful of minimalist rooms, decked out in neutral tones, pancake breakfasts and a large stone fireplace to gather around on cold day are some of the boons at this appealing B&B, a 5min walk from the centre. Friendly owners Elizabeth and Jorge are excellent sources of local info. US$120

Posada Karut Josh Calle 12 No. 1887 ☎02902 496444, ⓦcposadakarutjosh.com.ar. This guesthouse, a short walk from the centre, has several things going for it: a peaceful location, spacious rooms decorated in bright colours and, above all, the warmth and hospitality of Claudia and Federico, who go out of their way to make their guests feel welcome. US$83

HOSTELS

★ **América del Sur** Puerto Deseado 153 ☎02902 493525, ⓦamericahostel.com.ar. A well-designed, spacious and friendly place with wonderful views of Lago Argentino and knowledgeable staff who can help you organize a wide range of trips. The four-bed dorms and private rooms are clean and bright, with under-floor heating. It's a 10min uphill walk from the centre. Dorms US$21, doubles US$80

Hostal Schilling Gobernador Paradelo 141 ☎02902 491453, ⓦhostalschilling.com. Its vast lounge wall decorated by globetrotting guests of all ages, this professionally run guesthouse offers spacious, comfortable but featureless en-suite rooms and a single dorm. There's a bar on site, and the owner runs the excellent Glaciar Sur trips (see page 408). Dorms US$18, doubles US$41

Hostel del Glaciar Libertador Av Libertador 587 ☎02902 491792, ⓦglaciar.com. This enormous wooden house sleeps more than a hundred in spotless dorms with private bathrooms or lovely private rooms. Walls are thin, so you may feel as if you're in bed with your neighbours, and the service is professional if impersonal. Dorms US$18, doubles US$50

EATING

CAFÉS AND CHEAP EATS

Olivia Coffee Shop 9 de Julio 131 ☎02902 488038. The nicest of El Calafate's coffee shops, *Olivia* is the place to linger with a specialized brew, or a good spot for light lunch – they serve filled bagels (AR$120), wraps and Caesar salad. Daily 10am–8pm.

Viva La Pepa Amado 833 ☎02902 491880. Cheerful, whimsical café decorated with children's paintings and specializing in sweet and savoury crêpes (AR$120–160) – lamb with honey and rosemary, say, or chicken with blue cheese and pear, perhaps followed by *dulce de leche* with chocolate-covered banana – as well as soups, sandwiches, fresh juices and coffee. Mon–Sat 11am–11pm.

RESTAURANTS

Casimiro Biguá Av Libertador 963 ☎02902 492590, ⓦcasimirobigua.com. With formally attired waiters and a Patagonian barbecue pit in the window, this is the town's most upmarket steakhouse. You can order numerous offal dishes and sweet potato chips or grilled vegetables to go with the grilled meats, and their made-to-share plate of Patagonian appetizers, such as smoked trout and deer salami, is superb. Mains AR$268–525. Daily noon–4pm & 7.30pm–1am.

Mi Rancho Gobernador Moyano at 9 de Julio ☎02902 490540. All exposed brick and homely touches, this intimate little restaurant offers some wonderfully creative and surprisingly affordable dishes. Your taste buds will thank you for the pork with apple chutney and lamb T-bone with calafate sauce. Mains AR$300–380. Daily noon–3pm & 8pm–midnight.

Pura Vida Av Libertador 1876 ☎02902 493358. A 10min walk from the centre, this A-frame cabin is a godsend for vegetarians, though meat eaters can also enjoy the likes of "Granny's lentil stew", country chicken pie, lamb *empanadas* and gnocchi in saffron sauce. Save room for dessert. Mains AR$200–260. Mon, Tues & Thurs–Sun 7.30–11.30pm.

★**La Tablita** Rosales 28 ☎02902 491065, ⓦlatablita.com.ar. An El Calafate institution for almost thirty years, this large hall is popular with discerning carnivores who come for the spit-roasted Patagonian lamb, steak and traditional gaucho dishes, such as lamb chitterlings and sweetbreads. If there's two of you, go for "Mix Carnes" (AR$550). Daily noon–3.30pm & 7pm–midnight.

DRINKING

Borges & Alvarez Libro-bar Av Libertador 1015 ☎02902 491464. This small, warm café-bar with a cave-like, book-covered lounge and elevated outdoor terrace attracts bibliophiles and cocktail lovers alike. There's an extensive range of coffee-table books to flick through while perusing the long list of cocktails (AR$140–180) or sipping a regional craft beer or coffee. Daily 10am–3am.

★**La Zorra Taproom** Av Libertador 832 ☎02902 488042, ⓦcervezazorra.com. Its interior decked out with dozens of humorous beer-related posters, this wood-panelled tap room devoted to El Calafate's craft beer attracts a good mix of younger locals and travellers. There's a nice outdoor terrace, and the kitchen serves burgers, sandwiches and pizza to go with the dozen craft beers on tap. Mon 6pm–2am, Tues–Sun noon–2am.

Glaciar Perito Moreno

49km west of El Calafate along Ruta 11 • Daily 8am–7pm • AR$500

At the southern sector of the Parque Nacional Los Glaciares you'll find one of Argentina's leading attractions, the **Glaciar Perito Moreno**. The vast glacier – 30km long, 5km wide and 60m high – sweeps down off the ice cap in a great curve, a jagged mass of crevasses and towering, knife-edged obelisks of ice (seracs), almost unsullied by the streaks of dirty moraine; it's marbled in places with streaks of muddy grey and copper sulphate blue, while at the bottom the pressurized, de-oxygenated ice has a deep blue, waxy sheen.

When it collides with the southern arm of Lago Argentino, vast blocks of ice, some weighing hundreds of tonnes, detonate off the face of the glacier with the report of a small cannon and come crashing down into the waters of Canal de los Témpanos (Iceberg Channel) below. One of the world's few advancing glaciers, Perito Moreno periodically blocks off Lago Argentino, causing the waters to build up until they burst through the dam, creating a spectacular ice arch. The glacier tends to be more active in sunny weather and in the afternoons. Tour groups tend to be more plentiful in the mornings. You can admire the glacier from a series of boardwalks and viewpoints, take

9

one of the hourly boats up close to the face of the glacier for a greater appreciation of its vastness, or join an ice-trekking or full-day boat tour (see page 408).

Upsala and other glaciers

85km northwest of El Calafate • Accessible by catamaran excursion from Puerto Bandera along Lago Argentino's northern arm; tours run by Cruceros MarPatag and Southern Spirit (see page 408) • Full-day tours ARS2000–3950, plus park entry fee (ARS500)

Although receding fast, **Glaciar Upsala** remains the longest glacier in the park and indeed in South America. The same height as Perito Moreno (60m), Upsala is twice as long (roughly 60km), 7km wide and known for calving huge translucent, blue-tinged icebergs that bob around Lago Argentino like surreal art sculptures. Tours (see page 408), usually called "All Glaciers", also take in the **Spegazzini** and **Perito Moreno** glaciers. Note that Upsala is occasionally inaccessible when icebergs block the channels. The **Mayo** glacier, reachable via the Brazo de Mayo, and closest to the Perito Moreno glacier, has recently become accessible to the public; contact Southern Spirit (see page 408).

Lago Roca and Lago Frías

The southern arm of Lago Argentino, and also known as Brazo Sur, **Lago Roca** is fringed by dense forest and hemmed in by mountains. This is the least visited and the most serene corner of Parque Nacional Los Glaciares, and to reach the most spectacular part – an unnamed glacial lagoon full of enormous chunks of ice, fed by two glaciers and with Glaciar Dickson peeping from the border of Parque Nacional Torres del Paine (see page 398) – you have to join an **organized tour**. Glaciar Sur (see page 408) is the only company allowed to bring a group of up to fourteen people daily to this remote area. The tour involves a boat ride to the southern end of Brazo Sur, an hour's stiff hike to the smaller **Lago Frías**, a zodiac boat ride across and then a spectacular, mostly flat hike along a dried riverbed to the lagoon, with waterfalls cascading down the mountains on one side.

Fitz Roy Massif

The northernmost section of Argentina's Parque Nacional Los Glaciares contains the **Fitz Roy Massif**, boasting some of the most breathtakingly beautiful mountain peaks on the planet. Two concentric jaws of jagged teeth puncture the Patagonian sky, with the 3445m incisor of **Monte Fitz Roy** at the centre.

El Chaltén

Argentina's tiny trekking capital, **EL CHALTÉN**, sits at the confluence of two pristine rivers, with a healthy contingent of hikers and climbers flocking to this surprisingly cosmopolitan town of just over one thousand inhabitants for the summer season. El Chaltén means "smoking mountain", a name given to Monte Fitz Roy by the Tehuelche, who probably mistook the wisps of cloud around its summit for volcanic activity.

ARRIVAL AND DEPARTURE   EL CHALTÉN

By bus Chaltén Travel (☎ 02962 493092, ⓦ chaltentravel. com), Taqsa/Marga (☎ 02962 493068, ⓦ taqsa.com. ar) and Cal-tur (☎ 02962 493801, ⓦ caltur.com.ar) all run up to three buses daily to El Calafate. Chaltén Travel and Taqsa/Marga also run buses up Ruta 40 (Jan– April, Nov & Dec daily). Las Lengas (☎ 02962 493023, ⓦ transportelaslengas.com) runs shuttle services to El Calafate Airport, Lago del Desierto, Río Eléctrico and

Hostería El Pilar. All buses stop at the National Park information centre before arriving at the terminal at the south end of town. You have to return to El Calafate for all onwards connections to most other Argentine destinations. Buy tickets at least a day in advance for all services, especially in peak season, when demand outstrips supply.

Destinations Los Antiguos (daily; 10hr 30min); Bariloche (1–2 daily; around 23hr); El Calafate (3–9 daily, typically

TREKKING IN PARQUE NACIONAL LOS GLACIARES

One of the beauties of this park is that those with limited time can still make worthwhile **day hikes**, using **El Chaltén** as a base. For visitors who enjoy sleeping in the wild, there are free basic campsites at Laguna Torre, Laguna Capri, Laguna Toro and Poincenot, with Río Blanco reserved for climbers only.

SHORT WALKS

For a really **short hike**, you could take an hour's walk from the north end of town to Chorillo del Salto (waterfall). Alternatively, for a panoramic view of El Chaltén From the National Park information centre, take the Los Condores or Las Aguilas trails.

DAY HIKES

The most popular trail is the relatively flat hike to **Laguna Torre** (11km; 6hr round-trip), which follows the Río Fitz Roy to a silty lake resplendent with floating icebergs, overlooked by Cerro Torre. A more strenuous hike is to **Laguna de los Tres** (12.5km; 8hr), which ascends sharply to a glacial lake with in-your-face views of Fitz Roy; this is impassable in the winter. For the best panoramic views in the area – of Monte Fitz Roy and Cerro Torre as well as Lago Viedma – hike uphill to 1490m-high **Lomo del Pliegue Tumbado** (12km; 8hr).

MULTI-DAY TREKS

A classic multi-day hike is the **Monte Fitz Roy/Cerro Torre loop** (3 days, 2 nights), which leaves either from El Chaltén or just beyond the park's boundaries at *Hostería El Pilar* (15km north of town). There are three free **campsites** (with latrines only) along the route. A tough five-day, anticlockwise loop takes in Laguna Toro, Paso del Viento, amazing views of Glaciar Viedma, and Paso Huemul, before skirting **Lago Viedma** on the way back to town. Tougher still, and requiring a guide unless you're an experienced wilderness trekker, is the multi-day trek from **Río Eléctrico** that crosses **Glaciar Marconi** and involves overnighting at least twice on the Southern Icefield. Allow at least a week and get stamped out by the *carabineros* in El Chaltén, since the trek meanders over the Chilean border and back again.

HIKES AROUND LAGO DEL DESIERTO

If you exhaust your hiking options in the immediate vicinity of El Chaltén, take one of the daily transfers from the bus terminal to **Lago del Desierto** (37km away); there's an easy round-trip hike (2hr) to Glaciar Huemul and a trek (5hr) that skirts the side of the lake, heading towards the border with Chile (see page 378).

HIKES AROUND LOS HUEMULES

Lago del Desierto transfers pass the private **Reserva Los Huemules** (AR$200; ⓦloshuemules.com), 17km north of El Chaltén, and can drop you at the entrance. The reserve's 25km network of beautifully maintained trails includes those to Laguna Condor and Laguna Azul – easy, largely flat walks. You can also take a moderately easy, three-hour climb up to Laguna del Diablo and the Cagliero glacier, or a tough, steep hike, Lomo del Diablo, to a viewpoint overlooking the glacier and Laguna del Diablo.

8am, 1pm & 7.30pm; 3hr); El Calafate Airport (1–3 daily; 3hr); Perito Moreno (1–2 daily; 11hr 30min).
By car From El Calafate, head east along RN-11 for 30km, then turn left on Ruta 40 North, then northwest onto Ruta 23. The 220km road is completely paved but can be extremely windy.
By boat For the most direct route possible to Chile, take a combination of boat/hike or hike/boat (see page 378).

INFORMATION

Tourist office There's a helpful booth (daily 8am–8pm) inside the bus terminal. All the information – from lists of accommodation options to info on local tour operators – is there 24/7.
National Park information office At the village entrance (daily 9am–8pm in peak season, shorter hours rest of the year; ☎02962 493004, ⓦelchalten.com). Climbers *must* register here, as should anyone planning to stay at the Laguna Toro *refugio* and campsite to the south. Visitors are given an informative talk on hiking in the park and receive trail maps.

9

ACTIVITIES AND TOURS

Parque Nacional Los Glaciares has more to offer than just trekking. If you're looking for alternative adventure activities, try the following reputable operators.

Chaltén Mountain Guides San Martín 187 ☎02962 493320, ⓦchaltenmountainguides.com. These certified guides run ice climbing and rock climbing trips – from half-day introductions (US$50) to multi-day adventures.

Estancia Cerro Fitzroy Around 2km south of town, across the river ☎09 2966 344540, ⓔestanciacerrofitzroy@gmail.com. Fitzroy Madsen, the great-grandson of Andreas Madsen, the first Danish settler in the area, combines an easy, scenic walk with a tour of the restored Casa Madsen (US$25), telling you the story of his settler family, showing you the family graveyard and treating you to *mate* and biscuits afterwards. Call ahead to arrange.

Fitz Roy Expediciones San Martín 56 ☎02962 493078, ⓦfitzroyexpediciones.com.ar. Longstanding

local operator that offers a day-long trek to the Glaciar Cagliero, plus ice trekking on the glacier itself and a via ferrata section. Fit, active travellers only. AR$4100.

Patagonia Aventura San Martín 56B ☎02964 436424, ⓦpatagonia-aventura.com. Boat excursions across the lake to the snout of Glaciar Viedma (AR$1100) and trekking on the Peninsula Viedma (AR$2100).

Walk Patagonia Antonio Rojo 62 ☎02962 493275, ⓦwalkpatagonia.com. This energetic Argentinian/British husband-and-wife team organizes anything from tailor-made treks with an emphasis on local fauna, flora and history to guided day hikes (including the Argentina-Chile border crossing; US$100/person) and logistical support for visitors who want to do the longer treks in the area.

ACCOMMODATION

HOTELS AND GUESTHOUSES

Cabañas Aires del Fitz Ricardo Arbilla 124 ☎02962 493134, ⓦairesdelfitz.com.ar. An effusive hostess runs four split-level *cabañas* sleeping either two/three or six people. Each beautiful living space comes with a fully equipped kitchen, satellite TV in the common area, lofty bedrooms and nice touches such as blackout curtains and drying racks in bathrooms. US$120

Hostería Senderos Perito Moreno 35 ☎02962 493336, ⓦsenderoshosteria.com.ar. Catering to hikers who appreciate their creature comforts, this attractive lodge comes with 21 spacious rooms, most with king-size beds, all with bathtubs and half with views of Fitz Roy (US$30 extra). The attentive hostess goes out of her way to be helpful. The buffet breakfast is extensive. Closed May–Aug. US$170

Kaulem Av Antonio Rojo at Commandante Arrua ☎02962 493267, ⓦkaulem.com.ar. With just four doubles and a two-person *cabaña* – all with king-size beds – this intimate hotel with Fitz Roy views doubles as a gallery for local and regional artists, with exhibitions changing bi-monthly. Supported by a rough-hewn tree trunk, the lounge is full of light. The on-site café is open to non-guests. Breakfast includes freshly baked bread. Doubles US$155, *cabaña* US$135

HOSTELS

Albergue Aylen-Aike Trevisán 125 ☎02962 493311, ⓦelchalten.com/aylenaike/indexed.php. Particularly popular with those scaling Fitz Roy (check out the wall covered wtih photos of climbers), this intimate hostel has plenty of *buena onda*, courtesy of knowledgeable owner

Sebastian. The six-bed dorms are spacious enough as not to be stuffy, and guests can use the kitchen. Closed May–Aug. Dorms US$23

Hostel Pioneros del Valle San Martín 451 ☎02902 492217, ⓦcaltur.com.ar. Centrally located on the main street, this Cal Tur-affiliated behemoth offers professional if impersonal service. There's a large range of backpacker amenities, including currency exchange and bus pickup and drop-off. Guest rooms include sparsely decorated en suites and good-value rooms with private bathrooms. Dorms US$18, doubles US$60

★**Patagonia Travellers' Hostel** San Martín 493 ☎02962 493019, ⓦpatagoniahostel.com.ar. With its slate walls, a beautiful, airy common space with plasma TV and well-equipped guest kitchen, this chalet-like hiker refuge is the most appealing of the town's hostels. The downsides are the lockers located outside the simple four-person dorms and the school-gym-like communal bathrooms, though private rooms are en suite. Their biking tours from Lago del Desierto are justifiably popular. Closed mid-April to mid-Sept. Dorms US$17, doubles US$75

Puesto Cagliero Laguna Diablo ☎09 11 3242 5406, ⓦpuestocagliero.com. The only accommodation in Estancia Los Huemules (see page 411), this simple refuge, with snug en suite rooms with bunks, overlooks Laguna Diablo and the Cagliero glacier. It's a 2hr or 3hr hike to get here. Rates are full board; meals are simple and served communal-style. Guests can do the day-long ice trek on the glacier for US$182. Reserve ahead. Closed May–Aug. Dorms US$100, doubles US$320

Rancho Grande San Martín 520 ☎02962 493005, ⓦranchograndehostel.com. This large Chaltén Travel-affiliated hostel is a backpacker factory, but they're good at what they do. Pluses include snug four-bed dorms, a two-tiered dining/hangout area, an on-site café/bar, a small kitchen and a designated member of staff who helps you plan your stay. They also change currency, accept credit cards and sell onward bus tickets. Dorms US$23, doubles US$96

EATING

CAFÉS AND CHEAP EATS

Patagónicus Güemes at Madsen ☎ 02962 493025. Consistently the best pizza in town (twenty types, to be precise, including plenty of vegetarian ones), served at big wooden tables to encourage mingling among guests. The good range of beers includes their very own Chaltén and Patagónicus brews. Small/large pizza from AR$100/AR$200. Daily except Tues noon–11pm.

Prana San Martín. Indian wall hangings decorate the salmon-pink walls of this snug vegetarian bistro and delicious smells lure you in to try the likes of brown rice risotto, lentil stew and beetroot gnocchi stuffed with sheep's cheese. Fantastic selection of gourmet teas, too. Mains AR$140–180. Daily 9am–11pm.

Puesto La Nona Cabo San Martín s/n. Towards the northern end of town and with rusty farm machinery out front, this café serves good coffee, hearty breakfasts (from AR$120) such as French toast, chunky sandwiches and more. Daily 7.30am–9pm.

La Wafflería San Martín. Colourful and snug, *La Wafflería* offers waffles with toppings galore, from calafate ice cream with *dulce de leche* to blue cheese, black olives and nuts (AR$95–265). Tipples range from seven types of hot chocolate to El Chaltén's very own Supay brew. Daily 10.30am–10.30pm.

RESTAURANTS

El Muro San Martín 948 ☎ 02962 493248. Lasagne with lamb and mushrooms, trout in orange and almond sauce and sweet and sour ribs are just some of the tempting creations dished up at this hungry hiker's haven. There's a climbing wall out back to help you work up an appetite. Mains from AR$250. Daily noon–midnight.

La Oveja Negra Av San Martín 780 ☎ 02966 271437. Permeated with delicious smells of grilling meat, this bright, sleek meatery is all wood-panelled walls with a succinct menu of *lomo*, lamb, short ribs and skirt steak, cooked to your specifications and served with simple accompaniments. Mains AR$200–320. Daily 12.30–11.30pm.

La Tapera Av Antonio Rojo ☎ 02962 493195. Adorable, split-level log cabin with a roaring fire, packed full of hungry punters tucking into pork shoulder cooked with beer, some of the town's best steak, salmon with spring onion and ginger, a smattering of tapas and a couple of cold weather warmers: *locro* (classic lamb/chorizo/bacon stew) and lamb and lentil stew. Mains AR$97–192. Daily 12.30–11.30pm.

DRINKING

La Cervecería Av San Martín 564 ☎ 02962 493109. One of the most sociable spots in town, with locals and hikers perching on rough-hewn wooden seats to savour pints of bock or pilsner microbrews or tuck into ample portions of stew, pizza or pasta. There's a beer garden out back and you can visit the brewery during one of the daily tours. Daily 11am–midnight.

★ **La Vinería** Av Lago del Desierto 265 ☎ 02962 493301. This busy, buzzy little joint is the place to sample a couple of dozen regional craft beers as well as wines from all over Argentina, accompanied by sharing platters (AR$360) of cold cuts (think smoked venison, trout, black pudding) and local and imported cheeses, as well as gourmet sandwiches (AR$150). Hugely popular, with a usually packed outdoor terrace. Daily 3pm–2am.

DIRECTORY

Banks and exchange El Chaltén has one ATM at the bus station and two Banco de Santa Cruz ATMs just outside the bus station (though they're rumoured to swallow some foreign cards). Many restaurants and some businesses accept cash only, so bring plenty to cover your stay. Dollars, euros and Chilean pesos are widely accepted. If you are planning on crossing the border to the Chilean village of Villa O'Higgins (see page 378) and then travelling up the Carretera Austral, bring US dollars and plenty of Chilean pesos.

Camping equipment Camping Center, San Martín 56, or Patagonia Hikes, Lago del Desierto at Rojo.

Hospital El Puesto Sanitario (☎ 02962 493033) is extremely basic; for medical emergencies, go to El Calafate.

Tierra del Fuego

CLIMBING CERRO GUANACO, PARQUE NACIONAL TIERRA DEL FUEGO

Tierra del Fuego

At the bottom end of the South American continent, and divided between Chile and Argentina, Tierra del Fuego ("Land of Fire") is as fascinating to travellers as Patagonia, from which it is separated by the Magellan Strait. In fact, it was Magellan who dreamed up the dramatic and somewhat unlikely name, after sighting dozens of fires lit by the native Yámana. Though comprising a number of islands, it's more or less the sum of its most developed part, the Isla Grande, the biggest island in South America. The easternmost half of Isla Grande, plus Isla de los Estados (Staten Island) and a smattering of tiny islets to the south belong to Argentina; the rest is Chilean territory.

10

On the **Chilean side**, you'll find the isolated main town of **Porvenir**, which huddles on the Magellan Strait. Flat and dusty plains cover much of northern and central Isla Grande, but further south, the countryside becomes less barren, with thick woodland and crystalline rivers near **Camerón** stretching southeast towards a number of pristine lakes, including **Lago Blanco**. In the far south are the new **Parque Nacional Yendegaia** and the largely inaccessible 2000m peaks of the Cordillera Darwin. South of Isla Grande, across the Beagle Channel, lies **Isla Navarino**, home to tiny **Puerto Williams**, the southernmost permanently inhabited settlement in the world, plus one of the most challenging hiking trails in South America, the **Los Dientes Circuit**. Beyond Navarino is **Cabo de Hornos** (Cape Horn), the land's end of the Americas, accessible only by sea or air.

In the **Argentine** sector, the leading attraction is the city of **Ushuaia** on the south coast of Argentine Tierra del Fuego. It is *the* base for visiting the **Beagle Channel**, rich in **marine wildlife**, the lakes, forests and tundra of nearby **Parque Nacional Tierra del Fuego**, the historic **Estancia Harberton**, and, of course, **Antarctica**. It is also Tierra del Fuego's main tourist destination, with winter skiing and summer trekking high on the list of activities. Also in Argentine Tierra del Fuego, you'll find the scenic **Lago Fagnano**; from the lake to the 2985m **Paso Garibaldi**, the gateway to Ushuaia by road, you'll travel through patches of low, transitional, lichen-festooned **Fuegian woodland**.

Porvenir and around

A collection of brightly painted corrugated-iron houses lining a narrow bay, **PORVENIR** ("Future") is order stamped on nature, with neat topiary leading down the main street, Philippi, from an immaculate **Plaza de Armas** overflowing with native vegetation. The seafront **Parque del Recuerdo** sports a curve of flagpoles, the painted skeleton

CROSSING THE BEAGLE CHANNEL

Highlights

❶ Porvenir and around Visit Chile's Fuegian capital and explore the harsh land around it, which includes the remains of gold mines and a king penguin colony. See page 416

❷ Isla Navarino Fly or sail to Puerto Williams, the world's southernmost town, and – if you have the stamina – tackle one of the toughest hiking circuits in South America, the Dientes de Navarino. See page 422

❸ Cape Horn Sailing around the tip of South America in a ship or viewing its harsh beauty from the air is a memorable experience. See page 428

❹ Boat trip along the Beagle Channel Spot sea lions and penguins, cormorants and albatrosses, and maybe even killer whales, while enjoying spectacular mountain views. See page 434

❺ Winter sports around Ushuaia Zip down the slopes of this winter sports resort, dramatically located at the end of the world, or go sledging with huskies. See page 435

❻ Parque Nacional Tierra del Fuego Explore this fascinating and little-visited chunk of jagged mountains, beech forest, bogs, tundra and beautiful coast on foot. See page 436

HIGHLIGHTS ARE MARKED ON THE MAP ON PAGE 418

of a steam engine, the mounted stern of a boat and a statue of a Tehuelche man – a rare reminder of a culture brutally extinguished by the gold rush and boom in sheep farming. A twenty-minute walk along the coast takes you to **Cerro Mirador**, from where there are excellent views.

Exploring the area **around Porvenir** involves driving along the island's virtually empty roads and taking in the rolling pampas, the **lakes** teeming with birdlife, and the rusting hulks of old machinery that hint at Tierra del Fuego's gold rush past.

TIERRA DEL FUEGO

HIGHLIGHTS

1. Porvenir and around
2. Isla Navarino
3. Cape Horn
4. Boat trip along the Beagle Channel
5. Winter sports around Ushuaia
6. Parque Nacional Tierra del Fuego

A PLAGUE OF BEAVERS

As you travel around Tierra del Fuego, the sight of dead trees and beaver dams is depressingly common, a situation that owes everything to the crackpot decision made by the Argentine military in the 1940s to import 25 pairs of **Canadian beavers** in a bid to start a lucrative fur trade. This backfired catastrophically: the beavers multiplied like wildfire in the absence of natural predators, the fur trade never took off and today more than half a million buck-toothed descendants of the original beavers plague the whole of Tierra del Fuego as well as the neighbouring islands, wreaking environmental havoc, infecting lake and river water with giardia and threatening to spread to Patagonia.

At one point, the Chilean government offered US$5 per tail in order to curb the population, but it didn't have the desired result, so other options are being looked into. Rather belatedly, the Chilean and Argentinian governments launched major culls in 2016 and 2017. If they're not effective, Tierra del Fuego faces an **ecological disaster**.

In the meantime, beaver sightings have been confirmed in the Cabo Froward area (see page 392), meaning that they have now made landfall in mainland Patagonia.

10

Porvenir cemetery

Esmeralda at Damian Riobo • Daily 8am–6pm • Free

Porvenir started life in 1883 as a police outpost during the Fuegian gold rush and has since been settled by foreigners: first came the British managers of sheep farms, and then, after World War II, refugees from Croatia. You can read the history of the town in the names of the dead at the **Porvenir cemetery** four blocks north of the plaza, a smaller version of Punta Arenas' Cementerio Municipal (see page 388), where grand marble tombs intermix with modest stone slabs amid meticulously pruned cypresses.

Museo de Tierra del Fuego Fernando Cordero Rusque

Padre Mario Zavattaro 402 • Mon–Thurs 8am–5.15pm, Fri 9am–4pm, Sat & Sun 10am–1.30pm & 3–5pm • Free but donations welcomed

On the north corner of the plaza, with a 1928 Ford-T outside, the intriguing **Museo de Tierra del Fuego Fernando Cordero Rusque** ushers you into the harsh world that shaped Porvenir. Evocative black-and-white photos, dioramas and exhibits introduce visitors to the Fuegian gold rush, the lives of the now-extinct Tehuelche and the European conquest of Patagonia.

ARRIVAL AND INFORMATION

PORVENIR

By plane The aerodrome sits 5km north of town. Taxis charge around CH$4500 to Porvenir; Aerovías DAP (w dapairline.com) also has a shuttle bus. DAP's office is in the same building as those of Transbordadora Austral Broom (Tabsa), on the seafront on Calle Señoret. There's a maximum 10kg luggage limit.

Destinations Punta Arenas (Mon–Fri 3 daily, Sat 2; 15–20min).

By ferry Transbordadora Austral Broom ferries from Punta Arenas arrive at Bahía Chilota, 5km west of Porvenir. A taxi costs around CH$4000 or you can take a cheaper *colectivo*. Check schedule well ahead and purchase ferry tickets from Tabsa (see page 425; Mon–Fri 9.15am–12.15pm & 2.30–6.30pm, Sat 9am–12.15pm; passengers CH$6200; t 61 258 0089, w tabsa.cl).

Destinations Punta Arenas (Tues–Sun 1 daily; 2hr 20min).

By car The turn-off for Porvenir is 16km south of the Punta Delgada ferry crossing (see page 388). The gravel road has a few potholes, but the section near Porvenir is paved.

By bus There are no buses from Punta Arenas to Porvenir; services from Porvenir to Camerón depart from the DAP office.

Destinations Camerón (Tues & Fri, generally 6am & 4pm, returning 8.30am & 6pm on the same days; 2hr); Vicuña (2nd and 4th week of the month Wed & Thurs 6am, returning 10am the same day; 3hr 30min).

Tourist office Zavatarro 434 (officially Mon–Fri 9am–5pm, Sat & Sun 11am–5pm, though these hours aren't always kept; t 61 258 0094), next to the museum.

10

EXPLORING TIERRA DEL FUEGO ON FOUR WHEELS

Visitors with their own **vehicles** get far more out of a trip to Chilean Tierra del Fuego than those limited to Porvenir. Cars can be rented in Punta Arenas and brought over to the island on the car ferry. Most of the roads – with the exception of the stretch from Onaisín to Cerro Sombrero – are unpaved, but can be tackled without a 4WD if you drive carefully. You'll need a high-clearance vehicle for the coastal road south of Camerón to Puerto Arturo, though.

Fuegians rely only on themselves and on each other when it comes to **breakdowns** and all motorists will stop should you come to grief. Nevertheless, you should come prepared with a sleeping bag, food, water, a torch, warm clothes, a spare tyre and all necessary equipment. Always stop to help other motorists in need and plan your journey carefully: there are only two petrol stations – one in Porvenir and the other in Cerro Sombrero. If you wish to head south to Lago Blanco, you must take a spare can of petrol with you.

ACCOMMODATION

Hostal Los Canelos Croacia 356 ☎61 258 1949. Opposite the Catholic church, you'll find a handful of swing-a-cat rooms with twee decor; some also have private bathrooms. Breakfast features home-made *kuchen* and bread, and singles cost exactly half of a double – a rarity in Chile. **CH$30,000**

★ Hostería Yendegaia Croacia 702 ☎61 258 1919, ☯yendegaiahouse.com. This large, creaky, yellow-painted wooden house is the best place to stay in town, offering spacious rooms with high ceilings, appealing splashes of colour and TVs. Its congenial owners specialize in birding and penguin-watching tours (see page 421) in Tierra del Fuego, and bike rental is available. **US$100**

Hotel Barlovento John Williams 2 ☎61 258 0046, ☯hotelbarlovento.cl. Located on the outskirts of town, Porvenir's smartest hotel has well-equipped en suites, a gym, friendly staff and even an indoor football pitch. The attached restaurant-bar offers several exotic-sounding dishes, but the Chilean standards are the most reliable options. **CH$70,000**

Hotel España Croacia 698 ☎61 258 0160, ☯hotelespana.cl. This deceptively large old building, run by a friendly, formidable hostess, is an acceptable fall-back for a night, with large but drab rooms with TVs. The downstairs restaurant serves good seafood dishes, such as *palta Porvenir* (avocado stuffed with king crab). **CH$35,000**

EATING

Club Croata Señoret 542 ☎61 258 0053. There's a Croatian coat of arms above the doorway, and the menu at this grand old club focuses mainly on fresh fish and seafood. The house special is the *trilogia austral*: crêpes with *centolla* (king crab), oysters and mussels, and the service is decidedly old-school. Mains CH$8000–10,000. Tues–Sun 12.30–3.30pm & 7–11pm.

Hotel Rosas Croacia 698 ☎61 258 0088. Generous portions of well-prepared seafood and fish are served at this informal restaurant, popular with locals. The lunchtime set menu is good value (around CH$6000) and the owner is extremely knowledgeable about the mining history of the area. Daily 12.30–3pm & 7–11pm.

DIRECTORY

Banks and exchange Bring plenty of cash as the single Banco Estado ATM only accepts Chilean MasterCard.

Hospital Carlos Wood between Av Manuel Señoret and Guerrero (☎61 258 0034).

Bahía Azul

Ferry summer every 45min, 8.30am–11pm; rest of year less often; 20min

The first 20km out of Porvenir heading north is lined with large shallow **lakes**, ranging in colour from turquoise to sapphire and often adorned with dazzling pink flamingos. Some 43km north of the oil settlement of Cerro Sombrero (139km from Porvenir), the **ferry** that connects Tierra del Fuego with Patagonia crosses the Primera Angostura from a place known locally as **BAHÍA AZUL** (Puerto Espora). During the crossing you may see schools of Commerson's dolphins.

Baquedano Hills

A little-used road heads east from Porvenir across the **Baquedano Hills**, where most of the region's gold was discovered; you pass the rusted remains of dredges along the way. The road meets the main Porvenir–San Sebastián road and, after another 84km of rolling pampas, reaches the **San Sebastián frontier** (see page 422). Ten kilometres southeast of San Sebastián lies "**Las Onas**" hill, the site of the oldest inhabited place on the island, estimated to be 11,880 years old.

10

Bahía Inútil

A pretty road follows the coast from **Bahía Inútil**, a wide bay that got its name by being a useless anchorage for sailing ships. After 99km you reach a crossroads; turn south, and a little past the village of **Onaisín** you pass a small **British cemetery**. The gravestones have English inscriptions that suggest tragic stories: "killed by Indians", "accidentally drowned" and "died in a storm".

When the tide's out, you can see an ancient way of catching fish – underwater stone *corrales* (pens) built by the Selk'nam to trap fish when the tide turned. Just before the village of Camerón, the road turns inland and leaves the bay, while a rough track carries on south along the coast to Puerto Arturo, a small stockbreeding settlement.

Camerón and around

From the small settlement of **CAMERÓN**, a former Scottish sheep ranch, a road leads through Magellanic forest, occasionally interspersed with open grassland, to a fork in the road: it heads north to San Sebastián and south to Río Grande.

ACCOMMODATION   CAMERÓN AND AROUND

Estancia Camerón Lodge Near Camerón ☎2 2520 2024 or ☎61 221 5029, ⓦestanciacameronlodge. com. This cosy lodge, built of native wood and stone and overlooking the Río Grande, was designed with serious anglers in mind; Lu, the host, is an extremely knowledgeable fishing guide. The four rooms are comfortable and centrally heated. Rates include full board and tours/activities. Closed mid-April to Dec. US$800

Lago Blanco and beyond

Some 21km south of Río Grande lies **Lago Blanco**, surrounded by steeply forested hills and snow-covered mountains. From the lake the road continues further south, past **Lago Deseado**, currently ending just beyond the majestic **Lago Fagnano**, part of Parque Nacional Tierra del Fuego. The Chilean government plans to build a new settlement on the shores of the lake, thus providing easier access to the natural attractions on the Argentinian side. A rough gravel road now reaches the western shore of Lago Fagnano (4WD only) and it may be possible to cross over to Argentina via Paso Bellavista (Dec–March only); check with local *carabineros*.

KING PENGUINS IN TIERRA DEL FUEGO

A number of **king penguins**, whose colonies have previously not been found further north than the South Georgia islands and Antarctica, have made Chile's Tierra del Fuego their home. The originally sixteen or so penguins have now increased in number, making this a permanent colony. The location, 15km south of the crossroads with the turn-off for Onaisín along the coastal road, is accessed via Estancia San Clemente, which is doing its best to protect the penguins. The owners of San Clemente are working together with a Punta Arenas-based interest group keen to study the penguins' behaviour. Visitors coming by car will see the sign for **Parque Pingüino Rey** (Tues–Sun 11am–6pm; CH$12,000; ⓦpinguinorey.com). Tours are run by *Hostería Yendegaia* in Porvenir (see page 420).

10

CROSSING THE ARGENTINE BORDER

Note that there are two **San Sebastiáns**. One is the **Chilean border post** (daily 8am–10pm) with a periodically open fast-food stall and not much else; the other is a fully fledged village further on in Argentina.

ACCOMMODATION   **LAGO BLANCO AND BEYOND**

Lodge Deseado Lago Deseado ☎09 9165 2564, ⓦlodgedeseado.cl. This intimate lodge consists of four cosy *cabañas* for a total of twelve guests. Excursions range from brown trout fishing on lakes Fagnano and Deseado to snoeshoeing and cross-country skiing in winter. It was closed for renovation at the time of research, but is due to re-open in late 2018.

Parque Nacional Yendegaia

A former Tompkins' conservation project (see page 350), **Parque Nacional Yendegaia** is a 38,500-square-kilometre swathe of native Fuegian forest, native grasslands, snow-tipped crags and icy waters, sitting by the Beagle Channel amid the Cordillera Darwin. Originally a cattle ranch, this piece of land had been turned into a nature reserve and great efforts have been made to restore its original ecosystem, in spite of the presence of feral horses and cows. In 2014, Yendegaia was donated to the Chilean government as a new **national park** and its location directly between Chile's Parque Nacional Alberto de Agostini and Argentina's Parque Nacional Tierra del Fuego (see page 436) acts as a wildlife corridor. Though it is conceivable that visitors to the latter may eventually be able to cross over to Yendegaia, at the time of research Yendegaia was only accessible by boat (you can ask the weekly ferry between Puerto Williams and Punta Arenas to drop you off); you have to bring all your supplies with you and camping wild is the only option.

The horse trail that runs south from Lago Fagnano to Yendegaia is due to be turned into a proper road, ostensibly to connect the rest of Tierra del Fuego to Puerto Williams by regular ferry and to give visitors easier access to the southern fjords. The construction of the road is yet to start.

Isla Navarino

Apart from compact **Puerto Williams** and the even tinier fishing village of **Puerto Toro**, **Isla Navarino**, the largish island to the south of Isla Grande, is an uninhabited wilderness studded with barren peaks and isolated valleys. Navarino is dominated by a dramatic range of peaks, the **Dientes del Navarino**, through which weaves a 70km hiking trail called the **Los Dientes Circuit**. What has spoiled some of the landscape, especially the woodland, however, is the devastation – including infecting lake and river water with giardia – brought about by feral **beavers** (see page 419).

ARRIVAL AND DEPARTURE   **ISLA NAVARINO**

By plane Aerovías DAP (ⓦdapairline.com) has flights from Punta Arenas to Puerto Williams (summer Mon–Sat 10am; winter less frequent). Note that there's a maximum 10kg luggage limit, though you can pay extra for more weight.

By boat Tabsa (ⓦtabsa.cl) ferries sail between Punta Arenas and Puerto Williams (2–3 weekly; 30hr; seat CH$108,000, berth CH$151,000). COMAPA (ⓦcomapa.com) also runs a four-day luxury cruise on the *Mare Australis* and the *Via Australis* (cheapest cabin from US$1440/person), dropping anchor in Isla Navarino's Wulaia Bay. From Ushuaia, a handful of companies (see page 430) run (generally) daily boats in spring andd summer (around 40min; from US$120 one way).

Puerto Williams and around

Although Ushuaia loudly proclaims its "end of the world" status, it suffers from geographical envy when it comes to **PUERTO WILLIAMS**. The town nestles in a small bay on the north shore of Isla Navarino, 82km due east and slightly south of Ushuaia across the Beagle Channel, home to around three thousand people. Originally a military outpost, it's officially the capital of Chilean Antarctica. The compact, windblown settlement has a desolate quality even in the height of the brief summer, but the people are exceptionally warm and welcoming and you get a real sense of a close-knit community, brought together by isolation from the rest of Chile. Most businesses are in the pedestrianized **Centro Comercial**, near the Plaza O'Higgins.

Puerto Williams is also the jumping-off point for a challenging but spectacular hike, **Los Dientes de Navarino Circuit**.

Museo Antropológico Martín Gusinde

Aragay at Gusinde • Tues–Fri 9.30am–1pm & 3–6pm, Sat & Sun 2.30–6.30pm • Free but donations welcomed • ☎ 61 262 1043, ⓦ museomartingusinde.cl

In a smart building with a replica Yámana hut and a whale skeleton outside, the excellent **Museo Antropológico Martín Gusinde**, named after the clergyman and anthropologist who spent a great deal of time among the indigenous peoples of Tierra del Fuego, has a host of beautifully presented displays on the history, culture, fauna and flora of the area.

The highlights are the exhibits on Yámana life, complete with artefacts, photographs and accounts of their legends; an obligatory stuffed Fuegian fauna section; and maps that chart the exploration of the region, from the days of indigenous settlements, through the gold rush, to the commercial shipping of today. The spiral staircase is decorated with stunning close-ups of local wildlife. Staff can also let you into the nearby Casa Stirling, the former home of a nineteenth-century British missionary.

Villa Ukika

Around 2.5km east of the town centre, just beyond the new ferry ramp

On the edge of town is the hamlet of **Villa Ukika**, home to the last descendants of the Yámana peoples. Among them is Cristina Calderón, the last speaker of the Yámana

---

THE YÁMANA, THE SELK'NAM, THE MÁNEKENK AND THE KAWÉSHKAR

Tierra del Fuego and Isla Navarino were originally home to the **Yámana (Yaghan),** the **Selk'nam (Ona)**, the **Kawéshkar (Alacalúf)** and the Mánekenk (Haush). The Kawéshkar inhabited the Magellan Strait and the western fjords; the Selk'nam dominated Tierra del Fuego, the Mánekenk favoured Tierra del Fuego's southeastern tip, while the Yámana resided in the southern fjords and Isla Navarino. Unlike the hunter-gatherer Selk'nam and Mánekenk, the Yámana and the Kawéskar were both nomadic "Canoe Indians", living off fish, shellfish and marine animals. European sealing and whaling activities from the nineteenth century onwards tremendously depleted their main sources of nourishment and European-borne diseases decimated the indigenous population. The last Yámana speaker, Cristina Calderón, lives outside Puerto Williams while the remote Puerto Edén is populated by the remaining Kawéshkar, and the descendants of the Selk'nam survive in Tolhuin and Río Grande in Argentina.

Though dismissed by European explorers as savages, the indigenous peoples had complex rituals. The Selk'nam performed a sophisticated **male initiation ceremony**, the *Hain*, during which the young male initiates, or *kloketens*, confronted and unmasked malevolent spirits that they had been taught to fear since their youth, emerging as *maars* (adults). Father Martín Gusinde was present at the last *Hain* ceremony in 1923, and managed to capture the event in a series of remarkable photographs, copies of which circulate as postcards today. Italian mountaineering priest and photographer, Alberto de Agostini, also sustained a long and fruitful relationship with the indigenous peoples of Tierra del Fuego.

LOS DIENTES DE NAVARINO CIRCUIT

Many travellers come to Puerto Williams to complete the **Los Dientes de Navarino Circuit** challenge, a strenuous four- to seven-day hike in the Isla Navarino wilderness, where there is no infrastructure, and you are faced with unpredictable weather as well as the rigours of the trail. This is for experienced hikers only and not to be attempted alone.

THE TRAIL

Follow Vía Uno west out of town; the trail starts behind the statue of the Virgin Mary in a grassy clearing. The road leads uphill to a waterfall and reservoir, from where a marked trail climbs steadily through the *coigüe* and *ñire* forest. It is a two-hour ascent to **Cerro Bandera**, a *mirador* with a wonderful view of the town, the Beagle Channel and the nearby mountains, and the Dientes de Navarino themselves. The rest of the trail is not very well marked; there are 38 trail markers (rock piles) spread out over the 53km route, which entails crossing four significant passes and negotiating beaver dams in between.

Once past the starkly beautiful **Laguna El Salto**, either cross a fairly steep pass and make a detour to the south, to the remote expanse of Lago Windward, or head west to **Laguna de los Dientes**. Continue west past Lagunas Escondido, Hermosa and Matrillo before reaching the particularly steep and treacherous descent of **Arroyo Virginia**; beware of loose rocks. The trail markers end before Bahía Virginia, and you have to make your own way over pastures and through scrubland to the main road. The trail officially finishes 12km out of town, behind a former *estancia* owned by the MacLean family, which has been developed into a *centolla*- and shellfish-processing factory. From here you can follow the main road back to Puerto Williams or hitch a lift.

MAPS AND ESSENTIALS

The best **map** is the *Tierra del Fuego & Isla Navarino* satellite map by Zagier & Urruty Publications, available in Ushuaia. Make sure you have plentiful food and **water** supplies (water on the island is not drinkable owing to the giardia carried by the beavers), sunscreen and warm and waterproof outdoor gear, and inform people in town of your plans before leaving.

GUIDED TREKS

If you prefer to have the benefit of a professional guide and logistical support, contact **Fuegia & Co** (see page 426), who can advise on trail conditions and offers guided four-day treks for around CH$350,000 per person.

10

language, who was aged 89 at the time of writing. In 2005 she published a book of Yámana stories with the help of her granddaughter. The only object of note in Villa Ukika is the replica of a traditional dwelling – the **Kipa-Akar** (House of Woman). It's open to visitors who can purchase traditional handicrafts – from miniature canoes to whalebone harpoons; ask around if you find it closed.

ARRIVAL AND INFORMATION   PUERTO WILLIAMS

By plane The tiny airport is a 2.5km drive west of town; most guesthouses provide a pick-up/drop-off service. Aerovías DAP has its office at Centro Comercial Sur 151 (☎61 262 1114, ⓦdapairline.com); confirm flight departure times here. Book well ahead for the Dec and Feb peak seasons.
Destinations Punta Arenas (Nov–March Mon–Sat 1 daily; otherwise 3 weekly; 45min–1hr 20min).
By boat From Punta Arenas, you'll arrive at the ferry ramp on Av Costanera. Boats from Ushuaia (see page 430) disembark at Puerto Navarino on the west side of the island, where you pass through Chilean customs before an hour's ride in a minibus to Puerto Williams. The Puerto Williams ferry continues to Puerto Toro once

a month. The Tabsa office at Costanera 435 (☎61 262 1015, ⓦtabsa.cl) sells tickets for the Punta Arenas-bound ferry (CH$108,000/151,000 for *semi-cama/cama* seats). A minibus picks up passengers at their *hospedaje* to take them to Puerto Navarino in time to catch a boat to Ushuaia (weather permitting).
Destinations Punta Arenas (1 weekly; 32hr); Ushuaia (Dec–Feb 1–3 daily, weather permitting; 45min–1hr).
Tourist office Next to the post office at Centro Comercial Sur s/n (theoretically Mon–Fri 8.30am–1pm & 2–5pm, though it doesn't always keep these hours; ☎61 241 2125). It has brochures on Puerto Williams and Cape Horn, but no maps of the Dientes de Navarino circuit.

10

ACTIVITIES AND TOURS

Fuegia & Co Patrullero Ortiz 49 ☎61 262 1251, ✉fuegia@usa.net. Guided treks and logistical support in the Dientes de Navarino.

Shila Turismo Aventura O'Higgins 220 ☎7897 2005, ⊛turismoshila.cl. As well as stocking basic maps of the Dientes de Navarino, Shila handles bookings for the boat to Ushuaia (see page 430), offers tours and rents out bikes and camping and fishing equipment.

SIM Expeditions Ricardo Maragaño 168 ☎61 262 1150, ⊛simexpeditions.com. This intrepid German/Venezuelan operator runs highly recommended two- to three-week sailing trips to Cape Horn, South Georgia and Antarctica, plus jaunts on the Beagle Channel.

Victory Adventure Expeditions ☎61 222 7098, ⊛victory-cruises.com. Sailing expeditions around Cape Horn, along the Beagle Channel and even to Antarctica, run by Californian Ben Garrett, who is based in Punta Arenas.

ACCOMMODATION

Except Errante Ecolodge and *Hotel Lakutaia* (see page 426), **accommodation** in Puerto Williams consists of rustic rooms/dorms in family homes. Peak **hiking** season lasts from January to March, when booking in advance is advised. Most places offer free airport pick-ups/drop-offs.

Errante Ecolodge 5.5km west of Puerto Williams ⊛errantecolodge.com. Promising an "off-grid" experience, this new hostel/guesthouse offers spacious eight-bed dorms and a couple of private doubles/twins, all with huge windows and expansive views. The owners are friendly and informed, and food and tours are on offer. The only downside is the long trek into town, though bikes are available and the owners often offer lifts. Dorms US$50, doubles US$200

Hostal Akainij Austral 22 ☎61 262 1173, ⊛turismoakainij.cl. Cosy en-suite rooms with down duvets, a cheerful living room filled with plants, and friendly owners happy to arrange a plethora of excursions make this an ideal mid-range guesthouse base. CH$50,000

Hotel Lakutaia Near the airport, 2km west of Puerto Williams ☎61 262 1721, ⊛lakutaia.cl. Somewhat isolated from Puerto Williams proper, the island's only hotel attracts active, well-heeled tourists with its multi-

day wilderness excursions around the island – these include heliskiing in winter, guided hikes in the Dientes de Navarino and flights and sailing trips around Cape Horn. Rooms are comfortable and the restaurant is good. US$292

Refugio El Padrino Av Costanera 276 ☎61 262 1136 or ☎09 8438 0843, ✉ceciliamancillao@yahoo.com.ar. A snug backpacker haven, this colourful hostel has a sign on the door inviting you to let yourself in and decide if you wish to stay. Most do; Cecilia, the owner, may not speak much English, but her genuine warmth transcends language barriers. Dorms CH$12,000

Residencial Pusaki Piloto Pardo 222 ☎61 262 1116, ✉pattypusaki@yahoo.es. A perrenial traveller favourite, with a warm family atmosphere and excellent home-cooked food (the *centolla* dishes are particularly good). Non-guests can come for dinner, provided you give owner Patty a few hours' warning. Dorms CH$15,000, doubles CH$35,000

EATING

For those who wish to do their bit for the environment, Cecilia of *Refugio El Padrino* (see above) can arrange for you to dine on **beaver** meat at a local family home.

★ **Puerto Luisa Cafe** Av Costanera 317 ☎9934 0849. By the new ferry dock, in a bright orange building, this charming café offers views across the Beagle Channel, good coffee, cakes, toasted sandwiches, omelettes and breakfast options, plus a selection of souvenirs and wi-fi. Mon–Fri 10am–1pm & 4–9pm, Sat 8am–9pm.

Restaurant Diente de Navarino Centro Comercial. Providing Puerto Williams with a touch of the Caribbean, this Colombian-run restaurant is decked out with flags, football scarves and pictures of Bogotá and Cartagena. As well as a good-value set lunch (CH$7000), *arepas*, seafood rice, and fried chicken are on the menu. Mon–Sat 12.30–3.30pm & 8–10pm.

Restaurant Wulaia Centro Comercial ☎61 253 9675. There's a real maritime feel to this restaurant, whose walls are covered with porthole mirrors, oars and shipping flags. The menu ranges from huge sandwiches (from CH$4500) to fish and seafood (mains from CH$9000). There's an attached souvenir shop, and staff are a good source of local info. Daily 12.30–3pm & 7–11pm.

El Resto del Sur Ricardo Maragano 146. The smartest restaurant in town, offering a concise mix of pasta (CH$6500–10,000; try the *centolla* ravioli) and pizza (CH$9000–13,000), and a range of drinks, including a refreshing calafate sour. Daily 12.30–3.30pm & 8–11pm.

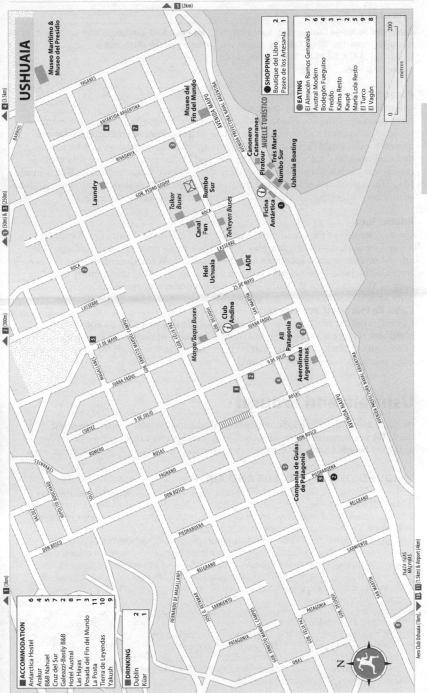

USHUAIA

10

ACCOMMODATION
Antarctica Hostel	6
Arakur	4
B&B Nahuel	5
Cruz del Sur	7
Galeazzi-Basily B&B	2
Hotel Austral	8
Las Hayas	1
Posada del Fin del Mundo	3
La Posta	11
Tierra de Leyendas	10
Yakush	9

DRINKING
Dublin	2
Küar	1

SHOPPING
Boutique del Libro	2
Paseo de los Artesanía	1

EATING
El Almacén Ramos Generales	7
Austral Modern	6
Bodegón Fueguino	4
Freddo	3
Kalma Resto	1
Kaupé	2
María Lola Resto	5
El Turco	9
El Vagón	8

DIRECTORY

Banks and exchange Banco de Chile, down a narrow passageway from the Centro Comercial towards the seafront, has an ATM, but it's best to bring plenty of cash to be on the safe side.

Internet Most guesthouses offer patchy wi-fi, as do *Puerto Luisa Cafe* and the museum.

Parque Etnobotánico Omora

Daylight hours • Free but donation expected • ⓦ umag.cl

Near the start of the Los Dientes trail, 3km west of Puerto Williams, is the entrance to the experimental part-state, part-private enterprise **Parque Etnobotánico Omora**, named for the world's southernmost hummingbird. The park plays an educational and environmental role, protecting the *ñire* and *lenga* forest by, among other things, encouraging locals to cull beavers for their meat. Native birds, including the red-headed Magellanic woodpecker (*lana*) and the ruffed-legged owl (*kujurj*), are monitored, along with other endangered species of flora, fauna and plants along the trails.

Puerto Toro

On the east side of the island, 46km southeast of Puerto Williams, lies **Puerto Toro**, a tiny fishing post – complete with a tiny school and a police station – inhabited by around seventy *centolla* fishermen and their families. At the time of writing, it was only reachable by boat – visitors can come on a day-trip by taking the monthly ferry (see page 425) from Puerto Williams – but a road is under construction.

Cabo de Hornos (Cape Horn)

Directly south of Isla Navarino lies a cluster of islands, part of the **Cabo de Hornos biosphere reserve** – a staggering five million hectares of native forest, tundra, glaciers, fjords and tall black cliffs. This pristine marine habitat is set aside for strict conservation only; overnight stays are not permitted.

Ushuaia and around

Its name meaning "westward-looking bay" in the indigenous Yámana language, **USHUAIA** lies hemmed in between the Sierra Venciguerra range and the deep blue of the icy **Beagle Channel** – the most dramatic location of any Argentine cities, with

---

ROUND THE HORN BY SEA AND AIR

In January 1616, the cape was christened Hoorn by the Dutchmen **Willem Schouten** and **Jacob Le Maire** who passed by aboard the *Unity*, in honour of another ship of theirs that got shipwrecked off the coast of Argentina. In time, the Spanish changed the name to **Cabo de Hornos**, which was corrupted in turn to Cape Horn.

For centuries the treacherous icy waters surrounding the Horn's islands captured the imagination of sailors and adventurers, not least because they constitute the biggest ship graveyard in the Americas: on old nautical maps, the waters around the islands are littered with tiny pictures of sunken vessels. Today, Cape Horn still presents a sizeable challenge for experienced sailors and travellers alike, many of whom, having come this far south, can't resist going all the way round.

SIM (see page 426) and Victory Adventure Expeditions (see page 426) are good places to enquire about **sailing trips**. Weather permitting, you can visit the tiny Chilean naval base, lighthouse and chapel; a statue of an albatross overlooks the stormy waters beyond. Aerovias DAP (see page 422) and the local flying clubs run expensive (around CH$650,000/small chartered plane) thirty-minute flights from Punta Arenas and Puerto Williams that do a loop and return without landing. These air excursions treat you to incredible views of Isla Navarino and the Darwin peaks. Weather is a vital factor.

colourful houses tumbling down the hillside to the wide, encircling arm of land that protects its bay from the southwesterly winds. San Martín is the city's main thoroughfare, and most visitors without their own transport stick to the compact grid of streets in Ushuaia's centre.

Around Ushuaia, the nature trails of **Parque Nacional Tierra del Fuego**, the spectacular **Beagle Channel**, the historic **Estancia Harberton** and the snow-covered slopes of **Cerro Castor** offer plenty of activities for travellers throughout the year.

Brief history

In 1869, Reverend Waite Stirling became Tierra del Fuego's first white settler when he founded his **Anglican mission** among the Yámana here. Stirling stayed for six months before being recalled to the Falklands Islands to be appointed Anglican bishop for South America. Thomas Bridges, his assistant, returned to take over the mission in 1871, after which time Ushuaia began to figure on mariners' charts as a place of refuge in the event of shipwreck. In 1896, in order to consolidate its sovereignty and open up the region to wider colonization, the Argentine government used a popular nineteenth-century tactic and established a **penal colony** here, eventually closed by Perón in 1947.

Museo del Fin del Mundo

Maipú 173 • Mon–Fri 10am–5pm, Sat 2–6pm • Free

The small **Museo del Fin del Mundo** has exhibits on the region's indigenous peoples and arrival of European missionaries. There's a thorough section on birdlife, and a rare example of the Selk'nam–Spanish dictionary written by Salesian missionary José María Beauvoir. The ghostly figurehead of the *Duchess of Albany*, a ship wrecked on the eastern end of the island in 1893, looks on overhead.

Museo Marítimo and Museo del Presidio

Yaganes at Gobernador Paz • Daily: Jan & Feb 9am–8pm; March–Dec 10am–8pm • AR$400 • ℗ museomaritimo.com

The star attraction in Ushuaia itself is undoubtedly the imposing former **prison**, built by convicts between 1902 and 1920 and now home to the **Museo Marítimo & Museo del Presidio**. Its exhibits, ranging from Antarctic wildlife and exploration of the last continent to everyday life in the prison and its most notorious inhabitants, are arranged inside the cells along three of the five wings that radiate from the central chamber like spokes from a half-wheel. Most engaging are the scale models of famous ships from the island's history; spot a ship made entirely out of matchsticks by one of the inmates. The most celebrated prisoner to stay here was early twentieth-century anarchist Simón Radowitzky, whose story is recounted by Bruce Chatwin in *In Patagonia*.

ARRIVAL AND DEPARTURE   USHUAIA

In peak season it's a good idea to book your bus or plane ticket well in advance, as demand frequently outstrips supply.

By plane The international airport, Malvinas Argentinas, lies 4km southwest of town; a taxi to the centre costs about AR$180. Aerolineas Argentinas (℗ aerolineas.com.ar) and LATAM (℗ latam.com) serve destinations in Argentina; Aerovias DAP (℗ dapairline.com) has flights to Punta Arenas in Chile.
Destinations Buenos Aires (4–8 daily; 3hr 20min); El Calafate (2–3 daily; 1hr 20min); Punta Arenas (Chile; Nov–March 2 weekly; 2hr); Trelew (1 daily; 2hr 10min).
By bus Frequent bus services run via Chile to both Argentine and Chilean destinations. All long-distance bus rides entail

a short ferry crossing at Primera Angostura. Buses arrive and depart from their companies' respective offices. Buses Pacheco and Bus Sur (book both through Tolkeyen at San Martín 409; ℗ 02901 437073, ℗ tolkeyenpatagonia. com) and Tecni Austral (book through Tolkar at Roca 157; ℗ 02901 431412, ℗ tolkarturismo.tur.ar) run to Punta Arenas; Bus Sur carries on to Puerto Natales; Río Gallegos is served by Taqsa (Fadul 126; ℗ 02901 435453, ℗ taqsa. com.ar); change there for buses to El Calafate. These are high-season schedules; services are reduced at other times of the year – check at the tourist office.

10

ANTARCTICA – THE REMOTEST CONTINENT

Ushuaia lies 1000km north of **Antarctica**, but is still the world's closest port to the white continent. Most tourists pass through the city to make their journey across **Drake's Passage**, the wild stretch of ocean that separates it from South America; the two-day crossing is notoriously rough.

The grandeur of Antarctica's pack ice, rugged mountains and phenomenal bird and marine life will leave you breathless: whales, elephant and fur seals, albatrosses and numerous varieties of penguin – including king, gentoo, Adélie, and chinstrap – are just some of the species you can see. Kayaking, hiking, Zodiac boat trips, diving and snorkelling, cross-country skiing, snowshoeing and mountaineering are among the activities on offer.

Regular **cruise ships** depart from November to March; most cruises last between eight and 21 days. Some of the longer cruises also stop at the **South Atlantic islands** (Islas Malvinas/ Falklands, South Georgia, the South Orkneys, Elephant Island and the South Shetlands) en route. Some of the ships are huge, carrying five hundred passengers or more; travellers generally report a better experience on one of the smaller vessels, plus the biggest ships are banned from landing passengers on Antarctica.

As an alternative to the cruises, several agencies, including Quark (see below), also offer packages in which you fly from Punta Arenas in Chile to Antarctica, explore by Zodiac boat for several days, and then fly back.

BOOKING A CRUISE

Cruises are very expensive, but you can sometimes get last-minute discounts (in some cases bringing trips to around US$4000/person) in Ushuaia, especially on the newest ships. Ushuaia's **Oficina Antártica**, next to the tourist office (Jan–March, Nov & Dec Mon–Fri 8am–6pm, Sat & Sun 9am–6pm; April–Oct Mon–Fri 9am–5pm; ☎02901 430015, ☷tierradelfuego.org.ar/ antartida/oficina_antartica), is a useful source of information. Otherwise, try contacting the following agencies: Antarpply, at Gob. Paz 633 (☎02901 436747, ☷antarpply.com), Canal Fun & Nature (see page 432), Rumbo Sur (see below) or SIM Expeditions (see page 426).

Whoever you book with, make sure they are a member of the International Association of Antarctica Tour Operators (IAATO; ☷iaato.org), which promotes safe and environmentally responsible travel.

OPERATORS

Polar Latitudes Based in the USA ☷polar-latitudes.com. Highly regarded company with an extensive range of itineraries lasting 11–22 days on luxurious ships. Kayaking beside icebergs, camping on the ice and "citizen scientist" projects are among the memorable activities on offer.

Quark Expeditions Based in the UK ☷quarkexpeditions.com. Quark offers a number of cruises lasting 10–20 days; prices start at US$6000/ person. Some vessels take as few at twelve passengers, giving you a more private and intimate experience, though you have to pay more.

Destinations Punta Arenas (2–3 daily; 12hr); Puerto Natales (1 daily via Punta Arenas; 15hr); Río Gallegos (3 daily; 12hr).

By ferry and boat Cruceros Australis (☷australis.com) runs scheduled luxury cruises (at least 1 weekly) to Punta Arenas, with three-, four-, seven- and eight-day trips, including one retracing the route of Charles Darwin. To cross from Ushuaia to Puerto Williams, Isla Navarino, the only option is to take a small boat with a company such as Piratour (☎02901 424834, ☷piratour.com.ar), Rumbo Sur

(☎02901 421139, ☷rumbosur.com.ar) or Ushuaia Boating (closed at the time of research but due to re-open; ☎02901 436193, ☷ushuaiaboating.com); all have offices in the Muelle Touristico. One-way tickets cost from US$120 and the boats are notoriously weather-dependent; crossings can be a rollercoaster ride and if it's too windy, they can be delayed for hours and sometimes days. Note that there's an ARS$60 embarkation tax for international boats.

Destinations Puerto Williams (Nov–April generally daily; 45min 1hr).

GETTING AROUND AND INFORMATION

Car rental Avis (☎02901 433323, ☷avis.com) and Hertz (☎02901 432429, ☷hertz.com) have offices at the airport.

Most companies do not permit you to take your rental car out of Argentina. Roads are fairly reliable from Oct to early

May; outside this period, carry snow chains and drive with caution.

Tourist office The main tourist office is at Av Prefectura Naval Argentina 470 (daily 9am–8pm; ☎02901 437666, ⓦturismoushuaia.com), by the passenger boat terminal: handily it has free wi-fi and toilets. There's also an information kiosk (☎02901 423970) at the airport that opens to meet incoming flights.

Club Andino Fadúl 50 (Mon–Fri 10am–12.30 & 3–8.30pm; ☎02901 422335, ⓦwww.clubandinoushuaia.com.ar). Provides information on trekking, climbing and winter sports.

ACTIVITIES AND TOURS

Ushuaia is an **outdoor activity hub** and a number of companies offer everything from conventional city tours and boat outings on the Beagle Channel to rock climbing, 4WD adventures, horseriding and diving.

Aero Club Ushuaia Luis Pedro Fique 151 ☎02901 421717, ⓦaeroclubushuaia.com.ar. Offers 15min, 30min and 1hr flights over the national park, the Faro Les Éclaireurs, the Beagle Channel, Estancia Harberton and parts of Lago Fagnano and Lago Escondido.

Canal Fun Roca 136 ☎02901 435777, ⓦcanalfun.com. A wide range of activities, including 4WD trips to Lago Fagnano, kayaking trips, horseriding and much more.

Canoero Catamaranes Ushuaia Muelle Turístico ☎02901 433893, ⓦcatamaranescanoero.com.ar. High-quality trips on a two-tiered catamaran along the Beagle Channel, taking in the birdlife of Isla de Pájaros, a sea-lion colony, Estancia Harberton and the penguins of Isla Martillo, and the Faro Les Éclaireurs.

Compañía de Guías de Patagonia San Martín 628 ☎02901 437753, ⓦcompaniadeguias.tur.ar. Experienced agency that runs multi-day trekking trips in Tierra del Fuego and arranges ice- and rock-climbing, kayaking and mountain-biking.

Heli Ushuaia San Martín at Lasserre ☎02901 444444, ⓦheliushuaia.com.ar. Scenic helicopter circuits (7–45min), the shortest covering the city highlights, and the other three taking in various combinations of natural highlights around Ushuaia.

Piratour Muelle Turístico ☎02901 424834, ⓦpiratour.net. The only company authorized to offer a walk with the Magellanic penguins on Isla Martillo, which allows you to see the birds up close.

Tres Marías Muelle Turístico ☎02901 436416, ⓦtresmariasweb.com. This is the only boat company allowed to land on Isla H, taking just eight passengers at a time on hiking/birding excursions.

Ushuaia Divers ☎02901 444701, ⓦushuaiadivers.com. Reputable operator running diving trips in the frigid Beagle Channel to see shipwrecks, sea lions and king crabs.

ACCOMMODATION

Ushuaia has a good but pricey range of hotels and hostels. December to February is peak season, when you should book **accommodation** well in advance.

HOTELS AND B&BS

★ **Arakur** 4km northeast of the city centre ☎02901 442900, ⓦarakur.com; map p.427. The top hotel in Ushuaia – literally and figuratively. Atop Cerro Alarken, flanked by a private nature reserve, and with stupendous views, Arakur boasts modern en suites – curtains open and close at the press of a button – smart service, a well-equipped spa (with heated indoor and outdoor pools) and a great restaurant; if you can, opt for a Beagle Channel-facing room. US$315

B&B Nahuel 25 de Mayo 440 ☎02901 423068, ⓦbybnahuel.com.ar; map p.427. A bright green exterior makes this guesthouse easy to spot; inside are homely, rather frilly rooms (one of which has shocking-pink walls you'll either love or hate) with shared or private bathrooms. There's a TV lounge. US$91

★ **Galeazzi-Basily B&B** Gob Valdéz 323 ☎02901 423213, ⓦavesdelsur.com.ar; map p.427. This guesthouse, run by the warm and hospitable, English- and French-speaking Frances and Alejandro, is an excellent place to meet fellow travellers without sacrificing comfort or privacy. Besides the twin and a double there are two fully equipped *cabañas* which sleep up to four. Doubles US$80, *cabañas* US$140

Hotel Austral 9 de Julio 250 ☎02901 422223, ⓦhotelaustral.com.ar; map p.427. One of the better mid-range options in a town painfully short of them, Austral has a conveniently central location, very comfortable en-suite rooms with bright decor, queen-sized beds and TVs, and friendly service. Book well in advance. US$131

Las Hayas Luis F. Martial 1650 ☎02901 442000, ⓦlashayas.com.ar; map p.427. Located on the road to the Martial Glacier, this handsome top-end hotel has large en suites, efficient staff, a heated indoor pool, a good spa, a bar and a fine dining restaurant. Free shuttles run guests to/from the city centre (some 4.5km away). US$170

Posada del Fin del Mundo Rivadavia and Gob. Valdez ☎02901 435062, ⓦposadadelfindelmundo.com.ar; map p.427. Homely rooms – all with private bathrooms, flowery curtains, and TVs – good views, and a friendly welcome greet you at this guesthouse, a 10min walk uphill from the city centre. US$110

★ **Tierra de Leyendas** Tierra de Vientos 2448 ☎02901 446565, ⓦtierradeleyendas.com.ar; map p.427. A short drive southwest of the city centre, this small boutique hotel gives you a choice between two views: the sea or the mountains. Besides the splendid location, the deluxe rooms all come with jacuzzis and there's a superb on-site restaurant. US$172

HOSTELS

Antarctica Hostel Antártida Argentina 270 ☎02901 435774, ⓦantarcticahostel.com; map p.427. This hostel's best feature is the huge, light-drenched lounge with colourful wall hangings, mini-library, guitars for guest use and a bona fide bar serving a good range of drinks. However, the plain upstairs six-bed dorms are a bit of a hike from the downstairs bathrooms. Dorms US$22, doubles US$86

Cruz del Sur Gob. Deloqui 242 ☎02901 434099; map p.427. Although it lags a bit behind the other

hostels reviewed here, the "Southern Cross" is a reliable if unexciting choice. It has a well-equipped kitchen, a relaxed lounge area and a small library. The four- to eight-bed dorms are warm and clean, but rather compact. US$23

★ **La Posta** Perón Sur 864, 3km southwest of downtown ☎02901 444650, ⓦlapostahostel.com. ar; map p.427. Lovely family-run hostel with facilities more akin to a hotel than a backpacker joint: two kitchens, free laundry, well-scrubbed dorms with five to eight beds, private rooms and apartments with kitchenettes. There's a tangible sense of guest camaraderie and the owners are treasure troves of information. Dorms US$22, doubles US$75, apartments US$115

Yakush Piedrabuena 118 ☎02901 435807, ⓦhostelyakush.com; map p.427. One of the best hostels in Ushuaia, in a central location. It gets high marks for its good communal areas, sociable atmosphere and economical four- to six-bed dorms and private rooms. Dorms US$28, doubles US$90

10

EATING

CAFÉS AND CHEAP EATS

El Almacén Ramos Generales Av Maipú 749 ☎02901 424317; map p.427. At this half-museum, half-café/bakery, the antique-dotted surroundings are as much of a draw as the hearty soups, filled baguettes and mains (AR$260–450) such as goulash; you can also get appealing croissants and *pains au chocolat*. Daily 9am–midnight.

Austral Modern 9 de julio 74; map p.427. This café aims for a hip, Scandinavian aesthetic, with minimalist decor and a window filled with Fjällräven rucksacks, but it also produces fine coffee (AR$45–85), plus a short but sweet range of sandwiches, cakes and snacks. Tasteful TDF-themed souvenirs, too. Mon–Sat 9am–1.30pm & 4–8.30pm.

Freddo San Martín and Rivadavia ⓦfreddo.com. ar; map p.427. This famous Argentine chain serves up excellent, and very moreish, ice cream (from AR$60): you can't go wrong with any of the various dulce de leche flavours. Hot drinks and snacks, including *medialunas* (sweet, doughy croissants), are available too. Mon–Thurs & Sun 10am–12.30am, Fri 10am–1am, Sat 10am–1.30am.

El Vagón Av Maipú 771 ☎02901 421480, ⓦelvagonushuaia.com.ar; map p.427. Decked out like an antique, wood-panelled train carriage, with glimpses of labouring convicts out of the "windows", this café offers "passengers" a relatively economical (for Ushuaia) menu of pizzas (from AR$120), pastas (AR$170–250), stir fries and snacks. Mon–Fri 8am–midnight, Sat 10am–midnight.

RESTAURANTS

Bodegón Fueguino San Martín 859 ☎02901 431972, ⓦtierradehumos.com; map p.427. Park yourself on a sheepskin-draped wooden bench in this historic wooden house (built in 1896) and order the likes of lamb in red wine sauce or pork leg with orange and honey sauce (mains AR$250–350). Good TDF-brewed beer (from AR$60), too. Tues–Sun noon–2.45pm & 7.45–11.45pm, Mon 7.45–11.45pm.

★ **Kalma Resto** Gob. Valdez 293 ☎02901 425786, ⓦkalmaresto.com.ar; map p.427. In a new location, but still the culinary king of Ushuaia. Chef Jorge's menu changes depending on seasonal availability of local ingredients, but you may be treated to the likes of king crab with apple, peppers and "sea air" and a deconstructed *chocotorta*. The presentation and service is flawless; if you're going to splurge on a meal (five-course set menu AR$950) in Argentina, do it here. Reservations essential. Mon–Sat 7–11pm.

★ **Kaupé** Roca 470 ☎02901 422704, ⓦkaupe.com. ar; map p.427. This stylish, well-established hilltop restaurant holds its own against the newcomers thanks to the efforts of chef Ernesto, who works wonders with *centolla* and *merluza negra* dishes, and the extensive wine list. The king crab crêpes in saffron sauce are particularly good (mains AR$250–400). Reservations recommended. Mon–Sat noon–2pm & 6.30–11pm.

María Lola Resto Deloqui 1048 ☎02901 421185, ⓦmarialolaresto.com.ar; map p.427. Besides its superlative views of the bay, this slick, professional restaurant delivers creative and classic dishes: think linguine with king crab and scallops, or Fuegian lamb with sauteed vegetables (mains from AR$240); each dish is thoughtfully paired with a suggested wine. Mon–Sat 12.30–2.30pm & 8–11pm.

El Turco San Martín 1410 ☎02901 424711; map p.427. No-frills local restaurant that provides hearty (if not especially exciting) meals at relatively low (for Ushuaia) prices. The menu features *milanesas*, pizzas, pastas and steaks, plus a selection of fish dishes (mains AR$110–320). Mon–Sat noon–3pm & 8pm–midnight.

DRINKING

Dublín 9 de Julio 168 ☎02901 430744; map p.427. This green-walled, red-roofed pub is a good place for a draught beer (AR$80 plus), with a buzzing atmosphere and occasional live music. Apart from the Guinness posters, however, there isn't much in the way of Irish trappings. Daily 7pm–4am.

Küar Perito Moreno 2232 ☎02901 437396, ☻kuar.com.ar; map p.427. Set in an attractive stone-and-timber building right on the seafront, on the road towards Río Grande, this youthful bar-restaurant has stupendous views and a blazing fire, as well as heaped picadas, snacks, main meals and a wide range of beers, cocktails and wine (alcoholic drinks from AR$80). It has another, less scenically located city centre branch (San Martín 471). Mon–Sat 12.30–3.30pm & 6.30pm–midnight.

SHOPPING

In addition to the options reviewed here, **Austral Modern** (see page 433) has a small, tasteful collection of pottery, bags and purses, while **Ramos Generales** (see page 433) sells kitsch and very Argentine penguin-shaped jugs (used typically for wine).

Boutique del Libro San Martín 1120 ☎02901 424750, ☻boutiquedellibro.com.ar; map p.427. Easily the best bookshop in Ushuaia, with a range of English-language fiction and non-fiction titles, including several on Tierra del Fuego and numerous on Antarctica. Mon–Sat 10am–1pm & 3.30–8.30pm.

Paseo de los Artesanía Maipú and Lassere; map p.427. Near the tourist office and, for some reason, pumping out Argentine rock throughout the day, this collection of craft and art stalls is a handy place to pick up a souvenir or two. Daily 10am–7pm.

DIRECTORY

Banks and exchange There are ATMs at most banks, most of which are along San Martín; there's also the HSBC at Maipú and Godoy. Note, however, that they often run low on cash on and immediately after the weekend.

Hospital The regional hospital is at 12 de Octubre, between Maipú and Fitz Roy (☎02901 423200 or ☎02901 441000).

Laundry Soles del Milenio (Gob. Paz 219; Mon–Fri 9.30am–1.30pm & 4–8pm, Sat 10am–2pm; ☎02901 424108).

Cerro Martial and Glaciar Martial

Chair lift closed indefinitely for maintenance at the time of writing • A taxi from Ushuaia centre costs around AR$130

There are lofty views from the base of **Glaciar Martial**, a receding glacier that's accessed from the top of the 7km road that winds up **Cerro Martial** from the city. From the car park, it may be possible to take the chair lift part of the way; it's then a further ninety-minute uphill hike (or a two-hour hike up without the chair lift) and scramble to the base of the glacier. Views of the channel below are even better than the glacier itself. A charming *refugio* sells snacks at the bottom of the chair lift and canopy tours are on offer in peak season (☻canopyushuaia.com.ar; AR$450–600).

Beagle Channel

Boats depart from Ushuaia's Muelle Turístico; several companies run tours (around AR$1300; plus AR$20 embarkation tax) of the channel (see page 432)

No visit to Ushuaia is complete without a boat trip on the **Beagle Channel**, the majestic, mountain-fringed sea passage south of the city. Most tours visit Les Éclaireurs

WINTER SPORTS AROUND USHUAIA

To ski at the end of the world, come sometime between June and early September (though not in July if you wish to avoid the holidaying crowds) and head for **Cerro Castór** (day tickets AR$560–1280; ☎02901 499301, ⓦcerrocastor.com), the only alpine ski resort in the area, 26km from Ushuaia along the RN-3 and boasting powder snow as well as 24km of ski runs. The fifteen slopes feature a good mix of runs, and you can rent equipment at the resort (AR$665–735/day for full ski/snowboard gear). Ask at the tourist office about transport to and from Ushuaia. If cross-country skiing is your passion, you won't want to miss the annual **Marcha Blanca** (ⓦmarchablanca.com) ski marathon.

Around 20km northeast of Ushuaia is the **Valle de Lobos** (☎015 612319, ⓦvalledelobos. com). This husky breeding centre offers dog-sledding, snowmobile rides and off-road safaris, depending on the season.

10

Lighthouse – once thought to be the "Lighthouse at the End of the World" from Jules Verne's eponymous novel. Other popular destinations include Isla de los Pájaros, Isla de los Lobos, Estancia Harberton, the penguin colony on Isla Martillo and Parque Nacional Tierra del Fuego. The main draw is the chance to spot **marine wildlife**, including albatrosses, giant petrels, skuas, cormorants, South American terns and Magellanic penguins; resident sea mammals are sea lions, Peale's dolphins, minke whales and, if you're lucky, killer whales. Tours returning by land from Estancia Harberton stop by the **árboles banderas** – trees bent sideways by the fierce Patagonian wind, the *Escoba de Díos* (God's Broom).

Estancia Harberton and around

85km east of Ushuaia along the scenic RN-3 then Route J (Ruta 33) • Jan to mid-April & Oct–Dec daily 10am–7pm • $240 (includes a 2hr guided walking tour of the homestead and the museum) • ⓦestanciaharberton.com • From mid-Oct to March several travel agencies (mostly based at the Muelle Turístico) run buses from Ushuaia to Harberton (1hr 30min–2hr); a taxi from Ushuaia costs around AR$3345 one way

Patagonia's most historic ranch, **Estancia Harberton** is an ordered assortment of whitewashed buildings on the shores of a sheltered bay. Built by Reverend Thomas Bridges, the man who authored one of the two seminal Fuegian texts, the *Yámana–English Dictionary*, it was the inspiration for the other, Lucas Bridges' classic, *Uttermost Part of the Earth*. As well as being a place where scientists and shipwrecked sailors were assured assistance, Harberton provided sanctuary for indigenous groups.

Today the *estancia* is owned by the fourth- and fifth-generation descendants of Thomas Bridges, and is open for **guided tours** that take in the copse on the hill – Tierra del Fuego's first nature reserve – where you learn about the island's plant life, authentic reconstructions of Yámana dwellings, the family cemetery and the old shearing shed. Housed in a building at the entrance to the farmstead is an impressive marine-mammal museum, **Museo Acatushún**.

Isla Martillo

While at Harberton you can cross to the Reserva Yecapasela on **Isla Martillo**, the only island in the Beagle Channel that **penguins** call home. There are large colonies of two species – Magellanic and the orange-beaked sub-Antarctic Gentoo. In recent years a few king penguins have also arrived. The sensitively run tours are a wonderful way to view the creatures.

Lucas Bridges Trail

Opened in 1898 to drive herds of sheep from Harberton over the mountains to a new *estancia*, Viamonte, on the Atlantic coast, the **Lucas Bridges Trail** is a rewarding challenge for hardy travellers. Although you can attempt the trek on your own, it is

10

not to be taken lightly: register first at Harberton, where you can obtain a basic map (there's also more info on the website). Forest fires are a real danger here: don't start a fire and be extremely careful with cigarettes. You can take a guided tour with Luis Turi (☎02901 437753, ⓦcompaniadeguias.com.ar).

ARRIVAL AND DEPARTURE

ESTANCIA HARBERTON AND AROUND

By tour Travel agencies offer guided day-trips to Harberton, often combined with a tour of the Beagle Channel. The only operator permitted to land boats on Isla Martillo is Piratour (see page 432); its half-day bus and boat trips depart from Ushuaia via Harberton but don't really visit the *estancia*.

ACCOMMODATION AND EATING

★ **Estancia Harberton** 85km east of Ushuaia, Skype estanciaharberton.turismo, ⓦestanciaharberton. com. Comfortable accommodation is provided in the old *Shepherd House*, which has en-suite rooms sleeping up to three people, a shared kitchenette and a large porch; more basic accommodation – three small private rooms with a shared bathroom and kitchenette – is on offer in the *Foreman's House Hostel*. Rates for the former include full board, an Isla Martillo trip, an *estancia* tour and a museum visit (half-board packages also available); rates for the latter include breakfast, the *estancia* tour and the museum visit. Free camping is permitted, though there are no facilities; register first at the *estancia*. There is a lovely teashop and restaurant. *Foreman's House Hostel* US$100, *Shepherd House* US$580

Parque Nacional Tierra del Fuego

12km west of Ushuaia • Summer daily 8am–8pm; rest of year reduced hours • ARS350

Parque Nacional Tierra del Fuego protects 630 square kilometres of jagged mountains, intricate lakes, southern beech forest, swampy peat bog, sub-Antarctic tundra and verdant coastline. The park stretches along the frontier with Chile, from the Beagle Channel to the **Sierra de Injugoyen** north of Lago Fagnano, but only the southernmost quarter is open to the public, accessed by the RN-3 from Ushuaia.

There are three main sectors: **Bahía Ensenada** and **Río Pipo** in the east; **Lago Roca** further to the west; and the **Lapataia** area to the south of Lago Roca, which includes Laguna Verde and, at the end of RN-3, Bahía Lapataia on the Beagle Channel. Here you may see **birds** such as Magellanic woodpeckers, condors, torrent ducks, steamer ducks, upland geese and buff-necked ibises, and **mammals** such as guanacos, the rare sea otter, Patagonian grey foxes and their larger, endangered cousin, the native Fuegian fox once heavily hunted for its pelt. Introduced Canadian beavers (see page 419) and European rabbits also run amok, wreaking environmental havoc.

The park offers several beautiful **trails**, ideal for short excursions or day-hikes.

Bahía Ensenada and Senda Costera

The small **Bahía Ensenada**, 2km south of the crossroads by the Tren del Fin del Mundo train station, is where you'll find the jetty for boats (no fixed schedule) to Lapataia and the Isla Redonda. It's also the trailhead for one of the most pleasant walks in the park, the **Senda Costera** (8km; 3–4hr), which starts at the jetty and follows the shore of Bahía Ensenada through dense coastal forest of evergreen beech, winter's bark and *lenga*, meeting the RN-3 near the Lapataia park administration centre. It affords spectacular views of the Beagle Channel, passing grass-covered mounds that were former campsites of the indigenous Yámana.

Cerro Guanaco

The climb up **Cerro Guanaco** (8km; 7hr return), the 970m-high mountain ridge on the north side of Lago Roca, is relatively challenging. Take the Hito XXIV path from the car park at Lago Roca and after ten minutes you'll cross a small bridge over a stream. Immediately afterwards, the path forks: to the left, **Senda Hito XXIV** runs along the northeastern shore of Lago Roca to an obelisk that marks Argentina's border with Chile

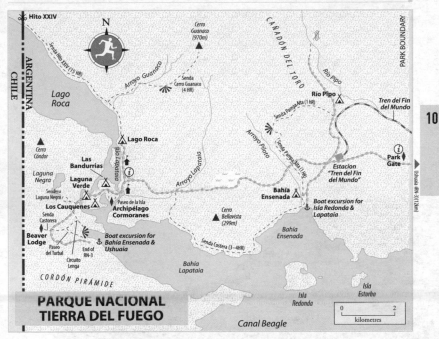

PARQUE NACIONAL TIERRA DEL FUEGO

(3.5km; 1hr 30min one way). To the right, **Senda Cerro Guanaco** runs up the slope to the summit of its namesake peak.

The path up the forested mountainside is steep, and parts are boggy. The view from the crest to the south is memorable: the tangle of islands and rivers of the Archipiélago Cormoranes, Lapataia's sinuous curves, the Isla Redonda in the Beagle Channel, and across to the Chilean islands, Hoste and Navarino, separated by the Murray Narrows.

ARRIVAL AND INFORMATION

PARQUE NACIONAL TIERRA DEL FUEGO

By bus High-season private buses (daily 9am–5pm; hourly; 20–30min; AR$500 return) depart from the bus stand on the corner of Maipú and Fadúl in Ushuaia for various points in the park. Services are reduced off season.

By train The Tren del Fin del Mundo is a scenic narrow-gauge train. It departs from its main station, 8km west of Ushuaia (daily: Jan–April & Sept–Dec 9.30am, noon & 3pm; May–Aug 10am, 12.30pm – if there's enough demand – & 3pm; 50min each way; AR$790 return; ☎02901 431600, ⓦtrendelfindelmundo.com.ar) and arrives at the park station, 2km from the main gate. A taxi from Ushuaia to the main station costs AR$650.

By taxi It's only worth taking a taxi from Ushuaia (AR$930 to Lago Roca or AR$1115 to Bahía Lapataia, both one way; AR$2230 return with 3hr waiting time) if there are four of you.

Park office By the park entrance (summer daily 8am–8pm; rest of year reduced hours). Offers a park map in exchange for your entrance fee (AR$350); if you're planning to come back the following day, let the staff know, and you won't have to pay the fee twice. There's also a visitor centre, the Alakush (same opening hours; ⓦcentroalakush.com.ar), with a restaurant, on Ruta 3, near the western end of the Senda Costera.

Easter Island and the Juan Fernández Archipelago

MOAI AT AHU TONGARIKI, EASTER ISLAND

Easter Island and the Juan Fernández Archipelago

Chile's two remote island territories, enchanting Easter Island and the little-known Juan Fernández Archipelago, are collectively referred to as the Islas Esporádicas ("Far Flung Isles"). Both are national parks and have been singled out by UNESCO for special protection. Both are expensive to visit, and most travellers never do, but anyone lucky enough to make the journeys will find their efforts and expenditure richly rewarded with a set of tantalizingly enigmatic statues and one of the world's most precarious ecosystems, respectively.

11

Lost in the vastness of the ocean, tiny **Easter Island** (or, in Spanish, Isla de Pascua) remains a world unto itself, its closest inhabited neighbour being Pitcairn Island, 2250km northwest. Spanning just 23km at its longest stretch, the island is triangular, with low-lying extinct volcanoes rising out of each corner. Scattered between these points are dozens of **moai**, the intriguing monolithic stone **statues** that have made the island universally famous.

Much closer to the mainland, at a mere 675km west of Valparaíso, but still relatively unknown, the **Juan Fernández Archipelago** is, ironically, far more difficult to reach. With their sharp, jagged peaks, coated in lush, deep-green foliage, the islands boast a topography that is among the most spectacular in Chile. The archipelago's largest and only permanently inhabited island – **Isla Robinson Crusoe** – started out as a pirates' refuge. In 1709 it was brought to public attention when Scottish seaman Alexander Selkirk was rescued from its shores after being marooned there for more than four years – his story was used as the basis for *The Adventures of Robinson Crusoe* (see page 459).

Easter Island

One of the most remote places on earth, tiny **Easter Island** is home to around seven thousand people. Around half are indigenous (who generally call themselves Rapa Nui; mainland Chileans refer to them as *pascuenses*), with the rest predominantly *continentales* (mainland Chilean immigrants). The Rapa Nui have Polynesian features and speak their own Polynesian-based language (also called Rapa Nui) in addition to Spanish. Virtually the entire population lives in the island's single settlement, **Hanga Roa**, and most islanders make their living from tourism, which has been growing steadily since an airstrip was built here in 1968.

The key points of interest are found within **Parque Nacional Rapa Nui**, which comprises all of the island but Hanga Roa. Highlights include **Rano Kau**, a huge volcanic crater and site of the ceremonial village of **Orongo**; the **Rano Raraku** quarry,

TAPATI RAPA NUI FESTIVAL, EASTER ISLAND

Highlights

❶ Tapati Rapa Nui festival Discover the mysterious roots of Easter Island's ancient culture at its carnival (late January/early February), which features everything from traditional dancing and singing to hurtling down volcanic slopes on banana trunks. See page 449

❷ Ahu Tongariki Fifteen impeccably restored *moai* (giant statues) lined up to be admired against a backdrop of green cliffs and roaring waves. Watching the sun rise here is one of the most memorable experiences you'll have on the island – or anywhere. See page 450

❸ Rano Raraku This mighty mountain at the heart of Easter Island is where the *moai* were quarried. Some, too big to move, never left the rock where they were hewn – including El Gigante, the biggest *moai* ever carved. See page 451

❹ Orongo Imagine the mind-boggling rituals of the Birdman cult as you gaze out at craggy islets in a sapphire-blue ocean or inwards to a reed-filled crater at one of Easter Island's most breathtaking natural sites. See page 456

❺ Juan Fernández flora and fauna Frolic underwater with fish and sea lions, watch the antics of hummingbirds and observe dozens of endemic species of plant on this treasure island of unique (and painfully fragile) wildlife. See page 456

HIGHLIGHTS ARE MARKED ON THE MAPS ON PAGES 442 AND 458

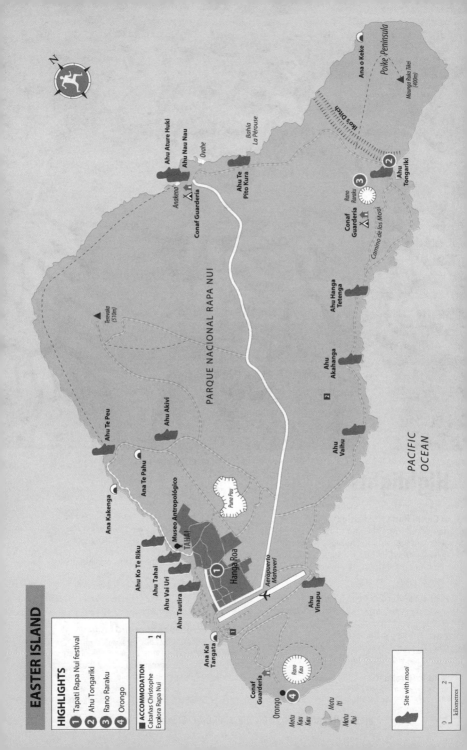

EASTER ISLAND

HIGHLIGHTS

1. Tapati Rapa Nui festival
2. Ahu Tongariki
3. Rano Raraku
4. Orongo

■ ACCOMMODATION

Cabañas Christophe	1
Explora Rapa Nui	2

Ana Kakenga

Ahu Te Peu

Ahu Akivi

Ana Te Pahu

Terevaka
(510m)

PARQUE NACIONAL RAPA NUI

Ahu Ko Te Riku

Ahu Tahai

Museo Antropológico

TAHAI

Ahu Vai Uri

Ahu Tautira

Ana Kai Tangata

Hanga Roa

Pana Pau

Aeropuerto
Mataveri

Conaf Guarderia

Orongo

Rano
Kau

Motu
Kau Kau

Motu
Iti

Motu
Nui

Ahu Vinapu

Ahu Vaihu

Ahu Akahanga

Ahu Hanga
Tetenga

Camino de los Moai

Conaf
Guarderia

Rano
Raraku

Ahu
Tongariki

Ahu Te
Pito Kura

Bahía
La Pérouse

Conaf Guarderia

Anakena

Ovahe

Ahu Nau Nau

Ahu Ature Huki

Iko's Ditch

Poike Peninsula

Ana o Keke

Maunga Puka Tiket
(400m)

PACIFIC
OCEAN

Site with moai

0   2
kilometres

where almost all the *moai* were carved; and the largest *ahu* (platform) on the island, **Ahu Tongariki**, which boasts fifteen *moai*. Archeological treasures aside, Easter Island has much to offer outdoor enthusiasts, from **diving** in waters with arguably the best visibility in the world to **surfing** major waves.

Easter Island is two hours behind mainland Chile. The weather is fairly constant year-round, with an average temperature of around 23°C (73°F) in January and February, and 18°C (64°F) in July and August. Late January and early February is the busiest time, thanks to the annual **Tapati Rapa Nui festival**. A warning: many places don't accept **credit cards**, so bring plenty of cash with you. US dollars are widely accepted.

Brief history
Easter Island was "discovered" and named by Dutch naval commander **Jacob Roggeveen** on Easter Sunday, 1722. In the absence of any written records left by the islanders, Roggeveen's **log** is the earliest written account of the island. His party spent only a day on land, long enough to observe the "particularly high erected stone images". After their departure, it was another 48 years before Easter Island

11

WHERE DID THE RAPA NUI COME FROM?

The islanders' oral history claims Easter Island's original colonizer was **Hotu Matu'a**, a great *ariki henua* (chief) who lived possibly in Polynesia or the Marquesas. It had been revealed to Hotu Matu'a's tattooist, in a dream, that an island with craters and fine beaches awaited his master. The chief dispatched a reconnaissance party to find this promised land, following some time later with his family and fellow colonists. He arrived on Anakena beach, just as his wife was giving birth to their first son.

As *ariki henua*, Hotu Matu'a was not a political leader, but a revered and important person with great supernatural qualities (*mana*). Accordingly, he and his home were *tapu* (sacred and untouchable), and so Hotu Matu'a and his family lived at Anakena while the rest of his party dispersed around the island. Their families eventually grew into eight separate kin-groups, and as time passed, these groups became more sophisticated and stratified.

THOR HEYERDAHL AND THE SOUTH AMERICAN THEORY

Central to any discussion of Easter Island's settlement are the controversial theories of **Thor Heyerdahl**, the Norwegian explorer-archeologist whose widely publicized expeditions and books generated enormous interest in the island. Heyerdahl was convinced the island had been colonized by South American settlers and, in 1948, he proved, spectacularly, that such a voyage was possible when he and five companions successfully sailed a traditional balsa raft (the *Kon Tiki*) from Peru to an island east of Tahiti.

He backed up his theory with some persuasive but highly selective details, concentrating on the fact that Pacific winds and currents move in a westward direction; the presence in Polynesia of the sweet potato, indisputably of South American origin; the resemblance between the stonework of some Easter Island platforms and certain types of Inca masonry; and the ancient Peruvian custom of artificially extending the ear lobes, just like the islanders at the time of European contact. He failed to explain, however, the total absence of South American pottery and textiles in Polynesia, and the fact that no trace of any indigenous South American language had been found there.

WHAT THE EXPERTS SAY

The view of most experts is that Easter Island was colonized by Polynesians from the west – an opinion backed by linguistic evidence, physical anthropology and the proliferation of Polynesian plants. Which part of Polynesia these settlers came from is still open to debate, though the **Marquesas** is thought the most likely.

As for the date of the settlers' arrival, all we can be sure of is that they were constructing *ahu* (ceremonial platforms) by 800 AD. No one knows for sure if this culture developed in complete isolation, or if another wave of colonists arrived later, as suggested in some of the oral traditions.

was revisited, this time by Spanish commander **Felipe González**, who mapped the island and claimed it for King Carlos III of Spain during a six-day stay.

Four years later, **Captain Cook** anchored here in the hope of restoring the health of his scurvy-ridden crew. He, too, observed with incredulity the "stupendous figures", though he noted some lay strewn on the ground, toppled from their platforms. Later visitors reported an increasing number of **fallen statues**, and by 1825 all of the *moai* on Hanga Roa bay had been destroyed.

The arrival of the slave traders

In 1805, the island was raided by the first of the **slave traders**, when an American schooner captured 22 men and women to be used as seal hunters on the Juan Fernández Islands. After three days at sea, the prisoners were allowed onto the deck, whereupon they promptly threw themselves overboard and drowned in a desperate attempt to swim back to the island. Between 1862 and 1864, Peruvian sailors captured over two thousand five hundred islanders, who were shipped off to work as slaves in the guano mines.

After many of the islanders had died from disease and the appalling conditions in the mines, the Bishop of Tahiti finally managed to persuade the Peruvian government to repatriate the remaining prisoners – most of whom died on the voyage home. Tragically, the sixteen who made it back infected the rest of the islanders with smallpox and TB, reducing the population to around one hundred. Critically, the loss of life was accompanied by the loss of a crucial part of the island's culture and collective memory, for the last *ariki henua* (high chief), *moari* (keepers of sacred knowledge) and *tangata rongo rongo* (specialist readers) were among those who perished.

Missionaries and plantations

A certain degree of stability came when the first missionary, **Eugène Eyraud**, arrived in 1864 and set to converting the islanders to Christianity, a mission fully accomplished by the time of his death, four years later. The peace was disrupted, however, when a French plantation owner, **Jean-Baptiste Onésime Dutrou-Bornier**, bought up large tracts of land and proceeded to run the island as his personal ranch, paying the islanders a pittance for their hard labour and resorting to violence when they wouldn't cooperate. When the missionaries opposed Doutrou-Bornier's exploitation, he attacked their

RONGO RONGO: EASTER ISLAND'S MYSTERIOUS SCRIPT

In 1864, French missionary **Eugène Eyraud** wrote of "tablets or staff of wood covered with hieroglyphics" that he'd found in the islanders' homes. This was the first the outside world had heard of *ko hau motu mo rongo rongo* or "lines of script for recitation". The **rongo rongo** tablets remained firmly beyond the grasp of the scholars who came to study them, for none of the islanders knew how to read them. Almost 150 years later, no one has succeeded in deciphering them.

The script consists of tiny, tightly packed symbols carved in straight lines across the wooden boards. The symbols, which include representations of people, animals, birds and plants, are upside down on each alternate line. Late nineteenth-century oral testimonies suggest the tablets contained records of genealogies, myths, wars, deaths and religious hymns.

POPULAR THEORIES

Some modern scholars believe the script was developed after the first European contact, inspired by the written documents the Spaniards made the chiefs sign in 1770; others believe it is only one of four written languages in the world to have developed entirely independently of outside influence. The most widely accepted theory is that the symbols were **mnemonics** for use in recitals and chanting.

Today, fewer than thirty *rongo rongo* tablets remain in existence, all of them spirited off to overseas museums in Santiago, Rome, London and Washington, DC.

PARQUE NACIONAL RAPA NUI

There is a US$80 fee to enter **Parque Nacional Rapa Nui**, which covers most of the island's archeological sites. You buy the entry permit – which lasts for ten days – from the kiosk at the airport immediately after you land, and it will be checked at most of the sites. Note thata you can only visit Orongo and Rano Raraku once each; you can visit the rest of the sites as many times as you want.

Along with the permit, you'll receive a leaflet map warning you not to touch or interfere in any way with the *moai* or the other archeological sites. These rules are not to be taken lightly: an idiotic Finnish tourist was arrested, fined and banned from Chile for three years after chipping off the earlobe of a *moai* in 2008.

---

missions, forcing them to flee the island. He dealt a further blow to the island's slowly recovering population by sending all but a hundred islanders to Tahiti to work on his partner's plantation, before finally being murdered in 1877 by the oppressed islanders.

Annexation

The **Chilean government** acquired first Doutrou-Bornier's lands, and then most of the remaining land on the island, leaving only the village of **Hanga Roa** in the possession of the islanders. Then, on September 9, 1888, the Chilean Navy controversially **annexed** Easter Island, declaring it Chilean territory. Chile subsequently leased it to British wool-trading company Williamson Balfour, which virtually governed the island according to its own needs and interests.

In 1953, the company's lease was revoked and the Chilean Navy stepped in to resume command, though the islanders were given no say in the running of the island. It was not until 1964 that they were allowed outside Hanga Roa (let alone off the island), and granted full citizenship and the right to vote.

The drive towards autonomy

In recent years the management of some local affairs, including education (which is bilingual), has been transferred to the islanders. However, many continue to call for greater autonomy and even **secession**, expressing concern over issues including the pace of development and its effect on the environment, the impact of the growing tourist industry (around eighty thousand people visit each year), and the increasing numbers of mainland Chileans settling on the island. Overfishing and inadequate waste-disposal facilities are further problems.

While many of these problems remain unresolved, some positive steps were taken in 2017: the Chilean government gave the local community partial control of Parque Nacional Rapa Nui, and one of the world's largest **marine parks** – the 740,000-square-km **Rapa Nui Rahui Marine Protected Area** – was created offshore, protecting 142 endemic species, including 27 at risk of extinction.

INFORMATION **EASTER ISLAND**

A Companion to Easter Island, by James Grant-Peterkin of Easter Island Spirit (see page 447) is an informative guide to Rapa Nui and its attractions, while ⓦ imaginaisladepascua. com is a handy Spanish/English website.

Hanga Roa

The laidback town of **HANGA ROA** has been the island's only residential sector since the 1860s, when Catholic missionaries relocated the islanders here to facilitate their conversion. Its long, sprawling streets are lined with single-storey houses and fragrant eucalyptus trees, giving the place the feel of a recently settled frontier town.

Atamu Tekena is the main road, lined with souvenir shops, restaurants and tour agencies. Most of the action is centred around the Caleta Hanga Roa harbour, overlooked

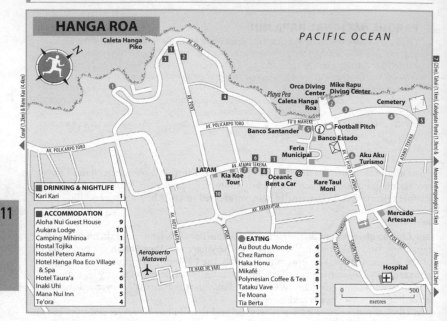

by Ahu Tautira, the only *moai* in the town proper. Restaurants stretch from here along oceanside **Policarpo Toro**, parallel to Atamu Tekena. East–west **Te Pito O Te Henua** connects the two, ending at the church, where islanders still congregate every Sunday morning. Just south of the pier lies tiny **Playa Pea**, where a rock pool safe for swimming is cordoned off from the stretch of ocean popular with surfers and body boarders.

ARRIVAL AND DEPARTURE

HANGA ROA

By plane LATAM (Atamu Tekena and Pont; ☎ 32 210 0279, ⓦ latam.com) flies to/from Santiago (1 or 2 daily; 4hr 50min–5hr 40min), and to/from Papeete, Tahiti (1 weekly;

5hr 50min). Mataveri airport is on the southern edge of Hanga Roa, 1km from the centre. Most hotels pick you up for free; a taxi to the centre costs around US$10.

GETTING AROUND

The easiest way to explore is on a **guided tour** (see page 447), though some of the less expensive ones feel a bit crowded and rushed.

By car/motorbike Many travellers rent a car (from around CH$45,000/day), motorbike (from CH$25,000/day) or even a quad bike (around CH$40,000/day) to explore the island. Book a vehicle as soon as you can after arrival (or before). Outlets include Aku Aku Turismo (see page 447) and Oceanic Rent a Car, Atamu Tekena s/n (☎ 32 210 0985, ⓦ rentacaroceanic.cl). Two things to note: there's no car

insurance on the island; and the many free-roaming horses can be a hazard, especially at night.
By bike/on foot You can visit some of the sites closest to Hanga Roa on a mountain bike or on foot, though travelling around the whole island under your own steam would be quite a challenge. Stores on Atamu Tekena, many hotels and Oceanic Rent a Car (see above) rent bikes (CH$10,000–15,000/day).

INFORMATION

Tourist office Tu'u Maheke and Policarpo Toro (Mon–Thurs 8.30am–5.30pm, Fri 9am–5pm; ☎ 32 210 0255, ⓦ sernatur.cl).

Conaf Mataveri s/n, on the outskirts of Hanga Roa (Jan–March & Dec 9am–7pm; April–Nov 9am–6pm; ☎ 32 210 0236, ⓦ conaf.cl); there is also a visitors' centre at Orongo (see page 456).

EASTER ISLAND TOURS AND ACTIVITIES

There are several ways to explore Easter Island, whether you want to get active or take a guided tour; the following **operators** are reliable. Almost all the hotels, and many of the guesthouses, offer tours, notably *Hotel Taura'a* and *Aukara Lodge* (see below).

Aku Aku Turismo Av Atamu Tekena s/n ☎32 210 0770, ⊛akuakuturismo.cl. Bilingual tours to all the main sites (from CH$26,000).

Cabalgatas Pantu Pikerauri Eco Lodge, Tekerera s/n ☎32 210 0577, ⊛pikerauri.com. Horseback tours (from US$55) of the west and north coasts, including the ascent of Maunga Terevaka, the island's highest point, plus overnight camping trips.

Easter Island Spirit ☎09 8741 5166, ⊛easterislandspirit.com. Excellent private tours (from US$140) that take in both the main sights and little-explored places; they are particularly good for keen photographers. Book online.

Kava Kava Tours ☎09 7216 5015, ⊛kavakavatours.com. Recommended private tours throughout the island, including sunrise and sunset excursions. Book online.

Kia Koe Tour Av Atamu Tekena s/n ☎32 210 0282, ⊛kiakoetour.cl. Bilingual tours to sites across the island (from CH$26,000).

Mike Rapu Diving Centre On the caleta ☎32 255 1055, ⊛mikerapu.cl. A range of scuba diving (from CH$35,000) and snorkelling (CH$20,000–25,000) trips. They also rent out kayaks (CH$15,000/3hr) and offer boat tours (CH$20,000).

Orca Diving Center On the caleta ☎32 255 0877 or ☎32 255 0375, ⊛orcadivingcenter.cl. The well-established outfit offers scuba diving (from CH$35,000) and snorkelling (CH$20,000–25,000) trips. Hare Orca, next door and attached to the centre, rents surfboards (CH$15,000/4hr), boogie boards (CH$10,000/4hr) and snorkelling gear (CH$10,000/8hr); the shop can put you in touch with surfing instructors.

11

ACCOMMODATION

Though there are some budget options, **accommodation** is more expensive than on the mainland. Book well in advance during busy times, such as Tapati (see page 449).

HANGA ROA
HOTELS AND GUESTHOUSES
Aloha Nui Guest House Av Atamu Tekena s/n ☎32 210 0274, ✉haumakatours@gmail.com; map p.446. Run by a charming couple, this tastefully decorated guesthouse has six clean and comfortable en suites, a tropical garden and a library filled with books, music and artwork. Excellent tours on offer, too. <u>CH$80,000</u>

Aukara Lodge Pont s/n ☎32 210 0539, ⊛aukara.com; map p.446. Follow the signs for the Aukara art gallery, which showcases the owner's pieces, to this small guesthouse, surrounded by a lush garden. As well as simple, comfortable rooms, there's a small kitchen for guests, and tours are available. <u>CH$85,000</u>

Hotel Hanga Roa Eco Village & Spa Av Pont s/n ☎32 255 3700, ⊛hangaroa.cl; map p.446. The smartest hotel in Hanga Roa, with spacious en suites with distinctive tree trunk designs, private terraces, minibars and huge beds. There's also a pool, a top-class restaurant-bar and a well-equipped spa. Half- and full-board options with tours available. Discounts for stays of more than two nights. <u>US$620</u>

Hotel Taura'a Av Atamu Tekena s/n ☎32 210 0463; map p.446. This reliable hotel, right in the heart of town, boasts spacious, airy a/c rooms and an attractive garden.

English and French are spoken, and the congenial owners run a good tour agency. <u>CH$114,000</u>

Inaki Uhi Av Atamu Tekena s/n ☎32 210 0231, ⊛inakiuhi.cl; map p.446. Very central guesthouse with sizeable, modern en suites with mini-fridges and plenty of wood panelling, a guest kitchen, a shady garden and friendly staff. <u>CH$85,000</u>

CABAÑAS
Hostal Tojika Apina s/n ☎9 9215 2167, ⊛tojika.com; map p.446. An excellent, economical choice, *Hostal Tojika* has a collection of simple, clean en-suite rooms sleeping up to five; the larger ones come with kitchenettes and are ideal for groups and families. <u>CH$55,000</u>

Mana Nui Inn Tahai s/n ☎32 210 0811, ⊛mananui.cl; map p.446. Boasting a peaceful location away from the town centre, and great sea views, *Mana Nui Inn* is a good mid-range option. There's a choice of *cabañas* with kitchenettes sleeping up to seven; all have private bathrooms, TVs, fridges and fans. Guests can also use the barbecue and laundry facilities. *Cabañas* <u>CH$92,000</u>

Te'ora Apina s/n ✉info@rapanuiteora.com, ⊛easterislandteora.bizland.com; map p.446. This friendly, good-value Canadian-run place has, amid its gardens, a trio of delightful, spotless *cabañas*; all come with kitchenettes, private patios and sea views. Laundry service (CH$5000/load) available. CH$40,000

HOSTEL AND CAMPSITE

Camping Mihinoa Pont s/n ☎ 32 255 1593, ⓦ mihinoa. com; map p.446. Probably the best budget option on the island, this large campsite offers excellent ocean views and is run by a friendly family. Showers, kitchen facilities, dining room and car, scooter and bike rental available; the lack of shade is the only drawback. The adjoining guesthouse has simple rooms and a five-bed dorm. Camping CH$10,500, dorms CH$16,000, doubles CH$40,000

Hostel Petero Atamu Petero Atamu s/n ☎ 32 255 1823, ⓦ hostalpeteroatamu.com; map p.446. Easter Island is a challenge for backpackers, but this hostel is a reasonable choice: the dorms and private rooms are tight, and the lime green colour scheme isn't for everyone, but the rates are hard to beat. Dorms CH$S16,000, doubles CH$25,000

AROUND HANGA ROA

Cabañas Christophe Policarpo Toro s/n ☎ 32 210 0826, ⓦ cabanaschristophe.com; map p.442. This good-value lodge is near the start of the trail up to Orongo, 2km southwest of Hanga Roa, so is best suited to travellers with their own transport. The rooms and cabins are en suite, with fridges and TVs; the latter sleep up to five people. Doubles CH$64,000, cabins CH$160,000

★ **Explora Rapa Nui** 8km east of Hanga Roa; reservations ☎ 2 2395 2800, ⓦ explora.com; map p.442. The most luxurious hotel on the island, and one of the most memorable places to stay in Chile, the tranquil, ecofriendly *Explora* has elegant, spacious en suites with all the creature comforts. There's also a wonderful pool and spa, classy restaurant and bar, and expert guides to help you explore (activities include diving, snorkelling, hiking and cycling). Rates are full board, including two daily excursions; minimum three-night stay. US$1126

EATING

Prices are higher than on the mainland. **Seafood** is a highlight, particularly the fresh tuna and lobster.

Au Bout du Monde Av Policarpo Toro s/n ☎ 32 255 2060; map p.446. A Belgian chef is at the helm at this charming restaurant, and the inventive menu features excellent food (mains CH$12,000–18,000) such as tuna in a Tahitian vanilla sauce, fresh pasta and a delectable chocolate mousse. Mon & Wed–Sun 12.30–3pm & 6.30–10.30pm.

Chez Ramon Av Te Pito Te Henua s/n ☎ 32 210 0833; map p.446. This low-key restaurant has an overgrown garden, friendly service and a short, straightforward menu: think fish soup, tuna *ceviche* and steak and chips. Dish of the day around CH$7000: good value for Easter Island. Mon–Sat noon–3pm & 7.30–10pm.

Haka Honu Av Policarpo Toro ☎ 32 255 1677; map p.446. This super-friendly, open-fronted restaurant has a breezy location looking out to sea. Excellent fish and seafood includes *pastel de jaiba* (crab gratin), *ceviche* and grilled fish with papaya chutney (mains CH$12,000–16,000). It's a great place for a sundowner. Tues–Sun 12.30–11pm.

★ **Mikafé** La Caleta; map p.446. This tiny café, with just a handful of tables outside, serves delicious home-made ice cream (from CH$2100) – banana split, blueberry and even beer are among the flavours – as well as cakes, muffins, pastries and some of the best coffee on the island. Mon–Sat 9am 9pm.

Polynesian Coffee & Tea Av Atamu Tekena; map p.446. Delightful café, on the main strip, serving hot drinks (CH$1500–4000), breakfast options and cakes. If you've over-indulged, opt for a wheatgrass shot and a bowl of acai, yoghurt and granola. Daily 7am–2pm & 5–9pm.

Tataku Vave Hanga Piko s/n ☎ 32 255 1544, ⓦ facebook.com/tatakuvave; map p.446. On the edge of town, with stunning sea views, particularly at sunset, this is a popular place for a drink or a meal: the cocktails and the *ceviche* are among the highlights. Mains CH$12,000–18,000. Mon–Sat noon–11pm.

Te Moana Av Policarpo Toro s/n, near the caleta ☎ 32 255 1578, ⓦ facebook.com/TeMoana.Restaurante; map p.446. Smart restaurant-bar, right on the front and perfect for a sundowner: there's a good range of cocktails (CH$5000–8000) and beers (including the Tahitian lager, Hinano). The food (mains CH$14,000–18,000) is good, too, but service can let the side down. Mon–Sat 12.30–11pm/midnight.

★ **Tia Berta** Av Atamu Tekena s/n ☎ 9 7979 6953; map p.446. Service may be a bit slack, but this popular local joint is a hit. Steer past the standard mains, and go for a delicious – and huge – seafood *empanada* (CH$3000–3500) with a cold Mahina beer (CH$4000). Mon–Sat noon–4pm.

DRINKING AND NIGHTLIFE

Hanga Roa has a shortage of genuine drinking spots; instead most restaurants double up as **bars** in the evening. Thanks to their locations, *Haka Honu*, *Tataku Vave* and *Te Moana* (see above) are all great sunset spots. Keep an eye out for the island's craft beer, Mahina: the IPA is particularly good.

EASTER ISLAND FESTIVALS

Tapati Rapa Nui is a ten-day cultural celebration in late January/early February. Celebrating Rapa Nui culture, tradition and history, the festival features dancing, body painting, statue carving, choral recitals, surfing displays, canoe races, re-enactments of old legends and huge *curanto* feasts. **Semana Santa** (Easter week) features lively celebrations at Hanga Roa's church. The **Ceremonia Culto al Sol** is a feast that takes place on June 21 for the winter solstice, while **Día de la Lengua Rapa Nui**, a celebration of the Rapa Nui language, is held in late November.

Kari Kari Av Atamu Tekena s/n ☏32 210 0767, ⓦfacebook.com/karikari.balletcultural; map p.446. The longest-running traditional dance-and-music show (1hr) on the island, featuring talented young performers in elaborate costumes. Entry US$25; with traditional *curanto* dinner US$60. Tues, Thurs & Sat 9pm.

DIRECTORY

Banks and exchange There are a couple of ATMs: Banco Estado, Tu'u Maheke s/n and Banco Santander, Policarpo Toro s/n; the latter is generally more reliable. Both also offer cash advances on credit cards. Several places change cash (generally at poor rates), and US dollars are widely accepted. Bring a stash of pesos/dollars from the mainland to be on the safe side.

Honorary counsel British honorary counsel James Grant-Peterkin (☏09 8741 5166, ⓦeasterislandspirit.com) can support travellers from the UK (and elsewhere) who get into trouble on Rapa Nui.

Hospital Hospital Hanga Roa on Simón Paoa s/n (☏32 210 0183), southeast of the church, has basic medical facilities.

Internet and wi-fi Most hotels and guesthouses offer wi-fi. There are also free hotspots around town, including by the tourist office (see page 446) and in the square at the corner of Av Atamu Tekena and Av Te Pito Ote Henua. Connections are slow.

The southeastern circuit

The loop formed by the 16km southern coast road and the 30km paved road from Anakena to Hanga Roa lends itself to a convenient sightseeing route that takes in some of the island's most impressive sights – including **Ahu Vinapu**, **Ahu Tongariki**, **Rano Raraku** and **Anakena**.

Ahu Vinapu

From Hanga Roa, follow Avenida Hotu Matu'a down to the southern coast road then turn right, just after the white oil containers, and you'll reach **Ahu Vinapu**, the site of two large *ahus*, with *moai* lying in fragments behind the platforms. Anyone who's seen Machu Picchu or other Inca ruins will be amazed by the similarity of the masonry of Vinapu's main *ahu*, made of huge, mortarless blocks of stone "fitted carefully to one another without a crack or a hole". Close to this platform, known as Vinapu I, is another *ahu*, Vinapu II, whose stonework is vastly inferior to its neighbour.

Thor Heyerdahl's expedition was the first to excavate the site and, with radiocarbon dating, concluded that the precisely carved Vinapu I was among the earliest built on the island, and that Vinapu II was a much later construction, suggesting that the island's first settlers imported the highly specialized stone-carving techniques of Peru, and that later platforms were built by "far less capable architects, who were no longer masters of the complicated Inca technique". Modern archeologists, however, believe that this impressive masonry is simply a perfected example of a style developed locally on Easter Island, and more recent radiocarbon tests have given Vinapu I a new date of 1516 AD, and Vinapu II a date of 857 AD – the reverse of Heyerdahl's sequence.

Sites along the southern coast

East from Vinapu on the coast road, the first site you pass is **Ahu Vaihu**, where eight tall statues lie face-down on the ground, their red stone topknots strewn along the coast. Three kilometres further along, **Ahu Akahanga** presents an equally mournful picture of a row of fallen *moai*; according to some oral traditions, it's also the burial place of Hotu

THE MOAI OF EASTER ISLAND

Easter Island's enduring symbol is the **moai**. A **Neolithic statue cult** on this scale would impress in any location, but the fact it developed in total isolation on a tiny island in the middle of the Pacific almost defies belief. There are some four hundred finished statues scattered around the island, and almost as many in the quarry, in varying stages of completion. The *moai* range in height from 2m to about 20m, and though styles evolved over time, all are carved in a **highly stylized** manner. Their bellies are gently rounded, and their arms are held tightly by their sides, with their strange, long-fingered hands placed across their abdomens. Their heads are long and rectangular, with pointed chins, prominent, angular noses and thin, tight lips.

FUNCTION AND FORM

According to the islanders' assertions, which are consistent with widespread Polynesian tradition, these figures represented important **ancestors**, and were erected on the ancestral land of their kin-groups, which they would watch over and protect with their *mana* (almost all the *moai* face inland). Archeologists have proposed tentative dates of around 1000 AD for the carving of the early statues, and around the **fifteenth century** for the bulk of the statues, when production peaked. Rano Raraku's unfinished statues demonstrate how their forms were chiselled out of the rock face until they were attached to it by just a thin keel running down their spine. When all was completed but their eye sockets, they were freed from their keel and slid down the quarry's slope, then temporarily erected in a pit until they were transported to their *ahus*.

TRANSPORTATION

The island's oral histories offer no clues as to how the **20- to 25-tonne statues** were moved, claiming the statues' *mana* enabled them to walk short distances each day until they reached their platforms. Modern theories have included horizontal and vertical swivelling, but since it was established in the 1980s that the island was once densely covered by trees, it's been assumed that they were dragged on wooden sledges or on top of rollers.

RAISING THE MOAI

How the statues were **erected** onto their platforms in the absence of any type of machinery is another enigma, though in 1955, Thor Heyerdahl challenged the island's mayor to raise a fallen, 25-tonne statue at Anakena Beach and, under the mayor's supervision, twelve islanders raised the statue in eighteen days, using two levers and slipping layer after layer of stones underneath

Matu'a. Further up the coast, **Ahu Hanga Tetenga** is the site of the tallest *moai* (9.94m) ever transported to a platform.

Just beyond Ahu Hanga Tetenga, the road forks. The left-hand branch (**Camino de los Moai**) leads to the quarry of Rano Raraku. It's thought to have been the main roadway along which the statues were transported from the quarry. The right-hand branch continues up the coast to the magnificent Ahu Tongariki.

Ahu Tongariki

The fifteen colossal *moai* lined up on **Ahu Tongariki** make a sensational sight. This was the largest number of *moai* ever erected on a single *ahu*, which, at 200m long, was the largest built on the island. It was destroyed in 1960 when a massive tsunami, triggered by an earthquake in Chile, swept across this corner of the island, dragging the platform blocks and the statues 90m inland – a remarkable distance, given that the statues weigh up to 30 tonnes each.

In November 1988, Sergio Rapu, a former Governor of Easter Island, stated during an interview for a Japanese TV show that if they had a crane they could save the *moai*; a Japanese man watching the show decided to act and a committee was established. The restoration of the *ahu* involved Chilean archeologists Claudio Cristino and Patricia Vargas, a group of forty islanders, specialists from the Nara Institute of Japan and recognized international experts in stone conservation. The five-year project was completed in 1995.

the horizontal statue. Little by little, it was raised on the bed of stones until it was level with its platform; at this point, the layers of pebbles were placed only under its head, until the statue was nearly vertical and could be slipped into place. Archeologists agree this method is highly likely to have been used to raise the statues. In contrast, no one has been able to demonstrate how the large, heavy "topknots" were placed on the raised statues' heads – a monumental feat, achieved only with a crane in modern times.

THE STATUE-CARVERS

Easter Island society was based around independent clans, or **kin-groups**, each with its own high-ranking members. The statue-carvers were highly revered members of a privileged class who were exempt from food production and were supported by farmers and fishermen. Such a system must have involved a great deal of economic cooperation, which appears to have been successfully maintained for centuries.

THE BEGINNING OF THE END

Then, in the later stages of the island's prehistory, the system collapsed, and the island became engulfed by warfare. Archeological records reveal a sudden, dramatic proliferation of obsidian **weapons** during the eighteenth century, as well as the remains of violently beaten skulls, and evidence of the widespread use of caves as refuges. Archeologists have also found possible evidence of cannibalism – which featured prominently in the island's oral traditions. The most dramatic testimony of this period, however, is provided by the hundreds of fallen statues littering the island, deliberately toppled as enemy groups set out to desecrate each other's sacred sites.

SO WHAT WENT WRONG?

It seems likely the seeds of **social collapse** lay in the extremes the statue cult was taken to by the islanders. As the impulse to produce *moai* required more and more hands, the delicate balance between food distribution and statue-carving was destroyed. This situation was profoundly aggravated by the growing scarcity of food brought about by overpopulation, and deforestation, following centuries of logging for boat-building, fuel consumption and statue-transportation. This must have had a catastrophic effect on the islanders' ability to feed themselves: deep-sea fishing became increasingly difficult, and eventually impossible, owing to the lack of wood available for new canoes, and even land cultivation was affected, as the deforestation caused soil erosion. In this climate of encroaching deprivation, the Easter Island civilization descended into anarchy, dragging its majestic monuments with it.

Rano Raraku

Around 1km northwest of Tongariki • Daily: Jan–March & Dec 9am–7pm; April–Nov 9am–5.30pm

North of Tongariki, **Rano Raraku** rises from the land in a hulking mass of volcanic stone. This crag is where almost all of the island's statues were produced, carved directly from the "tuff" (compacted volcanic ash) of the crater's outer slopes. The first surprise, on approaching the crater from the car park, are the dozens of **giant heads** sprouting from the ground. They are, in fact, finished *moai* brought down from the quarry, which were probably placed in shallow pits (that gradually built up) until they could be transported to their *ahu*. One of them bears an image on its chest of a three-masted sailing ship, suggesting that they were carved after European contact.

Among this mass of shapes, still attached to the rock face, is **El Gigante**, the biggest *moai* ever carved, stretching over 20m from top to bottom. Experts believe that it would have been impossible to transport, let alone erect.

The east end of the trail culminates in the kneeling, round-headed **Moai Tukuturi**, the only one of its kind, discovered by Thor Heyerdahl's expedition in 1955. To the west, the trail winds its way up between wild guava trees into the crater itself, with several dirt paths running through knee-high shrubbery alongside the large reed-strewn, freshwater lake. If you follow the trails all the way up to the crater's eastern rim (avoid treading on the toppled *moai* at the top) you are rewarded with unparalleled views of the bay and Ahu Tongariki in the distance.

THE MYTH OF THE "LONG EARS" AND THE "SHORT EARS"

An oft-repeated oral tradition has it that the island's population, in the time just before the toppling of the statues, was divided into two principal groups, the **"Short Ears"** and the **"Long Ears"**. In fact, the whole myth is based on a mistranslation. It seems the two clans were really the *Hanau eepe* ("short and stocky") and the *Hanau momoko* ("tall and slim"); the strange mix-up came from mistranslating *eepe* – short and stocky – as "ear" ("*epe*" in Rapa Nui).

The Long Ears, who saw themselves as more aristocratic, were extremely domineering, and the Short Ears resented them intensely. The Short Ears rebelled when forced to clear rocks off the land, forcing the Long Ears to retreat to the **Poike Peninsula**. Here they dug deep ditches, and filled them with branches and grass, intending to force their enemies inside and set them alight. However, a Short Ears woman who was married to one of the Long Ears alerted her people, and allowed them to surround their enemies while they were sleeping. When they attacked, the Long Ears ran straight into their own ditch, which was set alight. Most of the Long Ears burned to death, but three escaped. Two of them were caught and executed, but one, **Ororoina**, was allowed to live, and went on to father many children – whose descendants, to this day, are proud of their *Hanau momoko* heritage.

11

The Poike Peninsula

East of Rano Raraku, the seldom-visited **Poike Peninsula** is a green, gently rounded plateau bounded by steep cliffs. You can walk round the edge of the peninsula in about four hours, but there's no shade and no path.

Ana o Keke

Poike's main interest lies in the myths and legends associated with it. One tells of the cave of the virgins, **Ana o Keke**, where a number of young girls were confined for months on end so that their skin would remain as pale as possible. Access to Ana o Keke is treacherous, however, and should only be attempted with a guide.

Iko's ditch

More famous than Ana o Keke is the myth of the battle of the **"Long Ears" and "Short Ears"** (see above). This battle is supposed to have taken place in the 3.5km-long ditch separating the peninsula from the rest of the island, known as Ko te Ava o Iko, or **"Iko's ditch"**.

Ahu te Pito Kura

From the southern coast, the road turns inland, cutting past the Poike Peninsula, and leads directly to Ovahe and Anakena. On the way, look out for **Ahu te Pito Kura**, down by Bahía La Pérouse (signposted). This is the site of **Paro**, at 9.8m tall probably the largest *moai* successfully erected on a platform. Paro is thought to have been one of the last *moai* to be moved and erected, and is estimated to weigh a staggering 90 tonnes. No one has attempted to restore and re-erect the giant, which still lies face down before its *ahu*, surrounded by rubble.

Ovahe

North of Paro, **Ovahe** is a tiny, secluded and exquisite beach, its white sands lapped by crystal-clear waters at the foot of a large volcanic cliff, very popular with locals who come to picnic, swim and snorkel. It's best earlier in the day, before the cliff blocks the afternoon sun.

Playa Anakena and around

Up the coast from Ovahe, **Playa Anakena** is much larger, and presents a picture-postcard scene of powdery golden sands fringed by swaying palm trees, great for

FISHERMAN HOLDING LOBSTER, ISLA ROBINSON CRUSOE

an afternoon of swimming or sunbathing. Several snack stands offer drinks and sandwiches, though they're not always open, so bring some food and water with you. **Anakena** has a special place in Rapa Nui oral history, which holds it to be the landing site and dwelling place of Hotu Matu'a, the island's first colonizer (see page 443). It's also home to the splendid *moai* of **Ahu Nau Nau**, which were so deeply covered in sand until their restoration, led by local archeologist Sergio Rapu Haoa in 1978, that they were largely protected from the effects of weathering.

Ahu Ature Huki

Just up the hillside by the beach you'll find the squat and corpulent *moai* of **Ahu Ature Huki**. This was the first *moai* to be re-erected on the island in the experiment carried out by Thor Heyerdahl in 1955, when twelve strong islanders showed they could raise a 25-tonne statue in eighteen days (see page 443).

11 The northern circuit

Although the triangle formed by Vinapu, Tongariki and Anakena contains the densest concentration of sites, the western and northern parts of the island are also well worth exploring. Attractions include the impressive *moai* of **Tahai** and **Ahu Akivi**, plus a network of underground **caves**.

Tahai and around

If you walk north from the *caleta* past the cemetery, taking the road that hugs the coast, after about ten minutes you'll reach the ceremonial centre of **TAHAI**, composed of three *ahus*, a favourite spot for viewing colourful sunsets. The first, **Ahu Vai Uri**, supports four broad, squat *moai*, two of which have badly damaged heads, and the stump of a fifth statue. In front of the *ahu* is the outline of a flattened esplanade, presumed to have been used as a ceremonial site.

Archeological remains suggest some individuals – possibly chiefs and priests – used to live near these ceremonial sites, in several locations on the island, in stone, oval houses called *hare paenga* that looked like an upturned canoe. You can see the foundations of one of these houses near Ahu Vai Uri. The second platform is **Ahu Tahai** itself, topped by a lone, weathered *moai*. Finally, **Ahu Ko Te Riku** is the site of a well-preserved *moai* fitted with white, glinting eyes and a red topknot.

Museo Antropológico Sebastián Englert

500m north of Tahai, set well back from the coastal path • Tues–Fri 9.30am–5.30pm, Sat & Sun 9.30am–12.30pm • Free • ☎ 32 255 1020, ⓦ museorapanui.cl

The unmissable **Museo Antropológico Sebastián Englert** gives a thorough introduction to the island's geography, history and society, covering the **Birdman cult** (see page 456) and the origins and significance of the *moai*. The displays, well labelled in Spanish and English, include an evocative collection of black-and-white photographs of islanders from about 1915 onwards, a rare female *moai* and replica *rongo rongo* tablets.

Ana Kakenga

On the coastal road, around 3km north of the Museo Antropológico (see above), you reach the point where you're opposite two little islands. A stone cairn by the left-hand side of the road signals a track down towards the cliffs; it's not easy to spot. At the end of the track, a tiny opening in the ground is the entrance to a pitch-black passage (take a torch), which continues 50m underground to the adjoining **Ana Kakenga** (Dos Ventanas Caves). Both caves are flooded with light streaming in from the "windows", or gaping holes, that open out of the cliff wall. Prepare for a rush of adrenaline as you approach the edges, as both drop vertically down to a bed of sharp rocks and pounding waves many metres below.

Ahu Te Peu

About 1km further up the coast from the Dos Ventanas Caves is **Ahu Te Peu**. The *moai* that once stood on the *ahu* still lie flat on the ground, left as they were during the period of warfare. Scattered around are the remains of many boat-shaped *hare paenga*, including one that's 60m long. It's thought this was the site of the village of the Miru clan, the direct descendants of Hotu Matu'a.

At Ahu Te Peu, most people join up with the inland road and head back to Hanga Roa via Ahu Akivi. You can, however, continue north, either heading up the gentle volcanic cone of **Terevaka**, where you'll be rewarded with fine views across the island from its 510m summit, the highest point of the island (no path; 1hr up), or else follow the coastline round to Playa Anakena (4–5hr on foot; sunscreen is absolutely essential and you must take plenty of water). On the way, you'll pass many fallen *moai*, none of them restored, as well as the ruins of stone houses and chicken pens.

Inland to Puna Pau

From Hanga Roa, heading up the inland road to Ahu Akivi (first left from the paved road to Anakena) you'll pass a signed track branching left to **Puna Pau**, a low volcanic crater made of rusty-coloured rock, known as *scoria*, where the islanders carved the **pukao** the cylindrical "topknots" worn by up to seventy of the *moai* standing on *ahu*. No one knows for sure what these cylinders represented, though suggestions include topknots (of hair) and feather headdresses. Up in the quarry, and along the track to the top, you can see thirty or so finished *pukao* lying on the ground.

Ahu Akivi

On the inland road north of Puna Pau, the seven *moai* at **Ahu Akivi** are the only ones to have been erected inland, and the only ones that look towards the sea. It's been discovered that they are oriented directly towards the rising summer solstice, along with several other *ahu*, suggesting that solar positions were of significance to the islanders. The Ahu Akivi *moai* were raised in 1960 by William Mulloy and Gonzalo Figueroa, two archeologists recruited by Heyerdahl in 1955, both of whom devoted their careers to Easter Island.

Ana Te Pahu

From Ahu Akivi, the road turns towards the coast, where it meets Ahu Te Peu. On the way, a second path branches left from the main road, leading towards the **Ana Te Pahu** caves. If you clamber down, you'll see some tall bamboo trees growing in a magical underground garden, along with sweet potatoes, taro, avocados, lemons and sugarcane. This cave is connected to another huge cave (once used as a dwelling) by a long lava tube.

South of Hanga Roa: Rano Kau

South of Hanga Roa, a dirt road climbs steeply past a *mirador* offering an excellent view of Hanga Roa up to one of the most awe-inspiring spots on the island – the giant crater of the extinct **Rano Kau** volcano, and the ceremonial village of **Orongo**, perched high on its rim. The dull waters of the volcano's reed-choked lake contrast sharply with the brilliant blue of the Pacific, stretching as far as the eye can see, visible where a great chunk of the crater wall is missing. Just before you reach Orongo, a path disappears into the lush vegetation around the crater's edge; it is possible to follow this around the crater as a leisurely day's walk, but bring plenty of water.

11

THE BIRDMAN CEREMONY

A great deal is known about the **Birdman ceremony**, which was practised right up to 1878. It took place annually at the September **equinox**, when the chiefs of the various kin-groups assembled at Orongo to compete. The aim was to find the first egg laid by the sooty tern (a migratory bird) on Motu Nui, the largest of three islets sitting opposite Orongo, 2km out to sea. Each chief would choose a representative, or *hopu*, who would scale down the sheer cliff to the ocean and swim through shark-infested waters to the islet. It could take several weeks for the egg to be found; meanwhile, the chiefs would remain in Orongo, where they participated in ritual dances, songs and prayers.

Once the egg was finally found, whoever discovered it would bellow the name of his master and then swim back to the island with the egg tucked into a headband. The victorious chief now became the new *tangata manu*, or **Birdman**. The new Birdman would first have all the hair shaved off his head; he would then live in strict seclusion for a whole year in a sacred house at the foot of Rano Raraku, eating only certain foods, and forbidden to bathe himself or cut his nails. His kin-group, meanwhile, was endowed with a special, high status, which was often taken as an excuse for members to dominate and bully their rival groups.

11

Orongo

Just west of Rano Kau • Daily: Jan–March & Dec 9am–7pm; April–Nov 9am–5.30pm; your entry permit will be checked at the ranger's office here • Car or taxi (around CH$20,000, including waiting time) from Hanga Roa (10min), or on foot (1hr)

ORONGO, just beyond the Conaf visitor centre, consists of the partially restored remains of some 48 low-lying, oval-shaped huts made of thin stone slabs, each with a tiny entrance just large enough to crawl through (don't try). A few steps from the houses, on the face of some basalt outcrops looking out to sea, a dense group of exquisitely carved **petroglyphs** depict curled-up human figures with birds' heads and long curved beaks. These images honour an important annual ceremony dedicated to the **cult of the Birdman** (see above).

The Juan Fernández Archipelago

The **Juan Fernández Archipelago** is made up of three islands and numerous rocky islets. It is named after **João Fernandes**, the Portuguese sailor who discovered it on November 22, 1574, while straying out to sea to avoid coastal winds and currents in an attempt to shorten the journey between Lima and Valparaíso. The more easterly of the two main islands was originally called **Más a Tierra** ("Nearer Land"); the other, 187km further west, was known as **Más Afuera** ("Farther Out"). The few tourists who make it here generally arrive between October and March, when the climate is warm and mostly dry and the sea is perfect for swimming.

Brief history

João Fernandes made a brief attempt to colonize the three uninhabited islands, introducing vegetables and goats, which multiplied in great numbers (the third, smallest, island was later known as Goat Island, though officially Isla Santa Clara). These were still flourishing when British buccaneers started making occasional calls to stock up on water and fresh meat between their raids on the mainland.

Following Alexander Selkirk's much-publicized rescue (see page 459) buccaneers began calling at the islands more frequently, prompting the Spanish Crown to take official possession of the archipelago in 1742, building a series of forts around **Más a Tierra**. The island was then used as a **penal colony** for many years, and it wasn't until the mid-nineteenth century that Chilean and European colonizers formed a permanent settlement. In 1966, with an eye on the islands' potential as a tourist destination, the Chilean government changed Más a Tierra's name to **Isla Robinson Crusoe**, while

Más Afuera became **Isla Alejandro Selkirk**, seasonal home to lobster fishermen and very difficult to reach. In 2015, ministers created the new 301,000-square-km **Juan Fernández Marine Protected Area** off the coast of the archipelago, currently the second-largest of its kind in South America.

Isla Robinson Crusoe

Twenty-two kilometres long, and 7km at its widest point, **Isla Robinson Crusoe** is the archipelago's only permanently inhabited island. Most islanders – some of them descendants of the Swiss Baron de Rodt and his compatriots who settled the island at the end of the nineteenth century – live in the little village of **San Juan Bautista**, on sheltered Bahía Cumberland. The main economic activity is trapping **lobsters**, and one of the highlights of a stay is helping a fisherman haul in his catch (and sampling it).

Lobsters aside, the island's two principal attractions are associated with **Alexander Selkirk** and the richness of its flora and fauna. Of the 146 plant species, 101 are endemic to the island (the second-highest proportion in the world after Hawaii), which is a national park and UNESCO World Biosphere Reserve. Most prolific, and stunning, is the luxuriant rainforest that covers the higher slopes.

The local fauna also comprises numerous endemic species, such as the **Juan Fernández fur seal**, which has made a comeback after being hunted to near extinction in the eighteenth century, and the Firecrown hummingbird, as well as seabirds such as the giant petrel. Meanwhile, diving at sites around Isla Robinson Crusoe is an excellent way to appreciate the wealth of its marine life. **Mosquitoes** abound, so bring plenty of repellent.

11

San Juan Bautista and around

Huddled by the shores of Bahía Cumberland, at the foot of a green curtain of mountains, **SAN JUAN BAUTISTA** is the island's only settlement. A spread-out village with simple houses, for most people "El Pueblo" is just a base from which to explore the island's interior and coastline. That said, there are several curious relics here. At the southern end of the bay, a 5min walk from the village, the small rocky beach of **El Palillo** is a good swimming spot.

Fuerte Santa Barbara, a small stone fort, is perched on a hillside just north of the plaza. Heavily restored in 1974, it was originally built by the Spanish in 1749 in an attempt to prevent buccaneers from using the island as a watering point.

THE 2010 TSUNAMI

In the early hours of February 27, 2010, a **tsunami** triggered by the 8.8 magnitude **earthquake** on mainland Chile struck the Juan Fernández Archipelago. A wave of around 20m in height swept 300m into **Isla Robinson Crusoe**, destroying much of San Juan Bautista and killing sixteen. A mix-up between the Chilean Navy and the tsunami alert services meant the islanders received no official warning, and the death toll would have been much higher but for a 12-year-old girl: awake at night, Martina Maturana spotted the fishing boats bobbing violently, and ran from her home to ring the emergency bell in the town square to warn the island's six hundred or so inhabitants.

Following the disaster, the island's population fell by about a third, as many people left for the mainland. Islanders, angry at the lack of official warning, launched a court case against the government. Meanwhile, **rebuilding** efforts – the tsunami destroyed the library, town hall, museum, cultural centre, naval offices, post office, school and every shop, plus many homes and hotels – are ongoing.

To compound matters, on September 2, 2011, 21 passengers were killed after an air force **plane crashed** into the sea after twice failing to land in windy conditions. Among those killed was TV presenter Felipe Camiroaga, who was making a film on the reconstruction efforts.

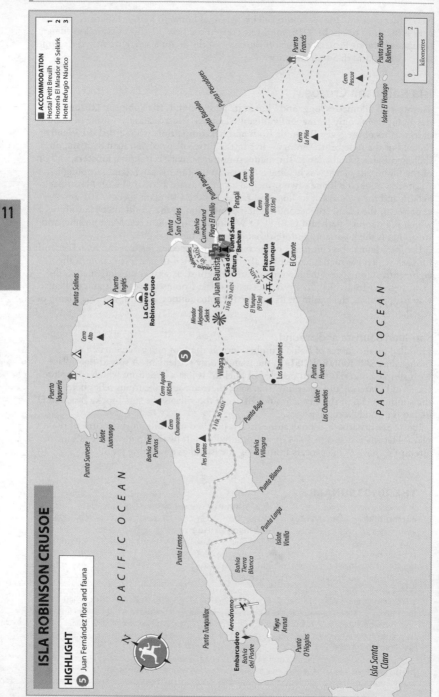

ISLA ROBINSON CRUSOE

HIGHLIGHT

5 Juan Fernández flora and fauna

■ ACCOMMODATION
Hostal Petit Breuilh — 1
Hostería El Mirador de Selkirk — 2
Hotel Refugio Náutico — 3

0 — 2 kilometres

11

PACIFIC OCEAN

Punta Hueso
Ballena

Puerto
Francés

Cerro
Pascua ▲

Islote El Verdugo

Cerro
La Piña ▲

Punta Pesقdores

Punta Bacalao

Cerro
Centinela ▲

Pangal ●

Cerro
Damajuana
(635m) ▲

Playa El Palillo
Bahía
Cumberland
Punta
San Carlos

Fuerte Santa
Bárbara

El Camote ▲

Plazoleta
△ ⛺ El Yunque
45 MIN

Casa de
Cultura

San Juan Bautista
❋ 1 HR 30 MIN

Cerro
El Yunque
(915m) ▲

Mirador
Alejandro
Selkirk

Puerto
Inglés △

Cerro
Alto ▲

5

Villagra ●

Los Ramplones ▲

Punta
Hueca

Islote
Los Chamelos ○

Punta Salinas

PACIFIC OCEAN

Puerto
Vaquería ⛴

Islote
Juanango ○

Bahía Tres
Puntas

Cerro Agudo
(685m) ▲

Cerro
Chumacera ▲

3 HR 30 MIN
Cerro
Tres Puntas ▲

Punta Suroeste

Punta Lemos

PACIFIC OCEAN

Punta Baja

Bahía
Villagra

Punta Blanco

Punta Larga

Islote
Vinillo ○

Punta Turquillax

Embarcadero
Bahía
del Padre

Aerodromo ✈

Playa
Arenal

Punta
O'Higgins

Bahía
Tierra
Blanca

N

Isla Santa
Clara

PACIFIC OCEAN

ALEXANDER SELKIRK

Daniel Defoe's story of Robinson Crusoe, the world's most famous literary castaway, was inspired by the misadventures of the real-life Scottish mariner **Alexander Selkirk**, who was marooned on Isla Robinson Crusoe (then Más a Tierra) in 1704 while crossing the Pacific on a privateering expedition. Unlike Crusoe, who was shipwrecked, Selkirk actually asked to be put ashore after quarreling with his captain. The irascible sailor regretted his decision as soon he was deposited on the beach with a few scanty supplies, but his cries to be taken back onboard were ignored. Selkirk spent four years and four months on the island, with only his Bible and dozens of wild goats for company. During that time he was transformed into an extraordinary athlete, as he hunted the goats on foot, and a devout Christian.

Following his **rescue** by a British ship in 1709, however, Selkirk reverted to his buccaneering ways, joining in attacks on Spanish vessels all the way home. Back in Fife, the former castaway became something of a celebrity and threw himself into a life of drink and women. Fourteen years after his rescue, Selkirk finally met his end when he took up the seafaring life once more, set off on another privateering expedition and died of fever in the tropics.

A short walk north of Fuerte Santa Barbara takes you to the **Cuevas de los Patriotas**, a group of seven fern-covered caves allegedly inhabited by 42 independence fighters who were banished to Más a Tierra after the Battle of Rancagua in 1814.

On the shore, follow the path to the north end of the bay and you'll reach the cliffs of the **Punta San Carlos**, embedded with unexploded shells fired by British warships at the German *Dresden* during World War I. The Germans surrendered, but sank their ship rather than let it go to the British, and the wreck still lies 70m under the sea, in Bahía Cumberland. Nearby are the graves of the naval battle's casualties in the **cemetery**, next to the lighthouse, and **photos** of the incident at the **Casa de la Cultura**, on Vicente González.

Hikes on Isla Robinson Crusoe

There are numerous good **hikes**, though some are unmarked; you will need guides for all those in the east of the island, as well as between Bahía Inglés and Puerto Vaquería. Some destinations are reachable by boat with a fisherman, who can drop you off in the morning and pick you up at the end of their day.

Sendero Salsipuedes

Excellent short hikes from San Juan Bautista include the fairly steep **Sendero Salsipuedes** ("Get out if you can"), which leads from the village's Calle La Pólvora through pine and eucalyptus forest up to the *mirador* overlooking Bahía Cumberland from the northwest side. Allow an hour's round trip and beware of loose scree. The views of San Juan Bautista spread out below are excellent. From here, though, landslides render it dangerous to navigate.

Plazoleta El Yunque

A sometimes muddy 3km trail leads from the village (continuing from Calle Lord Anson; 1hr 30min return) through native forest to **Plazoleta El Yunque**, a lookout point and an attractive shaded **campsite** at the foot of Cerro El Yunque, the island's tallest mountain (915m). The nearby stone ruins are the remains of the house of Hugo Weber, the "German Robinson Crusoe", who spent twelve years here after escaping from the *Dresden* (see above). From the campsite, the pleasant trail loops through native vegetation, including giant *nalca* (rhubarb) and ferns, before finishing back at the campsite. From the Plazoleta, it is possible to make the steep ascent through thick native forest to **El Camote**, a peak offering spectacular views of the island, though this requires a guide.

BOAT TRIPS FROM SAN JUAN BAUTISTA

A fifteen-minute boat ride from San Juan Bautista is **Puerto Inglés**, where there's a good camping spot and a mock-up of Selkirk's cave (see page 459). Other destinations include **Puerto Vaquería**, west of Bahía Inglés, a popular spot to snorkel with seals; **Puerto Francés**, in the east of the island, where you'll see Spanish ramparts built to deter French pirates; and **Playa Arenal**, the island's only sandy beach, which lies 2hr 30min away by boat through islets and seal colonies, just south of the airstrip.

Cerro Centinela

A 45min walk south of San Juan Bautista, and then a 362m hike up a trail, takes you to the top of **Cerro Centinela**, which offers expansive views of Bahía Cumberland and Bahía El Pangál. From here, an unmarked trail zigzags its way along the coast to **Puerto Francés** (see above), a route only to be attempted with a knowledgeable local.

The cross-island hike

The island's best trek is the **cross-island hike** running from the airstrip to San Juan Bautista, via the Mirador Alejandro Selkirk; bring plenty of water and allow at least five hours. Arrange to be dropped off by a fisherman at the **Bahía del Padre**, the launching place for the boat that picks you up from the airstrip, and home to a large fur seal colony. Outside breeding season, they are not dangerous and you can swim with them. The largest fur seal colony lies at **Bahía Tierra Blanca**, the first bay you come to along the trail.

Follow the road uphill and take the well-marked trail running from the airstrip. The path skirts the zigzagging coastline, with turquoise bays appearing around every corner, the barking of sea lions echoing from below and the landscape gradually changing from arid desert-like hills with their vividly multicoloured soil to steep pasture land to jagged mountains covered in dense endemic vegetation. For the most part, it's wide enough to take a vehicle, ascending very gradually until you reach **Villagra**, a couple of houses with a corral for animals, where the rodeo is held in February.

Mirador Alejandro Selkirk

At Villagra, the cross-island track divides; take the rocky footpath overgrown with vegetation, which climbs steeply uphill until it reaches the **Mirador Alejandro Selkirk**, the famous lookout point where, according to a disputed story, Selkirk lit his daily smoke signals and scoured the horizon for ships (see page 459). You'll be rewarded with stunning panoramic views. Note the two memorial plaques, one donated by the officers of HMS *Topaze* in 1868, the other by one of Selkirk's descendants in 1983, pledging to remember his forefather "Till a' the seas gang dry and the rocks melt i' the sun."

You could also reach the *mirador* from the village, though it's a steeper climb (around 90min); the path starts north of the plaza.

ARRIVAL AND DEPARTURE   ISLA ROBINSON CRUSOE

By plane Getting to Isla Robinson Crusoe is an adventure, involving a bumpy flight on a seven-seater plane. Three airlines serve the island, usually once or twice weekly, depending on demand: ATA (☏2 2275 0363, ⊛aerolineasata.cl), LASSA (☏2 2273 5209, ✉lassa@terra.cl) and Aerocardal (☏2 2377 7444, ⊛aerocardal.com), all based at Aeródromo Tobalaba, Av Larraín 7941, Santiago. They have a 10kg luggage allowance and charge around US$860 return from Santiago. It is a bit cheaper to organize a charter flight, if you can get a group of

at least six together; contact Santiago FBO (☏2 2674 4000, ⊛santiagofbo.cl) for details. Flights are weather-dependent, so be prepared to spend an extra day or two on the island. The airstrip is 13km from San Juan Bautista; a speedboat (included in the flight ticket) transfers you to the village – it can be a rough ride.

By boat Transmarko (☏09 6157 7480, ⊛transmarko.cl) has irregular services from Valparaíso (return ticket, including full board, CH$170,500; 30–60hr); the boat spends five to seven days on the island. Book well in advance. There is also a monthly Navy supply boat from Valparaíso, which spends around 72hr on the island; a one-way ticket costs around CH$30,000. Book with the Comando de Transporte at the Primera Zona Naval, Plaza Sotomayor 592, Valparaíso (☎32 250 6354), but note that departure dates change regularly and preference is given to islanders.

INFORMATION AND TOURS

Tourist information The Municipalidad (☎32 270 1045, ⓦcomunajuanfernandez.cl) and Conaf (☎32 268 0381, ⓦconaf.cl), in a small kiosk near the plaza, provide information on the island.

Entry permits National park entry permits (necessary for most activities on the island) are CH$5000, valid for a week, and available from the Municipalidad and Conaf.

Website The bilingual ⓦexperiencerobinson.com has information on accommodation, transport and activities.

Tours *Hotel Refugio Náutico* (see below) offers hikes, historical tours, fishing trips (including for lobster), diving, snorkelling, surfing and birdwatching; ⓦcomunajuanfernandez.cl has a list of local guides.

ACCOMMODATION

There is a list of **accommodation** on the municipal website (ⓦcomunajuanfernandez.cl). Most people eat at their hotel.

11

Hostal Petit Breuilh Vicente Rozales 80 ☎09 9549 9033, ✉crusoepetit@hotmail.com; map p.458. Located 300m from the dock, this guesthouse has simple en-suite rooms with fridges and TVs, as well as a bar-restaurant and laundry service. The owners can help arrange local guides and excursions. Full board. **CH$50,000**

Hostería El Mirador de Selkirk Castillo 251 ☎09 9550 3305, ✉hosteriaselkirk@gmail.com; map p.458. Attractive guesthouse with good views and a handful of comfy rooms. The owner is a third-generation islander –

she is happy to talk about her family history – and a good cook. Full board. **CH$50,000**

Hotel Refugio Náutico Southeastern edge of the village ☎09 7483 5014, ⓦislarobinsoncrusoe.cl; map p.458. Bright and airy en suites, a good bar-restaurant with outdoor terraces (the lobster, octopus or golden crab dishes are hits) and a hot tub. Staff can arrange excursions and activities, and guests can use the kayaks and snorkelling gear. B&B and half- and full-board packages are available. **CH$134,000**

DIRECTORY

Banks and exchange There are no banks or *cambios*, so bring plenty of cash; bear in mind that poor weather may delay your flight by a day or two.

Hospital The Posta Rural, Vicente González s/n, deals with minor medical issues; anyone requiring serious treatment has to be flown to the mainland.

Isla Alejandro Selkirk

If you have plenty of time and energy to spare, consider attempting to reach the even more remote and ruggedly mountainous **Isla Alejandro Selkirk**. During the October to May lobster season, it is home to around forty to fifty people, a few conservationists and some feral goats. Bring all food and gear with you, including a tent.

ARRIVAL AND DEPARTURE   ISLA ALEJANDRO SELKIRK

By boat An irregular supply boat (roughly 17hr; CH$60,000–70,000), and fishermen, ply the waters between Isla Robinson Crusoe and Isla Alejandro Selkirk.

Contact the Municipalidad about passage; if you don't arrange a return trip, you could find yourself marooned.

ILLUSTRATION OF ANDACOLLO

Contexts

History

Enveloped by the Andes, the Atacama Desert and the Pacific Ocean, Chile has evolved almost as an island, relatively undisturbed by the turbulence that has raged through much of South America's history. Though the country has been inhabited for millennia by indigenous peoples, its recorded history begins with the sixteenth-century arrival of the Spaniards. The colonial society that emerged and the ensuing struggle for independence resemble those of the whole continent, but from its early days as a republic, Chile took on its own political shape, distinct from that of its neighbours. With its largely ordered, constitutional model of government, and healthy respect for the law, Chile earned itself the sobriquet "the England of South America" in the nineteenth century, which is why it was so surprising when it returned to the attention of the outside world with the repressive military regime of General Augusto Pinochet during the 1970s and 1980s. Today, with democracy firmly back in place, Chile is an outward-looking nation boasting political and economic stability, albeit with some serious social inequalities and unresolved political legacies lurking beneath the surface.

The Ice Age and beyond

Chile's anthropological record, like that of all the Americas, began when the first groups of Asians crossed the land bridge connecting Siberia to Alaska before the end of the last Ice Age, when the sea level was 70–100m lower than it is today. Archeologists are unable to tell us exactly when this **first migration** occurred, but it's generally thought to have been between 25,000 and 40,000 years ago.

What *is* known is that by 12,000 BC the descendants of these people, supplemented by further waves of migration from Asia, had spread down the whole of North and South America as far as the southern tip of Patagonia. While some devoted themselves to fishing, the majority were probably nomadic hunters living off the animals that inhabited the region at the time – mastodons (prehistoric elephants), mammoths, giant armadillos and wild horses. When the last Ice Age came to an end around 11,000 BC, the climate changed abruptly and many of these animals became extinct. The hunters were forced to adapt, supplementing their diet by gathering fruits and seeds. Eventually this led to the deliberate cultivation of foodstuffs and the domestication of animals; along with these incipient agricultural practices came more stable communities and important developments, such as pottery and burial customs. Slowly, distinct cultural groups emerged, shaped by their very different environments and the resources available to them.

12,500 BC	5000 BC	1463 AD
Carbon dating places the first inhabited site in South America just outside Chile's Puerto Montt.	Mummification technique developed by the Chinchorro people.	The Incas conquer a huge part of Chile up to the Río Maule.

The pre-Columbian cultures

In the absence of written records, archeologists have had to piece together information about Chile's **pre-Columbian cultures** from what these groups left behind, principally funerary offerings found in burial sites and domestic objects left in former dwelling places. The strata in which the remains are buried (plus the use of radiocarbon dating) indicate the chronology in which these developments took place. However, variations in Chile's geography from north to south present unequal conditions for the preservation of artefacts and have led to a far greater knowledge of the cultures of the north than those of the south.

Mummies and hallucinogens: El Norte Grande

More is known about the pre-Columbian cultures of Chile's Norte Grande – the Far North – than of any other part of the country. The extreme dryness of the Atacama Desert preserved archeological remains for thousands of years. One of the earliest groups of people to leave its mark was the **Chinchorro culture**, a collection of nomadic fishing communities that lived along the desert coast some eight thousand years ago. By 5000 BC, the Chinchorro had developed the practice of **mummifying their dead** (see page 208) – two thousand years earlier than the Egyptians. Their technique, which involved removing internal organs and tissues and replacing them with vegetable fibres and mud, survived for four thousand years and is the oldest known in the world.

By around 500 BC, life in El Norte Grande was based largely on agriculture, supplemented by fishing in the coastal areas, and herding llamas and alpacas in the Andean highlands. Although vast tracts of the region are taken up by barren desert, a number of oases provided fertile land where agricultural communities were able to dedicate themselves to the cultivation of maize, beans, squash, chillies and potatoes. They lived in permanent dwellings, usually consisting of circular huts surrounding a shared patio, and often with a cemetery nearby.

Among the most important (and longest-lasting) of these early agricultural groups was the **San Pedro culture** (or Atacameño culture), which settled along the salt-flat oases around San Pedro de Atacama in around 500 BC. They produced ceramics, textiles and objects in copper and stone, along with delicately carved wooden snuff tablets and tubes used for inhaling hallucinogenic substances – a custom probably introduced by the **Tihuanaco culture** in around 300 AD. This latter was a powerful religious state based near the southern shores of Lake Titicaca in present-day Bolivia, whose influence extended over most of northern Chile and much of Peru for many centuries. The Tihuanaco impact was most visible in the spread of its ceramics and textiles, often decorated with images of cats, condors and snakes, which probably had religious significance. The Tihuanaco also fostered an active trading system, encouraging the exchange of goods between regions, and bringing about increased social stratification, with those at the top controlling the commercial traffic.

Sometime between 900 and 1200 AD, for unknown reasons, the Tihuanaco culture declined and collapsed. The regional cultures of the Norte Grande were then free to reassert their individual authority and identity, expressing their independence with a series of *pukarás* (fortresses) dotted around the altiplano. This period of *desarrollo regional* ("regional development"), as it is known, was halted only by the arrival of the Inca in the late fifteenth century.

1520	1535	1535–1880
The first European to reach Chile, Ferdinand Magellan, sails through the strait now named after him.	The first Spanish venture into Chile, under the command of Diego de Almagro, ends in failure.	The Arauco War: the Mapuche resist all attempts at conquest from their stronghold south of the Río Bío Bío.

Llamas and ceramics: El Norte Chico

Around 300 AD, when the peoples of the Norte Grande had been living in fixed agricultural communities for several centuries, those of the Norte Chico were just beginning to abandon their lives of hunting and gathering, and turn to cattle herding and farming. The resulting **El Molle culture** was composed of communities that settled along the river valleys between Copiapó and Illapel, where they developed a system of artificial irrigation to cultivate maize, beans, squash and possibly cotton. They also herded llamas, a practice recorded in numerous petroglyphs, and produced the first ceramics of the Norte Chico. Between 700 and 800 AD the El Molle culture declined and was replaced by a new cultural group known as **Las Animas**, which probably originated in the Argentine highlands. The changes introduced by this culture included rapid developments in metalworking; new, more decorative, styles of pottery, and – most curiously – the custom of ritual sacrifice of llamas.

Towards 1000 AD, the important **Diaguita culture** appeared in the Norte Chico, dominating the region over the next five centuries until the Spanish invasion. The Diaguita tended to live in large villages along the river valleys, presided over by a chief and a shaman. Each valley was divided into two sections: a "lower" section, towards the coast, which was ruled by one chief, and a "higher" section, towards the mountains, ruled by another. Their economy was based on agriculture, herding, mining and metalworking, and was supplemented by fishing on the coast, aided by the invention of inflated sealskin rafts. The Diaguita's greatest achievement, however, was their outstandingly fine pottery, characterized by intricate white, black and red geometric patterns.

Burial urns and mud huts: central Chile

The first agricultural groups to settle in central Chile were the **El Bato** and **Llolleo** peoples, from around 300 AD. The El Bato group occupied the zone between the Río Choapa (near Illapel) and the Río Maipo (south of Santiago); its highly polished monochrome pottery indicates that it was strongly influenced by the El Molle culture from the Norte Chico. The Llolleo settlements were spread along the coastal plains between the Río Aconcagua (just north of Santiago) and the Río Maule (near Talca). One of the most striking characteristics of this culture was their custom of burying their dead under their own houses; small children were buried in clay urns.

Later, around 900 AD, the **Aconcagua** emerged as the dominant culture in Central Chile. These people lived in houses made of branches and mud and dedicated themselves to growing beans, maize, squash and potatoes; they also developed far more specialized ceramics than had previously existed in the region.

Nomads and hunters: Araucania

While relatively little is known about the development of the cultures in the south of Chile, owing to a paucity of archeological remains, it's generally agreed that the first group to adopt cultivation was the **Pitrén culture**, around 600 AD. This comprised small family groups spread between the Bio Bío and Lago Llanquihue, where they grew maize and potatoes on a small scale, as well as hunting and gathering. They also produced ceramics, often decorated with zoomorphic and anthropomorphic images, which they usually buried with their dead.

1541	1553	1554
Conquistador Pedro de Valdivia reaches the Mapocho Valley and founds the city of Santiago de Nueva Extremadura on February 12.	Lautaro, a famous Mapuche chief, kills Pedro de Valdivia in a particularly gruesome manner during the Battle of Tucapel.	Conquistadors bring the first vines to Chile, marking the beginning of wine production.

Around 1000 AD a new community, known as **El Vergel**, emerged in the region between Angol and Temuco. Its economy combined hunting and gathering with the cultivation of potatoes, maize, beans and squash, and it is likely that its people were the first to domesticate guanacos. Other practices they brought to the region included burying their dead in ceramic urns, decorated with red and white paint. They also developed a very beautiful style of pottery, now known as Valdivia pottery, characterized by parallel zigzag lines and shaded triangles.

Sometime in the fourteenth century a group of nomadic hunters called the *moluche* ("people of war") arrived from Argentina and occupied the land between the Itata and Toltén rivers. They absorbed the existing Pitrén and El Vergel cultures to form a new entity called **Mapuche** ("people of the land"). While engaging in fishing, hunting and gathering, their lifestyle was based principally on herding and farming – labour was divided between the sexes, with men responsible for preparing the fields, and women for sowing and harvesting. The basic social unit was the family clan, or "lov", which were independent from each other and autonomous. Its isolation meant the Mapuche culture didn't develop any further until it was forced to unite in the face of the Spanish invasion.

Canoe fishermen and hunters: the far south

The narrow channels, fjords, impenetrable jungles and wild steppes of the far south have never encouraged communities to settle in one place. Accordingly, the peoples that inhabited this region led a more primitive lifestyle than those further north – they could not adopt agriculture as their main economy, and so maintained their tradition of hunting and fishing in nomadic groups. Groups like the **Selk'nam** and the **Tehuelche** hunted guanaco and rhea on the Patagonian steppes, and lived in temporary wigwam-like structures covered in guanaco skins. The **Yámana** and **Chono** people hunted seals, otters, birds and gathered shellfish in their canoes, constantly moving from place to place. None of the Patagonian or Fuegian groups produced ceramics, manufacturing instead bows, arrows, lassos, baskets and warm skin capes. Their understanding of the world was rich in mythology and symbolism. The Selk'nam, for instance, believed that many birds and animals were spirits that had once been human; they also practised elaborate initiation rites marking the passage from boyhood into manhood, involving physical tests and secret ceremonies. Unlike the other native peoples of Chile, these groups were never incorporated into Spanish colonial society, and their lifestyles remained virtually unchanged until the twentieth century, when clashes with seal hunters and sheep farmers led to their disappearance.

The Inca conquest

While the native peoples of Chile were developing relatively simple communities based on agriculture, herding and fishing, a great civilization was emerging further to the north – that of the **Inca**. These people arrived in Cusco around 1200 AD, and by the fifteenth century had developed a sophisticated and highly organized society that boasted palaces, temples and fortresses of great architectural sophistication. In 1463, the Inca emperor, Pachacuti, initiated a period of massive **expansion** that saw the

1561	1593	1598
Governor Don García Hurtado de Mendoza is sent from Peru to subjugate the natives in central Chile.	The first Jesuit order arrives in Chile and sets about converting locals and appropriating large amounts of land.	The Great Uprising removes all Spanish presence south of the Río Bío Bío, and the river becomes the Spanish–Mapuche frontier.

LA LUCHA DE MAPUCHE

The **Mapuche**, or "people of the land" from "che" (people) and "mapu" (of the land), have been in constant conflict with invaders since the arrival of the Spanish. That conflict continues today. Though they have put up the bravest resistance out of all the indigenous people of the Americas, the Mapuche have nevertheless seen their original homeland of over 100,000 square kilometres shrink to just 5000 square kilometres. While Chile's left-wing governments tried to address the **land issue**, any improvements made between 1965 and 1973 were reversed by Pinochet's government, which went a step further by signing into law an anti-terrorist act aimed squarely at any Mapuche attempt to assert themselves and pursue their rights. Crimes such as arson were punished with excessively long prison sentences, torture and harassment of families.

While some progress has been made since the return of democracy in the dispute over their historical **ancestral territory** (known as *Wallmapu*), many Mapuche feel that the concessions made by the Chilean government fall far short, and that their lands remain under constant threat from powerful business interests. Today, the Mapuche lead a largely marginalized existence in Chile's Lake District, living mostly in cities – Temuco in particular – or rural *reducciones* (settlements), and making a living from small-scale agriculture and selling handicrafts. Though their language, *Mapundungun*, is no longer outlawed as it was under Pinochet, there is nevertheless constant pressure to assimilate.

Though not as actively endorsed by the Chilean government as under Pinochet, police persecution of Mapuche communities (and those sympathetic to the Mapuche cause, such as foreign journalists) has nevertheless been brought to the attention of various human rights organizations in recent years. **Clashes** between the Mapuche and the police are commonplace and abuses have ranged from harassment, such as tear gas grenades thrown into Mapuche houses, to holding the likes of 12-year-old Luis Marileo – accused of belonging to an "illegal terrorist organization" – in a detention centre and shooting 17-year-old Alex Lemun in the head during a violent eviction. In 2012, indigenous Mapuche activists were accused of deliberately starting forest fires in the Bío Bío region, killing seven firemen and prompting President Sebastian Piñera to invoke an **anti-terror law**. On coming home after attending the funeral of a fire fighter who died in the forest fire, a Mapuche leader found his house had been deliberately burned down.

Tensions remain high. In 2017, a Mapuche sympathizer, Santiago Maldonado, was killed in Argentina, while there was a series of protests against the Pope's January 2018 visit to Araucania, and several Mapuche prisoners went on hunger strike.

For more information on the ongoing struggle of the Mapuche, visit Ⓦmapuche-nation.org.

---

conquest of lands stretching north to modern-day Quito and south as far as the Río Maule in Chile, where its progress was halted by the fierce Mapuche resistance.

The Inca effect

The impact of the Inca in Chile was considerable. They constructed a breathtaking network of roads connecting conquered territory to the capital of the empire in Cusco (which later proved to be very useful to the Spanish conquistadors), as well as forcing subjugated peoples to pay tribute to the Inca ruler and use **Quechua** as their official language. While the Inca tolerated indigenous cults, they required their subjects also to adopt the **cult of the sun**, a central tenet of Inca religion. Sun worship usually took place at altars built on high mountain peaks where the sun's first rays were received;

1600s	Late 1600s	1759–88
The *encomienda* system is established, which involves parcelling out land to settlers and using natives as slaves.	Owing to the decimation of the native population, mestizos are used as hacienda labourers.	Charles III takes the Spanish throne and lifts trade restrictions in order to increase Chile's revenue and then tax it.

it sometimes involved human sacrifice, but more commonly animals or objects like silver figurines were offered as substitutes. Remains of Inca worship sites have been found on numerous mountains in Chile, the most famous being Cerro El Plomo, near Santiago, where the frozen body of a small child, undoubtedly offered as a sacrifice, was discovered in 1954. The Inca occupation of Chile spanned a relatively short period of time – about seventy years in the Norte Grande and perhaps just thirty in Central Chile. It was interrupted first by civil war in Cusco, caused by the struggle between two rivals over succession to the throne. Then, in 1532, the Spanish arrived in Peru, marking the beginning of the end of the Inca empire.

Enter the Spanish

It was while seeking a westward route to Asia across the Atlantic that **Christopher Columbus** inadvertently "discovered" the Americas in 1492. His patron, Queen Isabella of Spain, supported him on two further expeditions, and sent settlers to colonize the Caribbean island of Hispaniola (today's Haiti and Dominican Republic). It gradually became apparent that the islands were not part of Asia, and that a giant landmass – indeed a whole continent – separated them from the East. After colonizing several other islands, the explorers and adventurers, backed by the Spanish Crown, turned their attention to the mainland, and the period of conquest began in earnest.

The conquest of Peru and venture into Chile

In 1521 **Hernán Cortés** defeated the great **Aztec Empire** in Mexico. Then in 1524 **Francisco Pizarro** and his partner **Diego de Almagro** set out to find the rich empire they had been told lay further south. After several failed attempts, they finally landed on the coast of **Peru** in 1532, where they found the great **Inca Empire** racked by civil war. Pizarro speedily conquered the empire, aided by advanced military weapons and tactics, a frenzied desire for gold and glory and, most significantly, the devastating effect of Old World diseases on the indigenous population. Within a few years, Peru was firmly in Spanish hands.

Diego de Almagro was entrusted with the mission of carrying the conquest further south to the region named **Chile**, spoken of by the Peruvian natives as a land rich in gold and silver. In 1535, Almagro and his four hundred men set off from Cusco and followed an Inca road down the spine of the Andes as far as the Aconcagua Valley, suffering extreme deprivation and hardship along the way. To make matters worse, the conquistador found none of the riches the Peruvians had spoken of. Bitterly disappointed, Almagro returned to Cusco, where his deteriorating relations with Pizarro led to armed combat and death at the hands of Pizarro's brothers.

Colonization of Chile and clashes with the Mapuche

Three years later, **Pedro de Valdivia**, one of Pizarro's most trusted officers, was granted license to colonize Chile. Owing to its lack of gold and the miseries of the first expedition, Chile was not an attractive destination, so when Valdivia set off from Cusco in 1540 he was accompanied by just ten compatriots, a group of native porters and his mistress, Inés Suarez. Almost a year later, having picked up 150 extra men en route, Valdivia reached the Río Mapocho in the Aconcagua Valley, where he founded

1767	1777–78	1810
Believing them to be too powerful, the Spanish Crown expels the Jesuits from Chile and other Spanish colonies.	Chile's first general census indicates that the country's population consists of 259,646 inhabitants.	A national junta is established to govern Chile in place of the deposed King Ferdinand VII.

Santiago de la Nueva Extremadura on February 12, 1541. The new "city" was hastily put together, with all the trappings of a colonial capital, including church, prison, court and *cabildo* (town council), which elected Valdivia as governor. It was a humble affair, regularly attacked and destroyed by local Picunche, but the new colonists were determined to stay, and did not return to Peru.

Over the next decade, Valdivia attempted to expand the colony, founding the cities of **La Serena** in the north in 1544 and **Concepción** in the south in 1550, followed by a handful of other centres in the south. It was there that the Spaniards faced the fierce resistance of the **Mapuche** (known by the Spanish as the Araucanians), who successfully prevented the spread of colonization south of the Río Bio Bío, thereafter known as **La Frontera**. Valdivia met his death there in 1553, in a confrontation with the Mapuche, at the hands of the famous chief **Lautaro**. The details of Valdivia's execution are believed to be particularly grisly – some versions claim he was forced to swallow molten gold, others that he was lanced to death by a crowd of warriors, one of whom sliced through his breast and ripped out his heart.

In the panic caused by Valdivia's death, the southern colonists retreated to Santiago, leaving only Concepción as a garrison outpost, occupied mainly by soldiers guarding La Frontera. A new governor – Don García Hurtado de Mendoza – was dispatched from Peru. By the time his term of office ended, in 1561, the natives in the central region had been subjugated, though the south would remain a no-go area for another three centuries.

Colonial society

The new colony was a marginal, isolated and unprofitable addition to Spain's empire in the Americas, which revolved around the viceroyalties of Mexico and Peru. The need to maintain a standing army to guard La Frontera, and the absence of large quantities of precious metals to fund it, meant that Chile ran at a deficit for most of the colonial period. Administratively, it was designated a "**captaincy-general**", ruled by a governor with the help of an *audiencia* (a high court, whose function included advising the governor). All high officials were sent from Spain as representatives of the king, whose authority was absolute, and whose instructions were communicated via the *Consejo de Indias* (Council of the Indies). Chile, however, received little attention and, enclosed within the mighty barriers of the Atacama desert and Andean cordillera, was largely left to its own devices.

Haciendas and encomiendas

Growth was very slow, amounting to no more than five thousand settlers by 1600. Most of these lived from the farming of land handed out by the governor in grants known as **mercedes de tierra**, spreading over the valleys near Santiago and in the Central Valley. At the same time, large "grants" of indigenous people were given to the colonists in what was known as the **encomienda** system – the *encomienda* being the group of natives allocated to an *encomendero* as a force of effectively slave labour (see page 470).

During the **seventeenth century** this pattern became more clearly defined with the emergence and economic dominance of the **hacienda**. Enclosed within thick,

1818	1821	1826
José de San Martín liberates Santiago, and Bernardo O'Higgins becomes "supreme director" of the new Chilean republic.	Spanish troops around Valdivia are defeated by British privateer Thomas Cochrane, who sails in under a Spanish flag.	The remaining Spanish troops on Chiloé surrender, marking the end of the Spanish presence in Chile.

THE LIE OF THE LAND

In theory, the land-owning **encomenderos** of the colonial system were supposed to look after the wellbeing of their charges and convert them to Christianity in exchange for tribute (by means of work) offered to the Spanish Crown. In reality, the system simply provided the colonists with a large **slave workforce** that they could treat however they pleased, which was often appallingly. From the very beginning, then, the *mercedes de tierra* and *encomiendas* established a pattern that was to dominate Chile's rural society until modern times: namely, large estates owned by seignorial landlords at the head of a dependent, disempowered workforce.

---

protective walls, haciendas were self-sufficient, self-contained entities, whose buildings – arranged around numerous courtyards – comprised workshops, wine *bodegas*, dairies, a chapel and the *casa patronal*, the landowner's home. Initially the workforce was provided by *encomiendas*, but, with tragic inevitability, the indigenous population rapidly decreased through exposure to Old World diseases. In its place there sprang up a new generation of **mestizos**, the result of relationships between the Spanish colonists (initially almost exclusively male) and indigenous women.

In time, a more or less homogeneous mestizo population came to make up the bulk of the Chilean workforce, presided over by a ruling, land-owning elite made up of **peninsulares** (Spaniards born in Spain) and **criollos** (those of Spanish blood born in the colony). Most mestizos were incorporated into the haciendas either as peons or as **inquilinos** – labourers allowed to farm a small plot of land in return for year-round service (a practice that continued until the twentieth century).

The rise of the Catholic Church

Along with the haciendas, the other main shaping force in Chilean society was the **Catholic Church**. From the colony's earliest days, missionaries from most orders poured into Chile and embarked on a zealous programme of conversion in the farthest flung corners of the territory, which further helped to decimate the native population through the introduction of European-borne diseases. The missionaries' success was rapid and set the seal on the "pacification" of the indigenous people, who were less likely to cause trouble if they could be incorporated into the Hispanic culture and their sense of separate identity diminished. The Catholicism that emerged wasn't an altogether orthodox version, as many indigenous elements of worship – such as ritual dancing and sacrificial offerings – were incorporated into this new religion, and even now survive in Chile's more remote communities, especially in the north. Nonetheless, both *indígenas* and mestizos embraced the symbolic elements of the Catholic faith with enthusiasm, and several cults sprang up around supposedly miraculous icons, such as the **Cristo de Mayo** in Santiago, believed to have bled real blood after an earthquake in 1647.

Expansion of trade

The reign of **Charles III**, from 1759 to 1788, brought great changes to the colony. The most progressive of the Bourbon monarchs (who had replaced the Habsburg dynasty in Spain in 1700), the king set about improving the management of the American

1833	1834–35	1848–58
Diego Portales is the architect of Chile's first Constitution, which grants enormous powers to the president.	Charles Darwin sails along Chile's coast in HMS *Beagle* and seizes three Fuegian natives.	The port of Valparaíso becomes a crucial supply stop for ships en route to California during the California Gold Rush.

THE RISE AND FALL OF THE JESUITS

The most influential element of the Catholic Church in Chile, the **Jesuit order** (Compañia de Jesús), arrived in 1593 and quickly established itself as one of the colony's largest landowners.

In a paternalistic arrangement, the **Jesuits** gathered hundreds of indigenous families to their **missions**, where they were fed, clothed, converted, taught Spanish and instructed in skills ranging from weaving to glass manufacturing. As a result, and as throughout Spanish America, the order's numerous **workshops** were the most productive and profitable in the country. However, the Crown was eventually persuaded that the Jesuits had become too powerful to be tolerated, and they were abruptly **expelled** from the Spanish Empire in 1767.

colonies and increasing their productivity, so as to augment revenues. Among his reforms was the relaxation of the stifling trade restrictions that had hampered economic growth throughout much of Spanish America. Suddenly, the colonies were able to trade freely with each other and with Spain. There was no overnight miracle, but Chilean trade did expand considerably, particularly with neighbouring Río de la Plata (future Argentina).

At the same time, imports soared, and the need to pay for them in gold or silver stimulated a small **mining boom** in the Norte Chico. Settlements sprang up around the mining centres, and some, such as Copiapó, Vallenar and Illapel, were granted official city status. All in all, there was an emerging spirit of change and progress, which gave a sense of empowerment to Chile's *criollos*, who had always been barred from the highest colonial offices. But while Chile's commercial horizons were widening, the king's administrative shake-ups – which involved sending a number of *intendants* to the colonies to tighten up administration and eradicate abuses of local power – were experienced as unwanted interference. The resulting tension would soon find a more focused channel.

The struggle for independence

Chile entered the **nineteenth century** with a burgeoning sense of its own identity. The *criollo* elite (Chile-born Spanish), while fiercely loyal to the Spanish king, was becoming increasingly alienated from the *intendants* dispatched from Spain to administer the colony, and the gap between them was widening with each successive generation. *Criollo* aspirations of playing a more active role in government (and thus of looking after their own interests, not just the Crown's) were given a sudden, unexpected opportunity for fulfilment when Napoleon invaded Spain in 1808 and deposed Ferdinand VII. **Local juntas** sprang up in Spain's main cities to organize resistance to Napoleon, and they were soon followed by a number of locally elected juntas in the American colonies. In Chile, over four hundred leading citizens gathered in Santiago on September 18, 1810, and elected a six-man **junta**, made up of Chileans. It must be stressed that the junta's initial objective was to "preserve the sovereignty of Ferdinand VII" in the absence of legitimate authority, and few entertained thoughts of independence at this stage. The junta did, however, go on to implement several far-reaching reforms: trade was liberalized; a Congress was elected; and the *real audiencia* (royal court) was replaced by a tribunal with Chilean judges.

1860	1865	1879–84
Orélie-Antoine de Tounens, an eccentric Frenchman, befriends Mapuche leaders and is crowned King of Araucanía.	A wool boom heralds a prosperous new era in Patagonia after the introduction of sheep from the Falklands brings wealth.	Chile goes to war with Bolivia and Peru in the War of the Pacific and emerges victorious.

The first stirrings of independence

Soon, a minority of *criollos* began to seek a far greater degree of autonomy for the colony, and whispers of independence grew. This small tide was given dramatic impetus in November 1811, when **José Miguel Carrera**, a member of one of the wealthiest and most influential *criollo* families, seized power, dissolving Congress and appointing himself head of a new, more radical, junta. His actions were swift and bold, and included the creation of a Chilean flag and the drafting of a provisional constitution that declared all rulings issued outside Chile to be illegitimate. Greatly alarmed, the viceroy of Peru – where the colonial machinery remained intact – sent troops in early 1813 down to the old-guard strongholds of Chiloé and Valdivia to prepare for an assault on Santiago. In response, Carrera charged down to confront them with Chilean troops (whose generals included Bernardo O'Higgins, the son of a former viceroy of Peru), and war was effectively declared. Loyalties were now thrown sharply into focus with the **Royalists** on one side, made up of Spaniards and pro-Spanish Chileans, and the **Patriots** on the other, made up of *criollos* who supported some form of self-government.

The liberators: Bernardo O'Higgins and José de San Martín

When Carrera's military leadership did not produce impressive results, the junta voted to replace him with **Bernardo O'Higgins**, who proved far more adept at holding off the Royalist forces. In July 1814, the power-hungry Carrera returned to Santiago and overthrew the government once more, reinstating himself at its head and causing considerable upheaval. In October of that year, Royalist troops, taking advantage of the chaos, began to advance on Santiago and, after a showdown at Rancagua (see page 473), ultimately won out.

The victory coincided with the defeat of Napoleon in Spain and the restoration of Ferdinand VII, who immediately set out to crack down on all insurgent elements in his American colonies. In Chile, some forty Patriot *criollos* were exiled to the Juan Fernández Islands, and every reform instigated by the junta was reversed. The Spanish Crown's attempt to turn back the clock and revert to a centralized, interventionist colonial government was felt as repressive and authoritarian by *criollos* throughout the continent.

Just as the great general **Simón Bolívar** was preparing anti-Spanish campaigns in Venezuela that would liberate the northern half of the continent, **José de San Martín**, the Argentine general, was drawing plans for South American emancipation from his base in Mendoza, near the Chilean border. San Martín knew that independence could never be assured until the Spanish were ejected from their heartland in Peru, which he planned to achieve by first liberating Chile, from where he would launch a naval attack on Lima.

The final push

With O'Higgins in command of the Chilean division, San Martín's army scaled the cordillera over four different passes in February 1817. On February 12, Patriot forces surprised the Spaniards and defeated them at the Battle of Chacabuco, just north of Santiago. The Royalists fled to the south, and the Patriots entered the capital in triumph. Fighting continued after Royalist reinforcements were sent from Peru, but

1881–83	1883–1909	1888
The last big Mapuche uprising is defeated in the "Pacification of Araucanía"; Mapuche children are enslaved.	Gold is discovered in Tierra del Fuego, prompting mass immigration by fortune seekers and horrific abuse of the indigenous population.	Chile claims Easter Island; the island is turned into a sheep farm and islanders are confined to Hanga Roa.

THE DISASTER OF RANCAGUA

As Royalist troops neared Santiago in the autumn of 1814, **Bernardo O'Higgins** mounted a desperate and heroic defence at Rancagua. Promised reinforcements never arrived, however, and the Patriots were overwhelmingly defeated. The "**Disaster of Rancagua**", as it is known, marked the end of **La Patria Vieja** (the name given to the fledgling independent nation) and its leaders fled across the Andean border to Mendoza in Argentina, as the Royalist troops marched triumphantly into the capital.

when San Martín inflicted devastating losses on their army at the Battle of Maipú in April 1818, the Patriot victory was complete, setting the final seal on Chilean independence. Leadership of the new country was offered to San Martín, but he declined – instead, the job went to Bernardo O'Higgins, who was elected Supreme Director by an assembly of Chile's leading *criollos*.

O'Higgins' immediate task was to put together a national navy with which to clear the southern coast of remaining Royalist troublemakers and launch the seaborne attack on Peru. A flotilla was equipped and placed under the command of a British admiral, **Lord Thomas Cochrane**, who successfully captured Callao, the port of Lima, in 1820. With the colonial nerve centre effectively toppled, the days of the Spanish Empire in the Americas were numbered.

The building of a nation

The transition from colony to republic was not smooth. During its first thirteen years of independence, marked by continual tussles between **Liberal** and **Conservative** factions, Chile got through five constitutions and eleven changes of government. Then, in 1829, the Conservatives, with the support of the army, imposed an authoritarian government that ushered in a long period of political stability, making Chile the envy of Latin America. The chief architect of the regime, **Diego Portales**, never stood for the presidency, preferring to run the show from various cabinet posts. Convinced Chile could only move forward under a strong, centralist government able to maintain rigorous order, Portales designed, in 1833, the **Constitution** that was to underpin Chilean government for 92 years. It granted enormous powers to the president, allowing him, for instance, to veto any legislation passed by Congress, and protecting him from impeachment. Portales was not, however, without his detractors, and in 1837, in protest at the government's invasion of Peru (forcibly annexed by the Bolivian president), he was brutally gunned down by political opponents. This atrocity led to increased support for the government, which went on to defeat the Peru–Bolivia Confederation – to the great pride of Chilean citizens.

Growth and prosperity

The growing self-confidence of the nation, together with its political and social stability, created conditions that were favourable to growth. International trade took off rapidly between the 1830s and 1870s, with hugely increased wheat exports fuelled by the Californian and Australian gold rushes, and, more significantly, **a silver- and copper-mining boom** in the Norte Chico. At the same time, advances in technology

1890–91	1904	1907
Civil war erupts when Congress revolts over President José Manuel Balmaceda's wealth redistribution reforms, resulting in 10,000 deaths.	Neftalí Ricardo Reyes Basoalto, better known as Pablo Neruda, is born on July 12.	The Chilean army massacres over five hundred saltpetre miners, their wives and children in Iquique.

and communications saw railways, roads, steamships and a telegraph network open up the country. Its populated territory expanded, too: a government programme encouraged Europeans to come over and settle the lakeland region of the south, which was duly cleared and farmed by four thousand German immigrants. Meanwhile, Santiago and Valparaíso were being transformed, with avenues, parks, palaces and mansions, and a growing population.

Rise of the Liberals

In time, Chileans began to tire of the authoritarian model of government established by Portales, and the influence of Liberal politics began to gain ground. In 1871 the election of **Federico Errázuriz Zañartu** as president marked the start of twenty years of Liberal government. Many of the Liberals' reforms were aimed at reducing the undiminished power of the Church. They legalized free worship in private places; introduced civil cemeteries, where persons of any faith could be buried; and instituted civil marriages and registries. The Liberals also went some way towards reducing the individual power of the president, and giving Congress a stronger role in government. The breath of fresh air and sense of optimism produced by these reforms suffered a deathblow, however, when a world recession between 1876 and 1878 sent copper and silver prices tumbling, and brought wheat exports to a virtual halt, plunging Chile into economic crisis.

The War of the Pacific

Rescue was at hand in what at first appeared to be yet another calamitous situation. Ever since the 1860s, when two enterprising Chileans started exploiting the vast nitrate deposits of the Atacama desert, Chilean capital and labour had dominated the region's growing **nitrate** industry (see page 193). Most activity took place on the pampas around Antofagasta, which Chile had formally acknowledged as Bolivian territory in 1874 – following lengthy border disputes – in exchange for an assurance from Bolivia that export tariffs would not be raised for 25 years. Many of Chile's most prominent politicians owned shares in the nitrate companies, so when Bolivia flouted its agreement by raising export taxes in 1878 – directly hitting shareholders' pockets – they were up in arms, and determined to take action.

With tension mounting, Chilean troops invaded Antofagasta in February 1879 and soon took control of the surrounding coastal strip. Within two weeks Chile and Bolivia were at war, with Peru drawn into the conflict on Bolivia's side within a couple of months. It soon became clear that success would depend on **naval supremacy** – Bolivia did not have a navy, leaving Peru and Chile pitted against each other, and fairly evenly matched. Following a series of early losses, Chile secured an overwhelming maritime victory in August 1879, when it captured Peru's principal warship, the *Huáscar*. The coast was now clear for the invasion of Peru's nitrate territories, and the emphasis shifted to land fighting. Casualties were heavy on both sides, but by June 1880 Chile had secured control of these areas with a resounding victory at El Morro, Arica.

With the nitrate fields theirs, the Chilean government would doubtless have been happy to bring the war to a close, but the public was clamouring for blood: it wanted Peru brought to its knees with the capture of Lima. In January 1881 Peru's humiliation

1914	1924	1925
The creation of the Panama Canal deals a huge blow to Chile's economy. Punta Arenas and Valparaíso go into decline.	President Arturo Alessandri appoints military figures to key cabinet positions and puts pressure on Congress to pass social reforms.	The new Constitution is drafted, restoring authority to the president, and incorporating welfare measures to quell protests.

> **ARTURO PRAT – A NAVAL TRAGEDY**
>
> Nothing has captured the Chilean imagination like the heroic, and tragic, efforts of **Arturo Prat** in the Battle of Iquique. On the morning of May 21, 1879, the *Esmeralda* – an old wooden boat under Prat's command – found itself under attack from Peruvian artillery on one side, and from the ironclad warship, the *Huáscar*, on the other. The two vessels could not have been more unevenly matched: the *Huáscar* boasted 300lb cannon, while those of the *Esmeralda* were only 40lb. When the *Huáscar* rammed the *Esmeralda*, Prat refused to give in, instead leaping aboard the enemy's vessel, sword in hand, determined to fight to the end. The gesture was futile, and Prat was killed on the warship's deck, but the commander's dignity and self-sacrifice have made him Chile's favourite national hero, in whose honour a thousand avenues and squares have been named.

was complete when Chilean troops occupied the capital. Peru was still not ready to give up, though, and the war dragged on for two more years, exhausting both sides and resulting in heavy human loss. Eventually, Peru accepted defeat, sealed by the **Treaty of Ancón** in October 1883 (an official truce with Bolivia was not signed until the following April).

By the end of the war, Chile had extended its territory by one-third, acquiring the Peruvian province of Tarapacá, and the Bolivian littoral (depriving Bolivia of sea access). Its new, nitrate-rich pampas yielded enormous, almost overnight wealth, refilling government coffers and restoring national confidence.

Civil war

By 1890, with the nitrate industry booming in earnest, export taxes were providing over fifty percent of government revenue. With national confidence running high and the economy in such good shape, the government's position looked unassailable. Within a short time, however, cracks began to appear in the constitutional framework, expressed by mounting tension between the legislature and the executive branch.

The conflict came to a dramatic head under the presidency of **José Manuel Balmaceda** (1886–91), a Liberal but autocratic leader who passionately believed in the president's right to run a strong executive branch – an approach jarringly at odds with the political trend of the previous couple of decades. One of the unifying objectives of the various Liberal parties was the elimination of electoral intervention, and when Balmaceda was seen to influence Congressional elections in 1886, many Liberals were outraged and withdrew their support. Equally polarizing was the president's determination to insist on his right to pick and choose his cabinet, without the approval of Congress. Their response was to refuse to pass legislation authorizing the following year's budget until Balmaceda agreed to appoint a cabinet in which they had confidence.

Neither side would give way, and as the deadline for budget approval drew close, it became obvious that Balmaceda would either have to give in to Congress's demands, or act against the Constitution. When he chose the latter option, declaring that he would carry the 1890 budget through to 1891, Congress revolted, propelling the two sides into war. Balmaceda held the army's support, while Congress secured the backing of the navy. Operating out of Iquique, where they established a junta, Congress was able

1927–31	1931	1938–46
General Carlos Ibañez passes far-reaching reforms before being ousted on a wave of Great Depression-related discontent.	Mountaineering priest Alberto de Agostini is the first man to cross the Patagonian Ice Fields.	The unionized labour movement lends its support to the Popular Front – a coalition of socialists, communists and radicals.

to use nitrate funds to recruit and train an army. In August that year, its troops landed near Valparaíso, where they defeated Balmaceda's army in two long, bloody battles. The president, whose refusal to give in was absolute, fled to the Argentine embassy, where he wrote poignant farewell notes to his family and friends before shooting himself in the head.

The Parliamentary Republic

The authoritarian model of government established by Diego Portales in the 1830s, already undermined over the previous two decades, had now collapsed. Taking its place was a system – dubbed the **Parliamentary Republic** – based on an all-powerful legislature and an extremely weak executive. Now it was Congress who imposed cabinets on the president, not the other way round, with frequent clashes and constantly shifting allegiances seeing cabinets formed and dissolved with breathtaking frequency – between 1891 and 1915 the government got through more than sixty ministries. This chronic instability seriously hampered government action, although, ironically, the one arena where great progress was made was the public works programme vigorously promoted by Balmaceda, which saw rapid construction of state railways, roads, bridges, schools, hospitals, prisons and town halls.

Industrial development and unrest

All this took place against a background of momentous social and economic change that the government, bound up with its continual infighting, seemed scarcely aware of. One of the by-products of the nitrate industry was increased **industrialization** elsewhere in Chile, as manufacturing stepped up to service increased production in the north. This, combined with the growth of railways, coal mining, education, construction and banking, saw a period of rapid **social diversification**. A new group of merchants, managers, bureaucrats and teachers formed an emerging middle class, while the increasingly urban workforce – usually living in dire poverty – formed a new working class more visible than its counterpart on the large rural estates.

It was in the nitrate fields of the north that an embryonic **labour movement** began to take root, as workers protested against the appalling conditions they were forced to live and work in. With no political representation to voice these grievances, **strikes** became the main form of protest, spreading from the mining cities of the north to the docks of Valparaíso. The government's heavy-handed attempts to suppress the strikes – reaching a peak of brutality when almost two hundred men, women and children were shot dead in Iquique in 1907 – were symptomatic of its inability to deal with the social changes taking place in the country. When the nitrate industry entered a rapid decline with the outbreak of World War I in 1914, leaving thousands of workers unemployed and causing inflation to soar, Chile's domestic situation deteriorated further.

Military intervention

The first leader committed to dealing with the republic's mounting social problems was **Arturo Alessandri**, elected in 1920 on the strength of an ambitious reform programme. The weakness of his position, however, in the face of an all-powerful and obstructive

1945	1947	1960
Gabriela Mistral – poet, educator and diplomat – becomes the first Latin American to win the Nobel prize for literature.	Chile establishes its first permanent Antarctic research station – Captain Arturo Prat Base – on Greenwich Island.	The tsunami caused by the Great Chilean Earthquake, the most powerful ever recorded (9.5 on the Richter Scale) devastates Valdivia.

Congress, prevented him from putting any of his plans into action, and after four years hardly anything had been achieved. Then, in 1924, a strange set of events was set in motion when an army junta – frustrated by the lack of government action – forced the cabinet to resign and had Alessandri appoint military men to key cabinet positions. The president appeared quite willing to accommodate the junta, which used its muscle to ensure that Congress swiftly passed a series of social reform laws, including legislation to protect workers' rights. After several months, however, the relationship between the president and his military cabinet began to unravel and Alessandri fled to exile in Argentina.

More drama was to follow when, on January 23, 1925, a rival junta led by General **Carlos Ibáñez** staged a coup, deposed the government and invited Alessandri to return to Chile to complete his term of office. With Ibáñez's weight behind him, Alessandri set about redrafting the Constitution, with the aim of restoring authority to the president and reducing the power of Congress. This was achieved with the **Constitution of 1925**, a radical departure from the one of 1833, incorporating protective welfare measures among other reforms. Despite this victory, however, tensions between Ibáñez and Alessandri led to the president's resignation. The way was now clear for the military strongman, Ibáñez, to get himself elected as president in May 1927.

Boom to bust

Ibáñez's presidency was a curious contradiction, both highly autocratic, with severe restrictions on freedom of expression, and refreshingly progressive, ushering in badly needed reforms promoting agriculture, industry and education. His early years were successful, bringing about improvements in living standards across society, and stimulating national prosperity. But when the Wall Street crash of 1929 sparked off a worldwide depression, Chile's economy collapsed virtually overnight, producing deep social unrest. Faced with a wave of street demonstrations and strikes, Ibáñez was forced to resign in July 1931. The task of restoring stability to the nation fell to the old populist, Alessandri, who was re-elected in 1932.

The rise of the multi-party system

Military interference in government affairs was now at an end – for a few decades, at least – and the country settled down to a period of orderly political evolution, no longer held back by a weak executive. What emerged was a highly diverse multi-party system embracing a wide spectrum of political persuasions. After 1938, the government was dominated by the **Radical Party**, a centre-right group principally representing the middle classes. Radical presidents such as Pedro Aguirre Cerda, Juan Antonio Ríos and Gabriel González Videla took an active role in regenerating Chile's economy, investing in state-sponsored steelworks, copper refineries, fisheries and power supplies. During the 1950s, as the voting franchise widened, left-wing groups gained considerable ground, but old-guard landowners were able to counter this by controlling the votes of the thousands of peasants who depended on them for their survival, thus ensuring a firm swing back to the right. Nonetheless, it was by a very narrow margin that the socialist Salvador Allende was defeated by the Conservative Jorge Alessandri (son of Arturo) in the 1958 elections, causing widespread alarm among the wealthy

1964

1970

Easter Islanders are finally granted Chilean citizenship and given the right to vote. Christian Democrat Eduardo Frei is elected president; he initiates far-reaching social and economic reforms.

Salvador Allende becomes the first democratically elected Marxist president in the world, winning by a tiny margin.

elite. As the next election approached in 1964, the upper classes, with the discreet backing of the USA (still reeling from the Cuban missile crisis), threw all their efforts into securing the election of **Eduardo Frei**, the candidate of the rising young **Christian Democrat Party**.

From right-wing to left

In power, Frei proved a good deal more progressive than his right-wing supporters could have imagined, initiating – to their horror – bold **agrarian reforms** that allowed the expropriation of all farms of more than 1.8 square kilometres. He also prompted the "Chileanization" of the **copper industry**, which had replaced nitrates as the country's dominant source of revenue, and which was almost exclusively in the hands of North American corporations. Frei's policy gave the state a 51 percent stake in all the major copper mines, providing instant revenues to fund his social reform programme. These included the introduction of a minimum wage and impressive improvements in education, and made Frei's government popular with the working classes, though his reforms were unable to keep pace with the rush of expectations and demands. At the same time, Conservative groups became increasingly alarmed at the direction Frei was steering the country, prompting Liberals and Conservatives to join forces and form the new **National Party**, aimed at putting a check on reform. As Chile approached the 1970s, its population grew sharply polarized between those who clamoured for further social reform and greater representation of the working class, and those to whom this was anathema and to be reversed at all costs.

Salvador Allende's rise to power

On September 4, 1970, **Salvador Allende** was elected as Chile's first socialist president, heading a coalition of six left-wing parties, known as the **Unidad Popular** (UP). His majority, however, was tiny, and while half the country rejoiced, full of hopes for a better future, the other half feared a slide towards communism. Allende was passionately committed to improving the lot of the poorest sectors of society, whose appalling living conditions had shocked him during his training as a doctor. His government pledged, among other things, to nationalize Chilean industries, redistribute the nation's wealth, increase popular participation in government, and speed up agrarian reform, though there were disagreements as to how fast these changes should be made.

Within a year, over eighty major companies were nationalized, including the copper mines, which were expropriated without compensation. The following year, radical agrarian reform was enforced, with over sixty percent of irrigated land – including all haciendas with more than 0.8 square kilometres – taken into government hands for redistribution among the rural workforce. In one fell swoop, the *latifundia* system (where landed estate utilized forced indigenous labour) that had dominated rural Chile for more than four hundred years was irrevocably dismantled.

In the short term, Allende's government was both successful and popular, presiding as it did over a period of economic growth, rising wages and falling unemployment. But it wasn't long before strains began to be felt. Government expenditure soon exceeded income by a huge margin, creating an enormous deficit. The looming economic crisis

1970–73	1973	1973
Allende's radical reforms – the nationalization of industry and land redistribution – are crippled by overspending and uncontrollable inflation.	Military coup led by Augusto Pinochet overthrows Allende's government on September 11; Allende dies during the siege of La Moneda.	Pablo Neruda dies on September 23; thousands of people defy Pinochet by mourning in the streets.

THIS DARK AND BITTER MOMENT: ALLENDE'S LAST STAND

Refusing a safe passage to exile, Salvador Allende ordered his soldiers to drag away his daughter (who wanted to remain with him in the besieged presidential palace) and, in an emotional **speech** broadcast live on radio, vowed that he would never give up, and that he was ready to repay the loyalty of the Chilean people with his life. In this unique moment of history, citizens heard their president declare "I have faith in Chile and in its destiny. Other men will overcome this dark and bitter moment…You must go on, safe in the knowledge that sooner rather than later, the great avenues will open once more, and free men will march along them to create a better society…These are my last words, but I am sure that my sacrifice will not be in vain." Shortly afterwards, the signals were cut short, and jets began to drop their bombs. At the end of the day, Allende was found dead in the ruins of the palace, clutching a submachine gun, with which, it is widely believed, he had killed himself.

---

was dramatically accelerated when the world copper price fell by 27 percent, cutting government revenue still further. Inflation began to rise uncontrollably, with wages unable to keep pace, and food shortages soon became commonplace.

The cracks appear

Part of the UP's failure stemmed from the sharp divisions within the coalition, particularly between those who, like Allende, were in favour of a measured pace of reform, and those pressing for rapid, revolutionary change. This internal disunity led to a lack of coordination in implementing policy, and an irreversible slide towards political chaos. Making matters worse were the extremist far-left groups outside the government – notably the Revolutionary Left Movement (**MIR**) – which urged the workers to take reform into their own hands by seizing possession of the haciendas and factories where they worked.

Opposition to the government rose sharply during 1972, both from political parties outside the coalition (such as the Christian Democrats, who had previously supported Allende) and sectors of the public. Panic was fuelled by the right-wing press and reinforced behind the scenes by the CIA, who, it later emerged, had a US$8 million budget to destabilize the Allende government. Strikes broke out, culminating in the truckers' stoppage of October 1972, which virtually paralysed the economy. By 1973, with the country rocked by civil disorder, it was clear to all that the government could not survive for much longer. On the morning of September 11, 1973, tanks rolled through the capital and surrounded the presidential palace, La Moneda, marking the beginning of the **military coup** that Chile had been expecting for months, and the end of both Salvador Allende's reign and his life (see above).

The Pinochet years

The military coup was headed by a four-man junta of whom **General Augusto Pinochet**, chief of the army, quickly emerged as the dominant figure. Although Chile had seen military intervention in government affairs on two occasions in the past, these had been the exception to a highly constitutional norm. Nothing in the country's political history prepared its people for the brutality of this operation. In the days and weeks

1973	**1973–89**	**1976–81**
In September and October, the Caravan of Death army death squad travels the length of Chile, murdering Pinochet's opponents.	Pinochet dissolves Congress, indefinitely suspends all political parties and rules by decree; thousands are tortured and at least 3065 killed.	The rapid growth of Chile's free-market economy, spurred on by elimination of price controls, is dubbed the "Chilean Miracle".

following the takeover, the **Caravan of Death** – a Chilean army death squad – travelled the length of Chile, executing 97 people. At least seven thousand people – journalists, politicians, socialists, trade union organizers and others – were herded into the national football stadium, where many were executed; tens of thousands more were tortured. Curfews were imposed, the press was placed under the strict control of the junta, and military officers were sent in to take charge of factories, universities and other seats of socialist support. Before long, Congress had been dissolved, opposition parties and trade unions banned, and over thirty thousand Chileans had fled the country.

Death and the free market

At the same time as his henchmen were murdering the opposition (see page 481), General Pinochet saw his mission – one supported by a sizeable portion of the population – as being that of rescuing Chile from the Left and, by extension, from the economic and political chaos into which it had undoubtedly fallen. To achieve this, he planned not to hand the country over to a right-wing political party of his approval, but to take it into his own hands and rule it himself. His key strategy was to be the adoption of a radical **free-market economy**, which involved a complete reversal of Allende's policies and a drastic restructuring of government and society. In this he was influenced by a group of Chilean economists known as "the Chicago boys", who had carried out postgraduate studies at the University of Chicago, where they'd come into contact with the monetarist theories of Milton Friedman. Almost immediately, price controls were abolished, government expenditure was slashed, most state-owned companies were privatized, import tariffs were reduced, and attempts were made to liberalize investment and attract foreign capital.

Such measures would take time to work, and called for a period of intense austerity. Sure enough, unemployment soared, wages plummeted, industrial output dropped, and the lower and middle classes became significantly poorer. At the same time, as Pinochet strove to reduce the role of the state in society, social welfare became increasingly neglected, particularly health and education. By the late 1970s, the economy was showing signs of growth and inflation was finally beginning to drop – from an annual rate of nine hundred percent in 1973 to 65 percent in 1977 and down to a respectable 9.5 percent in 1981. Soon, there was talk of the Chilean "economic miracle" in international circles.

The boom did not last, and in 1982, Chile found itself, along with much of Latin America, in the grip of a serious **debt crisis** which swept away the previous advances: the country was plunged into recession, with hundreds of private enterprises going bankrupt and unemployment rising to over thirty percent. It wasn't until the late 1980s that the economy recovered and Pinochet's free-market policies achieved the results he sought, with sustained growth, controlled inflation, booming, diversified exports and reduced unemployment. This prosperity, however, did not benefit all Chileans, and 49 percent of Chile's private wealth remained in the hands of ten percent of its population.

The beginning of the end

Pinochet held the country in such a tight personal grip – famously claiming "there is not a leaf that stirs in Chile without my knowing it" – that it doubtless became difficult for him to conceive of an end to his authority. The Constitution that he had drawn up

1980	1982	1988
A controversial new constitution is passed, giving Pinochet extended powers and an eight-year term.	Isabel Allende's debut novel, *The House of the Spirits*, is published, bringing her international fame.	Fifty-six percent of the population vote against Pinochet's continuing presidency in a plebiscite, leading to a democratic election.

> **STATE-SPONSORED TERROR**
>
> Pinochet's free-market experiment had only been possible with the tools of ruthless repression at his disposal. His chief instrument was the secret police known as the **DINA**, which carried out surveillance on civilian (and even military) society, brutally silencing all opposition. Although the wholesale repression that followed the coup diminished in scale after the first year, regular "disappearances", torture and executions continued throughout Pinochet's regime. The regime was actively, if clandestinely, supported by the US, through the CIA, which even helped with the elimination of dissidents. In the absence of any organized political opposition, only the Catholic Church spoke out against the government's human rights violations, providing assistance and sanctuary to those who suffered, and vigilantly documenting all reports of abuse.

in 1980 – ratified by a tightly controlled **plebiscite** – guaranteed him power until 1988, at which point the public would be given the chance either to accept military rule for another eight years, or else call for elections.

From the mid-1980s, **public protest** against Pinochet's regime began to be voiced, both in regular street demonstrations and with the reformation of political opposition parties (still officially banned). Open repression was stepped down as international attention became increasingly focused on the Chilean government's behaviour, and the US (a major source of foreign investment) made clear that it favoured a return to democracy. In this climate, the opposition parties were able to develop a united strategy in their efforts to oust the dictator. As the referendum in which Chile would decide whether or not to reject military rule drew closer, the opposition forces banded together to lead a highly professional and convincing "no" campaign. Pinochet remained convinced of his own victory, and with control of all media, and the intimidation tactics of a powerful police state at his disposal, it is easy to see why. But when the plebiscite took place on **October 5, 1988**, 55 percent of the nation voted "no" to continued military rule.

Pinochet goes quietly

After sixteen years in power, the writing was on the wall for Pinochet's dictatorship. Much to everyone's surprise, he accepted his defeat without resistance and prepared to step down. But the handover system gave him one more year in power before democratic elections would be held – a year in which he hastily prepared **amnesty laws** that would protect both himself and the military from facing any charges of human rights abuses levied by the new government, and that would make his constitutional model extremely difficult to amend. A year later, on December 14, 1989, the Christian Democrat Patricio Aylwin, at the head of a seventeen-party centre-ground coalition called the **Concertación de los Partidos por la Democracia**, became Chile's first democratically elected president in seventeen years.

Return to democracy

The handover of power was smooth and handled with cautious goodwill on all sides, including the military. **Patricio Aylwin** was in the fortunate position of inheriting a robust economy and an optimistic public. Yet he faced serious challenges, including

1989	1990	1998
The first free elections since 1970 result in a victory for moderate Christian Democrat Patricio Aylwyn.	Pinochet steps down, but not before obtaining immunity from prosecution for himself and his cronies in the military.	Pinochet arrested in the UK – the first former head of state to be arrested on the principle of universal jurisdiction.

JUSTICE FOR SOME

One of the new Patricio Aylwin government's first actions was to establish a **National Commission for Truth and Reconciliation** to investigate and document the abuses committed by the military regime. Its 1991 report confirmed 2279 executions, disappearances and deaths caused by torture, and listed a further 641 suspected cases. Although compensation was paid to the families of the victims, the few attempts made to bring the perpetrators to justice were unsuccessful, owing to the protective **amnesty laws** passed by Pinochet before he relinquished power.

By 1995, however, the courts were finally willing to find ways of getting round Pinochet's amnesty laws. There were breakthrough convictions of six former *carabineros*, two former DINA (secret police) agents and most significantly, of General Manuel Contreras and Brigadier Pedro Espinoza, both sentenced to **life imprisonment** in "Punta Peuco", a jail built purposely for high-profile human rights criminals. Several more cases resulted in prison sentences for violators, though the government controversially approved measures aimed at imposing a time limit on human rights investigations, which some claimed were dragging on excessively. In spectacular circumstances, former secret police chief **Manuel Contreras**, who had already served part of an earlier life sentence, was arrested in early 2005 on fresh charges – he allegedly tried to shoot the officers who went to his house to detain him.

the need to channel substantial funds into those areas neglected by the previous regime while sustaining economic growth, and to address human rights abuses without antagonizing the military and endangering the transition to democracy.

Pinochet's **economic** model was barely contested, and was vigorously applied in an effort to promote "growth with equity" (the Concertación's electoral slogan). Foreign investment poured into the country and exports continued to rise, keeping economic growth at high levels and allowing Aylwin to divert resources into health and education. He was also felt to be making genuine efforts to alleviate the problems faced by the poorest members of society.

Return of Eduardo Frei (Jr)

After a successful four-year term, the Concertación was in 1993 once again elected to power, headed by the Christian Democrat **Eduardo Frei** (son of the 1964–70 president). Frei's policies were essentially a continuation of his predecessors', with a firmer emphasis on tackling human rights issues (see above) and eradicating severe poverty. His success was mixed. His National Programme for Overcoming Poverty, established in 1994, was seen as inconsistent and ineffective. In its last couple of years, Frei's government ran into unexpected problems. First, the Asian economic crisis of 1998 had serious repercussions on the Chilean economy, hitting exports, foreign investment (much of which came from Southeast Asia) and the value of the peso, which has been sliding gradually ever since. At the same time, the unresolved tensions over lack of justice for Pinochet erupted afresh when the general retired from his position of commander-in-chief of the army in early 1998 but immediately took up a seat in Congress as a life senator. More controversy followed later the same year as he was dramatically thrust into the international spotlight following his arrest in a London

2000	2004
Ricardo Lagos, a moderate leftist, is elected president – one of several leftist leaders in South America. Pinochet is released on medical grounds and sent back to Chile, disappointing those demanding justice for his victims.	Despite being a predominantly Catholic country, Chile finally legalizes divorce; courts are flooded with thousands of cases.

WILL HE OR WON'T HE: THE PINOCHET AFFAIR

On October 16, 1998, justice finally caught up with Augusto Pinochet who was arrested in a London hospital after Spain had requested his extradition. The arrest provoked strong reactions in Chile. Families of Pinochet's victims rejoiced euphorically, while supporters of the general were outraged, burning British flags in the streets. The government, in a difficult position, denounced the arrest as an affront to national sovereignty and demanded Pinochet's immediate return to Chile – whereupon, they claimed, his alleged crimes would be dealt with in the Chilean courts. After a protracted and complex legal battle, during which the British judiciary ruled both for and against Pinochet, Britain's Home Secretary, **Jack Straw**, announced in 1999 that proceedings could go ahead. They again got bogged down, this time over whether the former dictator was fit to stand trial.

Straw finally decided to send Pinochet back to Chile in March 2000, just before Ricardo Lagos was sworn in at La Moneda. There was an international outcry when he was welcomed back with pomp and circumstance by the armed forces, and Congress granted all former heads of state **lifelong immunity** from prosecution. Even Lagos expressed support for such a move, to quell any stirrings in the military. Yet the former dictator was stripped of his immunity in June and by Christmas 2000 he had faced charges for kidnapping opponents. Early in 2001 he was judged mentally fit for trial, and, at the end of January Chilean judge **Juan Guzmán** ordered Pinochet's house arrest. But within months the case fizzled out yet again, and in July 2001 all charges against Pinochet were dropped after a Santiago court decided he was, after all, unfit to stand trial. Nevertheless, like the former tyrant himself, the case would not lie down and die. Further appeals and counter-appeals meant that the affair dragged on for one more year. Finally the country's Supreme Court ruled, in 2002, that Pinochet was indeed unfit to stand trial on mental-health grounds. He responded by resigning as life senator from Chile's Congress and was reported as saying that he did so "with a clear conscience", unleashing a furore among his opponents.

CORRUPTION CHARGES

Spectre-like, Pinochet returned to the fore once more amid a **financial scandal** in 2005. Though the ex-dictator had always claimed that, unlike many of his peers, his only interest was the wellbeing of his country and not of his pocket, it transpired that he and/or his relatives had creamed off tens of millions of dollars in murky wheeling and dealing, and carefully stashed the laundered booty in US bank accounts, one of them at Riggs Bank; cooperation with the US financial authorities revealed the existence of the funds, a very generous nest egg for his family. In February 2005, Riggs donated $8 million to a pension fund set up for the families of three thousand victims of human rights abuses under the general's regime. In June of the same year, the courts decided that he was fit to stand trial to answer the corruption charges yet mortality was to intervene before any sentence could ever be passed (see page 484).

hospital on October 16, following a request for his **extradition** to Spain to face charges of murder and torture (see above).

The rise of the left

In December 1999, the first round of presidential elections left two front-runners neck and neck in the second round: the Concertación's candidate, socialist **Ricardo**

2005	2006
Constitutional reforms fully restore democracy, dispensing with military commanders and non-electe senators-for-life such as Pinochet.	In January, Chile elects its first female president, Michelle Bachelet, to lead the centre-left Concertación coalition. Pinochet dies without ever standing trial for his crimes and is denied a state funeral. Bachelet does not attend.

JUSTICE DENIED: THE DEATH OF PINOCHET

Chile was once more convulsed with polarized passions following **Pinochet's death** from a heart attack in December 2006, symbolically enough on International Human Rights' Day. At the time of his death, he was under house arrest and facing trial over charges in Chilean courts relating to one financial enquiry and five human rights cases. In October 2006, an appeal court had dropped corruption charges brought against his wife and five children who had been accused of sending state funds illegally to foreign bank accounts in the US. They say that for Chileans there's no middle ground on Pinochet – they either love him or hate him. This never appeared so true than in the days following his death. While jubilant opponents danced in the centre of the capital, his supporters mourned outside the military hospital where he died, loving the man they insisted had saved the country from Marxism and put Chile on the path of strong economic growth.

Bachelet **refused to authorize** the type of state funeral normally granted to former presidents, saying it would be "a violation of my conscience" to do so and did not attend. Instead, Pinochet was allowed only military honours as a former head of the Chilean army. For many, there is still anger and frustration that the former dictator never faced trial for his crimes. Though it may be little solace, in the words of Uruguayan writer Mario Benedetti: "Formal justice may remain incomplete, but history has judged him and condemned him."

Lagos, a former education minister under Aylwin who had famously voiced criticism of Pinochet in the late 1980s, and **Joaquín Lavín**, who had served under the general and was standing on a firmly right-wing platform. Lagos pulled off an eleventh-hour victory on January 16, 2000, beating his opponent narrowly – by 51 to 49 percent.

Social and land reform

Determined to continue with his predecessors' overhaul of two main areas of social policy, namely **health and education**, the highly popular Lagos implemented an ambitious programme based on reforming the state. A push towards universal free medical care initiated by Lagos has now mostly been achieved, with free treatment for low-income earners and people over 60, and with the rest paying a contribution dictated by their earnings. Hospitals and other services, mostly in a pitiful state after years of neglect, were improved, too. After compulsory schooling, shortened to the bare minimum by Pinochet, was dramatically lengthened, plans to recruit more teachers, improve their training and raise their salaries were implemented. **Divorce** was finally legalized in 2004, despite opposition by the Church, which has said it will do all it can to obstruct the new, democratically enacted law. Abortion remains utterly taboo.

Lagos also tried to tackle the thorny issue of **indigenous peoples' rights**, handing back tracts of land to the Mapuche and others early on in his presidency. However, emboldened *indígenas* demanded more of their land back, resulting in some ugly clashes with the police in 2002, when demonstrators tried to block the construction of a new road through land claimed by the Mapuche; there have been several similar incidents in recent years.

2007

The DNA of a Polynesian chicken is found at the Mapuche settlement of El Arenal, suggesting new human migration theories.

WOMEN'S RIGHTS IN THE NEW CHILE

In a country with fewer **women** in the workforce than anywhere else in Latin America, Bachelet promised to champion women's causes. In her first year, she delivered not only the breast-feeding law but also set up hundreds of nurseries and shelters for victims of domestic violence. By presidential decree, and to the disgust of the Catholic Church, she made the **morning-after pill** available free to girls as young as 14. In 2017, in a landmark move, the Bachelet government finally pushed through a partial legalization of abortion.

Trouble abroad

International relations, in particular with the country's neighbours, were decidedly rocky as Lagos headed towards the end of his term of office. His dismissive remarks plus chauvinistic Chilean media coverage following the arrest of two young Chileans accused of defacing an ancient wall in the Inca city of Cusco, did little to smooth relations with **Peru**, Chile's traditional rival to the north. Chile's refusal to negotiate a guaranteed ocean access for landlocked **Bolivia**, meanwhile, further soured relations with another long-time foe. And **Argentina**'s decision to prioritize its domestic gas demand, at the risk of cutting supplies to Chile, increased trans-Andean tensions.

South America's first female president

From March 2006, Chile had a woman president, socialist **Michelle Bachelet**, elected by a comfortable margin in the second-round run-off in January that year. She had stood against charismatic businessman and current president Sebastián Piñera, of the centre-right National Renewal Party, in the *balotaje* (decisive second round). Furious at his decision to run and split the right-wing vote, Lavín supporters likened Piñera – billionaire owner of the TV channel Chilevisión, and president of LAN (now LATAM), the national airline – to Italy's Silvio Berlusconi. Bachelet, by contrast, was a physician who'd gone into exile in Australia and East Germany in the 1970s after her father, a moderate Air Force general, was assassinated under Pinochet. In her victory speech she said that a **feminine touch** was needed to smooth international relations and promised to work for greater friendship between Chile and its neighbours, particularly Argentina.

Bachelet in office

Bachelet's election as Chile's first female head of state also made her the first woman to be directly and democratically elected in South American history. Indeed, one of outgoing President Lagos' stated aims had been to reduce the acute **gender inequality** in the country, and he appointed Chile's first female ministers for defence (Bachelet herself) and foreign affairs (her erstwhile rival in the presidential race, Soledad Alvear). The number of women in the principal judicial bodies has also risen, while the House of Deputies had two woman speakers at the beginning of the millennium, and during Bachelet's presidency the Cabinet of Chile had equal numbers of male and female ministers.

2010

On February 27, a powerful earthquake damages Concepción, and the resulting tsunami devastates the island of Juan Fernández. Sebastián Piñera comes to power in January's elections in the first democratic victory for Chile's right-wing movement since Pinochet's coup, and in August, the collapse of a copper-gold mine leaves 33 miners trapped underground for 69 days.

Criticized during the campaign for her vague policies and indecision, Bachelet nevertheless started her presidency with a strong mandate, a supportive parliament and many expectations. She promised a new, participatory style of government that would continue pro-market economic policies begun under the dictatorship of Augusto Pinochet, but with an accent on empowering ordinary Chileans. The fact that she was detained and tortured, along with her mother, in the early Pinochet years before her family was allowed to leave the country, enhanced her popularity on the left; but her **progressive stance** on issues such as divorce, human rights and religion (she is a professed agnostic) and the fact that she is separated from her husband and did not marry the father of her third child, put off many traditional voters even in her own camp. All that said, she was staunchly opposed to gay marriage (but not to some kind of official recognition of same-sex couples).

Although Bachelet enjoyed 62 percent approval shortly after taking office, it didn't take long for the inherited hangovers from the previous administrations to reassert themselves: labour protests, social unrest from students complaining about the poor quality of public education and a botched overhaul of Santiago's transport caused her public standing to plummet. During the first two and a half years of her presidency, Chile's economy ticked along nicely, thanks largely to Asian demand delivering booming revenues for Chile's chief export, copper. But amid the **global financial crisis** that took hold in mid-2008, the price of copper halved in the space of four months.

Diplomatic manoeuvres

Bachelet aimed to focus foreign policy on improving **international relations** with Chile's neighbours. In a move seen as a chance to improve strained ties between Bolivia and Chile, Bachelet made a rare trip to **Bolivia** in 2007 for talks with President Evo Morales and the president of Brazil in La Paz. There they agreed ambitious plans to build a highway linking the Atlantic and Pacific coasts of South America from Santos in Brazil to Iquique in Chile. The highway was completed in 2012 and promises to be economically advantageous for all parties. However, though the countries might appear friendlier towards each other, the territorial dispute still rumbles on. The same old tensions continued to shape relations between Chile and **Argentina**; when President Cristina Fernández de Kirchner, a friend of Bachelet, was elected, diplomatic relations improved, though the two countries had still not formally agreed on border issues. In 2007, however, during one of South America's coldest winters, Argentina cut supplies of natural gas along pipelines to Chile, a move that led inevitably to frostier relations between the two. Bachelet was keen to emphasize Chile's long-term energy option of diversifying its energy supplies thereby reducing future dependence on Argentina for fuel.

In 2009, Bachelet and Fernández signed the Maipú Treaty of Integration and Cooperation, and Argentina's assistance after Chile's earthquake of 2010 was followed by Piñera's visit to Argentina and his expression of deep commitment to good relations between the two countries. The only fly in the ointment remains the disputed demarcation of the limit of the Southern Ice Field (a closed issue as far as Chile is concerned). Relations with **Peru** meanwhile, soured in 2008 when it filed a lawsuit at the International Court of Justice in a bid to settle the long-standing dispute over

2011	2011–12
The ALMA telescope – the most complex in the world – begins its quest to study the "Cosmic Dawn".	Chilean Education Conflict: thousands of students stage demonstrations and occupy universities and schools in protest against expensive, inadequate education. A forest fire in Torres del Paine National Park, caused by human negligence, sparks anger at the government's slowness of response.

maritime boundaries; the court pronounced its verdict in 2014 and both countries said that they'd abide by the ruling.

Natural disaster and a swing to the right

Despite Michelle Bachelet's efforts, the Chilean public was growing disillusioned with the centre-left coalition amid allegations of incompetence and large-scale corruption. By 2009, the main opposition to Bachelet's governing party, the right-wing Alliance for Chile coalition, gained ground in local elections. It won mayoral contests in key cities so that, for the first time, the right had more mayors in office than the ruling coalition. Led by billionaire businessman **Sebastián Piñera** – who narrowly lost to Bachelet in 2006 – the Alliance finally translated these gains into success at the January 2010 presidential poll, winning 52 percent of the vote.

While Piñera inherited his share of problems, he doubtless didn't anticipate the global media frenzy Chile would find itself at the centre of after suffering two major disasters within months of his taking office. On Saturday, February 27, 2010, a powerful **earthquake** – 8.8 on the Richter scale – occurred off the coast of Chile, causing particular destruction in the coastal city of Concepción and affecting the southern half of the country. The death toll numbered 525, with a countrywide blackout and half a million homes rendered uninhabitable. An attendant **tsunami** compounded the misery, wreaking havoc in south-central Chile and causing over twenty deaths on the tiny island fishing community of San Juan Bautista alone – an immeasurable loss for a community of only six hundred people. Half of the country was declared a "disaster zone" and Piñera's government came under criticism for its inadequately fast response in dealing with the aftermath. Mobs of post-earthquake looters converged on supermarkets in Concepción to steal electrical goods as well as food, necessitating deployment of a special force of *carabineros* (policemen) wielding water cannons and tear gas. A prison riot in Concepción, meanwhile, required the intervention of the armed forces, and prison escapees in Chillán wreaked havoc further south.

Chile's *annus horribilis* continued later that year when, on August 5, a major cave-in was reported at the 121-year-old San José copper gold mine near the town of Copiapó, trapping 33 men (who came to be known as "Los 33") 700m underground. Given the mine's troubled history, it was originally thought that the miners would not survive or would not be found in time (see page 157). However, seventeen days after the accident, with successful exploratory drilling having pinpointed the trapped miners' location, president Piñera himself held up a note for the jubilant public to see: "*Estamos bien en el refugio, los 33.*" In the wake of the criticism directed at the Chilean government for its handling of the earthquake and tsunami, Piñera cut short official business especially to visit the mine and was there to greet the miners when they were freed through international efforts, thus giving a much-needed boost to his government's ratings.

Economy, education and Piñera's woes

While the Chilean economy had remained relatively stable throughout the economic crisis which affected much of the world, growing **student unrest** exploded in a series of protests in 2011 (some of them violent) over the high price and poor quality of state

2012

An anti-discrimination law is passed which forbids discriminating against employees due to their sexual orientation. Eight former army officers who allegedly took part in the 1973 murder of singer Victor Jara are arrested.

education, and greatly contributed to the fall of Piñera's ratings to 26 percent – the lowest of any post-dictatorship Chilean president. With regard to indigenous rights, there was ongoing unrest as well (see page 467), and on the environmental front Piñera's government came under heavy criticism for their environmentally unfriendly decision to approve plans for five major hydroelectric dams in Patagonia to feed Santiago and the northern mines' insatiable need for energy. The Piñera government's controversial parting gesture was to finally approve the construction of South America's largest suspension bridge by an international consortium, due to link Chiloé to the mainland within a decade. The opinion of Chiloé's residents wasn't sought, and many protested that the money would be better spent on establishing essential services on the island, such as a proper hospital.

Environmental progress and the fall of Bachelet

The student protests continued well into 2013, and **Michelle Bachelet** won a second term as Chile's president. One of her promises was to establish a system of universal and free higher education within six years. In a decision applauded by environmentalists both in Chile and around the world, in 2014 the Chilean government sided with the majority of Chileans, as well as a coalition of over seventy Chilean and international organizations, and rejected plans for the US$10 billion mega-dam project that was due to go ahead on two of Patagonia's wildest rivers, as well as cancelling an environmental permit to build five dams on the Pascua and Baker rivers that was granted in 2011.

In March 2017, the government signed an historic deal to create around 40,000 square kilometres of new and expanded **national parks** (see page 42). Later in the year, Bachelet secured a major achievement in the social sphere, with the **legalization of abortion** in certain circumstances.

In the 2017 presidential elections, however, Chile seesawed back to the right. With Bachelet unable to stand again, **Sebastian Piñera** beat centre-left opponent Alejandro Guillier in the run-off, 54.6 percent to 45.4 percent. During the campaign, Piñera argued that social reforms had gone too far and accused his predecessor of economic mismanagement. Whether his conservative agenda is any more successful second time around remains to be seen.

2013	2017
An official apology is made by the body representing Chilean judges for its members' actions during Pinochet's rule in failing to protect victims of state abuse. Michelle Bachelet wins second term as president in the December election.	In a landmark move, the constitutional court approves a bill legalizing abortion in certain circumstances. Sebastián Piñera returns for a second spell as president, claiming 54.6 percent of the vote.

Landscape and the environment

Chile is roughly the same size as France and Britain combined – but stretched over a distance equivalent to that from Vancouver to Panama. This strange long sliver of a country, on average just 180km across, spans 4350km from the desert of the north to the sub-Antarctic ice-fields in the south, and encompasses almost every kind of natural habitat along the way.

Geography

Geographically, Chile is divided into a number of latitudinal **zones**, each of which shows clear differences in climate, vegetation and fauna. These zones only tell part of the story, though, with Chile's three principal landforms – the Andes, the central depression and the coastal range, running the length of the country – all having a significant impact on the local ecology. The **Andes**, in particular, straddles all of Chile's disparate regions. Characterized by precipitous slopes with ravines cut deep into the rock, at points the range acts as a great, impenetrable wall dividing Chile from neighbouring Argentina and Bolivia. Scores of **volcanoes**, many topping 6000m, line these borders, where episodic eruptions and seismic activity are everyday realities. The country's highest peak, Ojos del Salado (6893m), is also the world's highest active volcano; Aconcagua (6959m), the tallest peak outside the Himalayas, lies a few kilometres over the Argentine border.

Desert and volcanoes: Norte Grande

In the far north, the **Norte Grande** region stretches from the Peruvian border over 1000km south to the Copiapó river valley. Covering the central depression between the Andes and the coastal range lies the **Atacama Desert**, thought to be the driest place on earth. Surprisingly, the desert is unusually temperate, owing to the moderating influence of the Humboldt Current, a cold-water sea current just off the coast. While thick fog banks, known as *camanchaca*, accumulate along the coast where the cold water meets the warm air, a high-pressure zone prevents the cloud from producing rain and moving inland.

A search for wildlife is a pretty fruitless activity in these barren northern wastes. The frustrated ornithologist A.W. Johnson remarked that the desert was "without doubt one of the most completely arid and utterly lifeless areas in the whole world". It's a very different story, however, up in the Andes bordering the Atacama, where a high plateau known as the **altiplano** is home to a diverse wildlife population and an otherworldly landscape of volcanoes, lakes and salt flats.

Mining and exotic fruit: Norte Chico

The semi-arid **Norte Chico**, bounded roughly by the Copiapó Valley and the Aconcagua Valley, just north of Santiago, forms a transitional zone, where the inhospitable northern desert gives way to scrubland and eventually forests further south, as precipitation levels increase. The heat of the sun here is tempered by air humidity, making the land suitable for irrigation farming. Tobacco and cotton, which predominated in the colonial era, have since been replaced by more lucrative exotic fruits, such as papaya and *chirimoya*. Throughout the north mining has also long been prevalent, thanks to the high levels of nitrates, copper, silver and other minerals.

Grapes and non-native trees: Central Valley

Beyond Santiago, the region known as the **Central Valley** extends south to the Río Bio Bío. Mineral-rich earth coupled with warm dry summers and short humid winters have provided ideal conditions here for growing grapes, peaches, pears, plums, mangoes, melons, apricots and avocados. As the country's primary agricultural zone, as well as a major centre of industry, it is no surprise that this region is home to around eighty percent of the country's population, almost half based in the capital.

Towards the southern end of the Central Valley, forests signal a marked increase in precipitation levels. Systematic **afforestation**, begun over a hundred years ago in Arauco province, has seen the introduction of a variety of foreign trees, such as eucalyptus and Australian myrrh. No species has flourished as well as the radiata pine, however, which far exceeded the rate of development normal in its native California; concern is mounting that its success is damaging Chile's fragile endemic forest habitats.

The Lake District, Patagonia and Tierra del Fuego

In the **Lake District**, between Temuco and Puerto Montt, precipitation reaches 2300mm a year, allowing luxuriant native forests to predominate over the rolling foothills of the coastal range. To the east, azure lakes, remnants of the last glacial age, are backed by conical, snowcapped **volcanoes**. Among the many volcanoes still active, both Villarrica and Llaima have erupted ten times in the last hundred years. On May 2, 2008, the Chaitén volcano, situated further south on the mainland across from Chiloé, began erupting for the first time in nine thousand years; a huge column of smoke and ash rose into the sky, coating the land around the volcano and reaching into neighbouring Argentina.

Beyond Puerto Montt, the central depression submerges into the sea, while the tops of the coastal mountains nudge through the water in a mosaic of **islands** and **fjords**. It is here, in this splintered and remote region, that continental Chile finally runs out of dry land: the Carretera Austral, the highway that runs south from Puerto Montt, is cut short after 1000km by two massive ice-fields, the largest in the southern hemisphere outside Antarctica. **Southern Patagonia** is a mostly inhospitable place, with continual westerly winds roaring off the sea and dumping up to seven metres of snow, sleet, hail and rain on the western slopes every year. Even so, the glaciated scenery, with its perfect U-shaped valleys and rugged mountains, has an indisputable grandeur. In stark contrast, the monotonous grasslands of the Patagonian pampa, which lies in the rain shadow on the eastern side of the Andes, describe the beginning of a quite different habitat.

Tierra del Fuego ("Land of Fire") is an archipelago separated from mainland Chile by the Magellan Strait. Mountains and forests dominate the south of the region, while the north hosts little more than windswept grasses. From Cape Horn, South America's southernmost point, Antarctica is a mere 1000km away.

Flora

Extraordinary diversity of altitude, latitude and precipitation inevitably leads to an extraordinary diversity of flora. Only humid tropical forest fails to feature in Chile's rich and varied ecology. The tropical area in the far north is stricken with aridity too severe to support most plant life, except at higher altitudes, where **xerophytes** ("dry growers"), such as **cacti**, begin to appear. Ninety percent of Chile's vascular plants are from the cactus family, many of them endemic and endangered. On the altiplano, **tough grasses** and **brush** associated with minimal rainfall support the herds of grazing alpaca.

Central Chilean flora

Moving south towards Central Chile, where the climate is more balanced and water less scarce, **sclerophyllous** ("rigid leaf") shrubs and trees feature leathery leaves that help them retain water. As rainfall increases towards the south, these plants begin to blend with **temperate rainforests**. In the heavily populated areas of this central region, such woodlands have suffered widespread deforestation as land has been cleared for farming and housing, and only patches remain. In Parque Nacional La Campana near Santiago, for example, stands the last forest of endangered **Chilean palm** (*Jubaea chilensis*), sole reminder of a time when millions of the trees covered the area, favoured as they were for the flavour of their sap.

Temperate tree species and Patagonian flora

Further south the **temperate rainforests** have fared a little better, constituting almost a quarter of this type of habitat worldwide. Over 95 percent of the fifty tree species found here are endemic, including the **araucaria** (*Araucaria araucana*), known in English as the **monkey puzzle**, Chile's national tree, and rare **southern beeches** (*Nothofagus*) – principally *coïgue, ñire, raulí* and *lenga* – which vie for sunlight, towering up to 40m into the air to break clear of the canopy. The **alerce**, or **Chilean false larch** (*Fitzroya cupressoides*), a relative of the North American sequoia, takes several hundred years to reach maturity and can live for four thousand years, providing the loggers don't get there first. The tree is best seen in the areas around Puerto Montt.

In Chilean Patagonia, **evergreen beeches** (*Nothofagus betuloides*) grow in the sheltered areas bordering the great fields of ice, while their **deciduous** cousins *Nothofagus pumilio* and *N. antarctica* prefer the drier eastern flanks of the Andes. Where the canopy is broken, dazzling scarlet *embothrium*, yellow *berberis* bedecked with mauve berries, and deep-red *Pernettya* emblazon the ground. Rare **orchids** and pink **oxalis** interweave in a tapestry of colour. Such brilliant displays are impossible on the coastal Magellanic **moorland**, where high levels of precipitation drown all but the sphagnum **bog** communities and **dwarf shrubs**. Here, the wind-beaten **Magellanic gunnera** grows only a few centimetres high, a tiny fraction of what its relatives are capable of in the Valdivian rainforest. Meanwhile, the rain shadow effect on the eastern Patagonian steppe supports little more than coarse tussocks of *festuca* grasses.

Environmental issues

The slow destruction of Chile's **environment** was set in motion by the Spanish in the sixteenth century, though it wasn't until the early twentieth century, with widespread settlement and increased industrialization, that the scale reached damaging levels. Today, although Chile has suffered less environmental degradation than many other countries with comparable resources, there are few habitats that have not been affected in some way by human activity, and it's debatable whether future governments will be prepared to prioritize protection over financial exploitation. While the Bachelet government overruled the decision made by the previous administration to allow the damming of Patagonia's wildest rivers, there is no guarantee that governments in the future won't counter-reverse this ruling.

Pollution

There was little interest in environmental issues in Chile until large-scale disruption caused by the appalling **smog in Santiago**, considered by Greenpeace to be the third most polluted city in Latin America, mobilized public concern. Most years the capital's schools are suspended for days on end and people are warned to stay indoors as a dense cloud of toxic gases hangs over the capital, caught between the two surrounding mountain ranges. The problem is worsened in dry weather, when the concentration of contaminated air is not dissolved by rain. Pressure from the urban middle classes has forced the government to introduce (weak) measures to lessen air pollution in Santiago and has encouraged politicians to include environmental elements to their policies.

The most important **environmental law**, following a guarantee in the 1980 Constitution that all Chileans have "the right to live in an environment free of pollution", was the Environmental Act of 1994, which has standardized procedures for

THE EL NIÑO EFFECT

Nature's footnote to the end of the millennium, the **1997–98 El Niño** wreaked havoc with global climate patterns and brought chaos to the world. In parts of Chile, Peru and Ecuador, floods and landslides engulfed people, animals, houses, farms and factories, while torrents swept away bridges, roads and railways. Elsewhere, severe droughts scorched the earth, drying up forests and bushland and creating the tinderbox conditions that sparked off raging fires. Clouds of poisonous smoke billowed into the atmosphere, affecting seventy million people in Southeast Asia, while millions of others risked starvation following widespread crop failure. As the Pacific countries affected by El Niño picked up the pieces, conservative estimates of the cost of reparation put it at around US$20 billion.

In Chile, **flooding** was the worst it had been for a decade, as eighty thousand people were made homeless in June 1998 alone. The warm coastal water associated with El Niño drove fish stocks to cooler places, crippling the fishing industry and killing millions of marine animals. But while some watched their crops and livestock drown, the rains also filled irrigation basins that had been at a critically low level for years, and water surges saved the hydroelectric companies from having to ration their power output. In the Atacama Desert, freak rainfall woke up the barren soil, causing it to burst into blossom. A relatively mild El Niño in early 2002, meanwhile, meant that while the ski season was one of the best in ten years, torrential rains in central Chile left fifty thousand people homeless and killed nine. At the time of writing, the most recent El Niño episode occurred in 2014–16: in 2016, the Atacama Desert received a year's worth of rain in a single day, yet overall the country endured its driest year in four decades.

THE METEOROLOGY BEHIND THE MAYHEM

The El Niño phenomenon occurs roughly every five years or so. Records document such events over four hundred years ago, but it was only in the 1960s that Norwegian meteorologist Jacob Bjerknes identified the processes that lead to such an event. He saw that El Niño (meaning "the Little Boy" or "the Christ Child", a name given by Peruvian fishermen to the body of warm water

assessing environmental damage, while encouraging public involvement by allowing citizens to bring charges against violators, even if they have not been directly affected by them. One successful application of this new law occurred in 1997, when the Chilean Supreme Court overturned a government-approved project involving the logging for woodchips of centuries-old, endangered forests of native *lenga*, a cherry-like beech found in Tierra del Fuego. In 2012 the creation of the new office of the Environment Superintendent, to the surprise and delight of environmentalists, promptly slapped a US$16 million fine on the Barrick Gold Corporation – the largest gold-mining company in the world – for water pollution and other violations, though inadequate funding for inspections and enforcement of its rulings is still an issue.

Forests under threat

Chile's precious **temperate rainforests** have been threatened for many years by intensive logging and the introduction of harmful foreign species, with large tracts razed in the free-for-all scramble to colonize remote areas. The worst damage occurred in the first half of the twentieth century, but illegal clearance is still common today. The *alerce*, an evergreen with a life span of four thousand years, has been a target of international campaigning as it continues to be logged because of the high commercial value of its wood, despite a law passed in 1976 making it illegal to cut live *alerces*. Yet landowners burn the trees or strip their bark to kill them first, thus evading the hands of the law. Many thousands of hectares of *alerce* forest are wiped out in this manner every year.

Meanwhile in the central regions native trees have been wiped out to make space for the commercial planting of more profitable foreign species. In many areas the practice has left only islands of indigenous forest in an ocean of introduced eucalyptus and radiata pine. The result is genetic isolation of both flora and fauna, leaving many mammals with distinct ecological needs imprisoned in small pockets of native

that would arrive around Christmas) was intimately connected to extremes in the so-called **Southern Oscillation**, a feature where atmospheric pressure between the eastern equatorial Pacific and the Indo-Australian areas behaves as a seesaw, one rising as the other falls.

In "normal" years easterly trade winds blow west across the Pacific, pushing warm surface water towards Indonesia, Australia and the Philippines, where the water becomes about 8°C warmer and about 50cm higher than on the other side of the ocean. In the east, the displacement of the sea allows cold, nutrient-rich water, known as the Humboldt or Peru Current, to swell up from the depths along the coast of South America, providing food for countless marine and bird species.

An El Niño event occurs when the trade winds fall off and the layer of warm water in the west laps back across the ocean, warming up the east Pacific and cooling the west. Consequently, air temperatures across the Pacific begin to even out, tipping the balance of the atmospheric pressure seesaw, which further reduces the strength of the trade winds. Thus the process is enhanced, as warm water continues to build up in the eastern Pacific, bringing with it abnormal amounts of rainfall to coastal South America, while completely starving other areas of precipitation. The warm water also forces the cold Humboldt Current and its micro-organisms to deeper levels, effectively removing a vital link in the marine food chain, killing innumerable fish, sea birds and mammals. Meanwhile, the upset in the Southern Oscillation disturbs weather systems all around the world, resulting in severe and unexpected weather.

EL NIÑO AND GLOBAL WARMING

Since 1980 or so, El Niño-Southern Oscillation (ENSO) events seem to have become stronger, longer and more frequent, leading many to suggest that human activity, such as the warming of the earth's atmosphere through the **greenhouse effect**, could well be having an influence. If this is true, failure to cut emissions of greenhouse gases may in the end cost the lives and livelihoods of millions of people across the world, though some schools of thought suggest that perhaps the stronger El Niño events occur only during the initial stage of global warming and that they will become weaker as the ocean becomes warmer. More research is required to provide a definitive answer.

woodland. The few thin strips that connect such pockets are the only way for many species to maintain communication with the rest of their population. If these corridors are destroyed, countless endemic organisms face extinction. However, efforts are made by the likes of Parque Tantauco and the various Tompkins' foundations (see page 351) to preserve unique ecosystems and to restore local ecosystems by hand if need be, pulling up aggressive non-indigenous species and planting indigenous plants in their stead.

Mining

In the north **mining** is a major cause of environmental concern. Chuquicamata, near Antofagasta, is the biggest open-pit copper mine in the world and it continues to grow. Now visible from space, the giant pit has effectively swallowed up the town that grew with it, as 600,000 tons of rock are dug up every day, spewing arsenic-rich dust into the air. Workers at the mine and their families have now been relocated from Chuquicamata to nearby Calama. The plume from the smelting works carries 200km to San Pedro de Atacama, a pre-colonial village in the east. The country's mines consume vast quantities of water, often contaminating it in the process. In tandem with agricultural irrigation, reckless water usage is taking its toll on wildlife, as animals find the search for drinking places increasingly difficult. Even the human population has been put out, relying in some northern villages on an ingenious invention that turns fog into drinking water.

Overexploitation of resources

Overexploitation of the land and sea has brought further problems. Incompetent or negligent farming, either through overgrazing or the clearing of vegetation, has resulted in extensive **desertification**, particularly in the north. Meanwhile, careless practices in the fishing industry are upsetting the fragile balance of Chile's **marine life**. A leaked government report shows that some fish stocks were depleted by as much as 96 percent between 1985 and 1993. On a global level, many believe human-induced climate change to be a leading cause of the **El Niño phenomenon**, which has badly damaged Chile's fisheries, agriculture and marine species (see page 492). Moreover, the large hole in the ozone layer over Antarctica has put many people, especially in Patagonia, on guard against the harmful ultraviolet rays that seep through it. Chile has been more effective than most Latin American countries in its opposition to the damage brought about by the excesses of unfettered capitalism, and awareness of the delicacy of the country's habitats and its unique species is growing. However, environmentalists continue to bemoan the lack of concerted pressure, claiming that many merely respond occasionally and emotionally to images churned out in the media rather than pushing consistently for action and reform.

Droughts and forest fires

Throughout its history, Chile has been affected by droughts on a fairly regular basis, but these have become more frequent and consistent in recent years as result of climate change. In March 2015, the southern region of Araucanía, which had been experiencing years of **drought**, was hit by **forest fires**. As the fires raged out of control, threatening centuries-old monkey puzzle trees in China Muerta National Reserve, Nalca Lolco National Reserve and Conguillío National Park, Chile declared a **national emergency**. Forest fires also threatened the port of Valparaíso, leading to the immediate evacuation of thousands of people. In response, Bachelet announced Chile would be investing millions of dollars in desalination plants to provide drinking water and to improve access to underground water.

Chilean music: nueva canción

Chile has produced a wide range of music genres, from cueca to bolero, but none has been as important or influential as nueva canción, the "new song" movement that developed in the 1960s along with parallel movements in Argentina, Uruguay and Cuba. Rooted in the guitar traditions of the troubadour, the songs could be love lyric or chronicle, lament or call to action and, as such, they have played an important part in Latin America's political and cultural struggles. The style was brought to international attention, above all, by theatre director and singer-songwriter Víctor Jara, who was murdered by Pinochet's thugs during the 1973 coup, while groups like Inti Illimani were forced into exile.

Pity the singer...

Nueva canción as a movement spans a period of more than thirty years, starting in the early 1960s when its musicians became part of the political struggle to bring about change and reform in their own countries. As a result of their activities, many were arrested or forced into exile by dictatorships which through murder, torture and disappearance wiped out so much of a generation. The sense of a movement grew as the musicians involved met each other at festivals in Cuba, Nicaragua, Peru, Mexico, Argentina and Brazil, visited each other's countries, and occasionally sang each other's songs. At the end of the 1990s, with the return to democracy on the continent, the singers continued to pursue their careers in different ways, while maintaining long-term friendships and exchanges.

The 1960s was a time of politics and idealism in South America – far more so even than in Europe or North America. There was a stark challenge presented by the continent's obvious inequalities, its inherited power and wealth, its corrupt regimes, and by the denial of literacy and education to much of the population. It is within this context that *nueva canción* singers and writers must be understood. With voice and guitar, they composed songs of their own hopes and experiences in places where many of those involved in struggles for change regularly met and socialized.

It is a music that feels now, in some ways, out of date, though its spirit, in keeping with the 1960s rhetoric of guitar as gun and song as bullet, is, in other ways, entirely appropriate to the current climate of global upheaval. These particular songs, though – poems written to be performed – are classic expressions of the years of hope and struggle for change, their beauty and truth later nurturing those suffering under dictatorship, and those forced into exile. They are still known by heart by audiences throughout the continent and exiled communities in Europe.

Nueva canción was an expression of politics in its widest sense. It was not "protest song" as such. The musicians involved were not card-carrying members of any international organization and were often independent of political parties – although in the early 1970s the Chilean musicians were closely linked with the Popular Unity government of Salvador Allende, the first socialist president and government to be legitimately elected through the ballot box (see page 478).

What linked these and other musicians of the movement was an ethical stance – a commitment to improve conditions for the majority of people in Latin America. To that end they sang not only in concerts and clubs but in factories, shanty towns, community centres and at political meetings and street demonstrations. People in protest the world over have joined in the Chilean street anthems *El Pueblo Unido Jamás Sera Vencido* (*The People United Will Never Be Defeated*) and *Venceremos* (*We Will Win*).

Yupanqui and Violeta Parra

The roots of *nueva canción* lie in the work of two key figures, whose music bridged rural and urban life and culture in the 1940s and 1950s: the Argentine **Atahualpa Yupanqui** (1908–92) and the Chilean **Violeta Parra** (1917–67). Each had a passionate interest in his or her nation's rural musical traditions, which had both an Iberian and Amerindian sensibility. Their work was in some respects paralleled by Cuba's Carlos Puebla.

Atahualpa Yupanqui spent much of his early life travelling around Argentina, collecting popular songs from itinerant *payadores* (improvising poets, Chile's indigenous rappers) and folk singers in rural areas. He also wrote his own songs, and during a long career introduced a new integrity to Argentine folk music – and an assertive political outlook that ultimately forced him into exile in Paris.

Violeta Parra's career in Chile mirrored that of Yupanqui. She travelled extensively, singing with and collecting songs from old *payadores* and preserved and popularized them through radio broadcasts and records. She also composed new material based on these rural song traditions, creating a model and repertoire for what became *nueva canción*. Her songs celebrated the rural and regional, the music of the peasant, the land-worker and the marginalized migrant.

Musically, Parra was also significant in her popularization of **Andean** or **Amerindian instruments** – the armadillo-shelled *charango* (small Andean lute), the *quena* (bamboo flute) and panpipes – and in her enthusiasm for the **French chanson** tradition. She spent time in Paris in the 1960s with her children Angel and Isabel, where she met Yupanqui, Edith Piaf and the flautist Gilbert Favre, who was to found the influential Andean band Los Jaivas, and with whom Parra fell in love. Returning to Buenos Aires, she performed in a tent in the district of La Reina, which came to be called the *Carpa de La Reina* (The Queen's Tent). However, with a long history of depression, she committed suicide in 1967.

Parra left behind a legacy of exquisite songs, many of them with a wry sense of humour, including the unparalleled *Gracias a la Vida* (*Thanks to Life*), later covered by Joan Baez and a host of others. Even her love songs seem informed by an awareness of poverty and injustice, while direct pieces like *Qué dirá el Santo Padre?* (*What Will the Sainted Pope Say?*) highlighted the Church's responsibility to take action. As Parra wrote (in the form she often used in her songs) in her autobiography:

I sing to the Chilean people
if I have something to say
I don't take up the guitar
to win applause
I sing of the difference there is
between what is certain
and what is false
otherwise I don't sing.

The movement takes off

Nueva canción emerged as a real force in the mid-1960s, when various governments on the continent were trying to effect democratic social change. The search for a Latin American cultural identity became a spontaneous part of this wider struggle for self-determination, and music was a part of the process.

The first crystallization of a *nueva canción* ideal in Chile emerged with the opening of a crucial new folk club. This was and is the legendary crucible of *nueva canción*, the **Peña de los Parra**, which **Angel and Isabel Parra**, inspired by the Paris *chanson* nightclubs, opened in downtown Santiago in 1965. Among the regular singer-songwriters who performed here were Víctor Jara and Patricio Manns. Their audiences, in the politically charged and optimistic period prior to the election of Allende's government, were enthusiastic activists and fellow musicians.

Víctor Jara

The great singer-songwriter and theatre director **Víctor Jara** took *nueva canción* onto a world stage. His songs, and his life, continue to reverberate, and he has been recorded by singers like Sting, Bruce Springsteen, Peter Gabriel and Jackson Brown, and (memorably) Robert Wyatt. All have been moved by Jara's story and inspired by his example.

Jara was born into a rural family who came to live in a shanty town on the barren outskirts of Santiago when his father died; Víctor was just 11. His mother sang as a *cantora* for births, marriages and deaths, keeping her family alive by running a food stall in the main Santiago market. It was from his mother and her work that Jara gained his intuitive knowledge of Chilean guitar and singing styles.

He began performing his songs in the early 1960s and from the beginning caused a furore. During the government of Eduardo Frei, for example, his playful version of a

---

PLEGARIA AUN LABRADOR (PRAYER TO A LABOURER)

Stand up and look at the mountain
From where the wind comes, the sun and the water
You who direct the courses of the rivers
You who have sown the flight of your soul
Stand up and look at your hands
So as to grow
Clasp your brother's, in your own
Together we will move united by blood
Today is the time that can become tomorrow

Deliver us from the one who dominates us
through misery
Bring to us your reign of justice and equality
Blow like the wind the flower of the canyon
Clean like fire the barrel of my gun
Let your will at last come about here on earth
Give to us your strength and valour so as to fight
Blow like the wind the flower of the canyon
Clean like fire the barrel of my gun

Stand up and look at your hands
So as to grow
Clasp your brother's, in your own
Together we will move united by blood
Now and in the hour of our death
Amen.

Víctor Jara

traditional piece, *La Beata* – a send-up of the desires of a nun – was banned, as was his accusatory *Preguntas por Puerto Montt* (*Questions for Puerto Montt*), which accused the minister of the interior of the massacre of poor landless peasants in the south of Chile. Working with Isabel Parra and the group **Huamari**, Jara went on to create a sequence of songs called *La Población*, based on the history and life of Santiago's shanty-town communities. His great gift was a deceptively simple and direct style applied to whatever he did.

One of Jara's best-loved songs, *Te recuerdo Amanda* (*I Remember You, Amanda*), is a good example of the simplicity of his craft. A hauntingly understated love song, it tells the story of a girl who goes to meet her man, Manuel, at the factory gates; he never appears because of an "accident", and Amanda waits for him in vain. In many of his songs, Jara subtly interwove allusions to his own life with the experiences of other ordinary people – Amanda and Manuel were the names of his parents.

Jara's influence was immense, both on *nueva canción* singers and the Andean-oriented groups like **Inti Illimani** and **Quilapayún** (see below), whom he worked with often, encouraging them to forge their own new performance styles. Enormously popular and fun-loving, he was nevertheless clear about his role as a singer: "The authentic revolutionary should be behind the guitar, so that the guitar becomes an instrument of struggle, so that it can also shoot like a gun." As he sang in 1972 in his song *Manifiesto*, a tender serenade which with hindsight has been seen as his testimony, "I don't sing just for love of singing, but for the statements made by my guitar, honest, its heart of earth, like the dove it goes flying … Song sung by a man who will die singing, truthfully singing his song".

Like many Chilean musicians, Jara was deeply involved with the Unidad Popular government of Salvador **Allende** who, in 1970, following his election, had appeared on an open-air stage in Santiago surrounded by musicians under a banner saying "There can be no revolution without song". Three years later, on September 11, 1973 – along with hundreds of others who had legitimately supported the government – Jara was arrested by the military and taken to the same downtown stadium in which he had won first prize at the First Festival of New Chilean Song in 1969. Tortured, his hands and wrists broken, his body was found with five others, riddled with machine-gun bullets, dumped alongside a wall of the Metropolitan Cemetery; his face was later recognized among a pile of unidentified bodies in one of the Santiago mortuaries by a worker. He was just 40.

Jara left behind a song composed during the final hours of his life, written down and remembered by those who were with him at the end, called as a poem of testimony *Estadio Chile* (*Chile Stadium*). It was later set a cappella to music as *Ay canto, que mal me sales*, by his friend and colleague Isabel Parra.

Exiles and Andean sounds

After the Pinochet coup anything remotely associated with the Allende government and its values came under censorship, including books and records, whose possession could be cause for arrest. The junta issued warnings to musicians and folklorists that it would be unwise for them to play *nueva canción*, or indeed any of the Andean instruments associated with its sound – *charangos*, panpipes and *quenas*.

It was not exactly a ban, but it was menacing enough to force the scene well underground – and abroad, where many Chilean musicians lived out the junta years in exile. Their numbers included the groups Inti Illimani and Quilapayún and later Illapu (see page 500), Sergio Ortega, Patricio Manns, Isabel and Angel Parra, and Patricio Castillo. They were not the only Latin Americans forced from their country. Other **exiled musician** of the 1970s included Brazilian MPB singers Chico Buarque, Caetano Veloso and Gilberto Gil; Uruguay's *nueva canción* singer Daniel Viglietti; and Argentina's Mercedes Sosa.

NUEVA CANCIÓN BANDS AND ALBUMS

Inti Illimani The foremost Chilean "new song" group, Inti Illimani (see page 498) began as students in 1967, bringing the Andean sound to Europe through their thousands of concerts in exile, and featuring the glorious-voiced José Séves. *Lejan'a* focuses on Andean themes in this celebration of the band's thirtieth anniversary and their original inspiration. *Arriesgaré la piel* is a celebration of the music the Intis grew up with, from creole-style tunes to Chilean *cuecas*, most lyrics by Patricio Manns with music by Salinas. This was the final album to be made with the core of the original band before Séves left. *Grandes Exitos* is a compilation of 17 songs and instrumental pieces taken from the band's history.

Llapu With a track record stretching back thirty years, and a big following in Chile, this band plays Andean instruments – panpipes, *quenas* and *charangos* – along with saxophones, electric bass and Caribbean percussion. Their music is rooted in the north of the country where most of the band hails from. *Sereno* is an enjoyable collection, which gives a pretty good idea of what Illapu have got up to over the years and includes strongly folkloric material, as well as dance pieces influenced by salsa, romantic ballads and the earlier styles of vocal harmony.

Quilapayún This key Chilean *nueva canción* group, who worked closely in their early years with Víctor Jara, split in 1973 into multiple groups in order to get their message across on as many stages as possible. They co-authored, with Sergio Ortega, the street anthem *El Pueblo Unido Jamás Sera Vencido* (*The People United Will Never Be Defeated*). Although they disbanded in the late 1990s, their influence lives on. *Santa María de Iquique*, Chilean composer Luis Advis's ground-breaking *Cantata*, composed for Quilapayún, tells the emblematic and heroic tale of the murder of unarmed nitrate workers and their families in 1907.

Various artists *Music of the Andes*. Despite the title, this is essentially a *nueva canción* disc, with key Chilean groups Inti Illimani, Quilapayún and Illapu to the fore. There is also an instrumental recording of *Tinku* attributed to Víctor Jara.

Víctor Jara *Manifesto* was reissued in 1998 to mark the 25th anniversary of the death of Víctor Jara, the leading singer-songwriter of his generation (see page 497); this is a key record of *nueva canción*, with *Te recuerdo Amanda*, *Canto libre*, *La Plegaria a un Labrador* and *Ay canto, que mal me sales*, the final poem written in the Estadio Chile before his death. *Vientos del Pueblo* is a generous 22-song compilation that includes most of the Jara milestones, including *Te recuerdo Amanda* and *Preguntas por Puerto Montt*, plus the wonderful revolutionary romp of *A cochabamba me voy*. Quilapayún provide backing on half the album. *Víctor Jara Complete* is the definitive Jara, featuring material from eight original LPs. Plane has also released an excellent selection of highlights. *La Población* is classic Jara: a project involving other musicians, but including most of all the lives and experiences of those celebrated here, who lived in various shanty towns (*poblaciones*) including the one where Jara himself grew up.

Violeta Parra *Canto a mi América* is an excellent introduction to one of South America's most significant folklorists and composers (see page 496), bringing you Parra's seminal songs. *Las Ultimas Composiciones* is a reissue of the 1965 release that turned out to be Parra's final songs ("*Ultimas*" means both "latest" and "last" in Spanish).

In Chile, the first acts of musical defiance took place behind church walls, where a group of musicians who called themselves **Barroco Andino** started to play baroque music with Andean instruments within months of the coup.

It was a brave act, for the use of Andean or Amerindian instruments and culture was instinctively linked with the *nueva canción* movement. Chilean groups like **Quilapayún** and **Inti Illimani** wore the traditional ponchos of the peasant and played Andean instruments such as panpipes, bamboo flutes and the *charango*, and the maracas and shakers of Central America and the Caribbean. That these were the instruments of the communities who had managed somehow to survive slavery, resist colonialism and its aftermath had a powerful symbolism. Both the "*los Intis*" and "*los Quilas*", as they became familiarly known, worked closely with Víctor Jara and also with popular classical composers Sergio Ortega and Luis Advis.

European exile

In 1973 Quilapayún and Inti Illimani travelled to **Europe** as official cultural ambassadors of the Allende government, actively seeking support from governments in

Europe at a time when the country was more or less besieged economically by a North American blockade, its economy being undermined by CIA activity. On September 11, when General Pinochet led the coup d'état in which Salvador Allende died, the Intis were in Italy and the Quilas in France. For the Intis, the tour ("the longest in history", as Intis member Jorge Coulon joked) turned into an exile of 15 years and 54 days for the group, an exile that put *nueva canción* and Amerindian music firmly on Europe's agenda of Latin American music.

The groups were the heart and soul of a worldwide Chilean (and Latin American) solidarity movement, performing almost daily for the first ten years. Both also recorded albums of new songs, the Intis influenced by their many years in Italy, creating some beautiful songs of exile, including the seminal song *Vuelvo* (*I Return*), with key singer-songwriter and musician **Patricio Manns**.

The impact of their high-profile campaigning against the military meant that the Intis were turned back on the airport tarmac long after politicians and trade union leaders were repatriated. They eventually returned on September 18, 1988, Chile's National Day, the day of one of the biggest meetings of supporters of the "No" vote to the plebiscite called by Pinochet to determine whether he should stay in office. Going straight from the airport to sing on a huge open-air stage and to dance the traditional *cueca* (Chile's National Day dance), the group had an emotional and timely homecoming. Though their line-up has somewhat changed over the years, the two groups are still going strong, performig together as Inti+Quila; various collaborative efforts have included a tour of South America and Europe and a release of their joint concerts.

The Andean instruments and rhythms used by Quilapayún (who disbanded in the 1980s) and Inti Illimani have been skilfully used by many other groups whose music is equally interesting – groups like **Illapu**, who remained popular throughout the 1980s (with a number of years in forced exile) and 1990s, and who released their most recent record, *Antología Viva*, in 2016.

The future and legacy

Times have changed in Chile and in Latin America generally, with revolutionary governments no longer in power, democracy restored after dictatorships, and even Pinochet dead and buried. The *nueva canción* movement, tied to an era of ideals and struggle, and then the brutal years of survival under dictatorship, would seem to have lost its relevance.

Its musicians have moved on to more individual concerns in their (always poetic) songwriting. But the *nueva canción* form, the inspiration of the song as message, and the rediscovery of Andean music and instruments, continue to have resonance and influence. The more recent generation of singers inspired by the history of "new song" includes **Carlos Varela** in Cuba, **Fernando Delgadillo** in Mexico, El Salvador's **Cutumay Camones**, Nicaragua's **Duo Guardabarranco** and the Bolivian singer **Emma Junaro**.

And there will be others. For Latin America, *nueva canción* is not only music but also history. As the Cuban press has said of the songs of Silvio Rodríguez: "We have here the great epic poems of our days." Or as the Dominican Republic's merengue superstar, Juan Luis Guerra, put it, "They are the master songwriters – they have influenced everyone."

Books

Unfortunately, a number of the best and most evocative books written on Chile have long been out of print, but we include some of them – mainly travel narratives or general accounts – below (marked by o/p in the parentheses after the title), as they can often be found in public libraries or on the internet. Modern publications are inevitably dominated by analyses and testimonies of the Pinochet years, much of which makes compelling reading. There are relatively few up-to-date general histories of Chile in English, with those available focusing more on the academic market than a general readership. Chilean fiction, meanwhile, is not very widely translated into English, with a few notable exceptions. Its poetry, or more specifically the poetry of its famous Nobel laureate Pablo Neruda, has been translated into many languages and is widely available. Books marked ★ are particularly recommended.

TRAVEL: GENERAL INTRODUCTIONS

Stephen Clissold *Chilean Scrapbook* (o/p). Beautifully and evocatively written, this book takes you from the top to the bottom of the country via a mixture of history, legend and anecdote.

Augustin Edwards *My Native Land* (o/p). Absorbing and vivid reflections on Chile's geography, history, folklore and literature.

Benjamin Subercaseaux *Chile: A Geographic Extravaganza* (o/p). This seductive, poetic meander through Chile's "mad geography" is still one of the most enjoyable general introductions to the country, if a little dated.

TRAVEL: NINETEENTH AND EARLY TWENTIETH CENTURY

Charles Darwin *Voyage of the Beagle*. This eminently readable (abridged) book contains some superb, evocative descriptions of nineteenth-century Chile, from Tierra del Fuego right up to Iquique.

Maria Graham *Journal of a Residence in Chile During the Year 1822* (o/p). The classic nineteenth-century travel narrative on Chile, written by a spirited, perceptive and amusing British woman.

Che Guevara *The Motorcycle Diaries*. Comic, picaresque narrative taken from the diaries of the future revolutionary as he and his friend, both just out of medical school, travelled around South America – including a large chunk of Chile – by motorbike.

Bea Howe *Child in Chile* (o/p). A charming description of the author's childhood in Valparaíso in the early 1900s, where her family formed part of the burgeoning British business community.

W.H. Hudson *Idle Days in Patagonia*. Drawn by the variety of fauna and the remarkable birdlife, the novelist and naturalist travelled to Patagonia at the end of the nineteenth century and wrote this series of charming, gentle observations.

George Musters *At Home with the Patagonians*. Remarkable account of time spent living with the Tehuelche people at the end of the nineteenth century that explodes the myth of the "noble savage" and provides a historically important picture of their vanishing way of life.

TRAVEL: MODERN AND CONTEMPORARY

★ **Bruce Chatwin** *In Patagonia*. The cult travel book that single-handedly enshrined Patagonia as the ultimate edge-of-the-world destination. Witty and captivating, this is essential reading for visitors to Patagonia, though it concentrates far more on the Argentine side.

Ariel Dorfman *Desert Memories*. Vivid depiction of desert life gleaned from Dorfman's travels through the Norte

Grande, which weaves past and present, memoir and meditation, history and family lore to provide an engaging chronicle of modern Chile.

Toby Green *Saddled with Darwin*. One hundred and sixty-five years after Charles Darwin embarked on the journey that produced the most radical theory of modern times, Green set out to retrace his footsteps on horseback.

The result is an epic journey across six countries, including Chile.

Alistair Horne *Small Earthquake in Chile*. Wry description of a visit to Chile during the turbulent months leading up to Pinochet's military coup, written by a British journalist.

John Pilkington *An Englishman in Patagonia* (o/p). A fun-to-read and sympathetic portrayal of Patagonia and its people. This book includes some wonderful black-and-white photographs.

Rosie Swale *Back to Cape Horn* (o/p). An extraordinary account of the author's epic 409-day journey on horseback from the Atacama Desert down to Cape Horn – which she'd last visited while sailing around the world ten years previously in 1972.

★ **Patrick Symmes** *Chasing Che*. The author undertakes an epic motorbike trip through South America – including hundreds of miles of Chile – following the route taken by a young Che, as chronicled in *The Motorcycle Diaries* (see page 501). A great mix of biography, history, politics and travel anecdotes, this is a sharply written and highly entertaining read.

Sara Wheeler *Chile: Travels in a Thin Country*. An entertaining account of the author's adventures in Chile as she travels from the Atacama to Antarctica.

HISTORY, POLITICS AND SOCIETY: GENERAL

Nick Caistor *In Focus: Chile*. Brief, potted introduction, highlighting the social problems bequeathed by Pinochet's economic model.

★ **Simon Collier and William Sater** *A History of Chile, 1801–1994*. Probably the best single-volume history of Chile from independence to the 1990s; thoroughly academic but enlivened by colourful detail along with the authors' clear fondness for the country and its people.

Brian Loveman *Chile: the Legacy of Hispanic Capitalism*. Solid analysis of Chile's history from the arrival of the Spanish in the 1540s to the 1973 military coup.

HISTORY, POLITICS AND SOCIETY: THE PINOCHET YEARS

★ **Andy Beckett** *Pinochet in Piccadilly: Britain and Chile's Hidden History*. A fascinating political travelogue that connects the past to the present as it explores the relationship between the two nations.

Sheila Cassidy *Audacity to Believe* (o/p). Distressing account of the imprisonment and horrific torture of a British doctor (the author) after she'd treated a wounded anti-Pinochet activist.

★ **Pamela Constable and Arturo Valenzuela** *A Nation of Enemies*. Written during the mid- to late 1980s, this is a superb look at the terror of everyday life in Chile at that time and the state apparatus used to annihilate free thinking and initiative. Essential reading if you want to understand contemporary Chile.

Marc Cooper *Pinochet and Me: A Chilean Anti-Memoir*. First-hand account of life under Pinochet in the early days of the coup, written by a young American who served as Allende's translator and narrowly escaped the death squads. Followed up by accounts of his periodic visits to Chile over the next quarter century.

John Dinges *The Condor Years: How Pinochet and His Allies Brought Terror to Three Continents*. Exhaustively researched book that examines the creation and use of international hit squads by the Pinochet regime.

Diana Kay *Chileans in Exile: Private Struggles, Public Lives*. Although written in a somewhat dry, academic style, this is nonetheless a fascinating study of Chilean exiles in Scotland, with a strong focus on women. The author looks at their attempts to reconstruct their lives, their sense of dislocation and the impact exile has had on their attitude to politics, marriage and the home.

Hugh O'Shaughnessy *Pinochet: The Politics of Torture*. Covering everything from the arrest of Pinochet in London to his secret plans to distribute sarin nerve gas to Chilean consulates abroad, this book provides an overview of the most influential man in Chilean politics in the years from 1973 to 1998.

Patricia Politzer *Fear in Chile, Lives Under Pinochet*. Award-winning account of the lives of Chileans during the dictatorship, and another insight into the repressive apparatus used to subdue Chileans.

Grino Rojo and John J Hasset (eds) *Chile, Dictatorship and the Struggle for Democracy*. A slim, accessible volume containing four essays written in the months approaching the 1988 plebiscite, in which the country would vote to reject or continue with military rule.

Jacobo Timerman *Chile: Death in the South* (o/p). Reflections on the Pinochet years by an Argentine journalist, written thirteen years into the military regime. Particularly compelling are the short personal testimonies of torture victims that intersperse the narrative.

Thomas Wright and Rody Oñate *Flight from Chile: Voices of Exile*. A detailed and affecting account of the exodus after the 1973 coup, when more than 200,000 Chileans fled their homeland.

SPECIAL-INTEREST STUDIES

Colin McEwan, Luis Borrero and Alfredo Prieto (eds) *Patagonia: Natural History, Prehistory and Ethnography* at the Uttermost End of the Earth. Brilliant account of the "human adaptation, survival and eventual extinction" of the native peoples of Patagonia, accompanied by dozens of haunting black-and-white photographs.

★ **Nick Reding** *The Last Cowboys at the End of the World: The Story of the Gauchos of Patagonia*. A brutally honest look at the end of the gaucho era in Patagonia. Excellent

exploration of how in the mid-1990s the gaucho culture crashed headlong into the advance of modern society.

William Sater *The Heroic Image in Chile* (o/p). Fascinating, scholarly look at the reasons behind the near-deification of Arturo Prat, the naval officer who died futilely in battle in 1879.

CHILEAN WOMEN

Marjorie Agosin (ed) *Scraps of Life: Chilean Arpilleras: Chilean Women and the Pinochet Dictatorship*. A sensitive portrayal of the women of Santiago's shanty towns who, during the dictatorship, scraped a living by sewing scraps of material together to make wall hangings, known as *arpilleras*, depicting scenes of violence and repression. The *arpilleras* became a symbol of their protest, and were later exhibited around the world.

Jo Fisher *Out of the Shadows*. Penetrating analysis of the emergence of the women's movement in Latin America, with a couple of chapters devoted to Chile.

Elizabeth Jelin (ed) *Women and Social Change in Latin America*. A series of intelligent essays examining the ways women's organizations have acted as mobilizing forces for social and political change in Latin America.

Alicia Partnoy (ed) *You Can't Drown the Fire: Latin American Women Writing in Exile*. Excellent anthology bringing together a mixture of short stories, poems and essays by exiled Latin American women, including Veronica de Negri, Cecila Vicuña, Marjorie Agosin and Isabel Morel Letelier from Chile.

FICTION

Marjorie Agosin (ed) *Landscapes of a New Land: Short Fiction by Latin American Women*. This anthology includes four short stories by Chilean women authors, including the acclaimed Marta Brunet (1901–67) and María Luisa Bombal (1910–80). Overall, the book creates a poetic, at times haunting, evocation of female life in a patriarchal world. Also edited by Agosin, *Secret Weavers: Stories of the Fantastic by Women of Argentina and Chile* (o/p) is a spellbinding collection of short stories interwoven with themes of magic, allegory, legend and fantasy.

★ **Isabel Allende** *The House of the Spirits* is the baroque, fantastical and best-selling novel by the niece of Salvador Allende, which chronicles the fortunes of several generations of a rich, landowning family in an unnamed but thinly disguised Chile, culminating with a brutal military coup and the murder of the president. *Of Love and Shadows* is set against a background of disappearances and dictatorship, including a fictional account of the real-life discovery of the bodies of fifteen executed workers in a Central Valley mine. Allende's more recent novel, *Maya's Notebook*, much of which is set in a remote community off the island of Chiloé, delves into traditional Chilote island life in the twenty-first century and the issues faced by the villagers.

Roberto Bolaño *Last Evenings on Earth*. The celebrated Chilean novelist's haunting first novel to be translated into English is set against the bleak backdrop of the Pinochet dictatorship, with its protagonists living on the fringes of society.

★ **José Donoso** *Curfew*. Gripping novel about an exiled folk singer's return to Santiago during the military dictatorship, by one of Chile's most outstanding twentieth-century writers. Other works by Donoso translated into

English include *Hell Has No Limits*, about the strange existence of a transvestite and his daughter in a Central Valley brothel, and *The Obscene Bird of Night*, a dislocated, fragmented novel narrated by a deaf-mute old man as he retreats into madness.

Ariel Dorfman *Hard Rain*. This complicated, thought-provoking novel is both an examination of the role of the writer in a revolutionary society, and a celebration of the "Chilean road to socialism" – not an easy read, but one that repays the effort. Dorfman later became internationally famous for his play *Death and the Maiden*, and has also written an account of the effort to prosecute Pinochet in *Exorcising Terror: The Incredible Unending Trial of Augusto Pinochet*.

Alberto Fuguet *Bad Vibes* (o/p). Two weeks in September 1980 as lived by a mixed-up Santiago rich kid. A sort of Chilean *Catcher In the Rye* set against the tensions of the military regime.

Luis Sepúlveda *The Name of a Bullfighter*. Fast-paced, rather macho thriller set in Hamburg, Santiago and Tierra del Fuego, by one of Chile's leading novelists.

Antonio Skármeta *The Postman*, formerly *Burning Patience*. Funny and poignant novel about a postman who delivers mail to the great poet Pablo Neruda. Neruda, in turn, helps him seduce the local beauty with the help of a few metaphors. It was also made into a successful film, *Il Postino*, with the action relocated to Capri. Also by Skármeta, *I Dreamt the Snow Was Burning* is a tense, dark novel evoking the suspicion and fear that permeated everyday life in the months surrounding the military coup, while *Watch Where the Wolf is Going* is a collection of short stories, some set in Chile.

POETRY

Vicente Huidobro *The Selected Poetry of Vicente Huidobro*. Intellectual, experimental and dynamic works by an early twentieth-century poet, highly acclaimed in his time (1893–1948) but often overlooked today.

Gabriela Mistral *Selected Poems*. Mistral is far less widely translated than her fellow Nobel laureate, Neruda, but this collection serves as an adequate English-language introduction to her quietly passionate and bittersweet poetry, much of which is inspired by the Elqui Valley.

Pablo Neruda *Twenty Love Poems and a Song of Despair; Canto General; Captain's Verses*. The doyen of Chilean poetry seems to be one of those poets people love or hate – his work is extravagantly lyrical, frequently verbose, but often very tender, particularly his love poetry. Neruda has been translated into many languages, and is widely available.

Nicanor Parra *Emergency Poems*. Both a physicist and poet, Parra pioneered the "anti-poem" in Chile during the 1980s: bald, un-lyrical, often satirical prose poems. A stimulating read.

BIOGRAPHY AND MEMOIRS

Fernando Alegría *Allende: A Novel*. Basically a biography, with fictional dialogue, of Salvador Allende, written by his former cultural attaché, who was busy researching the book while the president died in the coup. Also of note by Alegría is *The Chilean Spring*, a fictional diary of a young photographer coming to terms with the coup in Santiago.

Isabel Allende *My Invented Country – A Nostalgic Journey Through Chile*. A memoir that is an enthralling mix of fiction and biography and which describes the author's life in Chile up until the assassination of her uncle, president Salvador Allende. She provides a very personal view of her homeland and exhaustively examines the country, its terrain, people, customs and language.

Ariel Dorfman *Heading South, Looking North*. Memoir of one of Chile's most famous writers, in which he reflects on themes such as language, identity, guilt and politics. Intelligent and illuminating, with some interesting thoughts on the causes of the Unidad Popular's failures.

★ **Joan Jara** *Víctor: An Unfinished Song* (o/p). Poignant memoir written by the British wife of the famous Chilean folksinger Víctor Jara, describing their life together, the *nueva canción* movement (see page 495) and their optimism for Allende's new Chile. The final part, detailing Jara's imprisonment, torture and execution in Santiago's football stadium, is almost unbearably moving.

Luis Muñoz *Being Luis*. Account of a childhood spent growing up in 1960s–70s Chile that reflects recent history and leads to Muñoz's development as a left-wing activist, his arrest and torture by the military regime and eventual exile to England.

Pablo Neruda *Memoirs*. Though his occasional displays of vanity and compulsive name-dropping can be irritating, there's no doubt that this is an extraordinary man with a fascinating life. The book also serves as a useful outline of Chile's political movements from the 1930s to the 1970s.

PACIFIC ISLANDS

Sebastian Englert *Island at the Centre of the World* (o/p). Based on a series of lectures broadcast to the Chilean Navy serving in Antarctica, this is a clear and accessible (though dated) introduction to Easter Island, written by a genial German priest who lived there for 35 years from 1935.

Thor Heyerdahl *Aku Aku* (o/p). This account of Heyerdahl's famous expedition to Easter Island in 1955 is a cracking read, with an acute sense of adventure and mystery. Dubious as the author's archeological theories are, it's hard not to get swept along by his enthusiasm. In contrast, his *Reports of the Norwegian Archeological Expedition to Easter Island and the East Pacific* is a rigorous and respected documentation of the expedition's findings.

Catherine and Michel Orliac *The Silent Gods: Mysteries of Easter Island* (o/p). This pocket-sized paperback is densely packed with colour illustrations and surprisingly detailed background on the island's explorers, statues, myths and traditions.

★ **Katherine Routledge** *The Mystery of Easter Island*. Recently back in print, this compelling book chronicles one of the earliest archeological expeditions to the island, led by the author in 1914. Routledge interviewed many elderly islanders and recounts their oral testimonies as well as the discoveries of her excavations.

★ **Diana Souhami** *Selkirk's Island*. This gripping, award-winning account of the misadventures of Alexander Selkirk – the real life Robinson Crusoe, who spent four years marooned on a Chilean Pacific island – includes some vivid and evocative descriptions of what's now known as Isla Robinson Crusoe.

FLORA AND FAUNA

Sharon R. Chester *Birds of Chile* is a first-rate, easy-to-carry guide with more than three hundred colour illustrations of the birds of mainland Chile. *A Wildlife Guide to Chile* is the first comprehensive field guide in English that covers Chile's fauna, both on the mainland and its far-flung territories, including Antarctica and Easter Island.

Chilean Spanish

To get by in Chile, it's very helpful to equip yourself with a bit of basic Spanish. It's not a difficult language to pick up and there are numerous resources on the market, teaching to various levels – *Pimsleur Basic Latin American Spanish* is a very good starting point, the *Learn (Latin American) Spanish* app leave you with essential words and phrases at your fingertips, while for an old-fashioned, rigorous textbook, nothing beats H. Ramsden's *An Essential Course in Modern Spanish*, published in the UK by Nelson.

The snag is that Chilean Spanish does not conform to what you learn in the classroom or hear on your app, and even competent Spanish-speakers will find it takes a bit of getting used to. The first thing to contend with is the dizzying **speed** with which most Chileans speak; another is **pronunciation**, especially the habitual dropping of many consonants. In particular, "s" is frequently dropped from the end or middle of a word, so *dos* becomes *do*, *gracias* becomes *gracia*, and *fósforos* (matches) becomes *fohforo*. "D" has a habit of disappearing from past participles, so *comprado* is *comprao*, while the "gua" sound is commonly reduced to *wa*, making the city of Rancagua sound like *Rancawa*. The *-as* ending of the second person singular of verbs (*estás*, *viajas*, and so on) is transformed into *-ai*: hence *¿cómo estás?* usually comes out as "comehtai"; the classic *"¿cachai?"* ("get it?") is the second person singular form of the slang verb *cachar*, meaning to understand.

Another way in which Chilean differs from classic Castilian Spanish is its borrowing of words from indigenous languages, mainly Quechua, Aymara and Mapuche, but also from German (*kuchen*, for cake) and even English ("plumber" in Chile is inexplicably *el gasfíter*). Adding to the confusion is a widespread use of **slang** and **idiom**, much of which is unique to Chile. None of this, however, should put you off attempting to speak Spanish in Chile – Chileans will really appreciate your efforts, and even faltering beginners will be complimented on their language skills.

Pronunciation

The rules of **pronunciation** are pretty straightforward and, once you get to know them, strictly observed. Unless there's an accent, words ending in d, l, r, and z are **stressed** on the last syllable, all others on the second last. All **vowels** are pure and short.

A somewhere between the A sound of back and that of father.

E as in get.

I as in police.

O as in hot.

U as in rule.

C is soft before E and I, hard otherwise: *cerca* is pronounced "serka".

G works the same way, a slightly guttural H sound (between an aspirate "h" and the ch in loch) before E or I, a hard G elsewhere – *gigante* becomes "higante".

H is always silent.

J is guttural: *jamón* is pronounced "hamón".

LL sounds like an English Y: *tortilla* is pronounced "torteeya".

N is as in English unless it has a tilde (ñ) over it, when it becomes NY: *mañana* sounds like "manyana".

QU is pronounced like an English K (the "u" is silent).

R is rolled, RR doubly so.

V sounds more like B, *vino* becoming "beano".

X is slightly softer than in English – sometimes almost SH – except between vowels in place names where it has an H sound – for example *México* (Meh-Hee-Ko).

Z is the same as a soft C, so *cerveza* becomes "serbessa".

Below we've listed a few essential words and phrases, though if you're travelling for any length of time a dictionary or phrase book is obviously a worthwhile investment. If you're using a **dictionary**, bear in mind that in Spanish CH, LL, and Ñ count as separate letters and are traditionally listed in a special section after the Cs, Ls, and Ns respectively, though some newer dictionaries do not follow this rule.

WORDS AND PHRASES

The following should help you with your most basic day-to-day language needs; a menu reader and list of slang terms follows on.

BASICS

yes, no sí, no
please, thank you por favor, gracias
where, when? dónde, cuándo
what, how much? qué, cuánto
here, there aquí, allí
this, that este, eso
now, later ahora, más tarde

open, closed abierto/a, cerrado/a
with, without con, sin
good, bad buen(o)/a, mal(o)/a
big gran(de)
small pequeño/a, chico
more, less más, menos
today, tomorrow hoy, mañana
yesterday ayer

GREETINGS AND RESPONSES

Hello, Goodbye Hola, adiós (ciao/chau)
Good morning Buenos días
Good afternoon Buenas tardes
Good evening/night Buenas noches
See you later Hasta luego
Sorry Lo siento/discúlpeme (perdón)
Excuse me Con permiso/perdón
How are you? ¿Como está (usted)?
I (don't) understand (No) Entiendo
Not at all/You're welcome De nada
Do you speak English? ¿Habla (usted) inglés?

I (don't) speak Spanish (No) Hablo español
My name is... Me llamo...
What's your name? ¿Cómo se llama (usted)?
I am English Soy inglés (a)
...Irish ...irlandés (a)
...Scottish ...escocés (a)
...Welsh ...galés (a)
...American ...norte-americano (a)
...Australian ...australiano (a)
...Canadian ...canadiense
...New Zealander ...neozelandés (a)

ACCOMMODATION AND TRANSPORT

I want Quiero...
I'd like Quisiera...
Do you know... ¿Sabe...?
I don't know No sé
There is (is there?) (¿) Hay (?)
Give me... Deme...
...(one like that) ...(uno así)
Do you have... ¿Tiene...?
...the time ...la hora
...a room ...una habitación
...with two beds/double bed...con dos camas/cama matrimonial
...with private bath ...con baño privado
It's for one person (two people) es para una persona (dos personas)
For one night (one week) para una noche (una semana)
It's fine Está bien
How much is it? ¿Cuánto es?
It's too expensive Es demasiado caro
Don't you have anything cheaper? ¿No tiene algo más barato?
Can one...? ¿Se puede...?
...camp (near) here? ...acampar aquí (cerca)?

Is there a hotel nearby? ¿Hay un hotel aquí cerca?
How do I get to...? ¿Por dónde se va a...?
Left, right, straight on Izquierda, derecha, derecho
Where is...? ¿Dónde está...? **...the bus station** ...el terminal de buses **...the train station** ...la estación de ferrocarriles
the nearest bank el banco más cercano
the post office el correo
the toilet el baño
Where does the bus leave from? ¿De dónde sale el bus para...?
Is this the train for Santiago? ¿Es éste el tren para Santiago?
I'd like a (return) ticket to... Quisiera un pasaje (de ida y vuelta) para...
What time does it leave (arrive in...)? ¿A qué hora sale (llega en...)?
How long does the journey take? ¿Cuánto tiempo demora el viaje?
What is there to eat? ¿Qué hay para comer?
What's that? ¿Qué es eso?
What's this called in Spanish? ¿Como se llama esto en español?

IDIOM AND SLANG

As you travel through Chile you'll come across a lot of words and expressions that crop up again and again, many of which aren't in your dictionary, or, if they are, appear to have a different meaning from that given. Added to these day-to-day **chilenismos** is a very rich, exuberant and constantly expanding vocabulary of slang (*modismos*). Mastering a few of the most common examples will help you get by and raise a smile if you drop them into the conversation.

EVERYDAY WORDS AND EXPRESSIONS

Some of the words and expressions listed below are shared by neighbouring countries, while others are uniquely Chilean. As well as these peculiarities, we've listed a few other expressions you're likely to encounter very frequently.

Al tiro "right away", "immediately" – though this can mean anything up to several hours.

Boleta as Chilean law requires that customers must not leave shop premises without their *boleta* (receipt), you will frequently hear "*su boleta!*" yelled at you as you try to leave without it.

Calefónt (pronounced "*calefón*") water heater; not a real Chilean word, but one you'll need every day if you're staying in budget accommodation, where you'll have to remember to light the *calefónt* with *fósforos* (matches) before you take a shower.

Carné identity card.

Cédula interchangeable with *carné*.

Ciao (chau) by far the most common way of saying "goodbye" among friends; in slightly more formal situations, *hasta luego* is preferred over *adiós*.

Confort (pronounced "*confor*") a brand name but now the de facto word for toilet paper (which is correctly *papel higiénico*).

De repente in Spain this means "suddenly"; in Chile it means "maybe", "sometimes" or "occasionally".

Flojo "lazy", frequently invoked by northerners to describe southerners and southerners to describe northerners.

Guagua (pronounced "*wawa*") baby, derived from Quechua.

Harto "loads of" (for example *harto trabajo*, loads of work); a more widely used and idiomatic alternative to *mucho*.

Listo literally "ready", and used as a response to indicate agreement, or that what's been said is understood; something like "sure" or "right".

Plata literally "silver" but meaning "money", used far more commonly than *dinero*, except in formal situations.

Qué le vaya (muy) bien "May everything go (very) well for you", frequently said when saying goodbye to someone you probably won't see again.

Rico "good", "delicious", "tasty", usually to describe food and drink.

Ya Chilean equivalent of the Spanish *vale*; used universally to convey "OK", "fine", "sure" or (depending on the tone) "whatever", "hmm, I see".

SLANG

The few examples we give below barely scrape the surface of the living, constantly evolving lexicon of Chilean slang – for a crash course, get hold of the excellent *How to Survive in the Chilean Jungle* by John Brennan and Alvaro Baboada, available in the larger Santiago bookshops.

Buena onda "cool!"

Cachar "to understand"; hence "*¿cachai?*", "are you with me?", scattered ad nauseam through conversations.

Cocido drunk.

Cuico yuppie (especially in Santiago).

Huevón literally "huge testicle", meaning something like "asshole" or "fucker", but so commonly and enthusiastically used it's no longer particularly offensive. More like "jerk" or "idiot".

Los pacos the police.

Pololo/a boyfriend, girlfriend.

¡Sale! emphatically used to mean, "bullshit!" or "not a chance!"

Sí, po abbreviation of *sí, pues*, meaning "yeah", "sure" ("po" is tacked onto the end of just about every phrase, hence "*no po*", "*no sé po*").

Taco traffic jam.

NUMBERS AND DAYS

1 un/uno/una	30 treinta
2 dos	40 cuarenta
3 tres	50 cincuenta
4 cuatro	60 sesenta
5 cinco	70 setenta
6 seis	80 ochenta
7 siete	90 noventa
8 ocho	100 cien(to)
9 nueve	101 ciento uno
10 diez	200 doscientos (as)
11 once	201 doscientos (as) uno
12 doce	500 quinientos (as)
13 trece	1000 mil
14 catorce	2000 dos mil
15 quince	**first** primer(o)/a
16 dieciséis	**second** segundo/a
17 diecisiete	**third** tercer(o)/a
18 dieciocho	**Monday** lunes
19 diecinueve	**Tuesday** martes
20 veinte	**Wednesday** miércoles
21 veintiuno	**Thursday** jueves
	Friday viernes
	Saturday sábado
	Sunday domingo

USEFUL TRANSPORT VOCABULARY

4WD Doble tracción/cuatro por cuatro (4x4)
Aisle Pasillo
Car Auto
Car rental outlet Rentacar
Damages excess Deducible
Highway Carretera
Insurance Seguro
Jerry can Bidon
Left luggage Custodia
Luggage Equipaje
Non-4WD Tracción single/dos por dos (2x2)
Petrol Bencina
Petrol station Estación de bencina
Pick-up truck Camioneta
To rent Arrendar
Seat Asiento
Ticket Pasaje
Unlimited kilometres Kilometraje libre
Window Ventana

CHILEAN ROAD SIGNS

Curva peligrosa Dangerous bend
Desvío Detour
No adelantar No overtaking
Peligro Danger
Reduzca velocidad Reduce speed
Resbaladizo Slippery surface
Sin berma No hard shoulder

FOOD: A CHILEAN MENU READER

BASICS

Aceite Oil
Ají Chilli
Ajo Garlic
Arroz Rice
Azúcar Sugar
Huevos Eggs
Leche Milk
Mantequilla Butter
Mermelada Jam
Miel Honey
Mostaza Mustard
Pan Bread
Pimienta Pepper
Sal Salt

SOME COMMON TERMS

A la parrilla Grilled
A la plancha Grilled
A lo pobre Served with chips, onions and a fried egg
Ahumado Smoked
Al horno Oven-baked
Al vapor Steamed
Asado Roast or barbecued
Asado al palo Spit-roasted, barbecued
Crudo Raw
Frito Fried

Pastel Paste, purée, mince
Picante Spicy hot
Pil-pil Very spicy
Puré Mashed (potato)
Relleno Filled or stuffed

MEALS

Agregado Side order
Almuerzo Lunch
Cena Dinner
Comedor Dining room
Cuchara Spoon
Cuchillo Knife
Desayuno Breakfast
La carta The menu
La cuenta The bill
Menú del día Fixed-price set meal (usually lunch)
Once Afternoon tea
Plato vegetariano Vegetarian dish
Tenedor Fork

MEAT (CARNE) AND POULTRY (AVES)

Bistec Beef steak
Carne de vacuno Beef
Cerdo Pork
Chuleta Cutlet, chop (usually pork)
Churrasco Griddled beef, like a minute steak
Conejo Rabbit
Cordero Lamb steak
Escalopa Milanesa Breaded veal escalope
Filete Fillet steak
Jamón Ham
Lechón, cochinillo Suckling pig
Lomo General term for steak of indiscriminate cut
Pato Duck
Pavo Turkey
Pollo Chicken
Ternera Veal
Vienesa Hot-dog sausage

OFFAL (MENUDOS)

Chunchules Intestines
Guatitas Tripe
Lengua Tongue
Patas Feet, trotters
Pana Liver
Picante de conejo Curried rabbits' innards
Riñones Kidneys

FISH (PESCADO)

Albacora Albacore (a small, white-fleshed tuna)
Anchoveta Anchovy
Atún Tuna
Bonito Pacific bonito, similar to tuna

Ceviche Strips of fish marinated in lemon juice and onions
Congrio A large, superior member of the cod family known as conger eel
Corvina Sea bass (not the same as Chilean sea bass, which is under boycott)
Lenguado Sole
Merluza Hake
Reineta Similar to lemon sole
Salmón Salmon
Trucha Trout
Vidriola Firm-fleshed white fish from the Juan Fernández archipelago

SEAFOOD (MARISCOS)

Almeja Clam, cockle
Calamar Squid
Camarón Prawn
Centolla King crab
Choro, chorito Mussel
Erizo Sea urchin
Langosta Lobster
Langosta de Isla de Pascua Spiny lobster
Langosta de Juan Fernández Rock lobster fished near the Juan Fernández islands
Langostino Crayfish, red crab
Loco Abalone
Macha Razor clam
Mariscal Mixed shellfish, served chilled
Mejillones Mussels
Ostiones Scallops
Ostras Oysters
Paila marina Thick fish and seafood stew
Picoroco Giant barnacle with a single crab-like claw
Piure Scarlet-red, kidney-shaped animal with hair-like strands that lives inside a shell
Pulpo Octopus

VEGETABLES (VERDURAS)

Aceitunas Olives
Alcachofa Artichoke
Cebolla Onion
Champiñón Mushroom
Choclo Maize, sweetcorn
Chucrút Sauerkraut
Espinaca Spinach
Lechuga Lettuce
Palmito Palm heart
Palta Avocado
Papa Potato
Papas fritas Chips (French fries)
Poroto verde Green, French, runner bean
Tomate Tomato
Zapallo Squash

SOUPS AND STEWS

Caldillo Vegetables cooked in meat stock; between a stew and a soup
Caldo Quite bland, simple meat stock with loads of added salt
Charquicán Meat stew with lots of vegetables
Chupe Thick fish stew, topped with butter, breadcrumbs and grated cheese
Crema Creamy soup thickened with flour or egg yolks
Zarzuela Seafood stew (like bouillabaisse)

SALADS (ENSALADAS)

Ensalada chilena Tomatoes, shredded onion and vinaigrette
Ensalada primavera Hard-boiled eggs, sweetcorn, peas, carrot and beetroot
Ensalada rusa Diced vegetables and peas mixed in a thick mayonnaise
Ensalada surtida Mixed salad
Palta reina Avocado filled with tuna

SANDWICHES (SANWICHES)

Ave mayo Chicken and mayonnaise
Ave sola Chicken
Barros jarpa Ham and melted cheese
Barros luco Beef and melted cheese
Churrasco solo Griddled beef, like a minute steak
Completo Hot dog, sauerkraut, tomato and mayonnaise
Diplomático Beef, egg and melted cheese
Especial Hot dog with mayonnaise
Hamburguesa Hamburger

FRUIT (FRUTAS)

Albaricoque Apricot
Cereza Cherry
Chirimoya Custard apple
Ciruela Plum
Durazno Peach
Frambuesa Raspberry
Frutilla Strawberry
Higo Fig
Limón Lemon
Lúcuma Native fruit often used in ice cream and cakes
Manzana Apple
Membrillo Quince
Mora Mulberry
Naranja Orange

Pera Pear
Piña Pineapple
Plátano Banana
Pomelo Grapefruit
Sandía Watermelon
Tuna Prickly pear
Uva(s) Grape(s)

DESSERT (POSTRES)

When fruit is described as being "in juice" (*al jugo*) or "in syrup" (*en almíbar*), it will be out of a tin.

Flan Crème caramel
Helado Ice cream
Kuchen Cake
Macedonia Fruit salad
Manjar Very sweet caramel, made from condensed milk
Panqueques Pancakes
Torta Tart

DRINKS

Note that, owing to the Chileans' compulsive use of the diminutive (*ito* and *ita*), you'll hardly ever be asked if you want a *té* or *café*, but rather a *tecito* or *cafecito*.

ALCOHOLIC DRINKS

Cerveza Beer
Champán Champagne
Chicha (or sidra) Cider
Vino (tinto/blanco/ rosado) Wine (red/white/rosé)
 Hot drinks
Café Coffee
Descafeinado Decaff
Chocolate caliente Hot chocolate
Té Tea
Té de hierbas Herbal tea

SOFT DRINKS

Bebida Fizzy drink
 (en lata/botella) (in a can/bottle)
 (de máquina) (draught)
Jugo natural Juice (pure)
Néctar Juice (syrup)
Agua Water
Agua mineral Mineral water
 (con gas) (sparkling)
 (sin gas) (still)

Small print and index

A ROUGH GUIDE TO ROUGH GUIDES

Published in 1982, the first Rough Guide – to Greece – was a student scheme that became a publishing phenomenon. Mark Ellingham, a recent graduate in English from Bristol University, had been travelling in Greece the previous summer and couldn't find the right guidebook. With a small group of friends he wrote his own guide, combining a contemporary, journalistic style with a thoroughly practical approach to travellers' needs.

The immediate success of the book spawned a series that rapidly covered dozens of destinations. And, in addition to impecunious backpackers, Rough Guides soon acquired a much broader readership that relished the guides' wit and inquisitiveness as much as their enthusiastic, critical approach and value-for-money ethos. These days, Rough Guides include recommendations from budget to luxury and cover more than 120 destinations around the globe, from Amsterdam to Zanzibar, all regularly updated by our team of roaming writers.

Browse all our latest guides, read inspirational features and book your trip at **roughguides.com**.

Rough Guide credits

Editor: Samantha Cook
Cartography: Carte, Katie Bennett
Managing editor: Rachel Lawrence
Picture editor: Aude Vauconsant

Cover photo research: Phoebe Lowndes
Senior DTP coordinator: Dan May
Head of DTP and Pre-Press: Rebeka Davies

Publishing information

Seventh edition 2018

Distribution
UK, Ireland and Europe
Apa Publications (UK) Ltd; sales@roughguides.com
United States and Canada
Ingram Publisher Services; ips@ingramcontent.com
Australia and New Zealand
Woodslane; info@woodslane.com.au
Southeast Asia
Apa Publications (SN) Pte; sales@roughguides.com
Worldwide
Apa Publications (UK) Ltd; sales@roughguides.com
Special Sales, Content Licensing and CoPublishing
Rough Guides can be purchased in bulk quantities
at discounted prices. We can create special editions,
personalised jackets and corporate imprints tailored to
your needs. sales@roughguides.com.
roughguides.com

Printed in China by CTPS
All rights reserved
© 2018 Apa Digital (CH) AG
License edition © Apa Publications Ltd UK

Help us update

We've gone to a lot of effort to ensure that the seventh
edition of **The Rough Guide Chile and Easter Island** is
accurate and up-to-date. However, things change – places
get "discovered", opening hours are notoriously fickle,
restaurants and rooms raise prices or lower standards. If
you feel we've got it wrong or left something out, we'd like
to know, and if you can remember the address, the price,
the hours, the phone number, so much the better.

Please send your comments with the subject line
"Rough Guide Chile and Easter Island update" to mail@
uk.roughguides.com. We'll credit all contributions and
send a copy of the next edition (or any other Rough Guide
if you prefer) for the very best emails.

Reader's updates

Thanks to all the readers who have taken the time to write in with comments and suggestions (and apologies if we've
inadvertently omitted or misspelt anyone's name):

Andrew Coulthurst; Chris Dehondt; Anna Letts; Jeremy Marx; Corrie Moxon; Emma Maev O'Connell.

Acknowledgements

Nick Edwards Nick would like to thank the following
people for invaluable help and hospitality along the way:
Naomi McKee; Daniela and Macarena of *Oasis*; *Plaza San
Francisco*; *Rio Amazonas*; *Luciano K*; all at *Tierra Atacama*,
especially Claudia and Pablo; *Hostal Sonchek*; *Backpackers
Hostel Iquique*; and Ross of *Sunny Days* and Charlie of
Latinorizons in Arica. Thanks to Sam for silky smooth
editing. Love as always to Maria and Gandalf at base camp.
Anna Kaminski I would like to thank Mani and Ed, my
fellow authors and editor Sam, as well as the Erratic Rock
team; Patagonia Camp and EcoCamp Patagonia; Rob and
Monica; Sarina; Carolyn; Kevin; the drivers who fished my
car out of the mud in Hornopiren; Kris Tompkins; Amory
and Fernando; Marie and Fernando; Daniel; Silvie; Mariano;
Zoe and Leo; Maison Nomade; Patagonia House; and
everyone else who helped me along the way.
Shafik Meghji Many thanks to all the travellers and locals
who helped out along the way. A special muchas gracias

to: my fellow authors; Sam Cook for her sterling editing;
Mani Ramaswamy, Ed Aves and Becca Hallett; Naomi
McKee at Senderos; Simon Evans at Chimu Adventures;
Carolina Gutierrez Prado at Accor; Kristina Shreck of
Azure PR; Janak Jani in Valpo; Iain Hardy in Valpo; Cyril
Christensen of Chiloé Natural; all the staff at Tierra Chiloé;
James Grant-Peterkin of Easter Island Spirit; Lanny
Grossman; John Rees in Punta Arenas; Yamila Giserman
of Destino Argentina; Alberto Serrano in Puerto Williams;
Jean, Nizar and Nina Meghji; and Sioned Jones, for her love
and support.
Sorrel Moseley-Williams With thanks to Kristina Schreck
of Azure; Silvina Reusmann; the guys at Qapaq Raymi for
an Andean adventure when the car got altitude sickness;
the Argentines who let me ride out of the Andes with
them to Copiapó; Sonia from Hospedaje Sonia in Chillán;
Charlie Villard for the wine; and Allan Kelin.

ABOUT THE AUTHORS

Nick Edwards After studying Classics and Modern Greek at Oxford, Nick spent many years living in Athens and later Stateside in Pittsburgh, with lots of travelling in between, especially in India. When not researching Rough Guides to these places and newly discovered favourites – including Chile! – he lives in his native Southeast London with spouse Maria, devoting time to his beloved Spurs, obscure psychedelic music and trying to promote a bit of Oneness.

Anna Kaminski has been enamoured of this long, thin country ever since becoming hooked on Isabel Allende novels and Pablo Neruda's poetry while doing a degree on the history and literature of Latin America. Since then, she has travelled the entire length of Chile on several occasions – for research and pleasure – though it's the frozen south that entices her the most: she considers Patagonia her second home and finds herself returning year after year.

Shafik Meghji An award-winning travel writer, journalist and co-author of more than thirty Rough Guides, Shafik first visited Chile in 2004 and has since travelled throughout the country, from the Atacama desert to Tierra del Fuego. He writes for print and digital publications A fellow of the Royal Geographical Society, member of the British Guild of Travel Writers, and trustee of the Latin America Bureau, he blogs at ⓦunmappedroutes.com and tweets @ShafikMeghji.

Sorrel Moseley-Williams An award-winning journalist, based inArgentina since 2006. Also a sommelier, she navigates Latin America's southern cone to write about food, wine and travel, and edits her wine blog ⓦcomewinewith. me. She has written for several Rough Guides, including *The Rough Guide to South America on a Budget* and *The Rough Guide to Argentina*.

Index

Main references are in **bold** type

Map symbols

The symbols below are used on maps throughout the book

International border	★ Bus stop	Refugio (mountain lodge)	⚓ Port
Chapter boundary	Ⓜ Metro station	Cave	Volcano
Motorway	@ Internet café/access	Observatory	▲ Mountain peak
Main road	ⓘ Information office	Fortess	Mountain range
Unpaved road	⊞ Hospital	Castle	Museum
Minor road	⊠ Post office	⊙ Monument/statue	Building
Pedestrian road	Spring/spa	Church (regional maps)	Church (town maps)
Steps	Battlefield	Picnic area	Stadium
Path	Point of interest	Viewpoint	Market
Ferry	Ruin	Campsite	Salt pan
Funicular railway	Vineyard/winery	Swimming pool	Glacier
Railway	Mine	Surf beach	Beach
Cable car	Immigration/border crossing	Ski area	Park/reserve
✈ International airport	Guardería (ranger station)	Waterfall	Cemetery
Domestic airport			

Listings key

■ Accommodation
● Eating
■ Drinking/nightlife
● Shopping

A ROUGH GUIDE TO
ROUGH GUIDES

Published in 1982, the first Rough Guide – to Greece – was a student scheme that became a publishing phenomenon. Mark Ellingham, a recent graduate in English from Bristol University, had been travelling in Greece the previous summer and couldn't find the right guidebook. With a small group of friends he wrote his own guide, combining a highly contemporary, journalistic style with a thoroughly practical approach to travellers' needs.

The immediate success of the book spawned a series that rapidly covered dozens of destinations. And, in addition to impecunious backpackers, Rough Guides soon acquired a much broader readership that relished the guides' wit and inquisitiveness as much as their enthusiastic, critical approach and value-for-money ethos.

These days, Rough Guides include recommendations from budget to luxury and cover more than 120 destinations around the globe. Visit ⓦ roughguides .com for travel tips and inspiring features, to buy our latest ebooks and plan your next trip.

Long bus journey?
Phone run out of juice?

👉 **TEST YOUR KNOWLEDGE** WITH OUR ROUGH GUIDES TRAVEL QUIZ

1 Denim, the pencil, the stethoscope and the hot-air balloon were all invented in which country?

a. Italy
b. France
c. Germany
d. Switzerland

2 What is the currency of Vietnam?

a. Dong
b. Yuan
c. Baht
d. Kip

3 In which city would you find the Majorelle Garden?

a. Marseille
b. Marrakesh
c. Tunis
d. Malaga

4 What is the busiest airport in the world?

a. London Heathrow
b. Tokyo International
c. Chicago O'Hare
d. Hartsfield-Jackson
   Atlanta International

5 Which of these countries does not have the equator running through it?

a. Brazil
b. Tanzania
c. Indonesia
d. Colombia

6 Which country has the most UNESCO World Heritage Sites?

a. Mexico
b. France
c. Italy
d. India

7 What is the principal religion of Japan?

a. Confucianism
b. Buddhism
c. Jainism
d. Shinto

8 Every July in Sonkajärvi, central Finland, contestants gather for the World Championships of which sport?

a. Zorbing
b. Wife-carrying
c. Chess-boxing
d. Extreme ironing

9 What colour are post boxes in Germany?

a. Red
b. Green
c. Blue
d. Yellow

10 For three days each April during Songkran festival in Thailand, people take to the streets to throw what at each other?

a. Water
b. Oranges
c. Tomatoes
d. Underwear

ESCAPE THE EVERYDAY

ADVENTURE BECKONS

YOU JUST NEED TO KNOW WHERE TO LOOK

roughguides.com